# Consumer Economics

## Issues and Behaviors

### Elizabeth B. Goldsmith

PEARSON

Prentice
Hall

Upper Saddle River, New Jersey 07458

Library of Congress Cataloging-in-Publication Data

Goldsmith, Elizabeth B.
    Consumer economics  :  issues and behaviors  /  Elizabeth B. Goldsmith.—1st ed.
       p. cm.
    Includes bibliographical references and index.
    ISBN 0-13-098974-6
  1.  Consumer education.  2.  Consumption (Economics)  I. Title.
    TX335.G585 2005
    640'.7—dc22

                                                                    2004006258


**Executive Editor:** Vernon R. Anthony
**Editorial Assistant:** Beth Dyke
**Production Editor:** Patty Donovan, Pine Tree Composition, Inc.
**Production Liaison:** Janice Stangel
**Director of Manufacturing and Production:** Bruce Johnson
**Managing Editor:** Mary Carnis
**Manufacturing Manager:** Ilene Sanford
**Manufacturing Buyer:** Cathleen Petersen
**Creative Director:** Cheryl Asherman
**Senior Marketing Manager:** Ryan DeGrote
**Senior Marketing Coordinator:** Elizabeth Farrell
**Marketing Assistant:** Les Roberts
**Formatting and Interior Design:** Pine Tree Composition, Inc.
**Printing and Binding:** Courier Companies, Inc.
**Cover Design Coordinator:** Miguel Ortiz
**Cover Designer:** Wanda España
**Cover Photograph:** Courtesy of Comstock Images, Flat-rate Division

**Copyright © 2005 by Pearson Education, Inc., Upper Saddle River, New Jersey, 07458.**
Pearson Prentice Hall. All rights reserved. Printed in the United States of America. This publication is protected by Copyright and permission should be obtained from the publisher prior to any prohibited reproduction, storage in a retrieval system, or transmission in any form or by any means, electronic, mechanical, photocopying, recording, or likewise. For information regarding permission(s), write to: Rights and Permissions Department.

**Pearson Prentice Hall**™ is a trademark of Pearson Education, Inc.
**Pearson**® is a registered trademark of Pearson plc
**Prentice Hall**® is a registered trademark of Pearson Education, Inc.

Pearson Education LTD.
Pearson Education Singapore, Pte. Ltd
Pearson Education, Canada, Ltd
Pearson Education—Japan
Pearson Education Australia PTY, Limited
Pearson Education North Asia Ltd
Pearson Educaçion de Mexico, S.A. de C.V.
Pearson Education Malaysia, Pte. Ltd

10 9 8 7 6 5 4 3 2 1
ISBN 0-13-098974-6

# Contents

Contents

# PART 2  CONSUMER PERSPECTIVES

## Chapter 4    Consumer Responsibilities, Redress, and Law

## Chapter 5    Government Protection, Nongovernmental Proconsumer Groups, and Media

## PART 3   CONSUMERS IN THE MARKETPLACE

### Chapter 6   Buying Process, Brands, and Product Development

**Chapter 9    Health and Body Issues**                                    **235**

## PART 4   CONSUMERS IN THE FINANCIAL MARKETPLACE

### Chapter 12   Saving, Banking, Debt, and Credit Issues

## Chapter 13   Insurance and Investment Issues                                          355

# Preface

*We must be the change we wish to see in the world.*
Mahatma Gandhi

Consumer economics—since it mirrors social and economic change—is a very fast-paced discipline. The purpose of this book is to provide an updated look at the consumer movement and the intricacies of consumer behavior. It addresses who buys, what, how, when, and why. It also looks at the forces that impact consumer choice in an ever-changing and often turbulent world. Quality of life and well being are seen as end states, which consumers pursue in their decision making. Too often consumer books have focused on problems and complaints, and although these are addressed, solutions are also presented.

The 21st century has brought us a keen awareness of company frailties and less than perfect ethics. Exposure of company fraud and excesses is constantly in the news eroding consumer confidence. Personal bankruptcies and the number of consumer complaints have hit all time highs. In short, we have a way to go before we reach a truly functioning and fair marketplace. This book traces this pursuit through time and across countries. Adding to the global approach has been the Internet, which has pushed privacy issues to the forefront while at the same time opening up competition in products, information, and user practices. From the consumer point of view, competition is nearly always favorable. But in all things there are tradeoffs; and identity theft, which can happen in-person, or over the Internet, is the current number one consumer concern.

Today's consumer is operating in a much more complex marketplace than could ever have been envisioned by Adam Smith, founder of modern economics, who argued that consumers—not kings or parliaments—should rule nations. There is no doubt that the consumer is still sovereign, but controlling resources is becoming increasingly difficult. "New" consumers are about so much more than saving money and fighting the urge to buy on impulse. The following list highlights how the text's coverage seeks to explain the behavior and issues surrounding these new consumers.

- The text presents 14 chapters designed to be manageable in a semester long course, detailing the unique ideas and solutions that lead to more successful consumer experiences.
- Students like examples that relate to their own lives, so every effort has been made to give student-based examples such as landlord-tenant disputes, sorting through credit card and cellular phone offers, purchasing cars and vehicle repairs, and choosing travel and various other "deals" wisely.

- The Internet and e-commerce play very big roles in this text. The trend toward buying online or at least shopping around for information is well documented.
- More universities are incorporating consumer behavior into their consumer courses, and this combination is reflected in the title and the content. Advertising and media impacts are highlighted. At the same time, economics, environmental studies, public policy, and law are not neglected. The legal aspects of consumerism are especially emphasized.
- The text is unique in its introduction of a circular flow model and in its coverage of the process of consumption from beginning to end.
- A full chapter on consumption shifts and the consumer movement is also unique. It is amazing to see the types of products that consumers once used often to their detriment and how the government stepped in to make the marketplace safer. Personalities are included to add "faces" to the policy changes.
- What to eat and drink are daily consumption decisions we all make. The chapter provides state-of-the-art scientific and behavioral knowledge on diets, organically grown food, genetically altered food, additives, food-related disease, fast food versus the slow food movement, and bottled water consumption.
- Next, is a chapter on health and wellness, another keystone area in consumerism. Skyrocketing health care costs, recalls of medical devices, the latest in cosmetics and treatments, and alcohol and tobacco consumption patterns are all explored.
- Practical matters regarding purchasing homes, cars, insurance, and investments are covered. Warranties and guarantees are addressed as well as product safety and awareness of "get rich quick" schemes.
- The last chapter zeros in on identity theft and how to avoid it. Also covered are a variety of other topics such as vulnerable populations and global consumption and it finishes with a look toward the future.
- Since terms and words are so important in consumer economics, key terms are highlighted in the text and appear again in the Glossary to aid in study.
- Careers in consumer economics are mentioned throughout and again in the Appendices. When this book went to press the U.S. Securities and Exchange Commission announced they were hiring 800 new employees mostly as investigators. The career opportunities for those trained in consumer economics are boundless whether in community service, government service, corporate consumer affairs, association or trade organizations, education, or law.
- To aid instructors, ancillaries include an instructor's manual with a test item file and outlines and PowerPoints.

# Acknowledgments

When I began writing this book I knew I wanted it to be different, to inspire and motivate readers along their way towards a better life. Vern Anthony, Executive Editor at Prentice Hall, encouraged me from start to finish. Chris and Monica Ohlinger of Ohlinger Publishing Services took care of the finer points involved in bringing a book to press. My students at Florida State University always serve as a reality check and provide lively examples. One student complained about a faulty couch and not only did the department store give her a new couch, but also threw in a dinette set for free. The whole class cheered.

A textbook should be more than loosely tied together theories and facts; it should serve as a guide and a useful one at that. In this endeavor, the reviewer's contribution cannot be underestimated. Special thanks are given to:

| | |
|---|---|
| John R. Burton | Univeristy of Utah |
| Jane Kolodinsky | University of Vermont |
| Julia Marlowe | University of Georgia |
| Patricia Scheeserd | Indiana University of Pennsylvania |
| Anita Subramaniam | Montclair State University |
| Jing Jian Xiao | University of Rhode Island |

Mark Lino of the U.S. Department of Agriculture is thanked for his review of early drafts of Chapter Eight on *Food and Beverage Issues* and Chapter Nine on *Health and Body Issues*.

I'd also like to thank the government and journal editorial boards, which I serve on because I believe in consumer advocacy and try to live it. Particular thanks are extended to the Florida Motor Vehicle Repair Council, the Board of Trustees of the National Association of Insurance Commissioners, the U.S. Department of Justice Debtor Education Task Force, the *Journal of Family and Economic Issues*, and the *International Journal of Consumer Studies*.

Most of all I'd like to thank my family, my husband Ronald E. Goldsmith (the Richard M. Baker Professor of Marketing at Florida State University) and two sons, David and Andrew. They are the center of my life.

# PART 1

# Consumer Perspectives

**CHAPTER**

**1**

# Consumers in a Changing World

The world is so full of things, I'm sure we should all be happy as kings.
Steverson (1905)

**Learning Objectives**

1. Define consumer economics.
2. Explain the market economy.
3. Describe Adam Smith's contribution to consumer economics.
4. Explain the five steps in the consumption process.
5. Explain the three questions economies have to address.
6. Describe the three parts of the business cycle.

## INTRODUCTION

Written during the rise of the age of consumerism, Steverson's couplet highlights the importance of things and illustrates a childlike wonder about the possibilities set before us. If happiness is consumption, we should strive to acquire more and if all goes well, in the end, live as kings. Unfortunately, it is not as simple as that; even with endless consumption happiness is not so easily attained. What is the connection between happiness and consumption? What do consumers want? What motivates consumers to consume? How do they make choices?

This chapter introduces the fundamentals of consumerism and the changing world in which we live. Since we are all consumers, consumer economics is not esoteric; it is applicable every day. **Consumer economics** is the study of how people deal with scarcity, fulfill needs, and select among alternative goods, services, and actions. It provides an understanding of how the marketplace works, our role in it, and how our choices affect our lifestyles. Studying consumer economics:

- Enriches our lives by helping us get the things we want
- Increases our understanding of the factors influencing our choices and the choices of others
- Improves our understanding of how the marketplace works

An end result of studying consumer economics is improved decision making. Each person should be able to look back on decisions made and, for the most part, feel confident they were the right ones.

## WHY STUDY CONSUMER ECONOMICS?

The purpose of this text is to provide the reader with a usable understanding of consumer economics. By following the principles in this book, you will:

- Increase self-awareness
- Understand others' consumption patterns and perspectives
- Bring enthusiasm into daily living, a can-do spirit
- Overcome limitations and weaknesses by knowing your rights and responsibilities
- Improve your consumer behavior
- Participate in actions that bring fairness to the marketplace
- Take control of your happiness (at least as far as consumption is concerned)
- Find ways to profit, make your money stretch further
- Discover career options.

Most students in consumer economics classes aspire to careers working with people in education, law, business, community development, management, health, merchandising, design, government, communications, human resources, or marketing. Specific examples of careers involving consumer economics will be given throughout the book and in Appendix A.

As educated citizens, the challenge we face today is to overcome passivity and hesitation and to take the steps to join in, enter the marketplace, expect, receive, and provide fair treatment, and bring about improved lives. The main objective is to develop the ability to apply consumer economic knowledge to regulatory and social issues, as well as to personal buying decisions.

There is a certain passion, a sense of hope, that one brings to consumerism; it is not all reason and dry theory. Caring about the rights of others is central to the field. The consumer advocates and reformers, such as Erin Brockovich and Ralph Nader, that you'll read about were passionate about making people's lives better and safer. They gave stirring speeches and wrote popular books that changed the way cars and other goods were made in this country, and they crusaded for a cleaner environment. Brockovich exposed pollution in California and became famous in a 1990s movie directed by Steven Soderbergh for which Julia Roberts, playing the role of Brockovich, won an Academy Award. Brockovich and Nader symbolize how one person can make a difference which is another keystone concept in consumer economics. There are groups, individual leaders, and politicians such as Elliott Spitzer, attorney general of New York, who have led or fostered the consumer movement by exposing fraud and corruption. We have all benefited from their efforts. To summarize the role of passion in economic behavior, Alexander Pope wrote in *Moral Essays,* I:

> On life's vast ocean diversely we sail,
> Reason the card, but Passion is the gale.

## WHO CONSUMES AND WHY?

We need to consume to exist. **Consumers** are individuals or groups such as families who obtain, use, maintain, and dispose of products and services to increase life satisfaction and fulfill needs. Consumers are not always efficient in this process. For example, in one shopping study researchers found that many grocery products (usually ones bought for specific recipes or occasions) were never used (Wansink, Brasel, and Amjad, 2000). The usual reason given by respondents was that products were not used immediately after purchase and were slowly pushed to the back of the cabinet and forgotten. They called these products "cabinet castaways." It is estimated that about 12 percent of purchased products are never used and eventually thrown out (Wansink and Deshpande, 1994). Part of the reason for this is that preferences change as people learn and change. One of the subtopics in consumer economics is to increase the awareness of purchase and usage habits in order to save money and reduce waste. For example, information search is a good idea but it can be costly.

> About 12 percent of purchased products are never used and eventually thrown out.

Consumerism has many definitions. Sometimes the word is used to refer to the positive efforts of the consumer movement (essentially the consumer interest) while others times it refers to runaway materialism. For an excellent description of the word and all its permutations, see Roger Swagler's "Evolution and Applications of the Term Consumerism: Theme and Variations" listed in the reference section at the end of this chapter. For the purposes of this book, **consumerism** refers to the belief that goods give meaning to individuals and their roles in society. This combination of consumption, social roles, and politics was first voiced by Adam Smith (1723–1790), the founder of modern economics. He argued in his book *An Inquiry into the Nature and Causes of the Wealth of Nations* (1776) that the essential task of coordinating national economies should fall to consumers. He wrote

> Consumption is the sole end and purpose of all production; and the interest of the producer ought to be attended to only so far as it may be necessary for promoting that of the consumer. This maxim is so perfectly self-evident that it would be absurd to attempt to prove it. But in the mercantile system, the interest of the consumer is almost constantly sacrificed to that of the producer. (Helibroner, 1986, p. 284)

As a professor of moral philosophy at the University of Glasgow in Scotland, who taught classes several days a week (some as large as 90 with students ages 14 to 16), Smith knew consumers well. He did not sit isolated in a country mansion, and although he never married, he traveled and had many friends. He said his 3,000 books (a very sizable collection in that time) were his companions in life. Smith knew that consumers could make mistakes, but he thought for the most part that they could be counted on to be conscientious and careful spenders since this was in their best interest. He proposed that consumers be given freedom and authority in running their own economic affairs, and in the long run he felt this would benefit the nation as well. His doctrine, considered revolutionary in its time, was resisted by the English king and the business people of the day who dominated national decision making about trade. Across the ocean, his book was well received by many of the founders of the United States who were looking for more democratic ways to do things. They liked the idea of the consumer as king; it fit well into building a new country, welcoming new settlers, and encouraging expansion. In Smith's philosophy the wealth of nations was not based on gold and silver

Adam Smith (1723–1790) published An *Inquiry into the Nature and Causes of the Wealth of Nations* in 1776 laying the foundation of economics. He argued that the wealth of nations came from the goods and services produced and consumed. (Courtesy of Library of Congress.)

but rather on the goods and services produced and consumed by people. His philosophy of the "invisible hand" was directed as much against monopoly as government. He extolled the virtues of the acquisitive process and competitive markets. To put his philosophy into one phrase, Smith's understanding of human nature was that "to be human is to exchange freely."

In more modern times, consumerism expresses the cardinal political ideals of liberty and democracy because being able to choose among a vast array of commodities gives people a sense of freedom (Heilbronner, 1986). David Harris, author of *Cute, Quaint, Hungry and Romantic: The Aesthetics of Consumerism,* writes:

What, after all, would a world without consumerism be like?

Surely not one that I myself would choose to live in. There would be no cities because cities are dependent on trade, nor money because there would be nothing to buy. There would be no insurance companies because there would be no possessions, no realtors because there would be no houses, no lawyers because hunters and gatherers rarely have to untangle the red tape of copyright infringement or haggle over joint stock agreements or fax each other angry letters to cease and desist. To imagine a world without consumerism is to erase oneself. (p. 265)

## GOODS AND SERVICES

Buying and using goods and services is an act of faith; one assumes when purchasing something that the object (e.g., a sandwich) or service (e.g., dry cleaning) will provide satisfaction or fulfill a need. Goods are tangible objects: things you can see and feel. Services are intangible actions: work done to satisfy or provide for others such as a catering service. Because the general economic meaning of consumer goods encompasses consumer services, in this book when the word *goods* is used it implies both goods and services. In recent years the growth in the number of new consumer goods has been astounding—distance learning classes, technology-based cellular phones and Internet access, specialty coffee shops and Internet cafés, the proliferation of e-mail, and so forth. As an explanation, one author wrote:

> Consumer goods became a language, defining, redefining, and easing relationships between friends, family members, lovers, and strangers. Cars and clothes gave identity to young and old, female and male, ethnic majority and minority, telling others who they were and how they expected to be treated. Cosmetics and candy expressed both rebellion and authority, thus providing people with an understanding of themselves in an otherwise indifferent and sometimes unfriendly world. Moreover, goods redefined concepts of the past and future and gave a cadence to the rhythms of daily life when people purchased antiques and novelties and when Christmas became a shopping "season." (Harris, 2000, p. 265)

Not all our memories of consumption are such good ones. Consumerism is not always nostalgic. Have you ever purchased something that disappointed? What was

Shopping is an economic and social interaction experience. In this photo, three generations are shopping together. (Courtesy of Getty Images, Inc.—Taxi. Photo by Ken Chernus.)

it that did not bring you the degree of satisfaction that you hoped? Was it a ticket to a lousy movie or a printer that was always breaking? Perhaps most frustrating of all is a car that is constantly in the repair shop.

Not only does consumption not guarantee happiness, but it can also bring misery as the car in the repair shop example shows. The dark side of the marketplace exists. For example, according to government estimates, there are over 14,000 fraudulent telemarketing firms in the United States, bilking consumers, usually the elderly, out of $40 billion a year. This illustrates that consumerism is a multifaceted experience; it is attractive and pleasurable, but at the same time it can be fraught with deception. **Injurious consumption** happens when individuals or families make consumption decisions that will have negative consequences, affecting their quality of life in the long run.

> Every year over 10 million American consumers suffer financial losses from their addiction to gambling. . . . There are currently 10 million alcoholics and 80 million cigarette smokers in the United States. . . . Every year 25,000 people die as a result of alcohol-related traffic accidents. . . . All of these disturbing and disturbed behaviors result from consumption gone wrong. (Hirchman, 1991, p. 4)

**Caveat emptor**, translated as "may the buyer beware," is an integral part of the study of consumer economics, and you will see sections of chapters devoted to problems in the marketplace. Even knowing the pitfalls, consumers forge ahead looking for new and better products and enjoying discovering the latest fashions and electronics. A case in point is the refrigerator from LG, a Korean company, that has multifunctions such as a television screen and a keypad built-in with Internet capabilities. Why should a refrigerator, an appliance using energy 24 hours a day, have only one purpose, to keep food cold? Constant striving for improvement is part of consumer behavior.

## Human Needs

According to psychologist Abraham Maslow, humans have basic needs that have to be met before moving up to higher order needs (see Figure 1.1). In his hierarchy of needs, physiological needs such as hunger and thirst have to be at least partially met before safety, love and belongingness, esteem and self-actualization can be fulfilled (Maslow, 1954). Multiply these levels of needs across the population and you begin to realize the enormity of human demands and needs.

Only about 35 percent of U.S. families consist of a husband, wife, and children under age 18.

The last census revealed there are over 292 million people in the United States and over 80 million households. By U.S. Census Bureau definition, a **household** includes the related family members and all the unrelated persons who share a housing unit. According to the census, the "traditional" household, consisting of a husband, wife, and children under age 18, makes up only about 35 percent of all U.S. families. Today, one in eight households is "diverse" or "nontraditional" and includes childless married couples, empty nesters, singles living alone, adult live-togethers of one or both sexes, or single-parent families. Consumerism is an integral part of the household, national, and world economies.

Although consumerism received a boost in the twentieth century, it is not a time-bound concept since, as previously mentioned, humans need to consume to exist. Advertisements etched in stone in ancient Rome, Greece, and Egypt indicate that consumers have desired comfort and style for centuries. What has happened is

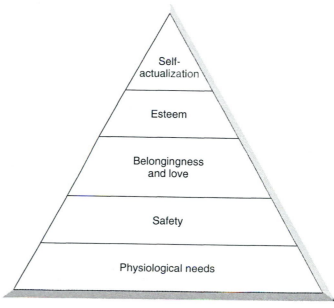

Maslow's Hierarchy of Needs

**Figure 1.1**   Maslow's Hierarchy of Needs. In this hierarchy of needs, basic physiological needs such as hunger and thirst have to be met before higher order needs.

that the rapid increase in worldwide populations and the market's response to meeting their needs has spurred the current surge in the growth of consumerism. Technological developments have played an important role as well, but it would be limited to say that consumerism is merely a result of increased populations and subsequent responses from merchandisers and advertisers. Consumerism is a way to define self, family, and community through the ownership of, use, and, ultimately, the disposal of goods. Owning a Lexus gives a far different message than owning a KIA.

## Demography and Demographics

Trying to calculate changes in human needs is an ongoing problem for marketers, educators, advertisers, public policy makers, and manufacturers. **Demography** is the study of human populations, including characteristics such as size, growth, density, distribution, movement, and other vital statistics. The world population is about 6.1 billion and the 50 most populous countries are listed in Table 1.1.

**Table 1.1**   The Eight Most Populous Countries

| | |
|---|---|
| China | 1,300 million |
| India | 1,000 million |
| United States | 292 million |
| Indonesia | 225 million |
| Brazil | 200 million |
| Russia | 190 million |
| Pakistan | 180 million |
| Japan | 175 million |

The World population is 6,344, 582,997 and growing

**Demographics** refer to data used to describe populations or subgroups. It is often applied to the study of consumers who are grouped by age, race, gender, income, educational level, marital status, zip code, renting versus owning housing, and number of children in the household. Marketers find these useful ways to segment consumers so they can reach them better than a scatter shot approach would provide, but they do not limit their advertising and distribution to demographic characteristics alone. Personality, tastes, and lifestyle (in essence, individuality) play a role in consumer behavior, as well as statistical groupings. Consumption of products gives people a way of identifying themselves in groups—displays, advertising, packaging all have ways of attracting certain groups based on the identity they have or that they seek. For example, a travel agency specializing in tours for those over age 55 may place ads in AARP publications or find that direct mailings to repeat customers works best. Another example is that short skirts sell better to younger women than to older women. If the demographic changes so that there is a shortage of young women then it seems prudent to consider this in clothing design if one is to reach the masses or to sway fashion in general. Failure to realize changes in demographics has been the downfall of many businesses.

## THE CONSUMPTION PROCESS

Consumer economics, since it has everyday uses for the individual, the family, and the household, is considered an applied social science. Something is going to happen rather than an idea that is merely discussed. In other words, consumer economics is not purely philosophical, it is a reality-based, action-oriented discipline. We are all consumers, we all have experience, and we all want to get better at this practical life skill. Because there are so many aspects to consumption, it can be thought of as a process. In terms of the individual making purchase decisions, the consumption process can be broken down into five parts:

1. Awareness
2. Thinking
3. Planning
4. Implementing/acting
5. Evaluating (see Figure 1.2)

The consumption process begins with an *awareness* that something is needed or desired. Perhaps the stimulus is that something has broken and needs to be replaced, or an occasion or event is coming up that requires new things or actions, or a new product has come on the market that could solve a problem or fulfill a need, want, or goal. Problems are questions or dilemmas and provide a stimulus to act. **Needs** are things that are deemed necessary, and **wants** are things wished for or desired, such as an expensive car. When consumers become aware, they

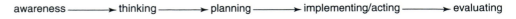

awareness ⟶ thinking ⟶ planning ⟶ implementing/acting ⟶ evaluating

**Figure 1.2**   Consumption Process.

begin to wonder about the benefits of a purchase and if certain services are better than others. For example, cars are not chosen simply to provide transportation; they provide status, identity, or prestige for their owners. Needs are few in number and very general (such as needing something to eat or a car to drive), but wants are limitless and often specific (such as a certain kind of food or car). Economic theory says that human wants are limitless although this concept can be challenged by individuals who say that the simpler life is better and that there is a level of contentment that can be reached. In other words, more is not always better. For instance, have you ever had too many clothes and needed to clean out your closet? Needs and wants are usually more immediate than goals. **Goals** are end-results, something you are striving for. Goals are based on values. The value of a good or service is subjective meaning that preferences differ dramatically between individuals.

After awareness of the need, want, or goal is complete, the process follows the next steps:

- *Thinking* is a mental exploration of the possibilities: weighing pros and cons and gathering information. Product image or features may be important at this stage.
- *Planning* revolves around deciding on an ordered set of steps of activities (Who do I need to call? Where do I need to go?)
- *Implementing/acting* means putting plans into action: doing something or going somewhere. This may involve sampling a product, visiting Web sites, getting an estimate or actually buying.
- *Evaluating* is the final step: a time for reflecting on outcomes. Individuals may ask, "Am I happy with what happened?" To be specific, "Do I like this brand of whole wheat bread or another brand better?" If I like another brand better, I'll act differently next time when I go to the grocery store. From the business point of view, evaluating can lead to repurchase behavior. Profitability increases with repeat business such as multiple haircuts over the course of several months versus a single visit so you may notice extra special treatment at the first visit. The wise barber or stylist tries to establish a relationship or rapport with the customer so that he or she will return and recommend the place to friends. This relationship can reduce choice for the consumer and makes purchasing decisions easier. By going to the same barber or stylist, the customer simplifies "the cognitive work and mental effort required for buying" (Hofacker, 2002, p. 46). "The benefits of choice reduction are especially prevalent when the product category is complex, where there is some risk associated with purchase, or if it is time-consuming or difficult for the consumer to specify his or her preferences" (Hofacker, 2002, p. 46).

To discuss the consumption process further, the steps of thinking and planning may seem like the same thing but they are not. Thinking involves a random set of thoughts: It is the accepting and rejecting of inputs and ideas, whereas planning is a more advanced stage of decision making wherein a specific course of action is set up. It is possible for someone to get stalled on the thinking stage and not move on to the others. Also, the process may be stopped at the awareness level if individuals are too busy to take the time to think or plan about a consumption decision. They may decide to wait before taking further steps.

## Place of Consumption

The first thought about consumption is that it takes place in a store between buyer and seller, but actually consumption takes place in a variety of settings, including at home, at school, at work, in the community, when traveling, and over the Internet. During the course of the day, you may consume water in several places: before leaving home, while walking or driving in the car, at lunch or dinner, and at work or school. Think how bottled water has revolutionized the places water can be consumed even to the point that an etiquette columnist was asked if it was all right for a guest to swig water from a bottle during a wedding. What do you think was the answer the columnist gave?

Businesses and governments consume as do individuals and households. There are all sorts of levels to consumption from the humble to the grand. It explains why in the marketplace there are bath towels that sell for $5 each and others that sell for $75: different markets, different consumers, different needs, and different incomes.

## Influences on Consumer Style

Consumers have a characteristic way of prebuying, buying, and postbuying that could be called their consumer style. It refers to patterns of behavior or ways of making financial decisions and acting. Factors that influence **consumer style** include:

1. Economics, the condition of national and worldwide economies during times of decision making. The economy is said to follow a business cycle (to be described in the next section).
2. History, the background of the person that influences the way decisions are made and acted upon. This includes immediate and past family history, and the history of the area or region or society in which the individual resides. Why is history an influence? The answer is that we can learn a great deal about consumer behavior from our past and from our general cultural past. In the *Life of Reason,* Santayan wrote, "Those who cannot remember the past are condemned to repeat it."
3. Culture, the groups and their behaviors or traditions that surround the individual or family. This group may be the overall culture and subcultures, including a consumer culture. Do you know what the manufacturer Lea & Perrins makes? You probably know it is Worcestershire sauce, a condiment. Can you even picture what the bottle looks like? It is a glass bottle wrapped in brown paper. This is part of a shared consumer culture.
4. Personality, the sum total of an individual's enduring traits, ways of relating, and characteristics, including reaction to risk and opportunity, likes and dislikes. Are you between the ages of twenty-five and fifty and interested in "natural," environmentally friendly products? If so, the Origins line of the Estee Lauder brand was created for you (Koehn, 2001).
5. Biology or environment, the physiology of individuals (their needs such as thirst, hunger) and the environment in which they live. You can see that the Origins line speaks not only to personality but also to environment. Successful products fulfill several areas of consumer needs or spheres of influence.
6. Technology, the methods and materials that individuals use to get what they want. Technology is a broad term that encompasses machines, techniques,

material objects, and processes. Certain individuals are more fascinated by technology than others. Entrepreneurs and inventors choose to lead in this area. Henry Ford led in automobiles and Michael Dell led in personal computers. Both were fascinated by new technology, constantly taking machines apart and reassembling them (Koehn, 2001).

7. Politics, voters, politicians, organizations, and bureaucrats affect the decisions that alter public policy.

To apply these influences to a specific purchase area, consider clothing. The style, color, and quality selected is affected by what is affordable and available (economics), what fits or has proven serviceable in the past (history), what others think or what friends wear (culture), what attracts (personality), what will keep a person warm or comfortable (biology or environment), what is the cut or weave (technology), and what sales tax is placed on the garment (politics).

Although, as stated earlier, consumers have a characteristic way of consuming, in recent times more variance in style has been observed by postmodernists. Whereas consumers in the past may have been fairly consistent in purchasing behavior (partly because they had fewer choices), in the twenty-first century there has been a more eclectic mix of goods that may sometimes seem inconsistent to outside observers.

> People do not always remain true to type. Depending on shifts of mood or shifts of situation, the same individual will behave like an upscale achiever one moment, like a downscale bargain hunter the next. The same consumer will buy part of her wardrobe at Bloomingdales and part at K-Mart. (Oglivy, 1990)

## ECONOMICS AND THE BUSINESS CYCLE

So far the chapter has focused on introducing consumerism and some beginning concepts about consumer behavior. Now, the chapter moves more into the economic side of consumption.

**Economics** is the study of or science of production, distribution, and consumption. It concerns itself with how wealth is created and managed in households, regions, countries, and businesses. Consumers participate in and react to movements in the economy. Their spending habits affect growth. One of the changes has been a decreased preference for shopping at malls. At least 300 older malls, each with one or two anchor stores, shut down between 1995 and 2001 (Greene, 2001). Another 300 to 500 such malls will follow suit. Why are so many older malls closing? Besides the economic problems the country is going through, another reason may be the glut in retail space. In 2000, the United States had 15 square feet of retail space in shopping centers for every man, woman, and child, up from 11 square feet in 1980 according to National Research Bureau data (Greene, 2001).

In 2000, there was 15 square feet of retail space for every man, woman, and child, up from 11 square feet in 1980.

Periodically, fluctuations occur in the **real gross domestic product (real GDP)** which is a measure of the value of all the goods and services newly produced in a country during some period of time, usually a year or a quarter, adjusted for inflation. **Inflation** is a steady increase in prices. **Deflation** indicates falling prices.

As a way to illustrate the usual expansions and contractions in the economy there is a **business cycle** (see Figure 1.3) made up of three stages:

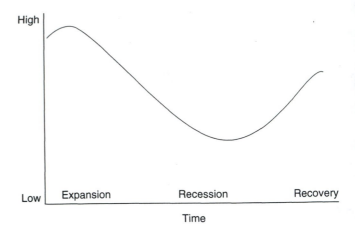

**Figure 1.3**    The Business Cycle. The economy goes through stages that tend to be cyclical. The stages reflect changes in employment, production, and consumption.

1. **Expansion**, the preferred stage in the business cycle, a period of prosperity, growth, higher output, low unemployment, increased retail sales and housing starts, in general economic activity, including investing, is growing, and interest rates are low or falling. With low interest rates, consumers find it easier to buy cars, homes, and other expensive goods on credit. For most of the 1990s, the United States was in a time of expansion.

2. **Recession**, a moderate and temporary decline or downturn in the economy. A recession is classically defined by the Bureau of Economic Research as a recurring period of decline in total output, income, employment, and trade, usually lasting from six months to a year and marked by widespread contractions in many economic areas. From 2001 to 2003, the United States was experiencing an economic slowdown. Consumer confidence declined and there were many layoffs; unemployment rose to 6.1 percent in June 2003. A very deep or prolonged recession is called a depression, and these are rare. The most notable one was the Great Depression of the 1930s which reached its greatest depth in 1933.

3. **Recovery**, the period in the business cycle when economic activity picks up, leading to expansion. Economic indicators show that when things are getting better, production and spending rises, consumer confidence improves, and employment picks up. Sometimes this stage includes a rise in interest rates. Signs of recovery were in evidence in 2004.

Although as illustrated these three stages run in a cycle, no one knows for sure how long each stage will last or how high or low the swings will go. Changes in the GDP are the main indicators, but unemployment and other factors play a role.

## Scarcity

Unlimited wants combined with limited supplies create **scarcity**, a condition in which there is an insufficient amount or supply, a shortage. Scarcity lies at the heart of production and consumption. A product may be in short supply, and the manufacturer cannot make enough of the product to meet consumer demand. For example, after the September 11, 2001, destruction of the World Trade Center in New York City and a section of the Pentagon in Washington, DC, there was a shortage of American flags in the United States. Demand far exceeded supply. It took several weeks for manufacturers and suppliers to catch up.

Scarcity exists on the consumer side as well. A consumer may not have enough money to buy what he or she wants. Scarcity often exists because we have unlimited wants but limited resources to pursue those wants. Scarcity is not the same as poverty. It can exist in a time of abundance and prosperity and it is relative to the individual. As we all know, some people are content living on very little, whereas others feel deprived if they cannot immediately get everything they want.

In economic theory, as long as a human need is not satisfied there is scarcity. In summary, scarcity is a normal part of life, unavoidable and individually defined, and it cycles and flows.

## Supply, Demand, and Equilibrium Price

The American flag shortage mentioned earlier is an example of a supply and demand situation. A worldwide shortage example is that of broadband Internet access. The demand far exceeds the supply and suppliers are hurrying up to catch up. According to Nielsen ratings systems, in the United States, Great Britain, and Canada, over 50 percent of the population has Internet access; worldwide about one-sixth of the world's population is online (*www.nua.ie*).

Over 50 percent of the U.S., Great Britain, and Canadian populations are online.

In economics, there are a number of theories that partially explain consumer reaction to prices. Some of these theories are elaborated upon in upcoming chapters, but for this introductory chapter, the most basic theory is that of **equilibrium price** which is reached when supply and demand are equal (see Figure 1.4). Scarcity affects supply. According to the **law of supply**, as the supply of a good or service goes up, the price comes down. In the **law of demand**, as the price of a good or service rises, the quantity demanded of that good or service falls. The price paid for goods and services reacts to these laws. For example, when a color goes out of style in furniture upholstery, goods in that color are less desired and the price decreases (the goods go on sale). Figure 1.5 gives more details about supply and demand, in particular what causes shifts in each. Supply represents the firms' side of transactions. Demand represents the consumers' side of transactions.

Prices based on supply and demand may be on actualities or only on perceptions. For example, in a natural disaster there may be plenty of gasoline available, but people may assume that is not the case and rush to the pumps to fill up. Word of mouth and news media can have a tremendous effect on people's perceptions.

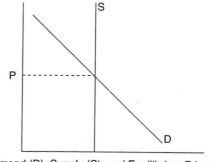

**Figure 1.4**   Demand, supply, and price are linked. A change in one affects changes in the others.

Demand (D), Supply (S), and Equilibrium Price (P)

Supply represents the firms' side of transactions.

Demand represents the customers' side of transactions.

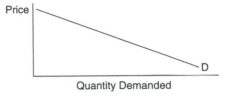

Supply shifts are due to:
- Number of competitors
- New inventions, "new and improved" driving out old
- Price of goods needed for production
- Future price expectations
- Government taxes, subsidies, legislation

Demand shifts are due to:
- Preferences
- Access: Ease of purchase
- Prices
- Number of competing buyers
- Consumer's ability to pay
- Expectations of shortages or rising prices
- Price of related goods that could be substituted (example, lamb chops cost more so person buys pork chops instead)

**Figure 1.5**   Supply and Demand Shifts.

An announcement of crop failures in peanuts will motivate consumers to buy whatever they perceive will be in short supply, such as peanut butter.

Figure 1.6 shows a diagram of how consumer demand affects supply and eventual resource use.

## SUPPLY, DEMAND, AND DEMOGRAPHICS

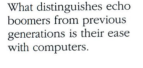

What distinguishes echo boomers from previous generations is their ease with computers.

Population changes affect consumption patterns. Demand can be explained as the relationship between price and the quantity demanded by consumers. If the number of consumers increases, then it follows that demand will increase and where populations choose to cluster makes a difference as well. Figure 1.7 shows an example of the spillover effect.

A successful supplier not only responds to changes but also anticipates buyers' changing preferences and, in the case of population shifts, responds to changes in movement patterns. Regarding U.S. population trends, during the first years of the twenty-first century there was a surge in the number of undergraduate students going to college, which affected demand for classes, dorm rooms, apartments, and the types of goods that people in their late teens and twenties buy.

Most readers of this book belong to the Generation Y or echo boomer generation, the 72 million people born between 1977 and 1994 (see Figure 1.8, unless

**Figure 1.6**   How Consumer Demand May Affect Supply and Eventual Resource Use.

**Figure 1.7**   How Moving Affects Others: The Spillover Effect.

otherwise noted the population figures given in this section are from the United States). This group peaked in 1988 when 3.9 million babies were born (the highest number since 1964). They are bringing another wave of high consumption through the nation as this generation goes through their teen years and early adulthood. What most distinguishes this group from previous groups is their computer fluency. Unfortunately, this group was coming of age when the country was going through tough economic times and more young American adults over age 18 were returning to the family nest. These young adults, called "boomerangers," were most likely to return home because of financial pressures (student loans, credit card bills, unemployment) or because they were marrying later. Nearly 4 million or 10.5 percent of the 25 to 34 age group (and 12 percent of those ages 25 to 29) were living in the family home (Gerider, 2001). This follows an historic trend: the number of boomerang kids rises when the economy sours. A November 2001 survey by Monstertrak.com found that 60 percent of college students planned to move back home after graduation and more than 20 percent will stay a year or more (Gerider, 2001).

The group called Generation X is composed of the 45 million people born between 1965 and 1976. As you can see from Figure 1.9, Generation X is a smaller group representing a shorter span of time than the groups before and after. This group cares about the environment; they like lower prices and a more functional look.

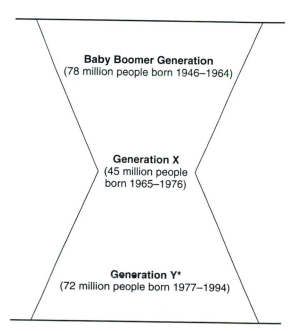

**Figure 1.8**   U.S. age distribution.
(Adapted from Kotler and Armstrong, *Principles of Marketing*)

*Also known as the baby boomlet generation. This group is still forming their preferences and behaviors.

At the other end of the spectrum, baby boomers (those 78 million born between 1946 and 1964) as they retire will require a different set of products and services. Companies have paid the most attention to the higher earners and more educated in this group. This attention was based on the notion that all things would go as planned and baby boomers would glide into a comfortable retirement. Instead what happened in 2001 was that there were massive layoffs that especially affected workers age 50 and older who not only lost their jobs but also their health insurance as well. Usually the ages 45 to 54 are the highest income earning years, but the recession made 50 to 64 year olds especially vulnerable (Nicholson, 2001). The point of presenting this information is not to depress the reader but to show that generalities can be made about consumption patterns by age group, but a marked upswing or downswing in the economy can change patterns overnight. If people, in any age group, feel vulnerable, they will change their spending and saving behaviors immediately unless they are in denial.

## Risk and Opportunity Costs

Two other economic concepts that greatly affect consumer purchasing behavior are risk and opportunity. Consumers weigh the risks and opportunities associated with decisions. An individual may be risk averse, risk attracted, or risk neutral.

**Risk** is the possibility or perception of harm, suffering, danger, or loss. In financial risk, this may include the fear of losing money in the stock market or from buying an inferior product. Most people are risk averse especially when it comes to their money. This is why discussions about how Social Security money should be invested or if consumers should be allowed to have more say in how their Social Security money should be invested turn into heated debate. Retirement is a time when people want to be secure and comfortable—no surprises.

The psychologist Abraham Maslow said that at any one time people are torn between growth and safety and that safety has the stronger pull. Given a choice, individuals are more drawn to the familiar and predictable. This is, of course, an overgeneralization, and it is difficult to completely type cast a person as risk averse, risk attracted, or risk neutral because much risk taking behavior is situational. Someone may be experimental when it comes to trying new food, but predictable when it comes to music or clothing. Usually, a risk averse person would be attracted to financial arrangements with fixed rates such as a fixed rate mortgage of 7 percent on a house versus an adjustable rate mortgage that could vary from 5 to 9 percent. They may be more worried about losing money than the prospect of gaining money. A risk attracted individual may be more drawn to the adjustable rate mortgage figuring the economy will go in their favor and the mortgage will stay at the lower end of the range and therefore be less costly than the fixed rate mortgage. A risk neutral individual could go either way. They are indifferent toward risk and uncertainty and would be drawn to expected rates of return.

Research indicates that women avoid risk more than men when it comes to investments. Women are more likely to say they are "careful with my money" (31 percent of women versus 24 percent of men), which is probably why they pick safer investments and let banks handle their accounts rather than keeping them with brokerages or mutual fund managers (Whelan, 2001). In the same nationwide study of 31,576 Americans, it was found that female college grads are more likely to put their money in investment products than those who graduated from high school.

In addition, there is true risk (i.e., a falling down bridge near collapsing) and there is perceived risk. What may be pleasurable to one person, such as a thrill ride at an amusement park, may be perceived as a dangerous risk to be avoided by another. In order to reduce perceived risk, individuals diminish their fears by finding out all they can about a product before purchasing it. For example, a person unsure about a thrill ride may watch it go around a few times and talk to others about it before standing in line to get on the ride. Another example is that people read about new car model ratings in *Consumer Reports* magazine or *Motor Trend* and talk with friends before purchasing a car. Another commonly used search mechanism to reduce risk is to gather information on the Internet.

Other types of risks include

- Time risk. Consumers do not want to waste time in finding and purchasing products.
- Security risk. Consumers may fear being a victim of crime, perhaps involving their credit card number or Social Security cards.
- Risk of privacy. Consumers may fear that their buying behavior or personal information is being reported and sold to companies.

**Opportunity** refers to a favorable outlook, a chance for progress, advancement, and action. Economics assumes that people will try to increase their satisfaction by taking advantage of opportunities. However, it is not always easy to tell when something is a risk or an opportunity such as a job offer in Idaho when you have lived all your life in Alabama. Is this the opportunity of a lifetime or is it a risky venture that will be regretted? Every choice made means that something else is given up. This is referred to in economics as **opportunity cost:** one alternative is selected over another and there is a cost attached to this choice. For example, Tiger Woods decided to drop out of Stanford University because he did not have the time to pursue his studies full time and golf full time. He joined the Pro Tour in 1996. He stunned the golfing world with huge victories in 1997, and by 1999 he was the top prizewinner on the Pro Tour. In Tiger's case, his scarce resource was time and taking a risk paid off.

Opportunity cost is related to the concept of trade-off. To get something desired, it is necessary to trade off something else because of scarcity (of time, of money, of energy). In **trade-offs,** something is sacrificed in order to obtain something else. Choosing to study one subject over another is an example of a trade-off, the maintenance of or improvement of a grade in the selected subject is the hoped-for outcome. Scarcity forces us to make these kinds of choices all the time. An economic principle is that if we worked harder and gave up leisure, we would produce more. Giving up one good or practice for another is the essence of trade-offs.

## Three Questions

Many of the previously mentioned examples are of an individual or personal choice nature, but large scale economies tackle similar issues. There are three problems or questions that economies must find a way to solve:

1. What is to be produced? Examples are trucks, television shows, computers, ice cream, and health care. A **product** is anything a consumer acquires or

Jubilant professional golfer Tiger Woods celebrates after hitting a hole in one on the fourteenth hole at the Greater Milwaukee Open. His decision to drop out of Stanford University to become a pro golfer is an example of opportunity costs, selecting one alternative over another. (Courtesy of AP/Wide World Photos.)

perceives to need. Over 15,000 new or improved products are introduced each year in grocery stores, not many will succeed.

2. How are these goods produced? Examples include what companies, what types of factories, and how much equipment, material, and labor are needed. International agreements such as NAFTA (North American Free Trade Agreement) have changed the level of competition and reduced international trade barriers. The Internet has also opened up exchange across borders. The general trend is toward freer exchange and less trade restraints which is usually a good thing for consumers. One of the few negatives is the problem of quality control since many countries in the world do not have strong consumer protection laws (i.e., copyright, trademark). Gucci purses, Louis Vuitton luggage, or CDs purchased abroad may be fakes.

3. For whom are the goods produced? Examples can range from the young to the old, from domestic markets to international.

## The Market Economy and Competition

Most economically developed countries, including the United States, Canada, Australia, Japan, and countries in Western Europe, are referred to as consumption societies. Consumers have a great deal of freedom to buy and sell products as they choose. In fact, people in consumption societies spend more time in consumption than nearly any other activity, including working and sleeping (both of which involve consuming). This is part of being a **market economy.** In a market economy, exchanges are controlled by marketplace forces of demand and supply rather

**A**                                                                                 **B**

Goods are produced and purchased for consumption. A: Courtesy of Getty Images Inc.—Stone Allstock. B: Courtesy of AP/Wide World Photos.

than by outside forces such as government control. This goes back to Adam Smith's philosophy that the market is a self-correcting mechanism; if left alone, it will function well. These exchanges do not exist in a vacuum, however, because untold numbers of dollars are spent on activities that encourage consumption such as attractive store environments, catalogs, and Web sites.

A market economy is characterized by the free exchange of goods and services in markets and by freely determined prices. This is contrasted with the **command or centrally planned economy** wherein most decisions about what, how, and for who to produce are made by those who control the government. An example would be the Soviet sphere for much of the twentieth century.

Connected to the market economy is the concept of **property rights**. These are the legal rights over the use, sale, and proceeds from a good or resource. Property rights are important because they allow people to buy and sell goods. If there were no property rights, anyone could take what you own and sell it. Imagine someone coming into your home, removing everything, and conducting a yard sale on your front lawn. Private property rights include the right to use, the right to protect, and the right to transfer use or ownership. These rights, however, are within the context of the greater society. For example, a homeowner cannot park a giant boat in his front yard if the homeowner's association of the street that he lives on prohibits it. If he lives in a rural area where there are no such rules, he can do what he wants.

In a total or absolute market economy, there would be no restraints placed on the economy by outside forces: There would be perfect competition and market sovereignty. Perfect competition means that many businesses could offer the same product at the same price. No company could be so large nor its brands so popular that they could ask a higher price.

## CONSUMER SOVEREIGNTY

**Consumer sovereignty,** mentioned earlier, refers to when consumers decide which goods will survive and to the idea that producers cannot dictate consumer tastes. Products do fall in and out of favor. Take the example of ketchup. Today, we are used to tomato ketchup but in the mid-nineteenth century walnut ketchup and mushroom ketchup as well as tomato ketchup were established seasonings in the United States (Koehn, 2001). Why did walnut ketchup and mushroom ketchup fall out of favor? Will they come back in style? As another example, people change their minds about what type of leisure activities they want to pursue. It is important to forecast trends in leisure because it is a $535 billion a year industry affecting fitness clubs, theme parks, marine and cruise industries, and motorcycle and motor sports businesses (Paul, 2001). Research indicates that the leisure activities on the rise include swimming, hiking, running, weight training, fishing, golf, hiking, and using aerobic machines. The activities on the decline include skateboarding, archery, surfing, and racquetball. When people are at home, the biggest leisure activities are reading, spending time with friends and family, and calling them on the phone. When they go out, the vast majority of Americans say eating out is their favorite leisure activity, and they plan to do more of it in the next two years (Paul, 2001).

The concept of consumer sovereignty is based on Adam Smith's philosophy that consumers should guide the economy, that *the consumer is king*. In many cases the consumer is king, but in looking at the total marketplace environment, consumer sovereignty does not always exist because of outside intervention such as government support for schools and postal services or government controls on imports and exports. For example, recent newspaper reports showed that the U.S. imports and sells far more Mexican beer than it exports because of consumer preference and policies making it difficult for U.S. beer to be delivered and sold easily in Mexico. So, each country sets up its own trade agreements and policies regarding imports and exports, and this greatly affects what the consumer can purchase. We do not live in a world where the only interaction is between the consumer and the market.

Sometimes, the government steps in to aid industry. For example, in 2001 the federal government gave billions of dollars to airlines to help bail them out when there was a decline in air traffic. In regional or national disasters, the normal balance of supply and demand is disrupted, and the government steps in to restore order and provide funds for rebuilding. This intervention is regarded as necessary for the good of the economy overall as well as for the good of the industry, employees, residents, or the region.

The United States waxes and wanes regarding how much intervention is needed. For example, in 2002 the federal government said they could not continue to bail out the airlines and aid lessened. Earlier, in the 1990s, a time of, for the most part, peace and prosperity, growth and expansion, the trend was toward less government intervention and an opening up of markets. This provided the climate for the passage of the international agreement NAFTA. During unsettled times the trend goes the other way, citizens turn internally looking to the government for increased control and protection.

# MONOPOLY

Government also becomes involved in the market economy by discouraging the growth of monopolies. The word "monopoly" comes from two Greek words meaning "single seller." A **monopoly** exists when there is only one producer and there is no substitute, such as there being only one airline or cruise ship line. The reason that monopolies are discouraged is that without competition, consumers may have no choice but to pay higher prices and it may discourage invention or the growth of new companies. The latter refers to high barriers to entry. New forces and businesses are discouraged. Rather than absolute, monopolies can be thought of as in degrees since it is rare for a monopoly to totally control a product or market. An example of a monopoly may be an electricity service in a particular area. It may not be practical to have competitors in this situation.

**Price** is the amount of money a person pays to buy or use a product. Setting the right price is essential in the consumer-market exchange. If a price is too low, it may indicate low quality; if it is too high, there will be few buyers. Price is affected by demand. For example, there is a higher demand for eggs at Easter time than at other times of the year. Sellers can decide whether to raise prices or to use increased holiday consumption as a ploy of attracting customers by reducing the price on eggs in the hopes they will buy other products in the store.

In consumer economics, a widely held principle is that *competition in the marketplace is good for consumers*. Sometimes it may not seem like much of a problem if a monopoly exists; a consumer may think I simply won't buy any more of that type of product (such as a food or drink item), but there are situations in which consumers have no choice such as a particular medicine that their doctor prescribes. If there are other brands or generic products, it would give the consumer a better range of choices and prices. In recent years, probably the most publicized monopoly case in the United States involved Microsoft.

A successful business has to have a thorough understanding of their competitor's goods, capabilities, and strategies. Part of their strategy may be to provide superior service, and other businesses will have to upgrade their customer services to compete.

## ECONOMIC SYSTEMS

To summarize the key point of the previous sections, it can be said that *for the most part we have a market economy*. In most ways, we are free as consumers to choose the products and services that we want. If we want to go to the store or go online to trade on eBay we do. If we choose not to purchase new clothes because we don't like the season's fashions, that is also consumer choice. A market economy is also referred to as **capitalism**, an economic system characterized by open competition in a free market. The ownership and control of resources and businesses are largely held by private individuals, and the forces of supply and demand are relied on to control the production of goods and services. Adam Smith called this perfect liberty which later became known as laissez-faire capitalism. Loosely translated it means hands off.

**Socialism** is an economic system in which the government (also referred to as "the state") centrally plans, owns, and controls most of the capital and makes decisions about prices and quantities. Capital refers to factories, stores, farms, and equipment. The degree of socialism varies by country. Scandinavian countries are generally regarded as more socialistic than the United States. Also, a country could have socialized medicine (such as Canada or the United Kingdom) but have a capitalistic structure in general. **Communism** is a social or an economic system in which nearly all capital is collectively owned, examples as of the writing of this book were North Korea and Cuba.

Since most of the world functions as a market economy, this economic system will form the backbone of this book. Today, most people and most nations prefer a high degree of consumer sovereignty.

## INTERNET AND E-COMMERCE

Economic systems cannot remain as isolated as they once were due to the high degree of the internationalization of business and the proliferation of the Internet. There is no question that the Internet has revolutionized the worldwide marketplace in terms of communication, entertainment, and exchange. The Internet provides an interactive medium as opposed to conventional venues of mass media such as TV, magazines, billboards, and radio. Mass media are unidirectional or one to many communication processes (Hofacker, 2000). The Internet provides a wide array of communication patterns between consumers and between consumers and firms.

The new buzz phrase in consumer marketing research is "**consumer mediated environments**" (CME) which refers to buying and selling over the Internet. **E-commerce** is a general term referring to exchange transactions that take place on the Internet. Examples are buying and selling goods, services, and information. This is in contrast to more conventional modes of exchange transactions, such as in-person, over the telephone, or by surface mail.

Characteristics of e-commerce include

- Pervasiveness of technology
- Speed
- Globalization

Many goods and services are sold on the basis of convenience and speed; buying over the Internet fulfills these needs. For example, at most universities you can buy your textbooks from the campus bookstore and have them delivered to your door or have them available for pickup rather than having to wait in long lines to find the books and purchase them. Campus bookstores had to do this in response to competition from Amazon and other online booksellers who were delivering books straight to dorm rooms and apartments.

E-commerce is such a huge concept that it is useful to break it into two parts:

1. *E-merchandise* is selling goods and services electronically and moving items through distribution channels, for example, through Internet shopping for groceries, cars, tickets, music, clothes, hardware, travel, books, flowers, or gifts.

2. *E-finance* is banking, debit cards, smart cards, banking machines, telephone and Internet banking, insurance, loans, financial services and mortgages online (Goldsmith and McGregor, 2000).

Of these, the most common uses of the Internet are for e-banking and for buying books, clothes, flowers, and gifts. Recently, there was a significant increase in more online car purchases (Forrester Research, 2001). As the media matures and as customers get more used to the idea, the list will expand to include items and services yet unforeseen.

Many stores have buildings and Internet sites. An example would be Britain's famous Harrods department store which has a large building in London and an Internet site (*www.harrods.com*). Internet retailers are referred to as e-tailers.

Although e-commerce has opened up new ways of trading, it is not without its risks, drawbacks, and critics. Some of the concerns center on the collection and dissemination of consumer information by marketers who participate in online retailing. Specific issues pertain to the privacy and security of consumer data and consumers' perception of such risks. Thirty-seven percent of online consumers say they would buy more online if they were not so concerned about privacy issues (Forrester Research, 2001). A more startling statistic was revealed in a survey by the UCLA Internet Project that found that 94.5 percent of consumers express some concern about credit-card security online. That number actually rose from 91.2 percent the previous year (Weber, 2001). The reality is that if a hacker steals your number and runs up your bill, you are out $50 at most if you report the credit card loss because of federal law. Banks will often let you off of the $50 charge as well. Credit card companies, banks, and consumer educators need to get this message out. Part of the reasons consumers are distrustful of computer transactions is that they know computers break, e-mail programs succumb to viruses, and Web pages deliver cryptic error messages. To allay fears it helps if consumers trust the companies they are dealing with and challenge any irregularities on their credit card bills. To protect consumers and online merchants, an innovation being tested is the use of a password, similar to the PIN codes used with ATM cards.

> When shoppers buy at a participating site, they will be prompted for the password. But the site won't ever see the secret code. Instead, it will be beamed to the credit card bank, which will then give the retailer an all-clear on the transaction. If it catches on, the approach could cut down on online fraud. (Weber, 2001, p. B1)

Issue: Should the government regulate online privacy?

A related concern is how much should government be involved in regulating online privacy. A nationwide survey revealed that 54 percent of respondents say government should regulate online privacy; this represented a decrease from the previous year of 61 percent (*Forrester Research,* 2001).

As may be expected, research studies indicate that higher levels of Internet experience lead to lower risk perceptions regarding online shopping (Miyazaki and Fernandez, 2001). In other words those using the Internet often perceive fewer risks than nonusers or less frequent users. Frequent users have found that their transactions have been protected and that the goods they ordered were delivered as expected. Much of the Internet shopping takes place during office hours and this phenomenon is being tracked internationally (*nua.com*).

In the third chapter there is more coverage on different types of media, including the Internet, and later in the book there is more coverage on legislation and regulation regarding maintaining privacy and security when buying and selling over the Internet. For this introductory chapter, the main point is that the use of the Internet is growing, and consumerism as we once knew it is rapidly changing. Economic growth increasingly depends on innovation and the spread of technology.

## SUMMARY

The study of consumer economics is about how people deal with scarcity and choose between alternative goods, services, and actions. Our task is to decide how to allocate limited resources to different competitive uses. Consumption has a purpose: it fulfills a need, want, or is used to fulfill or reach a goal. Consumerism is the belief that goods and services give meaning to individuals and their roles in society. According to Adam Smith, founder of modern economics, consumers guide the marketplace. The goods and services they produce and consume have more to do with the wealth of nations than silver and gold. This consumer power can be referred to as consumer sovereignty.

The chapter addressed the following questions:

Why consume?

Who consumes?

What affects consumption?

Consumption was explained as a process. The ever-changing nature of the marketplace and consumer demands has made consumer economics an increasingly necessary and important field to study. Given the demographic, economic, social, and technological changes in the world, the need for skilled consumption practices (more efficiency, less waste, risk minimalization, increased Internet access) at all levels has never been greater. The goal of reading this chapter is to feel part of the economy, to learn to think like a consumer economist (e.g., to understand why competition is good for consumers), to get an intuitive feel for how scarcity, choice, and economic systems interact.

## KEY POINTS

1. We are all consumers.
2. Consumption is a multistep process.
3. Everyone experiences scarcity, usually of time or money.
4. Scarcity leads to choice; a choice requires a consideration of opportunity costs or trade-offs.
5. Three questions that economies face are what, how, and for whom production takes place.

6. The business cycle has three parts: recovery, expansion, and recession.
7. The United States (and most of the world) has a market economy also referred to as capitalism. A market economy involves freely determined prices, property rights, freedom to trade, produce, and consume, and also includes a role for government.

## KEY TERMS

| | | |
|---|---|---|
| business cycle | demography | opportunity cost |
| capitalism | e-commerce | price |
| caveat emptor | economics | product |
| command or centrally controlled economy | equilibrium price | property rights |
| | expansion | real gross domestic product (real GDP) |
| communism | goals | |
| consumer economics | household | recession |
| consumerism | inflation | recovery |
| consumer mediated environment | injurious consumption | risk |
| | law of demand | scarcity |
| consumers | law of supply | socialism |
| consumer sovereignty | market economy | trade-offs |
| consumer style | monopoly | wants |
| deflation | needs | |
| demographics | opportunity | |

## DISCUSSION QUESTIONS

1. Consider the Duchess of Windsor who said, "I've been rich and I've been poor, rich is better." What do you think about that sentiment? In your opinion, what is the connection between happiness and consumption?
2. Tiger Wood's choice was to continue at Stanford or to potentially make millions of dollars by joining the golf Pro Tour. What would you have done?
3. Give an example of an opportunity cost in your own life. Why did you make the choice that you did?
4. A former head of Revlon said, "In the factory we make cosmetics, in the store we sell hope." What does this quote tell you about consumer needs?
5. Select one of the e-resource Web sites listed next. What did you find on that site?

## E-RESOURCES

The U.S. Census Report
www.census.gov

Government source, demographic, social, and economic data

| | |
|---|---|
| Electronic Commerce Policy www.ecommerce.gov | Government source, link to "Business America" about international trade and e-commerce |
| CNET www.cnet.com | News about e-business, computing, and the Internet |
| NUA Internet Surveys www.nua.ie | Research statistics on use of the Internet |

# REFERENCES

Cross, G. (2000). *An all-consuming century: Why commercialism won in modern America.* New York: Columbia University Press, p. 1.

*Forrester Research: Privacy issues inhibit online spending* (October 3, 2001), www.nua.ie.

Goldsmith, E., and S. McGregor. (2000). E-commerce: Consumer protection issues and implications for research and education. *Journal of Consumer Studies and Home Economics, 24* (2), 124–27.

Greene, K. (December 12, 2001). What a bleak Christmas may mean for older malls. *Wall Street Journal,* pp. B1, B8.

Greider, L. (December 2001). Hard times drive adult kids 'home.' *AARP Bulletin, 42* (11). Washington, DC.

Harris, D. (2000). *Cute, quaint, hungry and romantic: The aesthetics of consumerism.* New York: Basic Books, p. 265.

Hirschman, E. (1991). Secular mortality and the dark side of consumer behavior. In *Advances in Consumer Research XVIII,* ed. R. Holman and M. Solomon. Provo, UT: Association for Consumer Research, pp. 1–4.

Hofacker, C. (2000). *Internet marketing.* Dripping Springs, TX: Digital Springs, Inc., 8–9.

Hofacker, C. (2002). *Internet marketing,* 3d ed. New York: John Wiley.

Koehn, N. F. (2001). *Brand new: How entrepreneurs earned consumers' trust from Wedgwood to Dell.* Boston, MA: Harvard Business School Press, pp. 70, 260. Also quoted in Michael Dell with Catherine Fredman. *Direct from Dell: Strategies that revolutionized an industry.* New York: Harper Collins, 1999.

Maslow, A. (1954). *Motivation and personality.* New York: Harper & Row.

Miyazaki, A. D., and A. Fernandez. (2001). Consumer perceptions of privacy and security. *Journal of Consumer Affairs, 35* (1), 27–44.

Nicholson, T. (December 2001). You're out! More lose jobs, insurance. *AARP Bulletin, 42* (11). Washington, DC.

Oglivy, J. (1990). This postmodern business. *Marketing and Research Today,* February 4–21. See also E. C. Hirschman and M. Holbrook (1992), Hedonic consumption: Emerging concepts, methods, and propositions. *Journal of Marketing, 46,* 92–101.

Paul, Pamela (November 2001). Leisurely occupations. *American Demographics,* 14–15.

Smith, A. *An inquiry into the nature and causes of the wealth of nations,* 1776, as edited by Robert Heilbroner in *The essential Adam Smith.* New York: Norton, 1986, p. 284.

Swagler, R. (1994). Evolution and applications of the term consumerism: Theme and variations. *Journal of Consumer Affairs, 28* (2), 347–60.

Wansink, B, Brasel, A., and S. Amjad. (2000). The mystery of the cabinet castaway: Why we buy products we never use. *Journal of Family and Consumer Sciences, 92* (1), 233.

Wansink, B., and R. Deshpande. (1994). Out of sight, out of mind, Pantry stockpiling and brandage frequency. *Marketing Letters, 5* (1), 91–100.

Weber, T. (December 10, 2001). What do you risk using a credit card to shop on the net? *Wall Street Journal,* p. B1.

Whelan, David. (November 2001). Investing with care. *American Demographics,* 12–13.

# The Consumer Movement

In the 19th century novels we first see the caricature of capitalism:
the individual who lives for no other purpose than
maximizing his profits. How far this all is from Adam Smith.

William McGurn

**Learning Objectives:**

1. Trace the beginnings of the consumer movement.
2. Identify key presidents, writers, and scientists and their contributions to consumer protection legislation and reform.
3. Describe how the consumer movement changed from 1880 to present.

## INTRODUCTION

Adam Smith lived in the eighteenth century; by the nineteenth century, his writings about rational self-interest, freedom, and the marketplace were being challenged by a less noble approach to consumerism, that is, buy more to get ahead. "The expanding America of the post-Civil War era was the paradise of freebooting capitalists, untrammeled and untaxed. They demanded always a freehand in the marketplace, promising that in enriching themselves they would 'build up the country' for the benefit of all people. . . . Theirs is the story of a well-nigh irresistible drive toward monopoly" (Josephson, 1962).

In the United States we had a newly launched society, and as Mary Elizabeth Sherwood wrote in 1897, "the tendency to vulgarity is the great danger of a newly launched society." "Waves of immigrants brought their own manners to America, and on the frontier a spoon and fingers were sufficient for a tasty repast" (Crossen, 2001). In short, money and taste did not always go hand in hand, "as was demonstrated during the Gilded Age when wealthy American men collected diamond-encrusted daggers, and women carried 2,000 violet bouquets" (Crossen, 2001).

Smith promoted **rational self-interest** meaning that people will make choices that will give them the greatest amount of satisfaction at a particular time based on information they have at their disposal. As mentioned in the previous chapter not all consumption is based on reason, other factors come in to play such as status. **Conspicuous consumption** occurs when someone pays an extremely high price for a product for its prestige value leading to a much higher demand than a simple price-demand relation would indicate. A modern day example is when a consumer pays $200 for a designer name brand microfiber purse rather than $39 for a store brand microfiber purse. One of the difficulties in understanding rational self-interest is that there is a difference between it and being selfish. A person acting in their own rational self-interest is not necessarily selfish.

In the nineteenth century, more pragmatic views of life were evident. Many espoused that the main purpose was, as the opening quote shows, to maximize profits. Times were exciting but at the same time harsh, people relied less on families for support as the moved across oceans and across the country in their quest to establish new lives. The gap between the poor and the rich was growing. As a means of distinguishing rich from poor, conspicuous consumption gained in importance in clothes and homes. In cities, things were more crowded, people felt more competitive. Of course, in the nineteenth century you will find individuals who do not fit these generalizations, but an examination of novels and diaries in the nineteenth century reveal a decided switch in attitude from earlier times.

The reason it is important to begin this chapter on the consumer movement with a discussion of the nineteenth century is to provide a bridge between what Adam Smith and his contemporaries thought in the eighteenth century and what came about in the twentieth century. What we shall see is that the twentieth century brought another switch in attitude and historical events that necessitated increased government intervention in the form of subsidies and consumer protection. These previous developments and events led to the consumer climate in the twenty-first century which is filled with risks and opportunities.

## DEMOGRAPHIC AND CONSUMPTION SHIFTS

In 1776 the population of the 13 colonies was about 2.5 million (compare this with 292+ million today in the United States), and people were highly self-sustaining and individualistic—most lived in rural areas. By 1890, nearly 40 percent lived in cities. In 1776, pioneers wanted freedom and independence and were mostly self-sufficient, but by the 1890s citizens had less personal control over the production of goods and relied more on big companies for basics like food and soap. While this transition was taking place, there was a period of dangerous, untested products being sold to unsuspecting consumers. This dangerous period led to the consumer protection legislation discussed in this chapter.

The trend toward reliance on outside companies and businesses for our basic needs continues. Buyers today are more removed from the production of goods than ever before and confused by the array of products available and most specifically an understanding of how they work. Consider this perspective given by Daniel Harris, author of *Cute, Quaint, Hungry and Romantic: The Aesthetics of Consumerism:*

> My life is suspended above an abyss of ignorance. Virtually nothing I own makes sense to me. What happens when I flick on my light switch? Why does my refrigerator keep my food cold? How does my answering machine record the voices of my friends? When I delete a paragraph on my word processor, what makes it disappear and where in the world does it go? In the interest of saving time, as well as out of pure laziness, I, like most people, have deliberately chosen to leave these questions unanswered. . . . I live quite happily hemmed in on all sides by an impenetrable wall of technological riddles. (2000, p. ix)

During wartimes concerns about consumerism tend to take a backseat as the focus shifts to foreign policy over domestic policy. But, during quieter more prosperous times, a crisis such as massive illness or death caused by infected hamburgers or tampered with medicine bottles rallies the cause for consumer protection. A well-publicized safety problem or court case garners public support for reform.

## CONSUMERISM AND THE CONSUMER MOVEMENT DEFINED

As explained in Chapter 1, consumerism is defined as the understanding of self in society through goods. The **consumer movement** refers to policies aimed at regulating products, services, methods and standards of manufacture, selling, and advertising in the interests of the buyer. Regulations can be voluntary by industry or written laws or statutes. The movement involves not only policies but also the issues and the leaders that brought to the public the need for regulations. The objective of the consumer movement is to ensure that consumers pay a fair price for safe, effective, environmentally-sound, and need/want-satisfying goods and services.

"A narrow definition of the consumer interest might deal solely with safe, reasonably priced and accurately labeled products. To its credit the consumer movement has never defined the consumer interest so narrowly" (Aaker & Day, 1982, p. 32).

## CONSUMER MOVEMENT WORLDWIDE

For simplicity's sake, most of the coverage in this chapter is on the consumer movement in the United States. The United States is a recognized leader in consumer legislation, product testing, and advocacy. However, most countries also have a consumer movement history (meaning a progression of legislation designed to protect consumers and promote fair dealing in the marketplace) so that to be most accurate the consumer movement should be described as a worldwide movement.

One of the linkages between countries is that the substances most likely to be regulated in any country are food and drugs. Another common thread is legislation regarding labeling. For example, the Swedish system of labeling requires labels to describe the main characteristics of the product in easily understood language in under 200 words. Another linkage between countries is that legislation adopted in one country often leads to the adoption of similar legislation in another. As an example of this, in 1893 England passed a general law entitled the Sale of Goods Act that stated that whenever a buyer expressly or by implication makes known to the seller the particular purpose for which the goods are required, there is an implied expectation that the goods sold will be reasonably fit for their intended purpose. England also passed the Adulteration of Food and Drugs Act in 1872, many years before a similar act was passed in the United States. The United Kingdom continues to be a leader in safe food regulation and consumer protection in general.

Another linkage between countries is that news of a consumer fraud area or health risk spreads from one country to another. Information is borderless. Also consumer courses are commonly taught in many schools and universities around the world.

A further linkage is that countries that share borders such as the United States with Canada and Mexico usually set up cooperative agreements because so many goods transverse borders and workers cross borders for employment. In Europe there are many examples of cooperation between countries, especially those that share borders which may be rivers or coastlines, regarding water quality/pollution, fishing rights, and transportation issues.

As the global market grows and more goods transverse borders and are manufactured in several countries, more international cooperation and agreement will be sought on quality, labeling, trademark, copyright, finance, and safety issues. An example of international cooperation is the adoption of euro coins and notes replacing the mark, franc, and other currencies as legal tender in 12 European countries in 2002.

International consumer conferences and world trade conferences are held regularly to discuss issues, research, and policies. The *International Journal of Consumer Studies* based in the United Kingdom is a leading academic journal with authors and subscribers throughout the world. Names of other consumer journals are listed in Appendix B.

## DECADES OF CONSUMERISM

In the following sections, information is given about the lifestyles of the times and the consumer legislation that took place. The growth of the consumer movement is evidenced as are leaders and issues.

### 1880–1900

In the United States, the turn of the century was a time of great promise called "the gilded age." Railroads, appliances, and indoor plumbing became more common. Immigrants came in droves. The flow of immigrants after 1880 came from the Orient and Mexico, as well as from Eastern and Southern Europe and Russia, adding diversity to all aspects of American life, including religion and diet. An American style of manners, home design, and cuisine distinct from Western Europe developed. Life became easier for most, but not for all. To name just a few of the problems: coal miners worked under appalling conditions, gold rushes and land rushes often left people broke and stranded, and the Native American Nations were systematically moved against their will further west to reservations (Schlereth, 1991).

> From 1880–1900, the middle class grew. It was not unusual for middle class households to have servants or at least a hired girl in to do the laundry once a week. Domestics who lived in received a room usually in the attic or near the kitchen, board, a small wage, and sometimes used clothes. (Schlereth, 1991)

There was no income tax so a few very wealthy families emerged unfettered. They built palatial mansions with over 200 rooms, including Vanderbilt's "Biltmore" in Asheville, North Carolina. As of the writing of this book, this home is still the largest private home in the United States (although open to the public for tours it is owned by the Vanderbilt family). The Vanderbilt fortune was built on steamships.

The expansion of the United States: Conestoga wagons pulled by horses in a land rush circa 1910s. (Courtesy of Getty Images Inc.—Image Bank.)

Other famous rich and powerful men included J. P. Morgan (railroads, finance, and banking), Andrew Carnegie (steel), and John Rockefeller (oil). Their influence on the rise of industry and capitalism in this country cannot be overestimated.

There were a lot of food fads and **hucksterism** (extreme promotion) from 1880–1900. Food fads, including diet fads such as fasting, miracle foods, and Fletcherism (ritual overchewing of food), abounded. Fletcherism is named after Horace Fletcher who believed that chewing food 30 times or more would help people digest their food more easily and use it more effectively. Many patent medicines contained alcohol which is why they gave patients "a lift." Through school and community classes, home economists and dietitians stepped in to give a sensible voice to nutrition. With the growth of railroads, American consumers had far more access to a variety of fresh fruits and vegetables. So, in time the American diet became broader, relying less on meat. John Harvey Kellogg and C. W. Post launched their breakfast cereal empires in Battle Creek, Michigan. Kellogg recommended large doses of bran, granola, and graham crackers. Post developed Grape-Nuts (1898) and Post Toasties. Kellogg challenged Post Toasties with his own version named Kellogg's Toasted Corn Flakes.

## 1900s

In the twentieth century materialism and consumerism became more complex. The change began in the early part of the century when inventors and businesses brought many new goods to the market. There was less domestic help, women's roles began to change, and suburban and small town living replaced rural living for the masses. The former manners and ways of living including "calling cards, debutante balls, morning coats and finger bowls gave way to backyard barbecues, cocktail buffets and BYOB parties" as the century progressed (Crossen, 2001).

Early consumer protection legislation centered around the control of trade and monopoly and of products closely related to the home, namely, food and drugs. It is difficult to put consumer protection legislation into categories by decade because often the groundwork is laid in one decade and the legislation comes about in the next or even a later decade. A case in point is the fight for better food quality led by Harvey Wiley.

Because of his pioneering efforts, *Wiley is often called the founder of the modern consumer movement.* To give you some idea of his background, he began his career as a chemistry professor at Purdue University. He resigned his post to go to work for the Indiana Department of Agriculture. While there he tested the ingredients in bags of chemicals purchased by farmers to improve soil. From this experience he went a step further and thought that consumers should also have food products tested and took this quest to the U.S. Department of Agriculture. His role was to determine the safety of the U.S. food supply. In the 1880s he circulated his findings among other professionals, and in the 1890s he went public with his research, urging consumers to join in a campaign aimed at getting Congress to initiate laws on food quality.

**Historical Perspective.**   To set Harvey Wiley and his work in historical perspective, at the turn of the century things were developing so fast that there were very few regulations to manage production and distribution in a consistent way. Food was the largest expense for the factory laborer and for many middle-class families, which is different from today when housing is usually the most expensive item. So, the expense and purity of food was especially critical to the well-being of individuals and families. Inventions that we now take for granted had their start during these times: the airplane, the automobile, motion pictures, electric lights and appli-

Harvey Wiley, the founder of the consumer movement, was a pure food reformer. He encouraged the packaging of food to keep it clean. (Courtesy of the U.S. Food and Drug Administration.)

ances, radio, canned soups, detergents, and bottled soft drinks. Let us take, for example, the evolution of Coca-Cola.

> On May 8, 1886, the soft drink was invented by the Atlanta druggist John Pemberton primarily as a headache cure. He and a partner named it Coca-Cola because its ingredients included extracts derived from Peruvian coca leaves and African cola nuts (Schlereth, 1991).

> By 1891, it was one of the most popular soft drinks in the United States, and Asa Candler bought controlling shares.

> Between 1891 and 1929, Coke gained national distribution, selling for a nickel a bottle.

> By 1929, Coke was sold in 66 countries.

> In late 1930s, Pepsi-Cola became a serious challenger. The main way Pepsi challenged Coke was by selling at a lower price.

Coke and its competitors raised the question: Are brand names and advertising important? Yes, they are. "Coca-Cola stands today as the second most widely understood term in the world, after okay" (Tedlow, 1990, p. 24). The basic goal of the advertising campaign was to make consumers think of Coke when they were thirsty and to assure them that Coke was the best choice to quench that thirst (Tedlow, 1990, p. 48).

When Coca-Cola came of age, the timing could not have been better. Prosperity, affluence, and expansion ruled. Americans had more purchasing power than ever before and a growing array of goods to choose from and they also had more free time. The six-day workweek was common in 1900. Between 1900 and 1930 Americans extended their time in school going beyond the eighth grade, finishing high school became more the norm, and more students went on to college. More time in school meant more time for leisure, increased exposure to peer pressure, and a better educated citizenry. Home economists taught food and consumer classes in schools and communities and prepared pamphlets for the poor, based on the theory that educated consumers could combat high prices (Strasser, 1989). They publicized pure-food concerns in their classes (Strasser, 1989).

Another invention, the automobile, liberated middle-class youth as well as families. In short, in the early twentieth century to consume took on whole new meanings and luxury was part of it (Cross, 2000). "Materialism became Americanism" (Schlereth, 1991, p. 302).

However, before we go any further, it should be pointed out that laboratory testing methods in the late nineteenth and early twentieth centuries were primitive compared with today. In 1902, in order to test food additives, Wiley set up a group called the "Poison Squad." The squad was made up of healthy young adults, mostly college students, who ate unadulterated food and also ate the same diet with food additives over a five-year period. He compared their weight and physical condition and found that preservatives readministered continuously in small doses negatively affected their digestion, appetite, and general health. "The men, of course, knew they were eating potential poisons. They didn't know, however, which foods contained the substances. At first borax was added to butter, to which the men developed a sudden distaste. Wiley then tried it in milk, meat, and coffee. Borax is a hydrated sodium borate (borate is a salt of boricacid used as a preservative). Evidently, as the men determined which food contained the substances, they began eating less of it and eventually avoided that food altogether" (White, 2002, p. 14). Wiley observing this eventually changed to putting preservatives inside gelatin capsules. The Poison Squad became a sensation with the press and the public. Reporters were interviewing the chef through a basement window. Wiley decided he better cooperate so he ended up sharing the details of the experiments with reporters. The experiments stopped when the men couldn't function or work. His efforts led to the regulation of food additives. What happened to the Poison Squad? There are no scientific reports, but anecdotal reports indicate that none were harmed. William O. Robinson of Falls Church, VA, a member of the Squad, lived to be 94 years old.

Not everyone backed Harvey Wiley's quest for better food safety. Some business groups said his work was antibusiness—even anti-American.

Wiley became the symbol of food and drug reform. Reformers were interested in two main issues: fraud and poison. The kinds of frauds included the extension of flour, mustard, and ground coffee with cheap fillers, including sawdust and chalk (Strasser, 1989). Besides the alcohol already mentioned, patent medicines were found to contain cocaine and opium.

His results caught the attention of the American Medical Association (AMA) who began analyzing drugs and medicines. Not everyone rallied behind Wiley and the AMA; many business groups said the research was antibusiness and even anti-American. Business was a tremendous force during this era. It was the golden age of national name brands such as Ralston Purina and Quaker Oats. Improvements were made in transportation, advertising, packaging, machinery, and corporate growth and coordination (Cross, 2000, p. 31). As an example, cereals were no longer just breakfast foods. They were promoted as having all kinds of health benefits, including inspiring confidence, providing a good start to one's day. So, Wiley was up against a formidable enemy. He persevered and his work paved the way for the Pure Food and Drugs Act of 1906 which was considered the first federal

The Pure Food and Drugs Act of 1906 was the first federal law in U.S. history specifically enacted to protect consumers.

The Poison Squad. (Courtesy of the U.S. Food and Drug Administration.)

law in U.S. history specifically enacted to protect consumers. This act dealt with the production, transportation, and sale of food and drugs in the United States.

**Upton Sinclair and President Theodore Roosevelt.**　　Another piece of legislation came to the forefront, but the source was not the laboratory, but a stirring novel written by a journalist. In 1906, public uproar over the expose of the Chicago meat-packing industry depicted in the novel *The Jungle* by Upton Sinclair led to the passage of the Meat Inspections Act. Sinclair graduated from the College of the City of New York in 1897 and went to graduate school at Columbia University. He supported himself by journalistic writing, and *The Jungle* was his sixth novel. His purpose was to write about immigrant families and their struggle but his story of the squalor and impurities in processed meats aroused widespread public indignation. He said, "I aimed at the public's heart and by accident I hit in the stomach." Here is a passage from the book:

> There was never the least attention paid to what was cut up for sausage; there would come all the way back from Europe old sausage that had been rejected, and that was mouldy and white—it would be dosed with borax and glycerine, and dumped into the hoppers, and made over again for home consumption. There would be meat that

American author Upton Sinclair writing by the light of his desk at home in California. His most famous book was *The Jungle,* which exposed wrongdoing in the meat packing industry. (Courtesy of Getty Images Inc.— Hulton Archive Photos. Photo by Murray Garrett.)

had tumbled out on the floor, in the dirt and sawdust, where the workers had tramped and spit uncounted billions of consumption germs . . . rats were nuisances and the packers would put poisoned bread out for them, they would die, and then rats, bread, and meat would go into the hoppers together. (p. 136)

Sinclair became known as a **muckraker** which is a term for writers, politicians, journalists, and public speakers who search out and expose political or commercial corruption. *The Jungle,* which is still in print today, was first published at Sinclair's own expense and became a best seller. He wrote more books, including *Oil!* (1927) which was based on the Teapot Dome Scandal and *Boston* (1928) which was based on the Sacco-Vanzetti case, but none had the enduring impact of *The Jungle*. His works were popular abroad, including in Russia before and after the Revolution of 1917. In later years he ran as Democratic candidate for governor of California and lost. He was known throughout his life as a fighter for social causes. Sinclair was not alone in his crusade. He was joined by many others who formed the first Consumer's League in 1891. In 1899, this was followed by the National Consumers League that fought for justice in the marketplace. What was happening was the development of a consumer consciousness. There is no question that consumer consciousness—through organizations, books, the press, and word of mouth—was raised during this era.

President Theodore Roosevelt, writer, rancher, explorer, and soldier whose years in office were 1901–1909, was outraged by *The Jungle* and called for an investigation just as he had earlier by assigning eminent chemists to review Wiley's work (Strasser, 1989). Food reformers had a friend in Roosevelt who had testified before a Senate investigating committee that he would just as soon as eaten his old hat as the canned food that, under a government contract, had been shipped to the soldiers in Cuba during the Spanish-American War (Downs, 1963, p. 344). The investigation of the Chicago meat-packing industry revealed that the book did not exaggerate. In fact, conditions were worse than Sinclair had reported. Based on this Roosevelt joined Congress in calling for federal legislation to correct the matter. On June 30, 1906, he signed both the Pure Food and Drugs Act and the Meat Inspection Act.

Theodore Roosevelt, a Republican, is known as a president who expanded the powers of the federal government on the side of public interest in conflicts between big business and big labor. In 1902 he established a Bureau of Corporations with powers to inspect the books of all businesses engaged in interstate commerce. He was also a trust-buster, bringing suit against 44 major corporations during his presidency.

His most successful suit was against the Northern Securities Company using the Sherman Anti-Trust Act which was passed in 1890 but largely ignored until Roosevelt invoked its power. **Antitrust laws** prevent business monopolies. They are aimed at establishing and maintaining competition so that consumers get fair prices and goods in adequate quantities. The rights of buyers and competitors fall under the general category of **common law,** based on custom, which is the unwritten system of law that is the foundation of both the U.S. and English legal systems (excluding Louisiana whose laws are based on Napoleonic Code). The Sherman Anti-Trust Act made monopoly and price fixing illegal so that firms are prevented from unfairly harming their competitors. Roosevelt is considered a leader in the modern concept of consumer protection. He was first and foremost a crusader, a person

Theodore Roosevelt, the twenty-sixth president of the United States, sitting at his desk working. He was a champion of consumer rights, and an antimonopolist. (Courtesy of Getty Images, Inc.—Hulton Archive Photos.)

who overcame physical weakness in his youth, to become a lifelong competitor and adventurer.

In 1908 the first court case using the Pure Food and Drugs Act was tried. The product under investigation was deemed worthless. It did not cure the headaches it was supposed to nor did its usage make consumers more intelligent. The manufacturer was ordered to change the label and was charged a $700 fine. As is common, this fine was a mere slap on the wrist as the manufacturer had already made millions of dollars. This is an ongoing problem in consumer protection that the fines are often minuscule compared with the profits. By the time an advertisement is pulled or a company sent to court, they have already made all the money they set out to make. Another problem is that corporate lawyers are usually better paid and have more staff support than government lawyers, which makes for uneven battles.

## 1910s

More consumer legislation followed. In 1914 the Federal Trade Commission (FTC) Act was passed to enforce antitrust laws and to spell out unfair methods of competition including deceptive advertising. The FTC, for example, can issue a **cease-and-desist order** which is an administrative or judicial order ordering a business to cease "unfair or deceptive acts or practices." For a listing of key consumer laws passed during 1880–1929 see Box 2.1. Also in 1914 Christine Frederick published *The New Housekeeping: Efficiency Studies in Home Management* which extolled the virtues of an orderly, labor-saving home and the need for more packaged goods and fairer deals in the marketplace. She testified before Congress on behalf of consumers.

---

**BOX 2.1    Key Consumer Legislation 1880–1929. During this time period over 50 consumer laws were passed in the United States, here is a sample:**

1887 Interstate Commerce Act
Power to regulate commerce was reserved to the States.

1890 Sherman Anti-Trust Act
Prohibits monopolies and price fixing, encourages competition.

1906 Pure Food and Drug Act
Prohibits adulteration of food and drugs and mislabeling of such sold in interstate commerce. Requires disclosure of narcotics and alcohol contents on patent medicine labels. Prohibits manufacturers from claiming ingredients that are not present.

1906 Meat Inspection Act
Provides for meat inspection. There had been an earlier act in 1891 that set up the Federal Meat Inspection Service.

1914 Federal Trade Commission Act
Prohibits deceptive advertising and unfair and deceptive trade practices. The FTC Act was used in the battle against trusts. Examples of early trusts (combinations of firms that got together to reduce competitions and control supplies and/or prices in an industry or region) included sugar, whiskey, matches, and fuel.

---

The Federal Bureau of Standards established a national system of weights and measures; as its name implies it standardized how goods were weighed and sold. To raise consumer awareness, at food expositions and state and county fairs consumers were shown measuring devices with false bottoms and nonregulation size milk bottles and bushel baskets (Strasser, 1989, p. 262).

Other developments include the establishment of the Better Business Bureaus (BBBs) in 1912 which discouraged dishonest business practices. In 1913 the Sixteenth Amendment to the U.S. Constitution was passed giving Congress the right to collect income taxes. The Amendment stated, "The Congress shall have the power to lay and collect taxes on income." The first tax was only one percent of income. By 1915, to be middle class meant to have electricity, and the expression "chain" store came into being. Chain stores that bought in bulk passed savings on to consumers. It was more common for people to eat cereal out of a box for breakfast instead of the previous home-cooked breakfast of beefsteak, bacon and eggs, fried potatoes, wheatcakes and sausage, porridge, donuts, and fruits (Schlereth, 1991).

In 1917, the United States became involved in World War I and concern switched to international affairs over domestic ones. The war led to a quiet period in the consumer movement.

*The Sixteenth Amendment was added to the U.S. Constitution in 1913 allowing for the collection of income tax.*

## 1920s

The decade began with relief that the war was over. Parties, extravagant lifestyles, gambling, bobbed hair, and flapper dresses marked the first years. Consumer incomes rose steadily while prices remained stable. However, by 1928 discontent was expressed in *Your Money's Worth* by Stuart Chase and F. J. Schlink. The authors exposed false advertising and high-pressure sales techniques. They called for more testing of products and improved standards. As a result in 1929 Consumers'

Research, Inc. (of which Schlink became technical director) was formed to perform testing work. Although there was a dearth of consumer protection legislation during this decade, the government was actively involved in testing the effectiveness of "germ-killing" products and enforcing the 1906 Food and Drugs Act, seizing defective food and drugs before they were shipped. In October 1929 the stock market crashed in the United States, and a depression began not only in this country but also worldwide. A **depression** is characterized as a drastic and long-lasting decline in the economy with high unemployment, falling prices, and decreasing business activity.

## 1930s

The lowest point of the depression was in 1933. Although there was a panic and a run on the banks in late 1929, no one really knew what was happening until well into the 1930s, and more important at first no one really knew what to do about it. There was no question that people lost faith in American industry and in American banks.

> The Depression hit America like a typhoon. One half the value of all production simply disappeared. One quarter of the working force lost its jobs. Over a million urban families found their mortgages foreclosed, their houses lost to the bank. Nine million savings accounts went down the drain when banks closed, many for good.
>
> Against this terrible reality of joblessness and loss of income, the economics profession, like the business world or government advisers, had nothing to offer. Fundamentally, economists were as perplexed at the behavior of the economy as were the American people themselves. (Heilbroner and Thurow, 1998, p. 30)

**Economist John Maynard Keynes.**   During these troubled times, English economist John Maynard Keynes's (pronounced "canes") published in 1936 *The General Theory of Employment, Interest and Money,* a more complicated and technical book than Adam Smith's *The Wealth of Nation.* It had a central message that was easy to grasp that economic activity in a capitalist system is determined by the willingness of its entrepreneurs to make capital investments (Heilbroner and Thurow, 1998). Sometimes this willingness is blocked, and the import of his theory was that if there is no self-correcting property in the market system, such as prolific business investment to keep capitalism growing, other solutions have to be found. The solution in this case was increased government spending on public works. Since his book was published during the depression, it influenced President Franklin D. Roosevelt and his economic/political advisors and the policies forthwith. Keynes influence extends to today. He founded a school of thought called Keynesian economics that emphasizes the role government plays in stabilizing the economy.

**President Franklin D. Roosevelt.**   Franklin Delano Roosevelt (FDR), a Democrat, who became president in 1933, rose to the challenge that the depression presented. As evidence of his popularity and effectiveness, he is the only president to be reelected three times. His years in office were 1933–1945 (a complete list of U.S. presidents and their terms in office are given in Appendix C). He used the federal government's powers to bring about a national economic recovery which was called the New Deal, and he was president during World War II. Therefore, during his administration his policies were not of the hands-off kind of government rec-

FDR signed into law the 44 hour workweek in 1938 and reduced it to 40 hours in 1941.

ommended by Adam Smith; quite the contrary he thought that the crisis demanded a more hands-on approach, and Keynes's book provided the theoretical background for much of the approach that was taken. Examples of Roosevelt's policies include signing the Fair Labor Standards Act in 1938 which established the 44-hour workweek. In 1941 this was reduced to the standard 40-hour workweek that we use today.

By way of background, Roosevelt went to Harvard and studied law at Columbia University. In 1905, he married Eleanor Roosevelt, an outspoken consumer advocate and the niece of Theodore Roosevelt. In 1910 he was elected to the New York Senate and later became governor of New York. He rose up through the ranks, and as president he promoted sweeping economic programs that provided relief, loans, and jobs through federal agencies.

During his years in office many consumer laws were passed. He called for the passage of the Food, Drug, and Cosmetics Act of 1938. This act amended the 1906 act by adding cosmetics and allowing inspectors to remove dangerous products from store shelves while tests were being completed. Congressional leaders and Roosevelt were horrified by the disfigurements, and nearly 100 deaths caused by the new sulfa wonder drug named Elixir Sulfanilamide.

There were other problem products as well. The respectability in the use of cosmetics and beauty salons grew tremendously in the 1930s, but with it came abuse

President Franklin D. Roosevelt raises his hat while riding in a convertible with his wife Eleanor Roosevelt. They were both consumer activists who fought for better working conditions and product safety. (Courtesy of Corbis/ Bettmann.)

in the form of face creams that burned and dyes that caused hair to fall out. As an example, a "once pretty matron was blinded by Lashlure, an eyelash dye" (Aaker & Day, 1982, p. 27). Adding fuel to the fire was the 1933 *100,000,000 Guinea Pigs* by Arthur Kallet and F. J. Schlink. They introduced the public to a number of cosmetic, food, and drug problems, including the use of a well-known rat poison as the active ingredient in the depilatory cream, Koremlu. The book gave the following case first documented in the Journal of the American Medical Association about a woman, aged 24, who

> came to the Cleveland Clinic complaining of severe pains over the soles of both feet and ankles, weakness of both feet and legs, and intense burning of both feet. . . . Four and one-half months prior to entering the clinic, the patient had first noticed intermittent epigastric [abdominal] pains which gradually increased in severity to sharp, cramp-like pains throughout the entire abdomen. . . . The patient had become very nervous, cried easily, had lost about ten pounds, and felt continually tired. . . .
>
> It was discovered that she had been using a depilatory cream, "Koremlu," nightly for the preceding five months, beginning its use two weeks before the appearance of the first symptoms. A quantity sufficient only to cover the upper lip and the chin had been used on each occasion. (p. 82)

Kallett and Schlink made the point that:

> Purchasers of ordinary foods and drugs have little enough assurance of safety, despite the control (as some term it) provided by the Federal Food and Drugs Act and by various state agencies. The purchaser of cosmetics has no protection whatever. No Federal agency has jurisdiction over cold creams, depilatories, skin lotions, hair dyes, or any other substance intended for external use and not for the treatment of disease. (p. 78)

Although there was a depression and news of fraudulent products abounded, consumers still bought what they could. Inexpensive treats like nickel movies and gum sold well. The Snickers candy bar was introduced in 1930.

> There were signs of downscaling. Sales of men's suits dropped sharply. . . . Thin wallets led to record sales of glass jars for home canning. The "live at home movement" meant foregoing the night on the town and instead listening to the radio. . . . As common as cutting back, however, was a very different response—a refusal to retrench. Many Depression-era Americans were unwilling to abandon the "luxuries" of the 1920s. Cigarette smokers could not give up the habit. . . . Americans held on to their old Model Ts. (Cross, 2000, p. 69)

**Economist John Kenneth Galbraith.**   FDR rode out the storm very well. He was highly regarded by contemporaries and the general populace. John Kenneth Galbraith, the Paul Warburg professor of economics emeritus at Harvard University, at age 93 had this to say: "Franklin D. Roosevelt was good on great issues or small. A great war. A great depression. He presided over both. No question about it—he's the person who most impressed me. In my life, he had no close competitor" (Fussman, 2002, p. 60).

John Kenneth Galbraith (1908–) is a Canadian born economist who lived most of his life in the United States and is a well-known Harvard University professor emeritus known for liberal views. A prolific writer, one of his most famous books was *The Affluent Society* published in 1958. In this book he called for less emphasis on production and more emphasis on public service. He was a key advisor to John

F. Kennedy and served as ambassador to India (1961–1963) before returning to Harvard. During the FDR years, he served in several government posts.

## 1940s

World War II turned everyone's attention to the war front and interest in consumer legislation faded. Food and gasoline were rationed here and abroad so people were more interested in getting goods rather than worrying about their quality. "Here is a partial list of what you could not get for Christmas in 1943: beer mugs, bird cages, cocktail shakers, radios, doll carriages, rubber boots, bicycles or tricycles, typewriters, griddles, toasters, hair curlers, phonographs, alarm clocks or balls that bounced. America's armed forces, who were fighting overseas, needed all the metal, rubber, chemicals and food they could get" (Crossen, 2002, B1). Because household income had grown substantially from the depression years, for many men and women working at jobs in the United States this was the first time they could not buy something they were able to afford. According to recorded oral histories and exhibits at the D-Day Museum in New Orleans, this was the first time many women went to work outside the home, becoming welders and shipbuilders and, thus, earning their own wages. The economic freedom this provided was unprecedented and set the groundwork for the future expansion of women's employment.

Because of the wartime shortage of gasoline, travel was curtailed. The lack of basics like eggs, milk, and butter led to the development of recipes for cakes such as fruitcakes that used none of these ingredients. With shortages came a growing black market. To lessen hoarding and to provide fairly the federal government instituted rationing and price limits. "Every man, woman and child received a monthly ration book, giving them a certain number of red points (for meat, cheese, and oil) and blue points (for canned goods). A person might get 64 red points a month, but a pound of butter could require as many as 24. . . . So strict were the rules, that government employees would scan newspaper death notices and send letters to families asking them to return ration books. (Crossen, 2002, p. B1) Another response to the shortages was provided by the advertising industry. Instead of promoting consumption, they came up with slogans such as "Use it up, wear it out, make do or do without" (Crossen, 2002, B1).

Homeowners were encouraged to grow victory gardens for home-food consumption so that foods canned in factories could be shipped overseas. Nylon was used in the war effort so it could not be used for stockings. Women drew pencil lines up the back of their legs to simulate stocking seams. "In 1943, the season's most coveted gifts were a carton of cigarettes or a pair of nylon stockings" (Crossen, 2002, B1).

American homes were growing more technologically complex. Flush toilets were considered standard, telephones were owned by 36 percent of families, and refrigerators were in 91 percent of households (Cross, 2000, p. 89). Even though there were shortages, the average household improved substantially during the war years and immediately afterward.

The teen market was growing and paving the way for a resurgence of bobby-soxer power in the 1950s. *Seventeen* magazine was introduced in 1944.

Box 2.2 shows that no major federal consumer legislation was passed in the 1940s and only a few laws were passed during the 1950s. On the marketplace side of things, during the 1940s and 1950s advertising surged and demand for consumer goods was never higher. Production was more important than protection. Cigarette smoking was glamorized.

Advertisers gained respect when they produced effective propaganda for the war effort. "More important, they shaped popular opinion by addressing the critical question: 'What are we fighting for?' Their answer was well summarized by one ad: 'For years we have fought for a higher standard of living, and now we are fighting to protect it against those who are jealous of our national accomplishments'. A Nash-Kelvinator ad showed a paratrooper affirming, 'We have so many things, here in America, that belong only to a free people . . . warm, comfortable homes, automobiles and radios by the million'" (Cross, 2000, p. 84).

## 1950s

When the war ended in 1945, everyone wanted new houses, cars, furniture, washing machines, and every other kind of consumer good imaginable. The emphasis was on increasing production to meet these needs, and modern American business was born. For homeowners who already had washing machines, they upgraded from wringer washers to automatic washers and from clotheslines to electric dryers. Television grew tremendously during this decade. The Mickey Mouse Club premiered in 1955. College towns and campuses grew substantially during the late 1940s and the 1950s as the GI Bill allowed returning soldiers to go to college, swelling enrollments in universities. There was renewed interest in science and invention that would benefit homes and industry.

By 1954, Frigidaire was selling ten kinds of appliances; demand was high and consumers wanted choices (Tedlow, 1990, p. 313). Some of the innovations—especially the early dishwashers—were less than successful. To make them appear more useful, they were sold as multifunction appliances. For example, it was suggested that meat could be defrosted and cocktails (in shakers) could be mixed in the dishwashers while washing dishes.

The 1950s was a decade of private consumption, capitalism gone full tilt. To consume was to be free (Cross, 2000, p. 86). In the mid to late 1950s, loud was in, loud colors, loud television westerns, loud fashion, and loud music with rock'n' roll and Elvis Presley. Food preferences changed too, chips and dip replaced sandwiches for when guests dropped by (Cross, 2000, p. 91). The split level house was introduced as a change from the rectangular ranch. Inside unlikely combinations of the old and the new occurred such as knotty-pine cabinlike paneling and kitchen cabinets mixed with plastic formica tables and counters. The decade ends with the introduction of Mattel's Barbie in 1959.

Businesses became more sophisticated in their understanding of and use of market research. By the end of the decade, a new muckraker emerged, Vance Packard. His 1957 book *The Hidden Persuaders* exposed the manipulative methods that businesses use to stimulate sales. According to the book, "supermarket operators are pretty well agreed that men are easy marks for all sorts of impulse items and cite cases they've seen of husbands who are sent to the store for a loaf of bread and depart with both their arms loaded with their favorite snack items" (p. 95). Packard also reported that

An Indiana supermarket operator nationally recognized for his advanced psychological techniques told me he once sold a half ton of cheese in a few hours, just by get-

A Barbie doll from 1959 in a striped swimsuit. Barbie revolutionized the toy market and still is a top-seller worldwide although she now comes in countless variations. (Courtesy of AP/Wide World Photos.)

ting an enormous half-ton wheel of cheese and inviting customers to nibble slivers and cut off their own chunks for purchase. They could have their chunk free if they could guess its weight within an ounce. The mere massiveness of the cheese, he believes, was a powerful influence in making the sales. 'People like to see a lot of merchandise, he explained, 'When there are only three or four cans of an item on a shelf, they just won't move. (p. 94)

In 1959, the FDA seized boxes of Pillsbury Blueberry Pancake mix for misbranding. The ingredients list and the picture on the box included blueberries, but there were none in the product. Also, in 1959 a cranberry crop scare shook the nation. Cranberries were being sprayed with chemicals that caused cancer. The Food and Drug Administration (FDA) called for the end of distributing cranberries until this problem was solved. So, by the end of the 1950s with books like Packard's and the cranberry expose there was a return to interest in consumer protection. The groundwork was being laid for advances in the consumer movement in the 1960s.

## 1960s

In 1962, American biologist, Rachel Carson, founder of the modern environmental movement, exposed other environmental pollution problems in her book *Silent Spring*. **Pollution** refers to any undesirable change in biological, chemical, or

Rachel Carson (1907–1964) is considered the founder of the modern environmental movement. She was an American biologist who wrote *Silent Spring,* an exposé on pollution. (Courtesy of Magnum Photos, Inc. Photo by Erich Hartmann.)

physical characteristics of air, land, or water that harms activities, health, or survival of living organisms. Carson advocated the use of natural pests or deterrents rather than chemicals and questioned the soundness of run-away consumption.

Since the 1960s, **environmentalism** (defined as concern for the environment) has become a very important part of the modern consumer movement. Extensive media coverage of environmental ills, disappearing species, and a growing appreciation of the natural world spurred interest in environmentalism. And, there may be another reason as well: "Most consumers lack the scientific background to understand many environmental issues and few have relevant previous experience to guide them in assessing the relative environmental merits of market-place alternatives. Thus, the potential for consumer fraud and deception is great" (Cude, 1993, p. 207). President John F. Kennedy, a Democrat, read Carson's *Silent Spring* and decided to take action. His interest in her work led to his Consumer Message to Congress in March 1962. In the preamble, Kennedy gave the famous Consumer Bill of Rights:

1. The right to safety: to be protected from hazards to health and life
2. The right to be heard: to be protected from fraud, deceit, or grossly misleading information including advertising and labeling

3. The right to choose: to have access to a variety of products and services at competitive prices
4. The right to information: to be assured of fair and expeditious treatment from government and in policy formation

He particularly cited the need for revision of laws pertaining to food and drugs. Later presidents added the following rights:

5. The right to a decent environment (influenced by several presidents)
6. The right to consumer education (added by President Gerald Ford)
7. The right to reasonable redress for physical damages suffered from using a product (added by President Richard Nixon)

In January 1964, President Lyndon B. Johnson, (a Democrat), created the new White House post, special assistant for consumer affairs, and appointed outspoken consumer advocate Esther Peterson to fill it. He also promised he would support new consumer legislation.

In the 1960s the FDA seized bogus bust developers such as Lady Ample. The 1960s was the age of dominance of large national general merchandise and department stores over small, local mom and pop stores and the spread of fast food brands. In 1965, the leader in sales and profits was Sears, Roebuck & Company, followed by J.C. Penney and Montgomery Ward (Tedlow, 1990, p. 336). Ray Kroc bought out the McDonalds brothers in 1960 and franchised McDonald's restaurants.

Any discussion of consumer protection in the 1960s would be incomplete without recognizing the enormous contribution that muckraker Ralph Nader made in his 1965 book *Unsafe at Any Speed: The Designed-In Dangers in the American Automobile* which highlighted the need for more auto safety, including cushioning and seat belts. "The automobile had been around for seventy years before Ralph Nader got general recognition of the fact that autos included unsafe design features and sometimes were ill-engineered" according to authors David Aaker and George Day (1982, p. 31). A series of horrendous accidents caused by poorly manufactured cars led to a call for reform. Nader spoke out against industrial pollution and the abuse of corporate power not only in the car industry but also in the home repair industry, the food industry, and securities, to name a few. He testified extensively before Congress and advocates today on behalf of consumers, particularly regarding environmental concerns. He founded consumer groups that are still active. As this book went to press, Ralph Nader had declared himself a candidate for president in the 2004 election.

In 1968, Paul Erlich's *The Population Bomb* made the case that there are too many people, too many cars, too much of everything and if continued unchecked then famines and other catastrophes would occur. His book influenced the debate on the use of birth control methods and a reconsidering of optimal family size.

Another important book in 1968 was *The Dark Side of the Marketplace* by Senator Warren G. Magnuson and Jean Carper. The authors explained how the consumer movement had vastly expanded its scope, "from sales deceptions and safety standards to concern over the environment—air and water pollution—and the ominous trend toward economic concentration which threatens consumers' welfare" (1968, p. 2). In the first chapter, the authors explained how elderly couples were being bilked out of thousands of dollars by con men selling aluminum siding door-to-door. This influenced the passage of the 1973 FTC Door-to-Door Sales Rules Act. They asserted that deceptive selling by the unscrupulous few cheated Americans out of more money than is lost to "robbery, burglary, larceny, auto theft, embezzlement, and forgery combined" (p. 13). Their disturbing conclusion was that the public is not being adequately protected, including not knowing enough about the hazards of smoking. Their book influenced the passage of the 1970 Public Health Cigarette Smoking Act in Box 2.2; also notice the 1975 Act that bears Magnuson's name.

## 1970s

As Box 2.2 shows, there was a great deal of consumer protection legislation in the 1970s led by Presidents Richard Nixon (Republican), Gerald Ford (Republican), and Jimmy Carter (Democrat). Nixon, a lawyer by training, signed numerous pieces of consumer legislation into law and led the way to the development of small claims courts throughout the United States. Gerald Ford promoted consumer education. Carter called for conservation and reduction of energy consumption. He was personally interested in solar power and other environmental technologies. He appointed numerous strong consumer advocates to government posts, including Esther Peterson as special assistant for consumer affairs. Because of this and the legislation he supported, Carter is considered a strong proconsumer president.

Other developments during this decade included the end of the Vietnam War and changes in consumer buying patterns. Discount stores and malls grew and with them the growth in credit cards. More stores were open on Sundays.

Faux exercise devices including different models of the Relaxacizor were seized by the FDA several times during the 1970s. The FDA has a museum with collections of these types of devices, as well as cosmetics that came under regulation, biologic agents, foods, medical devices, and quack products of every sort. The

Consumer advocate and presidential candidate Ralph Nader shows off magazine cover that supports his platform outside the Franklin Pierce Law Center. Nader is a lifelong consumer activist. His famous book, *Unsafe at Any Speed,* revolutionized car safety. (Courtesy of Corbis/SABA Press Photos, Inc. Photo by Dan Habib/Concert Monitor.)

BOX 2.2    Key Consumer Legislation 1930–1979

1938 Federal Food, Drug, and Cosmetics Act
Extended coverage of earlier act added cosmetics. Gave federal agencies the power to re-
    move untested products from stores.

1938 Federal Trade Commission Act
Updated 1914 Act. Prohibits deceptive and unfair trading practices.

1939 Wool Products Labeling Act
Accurate labeling of wool products required.

1951 Fur Products Labeling Act
Requires proper labeling of fur products.

1953 Flammable Fabrics Act
Prohibits selling highly flammable clothes.

1957 Poultry Products Inspection Act
Requires inspection of poultry.

1958 Textile Fiber Products Identification Act
Covers advertising and labeling of all textiles products not covered in the Wool and Fur
    Products Labeling Act.

1960 Hazardous Substances Labeling Act
Requires warning labels on dangerous household products.

1964 Civil Rights Act*
Guarantees consumer choice, the "full and equal enjoyment of the goods, services, facili-
    ties, privileges, advantages, and accommodations of any place of public accommoda-
    tion."

1965 Cigarette Labeling Advertising Act
Warning labels required of possible health hazards (this act grew out of growing evi-
    dence that tobacco caused cancer).

1966 Child Protection and Toy Safety Act
Bans dangerous toys, requires childproof devices and special labeling.

1966 Fair Packaging and Labeling Act (more commonly known as Truth in Packaging
    Act) Requires that weight and content information must be given on product la-
    bels (thus enabling consumers to comparison shop).

1966 Child Protection and Toy Safety Act
Childproof devices and labeling required.

1966 National Traffic and Motor Vehicle Safety Act
New car dealers must be informed by manufacturers of any safety defects found after the
    manufacture and sale of autos.

1967 Wholesale Meat Act
Updates 1906 legislation, provides for higher standards in slaughter houses of red-meat
    animals.

1968 Interstate Land Sales Full Disclosure Act
Requires accuracy of information on interstate land sales.

**1968 Consumer Credit Protection Act (Truth in Lending Act)**
Protects and regulates credit transactions, demands that lenders inform debtors of annual interest rates, and limits the practice of garnishing wages.

**1970 Public Health Cigarette Smoking Act**
Prohibits cigarette advertising on television and radio.

**1970 Fair Credit Reporting Act**
Protects consumers' credit reports.

**1970 Clean Air Act**
Authorizes the Environmental Protection Agency to establish national air-quality standards. Requires states to develop plans for reducing pollution emissions by 90 percent in five years.

**1972 Consumer Product Safety Act**
Establishes Consumer Product Safety Commission, regulates hazardous items especially those related to the home such as toy, baby, and play equipment and household products. Provides for a continuous review of products.

**1972 Odometer Act**
Protects consumers about used car odometers, cannot be rolled back or disconnected.

**1972 Water Pollution Control Act**
Endeavors to make major waterways clean enough for fishing and swimming by 1983.

**1973 FTC** Door-to-Door Sales Rule**
FTC regulates door-to-door sales contracts.

**1973 FTC Rules of Negative Options**
Spells out FTC rules regarding book and record clubs.

**1974 Real Estate Settlement Procedures Act**
Requires the disclosure of home buying costs.

**1974 Equal Credit Opportunity Act**
Prohibits discrimination regarding credit.

**1974 Fair Credit Billing Act**
Protects against billing errors, establishes procedures for resolving mistakes on credit card bills.

**1975 Magnuson-Moss Warranty Act**
Governs content of warranties, including full and limited warranties. Warranty information must be given to the consumer before making a purchase.

**1977 Fair Debt Collection Practices Act**
Limits debt collectors and their methods, prohibits abuses such as harassment.

*This is far more than a consumer protection law. It was directed at ending racial discrimination and the humiliation of segregated facilities and denied access of consumer choice.
**Federal Trade Commission.

museum is part of the FDA History Office whose mission is to increase knowledge of the history, mission, and activities of the FDA and its predecessor, the Bureau of Chemistry of the U.S. Department of Agriculture. Besides this Washington-based museum, objects are on loan to the St. Louis Science Center, the Science Museum of Minnesota, and also in Washington's Smithsonian Institution.

Many of the 1970s Acts, because they are landmark legislation, are still influential today, for example, the Equal Credit Opportunity Act and the act establishing the Consumer Product Safety Commission. Especially significant was the previously mentioned 1973 FTC Door-to-Door Sales Rule which came about because high-pressure sales persons were rushing consumers into buying things they did not want, such as encyclopedias, magazine subscriptions, vacuum cleaners, and home improvements. Because consumers were approached at their homes, many people, particularly women and the elderly, felt threatened if they didn't sign for the product or felt vulnerable in some other way. With the legislation a consumer could cancel within a three-day cooling off period. The problem as the Consumer Alert box shows is that not all types of contracts were covered. This is often the case with consumer legislation, it stops some of the blatant abuses and while it is well intentioned, it only covers certain problem areas. Additionally, over time it becomes dated as new situations and products arise that were not anticipated and covered in the original legislation.

## 1980s

With President Ronald Reagan, a Republican, at the helm from 1981–1989, there was a renewed look at consumer protection in this country. Agencies were reorganized and some would say less powerful. As an advocate of supply side economics, Reagan mostly took the view that the market should regulate itself. He thought his predecessors may have been overzealous regarding reform, and there was evidence that citizens in the 1980s were tired of restrictions and conserving. The general attitude was that consuming, after all, is fun for most people, most of the time. Movies about greed and Wall Street abounded. College students flocked to business schools. Video games came into style for children. The term "yuppie" was used to describe trend-setting dual earner childless couples. Name brands such as BMWs and Ralph Lauren promised prestige.

Consumers were encouraged to use the laws already on the books. Nevertheless quite a bit of consumer protection legislation was passed during the Reagan term as shown in Box 2.3. According to public opinion polls, Reagan was a popular

---

**Consumer Alert (from the Federal Consumer Information Center)**

There is no universal three-day cooling off period. Do not be misled into thinking that you have an automatic three-day or other cancellation period for all purchases. Only a few types of contracts give you a right to cancel. Federal law, for example, gives you the right to cancel certain door-to-door contracts within three days, and some states provide cancellation periods for such things as health and dating club contracts. Check with your state and local consumer office for more information about cancellation rights.

president. He was followed by George Bush, 1989–1993, also a Republican who took a similar consumer protection stance.

During the 1980s, there was a corporate thrust behind consumer education. For-profit companies preferred consumer education to more legislation. Increased consumer education is worthwhile if it hits the right audience at the right time, but there is only so much it can do as the following quote makes clear. "Even genuine consumer education cannot, of course, solve consumer problems by itself. If all meat prices go up it's little help to tell consumers to buy the lower-price cuts. These usually go up the most. Nor can consumer education help much in restraining high mortgage interest rates or high medical and hospital fees"(Margolius, 1982, p. 56).

## 1990s

President Bush, the forty-first president, was followed by Bill Clinton, Democrat, 1993 to 2001. Although it is not considered consumer protection legislation per se, Clinton signed NAFTA (the North American Free Trade Agreement) which greatly impacted trade, employment in certain industries, and prices. His vice president, Al Gore, was known for his interest in environmental and family issues. He wrote the book *Earth in the Balance* which is about environmental problems. A modern-day muckraker, Erin Brockovich, was in the news, and there was an award-winning movie about her investigative work on exposing health-endangering pollution in a small town in California.

This was a decade of affluence, expansion, and low unemployment. The stock market rose steadily hitting century highs near the end of the decade. The Dow Jones Industrial Average of 30 major American companies hit a twentieth century high when it closed at 10,000 in 1999. At the same time there were a number of books, magazines, television shows, and writers advocating a simpler, less materialistic life. A book entitled *Affluenza* and public television documentaries *Affluenza* and *Escape from Affluenza* recommended that people go hiking, spend time with their families, or volunteer rather than go to the mall. Although not everyone chose to scale down their consumption, some did, and there was a nationwide switch to more recycling. School children were encouraged to participate. It became the American way in this decade and into the twenty-first century.

Holders of wealth changed greatly in the 1990s. By the time Sam Walton, founder of Wal-Mart, died in 1990, he was the richest man in the United States, but within a few years the richest man in the world (not just in the United States) was Bill Gates, founder of Microsoft. The consumption story of the 1990s cannot be told without a nod to computers and the Internet, the growth of e-mail and online buying and the trend toward working and shopping at home. Few consumer goods have become obsolete so fast: the "286" processor was replaced by the "386" then the "486" and then the Pentium in 1993 advancing to the Pentium IV and an operating system introduced by Microsoft called Windows XP, and the list goes on. To meet demand, office supply, computer, and/or electronic stores grew. As an alternative consumers could buy computers online, customizing the system that they wanted and getting home delivery.

To stay competitive, by the late 1990s most leading store chains, including department stores and gift shops, offered both **bricks and clicks**, meaning a physical store and an online store. The Mall of America opened in suburban Minneapolis in 1993, showing that entertainment, tourism, leisure, and shopping could all happen underneath one roof. The Mall sports two indoor lakes and an amusement park. Across the country, old malls were closing; there was a partial return to free-standing stores; grocery stores had their own delis and bakeries; and there were more superstores open 24 hours a day. Large mass market and department stores regrouped and some such as Kmart filed for bankruptcies and closed many of their stores. This trend continued into the 2000s.

## 2000s

A recession marked the beginning of the new century. One area of concern was the growth in unemployment which reached 6.1% in June 2003. More college grads put their dreams on hold as they took whatever job they could find to pay off student loans or added to their student loan debt by continuing on to graduate school. A 2003 study released by Collegiate Funding Services found that more than 30 percent of college graduates said they had to take a job other than the one they really wanted in order to pay off their loans. A year earlier the percentage was 20 percent (Kim, 2003, C1). The average debt increased to $20,000 from $17,000 with a range of $10,000 to $40,000 in student loans being common.

In 2000, consumer activist Ralph Nader at age 66 ran as the presidential candidate of the Green Party, garnering about 3 percent of the vote. To learn more about his views on politics, read his book *Crashing the Party: How to Tell the Truth and Still Run for President* (2002). A theme running throughout is that both major political parties "routinely savage the interests of the American people by ignoring such fundamental concerns as corporate control, environmental pollution and the widening gap between rich and poor" (Fund, 2002, p. A12).

As of the writing of this chapter, it was too soon to give a full report on the legacy of consumer protection legislation under George W. Bush, the forty-third president. During his presidency much of his attention has been drawn to the war on terrorism, the war in Iraq and problems with the nation's economy. His early years as president were marked by business scandals about financial mismanagement and improper reporting of funds. Corporate responsibility to employees and stockholders was questioned, as well as the adequacy of outside auditing procedures. In response, the Securities and Exchange Commission strengthened rules about reporting procedures and increased investigations.

President Bush supported health insurance reform that included more coverage of mental illness and caps (maximum amounts) on awards arising from malpractice cases so that doctors' malpractice insurance rates would drop or stabilize and they could continue practicing. Serious debate ensued about patients' rights. There are a number of ways to look at the malpractice issue from the consumer protection perspective, including the notion that the medical profession should do a better job of self-policing by removing bad physicians from practice. This would reduce the number of lawsuits since only a few physicians have, by far, the most. Since rising malpractice insurance rates have been a problem for years, this debate will continue at the state as well as at the federal level since most insurance regulation occurs at the state level.

During the Bush administration there were waves of mergers and turnovers in economic advisors. His Council of Economic Advisors noted that merger activity was well above average levels and had been growing for several decades. Mergers escalated because:

- Antitrust legislation was less enforced.
- Deregulation spread.
- Large companies benefited from mergers.
- A weakened economy made smaller companies more vulnerable, willing to sell.

Here are examples of mergers:

> Twenty years ago, cable television was dominated by a patchwork of thousands of tiny, family-operated companies. Today, a pending deal would leave three companies in control of nearly two-thirds of the market. In 1990, three big publishers of college textbooks accounted for 35% of industry sales. Today they have 62%. . . . In 1996, when Congress deregulated telecommunications, there were eight Baby Bells, today there are four, and dozens of small rivals are dead. ("Why the Sudden Rise in the Urge to Merge and Form Oligopolies?" February 25, 2002, *Wall Street Journal,* p. A1)

Regarding consumer organizations and issues during this decade, in 2002, Consumers Union launched Consumer WebWatch (*www.consumerwebwatch.org*), a project to help make Web sites more accountable for the accuracy of their information. The site provided news alerts for web-savvy consumers and research results. *The growth of the Internet as an information and selling source is a hallmark of the first decade of the twenty-first century.* Evidence of this was apparent in the passage of international legislation and the signing of treaties between countries regarding legalities and the Internet. The globalization of the economy continued with the spread of factories and sales. As evidence take a company such as Johnson & Johnson which had $36.3 billion in sales in 2002 as a world leader in health care products and as a provider of consumer, pharmaceutical, and medical devices and diagnostics markets. By 2003, it had 200 operating companies in 54 countries around the world, selling products in more than 175 companies (Mid-Year Report, 2003, preface).

---

**BOX 2.3    Key Consumer Legislation 1980–present**

**1981 FTC\* Used-Car Rule**
Requires used car dealers to disclose to consumers specified types of information.

**1984 FTC Funeral Home Rule**
Requires disclosure of prices and services.

**1984 Counterfeit Access Device and Computer Fraud and Abuse Act**
Prohibits counterfeit credit cards and other unauthorized access to credit.

**1984 Automobile Restraints**
Required all new cars sold after September 1, 1990, to have restraints (seat belts).

**1984 Toy Safety Act**
By this Act, CPSC\*\* can more quickly recall hazardous toys and equipment for children.

**1984 Generic Drug Act**
Allows FDA to speed up acceptance of generic drugs on which patents have expired on original drugs.

**1986 Smokeless Tobacco Act**
Requires labeling of hazards on smokeless tobacco products and prohibits advertising of these products on television and radio.

**1988 Home Equity Loan Consumer Protection Act**
Requires fuller disclosure of loans, prohibits lenders from changing contracts after signage.

**1990 Clean Air Act**
Updated 1970 Act, established new pollution limits and standards for automobile, power plant, and cancer-causing substance emissions.

**1990 Children's Advertising Act**
Directs FCC[†] to limit TV advertising directed at children.

**1990 Food Labeling Act**
Establishes new labeling standards.

**1993 Truth in Savings Act**
Requires that financial institutions report APY (Annual Percentage Yield) in the same way.

**1994 Dietary Supplement Health and Education Act**
Requires manufacturers to provide product safety information to FDA.[‡]

**1994 Fair Credit Reporting Act (Amended)**
Increases access to credit.

**1994 NAFTA (North American Free Trade Agreement)**
Gradually eliminates tariffs among Mexico, Canada, and the United States on most products. Agreement in full force in 2008. Included is a dispute resolution program.

**1998 The Digital Millennium Copyright Act**
Adapted U.S. legislation to the WIPO treaties. The World Intellectual Property Organization (WIPO) had two treaties, laid down in Geneva, that adapted copyright rules for e-commerce. Copyright laws cover physical copies, broadcasting, books, songs, and films distributed online. The treaties, ratified by 41 countries, went into effect in 2002.

*Federal Trade Commission.
**Consumer Product Safety Commission.
†Federal Communications Commission.
‡Food and Drug Administration.

## CONCLUSION OF THE DECADES OF CONSUMERISM

The more recent legislation and issues discussed in this chapter may ring a bell. Perhaps you heard about it on television or learned about it in school. Most of you probably do not remember a time when seat belts were not required or when food labels were not as extensive as they are today. Nor do you remember presidents much before Presidents Clinton and George W. Bush. To avoid fatiguing the reader, the chapter ends at this point with the intention of exploring the most current legislation and related issues further in upcoming chapters. It should also be noted that for brevity's sake not all the persons and organizations that contributed to consumer protection in the United States are mentioned. The consumer movement, much as the Internet, is borderless, free-ranging, and growing. Concerns come and go such as the SARS epidemic and Mad Cow disease to the point where people ask, "What next?"

Crises such as threats to our health draw attention to faulty products, health systems, or services that need correcting. The range of problems include everything from faulty tires to inadequate processing of food. The Food and Drug Administration has been enormously important in testing foods and seizing misbranded food, such as blueberry pancake mixes with no blueberries in them. Many of these seizures have been well publicized. We become aware of crises or misrepresentations through the news and the Internet. In the past, newspaper articles and books written by muckrakers rallied support for product or financial reform. Sometimes, reform has arisen out of invention or a natural evolution of things—new scientific discoveries disclose new ills or inventions such as computers or credit cards require new rules for handling their potential abuse.

This chapter focused on consumer rights and legislation, but this is only one side of the coin. The fourth chapter explores consumer responsibilities. The government cannot be everywhere, so how do consumers look out for themselves? What is their responsibility in the marketplace?

## SUMMARY

Unquestionably, the twentieth and twenty-first centuries can be seen as times of increasing affluence. But with affluence comes abuses in the marketplace which necessitate more consumer protection. The twenty-first century began with a rocky start as the nation's and the world's economy experienced a slowdown, and a series of corporate scandals led to a loss of faith in the dependability of American business standards and practices. Through it all the consumer movement has been active. In the United States, the modern consumer movement can be traced from the 1880s. The earliest concerns were about food quality, but over time many more product areas came under scrutiny, including drugs, cosmetics, toys, and broader social, technological, and financial concerns. The consumer movement embraced the environmental movement, and they are so coupled today it is difficult to separate them. The late 1960s and early 1970s were the heyday of environmental concerns spurred by well-publicized oil spills that wrecked coastlines and killed wildlife. In more recent decades, concerns shifted back to food quality and purity, as well as other health related issues.

Certain decades produced more consumer protection legislation than others; particularly active decades were the 1930s and the 1960s through the 1980s. Presidents from both the Republican and Democratic parties have provided leadership in consumer protection. Senators, scientists, writers, corporate employees, and organizations have stirred the public interest by bringing to light shoddy and questionable practices and products. Ralph Nader and other consumer activists provided leadership and put the spotlight on food, environmental, and car problems. Some may question whether the phrase "consumer movement" is the best term since it is no longer an ideological movement because consumerism is a regular part of our everyday experience. If a product breaks or causes injury, we expect remedy or justice; consumer protection is a given in our daily lives. We rely on regulation to facilitate our reasoned choice and, in particular, to protect the young, elderly, and defenseless from unscrupulous practices.

Consumer protection needs arise in response to:

- New technological developments
- Changing conceptions of the social responsibilities of consumers, businesses, and nations
- Exposés of the dishonest, greedy, and selfish fringe that break the rules and take advantage

In conclusion, as long as there are consumers there will be a need for consumer protection.

## KEY POINTS

1. From 1776—the year of the publication of Adam Smith's book—to the present there has been a growing trend of consumer reliance on business to provide goods. With the decrease in self-production of goods comes the necessity to rely on business or government to ensure quality and safety.
2. Abuses in the marketplace lead to the need for consumer protection legislation.
3. The consumer movement refers to policies aimed at providing regulations and standards.
4. Harvey Wiley, chemist, is the founder of the consumer movement, and some would say the founder of the FDA. He is famous for his Poison Squad experiments on the effects of food additives.
5. Food reformers were most concerned about fraud and poison.
6. World War II brought shortages and rationing. Consumer legislation took a backseat to concerns about obtaining goods. Immediately after the war, increased production for houses, household goods, and cars became paramount.
7. Rachel Carson, biologist and author of *Silent Spring,* is the founder of the modern environmental movement.
8. Muckrakers such as Upton Sinclair, author of *The Jungle,* led to reforms in meat processing, and Ralph Nader, author of *Unsafe at Any Speed,* led to reforms in car safety.
9. Two economists and their contributions were introduced in this chapter: John Maynard Keynes (whose book *The General Theory of Employment, Interest, and Money* was important during the depression, he made the case for more government intervention) and John Kenneth Galbraith (author of many books including *The Affluent Society*). Galbraith served in various government roles during World War II and after. As an advisor to John F. Kennedy and ambassador to India, he influenced public policy and promoted public service.
10. Several presidents were key figures in influencing consumer legislation. Particularly noteworthy is John F. Kennedy who, in his Consumer Message to Congress, outlined the four basic principles of consumer protection: the right to safety, to be heard, to choose, and to information.

11. Consumer legislation is necessary and well intentioned. However, loopholes nearly always exist, and the Acts or Rules do not cover everything. For example, the 1973 FTC Door-to-Door Sales Rule only allows a consumer to cancel a few types of contracts within three days. In all cases the phrase "caveat emptor" (meaning may the buyer beware) holds true.

## KEY TERMS

| | | |
|---|---|---|
| antitrust laws | consumer movement | muckraker |
| bricks and clicks | depression | pollution |
| cease-and-desist order | environmentalism | rational self-interest |
| common law | hucksterism | |
| conspicuous consumption | | |

## DISCUSSION QUESTIONS

1. If President John F. Kennedy was alive today, would he be pleased with the state of consumer protection in this country? List his four consumer rights, and give a current example of each from your own life or from a friend's or relative's experience.
2. After reading the excerpt from *The Jungle,* do you think reforms were necessary in the meat processing industry in 1906? Yes or no. Explain your answer. What was President Theodore Roosevelt's role in meat processing reform?
3. It isn't easy being a reformer. Who did not support the work of food safety reformer Harvey Wiley?
4. Select one of the e-resource Web sites listed next. What did you find on the site?

## E-RESOURCES

| | |
|---|---|
| Consumers Union<br>www.ConsumerReports.org | Consumers Union, the publisher of *Consumer Reports,* is a nonprofit organization chartered in 1936. Provides information on consumer goods such as toothpaste, toys, toasters, and cars, conducts tests. |
| Center for Science in the Public Interest<br>www.cspinet.org | A nonprofit, membership organization that conducts research, education, and advocacy on food safety, nutrition, health, and related issues. |
| FDA History Office<br>http://www.fda.gov/oc/history/resourceguide/office.html | Information about its evolution, function, the oral history program, the museum collection, and the staff. |

| Federal Trade Commission www.ftc.gov and www.consumer.gov | A government commission offering consumer information on many subjects, including labeling, advertisements, and monopoly. |
| North American Free Trade Agreement (NAFTA) www.mac.doc.gov/nafta/ | Issues and information are given on this Web site which is of use to exporters, public policy experts, and economists. |
| Consumer WebWatch www.consumerweb watch.org | A Consumers Union site, helps make Web sites more accountable for accuracy, provides research results and news alerts for consumers. |

# REFERENCES

Aaker, D., and G. Day. (1982). *Consumerism: Search for the consumer interest,* 4th ed. New York: Free Press.

Carson, R. (1962). *Silent Spring.* Boston: Houghton Mifflin.

Chase, S., and F. Schlink. (1928). *Your Money's Worth.* New York: Macmillan.

Cross, G. (2000). *An all-consuming century: Why commercialism won in modern America.* New York: Columbia University Press.

Crossen, C. (December 28, 2001). Etiquette for Americans today. *Wall Street Journal,* p. W13.

Crossen, C. (December 18, 2002). In wartime holidays of the past, patriots curbed their spending. *Wall Street Journal,* p. B1.

Cude, B. (1993). Consumer perceptions of environmental marketing claims: An exploratory study. *Journal of Consumer Studies and Home Economics 12,* 207–25.

Downs, R. B. (January 1963, 4th ed.). Afterword in Upton Sinclair's *The Jungle.* New York: New American Library, pp. 343–50.

Erlich, P. (1968). *The population bomb.* New York: Ballantine Books.

Frederick, C. (1914). *The new housekeeping: Efficiency studies in home management.* New York: Doubleday, Page.

Fund, J. (January 9, 2002). Bookshelf: From consumer grouch to White House wannabe. *Wall Street Journal,* p. A12.

Fussman, Cal (January 2002). Interview with John Kenneth Galbraith. *Esquire,* p. 60.

Galbraith, J. (1958). *The affluent society.* Boston: Houghton Mifflin.

Gore, A. (1992). *Earth in the balance.* New York: Penguin Books.

Harris, D. (2000). *Cute, quaint, hungry and romantic: The aesthetics of consumerism.* New York: Basic Books.

Heilbroner, R., and L. Thurow. (1998). *Economics explained.* New York: Simon and Schuster.

Josephson, M. (1962). *The robber barons.* New York: Harcourt, Brace & World.

Kallet, A., and F. Schlink. (1933). *100,000,000 guinea pigs.* New York: Grosset & Dunlap.

Keynes, J. (1936). *The general theory of employment, interest, and money.* London: Macmillan.

Kim, J. (September 2, 2003). More college graduates postpone their "dream jobs" to pay loans. *Wall Street Journal,* p. C1.

Magnuson, W., and J. Carper. (1968). *The dark side of the marketplace.* New York: Prentice Hall.

Margolius, S. (1982). The consumer's real needs. In *Consumerism: Search for the Consumer Interest, Fourth Edition* by David A. Aaker and George S. Day. New York: Free Press, pp. 48–56.

*Mid-Year Report* (2003). Johnson & Johnson: Scios Acquisition. New Brunswick, NJ.

Nader, R. (1966). *Unsafe at any speed*. New York: Pocket Books.

Nader, R. (2002). *Crashing the party: How to tell the truth and still run for president*. New York: Thomas Dunne Books, St. Martin's Press.

Packard, V. (1958). *The hidden persuaders*. New York: Pocket Books.

Schlereth, T. (1991). *Victorian America: Transformations in everyday life 1876–1915*. New York: Harper Collins.

Sinclair, U. (1905). *The Jungle*. New York: New American Library of World Literature.

Smith, A. (1776). An inquiry into the nature and causes of the wealth of nations, 1776, as edited by Robert A. Heilbroner in the essential Adam Smith, New York: Norton, p. 284.

Strasser, S. (1989). *Satisfaction guaranteed*. New York: Random House.

Tedlow, R. (1990). *New and Improved: The Story of Mass Marketing in America*. New York: Basic Books.

White, S. (November–December 2002). The "poison squad" and the advent of food and drug regulation. *FDA Consumer*.

Why the sudden rise in the urge to merge and form oligopolies? (February 25, 2002). *Wall Street Journal*, p. A1.

## CHAPTER 3

# Consumer Theories and Developing a Model

*If we do discover a complete theory, it should in time be understandable in broad principle by everyone, not just a few scientists.*

**Stephen Hawking**

### Learning Objectives

1. Explain different theories and their relevance to the study of consumer economics.
2. Describe the components of the circular flow model of consumer economics.
3. Explain factors that affect the model.
4. Explain how consumer wellbeing is defined and measured, including consumer confidence.
5. Describe the basic functions of business and the nature of entrepreneurship.

## INTRODUCTION

We learned in the first chapter that the founder of modern economics, Adam Smith, believed that "to be human is to exchange freely." That idea—of humans wanting the freedom to exchange unrestricted by outside forces—is a theory that Adam Smith espoused. He believed in an orderly, progressive, and harmonious commercial society.

In today's world, many economists follow the teachings of Smith (summarized as faith in the market) while others believe as did John Maynard Keynes that the more complicated world that we live in necessitates more government intervention. Economists generally agree that consumers are **rational** (meaning having the ability to reason) and **acquisitive** (meaning having a strong desire for things, ideas, and information). Recent developments in economic theory and research have questioned the nature of rationality. For example, the 2002 Nobel Prize in economics went to Daniel Kahneman and Amos Tversky who published an article highlighting the irrational nature of people when it comes to consumption. They represent a growing area of economics called **behavioral economics** which is "pushing the frontiers of research by introducing psychologically realistic models of economic agents into economic theory" (Robinson-Brown, 2002, p. 1). Their particular contribution about judgment, attitudes, and decision making are discussed in this chapter. Regarding the acquisitive nature of human behavior, Harvard

The rationality of consumers to the exclusion of other factors is being questioned by economists.

University Professor Juliet Schor (1998) wrote that what we acquire is tightly bound to our identity. Theories such as these form the bulk of this chapter which explores the nature of theories and their roles in consumption. The chapter ends with discussions of consumer well-being including measures of consumer confidence.

## THEORY AND EXCHANGE PROCESS DEFINED

*Theories are useful for guiding research and explaining consumer behavior.*

A **theory** is an organized system of ideas or beliefs that can be *measured*. Theories are essentially systems of principles or assumptions. Because of the measurement aspect, theories are useful in guiding research and explaining behavior. A research project may start with questions or hypotheses which are predictions of future occurrences. For example, a researcher might predict that if a consumer has bought Tide detergent for the last ten years that he or she will likely continue to do so. In consumer research it has been proven many times over that past behavior is a strong predictor of future behavior. Knowing this many companies work hard at building brand loyalty in young people. As an example, consider the number of credit cards that have been offered to you during your college years. Even though you may not have much money now, the credit card companies know that you will soon and you are unlikely to change credit cards once you graduate.

*A fundamental consumer theory backed by research is that past purchasing behavior is a strong predictor of future purchasing behavior.*

In the following pages, we explore various theories about how people plan, decide, buy and exchange goods given scarce resources. Several theories exist because many factors or groups impact different kinds of consumers, and as time goes on new theories are formulated to describe behavior. Consumers come in all shapes, sizes, ages, nationalities, income levels, and so forth, although discernible patterns and statistics are useful in determining these groupings. For example, in the United States, women account for about 80 percent of consumer spending (Allon, 2001). So, gender is a factor in consumption behavior. A specific example of this is that in the United States most women use body wash, but only 45 percent of men use body wash and "most are using women's products and half are using them secretly. Their partners typically do not know that they're using it" (Neff, 2002, p. 8). Hoping to change this behavior and directly market to men, Procter & Gamble Co. launched Old Spice High Endurance body wash in January 2003 to mass market to men. This is called a **brand extension** because Old Spice already comes in after-shave, antiperspirants, and deodorants. Note also the words "high endurance" which sounds masculine rather than feminine.

*In the United States, women account for about 80 percent of consumer spending.*

Since consumer economics can be described most simply as the study of exchange activities, it is important to define what this encompasses. The **exchange process** occurs when people (as individuals, as family members, employees, members of religious groups etc.) negotiate with a goal of reaching an agreement, such as an agreed upon price or date of delivery. When the exchange is fulfilled, it is called a **transaction**.

In summary, because consumption behavior is affected by so many variables, it is useful to organize it by means of theories and models. This chapter introduces several of these as a guide to explaining consumers' choices and the influences on their behavior.

# THE THEORY OF REASONED ACTION

Although consumers are generally considered to be rational, as explained in the introduction the newer thought is that they do not always behave rationally. And, if one looks back there is much evidence of irrationality in the past, consider this example:

> In the late 19th century, teacher-turned-snake-oil-seller Lydia E. Pinkham used her image and signature to help sell her eponymous vegetable compound as a cure-all for faintness, flatulence, depression and other "female" complaints. While her product may have been suspect—a main ingredient was alcohol—her marketing strategy was sound. Ads that appeared in newspapers and on barns were so persuasive that women wrote her detailing their aches and pains. They always received a letter back signed by Lydia—even long after the lady died, thanks to those who kept the company going. (Well, 2001, p. 124)

Was it rational for women to think of Lydia Pinkham, a person they never met, as a friend? Do women think of modern-day media moguls Oprah Winfrey or Martha Stewart as friends? Do their companies promote these relationships much as Lydia Pinkham's did? This connection between attitudes, social relationships, and consumer behavior has been explored by several theorists. Probably the most commonly cited theory of this kind is the **theory of reasoned action** developed by Martin Fishbein and Icek Ajzen (Ajzen and Fishbein, 1980). Their theory states that behavioral intentions are based on a combination of the attitude toward a specific behavior, the social or normative beliefs about the appropriateness of the behavior, and the motivation to comply with the normative beliefs (Sheppard, Hartwick, and Warshaw, 1988).

In the theory of reasoned action, what is important is the consumer's attitude toward behaving a certain way, and the consumer's subjective norm which is his or her belief about other's evaluations of his or her actions.

Regarding this second point, what the consumer believes to be a rational or reasonable purchase or course of action may or may not be shared by his or her family, coworkers, or friends. For example, if a 55-year-old bald man buys a red sports car, he may or may not wonder what others think. If he senses disapproval (i.e., he is perceived as having a midlife crisis), he may select another color or a pick-up truck instead. This middle-aged man is not alone. "Many of us are continually comparing our own lifestyle and possessions to those of a select group of people we respect and want to be like, people whose sense of what's important in life seems close to our own" (Schor, 1998, p. 3). The theory of reasoned action shows that consumption is based on beliefs and attitudes, has consequences, and that it takes place within a social context.

# PROSPECT THEORY AND THE THEORY OF MENTAL ACCOUNTING

As mentioned in the introduction, economists for the most part follow a central tenet that people are logical with their money and that the market operates sensibly. The problem is that when the stock market reverses and companies go bankrupt, economists and others wonder how sensible the market really is. It appears to be capable of irradict behavior, and the corollary to this is that consumers also act in illogical

Lydia Pinkham's vegetable compound. Marketed to women, the main ingredient was alcohol. (Courtesy of the Drug Enforcement Administration.)

ways. When people do not have all the answers or ways of systematically approaching decisions, it does not stop them; they proceed and do what they can. In other words, they do not let uncertainty get in the way of making decisions.

In 1979, Daniel Kahneman and Amos Terksky (who died in 1996) published "Prospect Theory: An Analysis of Decision Under Risk" in *Econometrica,* a journal of economics. In this article, they "argued that people's degree of pleasure (their 'utility' in social science-ese) is more dependent on the change in their condition than on the absolute level. In other words, a rich man who loses $10 is apt to feel bad, whereas a poor man who wins $100 is apt to feel rich. This concept broke ground with classical economics, which held that rich always feels better than poor" (Lowenstein, 2003, p. 42). This was called **prospect theory** and led to the idea of loss aversion, that people feel more pain from loss than pleasure from profit. This explains why people hold onto stocks that are performing poorly (they are doing so to avoid pain even if they can afford the loss). It would probably be more rational to sell the stocks and put the money into a better performing investment. In regard to Kahneman's contribution, his department chairman, Gene Grossman, said, "He's challenged the basic model of how individuals behave economically. The standard model is that everybody is rational, self-interested, calculating; he's suggested that more psychological motives determine people's behavior and that these motives are important for economic phenomena. . . . I think there is now a broader range of thinking about certain issues, especially savings behavior and participation in the stock market" (Robinson-Brown, 2002, p. 2).

Richard Thaler, who teaches at the University of Chicago, studied with Kahneman (a Princeton professor who teaches Psychology 101 and has never taken or taught a course in economics) and came up with the **endowment effect**. In experiments Thaler found that "[s]ubjects who have been given a present—they used a coffee mug—will demand a higher price to sell it than people who don't have the mug would be willing to pay for one" (Lowenstein, 2003, p. 42). This finding contradicts the widely held classical economist view that in a free market, one price fits all. Again, human behavior (in this case a sense of ownership) affects what people set as an appropriate price. Thaler took this a step further and developed the **theory of mental accounting** in which people frame or put into context their buying and selling. So that "people who obsess over saving $5 on groceries will happily blow $1,000 on a vacation because they account for it differently" (Lowenstein, 2003, p. 42). They are, therefore, uneven in their response to money. Thaler, other economists, and family and consumer economists around the country through surveys and experiments are exploring other dimensions of saving and spending behavior.

# INNOVATION THEORY

Innovators or early adopters of new products and services are of interest to consumer economists and marketers. Research surrounds the questions of:

- Who are these first people to buy?
- Why do they do it?
- Does the trend toward buying first affect all product categories or is it product specific?

**Innovators** are the earliest buyers of new brands, services, products, stores, or other market offerings, and they like new ideas or technologies as well. They are attracted to grand openings of stores, advertisements of new products, door prizes, and excitement. Does this describe you or someone you know? The theoretical background for this phenomena was provided by E. M. Rodgers, author of *Diffusion of Innovations*. He defined a process through which an individual . . . passes (1) from first knowledge of an innovation, (2) to forming an attitude toward the innovation, (3) to a decision to adopt or reject, (4) to implementation of the new idea, and (5) to confirmation of this decision (1995, p. 161). An innovative consumer is highly involved, they want to know about what is happening. They may be avid readers or followers of the news, talk with friends about new products and services. As mentioned in the introduction, economists believe that people are acquisitive, they need to know what is going on in the marketplace, to acquire or at least think about or look at new things such as cars, houses, or electronic items such as digital cameras and flat-screen televisions. Rogers posited that there is a theme in consumer behavior of adoption and diffusion of innovations.

What is curious about innovation adoption is that a person can be an innovator in one category such as the latest fashions but a laggard in another category such as going to see the latest movies. This makes common sense because it would be very expensive, time-consuming, and exhausting to be an innovator in all areas of consumption so people make choices where to put their time, effort, and money. Many choose to ignore the latest ideas or products altogether and prefer the tried and the true. One thinks of the expression, "if it ain't broke, don't fix it." An example is of a nutrition professor who has a 1980s Amana microwave oven in her home kitchen. The oven is huge, family and friends kid her about it, but it still works, she is used to it, and sees no reason to change.

A consumer innovator is more likely to take risks and be more venturesome than later buyers. If marketers can find the innovators in a particular product class, promotion and distribution should be directed to them first. Marketing researchers would want to know what magazines and newsletters innovators read, what clubs they belong to, what sporting events or arts events they attend, and so on. Generally, innovators are more upwardly mobile. They are less price sensitive than later adopters. A product class that attracts innovators is computers and computing services. The final public relations approach could involve advertising and direct marketing or holding a launch party for magazine editors or hosting exhibit booths at conventions to display new wares. More subtle approaches include such things as sponsoring community, cultural events, or bowling teams; contributing to high school yearbooks; or buying tickets to charity events. The parties or events may involve gift bags with the new product or at least a discount on its purchase.

An innovation may be new to one social or cultural group or country, whereas it may not be perceived as new by another. It can be said that the innovation *diffuses,* or moves through, a social system over time—some pick it up late, some pick it up early, and the vast majority fall somewhere in-between. People in the middle are interested in what is new, but wary of things that are brand new. They may think that if they wait the kinks will be worked out of the new product such as a car model or that the price will come down. Rogers developed a bell-shaped curve to illustrate the rate at which new products, services, or ideas are typically adopted. At the beginning is 2.5 percent of the population designated as the innovators. They are followed by 13.5 percent who are early adopters, followed by 34 percent who are early majority, then 34 percent who are called the late majority, ending with the last group to adopt called the laggards who are estimated at 16 percent of the population. The nutrition professor with the old microwave oven would be a laggard.

## THE SCIENTIFIC METHOD

At this juncture, it would be useful to describe the scientific method that consumer researchers follow as do biologists and chemists. The five steps in the scientific method are

1. Describe what is happening (recognize the problem or opportunity).
2. Explain why it is happening (make assumptions).
3. Develop a model.
4. Predict what will happen in the future.
5. Control, check, or test what is happening.

The problem may be "I need shoes." The opportunity may be "I need new shoes even though I already own 30 pairs." Assumptions are commonly held beliefs or statements that are accepted as true without proof. Someone may assume that the new pair of shoes will give more wear, satisfaction, and status than the shoes already owned. He or she may predict or imagine what will happen when wearing the shoes, what compliments they will get, what outfits the shoes will go with, and so on.

In step five in the scientific method, the word control refers to the things people do to check their courses of action or to test what they have purchased. Checking, tests, or trials are used to determine whether a theory is consistent with the facts or the outcomes. For example, if one theorized that saving money was better than spending it, they could set up an automatic deduction of $50 from their paycheck that goes directly into a savings account. The control aspect would be checking on how the savings account is building. Did it bring the desired effect? Did the person feel too limited by having the $50 deducted from each paycheck? When individuals make purchase or financial decisions they are trying to predict what will happen (how much pleasure or pain they will derive from the decision) and on the basis of that analysis change or alter their behavior accordingly.

**Models** are representations or schematics or illustrations of relationships. They take abstractions from the real world and allow us to visualize the connections between ideas or between people or institutions. A common model is a blueprint, which is a flat drawing of a house. Another way to visualize the building of a new house or the remodeling of an existing home is to use computer simulations of floorplans and elevations. In the next section of the chapter, frameworks (which are outlines, connections of ideas) are discussed first, followed by more theories and models. In the course of this discussion, a new consumer model is proposed and illustrated.

## THE FRAMEWORK'S BASIC PREMISE LEADING TO THE MODEL

Consumer economics involves processes of exchange between two or more parties. The process occurs when parties negotiate (this can be verbal or nonverbal) and reach an agreement. The fulfillment of the exchange process is called a transaction (as mentioned earlier) and is illustrated in Figure 3.1.

An everyday example of this is when a person goes to the grocery store to buy a gallon of milk and then pays for it—the exchange is completed. This is what happens on the surface, but the exchange process is not really that simple. Behind the scenes, many forces and parties are involved—the cow produces milk, the farmer and suppliers get the milk to market, and then there are regulators, grocers, marketers, and promoters. Public policy may be involved in the form of taxes, farm subsidies, exports, or regulation so that prices or supply are affected. A government agency reinforces the rules that regulate product dating so that the store will have to stamp the appropriate pull date on the milk. Government inspectors make sure this is done correctly and consistently.

Other relationships are formed in exchanges, as well, such as market-to-market transactions (businesses selling to each other) and consumer-to-consumer transactions such as yard sales or college students selling used textbooks to each other. Consumer-to-consumer relationships are often communicated by word of mouth or

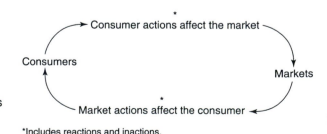

**Figure 3.1**   Exchange Process between Consumers and Markets.

referral networks such as local newspapers or signs. Because this book is about consumer economics, the focus is on where and how the majority of consumer transactions take place and that is between consumers and markets.

While most consumer-market exchanges are satisfactory in that both sides are satisfied, sometimes things go wrong, creating a **consumer-market conflict**. Getting agreement or reconciling differences may be difficult. Here is where public policy steps in. It anticipates potential areas of conflict and deals with it before, during, and after it has happened, and as such it plays a very important role in the consumer-market exchange and deserves a place in our model (see Figure 3.2).

## Public Policy

Figure 3.3 shows a traditional view of the consumer-market exchange wherein pubic policy serves as a moderator or mediator. The role of public policy is to make sure the exchange is fair in terms of competition, labeling, access, advertising, and pricing. The arrows in the model indicate relationships. As an example, the market (through for profit and nonprofit organizations) may hire lobbyists to sway public policy in their favor. The lobbying effort may lead to fewer restrictions on the organization or reduced taxes or the ability to advertise in new mediums.

Consumers want useful, safe, environmentally sound products at fair prices. They also want selection. **Public policy** is a plan or decision by government to act in a certain way or direction such as to keep products safe, open up competition, eliminate poverty, allocate more money to medical research or the space program, or to clean up the environment. It is in contrast to private matters or concerns such as how an individual or family acts. Public policy makers exist at all levels of government from the smallest town to federal government. They work in the executive, legislative, and judicial branches. Individuals and families get involved in public policy through an aspect of their consumer well-being referred to as political well-being. This is a reflection of the individual's internal sense of power and autonomy and of what is right and what is wrong. Freedom to make decisions, vote, and freely choose in the marketplace are part of political well-being.

Public policy responds to issues, problems that arise, causes, and influences such as those of voters, activist citizens, consumer organizations, and lobbyists. At any given time, one set of constituents' goals may be in conflict with another set of constituents' goals. They may not agree or support policies or actions proposed. When conflicts occur, difficult decisions have to be made usually in the interests of the greater good. Most public policy is designed to promote the general public interest, but it is influenced by politics and the support of certain individuals, groups, and organizations.

A common role of government is to regulate. Through regulation, society allows a bureaucracy to promote certain public or community interest causes or goals. An

**Figure 3.2**    This model shows the interaction between three fundamental components in the consumer exchange: consumer, public policy, and markets.

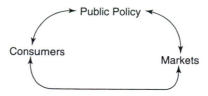

ongoing debate is how much regulatory power government should have versus allowing the market to exist unhampered. In the final analysis, it comes down to a series of trade-offs and decisions about how much regulation is in the best interest of consumers, including the costs involved in regulation.

## Consumer Organizations

Besides consumers, regulators, and markets, other groups such as consumer organizations come into play such as Consumers Union, National Consumers League, and AARP (the American Association of Retired Persons) (see Box 3.1 for a sample list of organizations). As their names imply, consumer organizations may cover a wide range of interests or may specialize in one area such as senior citizens' concerns. They may push for the passage of legislation in the public interest and send

*Consumer organizations assist, protect, and advocate for consumers.*

---

**BOX 3.1    Examples of National Consumer Organizations***

AARP (Consumer Issues Section)
AAFTEC (Alliance Against Fraud in Telemarketing and Electronic Commerce)
National Consumers League
American Council on Consumer Interests (ACCI)
American Council on Science and Health
Center for Science in the Public Interest
Center for the Study of Services
Coalition Against Insurance Fraud
Community Nutrition Institute
Consumer Action
Consumer Alert
Consumer Federation of America
Consumers for World Trade
Families USA Foundation
HALT: An Organization for Americans for Legal Reform
Health Research Group
Jump$tart Coalition for Personal Financial Literacy
National Association of Consumer Agency Administration
National Coalition for Consumer Education
National Community Reinvestment Coalition
National Consumer Law Center
National Consumers League
National Fraud Information Center/Internet Fraud Watch
National Institute for Consumer Education
Public Citizen, Inc.
Self Help for Hard of Hearing People (SHHH)
Society of Consumer Affairs Professionals in Business (SOCAP)
U.S. Public Interest Group (U.S. PIRG)
United Seniors Health Cooperative

*This is not a comprehensive list. More national organizations exist and some come and go. State, local, and international organizations also exist.

staff members to testify before Congress. They may also hire lobbyists or support people to run for political office in order to sway public policy their way. The main mission they have in common is to assist and protect consumers and provide consumer advocacy. Most try to improve the health and safety of consumers and better their lives, including improving their financial health and fair treatment in the marketplace. In the model, they could be placed under consumers as a subgroup, but not all consumers support or appreciate the work of consumer advocacy groups. In many ways, they are a force in and of themselves, so they deserve their own spot in the model. So, to update, a revised model includes other influences and groups such as trade and professional associations which are discussed next.

## Trade and Professional Associations

Companies that manufacture similar products or offer similar services often belong to trade and professional associations which serve to resolve problems between consumers and member companies. They also provide consumer information and education through Web sites and publications. An example is the American Bankers Association at *www.aba.com* which provides consumer education materials. Another example is the Food Marketing Institute at *www.fmi.org* which conducts programs in research, education, industry relations, and public affairs on behalf of its members—grocery retailers and wholesalers. Both of these associations are located in Washington, DC, as are many others. They offer career opportunities for those trained in consumer economics as well as those in public policy. Since trade and professional associations are most associated with markets, they are placed under markets in the model being developed in this chapter.

Besides these organizations, more has been added to the model shown in Figure 3.3 such as the influence or impact of environment (including technology and the economy). Each of these are discussed in the following sections.

## Environment

When we use the word environment in consumer economics, it refers to the space in which all transactions or potential transactions occur. Probably the best way to think of environments is external conditions, all encompassing. To give a specific example, a shopping mall is a consumer environment. An individual or family may window shop or they may actually buy a specific good. Prebuying, buying, and postbuying are all part of the consumption process. Environments affect what is being offered and how well it is received; thus, attractive displays and pleasant music are important. Consumption, therefore, takes place in an environmental context. Think of sitting in a dentist's chair or shopping in a grocery store and what music you hear—probably a preprogrammed tape with soothing instrumental music from old movies such as the *Sound of Music* or *Sleepless in Seattle*.

**Regional subcultures** exist in the United States due to differences in the natural environment and resources, characteristics of immigrant groups, and other social forces, including history and traditions. Beer consumption, advertisements, and formulas vary widely, hence the rise of microbreweries. To compete, large firms such as Anheuser-Busch have regional formulas and **targeted advertising**. For example, Anheuser-Busch divided Texas into regions and developed unique advertis-

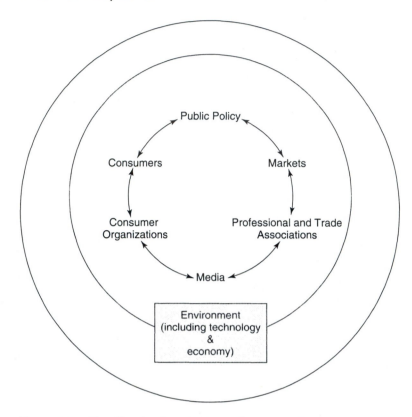

**Figure 3.3**    The Circular Flow Model of Consumer Economics.

ing for Budweiser in each. In the northern part of the state, it used a cowboy image, while in the southern part a Hispanic identity was stressed (Hawkins, Best, and Coney, 2001, p. 171). As other examples of environmental effects, hot donuts and coffee sell better in cold climates than in warm climates. Iced tea is on the menu year-round in the South, but may be a summer only item in New England and Canada. Around the world (partly because of the huge populations in Asia), tea is the most consumed beverage.

*Tea is the most consumed beverage in the world.*

If consumers do not like or need a product, they will not buy it, or they will try it once and reject it. It is estimated that 90 percent of new products fail. When this book went to press, it was yet to be seen if Old Spice High Endurance body wash would succeed or fail even though it had a better chance than average since it is a product extension and the product launch was backed by an estimated $15 million to $20 million in marketing support (Neff, 2002, p. 8).

*About 90 percent of new products fail.*

Failed products are an enormous expense to companies so every effort is made for them to succeed. Even very successful companies make mistakes. Examples of failed products by established businesses include Harley-Davidson wine coolers, Levi Strauss tailored suits for men, Life Savers gum, and Country Time apple cider (Hawkins, Best, and Coney, 2001). Each of these major product launches was an expensive loss. A new movie, for example, could cost millions of dollars to distribute, advertise, and merchandise. Why products fail is a subject of consumer research. One finding is that products are not pretested to the degree that they should be. Another is that manufacturers do not take into account regional differences or shifts in consumer preferences. Whatever the reason, a company has to be well capitalized to withstand the wins and the losses. In 1968 when Estee Lauder Inc. launched Clinique, a new line of skin care products and makeup, it lost money for several years before it became one of the market leaders that it is today (Koehn, 2001). Sometimes companies reinvent themselves, the restaurant chain Boston Chicken changed their name to Boston Market and became a wholly owned subsidiary of McDonald's Corporation, operating more than 650 company-owned restaurants in 28 states. They also sell a line of frozen entrees and jarred gravies and broths, manufactured by H. J. Heinz Co. Their newer restaurants or remodeled restaurants have booths and softer colors and lighting. Alyson Kim, communications manager for the Golden, Colorado–based chain, said, "Customers said they loved our home style food, but the dining experience didn't match it. . . . They wanted a warm, homey atmosphere" (Sams, 2001).

To conclude, the term environment is used in the model in its broadest sense referring to the environment in which consumer-market interactions take place. Environment encompasses the natural environment and human-made environment including the following: the cultural, educational, technological, physical, social, political, economic, situational, chemical, and biological influences. It is a view of the world in which we live and everything contained in it, including measures of time and place and all other external conditions affecting our lives.

Since environment is such a large concept, some theorists have divided it into two parts microenvironment (meaning close to the home and the individual) and macroenvironment (everything that surrounds the microenvironment). It used to be that the microenvironment was the context in which most production and consumption took place, but with the proliferation of world trade, radio, television, and the Internet, consumption even at the individual level is very much influenced by both parts of the environment. For example, you may buy a Hostess cupcake at the local convenience store, but the ingredients (wheat, sugar, and flavoring) and the packaging may have come from anywhere in the world—ingredients are listed on the package label not sources.

## Technology

**Technology** is the application of scientific knowledge to useful purposes. In the model, technology is considered part of the environment. An example of a consumer technology is the introduction of machine-read bar codes on products that are used in grocery and discount stores. Another example is the introduction of automatic teller machines (ATMs) used in financial transactions.

A paradox exists in technology in that most technologies save time while using time or taking time away from other technologies or behaviors. Paradoxes increase conflict or decision making; in other words they make life more complicated. Here is an example of a technology-based decision situation: Should you use a dishwasher to wash six dinner plates, glasses, and forks or should you hand wash them? What is the best use of your time? The trade-off between using a computer and cell phones versus other means of communicating or information search is another example. Research shows that time spent on the Internet and e-mailing—in the evening especially—is taking away from time spent watching television. As another example, American cell phone users age 25 to 34 are more than four times as likely to use their mobile phones as their primary phones than those over age 35 (Gardyn, 2001a).

If a product outdates soon after purchase or before it is worn out, a consumer experiences **technological obsolescence**. This is when products such as computers or video cameras lose value because they so rapidly become technologically out-of-date. No one can anticipate every new product or upgrade, the best one can do is to keep abreast of changes and/or buy equipment/devices that can be upgraded with add-ons. Or, in the case of the nutrition professor, hold on to old technologies and let the new technologies pass you by. New is not always better nor necessary.

## Media

**Media** is a means of mass communications as in newspapers, magazines, television, or the Internet, which has revolutionized human life in developed and developing countries the most in recent years. To get an idea of impact, it is useful to compare it with earlier technologies such as the radio and the television.

Radio exposed listeners to mass advertising, and television let them see it as well as hear it. The heyday of radio was from the 1920s through the 1940s. By the late 1940s it had a competitor in the form of television. By 1947, 200,000 U.S. homes had black-and-white television sets. In 1948, there were enough viewers to make a national audience for the *Ed Sullivan* and *Milton Berle* shows. By 1949, there were 2 million television sets in the United States, showing a very rapid adoption of this form of technology (Goldsmith, 2002). Although available in the 1950s, color television did not become common until the 1960s. In the late 1970s a device for projecting television onto a large screen became widely available. This technological advance was followed by VCRs (videocassette recorders). Presently, over 95 percent of U.S. homes have televisions.

In 1947 there were 200,000 tv sets in the United States; by 1949 there were 2 million.

The first radio shows often had only one sponsor, and the show was often named after that sponsor. Several early television shows also were named after their sponsor such as the 1940s and 1950s *The Texaco Star Theater,* but eventually television shows were so expensive to produce that they had multiple sponsors which is the format we are familiar with today. If we watch a televised football game, we expect to see many different advertisements (razor blades, cars, snack foods) rather than advertisements from a single company. The reason this is important to point out is that with only one sponsor the advertiser had quite a bit of control over program content and the show's stars and guests. Multiple sponsors provide more freedom of expression and a greater differentiation between the ads and the shows.

Today, radio and television can provide background noise, and the listener or viewer may only really notice it when a special song or an interesting show or announcement comes on. In this way, radio and television are different from print forms such as books and magazines that require more focus and usually require the reader to sit down. An exception to this is audio books that people listen to while driving.

With the advent of the remote control, people gained even more options because television and radio advertising could be muted and channels could be changed more quickly without getting up. Similarly Internet users can mute certain messages and ignore others and create musical tapes of only the songs that they want to hear. The Internet is different from radio and television in that it is still undergoing vast experimentation. Advertisements can be changed every few seconds versus a television advertisement that may take months to create and may repeat for months. Can you think of any advertisements that you are tired of or that you find irritating?

**Growth of the Internet.**　The development of the Internet is just part of the development and proliferation of computers. Significant years are as follows*:

| | |
|---|---|
| 1969 | Internet created as the result of a grant from the Advanced Research Projects Agency of the Pentagon. |
| 1977 | Apple II is available. |
| 1981 | IBM personal computer is available. |
| 1984 | Apple Macintosh has mouse and graphical user interface. |
| early 1990s | Internet passes from government to the private sector. |
| 1994 | World Wide Web emerges, a system of clients and servers. |
| 1997 | E-mail proliferates, documents sent from one Internet user to another. |
| 2003 | Nearly 100 percent of U.S. college students have Internet access |

The Internet can be seen as part of media. No one planned the Internet, and it still has few controls. Since no one company or government controls it, it is difficult to set policies or to screen what information is put on the World Wide Web, the information retrieval system.

**Internet Provides Interactivity.**　The Internet is useful in providing services and information, a communication exchange between customers and providers. It is interactive to a greater degree than most other forms of media. Billboards, magazines, radio, and television are mostly one-way exchanges from the publication, station, or program to the listener, viewer, or reader. An exception to this is that magazines have added the interactive feature of providing aftershave, perfume, or grapefruit samples (to increase grapefruit juice sales) that can be smelled. The addition of smell usually in scratch and sniff samples was a true innovation in print medium. Children's books have had similar interactive experiences for years (think of *Pat the Bunny*) before the magazines found a way to inexpensively mass market an interactive experience. Other examples of more interactivity are radio or television call-in or fax-in shows or the ones that allow e-mail messages to be sent and responded to on air.

An interesting mix of Internet and television can be experienced in shows like *Oprah* that continue after the show goes off the air with *oprah.com*. Viewers can go online and follow the discussion that takes place after the show is over. But, most typically television shows are one-way exchanges. You usually can't call in during the program and talk with the actors and suggest plot changes although some shows broadcast live and some stage plays have experimented with this format. In the plays, the characters are presented to the audience at the beginning of the

---

*Source:* Forrester Research, online.

show, and the audience votes as to who shall play what roles. Internet games allow for these types of interactivity so the general trend is for most forms of media to move to more interactivity. Higher involvement usually leads to more sales, so sponsors and advertisers want to encourage as much interactivity as possible. This is why they hand out perfume samples in department stores—if you try it, you are more likely to buy it.

Besides being a source for information and communication, the Internet is a useful tool for buying and selling financial services, software, tickets, collectibles, and computers. According to Connie Johnson, an analyst at Forrester Research, the top online retail stores are*

eBay 10 percent of all retail sales

Amazon 5 percent of all retail sales

Wal-Mart, Target, J. C. Penney, and most other major retailers each have one percent of the stake

The trend in Internet use for buying is upward. For example, Internet sales go up each holiday season. Consumers report that the main reason they shop online is that it is easier. The number of Americans shopping online was about 65 million in 2001 compared with 49 million in 2000, according to Jupiter Media Matrix Inc., a market-research firm. The total number of dollars was over $34 billion in 2001 compared with $24 billion the previous year (Landau, 2001). Since the numbers are constantly changing, memorizing the numbers is less important than witnessing the phenomenon—the upward trend in buying online.

**Media and the Model.** The purpose of media is to inform consumers about goods, services, news, and events and to provide purchase opportunities. Figure 3.4 illustrates the information-transaction process. Negotiations may include price, conditions, model, quantity, and delivery. The transaction is completed when both sides are satisfied and a purchase is made. This may involve an order, money, or a contract.

The two major media categories are

- print, which includes magazines, direct mail, newspapers, mass transit (i.e., signs in subways, buses), billboards, and dealer promotions such as free calendars
- broadcast, which includes the Internet, cable, television, and radio

The newspaper is the most basic of print media. Many national and international newspapers and magazines have regional editions so that advertising and stories can be targeted to certain markets. Newspapers or magazines may have special teen editions such as *Teen People* or *The Wall Street Journal Classroom Edition*. In economi-

---

The process can be diagrammed as:

information sent ⟶ information received ⟶ transaction negotiated ⟶ transaction completed

**Figure 3.4**   The Information-Transfer Process.

---

*\*Source:* Marketwatch.com/new, October 20, 2001.

cally developed nations, the most pervasive forms of media are radio and television. In some countries, radio and television are state run and accept no advertising, but may run government-sponsored spots announcing programs or events.

## CIRCULAR FLOW MODEL OF CONSUMER ECONOMICS

So far, the chapter has built a model of consumer economics that focuses on the transactions that take place between consumers and markets given other conditions and players. *Consumer economics can be described as a collection of activities, situations, or exchanges among several parties that take place within the environment.* It assumes that individuals seek to maximize their satisfaction from the decisions they make and that they seek fair trade and justice in the marketplace. It also assumes that, for the most part, consumers will gather information, a type of resource, before making decisions. The Circular Flow Model of Consumer Economics shows how all the pieces fit together. A circle is used instead of a square because the process involves a fluid motion, a feeling of constant motion rather than an angular or linear beginning and end-type exchange. Relationships are indicated by the arrows that serve as the channels or mediums for exchange.

Theory, research, and common sense suggest that consumers select what messages to receive and process.

The model incorporates theories from many areas. For example, consumers are bombarded daily with hundreds of messages. They cannot evaluate every message so they selectively choose the ones to listen to or read about. Much of this selection is automatic as new perceptions are made to fit comfortably existing knowledge or cognition (Foxall, Goldsmith, and Brown, 1998).

## CONSUMER DECISIONS AND EXPERIENCE

The relationships within the model are based on the fact that consumers hope to increase their well-being through consumption (something they have to do to exist) and that there are various indicators of well-being. One of these is environmental well-being. In consumer economics, we are concerned about the quality of the natural environment and the sustaining of it for future generations. Environmental well-being refers to a concern for society's role in the earth's diminishing resources, which affects the overall well-being of individuals, families, and communities.

Our consumer life is also influenced by our experiences. Think of all the experiences you have had visiting restaurants, hotels, theme parks, bakeries, national parks, grocery stores, schools, and the homes of friends. As a specific example, what have you observed about birthday cakes? At birthday parties, were the cakes store-bought or homemade? Which do you think is better? What is the tradition in your family? Do you blow out candles on the cake? Do you sing happy birthday? Or, do you ignore birthdays all together? Many of our traditions and consumer experiences have their roots in our early life.

Based on our childhood experiences, we make assumptions about how other people live. College is often a real awakening to the differences in how people live—what they eat, what they consider cleanliness, sleeping habits, and so forth.

For instance, one male student reported that his roommate bought a sack of potatoes and existed almost exclusively on baked potatoes. He said, "It freaked me out." Another male student reported that he ate cereal and bananas 90 percent of the time because it was easy to fix. An 18-year-old boy coming home from two college friends' apartment told his mother that all they had in the refrigerator was water and milk. He said, "Doesn't everyone at least have orange juice?" His assumption was based on his home refrigerator that was well stocked. Another way to look at the consumer experience is through the type of experiences that businesses provide such as Carnival describing themselves as "The Fun Ship" or "The Most Popular Cruise Line in the World." Many companies are not only selling products or services, but also they are selling experiences or entertainment such as those found in theme restaurants, for example, Rainforest Cafe, Hard Rock Cafe, or McDonald's. Note the use of the word café. What images does that word conjure up versus the words tearoom, roadhouse, or diner. When stores decorate for the holidays, they are also providing a fun shopping experience; they are getting customers in a shopping mood. Spas try to get their guests to relax through massages, creams, lotions, aromatherapy, and soft lighting and music.

How does experience relate to the remaining parts of the model: public policy and consumer organizations? Nearly everyone has experience with rules and regulations, with government, with elections and politics. Out of this experience comes opinions about who should be president, the right and wrong way to do things, and about what would be best for the greater good. Consumer organizations provide consumer education and advocate for change on behalf of consumers. In terms of public policy most legislation is based on previous laws and regulations. As the economy and consumers change, legislation and the causes that consumer organizations take up need to be updated.

## CONSUMERS

Although the model shows consumers as only one player in a series of players, they are the most important part. They drive the system, or, as noted in chapter 1 the consumer is sovereign or king. This is true, for the most part, but even kings don't always get their way. For example, a consumer may go to a store to buy a certain product and then learn that the store no longer carries that product nor does anyone else in town. In this situation, the consumer feels more like a pawn than a king. Given that it is an imperfect and complicated world and that the demands of the mass market have to be considered in the mix of goods that are offered, the individual consumer is shown as a player in an interactive environment rather than being placed at the center of the process.

In the model, consumers are placed directly across from markets because as the first illustration in this chapter shows the primary relationship or exchange is between consumers and markets. Consumers participate when they spend, save, barter, trade, and invest. They are involved in public policy when they vote or act to influence public policy in some other way. Consumers also use and dispose of goods, gather information and opinions, and react to media and other forms of communication. By behaviors such as voting and gathering information, consumers hope to improve their **quality of life,** which is their perception of and satisfaction with their lives. During lean economic times, Americans focus more energy and money on keeping their homes and families secure (Gardyn, 2001b).

**Consumption** refers to the using up of goods. Consumers have a **level of living** which is the way they are actually living but they aspire to a **standard of living** or quality of life. The difference is between how one actually lives and how one would like to live, actual versus ideal. This is connected to one's self-concept and self-concept is important in all cultures. There is the private self (how you see yourself) and the public or social self (how others see you). A strong disconnect between the private and public self can cause confusion. Public figures such as actors and politicians and their families are confronted with this all the time; most of the rest of us experience it to a lesser degree. **Lifestyle** is how one lives. It includes patterns of time use, living space, what is thought to be important and how money is spent. Have you ever heard the expressions "contented housewife," "business tycoons," or "social climber"? These are phrases that describe lifestyles.

Much of consumption behavior is directed toward improving one's lifestyle, which is linked to self-concept. For example, someone may say "next year I'm moving into a better apartment" or "someday when I'm working full time I'm going to buy Ralph Lauren clothes." When millions of consumers make similar choices, this is called **mass consumption** which has a tremendous impact on the general economy.

## Consumer Well-Being: Defined

As mentioned earlier, a key aspect of consumers' lives is their well-being. Well-being is made up of a variety of factors, including material, social, and spiritual dimensions (Chambers, 1999). In the introduction we said that consumers are acquisitive. This means they want more things, ideas, and information, and they have to replace things that are worn out or used up. People consume or spend money to take care of basic needs such as food, clothing, and shelter and to take care of future needs through investing in retirement plans, making estate plans or setting up trusts, and by buying insurance. Through such activities, they are providing for their own well-being and that of their family members.

Consumer well-being is an umbrella term including

1. *Economic well-being:* the degree to which individuals and families have economic adequacy and security. It is the desire for or extent of protection against the economic risks people face in their daily lives (loss of employment, illness, bankruptcy, bank failures, poverty, and destitution in old age). Economic well-being also includes an overriding sense of economic equity or economic justice. This involves concepts of fairness not only within one's own community and nation but also internationally. The setting of a minimum wage is an example of economic equity or justice. Another example is child labor laws.

2. *Physical well-being:* the right to safety and to goods and services that provide for one's physical needs. Threats to physical well-being include but are not limited to, unsafe and irresponsible personal conduct or the actions of a third party; illness, disease, and malnutrition; lack of or inappropriate exercise; dangerous and hazardous products; adulterated foods; incompetent and irresponsible service delivery; and environmental degradation (McGregor and Goldsmith, 1998, p. 122).

3. *Social well-being:* the social space of the family or the group that provides for a sense of emotional well-being, caring, and working together. "The crux of social

well-being is interpersonal relationships and the dynamics of familial interaction to fulfill six basic functions: procreation, socialization, economic consumption and production, social control, physical care and maintenance, and love and emotional support" (McGregor and Goldsmith, 1998, p. 123). **Socialization** refers to the process of learning to interact with others, forming cooperative relationships, participating in society, and learning the ways of daily life. Parents and family are very important in the socialization of children. As social beings, we have a need to belong and this need to belong leads us to join groups, form families and circles of friends, buy certain brands, or wear certain types of clothes or adornments.

4. *Psychological or emotional well-being:* the mental state of individuals within the family or other groups. The emphasis in social well-being is on the group whereas the emphasis in psychological or emotional well-being is on the individual. Emotions are strong feelings that affect one's behavior and attitudes, general temperament, and demeanor. Consumer socialization is part of emotional well-being as well as part of social well-being. Consumer and family life specialists are interested in how well people are socialized to be consumers such as how they process information and make decisions, how they react to advertising, and how they seek remedy or recourse when a consumer situation comes up. When something goes wrong, do they fly into a rage or do they follow the steps necessary to get a refund? Psychological or emotional well-being is associated with thought and reflection, a sense of self and self-preservation.

5. *Environmental well-being, political well-being, and spiritual well-being:* The first two realms were introduced in previous sections; spiritual well-being "captures a layer of well-being, a sense of insight, and ethereal, intangible evolution not readily imparted by either social or psychological well-being as conventionally defined" (McGregor and Goldsmith, 1998, p. 124). A very broad definition of spiritual well-being encompasses the joy and sense of completeness associated with a connectedness with the world, peace, hope, and faith gained from insights and moments of growth and enlightenment. It is not simply about organized religion although many people experience spiritual well-being in this way. Nearly 90 percent of Americans claim a religious affiliation (Kosmin and Lachman, 1993).

Nearly 90 percent of Americans claim a religious affiliation.

If we consider the concepts of trade-offs and opportunity costs introduced in chapter one, we can see where individuals may choose to spend their time in church versus in a mall or singing in a choir versus going to a movie, or walking in the woods and communing with nature versus choosing a more consumption-oriented activity, or giving to charities versus buying another $10 T-shirt. This is not to imply that spiritual well-being and consumption activities are always opposites. Someone may find looking at a beautiful Christmas display at a store to be a joyful, spirit-lifting experience. Another may get a lift from singing the school song or the national anthem at a football game. Spiritual well-being may include beauty or aesthetics, music, patriotism, an appreciation of nature, and all sorts of other qualities or reactions, individually defined and appreciated.

## Consumer Well-Being: Measured

Discussing well-being or the qualities that make up human welfare is one thing, measuring it is another since so much of it depends on attitudes and people's responses. The United Nations Development Programme's **Human Development**

**Table 3.1**   Human Development Index Scores for Selected Developing Nations

| Nation | Life Expect. (Years) | Adult Literacy (%) | School Enroll. Ratio | Real Per Capita GDP (PPP$)* | HDI Score |
|--------|----------------------|--------------------|----------------------|-----------------------------|-----------|
| Brazil    | 66.8 | 84.0 | 80 | 6,480 | 0.739 |
| Turkey    | 69.0 | 83.2 | 61 | 6,350 | 0.728 |
| Sri Lanka | 73.1 | 90.7 | 66 | 2,490 | 0.721 |
| Congo     | 50.8 | 70.7 | 39 |   880 | 0.479 |
| Pakistan  | 64.0 | 40.9 | 43 | 1,560 | 0.508 |

*PPP = purchasing power parity (a measure of domestic income in terms of goods purchasing power).
*Source:* UNDP, Human Development Report, 1999.

**Index (HDI)** puts a number on (quantifies) well-being by combining several measures of human well-being. The HDI is broader than consumer well-being per se, but it touches on it. The HDI compares the progress of nations by using the same measures of quality of life across the globe. The HDI uses an adjusted measure of real per capita gross domestic product (GDP) as one component of an index that includes school enrollment ratios, adult literacy, and life expectancy. Table 3.1 shows how five developing nations compared on HDI Index Scores.

## Other Factors Including the Consumer Price Index and the Consumer Expenditure Survey

Connected to the discussion of well-being are other factors that consumer psychologists and economists look to as indicators of the strength of the economy since consumers need confidence to buy high-ticket items such as consumer durables and homes. **Consumer durables** are products bought by consumers that are expected to last three years or more, including automobiles, appliances, and furniture. Because of the lasting nature of these products, consumers look for quality. Companies such as Maytag Corporation and Electrolux that make these types of products are considered consumer durables manufacturers. In contrast, consumer nondurables manufacturers make more immediately consumable items such as food or medicines. The market basket on which the consumer price index is based includes shelter, transportation, tires, utilities, entertainment, health care, clothing, and services. The **Consumer Price Index (CPI)** measures prices each month of a fixed basket of 400 goods and services (durables and nondurables) bought by a typical consumer. The CPI is published by the Bureau of Labor Statistics (BLS) in the Department of Labor and is based on 100 in 1982. "The process by which the Bureau measures price changes to consumers each month requires the efforts of hundreds of BLS employees and the patient cooperation of thousands of individuals in households and retail outlets throughout the country. The cycle begins during the first week of the month when BLS data collectors (called economic assistants) gather price information from selected department stores, supermarkets, service stations, doctors' offices, rental units, etc. For the entire month, about 80,000 prices are recorded in 87 urban areas" (*www.bls.gov*). During these monthly visits, the economic assistant collects price data on a specific good or service. If available, the economic assistant records the price. If not available or if there are changes in the quality of an item, the assistant selects a new item or records

*Consumer durables last three or more years.*

*The consumer price index provides a statistical measure of the nation's economic well-being.*

the quality change. This sampling technique is used because it would be impossible to gather the price of every good or service bought each month in the United States. The entire process takes about 20 days for the reviewing, analyzing, and publishing of the data. The CPI is widely held as a cost-of-living benchmark that affects adjustments in Social Security payments and other pay schedules and tax brackets. The thinking is that if it costs more to live then the government should respond by increasing payments, for example, to the elderly. The president, Congress, and the Federal Reserve Board note trends in the CPI and use them for formulating policy. The CPI is used to adjust wages and payments such as to keep pensions, rents, royalties, alimony, and child support payments in line with changing prices. At the headquarters in Washington, DC, and in regional offices, specialists check the incoming data for accuracy and consistency. Computer programs calculate the weighted changes in prices. By the time the CPI is reported on the television news, the process has started all over again, and the next month's data are being gathered.

The CPI is actually a series of interrelated samples. These include the **Consumer Expenditure Survey** collected from a national sample of over 30,000 families which provides detailed information on spending habits. "This enables BLS to construct the CPI market basket of goods and services to assign each item in the market basket a weight or importance based on total family expenditures. Another national sample of about 16,800 families serves as the basis for a Point-of-Purchase survey that identifies the places where households purchase various types of goods and services" (*www.bls.gov*). Also, the BLS uses census data to determine which urban areas are selected for price checks. BLS jobs openings, including positions for economic assistants, economists, and administrators as well as internships and summer employment, are listed on the *www.bls.gov* Web site.

## Measuring Consumer Confidence

Another measure of consumer well-being is consumer confidence. **Consumer confidence** is measured and nationally reported by two organizations:

1. The Conference Board, a New York-based organization
2. The University of Michigan's Survey Research Center in Ann Arbor

The Conference Board specializes in consumers' plans to buy cars, houses, appliances, and participate in activities such as traveling. They do this by sampling the attitudes of 5,000 consumers with multiple-choice type questions and analyzing the results. According to the Conference Board, consumer confidence was on a decline in October 2001, dropping to 85.5 from 114 in August—the steepest fall since October 1990. According to their survey, fewer than 1 in 5 consumers rated business conditions as favorable, down from more than 1 in 4 in the previous month (Paul, 2001).

During the same time period, The Survey Research Center found a similar drop in consumer confidence. The Survey Research Center measures a sample of 500 consumers' expectations about the economy and their own personal finances and tries to determine attitudes about consumption and changes and trends therein. Both these organizations seek to determine how consumers view the health and direction of the economy and how they are responding to it so the measures are very much about perception. Optimism about the economy makes the consumer feel more confident about spending and more willing to acquire debt (credit cards and loans). Consumer confidence levels are reported in the news and used by government and business so they can make better policies and plans of action.

To provide more updated figures, the Conference Board reported a high of 110.2 in March 2002 compared with the previous six months (Eisinger, 2002). Likewise, the U.S. Commerce Department reported that in March 2002, personal income, saving, and spending rose. The general thinking is that if consumer confidence appears to wobble, consumer spending will fall; if confidence is up, then spending goes up. Investors watching these figures react in terms of what companies they will invest in and what stocks they may sell. A large reported gain or dive will impact investor reaction more strongly than a slight dip or rise.

When consumer confidence is down, how might consumers and businesses respond? This is the type of question investors would ask themselves. During times of uncertainty, familiar brands such as Proctor & Gamble's Ivory soap provide reassurance. According to an article published after the economic downturn and the September 11, 2001, tragedies:

> Marketing messages should be straightforward, honest and down-to-earth. This is not the time for messages about luxury or indulgence, which can come across as insensitive and irrelevant. Neither is it the moment for cheap solutions and quick fixes. People want to feel confident that what they're getting is the "right" product, something they can count on, something that will deliver on its promise. (Paul, 2001, p. 23)

In contrast, how should businesses respond when consumer confidence is up? In 2002, consumers were marching to a different drummer than they were in 2001. Luxury became attractive again. Consumers were buying upscale appliances, cars, electronics, travel, and homes. "Millions of Americans who once made up the vast middle of the nation's $7 trillion consumer market migrated upscale toward premium and luxury goods" (White and Leung, 2002, p. A1). According to Helmut Panke, an executive at German auto maker BMW, "today's auto market is increasingly shaped like an hourglass," meaning that there are many high end and low end purchases and not many in the middle. When interviewed many consumers say for a few thousand more they would rather have a premium car than an ordinary car (White and Leung, 2002, p. A1). For another example of this trend toward high-end consumption, consider the following:

> Who would pay $2,200 for a washer-dryer set with stainless-steel drums, 12 different wash cycles, rounded styling, baby-blue trim and room for 22 bath towels? Whirlpool Corp. thought it knew the answer when it introduced its Duet line last year: a niche of affluent laundry-doers willing to pay about three times the price of the company's midrange machines. Whirlpool expected the Duet would make up only 5% of its North American washer and dryer sales. Instead, in its first six months on the market, the Duet line is on track to double Whirlpool's projections. (White and Leung, 2002, p. A1)

As an example of a typical family who bought a Duet, the Boyd family with four children, who live in suburban Chicago (the mother is a substitute teacher, the father is a field manager in a construction company) said they bought the Duet because "we find in the long run it's more cost-effective to have high-quality products," because they perform better and last longer (White and Leung, 2002, p. A8). As this book went to press consumer confidence was rising and luxury goods in many categories were selling well.

During uncertain times, consumers are drawn to familiar brands.

## MARKET/BUSINESS

The goal of business is to maximize profits.

As the preceding quotes illustrate, today's businesses need to be sensitive to consumers' perceptions and actions at any given point in time. The goal of business is to *maximize profits*. They pursue this goal while cooperating with government and listening to consumers and watching sales figures closely.

Businesses cannot get so stuck on current conditions and issues that they lose the bigger picture which is planning for the future. For example, Albertson's, a food and drug retailer based in Boise, Idaho, updates their grocery stores' appearance every ten years. When they plan their redesigns, they have to imagine what future grocery stores will look like. Will there be the usual 21-aisle store with freezer cases? Will we still push carts up and down the aisles or will groceries be ready for us at the door of the store or delivered directly to our homes? Experiments with both are taking place, and it is not yet clear what the future holds except that history shows us that we can expect changes not just in store design and layout, but also in products. The typical 1950s North American grocery shopper would not have known what zucchini squash was or sushi or pesto.

In ancient times, markets were actual places where consumers and producers came together to trade.

Taking it back several steps into our past, in ancient times most markets were physical locations where consumers and producers came together to make trades. Consumers and producers set prices by arguing over what would be the right price. In many countries today, including the United States, Northern Ireland, France, Finland, and Mexico, farmers markets coexist with modern grocery stores. Some markets allow or encourage bargaining; most have set prices. Other examples are the New York Stock Exchange and tobacco and cattle markets where buyers and sellers come together to buy and trade. The Internet and other modern telecommunications services and devices have made being in the same location less important than it was in the past.

## Functions of Typical Companies or Corporations

Average size grocery stores have 40,000–50,000 products.

In the old markets, selection was limited by season and availability. With modern transportation and growing methods, seasons are less important in terms of what is offered. A concern for the future is how much choice can consumers handle? For example, most large grocery stores and Home Depot supply stores offer 40,000–50,000 products, and some of the superstores go as high as 100,000. How much more selection do consumers need? Is there an optimum number of products or size of store?

To handle these sorts of questions, a typical company that markets to consumers has various divisions, including top management, marketing, finance, human relations, research and development (R&D), purchasing, manufacturing, and accounting and sometimes product design and in-house consumer or public/media relations or investor relations. Here are their functions:

- Management sets the goals, the missions, objectives, and strategies often answering to a board of directors.
- Marketing promotes, sells, conducts survey research, or conducts focus groups to gather consumer opinions, and distributes goods.
- Finance balances current funds and procures more funds. A chief financial officer (CFO) may visit banks to get loans for factory expansion or may give

presentations to mutual fund managers in hopes that they will buy substantial numbers of shares in his or her company.

- Human relations departments take care of employee needs such as hiring and benefits.
- Research and development focuses on developing new and exciting, yet safe and effective, products. An example is Post-it Notes used in offices developed in the R&D Department of 3M (Minnesota Mining and Manufacturing).
- Purchasing gets supplies and materials, such as raw materials at a good price.
- Manufacturing oversees the production of a quality product and handles quantity.
- Accounting watches the books, checks costs and expenditures. Sometimes a head tax accountant moves into the finance department, and there are other movements between the other groups within companies noted in this section.
- Product design may be part of marketing or R&D or may be free-standing.
- Large companies usually hire outside firms to do their major public relations campaigns, including advertising, but they may have an in-house division to handle day-to-day media inquiries such as a newspaper columnist asking for a media kit with press releases and photos or slides.
- Large companies that sell consumer goods or services have consumer relations departments to handle consumer inquiries and complaints and report consumer trends to higher management. Thousands of companies have such departments from airlines to toy and food manufacturers. Choose nearly any packaged food product off a shelf at the grocery store or at home, and on the label there will be the toll-free number and address of the consumer relations department. For example, on the back of a Progresso French Onion soup can it says: "Questions or Comments? Call 1-800-200-9377 weekdays 8–6 CT. Information from label and end of can will be helpful. Consumer Relations, P.O. Box 555, Vineland, NJ 98360."
- If the company has stock that is publicly traded (in other words the stock is available in a stock exchange), they may have an investor relations department. An investor owning stock or thinking of buying stock can contact the investor relations department to find out more about how the company is doing and in particular inquire about the influences on stock. Figure 3.5 shows all these components.

## Entrepreneurship

Business doesn't exist without leadership. Unique, industry changing leaders are called **entrepreneurs**. Entrepreneurs pursue new business opportunities relentlessly, without becoming deterred by the limited resources that he or she initially controlled (Stevenson, 1985). Few are called and even fewer succeed. Entrepreneurs such as Bill Gates or Michael Dell are rare, and timing is everything. When they started their computer businesses, only a small number of people owned a personal computer let alone one that was made to order or designed for their individual purposes. Many students enrolled in consumer economics classes are interested in forming their own business some day, selling a product, or offering a service. The opportunities are limitless.

**Figure 3.5**    Components of Typical Consumer Products Companies. Note that in a smaller company, many of these functions may be performed by one employee or outsourced to another company. For example, accounting, public relations, or marketing may be done by an outside firm. Manufacturing may take place in another country. In a large multinational company, top management and many other functions may be spread throughout the world.

The concept of entrepreneurship is not new. In 1759 in the midst of the Industrial Revolution, Josiah Wedgwood founded his own pottery workshop with the idea of making affordable but well-designed dinnerware for the masses. He noticed that with the improved economy, more people wanted consumer goods, including china, linens, clocks, tea, tobacco, chocolate, window curtains, books, and cutlery (Koehn, 2001, p. 24). China was fast replacing the wood and pewter dishes that Britons had used for centuries. Within a few years the Wedgwood brand was well established and continues to be a leading brand of quality china, house wares, and giftware today. Besides developing new methods of production, Wedgwood was a master at organizing. He gained good public relations by making special sets for royalty that were displayed at great events and exhibitions.

How did Josiah Wedgwood become a successful entrepreneur? What qualities or characteristics does one need to succeed in a competitive business environment? Nancy Koehn in her study of six entrepreneurs documented in *Brand New: How Entrepreneurs Earned Consumers' Trust from Wedgwood to Dell* writes that each entrepreneur "intended to make the most of the moment to construct a name, brand and organization that would endure, and each succeeded brilliantly, in substantial measure, for the following five reasons:

- They had deep knowledge and personal experience of their product or service.
- They learned quickly from their mistakes and made rapid adjustments.
- They created meaningful brands that distinguished their offerings and responded to consumers' changing priorities.
- They initiated a process of reciprocal learning with their customers that resulted from ongoing two-way communication with them.
- They created a range of organizational capabilities that delivered on the promises of their respective brands." (p. 320)

Their efforts have important consequences for businesses and for consumers. Without their energy, foresight, and sheer drive, products may have remained unchanged for many years, and needs gone unfulfilled.

## Women as Entrepreneurs and Business Owners

In the United States, most of the entrepreneurs have been men, but that trend is changing. As recently as 1973, women owned just 4.6 percent of the U.S. businesses. By 2000, that percentage rose to nearly 50 percent. Between 1987 and 2000, the number of women-owned businesses doubled from 4.5 million to 9.1 million in the United States (Allon, 2001). These businesses employ more people than the Fortune 500 companies. In other words, businesses run by women are flourishing and part of the reason may be that women understand the needs of female consumers better. This is important because as mentioned in the introduction women account for 80 percent of the consumer spending in this country. Go to the grocery store, who do you see? Go to the mall, who do you see? Go to a Gap for Kids, who do you see? One might assume most shoppers in Home Depot or Lowe's are male, but recent surveys show about one-half the shoppers in Home Depot and Lowe's are women.

## SUMMARY

Adam Smith, founder of modern economics, said that "to be human is to exchange freely." This chapter explored theories that explain or provide insight into consumer behavior and presented a new multifaceted circular flow model of consumer economics. It was also said that consumer researchers follow the scientific method, a manner of analyzing issues following five steps. They recognize problems, make assumptions, develop models, make predictions, and check, control, or test facts or outcomes. They are concerned about scarcity and how consumers make transactions in a complex market involving public policy inputs and others.

Theory and the exchange process were defined. Examples of various theories were given that explain consumer behavior and the variances thereof.

Consumer decisions take place in an overall environment including technology, and they are based on experience. When one makes a new purchase, it is influenced by past purchase experiences as well as media and other factors. Public policy serves as a mediator or rule maker. Consumer organizations seek to protect, educate, and advocate for consumers. Consumer well-being was introduced as an umbrella term referring to many aspects of life, including economic, psychological or emotional, environmental, political, and spiritual well-being. Measures of consumer well-being include the Human Development Index (HDI), the consumer price index, and consumer confidence. In business, unique leaders emerge called entrepreneurs who substantially change industries: examples are Michael Dell, Bill Gates, and Josiah Wedgwood.

Consumer economists are curious about why people behave as they do.

The last chapter's summary challenged you to think like a consumer economist. Here is another facet that this chapter has added: consumer economists are curious, they want to know why people spend money and behave as they do. This is what consumer economics is all about. Given scarce resources why do people buy what they do? How much are consumers influenced by family and friends? How can they become better consumers? How can we improve consumer well-being as part of the greater picture of improving human welfare? Theories help us predict future behavior and models help us visualize the interplay between various groups and influences including individuals' real and perceived self-concepts.

## KEY POINTS

1. The objective of consumer economics is to understand the real world and how it operates, how exchanges or transactions take place and the factors (such as environment and experience) that influence them.
2. Theories and models are abstractions of the real world; they are used to organize and visualize thoughts and connections or relationships.
3. The Theory of Reasoned Action is a consumer behavior theory that states that one's own attitudes and those of others matter when it comes to a purchase decision.
4. Prospect theory argues that people make consumption decisions even when they are uncertain. They are not always rational, self-interested, and calculating. Kahneman and Tversky, authors of prospect theory, won the Nobel Prize in recognition for their work integrating psychology with economics and in so doing laying the groundwork for behavioral economics.
5. Innovation theory is a consumer behavior theory that indicates that innovations diffuse through social systems and that some people are innovators (early buyers or adopters) whereas others are late adopters or laggards. Research indicates that the differences vary by product category.
6. A new model, the circular flow model of consumer economics, was introduced. In this model the key players are consumers, business, public policy, media, and consumer organizations interacting within an environmental and experiential context.
7. Consumer economics is an applied social science. Perceived wants are unlimited and resources to satisfy them are limited, hence consumers make decisions about how to allocate scarce resources.
8. Level of living (actual) is different from standard of living (ideal). Much of consumption behavior is directed at raising one's level of living. The consumer price index, conducted monthly by the Bureau of Labor Statistics, is a leading measure of inflation, buying power.

9. Consumer confidence is tracked each month by two main organizations: The Conference Board (New York City–based) and the University of Michigan's Survey Research Center. Consumer confidence fluctuates, and markets, to be successful, have to be responsive to changes in how consumers feel and act.

10. There are several components of consumer well-being. The United Nations has attempted to compare human welfare conditions (including PPP$ which refers to goods purchasing power in relation to income) across many nations using the Human Development Index (HDI).

11. In ancient times, markets were physical locations where buyers and producers haggled over prices. Some such markets such as farmers' markets still exist, but for the most part, consumers and producers do not physically meet—there are many middlemen in between. Modern businesses have numerous divisions that have specialized functions.

## KEY TERMS

| | | |
|---|---|---|
| acquisitive | exchange process | socialization |
| behavioral economics | Human Development | standard of living |
| brand extension | Index (HDI) | targeted advertising |
| consumer confidence | innovators | technology |
| consumer durables | level of living | technological |
| Consumer Expenditure | lifestyle | obsolescence |
| Survey | mass consumption | theory |
| consumer-market | media | theory of mental |
| conflict | models | accounting |
| consumer price index | prospect theory | theory of reasoned |
| (CPI) | public policy | action |
| consumption | quality of life | transaction |
| endowment effect | rational | |
| entrepreneurs | regional subcultures | |

## DISCUSSION QUESTIONS

1. What do you think of prospect theory? Give an example of when you were uncertain but went ahead and made a consumption decision anyway. Describe the outcome (positive or negative) of the decision.

2. Give an example of a product that you were an innovator in (an early buyer) and an example of a product that you have been a late majority or laggard in buying. Describe why you were an early buyer in one case, but a late buyer (or nonbuyer) in another.

3. According to Pamela Paul, "Americans want good quality and good value from good companies doing good things." Do you agree or disagree? Explain your answer. How does a declining economy affect consumers' behavior, especially their need for value?

4. Visit one of the Web sites in the E-Resources section and find what issues they discuss.

## E-RESOURCES

| | |
|---|---|
| The Federal Trade Commission www.ftc.gov | Government source, advertising, labeling |
| Center for Media Education www.cme.org/cme | Organization, children, and advertising |
| Better Business Bureau www.bbb.org | Organization supported by businesses, advertising, product, and service-quality issues |

## REFERENCES

Ajzen, I., and M. Fishbein, (1980). *Understanding attitudes and predicting social behavior.* Englewood Cliffs, NJ: Prentice Hall.

Allon, J. (2001). *Turn your passion into profits.* New York: Hearst Books.

Chambers, R. (1999). *Whose reality counts?* London: Intermediate Technology Place.

Eisinger, J. (April 30, 2002). Ahead of the tape: Today's market forecast. *Wall Street Journal,* p. C1.

Foxall, G., R. Goldsmith, and S. Brown. (1998). *Consumer psychology for marketing,* 2d ed. London: Thomson Business Press.

Gardyn, R. (December 2001a). Phone home. *American Demographics,* pp. 18–19.

Gardyn, R. (December 2001b). The home front. *American Demographics,* pp. 34–36.

Goldsmith, E. (2002). Colgate Palmolive. *Encyclopedia of Advertising,* NY: Fitzroy Dearborn.

Hawkins, D., R. Best, and K. Coney. (2001). *Consumer behavior,* 8th ed. Boston: Irwin McGraw Hill.

Koehn, N. (2001). *Brand new: How entrepreneurs earned consumers' trust from Wedgwood to Dell.* Boston: Harvard Business School Press.

Kosmin, B., and S. Lachman. (1993). *One nation under God.* New York: Harmony Books, pp. 88–93.

Landau, M. D. (October 22, 2001). Holiday hints. *Wall Street Journal,* p. R4.

Lowenstein, R. (January 2003). A salute to the irrational. *SmartMoney,* pp. 42–43.

McGregor, S., and E. Goldsmith. (Summer 1998). Expanding our understanding of quality of life, standard of living, and well-being. *Journal of Family and Consumer Sciences,* p. 122.

Neff, J. (December 30, 2002). P&G shores up Old Spice with body-wash extension. *Advertising Age,* p. 8.

Paul, P. (December 2001). Pulse: A critical look at American views. *American Demographics,* pp. 22–23.

Robinson-Brown, L. (December 19, 2002). *Daniel Kahneman wins Nobel Prize.* News from Princeton University, Office of Communication, Princeton, NJ.

Rogers, E. M. (1995). *Diffusion of innovation,* 4th ed., New York: Free Press.

Sams, R. (December 13, 2001). Third Boston Market on the way. *Tallahassee Democrat,* p. E1.

Schor, J. B. (1998). *The overspent American.* New York: Harper Perennial.

Sheppard, B., J. Hartwick, and P. Warshaw. (December 1988). The theory of reasoned action. *Journal of Consumer Research,* pp. 324–343.

Stevenson, H. (1985). A perspective on entrepreneurship. In *New Business Ventures and the Entrepreneur,* eds. H. H. Stevenson, Michael J. Roberts, and H. Irving Grousbeck. Homewood, IL: Richard D. Irwin, pp. 2–15. See also William A. Sahlman, Howard H. Stevenson, Michael J. Roberts, and Amar Bhide, eds. (1995). *The entrepreneurial venture.* Boston: Harvard Business School Press, p. 1.

United Nations Development Programme. *Human development report 2000.* Oxford, England: Oxford University Press.

Well, M. (December 10, 2001). Less than perfect pitch. *Forbes,* pp. 122–24.

White, G., and S. Leung. (March 29, 2002). Middle market shrinks as Americans migrate toward the high end. *Wall Street Journal,* pp. A1 and A8.

# PART 2

# Consumer Protection

# Consumer Responsibilities, Redress, and Law

*Why should there not be patient confidence in the ultimate justice of the people? Is there any better or equal hope in the world?*

Abraham Lincoln

## Learning Objectives

1. Define fraud and know that identity theft is the number one fraud.
2. Discuss consumer responsibilities.
3. Discuss consumer service problems.
4. Recognize steps to follow before buying.
5. Know the steps to follow to complain effectively.
6. Understand how small claims courts work.

## INTRODUCTION

The second chapter documented the growth of the consumer movement. The emphasis was on consumer protection legislation that was passed to remedy or curtail abuses in the marketplace. This chapter discusses the other side of the coin, the responsibilities that consumers have in the marketplace. For example, it is their responsibility to spend and invest wisely and to consider the environmental implications of their consumption not only for themselves but also for future generations. They also have a responsibility to carefully examine products and avoid falling victim to fraudulent schemes. This is easier said than done because consumers are exposed daily to get-rich quick schemes, miracle diets, and mechanical belts that shake off fat. Who buys these things, such as pharmaceutical-grade industrial strength olive oil pills to build muscles, especially when they know that they don't work? Nearly all of us are vulnerable to sales pitches, some more sophisticated than others, that promise improved appearance or increased bank accounts. If we can take a pill rather than exercise to build muscles that is pretty attractive. And, maybe it is true that people in the Mediterranean have the secrets to a long life and now their secret (olive oil) can be ours! Hope often triumphs over experience or common sense. This is not to say that hope is bad, a certain amount is important as the opening quote by Abraham Lincoln illustrates, but hope has to be tempered with a degree of skepticism. One of the sayings in consumerism is that if it sounds too good to be true, it probably isn't. What complicates the process of sorting the legitimate from the fraudulent is that often fraudulent products are sold by legitimate stores such as drug stores or pharmacies and that the fraudulent

*If it sounds too good to be true, it probably isn't.*

products may have some basis in fact although greatly exaggerated. In this chapter, the steps to follow if a person becomes a victim of any kind of fraud or buys a faulty product will be covered as well as ways to reduce the chances of it happening. This chapter also discusses the more general topic of customer service and the steps to follow in the complaint process regardless of the nature of the complaint. When all else fails the last resource is the court system.

## TOP CONSUMER FRAUD COMPLAINTS

Poor quality products need to be differentiated from fraud. A **fraud** is an intentional deception perpetrated to deprive another person of his or her assets. Consumers deal with many frauds, but the fraud area rising the fastest is identity theft. It is the leading consumer fraud complaint, far exceeding gripes about Internet auctions and services. Of the 380,000 complaints compiled by the Federal Trade Commission in 2002, 43 percent were about identity theft up from 42 percent the previous year (Ho, 2002). *The hijacking of a person's identity information, such as Social Security numbers or credit card numbers, to steal money or commit fraud is one of the fastest-growing crimes in the United States.* The number of people victimized is estimated at 700,000 a year and increasing. Most victims do not know how or when their identity was stolen. It costs the average victim more than $1,000 in expenses to cope with the damage to accounts and reputation. "This is a crime that is almost solely on the shoulders of the victim to resolve," said Beth Givens, director of the Privacy rights Clearinghouse. "They're beleaguered, they're tired, they're angry, and it takes them a good deal of time to recover." In some cases, recovery of one's financial identity can take as many as five years to get bank accounts and financial records straightened out. The most likely use of another person's identity is for credit card fraud. Other major categories include fraudulent bank and cell phone accounts. The top consumer fraud complaints compiled by the FTC (percent of complaints) are as follows:

Identity theft (43 percent)

Internet auctions (13 percent)

Internet services, computers (6 percent)

Advance fee loans, credit protection (5 percent)

Shop-at-home and catalog sales (5 percent)

Foreign money offers (4 percent)

Prizes, sweepstakes, lotteries (4 percent)

Business opportunities, work-at-home plans (3 percent)

Telephone services (2 percent)

Health care (2 percent)

Magazines, buyers clubs (2 percent)

Regarding shopping over the Internet as the second and third highest categories of complaints, not only are there real risks but also there are perceived risks of pri-

Identity theft tops list of frauds.

vacy and security risks for online shopping. Until these real and perceived risks are resolved, the use of the Internet for shopping will be used hesitantly by some consumers. Obviously, new methods of protecting one's identity are also needed, and credit card and bank companies are devising better methods of protecting their clients' identities.

## CONSUMER RESPONSIBILITIES

As discussed in the second chapter, President John F. Kennedy gave a list of consumer rights to Congress. Unfortunately, a formal list of consumer responsibilities does not exist, but over the years it has become evident that consumers can look out for themselves by:

1. *Being honest* with merchants and manufacturers. For example, consumers should be honest when filling out job applications, mortgage applications, warranty information, selling used cars, returning clothing, and so forth.

2. *Being realistic* in possible outcomes and expectations. Cologne or toothpaste will not dramatically change one's life regardless of what advertisements say.

Consuming takes time, complaining takes even more time.

3. *Avoiding nuisance or frivolous law suits.* File complaints or lawsuits only when necessary. Complaining takes time and Americans have less time today than they had thirty years ago (DeGraff, Wann, and Naylor, 2001; Schor, 1992). What is frivolous is in the eye of the beholder or more specifically in the mind and body of the sufferer and the lawyers that represent them. A widely publicized case was overweight people suing fast food restaurants, charging that their weight gain was a result of eating the fattening food served. See the case box about a particular lawsuit that was thrown out. Many people reading or hearing about this case thought it was frivolous since the decision to eat in these restaurants and what to choose to eat was a personal responsibility rather than a corporate responsibility. In another case it was the restaurant chain's responsibility when it said it fried potatoes in vegetable oil when it turned out there was beef lard in the frying oil which was not in keeping with the diet requirements of vegetarians. The restaurant had to own up to the practice and change their oil immediately to vegetable oil only. A very controversial legal area is asbestos (used in fireproofing, electrical insulations, and building materials) and its harmful effects. In 2002, 90,000 new asbestos claims were filed—triple the number filed two years previous. Asbestos lawsuits (usually about lung abnormalities) now run more than $200 billion. The amounts awarded are increasing. The claimants (some of whom are sick, others are neither sick nor impaired) and the tort lawyers are pitted against an ever-widening group of defendants (corporations, builders, and owners of buildings including schools and businesses). When it is not a legitimate claim (no illness or injury) it can be considered a fraud in and of itself. In response, some law professors are calling for Congress to limit fraudulent claiming, putting a cap on how much can be awarded (Brickman, 2003, p. A18). Others would say this is not a good idea and would like to continue the system wherein the courts decide on the amount of awards.

4. *Keeping within the law* when protesting or boycotting products or companies. Safety is paramount and there are many ways to affect change. Consumers

have the right to be heard and informed but not to injure themselves or others in the process as they exercise the First Amendment right to free speech.

5. *Reporting faulty goods.* Producers want to know when a product doesn't work, they want satisfied customers. And, there is a larger aspect to this; if cars or tires are faulty, reporting problems may save lives.

6. *Reporting crime* and wrongdoings to the proper authorities or government agencies as a way to protect oneself and others.

7. *Taking responsibility for ill-conceived actions.* If the garment label says to dry clean only and the consumer washes a sweater in hot water in a machine, the maker cannot be held responsible. Likewise, if signs at a National Park tell tourists not to go into certain areas because of lava or geysers, the tourist should obey or possibly suffer negative consequences.

8. *Realizing that consumption has an effect on the environment and future generations.* According to Juliet Schor (1998), "A necessary first step toward becoming an educated consumer is to learn about the impact your consumption has on the environment. Only then can you make responsible and informed choices" (p. 156).

9. *Getting referrals before signing a contact.* Check out their recommendations with local consumer protection agencies and the Better Business Bureau. The more substantial the investment or cost, the more time should be spent checking out the business.

10. *Getting estimates* from at least two companies in such areas as home improvements, removing trees, or moving furniture. Acquiring a firm understanding of all charges, licenses, and potential liabilities.

11. *Lessening the chances of identity theft* by not leaving credit card receipts where they can be found and not writing Social Security numbers or home phone numbers on checks. Being careful what one puts in a mailbox that anyone can get into, for example, checks can be stolen out of letters.

12. *Dealing with reputable, socially responsible companies.* More and more consumers expect companies to be **socially responsible**, a broad-based term referring to caring about the community and the environment (Mohr, Webb, & Harris, 2001).

What do all these consumer responsibilities add up to? They are really about using common sense, being aware of surroundings, business dealings, and the potential for victimization, and thinking about others as well as oneself.

---

**Case Box**

In 2003, a federal judge dismissed a class action lawsuit filed on behalf of New York children that claimed McDonald's food caused them to suffer health problems, including diabetes, high blood pressure, and obesity. "One necessary element of any potentially viable claim must be that McDonald's products involve a danger that is not within the common knowledge of consumers. Plaintiffs have failed to allege with any specificity that such a danger exists." U.S. District Court Judge Robert Sweet in a 65-page ruling (McDonald's, January 23, 2003, p. E1).

# CUSTOMER SERVICE

The consumer experience includes not only actual buying but also what happens during the entire shopping experience. Potential areas of complaint include problems with delivery and in-store customer service.

> Clueless clerks roaming the aisles at Home Depot. Flight attendants in need of "anger management" counseling. Telemarketers calling promptly at dinner time to sell long-distance service. These are just some of the consumer gripes that proved costly to companies in the third annual corporate reputation survey conducted by Harris Interactive Inc., an online market-research firm. (Alsop, 2002, p. B1)

Consumer gripes are costly to companies because dissatisfied shoppers can take their business elsewhere. "When a company provides great service, its reputation benefits from a stronger emotional connection with its customers, as well as from increased confidence that it will stand behind its products," said Joy Sever, a senior vice president at Harris. The survey of 21,630 revealed that emotional appeal is the primary driving force behind corporate reputation. Johnson & Johnson has held the No. 1 spot in the Harris polls for several years. It has cultivated a powerful image as "the caring company," associated with products for cuddly babies. Quality products and services play into how people responded in the survey. One of the respondents, a 42-year old grocery clerk, said he got a burgerless Big Mac from the drive-through window at his local McDonald's.

Besides Johnson & Johnson, companies that scored high in exemplary service were FedEx Corp., United Parcel Service Inc., Hewlett-Packard Co., and Target Corp. Since this survey is taken every year, the names on this list change, but the point is that customer service is part of the consumer experience and that an individual's buying experience as well as the company's reputation plays into customer satisfaction and expectations. The customer with the burgerless Big Mac says now he double checks his bag before driving off.

Smart companies react to these types of polls. When Home Depot dropped from nineteenth place in 2001 from fourth in 2000, it put some changes in place such as having salespeople unpack merchandise at night so they can help customers during prime shopping hours and put more employees on the floor on weekends. Table 4.1 lists the top companies and their reputation rankings.

**Table 4.1**    Corporate Reputation Survey—Top 10 Companies

| 2002 Rank | 2001 Rank | Company |
|:---------:|:---------:|---------|
| 1 | 1 | Johnson & Johnson |
| 2 | NA | Harley Davidson |
| 3 | 3 | Coca-Cola |
| 4 | 15 | United Parcel Service (UPS) |
| 5 | NA | General Mills |
| 6 | 9 | Maytag |
| 7 | NA | Eastman Kodak |
| 8 | 19 | Home Depot |
| 9 | 13 | Dell |
| 10 | 5 | 3M |

NA means not available.
*Source:* Harris Interactive, 2003 Reputation Quotient Survey. Used by permission.

## STEPS TO FOLLOW BEFORE BUYING

In subsequent chapters, there will be information on specific products and services such as buying houses or leasing cars. But, here are general buying guidelines that consumers can follow to avoid potential problems:

1. Deciding in advance what is needed and affordable.
2. Researching the product or service by using resources including the Internet to comparison shop or to find out rules and regulations governing goods or businesses, including if a company has a complaint record through the Better Business Bureau or local consumer affairs offices.
3. Asking friends, family, and coworkers. Getting recommendations about companies and products.
4. Shopping around in person, comparing quality and prices.
5. Reading and understanding contracts and warranties, labels and tags, checking licenses. For example, if you are hiring a contractor to repair your roof, you would make sure first that they are properly licensed to do roof repairs.
6. Finding out about refund and return policies.
7. Getting things such as receipts in writing, keeping credit card receipts.
8. Being wary of buying from door to door salespeople, off the side of the road, out of a motel room, or any other type of business without a permanent address, including wariness in buying over the Internet from unknown companies or private individuals. An example of this occurred when a woman felt bad for two men who stopped at her front door in early December selling steaks door to door from the back of their truck. One of the guys kept saying, "Help me out; I need to make this sale for my bonus." . . . "It was before Christmas," the woman said. "I did feel sorry for him" (Rosica, 2003, p. 1B). She wrote a check for $329.50, and the men filled her freezer with steaks. She paid for 120 steaks and got 117, but the main problem was the quality: some of the cuts could not be identified and much of the meat was hamburger patties and thin steaks rather than the steaks the men had shown her initially. When she complained she could not get her money back. Their out-of-town company would not return phone calls. They did not have a license to sell in her county, and she discovered from the Better Business Bureau in the company's city that they had an "unsatisfactory record . . . of no response to customer complaints brought to (the Bureau's) attention," according to the Bureau's Web site. As of the writing of this book, she was following further steps, but it was not promising because she waited a month before filing a complaint and the state has a three working days cooling off rule in which contracts can be cancelled from day of purchase. "The best thing to tell people is 'caveat emptor'—Latin for 'let the buyer beware,'" said Dr. James Varley, a food safety specialist with the state's Department of Agriculture and Consumer Services. When it comes to buying meat, he said, "You'd do better at a name-brand grocery store," where there's attention to cleanliness and keeping the meat properly frozen (Rosica, 2003, B1). The women said she learned a valuable lesson. "Shut the door," she said. "There's no point in trying to be polite to these people. And they are very aggressive" (Rosica, 2003, B1).

9. Not signing contracts until all blanks or changes are properly initialed or filled in.
10. Knowing that certain areas are complaint prone. Besides the identity theft already discussed, there are a number of other prominent fraud areas. Every year the Consumer Federation of America and the National Association of Consumer Agency Administrators survey government consumer protection offices to find out what transactions generate the most complaints. Most commonly on the list are:

  New and used car sales

  Auto repairs

  Home improvement

  Retail sales

  Credit and lending

  Mail order and on-line orders

  Auto leasing

## STEPS TO FOLLOW AFTER BUYING: CONSUMER REDRESS

Before using any new product, read the instructions or labels, send in the warranty card, and keep all contracts, sales receipts, cancelled checks, owner's manuals, and warranty documents. If even after acting in this responsible manner, there are problems with a product or service, consumers have the **right to redress** which is the right to seek and obtain satisfaction for damages incurred through the use of a product or service. Consumer redress means that the consumer could not foresee or protect themselves against faulty goods or services and after the fact seeks satisfaction for damages incurred.

Consumer redress is complicated because it is not always easy to determine fault and to decide who to approach for redress. Accidents may be the fault of many parties or manufacturers or of the consumer himself or herself. According to the 2000 Statistical Abstract of the United States (p. 146), the number of home accidents per year connected to consumer products includes:

1. Stairs, ramps, landing, and floors . . . 1,971,685 accidents
2. Bicycles . . . . . . . . . . . . . . . . . . . . . . . 566,085 accidents
3. Knives . . . . . . . . . . . . . . . . . . . . . . . . 444,604 accidents
4. Beds . . . . . . . . . . . . . . . . . . . . . . . . . 400,648 accidents*
5. Doors . . . . . . . . . . . . . . . . . . . . . . . . 318,185 accidents

### First Steps in Redress, How to Complain Effectively

Before hiring an attorney or running off to court, there are less time consuming and less expensive remedies to try first. Figure 4.1 gives a list of steps to follow when seeking redress.

---

*You may wonder how one get hurts by a bed; a common accident is a child getting hurt from falling off or jumping off of a top bunk bed.

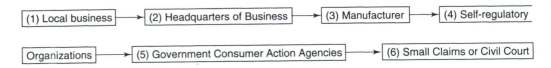

**Figure 4.1**    Steps to follow when bringing a complaint.

A description of each step follows.

1. *Local Business:* The first step is to go back to the local business where you bought the product such as returning rotten strawberries immediately to the store where you bought them and getting a refund. Before taking this step, make sure you have the paperwork. In the case of the strawberries, you may need the grocery receipt with the item circled and the strawberries. Go to the customer service desk at the grocery store, and get a cash refund. Many stores won't even require the receipt because the bar code on the plastic container has the price information that they need. A more expensive product such as a car is going to require more documentation, but still the first step is to *contact the business that sold you the item or performed the service. Most consumer complaints can be resolved at this level.*

2. *Headquarters: If the local business does not provide satisfaction, you may want to go directly to the headquarters* of the company. For example, if the local department store does not provide satisfaction, you would contact their headquarters by letter, e-mail, or phone call. To find most company's headquarters and their customer services office go to *www.companyname.com*, then click on customer service or a similar name and report the problem to them. Calmly and concisely describe the problem and what action you would like such as a refund, repair, or replacement. If you file a complaint by e-mail, there will be a form to fill out or a place to type in your complaint. This is easier than composing a formal letter and mailing it. The advantage of e-mail is that it is free, and it is 24–7 whereas many complaint toll-free phone lines are only open during normal business hours Monday through Friday. Increasingly, more people are using e-mail for complaint filing with companies or with government agencies. Companies and the government prefer e-mail to phone calls because they can manage the round-the-clock e-mails better than they can a surge of phone calls flooding the phone lines at certain times of the day.

3. *Manufacturer.* Another option is to go to the *manufacturer* or maker of the product. Let's say an electric ceiling fan does not work right, and the local home supply store where it was purchased will not give a refund. Besides going to the supply store's headquarters, an option would be to contact the manufacturer directly. There may be a regional office that will help you rather than a central office. Most products have a consumer complaint toll-free line or mailing or e-mail address on the box or product label. Telephone companies and libraries can also be assistance or check *www.standardandpoors.com* for their registry of manufacturers. At the manufacturers' main offices just as at retail stores' headquarters, there is a chain of command going from the entry level person you first contact all the way up to the president or chief executive officer (CEO) of the company. A last resort would be to send a letter and copy of receipts and/or correspondence to the president or CEO.

Over 1,500 companies have consumer affairs departments in the United States and Canada.

Consumer affairs or consumer relations departments are set up within companies because they want to hear from consumers. Many of the companies are members of the **Society of Consumer Affairs Professionals in Business (SOCAP).** Founded in 1973, this international professional organization offers training, conferences, and publications to encourage and maintain the integrity of businesses in their transactions with consumers and in communications with government regulatory groups and agencies. Their goal is to improve the marketplace for consumers through addressing their concerns with corporate structures. Examples of companies belonging to SOCAP are AAMCO Transmissions Inc., American Express Company, Ball Park Brands, and Campbell Soup Company.

As consumers go through these levels of complaint steps, they should keep a record of *efforts to resolve the problem.* When you e-mail or write to the company, describe the problem, what you have done so far to resolve it, and what solution you want. See Figure 4.2 for a sample complaint letter. When you call, keep notes of whom you spoke with and what they said and include dates.

An additional piece of advice is to allow time for the person you contacted to resolve your problem. Save copies of all letters to and from the company. Don't give up if you are not satisfied. There are self-regulatory organizations (discussed next), trade associations, media programs, national consumer organizations, and legal assistance programs listed throughout this book that may be able to assist you.

4. *Self-regulatory organizations* are also known as **third-party complaint handling sources** or dispute resolution groups. The reason they are called "third party" is because the consumer is involving someone besides themselves and the business. A third party is necessary when the local business, company headquarters or manufacturer refuses to do anything to resolve the complaint. Nonprofit third-party organizations exist to resolve disputes between buyers and sellers. Probably the best known of these is the Better Business Bureau (BBB) which has offices in about 150 larger communities in the United States. There are also 16 BBBs in Canada. BBBs are nonprofit organizations supported mostly by local business members. In other words, citizens are not paying taxes to run these organizations; rather legitimate businesses in the community pay to run them because they know it is good business to support an ethical marketplace and to provide an alternative place for dispute resolution. To find the office in your area go to *www.bbb.org.* Generally, BBBs offer the following:

- Consumer education materials that encourage honest advertising and selling practices and expose scams
- Answers to consumer questions
- Information about a business including whether there are unanswered or unsettled complaints or other marketplace problems.
- Help in resolving buyer/seller complaints against a business; including mediation and arbitration services
- Information about charities and other organizations that seek public donations

BBBs are nonprofit organizations supported by the business community that offer many services to consumers including dispute resolution.

What won't BBBs do? They do not judge or rate individual products or brands, handle employer/employee wage disputes, or give legal advice. Local BBBs are listed in the telephone directory, some offer 900 telephone numbers that charge a certain rate for the first four minutes, a lesser charge per minute afterward up to a maximum charge. Some numbers require a major credit card.

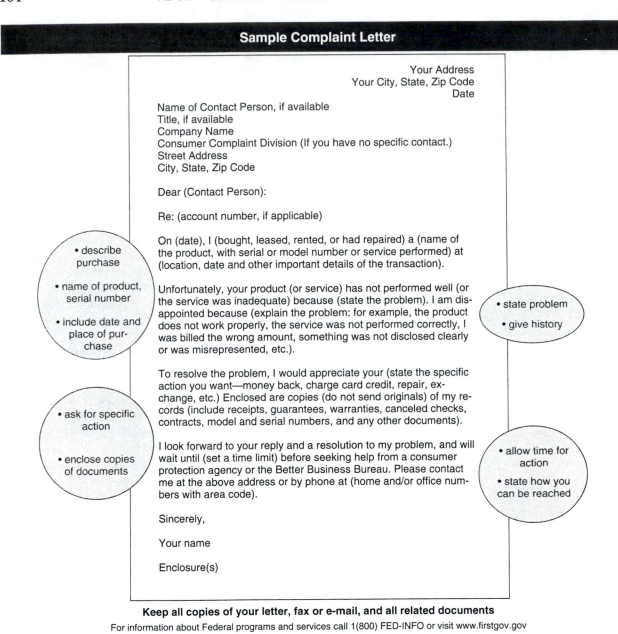

Figure 4.2    Sample Complaint Letter.

How do BBBs work exactly? The consumer calls or contacts the BBB. The BBB takes the consumer's records and takes up the complaint with the company involved. The company gets to tell their side of the transaction and what went wrong. A company could choose not to respond but this is unusual because the company does not want to have a bad record at the BBB and they do not want to have their membership dropped in the BBB. If the call or the letter from the BBB does not settle things, then the BBB may offer mediation or arbitration. **Mediation** is the process of negotiating to resolve differences, an attempt to bring about a peaceful settlement or compromise between the consumer and the business through the intervention of a third party. **Arbitration** is the process by which the parties in the dispute submit their differences to the judgment of an impartial person or group appointed by mutual consent. The arbitrator is the person chosen to settle the disagreement. He or she has the ability or power to make authoritative decisions. Mediation and arbitration are less expensive than legal proceedings.

So far the emphasis in this section has been on BBBs, but there are other organizations that offer mediation and arbitration. Another option is the consumer action panels (CAPs) that many industries have set up to handle industrywide complaints. Examples of CAPs dealing with automobile disputes are the:

- Automotive Consumer Action Program (AUTOCAP) at *www.nada.org*
- Center for Auto Safety (CAS) at *www.autosafety.org*
- BBB Auto Line at *infor@cbbb.bbb.org* or *www/bbb/org*

Besides arbitration and mediation, there is a third type of dispute resolution program, and that is conciliation. **Conciliation** means to reconcile, to make things pleasant again. A consumer offered a choice of these programs should select the one most appropriate by asking for a copy of the rules of the program before filing a case. The ruling may be binding for both the business and the consumer, or it may only apply to the business. If the program turns down your request, then the next step may be contacting consumer protection agencies or going to court.

5. *Government consumer protection agencies.* Some people may go to agencies before they go to the third-party dispute resolution organizations because they feel it is more appropriate or there is not a BBB in their community or for a variety of other reasons. So, although this is listed as the fifth step, it may very well be the fourth step.

Which level of government is appropriate varies by location and type of complaint. There are state, county, and city government consumer protection offices that

- Mediate complaints.
- Conduct investigations.
- Prosecute offenders of consumer laws.
- License and regulate a variety of professions and professionals. This varies by state but may include banking, insurance, securities, utilities, doctors, lawyers, home improvement contractors, auto repair, debt collection and child day care.
- Promote strong consumer protection legislation.
- Provide educational materials.
- Advocate in the consumer interest.

County and city offices may have a better idea of local problems and businesses so that would be the place to start. However, if a consumer does not have access to these then the next step is to contact the state consumer office or agency. Often these offices are part of the attorney general's office (this is the case in Arizona, Michigan, Minnesota, and Arkansas to name a few) or the governor's office; other times they are separate entities and still other times they could be part of another unit. See Box 4.1 for a list of the primary state offices dealing with consumer complaints. For example, Florida has a Division of Consumer Services within the Department of Agriculture and Consumer Services. They handle over 25,000 consumer complaints a month so that gives you an idea of volume. Florida also has other areas of state government that handle complaints such as the Department of Insurance and the Attorney General's Office to name two. To keep the list manageable, only one main source was given for each state. For example, for California the Department of Consumer Affairs is listed because it is the leading consumer department in a large and complex state with many consumer relations areas.

---

### BOX 4.1    State Consumer Protection Offices

Please note: Although states may have many consumer protection offices, the primary one for each state and the District of Columbia is listed here as a beginning contact. Also be aware that phone numbers and e-mail addresses change; the ones listed were accurate when this book went to press. In addition, most of the toll free numbers only work in the state; persons outside the state may have to pay for a phone call.

Alabama
Consumer Affairs Division
Office of the Attorney General
1 800 393 5658
www.ago.state.al.us

Alaska
Consumer Protection Unit
Office of the Attorney General
907 269 5100
www.law.state.ak.us

Arizona
Consumer Protection and Advocacy
    Section
Office of the Attorney General
1 800 352 8431
www.ag.state.az.us

Arkansas
Consumer Protection Division
Office of the Attorney General
1 800 482 8992
consumer@ag.state.ar.us

California
Department of Consumer Affairs
1 800 952 5210
www.dca.ca.gov

Colorado
Consumer Protection Division
Attorney General's Office
1 800 332 2071

Connecticut
Department of Consumer Protection

1 800 842 2649
www.state.ct.us/dcp/

Delaware
Fraud and Consumer Protection
    Division
Office of the Attorney General
1 800 220 5424
www.state.de.us/attgen/consumer.htm

District of Columbia
Office of the Corporation Counsel
202 442 9828

Florida
Consumer Services
Department of Agriculture and Consumer
    Services
1 800 435 7352
www.fl-ag.com

Georgia
Governor's Office of Consumer Affairs
1 800 869 1123
www2.state.ga.us/GaOCA

Hawaii
Office of Consumer Protection
Department of Commerce and Consumer
    Affairs
808 933 0910

Idaho
Consumer Protection Unit
Attorney General's Office
1 800 432 3545
www.state.id.us/ag

Illinois
Office of the Attorney General
1 800 243 0607

Indiana
Consumer Protection Division
Office of the Attorney General
1 800 382 5516
*inattgn@atg.state.in.us*
*www.ai.org/hoosieradvocate*

Iowa
Consumer Protection Division
Office of the Attorney General
515 281 5926
*cpmsiu,er@ag/state/oa/is*
*www/state/ia/us/government/ag/consumer.html*

Kansas
Consumer Protection Division
Office of the Attorney General
1-800-432-2310
*cprotect@ksag.org*
*www.ink.org/public/ksag*

Kentucky
Consumer Protection Division
Office of the Attorney General
1-888-432-9257
*attorney.general@law.state.ky.us*
*www.law.state.ky.us/cp*

Louisiana
Consumer Protection Division
Office of the Attorney General
1-800-351-4889
*www.laag.com*

Maine
Maine Attorney General's Consumer
Mediation Service
207-626-8800
*www.state.me.us/ag*

Maryland
Consumer Protection Division
Office of the Attorney General
410-528-8662
*consumer@oag.state.md.us*
*www.oag.state.md.us/consumer*

Massachusetts
Consumer Protection and Antitrust Division
Office of the Attorney General

617-727-8400
*http://www.aga.state.ma.us*

Michigan
Consumer Protection Division
Office of the Attorney General
517-373-1140
*www.ci.detroit.mi.us*

Minnesota
Consumer Services Division
Minnesota Attorney General's Office
1-800-657-3787
*consumer.ag@state.mn.us*
*www.ag.state.mn.us/consumer*

Mississippi
Consumer Protection Division of
the Mississippi Attorney General's Office
1-800-281-4418
*www.ago.state.ms.us/consprot.htm*

Missouri
Consumer Protection and Trade
Offense Division
1-800-392-8222
*attgenmail@moaga.org*
*www.ago.state.mo.us*

Montana
Consumer Affairs Unit
Department of Commerce
406-444-4312

Nebraska
Department of Justice
1-800-727-6432
*www.nol.org*

Nevada
Nevada Consumer Affairs Division
1-800-326-5202
*ncad@fyiconsumer.org*
*www.fyiconsumer.org*

New Hampshire
Office of the Attorney General
Consumer Protection and Antitrust Bureau
603-271-3641
*www.state.nh.us/nhdoj/Consumer/cpb.html*

New Jersey
New Jersey Consumer Affairs Division
973-504-6587
*browere@smtp.lps.state.nj.us*
*www.state.nj.us/lps/ca/home.htm*

New Mexico
Consumer Protection Division
Office of the Attorney General
1-800-678-1508
*www.ago.state.nm.us*

New York
New York State Consumer Protection
    Board
1-800-697-1220
*donna.ned@consumer.state.ny.us*
*www.consumer.state.ny.us*

North Carolina
Consumer Protection Section
Office of the Attorney General
919-716-6000
*www.jus.state.nc.us/cpframe.htm*

North Dakota
Office of the Attorney General
701-328-2210
*ndag@state.nd.us*
*www.ag.state.nd.us*

Ohio
Ohio State Attorney General's Office
1-800-282-0515
*consumer@ag.state.oh.us*
*www.ag.state.oh.us*

Oklahoma
Oklahoma Attorney General
1-800-448-4904
*www.oag.state.ok.us*

Oregon
Financial Fraud/Consumer Protection
    Section
Department of Justice
1-877-877-9392
*www.joj.state.or.us*

Pennsylvania
Office of the Consumer Advocate
Office of the Attorney General
1-800-684-6560
*paoca@ptd.net*
*www.oca.state.pa.us*

Puerto Rico
Department of Justice
787-721-2900
*Jalicea@caribe.net*

Rhode Island
Consumer Protection Unit
Department of Attorney General
1-800-852-7776
*www.creditcounseling.org*

South Carolina
SC Department of Consumer Affairs
1-800-922-1594
*scdca@infoave.net*
*www.state.sc.us/consumer*

South Dakota
Office of the Attorney General
1-800-300-1986

Tennessee
Division of Consumer Affairs
1-800-342-8385
*mwilliams2@mail.state.tn.us*
*www.state.tn.us/consumer*

Texas
Office of Public Insurance Counsel
512-322-4143
*rod.bordelon@mail.capnet.state.tx.us*
*www.opic.state.tx.us*

Utah
Division of Consumer Protection
Department of Commerce
801-530-6601
*commerce@br.state.ut.us*
*www.commerce.state.ut.us*

Vermont
Consumer Assistance Program
For Consumer Complaints
    & Questions
1-800-649-2424
*www.state.vt.us/atg*

Virginia
Office of Consumer Affairs
Department of Agriculture and Consumer
    Services
1-800-552-9963
*www.vdacs.state.va.us*

Washington
Consumer Resource Center
Office of the Attorney General
360-738-6185
*www.pan.ci.seattle.wa.us/esd/consumer*

West Virginia
Consumer Protection Division
Office of the Attorney General
1-800-368-8808
consumer@wvnet.edu
www.state.wv.us/wvag/index0816.html

Wisconsin
Division of Trade & Consumer Protection
Department of Agriculture

Trade and Consumer Protection
1-800-422-7128
www.badger.state.wi.us/agencies/datcp

Wyoming
Office of the Attorney General
Consumer Protection Unit
1-800-438-5799
cpetri@state.wy.us
www.state.wy.us/~ag/consumer.htm

When contacting a state department or office about a consumer complaint, the first contact should be a phone call on their toll-free line or by e-mail. The consumer hotline person or responder to e-mail will know how to direct your call or tell you what steps to take in filing a complaint. Investigators may be put onto cases involving several complaints such as travel fraud, auto repair, or health club fraud. They are interested in helping the consumer who has filed a complaint and also in preventing similar problems from happening.

How often do people file complaints? Although toll-free lines or e-mails gather tens of thousands of complaints a month in populous states, this is only the tip of the iceberg. An American Association of Retired Persons study found that less than 2 percent of consumers who believe they've experienced a major fraud complain to their state's attorney general's office (Sichelman, 2002). Why? The two most likely reasons are they don't want to bother or don't know where to turn for help.

Less than 2 percent of consumers who have experienced a fraud complain to their state's attorney general.

State consumer protection agencies may license and regulate a variety of professions and professionals. They may oversee boards that issue rules and regulations; prepare and give examinations; issue, deny, or revoke licenses; bring disciplinary actions; handle consumer complaints; and provide referral services. The agency may contact a professional on your behalf and might conduct an investigation and take disciplinary action which may include probation for that business, license suspension, or license revocation.

Regarding identity theft fraud, state governments as well as the FTC's consumer protection agency are actively investigating consumer complaints in this area, trying to lessen their occurrence and changing laws and procedures in the process. For example, in Florida, a statewide grand jury that is searching for ways to stop identity theft recommended tighter restrictions on the distribution of personal data, more frequent in-person driver license renewals, and a swifter response from law officials. Although identity theft is a growing national problem, certain areas are reporting more complaints than others. The District of Columbia had the highest rate of identity theft in 2001 with 77 victims for every 100,000 people; California and Nevada followed with 45 and 41 victims, respectively (Ho, 2002).

As mentioned previously, besides the general consumer protection office in the state, certain divisions may have their own toll-free lines or Web sites to handle complaints on specific areas such as insurance or auto repairs. If a consumer was having problems with a repair shop or an insurance agency or a policy and after they have tried to remedy the problem with the local company and headquarters and the BBB, they could call the Auto Repair Division or the Department of Insurance in their state and find out what they could do next. If there is a specialized agency such as this, the consumer should contact it first rather than the general consumer complaint agency.

The federal government may handle individual complaints in certain areas such as investment fraud on a national scale, but more likely the consumer should start at the city, county, or state level. For information and complaints regarding investments, a consumer could call the Securities and Exchange Commission (SEC) Office of Investor Education and Assistance toll free at 1-800-SEC-0330 or e-mail *www.sec.gov.*

Besides government agencies, on occasion private consumer organizations will try to help a member with a complaint, but generally consumer groups do not assist individual consumers with their complaints and encourage members to go through the steps previously outlined. For example, a group such as AARP has a consumer issues section that is mainly charged to examine those consumer problems and issues that impact the financial security of people 50 years of age or older, and to help its members protect themselves from marketplace fraud and deception. They employ a variety of strategies to keep members informed of wrongdoings, but they do not pursue individual complaints on a regular basis.

To avoid unnecessary duplication of effort, state consumer protection offices meet regularly to inform each other about scams that are drifting through the United States. It is common for states to form coalitions leveling charges of fraud or deception against a repeat-offender company. For example, the attorney generals of several states may charge a company with false and misleading claims. An out-of-court settlement may be reached wherein the company stops making such claims and pays each state an amount of money to cover the costs of their investigations and legal efforts. In so doing, the company is stopped, and the states bring issues to federal attention. It also takes the load off of courts.

Another way states have taken the load off of courts is that many have instituted systems of ombudspersons. The office of the **ombudsperson** mediates disputes, offers counseling and mediation services, and other out-of-court means to resolve conflict. Ombudspersons work with the court system to accelerate the bureaucratic process.

States also work together through the **Uniform Commercial Code (UCC)** whose main purpose is to set a standard by which merchants operating in more than one state can more easily comply with that state's laws. This statute has been adopted at least partially by all states and regulates most sales of goods. It makes it easier for sellers to conduct business in several states.

Lastly, a state attorney general or some other official may take the lead in a crusade for consumers that other states follow. For example, New York's Attorney General Eliot Spitzer used the threat of prosecution against stock analysts he accused of fraud. He said analysts gave investors bum advice, encouraging them to buy stocks of companies that the analysts' firms were wooing for investment banking business. His proof was private e-mails between analysts calling these same stocks dogs, disasters, and worse. He called it "a shocking betrayal of trust" (Gormley, 2002).

6. *Small claims court or civil court.* When all the previous steps have failed, a consumer can go to **small claims court** (in some places called conciliation court or magistrates court). This is a form of civil court that allows **litigants** claiming

---

**Case Study**

This a real story about a student and what happened to her in small claims court. The student was a middle-aged female who was an American citizen who had been born in Mexico. Her husband worked for the U.S. Post Office, and she was very proud of her family and American citizenship. One Christmas she was shopping for gifts at a store and left the gifts to be wrapped at the gift wrap department. On her return, the gifts were missing, and the store insisted she had made it all up and that she had not purchased anything. As the argument escalated, she was called racial epithets by the store managers. On the basis of her consumer economics class, she decided to go to small claims court. While waiting outside for her case to be called, the store managers said they wanted to settle out of court, and they would give her the money. She said, "No, I want my day in court" and went in. Not only was she awarded the money, but it turns out she exposed a ring that was working in the gift wrap department. They had an accomplice out the back door whom they would give the merchandise to when the shopper's back was turned. The judge awarded her the money she had lost. The student said had it not been for the class she would not have known what to do nor had the courage to do it. When she reported what had happened in class (she did not tell anyone at the time including her family because she did not know what would happen), they applauded and congratulated her. As a prevention technique, it was also discussed that shoppers should get proof that their gifts are being wrapped if they leave them (often stores have a ticket for this purpose) or keep their purchase receipt (what happened to this student is not only did the wrappers take the gifts but also took her receipt so she had no proof of purchase) or stay and wait for the gifts to be wrapped.

---

damages or resolving disputes that involve modest amounts of money. Each state sets the maximum allowed; in some states the maximum is $5,000. In small claims courts, consumers speak for themselves. The business also gives their side of the story. A judge listens and decides the outcome. It is rare, but some states have juries instead of judges. Usually the consumer wins. Often the business does not show up or tries to settle out the courtroom. The main reason they do not show up is because they can't spare the court time because usually there is some waiting time involved. A business owner's time may be worth more than the amount of money in dispute. Typical cases involve ruined clothes at dry cleaners, landlord-tenant disputes, and faulty home repairs. The judge, for example, may have the dry cleaner give a newlywed $1,000 for a ruined wedding dress. Cases involving more than the maximum allowed amounts or more complications would go to another civil court. The process that is usually followed in a small claims court is given in Box 4.2.

## CIVIL VS. CRIMINAL CASES

Civil court involves the hiring of attorneys, more formality, and more money than small claims court. If the litigant loses there are routes of appeal within the court system going all the way up to state supreme courts. This is a costly and time-

---

### BOX 4.2    Typical Small Claims Court Process

- First, the "wronged" consumer initiates the process by speaking with the clerk of the court (usually the consumer must live, work, or do business in the locale in question).
- If the clerk advises the consumer to proceed, he or she files a claim and becomes known as the **plaintiff** (the initiator of the law suit). Everything on the forms must be accurate. There may be a small fee for filing a claim. Businesses as well as consumers can file suits.
- Once the plaintiff files suit, the court issues a **summons** which is a notice to appear in court as a juror, defendant, or witness or a **subpoena** which is a legal writ requiring the appearance in court to give testimony. The **defendant** is the person required to answer the lawsuit. Upon receiving the summons, about one-quarter of the cases will settle out of court. In such an occurrence, the consumer should get the agreement in writing and file it with the court.
- If the case goes on and the defendant does not show up at court, then the court will often grant the claim by default. Usually no lawyers are involved unless there is a substantial amount of money. Some states prohibit lawyers from presenting at the cases. Generally, the setting is informal, and plaintiffs should be able to represent themselves. In preparation for a case, college students can often get free legal advice at their university. Call student services to find out if your college offers legal services to students. A common student problem is landlord-tenant disputes.
- If both sides show up at the court case, then they both give their sides of the story and present evidence in the form of photos, receipts, letters, contracts, cancelled checks, and so on. A calm, simple explanation is advised. Visitors, friends, and families can watch cases in progress.
- The judge usually decides the outcome right then; occasionally the judge may wait a few weeks and send the verdict by letter.

---

consuming process. If a person cannot afford a lawyer, he or she may qualify for free legal help from a Legal Aid or Legal Services Corporation (LSC) office or may receive help on a contingency basis. Telephone directories list the addresses and telephone numbers of Legal Aid offices or got to *www.nlada.org*. The LSC was created in 1974 by Congress to provide financial support for legal assistance in non-criminal proceedings for low-income consumers. They have offices in all 50 states, Guam, Puerto Rico, Micronesia, and the Virgin Islands. Their website is *www.lsc.gov*.

---

### Advice on Finding an Attorney

To find a lawyer ask family and friends for references and check with the lawyer referral services in your area. The bar association is listed in the telephone directory; also see e-resources section near the end of the chapter. As mentioned earlier, as a college student you may have access to free legal help on your campus. Contact student services.

---

Sometimes if the litigant wins and is awarded the money, the defendant refuses to pay. This may involve going back to court. **Civil cases** involve the settling of private conflicts between people or between businesses. Common cases involve landlord-tenant disputes, contract disputes, and ruined products. Usually the wrongdoer is asked to pay or remedy the situation in some way. Compensation is involved. A **tort** is a civil wrong that causes either (or both) emotional or physical injury. Torts can be intentional or negligent.

Crimes are acts that society forbids or punishes through legislative bodies or courts. **Criminal cases** involve prevention, punishment, and rehabilitation. In criminal cases, a violation is deemed to have taken place or an injustice committed against the government who brings charges against the person or persons who committed the crime. A person committing a crime is prosecuted and if found guilty is punished by the government according to its statutory laws.

## CONSUMER LAW

The law provides safeguards to buyers. Laws pertaining to consumers can be broken down into statutory law, regulatory law, common law, and constitutional law. There are hundreds of federal statutory and regulatory laws related to consumers. **Statutory laws** are laws enacted by the legislative branch of government which at the federal level means Congress. **Regulatory laws** are laws or rules or regulations enacted to protect consumers through agencies of the federal or state government. At the federal level, the Federal Trade Commission is often the agency that protects consumers, but there are over 100 federal government regulatory laws, and these involve many agencies from food safety to airline safety. Examples of other agencies are the Department of Agriculture and the Food and Drug Administration. At the state level, as shown in Box 4.1 the most likely agencies or offices are the state attorney general's office or Consumer Affairs Departments or Divisions.

**Common law** is based upon judicial decisions and embodied in reports of decided cases which have been administered by the common-law courts of England since the Middle Ages. These laws evolved into the type of legal system we now have in the United States and Canada, for the most part. The trend is away from common law to statutory law. **Constitutional law**, as the name implies, is based on the U.S. Constitution which is the fundamental law of the U.S. federal system of government. An example of a right discussed in the Constitution that affects consumers is the right to a fair trial.

## LICENSING BOARDS

Much of the state consumer protection activity takes place before it reaches the complaint level through state licensing boards. They issue licenses to professionals such as barbers, physicians, attorneys, and funeral directors. When you have had your hair cut, you have probably seen the license of the barber or cosmetologist prominently displayed. The boards have the power to issue and revoke licenses, charge fees, and in so doing protect the consumer from deceptive, harmful, or ineffective services. Critics of boards feel that some are not as consumer-oriented as they ought to be (depending on the makeup of the board and the kinds of information they are given this may or may not be true) and that they are inclined to be more in favor of the professional. Most boards try to do the right thing, and they perform important preventative services. Aren't you glad that someone has checked out your barber or cosmetologist before they take a scissor or razor to your head or use chemical dyes?

## WARRANTIES (GUARANTEES)

Many products offer warranties or guarantees. The terms warranty and guarantee can be used interchangeably according to the Magnuson-Moss Warranty Act which became law in 1977. This act requires that consumers be given warranty information, if it exists for a particular product or part of a product, before making a purchase. The act does not require that manufacturers give warranties, but if a warranty is given, it must be clearly stated as either a limited or a full warranty. See Box 4.3 for a list of what a full warranty promises and what a limited warranty means according to the Act.

A product such as a washing machine can have a full warranty on some parts and a limited warranty on others. Violations of the act should be reported to the Federal Trade Commission (*www.ftc.gov*).

Besides full and limited warranties, there are also implied and express (or written) warranties. Automobile manufacturers issue **written warranties** which are written promises that the character and quality of the product are as the manufacturer represent them. Usually the guarantee specifies what is covered for a specific number of miles or years (when leases are involved) or months. **Implied warranties** are not written but are inherently understood in the transaction. The **implied warranty of fitness** for a particular purpose means that the warranty holds for the correct use of the product. For example, the seller guarantees that a shampoo will clean hair, but he or she does not guarantee that it will clean car seat covers. The **implied warranty of merchantability** is more open than the implied warranty of purpose. The implied warranty of merchantability simply means that the product should work. It is salable and fit for the market. A blender that doesn't blend would be unmerchantable. Products delivered to your home should be as merchantable as they were in the store. The seller is obligated to deliver the product in a reasonable amount of time. Reasonable means what an average responsible adult would expect given the circumstances. A **reasonable person** is rational, attentive, knowledgeable, and capable of making judgments in his or her best interest.

## CONTRACTS

Agreements or promises that are legally enforceable are called **contracts**. Most significant contracts in consumer law are written, but they may also be oral or implied. Obviously, written contracts are more easily defended in court and in the

---

### BOX 4.3    The Magnuson-Moss Warranty Act

The Magnuson-Moss Warranty Act is the federal law passed by Congress in 1975 that governs consumer product warranties. It requires manufacturers and sellers of consumer products to provide consumers with detailed information about warranty coverage. In passing this act, Congress specified a number of requirements that warrantors must meet. The act affects the rights of consumers and the obligations of warrantors under written warranties. The following is a description of parts of the Act and its objectives, for further information go to *www.ftc.gov.*

The Act:

- Enables consumers to comparison shop for warranties.
- Encourages warranty competition.
- Promotes timely and complete performance of warranty obligations.
- Does not compel the consumer to be given a written warranty. (The act does not apply to oral warranties, only written warranties are covered.)
- Does not apply to warranties on services.
- Says that a product is "merchantable," meaning it is supposed to do what it claims. For example, one assumes that an oven will bake food at a controlled temperature selected by the buyer; if it does not heat or heats improperly, an implied warranty of merchantability would be breached.
- Implies warranty of fitness for a particular purpose, which means that customers rely on sellers to make a product for a specific use. An example given at the FTC Web site is that if an appliance manufacturer says that a washing machine will handle a 15-pound load, it should be able handle 15-pound loads.
- Implies a standard or level of performance at time of purchase. Implied warranties do not cover problems caused by abuse, misuse, ordinary wear, failure to follow directions, or improper maintenance. However, the normal durability of an appliance, for example, would be considered. Used merchandise may have implied warranties when the seller is a merchant who deals in such goods, not when a sale is made by a private individual.
- Discusses the concept of selling "as is." You cannot sell "as is" in some states; in others merchandise has to be clearly marked as defective or damaged. Sellers have to be careful when selling a product "as is" because they may be liable if it is dangerous or causes personal injury to someone.
- Distinguishes between a full warranty and the promises thereof and a limited warranty. In short, a limited warranty lets consumers know that the warranty offers less than a full warranty. Caution is advised, limited may mean only certain parts will be replaced for free or the buyer may have to pay for labor costs.

---

complaint process. A contract is an understanding reached between parties having the legal capacity to agree and something of value is exchanged between them. A contract is formed when the parties involved may be held liable or responsible. Contracts are made for the present and the future—not the past. The pros and cons of service contracts or extended warranties are covered in chapter 10; the present chapter's coverage serves as an introduction and emphasizes the legal ramifications of contracts.

A legally binding contract has:

- Mutual agreement.
- Competent participants, for example, the people must be of age, usually 18 or older. A person who is intoxicated or in some other way incapacitated is usually not legally held to contracts signed under those conditions.
- Legal subject matter.
- Consideration, implies an exchange of goods, money, or services; something is involved beyond words.
- Legal form, varies by state; in some states contracts have to be written.

## CONSUMER LEGAL TERMS

The chapter has already introduced some legal terminology and basic information about courts. Naturally, there is much more, and Box 4.4 lists other beginning definitions of legal terms. The intent of the chapter is not to turn you into an attorney, but to expose you to "legalese" relevant to the study of consumer economics. Many students who have found this part of the course interesting have gone on to law school or to graduate school in public administration or public policy; others work in businesses or nonprofit settings where they interact with lawyers so it is useful to have a beginning understanding of legal terminology.

## MEDIA SOURCES FOR REDRESS

At any point in the complaint process, a consumer may seek help from a media source. In most cities, there is a consumer reporter or a consumer segment on the radio or the evening television news programs and a hotline or action-line column in the newspaper. Many of the columnists or reporters will go to bat for wronged consumers and try to get answers. To find these services, contact the local newspaper. Usually the business section editor will know whom to contact, or you can call radio or television stations. Media are most likely to take up your cause if they feel it affects other viewers or readers as a public service. Newspapers and television news shows also perform a valuable public service by providing information about current fraud schemes, telling what is happening, and how to avoid being victimized. A well-known, long-standing national television program is *Sixty Minutes,* which for years has broadcast investigations into wrongdoings—many of which are consumer-linked, such as health fraud investigations, telemarketing and investment schemes, and so on.

Another media resource is Call for Action, Inc. (*www.callforaction.org*). It is a several decades old international nonprofit network of consumer hotlines operating in conjunction with broadcast partners. Their purpose is to educate and assist consumers and small businesses with consumer problems. Box 4.5 gives a list of their hotlines in major markets that are staffed with trained volunteers who at no cost offer advice and mediate complaints.

BOX 4.4    Consumer Legal Terms

Here are legal terms relevant to the study of consumer economics that have not already been defined in this chapter. These will not be listed in the Key Terms section at the end of the chapter because they are given mainly as a reference.

Action: a judicial proceeding, the lawsuit contested in court

Adversary Proceeding: legal procedure involving opposing parties such as a plaintiff and a defendant.

Adversary System: the system we are used to in the United States wherein there is a trial and the truth will emerge.

Answer: the defendant's written response to the plaintiff.

Breach of Contract: failure (without legal excuse) to fulfill any promise that is part of a contract.

Class Action: an action brought on by a group or class of plaintiffs or defendants who share the same interests in the litigation.

Complainant: the group or person who files a complaint.

Complaint: the initial pleading that begins a lawsuit includes allegations and remedies sought.

Default: failure to do something (such as pay a loan or show up in court), failure to comply.

Deposition: a statement or testimony made under oath.

Discovery: the methods used to obtain information held by the other party, can be used in civil or criminal actions.

Dismissal: the termination of an action or claim, end of a lawsuit.

Enjoin: to impose, constrain, attach, to stop a person from a specific act.

Fiduciary: acting on behalf of another (such as managing money or property), acting in good faith, such as being an executor of a will or guardian of a minor.

Garnishment: a device used by a creditor to get back money owed to them; a third party (such as an employer) can garnish wages of an employee and send that money through the court to the creditor.

Injunction: a remedy by a court order compelling a party to do or refrain from doing a specified act. An example would be the court ordering a person to leave a celebrity alone.

Joint and Several Liability: joint liability imposed on all the parties involved, if one party does not pay, the other parties must, may vary by jurisdiction and considerations of fault.

Joint Tenancy: two or more parties are held equally responsible, a form of legal co-ownership.

Liable: answerable according to law, being held responsible such as being an accomplice in a crime.

Negligence: failing to exercise the right amount of care in protecting others.

Rebuttal: giving evidence or arguments that rebuts or refutes previous testimony or evidence given by an adversary.

Settlement: an agreement reached, terminates the lawsuit

Verdict: decision of the jury, for the plaintiff or the defendant, or in criminal actions guilty or not guilty.

BOX 4.5 Call for Action, Inc. Hotlines in Major Markets (TV and Radio)

- Altoona, PA: WTAJ-TV Call for Action, 814 944 9336
- Atlanta, GA: WXIA-TV Call for Action, 678 422 8466
- Boston, MA: WBZ Radio Call for Action, 617 787 7070
- Buffalo, NY: WIVB-TV Call for Action, 716 879 4900
- Cleveland, OH: WJW-TV Call for Action, 216 578 0700
- Colorado Springs, CO: KKTV-TV Call for Action, 719 457 8211
- Dallas, TX: KTVT-TV Call for Action, Toll free 1 877 TEXAS11
- Detroit, MI: WXYZ-TV & WJR Radio Call for Action, 248 827 3362
- Fort Myers, FL: WINK-TV Call for Action, 941 334 4357
- Greensboro, NC: WFMY-TV Call for Action, 336 680 1000
- Kansas City, MO: KCTV-5 Call for Action, 913 831 1919
- Milwaukee, WI: WTMJ-TV Call for Action, 414 967 5495
- New York, NY: WABC Radio Call for Action, 212 268 5626
- Philadelphia, PA: WCAU-TV Call for Action, 866 978 4232
- Phoenix/Flagstaff, AZ: KPNX-TV and KNAZ-TV, 602 260 1212
- Pittsburgh, PA: WTAE-TV Call for Action, 412 333 4444
- St. Louis, MO: KTVI-TV Call for Action, 314 282 2222
- Salt Lake City, UT: KTVW-TV Call for Action, Toll-free 1 877 908 0444
- Toledo, OH: WTOL-TV Call for Action, 419 255 2255
- Washington, DC: WTOP AM & FM Call for Action, 301 652 4357

For phone number updates and additional stations, call the Network Hotline at Bethesda, MD, at 301 657 7490 or go to *www.callforaction.org.*

## SUMMARY

The study of consumer economics includes learning how to effectively complain and how to avoid fraud. Identity theft tops the list of consumer fraud complaints according to the Federal Trade Commission.

Legitimate businesses want satisfied customers (because they are more likely to return and provide good word of mouth to friends and family) so for the most part they will seek to remedy problems. This chapter gave a list of consumer responsibilities and steps to follow when seeking redress. The chapter addressed the following questions:

What do I do first if I have a faulty product or get poor service?

When is it appropriate to contact a third-party complaint handling organization such as a Better Business Bureau or a government consumer agency?

When is it appropriate to go to Small Claims Court or Civil Court?

The goal of reading this chapter is to help the reader feel in charge, to know what to do when a purchase goes wrong, how to complain effectively, and who to turn to for help.

Most consumers do not complain. An AARP study found that only 2 percent of consumers who experience a major fraud complain to their state attorney general's office.

Knowing legal terminology and basic consumer rights and responsibilities are useful consumer skills. Watching television programs and reading newspaper articles that expose fraud help keep one abreast of current scams. These are examples of knowledge is power. A lot of consumer complaints can be avoided by wariness (e.g., not buying from door to door sales people or off the side of the road), by making wise purchases, followed by the immediate return of faulty products or the canceling of contracts within three working days, if necessary.

## KEY POINTS

1. Consumers have responsibilities, for example to be honest in their dealings.
2. There are steps to follow in the complaint process. The recommended first step is to talk first to the people at the place the faulty product or service was purchased.
3. More people are using the Internet as a way to contact manufacturers and resolve complaints.
4. Most companies want good customer relations and will try to resolve complaints.
5. In most Small Claims Court cases, lawyers are not necessary, and there is usually a judge that decides instead of a jury.
6. Warranties, of which there are several kinds, protect consumers.
7. State government consumer protection departments and related units and media sources are ready to help consumers in their quest for complaint resolution.

## KEY TERMS

| | | |
|---|---|---|
| arbitration | litigants | subpoena |
| civil cases | mediation | summons |
| common law | ombudsperson | third-party complaint |
| conciliation | plaintiff | handling sources |
| constitutional law | reasonable person | tort |
| contracts | regulatory laws | Uniform Commercial |
| criminal cases | right to redress | Code (UCC) |
| defendant | small claims court | written warranties |
| fraud | socially responsible | |
| implied warranties | Society of Consumer | |
| implied warranty of | Affairs Professionals | |
| fitness | (SOCAP) | |
| implied warranty of | statutory laws | |
| merchantability | | |

## DISCUSSION QUESTIONS

1. Regarding the list of consumer responsibilities in the chapter, does it make any difference to you if a company that you buy from is socially responsible? For example, would you more likely shop in a department store that regularly gives

to charities and sponsors charity events than one that does not? If the prices were the same in competitive stores for the same pair of shoes that you are buying, would a store that is more community or environmentally responsible get your business? Explain your answers.

2. What has been your experience with customer service? Name one company that provided good service and one that did not. What happened in each case?

3. Do you know anyone who went to Small Claims Court? If so, what was their case about and what was the outcome?

4. Go to www.bbb.org and find the nearest Better Business Bureau to your campus. Also find out about a charity, select one and see what they say. Go to www.bbbonline.org and ask about an online business (e.g., eBay) and report on what you find out.

5. Go to refdesk.com and select a newspaper and find an article on consumer fraud. Print off the article and write a half-page summary of what the problem is and your solution (what you think should happen).

6. Go to lawyers.com and click on "Ask a lawyer" to try a question out or click on legal resources and find out more information beyond what the chapter covered.

## E-RESOURCES

| | |
|---|---|
| American Bar Association www.aba.org | Nonprofit organization source for legal help, information on dispute resolution |
| Better Business Bureau www.bbb.org | Nonprofit organization source for business and charity reports |
| search.bbb.org/search.html. | To check out a company on the BBB Web site |
| BBBOnLine www.bbbonline.org | Nonprofit organization source Verifies the legitimacy and privacy practices of on-line businesses |
| Lawyers.com | Web site offers definitions of legal terms and legal resources |
| refdesk.com | Web site that provides access to over 50 leading newspapers, including their consumer articles, fraud coverage |

## REFERENCES

Alsop, R. (January 16, 2002). Reputations rest on good service. *Wall Street Journal,* p. B1.

Brickman, L. (January 6, 2003). The great asbestos swindle. *Wall Street Journal,* p. A18.

DeGraff, J., D. Wann, and T. Naylor. (2001). *Affluenza: The all-consuming epidemic.* San Francisco, CA: Berrett-Koehler Publishers.

Gormley, M. (May 1, 2002). Associated Press release. His political stock rises as Wall Street shudders. *Tallahassee Democrat,* p. 6E.

Ho, D. (January 24, 2002). Identity theft tops list of frauds. *Tallahassee Democrat,* p. 1E.

Miyazaki, A., and A. Fernandez. (2001). Consumer perceptions of privacy and security risks for online shopping. *Journal of Consumer Affairs, 35* (1), 27–44.

McDonald's. (January 23, 2003). *Tallahassee Democrat,* p. E1.

Mohr, L., D. Webb, and K. Harris. (2001). Do consumers expect companies to be socially responsible? The impact of corporate social responsibility on buying behavior. *Journal of Consumer Affairs, 35* (1), 45–72.

Rosica, J. (January 7, 2003). Freezer full of unwanted steaks has woman steamed. *Tallahassee Democrat,* p. B1.

Schor, J. (1998). *The overspent American: Why we want what we don't need.* New York: Harper Perennial.

Schor, J. (1992). *The overworked American: The unexpected decline of leisure.* New York: Basic.

Sichelman, L. (January/February 2002). Protect your move. New York: *Century 21 House & Home,* a publication of Hachette Filipacchi Media U.S.

# Government Protection, Nongovernmental Proconsumer Groups, and Media

*Nothing is easier than spending the public money. It does not appear to belong to anybody. The temptation is overwhelming to bestow it on somebody.*

Calvin Coolidge

### Learning Objectives

1. Explain how to contact an elected official.
2. Understand the functions of government agencies most involved with protecting the consumer interest.
3. Discuss the reasons for regulation and deregulation.
4. Describe the three primary interests of nongovernmental proconsumer groups.
5. Explain the mission of consumer media.

## INTRODUCTION

Government spending goes up every year. "When consumer and corporate spending declines in difficult times, government spending acts as a buffer for the economy. And currently, the federal government has a major budget surplus, helping to ensure government spending can continue, even when tax receipts decline" (Lynch, 2001, A8). Perhaps you have an opinion on an issue such as government spending that you would like to share with an elected official. This chapter begins with a description of how to reach elected officials, including the president and vice president.

Although President Coolidge criticized those who loosely spend government money, we all need the services government provides and that includes consumer protection. In a recent American Customer Satisfaction Survey conducted by the University of Michigan, consumers were just as satisfied with services they received from federal government agencies as they were from services from private companies (Jones, 2002). A striking example was that respondents were more satisfied with the service from the Internal Revenue Service than from McDonald's.

This chapter builds on topics introduced earlier in the book: government, proconsumer groups, and media—all parts of the circular flow model of consumerism (see Figure 5.1). Some of the topics to be covered include product recalls, regulation and deregulation, and Web sites for information. And this latter point is important because we are living in an **information economy**. Those who produce, have access to, and influence the spread of information have power in the global society.

We are living in an information economy.

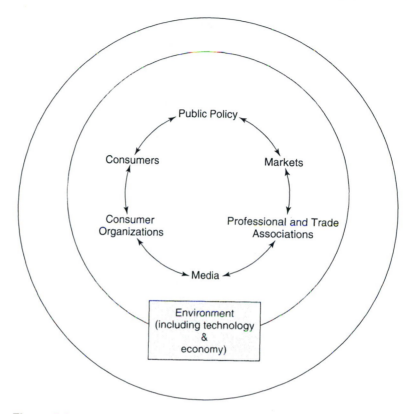

**Figure 5.1**    The Circular Flow Model of Consumer Economics.

## CONTACTING AN ELECTED OFFICIAL

It takes only a few minutes to write to an elected official, but it can make a difference if there is an issue that you care about. When elected officials receive enough letters from constituents or even a single stirring letter it will sway their vote or stance on an issue. Often elected officials will read out parts of the letters when they give testimony or make other types of public pronouncements. For greatest impact, follow these guidelines:

1. Use your own paper and your own words. Write clearly and concisely.
2. Focus on one subject per letter or e-mail.
3. Refer to specific legislation by name and/or number.
4. Request a specific action such as a vote in a particular way or suggest public hearings
5. If you work or live in the elected official's district say so.
6. Insulting words or lack of courtesy will not work. Polite wording will get more of the kind of attention and action that you want.

To find addresses of state and local representatives check your phone book. U.S. senators and representatives can be reached at the following addresses:

The Honorable _____          The Honorable _____

U.S. Senate                  U.S. House of Representatives

Washington, DC 20510         Washington, DC 20515

"The Honorable" in front of a person's name is a title of respect in the United States. It is reserved for those who hold or have held high office at the federal, state, or city levels. Members of Congress also have e-mail addresses and Web sites and local addresses in their districts. For a directory go to *http://lcweb.loc.gov/global/legislative/email.html*. The salutation on the email or letter should be Dear Senator _____ (the person's last name in the blank) or Dear Mr. _____ or Ms. _____ for a U.S. representative.

You can email the president at *president@whitehouse.gov* and the vice president at *vice.president@whitehouse.gov*. E-mails or letters should have the following salutation: Dear Mr. President or Dear Mr. Vice-President. In the event of a female president or vice president, it would be Dear Ms. President or Dear Ms. Vice President unless they announce another choice.

The correct salutation for a governor is Dear Governor or Dear Governor _____ (name). An e-mail or letter to a state governor would be addressed:

The Honorable

_____ (name)

Governor of _____

Address

For the closing of a business letter, "Sincerely" is always appropriate. For the president or another high official, it is appropriate to use "Respectfully yours." In a letter, skip three spaces down, and then type in your name. In the space above, handwrite your signature.

# AGENCIES/COMMISSIONS

## Federal

Several federal government agencies provide recall information, perform product tests and conduct research studies, and enforce product safety regulations. The agencies most involved with consumer protection are the Federal Trade Commission, the Consumer Product Safety Commission, the Food and Drug Administration, the U.S. Department of Agriculture, the Justice Department, the Securities and Exchange Commission, and the U.S. Department of Transportation. Also included in this section is the Federal Consumer Information Center (FCIC) who announces recalls and distributes the Consumer Action Handbook and booklets and pamphlets on specific consumer topics (see e-Resources for Web site).

**Federal Trade Commission (FTC).**    At the federal level, the Federal Trade Commission is the government's most aggressive official in rooting out fraud, violations of consumers' privacy, and deceptive marketing practices in the emerging point-and-click marketplace (Simons, 1999). The FTC was established in 1914 by the Federal Trade Commission Act, and since then their powers have broadened. In 1938, the Wheeler Lea Amendments clarified the FTC's role in regard to including "unfair or deceptive acts or practices." By these amendments, deceptive advertising came under the FTC's jurisdiction. Warranties and other trade-regulation rules were added under the 1977 Magnuson-Moss Warranty Act. This act also extended the FTC ability to enforce its rules (previously it had to go through the Department of Justice). In the 1980s, the FTC established an Office of Consumer and Competition Advocacy to identify and respond to issues regarding government intervention in the market. The FTC is continually balancing the need to protect legitimate business while going after fraudulent businesses as shown in the Consumer Alert.

This agency pursues Internet-related enforcement actions, including garden-variety fraud cases such as get rich-quick pyramid schemes and miracle weight-loss drugs. The FTC is also responsible for the laundering instructions sewn into every piece of clothing sold in the United States. They also wrestle with regulating television advertising and curbing telemarketing fraud. They have enforcement powers based on their statutes. The FTC, for example, can insist that advertisers run **corrective advertising**. This type of advertisement disclaims previously false advertising claims. It is advertising run by a firm to cause consumers to "unlearn" inaccurate information from prior advertisements. Here are two examples of corrective advertising messages:

- "Do you recall some of our past messages saying that Domino sugar gives you strength, energy, and stamina? Actually, Domino is not a special or unique source of strength, energy, and stamina. No sugar is, because what you need is a balanced diet and plenty of rest and exercise."
- "If you've wondered what some of our earlier advertising meant when we said Ocean Spray cranberry juice cocktail has more food energy than orange juice or tomato juice, let us make it clear: we didn't mean vitamins and minerals. Food energy means calories. Nothing more." (Hawkins, Best, and Coney, 2001, p. 728)

Although the effectiveness of corrective advertising has been questioned, the FTC continues in this effort as a means to bring accurate information to the public. In order for the FTC to insist on corrective advertising, the false impression that is

---

**Consumer Alert**

"Retirees! Moms! Earn extra cash while working at home!" We have all seen these classified ads that promote work-at-home scams in newspapers. The person answers the ad by sending money or charging a toll call to a credit card to get details. And what do they get in return? Instructions for running more ads or setting up a business or a box of trinkets to assemble or envelopes to stuff after which the person mails the items back at their own expense and supposedly earns a fee. Often the work is said to be shoddy, and the company offers more expensive kits or more likely the company has disappeared. Common sense should tell people that they will not be paid huge sums of money to sit at home and do simple work. This is where the FTC steps in; they warn people about misleading advertisements. To learn more about scams and how to spot them, log in to the Federal Trade Commission's Web site (*www.ftc.gov*), click on consumer protection, then go to Franchise & Business Opportunities.

The Federal Trade Commission enforces consumer protection laws against any illegal acts that are considered unfair methods of competition or unfair or deceptive practices. It was considerably strengthened in terms of enforcement power by the Magnuson-Moss Warranty Act.

made has to be very strong. Indirect effects or flattering words are difficult to define so puffery and fluff in advertising are legitimate and pervasive.

One of the FTC's biggest challenges is enforcing labeling and trade violations from overseas. With the advent of the Internet, more and more problems are coming from other countries where consumer laws are usually weaker. For example, Web sites abroad are offering prescription drugs without doctors or licensed pharmacies being involved.

One of its newer realms of coverage is dealing with telemarketers. The FTC steps in regarding violations of no-call requests. Box 5.1 gives information about how to reduce unwanted calls. Florida established the first state no-call list in 1991. To give you an idea about how such legislation comes about, this particular law was supported by Carl Carpenter, a state legislator, whose elderly, disabled mother could hardly get to the phone and then when she got to it the calls were from firms selling aluminum siding and bulk beef. She told him there should be a law to protect people from unsolicited sales calls so Carpenter fought for it and won.

Since the FTC's jurisdiction is so vast, they have divided their functions up into several divisions who are responsible for:

- Advertising
- Marketing
- Credit
- Enforcement
- Service industries

The FTC does not act on individual complaints; rather it looks for a pattern of complaints and then decides which ones to investigate. Complaints can come from a variety of sources, including consumers or consumer organizations, whistleblowers, congressional leaders, and scholars and institutes. If after an investigation the FTC believes that a business has violated the law, they will ask the business to stop a specific action and/or issue a complaint. If the business will not stop and no settlement is reached, the case may go forward. Formal hearings may take place, and an administrative law judge may issue a decision. Decisions can go all the way to the Supreme Court. Along the way an FTC rule may be challenged in a U.S. Court of Appeals. The rules or trade regulations are the FTC's most effective means of protecting consumers and legitimate businesses.

Another example of the jurisdiction of the FTC is that of monitoring mail-in rebate offers. For example, the FTC has taken action against electronic makers such

---

**BOX 5.1    Getting Relief from Telemarketers' Calls**

The National Do Not Call Registry is open for business, putting consumers in charge of the telemarketing calls they get at home. The Federal government created the national registry to make it easier and more efficient for you to stop getting telemarketing calls you don't want. You can register online at WWW.DONOTCALL.GOV or call toll-free, 1-888-382-1222 (TTY 1-866-290-4236), from the number you wish to register. Registration is free.

The Federal Trade Commission, the Federal Communications Commission, and the states are enforcing the National Do Not Call Registry. Placing your number on the registry will stop most, but not all, telemarketing calls.

as manufacturers of scanners who routinely paid out rebates months late or not at all (Spencer, 2002). More valuable rebates are the ones most often in question. Some offer as much as $400 off computer purchases, for example, while a charcoal rebate offer on a $4.99 bag of charcoal may be for only a $1 (when you take off the cost of the stamp that isn't much of a rebate). For the low-end offers, the percentage of consumers mailing in rebate coupons known as **claim rates** may be only 5 percent, but for the high end electronics offers the percentage may go as high as 40 percent (Spencer, 2002). The rebates attract customers and move merchandise, but they can trip a company up that does not plan wisely. One dot.com filed for bankruptcy court protection because it owed customers $90 million in rebates; one particularly enthusiastic shopper was owed $90,000 (Spencer, 2002).

The FTC also issues sets of guidelines such as voluntary guidelines for green claims (green meaning environmentally sound). Box 5.2 offers examples of these guidelines.

**Consumer Product Safety Commission (CPSC).**   The Consumer Product Safety Commission headquartered in Bethesda, MD (outside Washington, DC), was created in 1972 by Congress under the Consumer Product Safety Act; it began operating in 1973. It has three regional offices in New York City, Chicago, and Oakland, California. There are about 100 CPSC investigators, compliance officers, and consumer information specialists throughout the country. In total the CPSC has approximately 500 employees and monitors the safety of over 15,000 kinds of consumer products. It is an independent agency, meaning it doesn't report to nor is it part of any other federal department or agency. Its basic function is to protect consumers against injuries and deaths associated with consumer products. The kinds of products they are most involved in are toys, baby and sports equipment, and household products such as coffeemakers and lawn mowers, but they do not have jurisdiction over some categories of products such as automobiles, tires, boats, drugs, food, cosmetics, pesticides, and medical devices. According to the CPSC Web site, they:

- Develop voluntary standards with industry
- Issue and enforce mandatory standards or banning consumer products if no feasible standard would adequately protect the public
- Obtain the recall of products or arranging for their repair
- Conduct research on potential product hazards

*Consumers vary in their response to rebate offers from 5 percent to 40 percent, depending on the deal.*

*Trade regulations or rules are developed by federal and state agencies that define and prohibit various industry activities.*

---

BOX 5.2   Examples of Environmental Guidelines Issued by the Federal Trade Commission

- An ad calling a trash bag "recyclable" without qualification would be deemed misleading because bags aren't ordinarily separated from other trash at incinerators and landfills.
- A shampoo advertised as "biodegradable" without qualifications wouldn't be deceptive if there is reliable scientific support showing it will decompose in a short time.
- A "recycled" label on a bottle made from recycled material wouldn't be considered misleading even if the cap isn't made from recycled material

- Inform and educate consumers through the media, state and local governments, private organizations, and by responding to consumer inquiries

One of the problems involved in monitoring the safety of babies and young children is that because they live with adults and older brothers and sisters they are exposed to products that are not made for them. The worst case scenarios are that they suffocate in water beds, swallow parts from their older siblings' toys, and get strangled in window blind cords. Toy and household product manufacturers who are aware of such risks do what they can to reduce risks. For example, one leading window manufacturer places the blinds between two panes of glass and in so doing removes the blind cords as a safety measure for children. Parents and other caregivers have a responsibility to watch over children and to remove potential hazards. Seemingly safe products such as a bucket with wash water for floors can turn deadly if a toddler puts his or her head in, can't get out, and drowns. Child-proofing a house, yard, and pool area is essential coupled with active supervision. The CPSC offers suggestions on how to prevent accidental injuries in their publications and on their Web site.

The CPSC does not recommend brands or test products. It provides information to consumers on what safety features to look for in products and announces recalls.

***Information on Recalls by the CPSC.***   A product is recalled if it presents a significant risk to consumers either because the product may be defective or violates a mandatory standard issued by CPSC. If a product is recalled, you should stop using it, and find out from the CPSC what to do next by e-mailing *info@cpsc.gov* or calling 800 638 2772. If a toy, for example, is found to be unsafe, the recall may only apply to products manufactured and date coded at a specific time. When you check into a recall order, sometimes you get your money back, sometimes you don't. The CPSC regularly updates recall information on their Web site.

Examples of typical recalls by manufacturers in cooperation with the CPSC include strollers, activity gym toys, baby clothes, electric ranges, glue guns, dishwashers, and pull toys. To explain the types of problems that exist, in the case of strollers they often collapse and injure children who fall. To remedy this, the manufacturer sent a free repair kit so that the parent could make the stroller safer. In the case of gym toys that had detachable rattles that posed a choking hazard, a refund was offered from the store where purchased. The baby clothes had a zipper pull that posed a choking hazard, a refund was offered. In the electric ranges, when sparks or flames were possible a free in-home repair was offered. For glue guns that overheated, causing burn risks, a refund was offered. With dishwashers in question that could ignite, free rewiring or rebates were offered from the company. When pull toys had plastic connectors on string that could detach and put children at risk of choking, the manufacturer offered replacement.

***Reporting Injuries or Unsafe Products.***   If someone is hurt by a consumer product, the CPSC wants to know. It can be reported online at *hazard@cpsc.gov* or by phone 900 638 2772, extension 650 or by letter. What will happen next is a letter will be sent from CPSC's National Injury Information Clearinghouse. In response to the letter, CPSC will want to know more details and to confirm the accuracy of information already given. The complaint will be sent to the manufacturer.

It should be noted that not all complaints are investigated because CPSC receives reports of over 10,000 product-related injuries and deaths a year; due to a small staff size, they can only investigate some of these. Even if not investigated, the information sent is a valuable resource. It is put into the CPSC database and used to warn others, set up safety guidelines, and possibly influence rule making.

**Food and Drug Administration (FDA).**  The Food and Drug Administration (FDA) is an influential federal agency designed to protect consumers. Its mission is to promote and protect the public health by helping safe and effective products reach the market in a timely way, and monitoring products for continued safety after they are in use such as the example shown in the Consumer Alert.

> Every day, every American comes in contact with products that the FDA regulates.

The FDA considers its work as a blending of law and science aimed at protecting consumers. FDA-regulated products account for about 25 cents of every consumer dollar spent in the United States.

According to the FDA Web site, from the beginnings of civilization people have been concerned about the quality and safety of foods and medicines. In 1202, King John of England proclaimed the first English food law, the Assize of Bread, which prohibited adulteration of bread with such ingredients as ground beans or peas. In the United States, regulation of goods dates from early colonial days, and chapter 2 highlights legislation passed in the twentieth century. Remember the discussion of Dr. Harvey Wiley, the father of the Food and Drugs Act of 1906? He unified a variety of groups including the media and the public behind this federal law to prohibit the adulteration and misbranding of food and drugs.

Federal controls over the drug supply began with inspection of imported drugs in 1848. Most recently, in 1998, the Federal Food and Drug Administration Act was passed which offers gravely ill patients easier access to experimental drugs. It cut the waiting for approval time. More on the history of food, drug, and cosmetic controls is covered in an upcoming chapter focusing on health. The emphasis in this chapter is on the present and how these agencies function and affect our daily lives.

As the Consumer Alert shows, the FDA's jurisdiction encompasses human drugs, but as its name implies, it also oversees most food products (other than meat, poultry, and egg products). The FDA also is in charge of animal drugs, therapeutic agents of biological origin, medical devices, radiation-emitting products for consumers, medical, and occupational use, cosmetics, and animal feed. The staff size is approximately 9,100 employees (about one-third work in the Washington, DC, area), and it has a budget of over $1 billion. Agency scientists evaluate applications for new human drugs and biologics, medical devices, food and color additives, infant formulas, and animal drugs (Swann, 2002).

---

**Consumer Alert**

Shock your wrinkles away? Yes, this was a product promoted by actresses as the secret for younger-looking skin. Put this battery-operated device on your face every day, and the companies making the device suggest that the appearance of wrinkles will be reduced. The device sold for between $99 and $250 depending on the company. Testers who tried it said they felt pain and tingling. The FDA said the devices weren't authorized for removing wrinkles and sent warnings to the companies. The bottom line was that muscle stimulation may produce temporary swelling, but according to dermatologists, it cannot permanently remove wrinkles (GH Institute, 2001).

---

---

**Consumer Alert**

"They claimed their products could bolster the immune system and treat several serious diseases, including AIDS and cancer. But Allen J. Hoffman of Finksburg, Md., and a Virginia physician are now serving prison terms for fraudulently peddling an intravenous mixture containing aloe vera to treat autoimmune and other conditions." They billed up to $18,000 for a two-week treatment of intravenous aloe vera. Patients traveled from the United States to the Bahamas and Mexico for treatments. According to the investigator's report, "it is clear that some people were misled and defrauded into trying dangerous, unapproved and ineffective alternative treatments."

*Source:* Meadows, Michelle. (May–June 2002). Maryland man, Virginia physician sentenced for illegally marketing aloe vera "treatments." *FDA Consumer*, p. 34.

---

To give a broader picture, the types of products that the FDA regulates and the issues they get involved in include

Under Food: foodborne illness, nutrition, and dietary supplements

Under Drugs: prescription, over-the-counter, and generic

Under Medical Devices: pacemakers, contact lenses, and hearing aids

Under Biologics: vaccines and blood products

Under Animal Feed and Drugs: Livestock and pets

Under Cosmetics: Safety and labeling

Under Radiation-Emitting Products: Cell phones, lasers, and microwaves

Poisoning, much of it from food sources, is the nation's third most common form of unintentional death.

To give a specific example, the FDA announced a nationwide recall of Susie Brand imported cantaloupe due to salmonella (rod-shaped bacteria that can cause illness). It should be noted that poisoning, much of it from food sources, is the nation's third most common form of unintentional death. Other sources are household cleaning products and medicines usually swallowed by children. On the same day of the cantaloupe alert there were other recalls and alerts as well as recent approvals of new products. FDA is within the Department of Health and Human Services.

**Department of Agriculture (USDA).** The U.S. Department of Agriculture (USDA) headquartered in Washington, DC, has offices and testing centers throughout the United States. Examples of centers or divisions are given in Box 5.3. The USDA began in 1862 under President Abraham Lincoln when 48 percent of the people were farmers who needed good seeds and information to grow their crops. With less than 2 percent of the American population now living on farms, the mission and outreach of the USDA has broadened to include all segments of the population. Its range of activities has grown to include food and water safety, research, education, conservation, and overseeing a number of programs such as Food Stamps and School Breakfast and Lunch programs.

Regarding food, the USDA is responsible for the safety of meat, poultry, and egg products. This falls under Food Safety, a division that administers the federal meat and poultry inspection system and educates industry and consumers about food

BOX 5.3   Centers and Divisions within the U.S. Department
of Agriculture Most Related to Consumer Issues

- Animal and Plant Health Inspection Service, in Riverdale, MD, *www.aphis.usda.gov*
- Center for Nutrition Policy and Promotion in Washington, DC, *wwwusda.gov.cnpp*
- Cooperative State Research, Education and Extension Service, Washington, DC, *www.reeusda.gov* or consult country government listings in local telephone directories for the number of local Cooperative Extension Service offices
- Meat and Poultry Hotline, Washington, DC, *www.fsis.usda.gov*

The surface mail address for USDA and all its agencies:

U.S. Department of Agriculture
Washington, DC 20250

safety. Inspection of meat products is required by federal law. In 1996 the Meat and Poultry Rules were passed that allowed inspectors to use microscopes to detect *E. coli* and salmonella bacteria. This makes it much easier to determine if products carry these potentially deadly organisms. Another area of the USDA, The Food, Nutrition, & Consumer Service, runs the federal food assistance programs and coordinates nutrition research and policy.

The Cooperative State Research, Education, and Extension Service of the USDA has been a source of information and assistance to consumers for over a century. Educators are located in nearly every county to bring research-based knowledge directly to families and communities. Programs include personal finance issues, such as budgeting and retirement as well as programs on food and nutrition and safe housing. College students who have completed course work in consumer economics and related areas can consider the Cooperative Extension Service as a place for internships and employment, as well as the other agencies and commissions covered in this chapter.

**Department of Justice (DOJ).**   According to their Web site, the mission of the Department of Justice is to enforce the law and defend the interests of the United States according to the law, to provide federal leadership in preventing and controlling crime, to seek just punishment for those guilty of unlawful behavior, to administer and enforce the nation's immigration laws fairly and effectively, and to ensure fair and impartial administration of justice for all Americans. The part of the DOJ most connected to consumer economics is the Antitrust Division which promotes and protects the competitive process through the enforcement of antitrust laws. A more common way to refer to the Antitrust function is "trust busting." The practices that restrain trade include

- Price fixing conspiracies
- Corporate mergers likely to reduce the competitive vigor of particular markets
- Predatory acts designed to achieve or maintain monopoly power.

Monopolies occur when there is only one producer (a single firm) that controls or dominates an industry and for which there is no substitute. Because we live in a market economy we want to be free, as consumers, to choose the products and services that we want. We like selection. On the other hand, Adam Smith, founder of economics, recognized the desire of businessmen to monopolize trade by joining forces, and "although he was not able to specify what the monopoly price would be, he recognized that monopolists would extract a higher price by restricting output" (Landreth and Colander, 2002, p. 83). In other words, monopolies would ultimately result in higher costs to consumers and, thus, he encouraged competition. "He saw competition as fundamentally requiring a large number of sellers; a group of resource owners who were knowledgeable about profits, wages, and rents in the economy; and freedom of movement for resources among industries" (Landreth and Colander, 2002, pp. 82–83).

A **merger** occurs when two or more companies combine into a single unit. They can be classified by economic function such as horizontal, vertical, market, product or conglomerate. A **horizontal merger** combines direct competitors in the same product lines and markets. An example of a horizontal merger would be two department stores in the same town merging. A **vertical merger** combines supplier and company or customer and company. An example of a vertical merger is when a producer of a raw material also manufactures and wholesales the material. A **market extension merger** combines firms selling the same products in different markets. An example would when one grocery store distribution company buys another, increasing the area to which they distribute. A **product extension merger** combines firms selling different but related products in the same market. An example of this would be when a soft drink company acquires a snack food company thus extending or expanding their product line. The catch-all merger category is the **conglomerate merger** that combines companies with none of the previously mentioned relationships or similarities. An example of a conglomerate merger would be a beer manufacturer joining with a furniture company. Sometimes the federal government blocks or slows the growth of mergers, other times it lets them go by or only focuses on certain types. Many mergers involve small companies that do not have much consumer impact. The cases are costly in terms of personnel and money so the emphasis is on larger companies or precedent setting cases. There are a number of other factors as well, such as the general economic climate and the presidential administration. Now and then, Congress steps in (usually in response to a company scandal or consumer uproar) and insists on the need to strengthen antitrust laws.

Historically, the goal of antitrust laws is to protect economic freedom and opportunity through promoting competition. What are the benefits of competition?

- Competition provides businesses with the opportunity to compete on price and quality, on a level playing field, in an open market, unhampered.
- It tests and strengthens American companies at home, making them better able to succeed abroad.
- The bottom line is that competition within the United States or globally leads to lower prices, better quality, and greater choice for consumers.

The Antitrust Division prosecutes serious and willful violations of antitrust laws by filing criminal suits. Possible outcomes include fines and jail sentences. Civil action is also possible which would forbid future violations of the law. The statutes enforced by the Antitrust Division include

- The Sherman Antitrust Act (1890) deals with restraint of trade and monopolies. The main purpose of this act is to maintain a competitive economy. It was named after Senator John Sherman who was quoted on the Senate floor as saying, "If we will not endure a King as a political power, we should not endure a King over production, transportation, and sale of the necessaries of life." The first case tried under this act decided by the Supreme Court was *United States* v. *E. C. Knight Company* (1895). The American Sugar Refining Company controlled 98 percent of the U.S. sugar-refining industry. Cases since then have included monopolies in aluminum, oil, tobacco, steel, telephone, and computer industries.
- The Clayton Act (1914) includes statements about discrimination in price, services, or facilities. It discusses corporate mergers, exclusive contracts, and other processes that lessen competition.
- The Wilson Tariff Act has to do with imports and fairness of trade. There are also codes and statements regarding falsifying, concealing, or covering up by any trick, scheme, or device a material fact or in any other way misrepresentation, including frauds and swindles by mail, wire, radio, or television. Defrauding though the mails became a federal crime under the Mail Fraud Act of 1872.

**Securities and Exchange Commission (SEC).** The Securities and Exchange Commission (SEC) headquartered in Washington, DC, is the investor's advocate. Their primary mission is to protect investors and maintain the integrity of the securities (a word referring to stocks and bonds) markets. This agency was created by the Securities Exchange Act of 1934 to administer that act and the Securities Act of 1933, formerly the jurisdiction of the Federal Trade Commission. The SEC is composed of five commissioners who are appointed by the president on a rotating basis for five-year terms. The chairman of the SEC is designated by the president, and no more than three members of the commission may be of the same political party. The SEC supports full public disclosure and protects the investing public from malpractice in the securities market.

As the quote from the SEC web page in the Consumer Alert indicates, millions of Americans and foreign investors have money invested in the stock market either directly through individual stocks or mutual funds or through retirement accounts so the work of the SEC is crucial to their financial future. The SEC watches out for fraud and deception in the securities market and provides investor education. They

---

**Consumer Alert**

"As more and more first-time investors turn to the markets to secure their futures, pay for homes, and send children to college, these goals are more compelling than ever. The world of investing is fascinating, complex, and can be very fruitful. But unlike the banking world, where deposits are guaranteed by the federal government, stocks, bonds and other securities can lose value. There are no guarantees. That's why investing should not be a spectator sport; indeed, the principal way for investors to protect the money they put into the securities markets is to do research and ask questions" (*www.sec.gov*, May 23, 2002, What we do).

---

**Consumer Alert**

"Frank Gruttadauria, a star Lehman Brothers broker in Cleveland, siphoned an estimated $125 million from clients over 15 years, covering his tracks with forged account statements, federal regulators say. Where was the local Lehman official who was supposed to monitor his conduct? He reported to Mr. Gruttadauria. In Miami, R. Christopher Hanna used strikingly similar methods over 10 years to steal $15 million from his clients at Credit Suisse First Boston, regulators say. The former CFSB branch manager who was supposed to be overseeing Mr. Hanna may not have noticed because he was busy as a broker in his own right, handling accounts for wealthy customers" (Gasparino and Craig, May 23, 2002, p. A1).

may investigate allegations of wrongdoing on their own or join in with other groups. For example, in 2002 the SEC, New York Stock Exchange, and the regulatory arm of the National Association of Securities Dealers launched a joint examination of Wall Street compliance spurred by a broker in Cleveland who took an estimated $125 million from clients (see the Consumer Alert). Since other brokers were found to have committed similar fraud, the joint examination included a plan to canvass nearly 6,000 registered brokers to see if there were other gaps in monitoring the actions of brokers.

The laws and rules that govern the securities industry in the United States require public companies to disclose meaningful financial and other information to the public. The SEC promotes a steady flow of timely, comprehensive, and accurate information so investors can make sound decisions. The SEC oversees stock exchanges, broker-dealers, investment advisors, mutual funds, and public holding companies.

**National Highway Traffic Safety Administration (NHTSA).** The National Highway Traffic Safety Administration (NHTSA) in the Department of Transportation headquartered in Washington, DC, works to reduce injuries. It develops minimum performance standards by enforcing safety standards on motor vehicles, including bicycles, motorcycles, automobiles, trucks, buses, mopeds, recreational vehicles, and all accessories for these vehicles. For example, the safety belts come under their jurisdiction. Their goal is to reduce highway deaths, injuries, and property losses. Defects may require recalls so that corrections can be made. Visit their Web site for information on air bags, auto safety, child seat inspections, crash statistics, and crash tests.

**Federal Consumer Information Center (FCIC).** The Federal Consumer Information Center located in Pueblo, CO, is part of the U.S. General Services Administration. This center was established to help federal agencies and departments develop, promote, and distribute useful consumer information to the public. One of the ways they do this is by publishing a new Consumer Information Catalog four times a year. The center can also tell consumers who to contact for help with problems. FCIC enables consumers to send complaints directly to companies and agencies through its Web site (see E-Resources), but it does not handle consumer complaints. Their catalog lists more than 200 free or low-cost federal booklets on topics such as:

Cars including what to look for when buying new and used cars

Computers including how to avoid Internet investment scams

Education including financial planning for college

Employment including how to create resumes and cover letters

Family including resources for aging parents and black family research

Federal programs including public land for sale, disability rights laws

Food including diabetes recipes and reports on food allergies

Health including what you should know about drug interactions

Housing including how to buy a new home, information on indoor air hazards

Money including saving for a rainy day

Small business including where to get small loans

Travel including national park system maps, how to get a passport

And more, such as how to obtain vital records on births, deaths, marriage, and divorces

For a free catalog, go to *www.pueblo.gsa.gov.* At the Web site search for topics of interest, latest consumer news, and use the links to other federal agencies and consumer offices.

This concludes the federal government section of this chapter, but it should be noted that there are many other federal departments and commissions that affect consumers. For brevity's sake not all of them can be covered here, but many are covered in other areas of the book. For example, the Federal Reserve System (the "Fed") will be covered in the upcoming chapter on banking.

## State Consumer Protection Revisited

As mentioned in previous chapters, state governments provide consumer protection through agencies, commissions, boards, attorney generals' offices, Departments of Insurance, and Offices of Consumer Affairs and other units. They serve an important role in handling consumer complaints in their states. Some states have better protection measures than those of federal government agencies. In some cases, states handle the same sorts of complaints and cases as the federal government. In the earlier section on the FTC, it was noted that the FTC can go after companies who are consistently late in paying out rebates. Likewise, state government attorney generals can go after companies slow to pay up. Examples are Texas who settled with CompuServe and Florida who filed a complaint against the same company for failing to pay $400 rebates to dozens of customers who had signed up for three years of Internet service (Spencer, 2002). Box 5.4 gives a list of places to turn to if your rebate does not arrive in a reasonable time.

Certain fraud and deceptive practices tend to occur more often in specific areas of the country more than in others so in many cases localized solutions make more sense than federal intervention, and there is also a history in the United States of states' rights. Regarding targeted fraud, in Florida, California, and other states in the Sunbelt state governments are well aware that their high concentration of elderly makes them attractive to fraudsters, and so additional protections are needed. Con artists may come in the form of telemarketers, nursing homes salespersons,

> ### BOX 5.4    Where to Turn to When Your Rebate Fails to Come
>
> To move merchandise, companies are offering record numbers of rebates for everything to computers to charcoal. If your rebate is late beyond a reasonable amount of time, here are places to turn.
>
> - Your state attorney general office. To find the address and phone number go to *www.NAAG.org* which is the National Association of Attorneys General.
> - *www.FTC.com* You can file a complain on line or call 1-877-FTC-HELP.
> - Want to gripe or hear other people's horror stories? Try *www.RipOffReport.com* or *www.Planetfeedback.com*.
> - To track rebate offers on electronics and computers, go to *www.RebatePlace.com*.

financial planners, sellers of gold coins and foreign lottery tickets, roof repairers, and fortune-tellers. It is difficult to track financial crimes against the elderly because they are less obvious than product purchases, and the elderly are less likely to report frauds than the general population. Sometimes they simply don't know what happened to them, and other times they are too embarrassed to speak out. Other types of fraud common in the Sunbelt, desert areas, Hawaii, and mountain resort areas are phony land deals and tourist scams.

Besides the obvious consumer units, states have public health commissions that provide information on health care and look out for the health of citizens. They have other divisions that test foods grown within the state such as citrus fruit for diseases. States also have human rights commissions, boards of review, departments of transportation, and other departments similar to those at the federal level that handle consumer concerns. State and local courts also handle consumer cases, especially those involving contracts.

## Local Consumer Protection Including Police

Cities, counties, small towns, and military bases have their own consumer affairs, financial, or police departments that investigate consumer complaints, tenant-landlord disputes, conduct investigations, prosecute offenders of consumer laws, and advocate in the consumer interest. If there are criminal acts involving finances, threats, and scams, police become involved. Crimes of this type investigated by police may come under the category or division called bunco or more commonly **bunko** which refers to swindles in which an unsuspecting person or group of people are cheated. Police departments in recent years have had to spend more time on these types of crimes. This trend has been shaped by economic, legal, technological, and social forces along with the perennial problem of runaway greed. There are always people who want to get rich quick or get rich without working for it.

As readers of this book know by now, frauds are not new. "Old scams never die—they just change hands, passed along from one **grifter** to the next" (Adams, 2002, p. 240). A grifter is someone who uses his or her position to derive profit or advantages by unscrupulous means. **Extortion** is the illegal use of one's position, power, or knowledge to obtain money, goods, funds, or favors. In nine-

**Consumer Alert**

"In 1848 William Thompson came up with a disarmingly simple trick for separating New Yorkers from their assets. Well-dressed and polite, he approached a genteel-looking stranger on the street. After a bit of conversation, he asked, "Have you confidence in me to trust me with your watch until tomorrow? When a sucker did, Thompson walked off richer by a watch. This dodge gave birth to a new term: **'Confidence man'** or **con man** for short" (Adams, 2002, p. 240).

teenth- and twentieth-century novels, the main type of extortion was blackmail. The plot would revolve around the blackmailer holding a scandalous letter or photograph of a person. The blackmailer would then threaten to show the letter or photograph to interested parties unless he or she was paid money or given a position. With advancements in copy machines, this type of blackmail no longer makes sense since there can easily be more than one copy in circulation so that the victim would never know if his or her secret was safe by burning the original letter or photograph. More recently, tape recordings and e-mails have been used by blackmailers.

The terms "confidence man" or "con man" refers to a particular type of swindle in which victims are defrauded after their confidence has been won. The confidence or con game may take minutes, weeks, or years to pull off based on the amount of money involved and the complexity of the fraud. Movies have glamorized con games such as *Oceans 11* with George Clooney and *The Sting* with Paul Newman and Robert Redford, but in reality con games are not glamorous and can result in years in prison. Although the term "con men" is masculine, there are con women as well. A common crime is when female housekeepers or caregivers steal from the households that they are hired to clean or from the people they are hired to care for, especially the elderly. Besides stealing jewels and money, they may get a hold of the person's checkbook or credit card and scam undetected for a long time. Banks are on the lookout for any unusual moving around of large amounts of money and may report suspicious activity to the account holder. Before leaving the subject of con games, it should be pointed out that they occur in business as well as in personal life. Accountants or bookkeepers can siphon off company funds until caught. On the national scale, rigged television game shows and fake company sweepstakes have been exposed in the past. As a result, con games can be petty or involve millions of dollars. Regarding fraud directed at individuals, it is becoming more common for con people today to be less personal than the example in the Consumer Alert. The contact with the victim may more likely come through advertisements in newspapers, television, or over the telephone or the Internet.

In summary, as the marketplace becomes more complex so does the need for protection. It behooves all of us to pay more attention to what is occurring right in front of us, right now. We need to be curious about what is going on, what we are buying, and what we are eating and drinking. Being present in the moment will help us avoid injuries and frauds by being more careful of the environment that surrounds us which leads us to the next subject to be discussed—injurious consumption.

# INJURIOUS CONSUMPTION

The government agencies described in this chapter actively work to reduce injuries caused by consumer products and their use. **Injurious consumption** occurs when individuals or groups make consumption decisions that have negative consequences or misuse products in such a way as to cause injury to themselves or others. For example, every year 25,000 people die as a result of alcohol-related traffic accidents. Some of these people were drunk or alcohol impaired and others were innocent victims. There are about 10 million alcoholics and 80 million cigarette smokers in the United States (Hirschman, 1991; Faber, 1985). Companies promoting such products are often the culprit, but the government is not immune if one considers the number of state-sponsored gambling activities, including lotteries and companies that make potentially harmful products that are given subsidies or tax breaks.

In summary, consumers often engage in harmful activities and businesses and even the government can be the source of injurious consumption. "Economics is about events in the real world" (Landreth and Colander, 2002). So, even though it is difficult to point out that people consume for reasons that are not always healthy nor in their best interest, it has to be done. The Landreth and Colander quote points out that economics (and especially consumer economics) is about the real world and the outcomes of consumption are not always attractive.

# REGULATION AND DEREGULATION ISSUES

So far, this chapter has talked about rules, legislation, and agencies to protect consumers and some of the frauds and injuries that may befall consumers. Government, through its policies on taxes (e.g., placing high taxes on cigarettes) and spending, affects consumer behavior. It decides how schools will be funded and what roads will be built and if Social Security recipients will receive a raise each year and for how much. Once an agency is created, it has the authority to develop rules and regulations. It is usually easier to have rules and regulations set up than to have legislation pass through state legislatures and Congress. Besides developing rules, agencies have to see that they are enforced. In terms of consumerism, a rule or **regulation** is an attempt by government to control the workings of the marketplace. Regulations are necessary because policy makers believe that it is in the best interest of consumers and the overall economy as well as the development of certain industries if monopolies are held in check because they reduce competition in the marketplace. This reduction could lead to price fixing, poor service, and scarcer choice. This stance, of course, is opposed to the general philosophy of Adam Smith who argued that government interference, for the most part, is undesirable because it infringes upon the natural rights and liberties of individuals. However, his greatest concern was about the regulation of international trade rather than domestic trade (Landreth and Colander, 2002).

Rules and regulations relevant to consumer economics include those that:

- Educate consumers
- Protect consumers

- Regulate sellers, discouraging unfair or deceptive or dangerous practices
- Change the relationship between buyers and sellers so that certain practices or products are illegal

Many regulations protect children in terms of the advertising content and images targeted at them. For example, in 1996 the Federal Communications Commission issued new rules under the Children's Television Act that required stations to air three hours of educational programming targeting children 16-years-old and under per week and tightened the definition of what constitutes educational programming. Most people would agree that children need protection in the marketplace.

Regulations placed on products aimed strictly at adults are more controversial. Some economists and many corporations, especially those under investigation and those who represent them, feel that government intervention has gone too far. They would argue for more public choice. They believe that government regulation is ineffective or too restrictive of trade and agree with Adam Smith's philosophy of laissez-faire (let the marketplace run itself). Given the countless numbers of products and services available, it is safe to say that for the most part the marketplace is not regulated. For example, "supplements are largely unregulated by the federal government and are not monitored for potency, purity or correct dosage; older adults on other medications may be particularly susceptible to overdoses or adverse reactions" (Pope, 2002). Many in the population applaud government intervention and would like more of it, especially as new problems crop up. When it comes to the unknown and the untested, the public looks to government to serve as a protector. To summarize and extend the arguments already presented, as the marketplace becomes more impersonal with the disappearance of small local stores and consumers deal with sellers in an impersonal environment, fraud is more easily promulgated. Product complexity has also grown, requiring more knowledge of companies, products, and services. Advertising is more intrusive. All these factors make a case for the necessity for regulation.

Types of regulation include

- Pricing. For example, a maximum price may be set.
- Licensing. For example, licenses may be required to be an interior designer, nail technician, or a barber.
- Standard setting. Safety standards are set in factories or in how much beef should be in a can of beef noodle soup.
- Subsidies. Government can become involved in regulating supplies of imports such as oil and provide incentives or subsidies to grow certain crops or develop businesses.
- Privacy. For example, standards regarding financial transaction privacy.

In the 1970s, proponents of reform and some lawmakers began to question the wisdom of too much government regulation of industry. They argued that too much regulation was restricting trade and that in the long run consumers may gain from deregulation. **Deregulation** removes or reduces government intervention. It allows the free market to operate. Examples of deregulated industries include:

- Airlines: deregulated in 1978 in terms of fares, schedules, and routes. Under discussion, a passenger bill of rights, better airfare disclosures.
- Banking: deregulated in the 1980s, affecting savings rates, fees, and lending standards. The opening up of interstate banking came in 1994. When some

banks failed in the 1980s, some were bailed out by the government. Mergers ensued. In the United States, the top 25 banks controlled 51 percent of deposits in 1998, compared with 29 percent in 1980 ("Deregulated," 2002). Under discussion, more protection from unreasonable rate hikes especially use of ATM charges.

- Cable television: regulated and deregulated throughout the 1980s and 1990s affecting rates and services, an industry that often ranks low in consumer satisfaction surveys.
- Electricity: Deregulated in certain areas in the 1990s, controversial, problems with blackouts in California caused the state to suspend deregulation in 2001.
- Telephone: In 1984 telephone equipment was deregulated, long distance partly deregulated in 1984, and domestic service deregulated in the 1990s, continues. Problems with customer confusion over rates and services.

Box 5.5 provides a list of criteria to use in judging how well deregulation has worked.

If it works as intended, deregulation should lead to more competitive pricing, product and service innovation, and more options for consumers. In deregulation, sometimes smaller companies rise to the top such as Southwest Airlines (once a small, regional airline, now nationally known) that has consistently high consumer satisfaction ratings on service and prices. When deregulation does not work out well, there are the problems such as the blackouts in California noted in Box 5.5. So that in deregulation, services may suffer, prices may not decrease, and the number of choices can lead to customer confusion. An example of this is the confusion of many consumers over which telephone company or computer server to choose and arguments over improper or misleading charges. Because of the variance in industries and in consumer needs, each deregulated industry has to be judged individually. Traditionally it was assumed that for the most part, the positive aspects (in particular, better prices) far outweighed the negative aspects, but there have been

*Consumers need government protection through regulations and legislation, but they also can benefit from deregulation because of more competitive pricing.*

---

**BOX 5.5    Deregulation Criteria**

There are arguments for and against deregulation. In this chart, the usual criteria are listed to be used to decide if deregulation is working from a consumer point of view (adapted from "Deregulation," 2002). The reason a clear cut pro and con list cannot be given is that deregulation in certain industries may be better for urban dwellers that experience increased service and more competitive prices because they live in concentrated high-profit centers, whereas rural dwellers may experience less service and higher rates.

Choice:  Are consumers given more choices?
Consumer Rights:  Are consumers given more rights? Or, are the rights they already have upheld?
Innovation:  Are better products offered? Are new ways of manufacturing and production encouraged?
Safety:  Have security and safety increased?
Savings:  Are consumers saving money? Are prices lower?
Service:  Are consumers being served better? Are services dependable?

articles that question how much consumers really benefit from deregulation ("Deregulated," 2002). If an industry is deregulated, it does not mean that the government is no longer involved. Government watches for abuses in the system such as runaway rate hikes or discrimination and is prepared to step in when things get out of hand or existing laws are violated.

Another type of deregulation is when government turns to **privatizing**. This term means turning over some of the functions of government to business. The trend in many states is towards more privatization or outsourcing of formerly government-based work. This may involve government workers losing their jobs, being offered early retirement, or shifting them from government to business. There is debate on both sides (government and business) as to whether privatization leads to better service or in the long run to more efficiency and cost savings for citizens.

## SPECIAL INTERESTS

Business, organizations, and government do not operate in a vacuum they influence and are influenced by many groups. **Special interest groups** are units of two or more persons who have a common interest and seek to influence government policy and enforcement. They may do this by lobbying. **Lobbyists** represent special interest groups. A study by the Center for Public Integrity found that lobbyists vastly outnumber and overwhelm elected state officials. They are also a significant presence in Washington, DC. The top lobbying interests in the nation are given in Table 5.1. The number of lobbyists is highest for the insurance industry followed by those representing health services. There are different opinions about the worth and the functioning of lobbyists. Some call them swarming locusts, others call them useful resources. They definitely serve a function and that is to influence legislation on behalf of their client which may be an organization, industry, or employer. They are another voice in the legislative process. According to a study entitled "The Fourth Branch" by the Center in 2002, lobbyists spend more than $570 million per year influencing legislation in states across the country. States have laws regulating how much legislators can accept from lobbyists. In Florida, the limit is $100 per occurrence on how much a lobbyist can spend on a lawmaker. This can go for dinners, hunting trips, and sporting events tickets.

A study by Public Citizen and the Center for Responsive Politics in 2001 reported that the following two industries did the most political spending from

**Table 5.1**    Top Lobbying Interests in the United States

| Rank in Nation | |
|---|---|
| 1. Insurance | 6. Business services |
| 2. Health services | 7. Electric utilities |
| 3. Education | 8. Pharmaceuticals |
| 4. Local government | 9. Oil and gas |
| 5. Health professionals | 10. Lawyers/law firms |

*Source:* Center for Public Integrity, 2002 report, The fourth branch.

1999–2000: phamaceuticals ($177 million in lobbying, $20 million in campaign contributions) and insurance ($128 million in lobbying and $41 million in campaign contributions). So, there are a number of public action groups and centers monitoring political spending, including tracking advertisements and promotions. According to University of Pennsylvania's Annenberg Public Policy Center which tracks issue ads, "when it comes to issue advocacy money is indeed speech, with the largest bankroll having the loudest voice and the voice of those with limited means effectively drowned out" (Drugmakers, May 2002, p. 14).

## ENLIGHTENED COMPANIES AND CONSUMER PROTECTION

The activities of lobbyists, new laws and regulations, will continue to grow, but enlightened companies encourage their managers to look beyond what the rules say and simply "do the right thing." In other words, well-run companies will self-regulate. Socially responsible firms actively seek out ways to protect the long-run interests of their consumers and the environment (Kotler and Armstrong, 2002, p. 19). They do not rip off consumers by selling products that stop or reverse the aging process, for example. Since it is not currently possible, anyone who does this is lying even if they are a doctor according to S. Jay Olshansky, a demographer at the University of Chicago (Pope, 2002).

How businesses run themselves as well as the products they produce have come under public scrutiny. For example, recent well-publicized corporate scandals have drawn the public's attention to the pitfalls of poor business practices, including shoddy accounting. Businesses more than ever before are being expected to use common sense and have above reproach behavior. Many industries and professional associations have adopted a code of ethics or a set of guidelines for standards of behavior and accountability. The development of e-commerce and the Internet has pushed this agenda even further. Privacy issues have moved center stage. Legislators and company managers are asking: What are the rules in cyberspace? Written laws from the government have often not kept pace with this fast-moving technology, and existing laws are often difficult to apply or enforce.

If companies don't self-regulate, the government can and does step in. An example is that in 1998, America Online paid a $2.6 million penalty and agreed to update its business practices to settle a deceptive-marketing complaint brought forward by 44 state attorneys general. In the case, AOL failed to notify consumers clearly that the "50 free hours" in its online service's much-touted trial memberships must be used within a one-month period and that users would incur subscription fees after the first month (Kotler and Armstrong, 2002). Unethical marketing tactics are part of an area called social marketing. In **social marketing**, marketing strategies and tactics are applied to alter or create behaviors that have a positive effect or try to reverse negative outcomes for individuals, society, and the environment. For example, social marketing could be used to encourage recycling or to reduce smoking. In the case of smoking, this could be done through dramatic advertisements showing close-ups of the ruined teeth, wrinkled skin, or blackened lungs of lifelong smokers.

Leading corporations support social marketing by considering their own business practices and advertising and trying to help the communities in which they are located. They want consumers to have the information they need to make sound choices. Successful businesses know that good products, information, and word of mouth are essential to their continuing success in the marketplace. Smart consumers look for reliable companies whom they can trust. Legitimate businesses know it is in their best interest to have good relations with consumers and that is why they get involved in consumer protection. They provide full disclosure through warranties and labels, especially about health fields products. They want happy customers and repeat business. They also want to drive out illegitimate or quasi-legitimate businesses that give business a bad name. They may join Better Business Bureaus or associations whose primary goal is to help legitimate businesses maintain good reputations in communities by accepting consumer complaints.

As introduced in the previous chapter, over 2600 members representing over 1500 companies such as The Dial Corporation and Delta Air Lines, Inc. belong to the Society of Consumer Affairs Professionals International (SOCAP) which provides training, conferences, and publications. SOCAP exists to encourage and maintain the integrity of business in transactions with consumers; to encourage and promote effective communication and understanding among business, government and consumers; and to define and advance the consumer affairs profession. Contact information is given in the E-Resources section.

## NONGOVERNMENTAL PROCONSUMER GROUPS

There are literally thousands of nongovernmental proconsumer groups ranging from Centers for Economic Justice to Legal Aid Societies. Some have the word "consumer" in their titles and others don't, which makes some of them difficult to identify or classify until one examines closely the issues or the people that they represent. For example, the American Cancer Society would not be thought of primarily as a consumer organization, but they are a research and consumer advocacy group on the specific subject of cancer prevention and the search for cures. To summarize the main emphases, consumer groups are concerned with three things:

- Do consumers have full knowledge of what they are buying?
- Are products safe?
- Are products environmentally sound?

Chapter 3 provided information about leading national organizations that look out for the consumer interest. One of the oldest, largest, and most visible is Consumers Union of U.S. (CU) which publishes *Consumer Reports,* a monthly magazine, as well as other publications and media. The CU researches and tests consumer goods and services and publishes the results. CU is a nonprofit, independent organization.

The Consumer Federation of America (CFA), founded in 1968, is a large nationally recognized advocacy organization, working to advance proconsumer initiatives. CFA focuses much of its advocacy on the areas of:

- Financial services
- Utilities
- Product safety
- Transportation

**Table 5.2**    There are thousands of nongovernmental proconsumer groups; several of these were mentioned in Chapter 3. Here are some of the largest and most visible groups and their primary functions.

| Group | Function |
|---|---|
| American Association of Retired Persons | Information especially for those 50 and up lobbying, research, publications |
| American Council on Consumer Interests | Academic-based, information, journal |
| American Standards Association | Research on products, standard setting |
| Better Business Bureaus | Business supported, consumer protection |
| Center for Auto Safety | Car complaints, testing, lobbying |
| Center for Science in the Public Interest | Legal-based, lobbying, nutrition |
| Center for Study of Responsive Law | Legal-based, lobbying |
| Consumers Union | Testing, publications |
| Consumer Federation of America | Coordinating, lobbying |
| Public Citizen | Legal defense, lobbying, information |
|    Includes subgroups such as Congress Watch | |
|    Tax Reform Research Group | |
| Public Interest Research Groups (PIRGs) | Lobbying, research, on some college campuses |

- Health care
- Food safety

Located in Washington, DC, it mainly serves as a lobbying federation. Staff members testify before Congress, the White House, federal and state regulatory agencies, and the courts on consumer issues. Testimony is based on facts gathered and issue analysis. CFA also is an educational organization and coordinates the efforts of over 285 organizations reaching trade unions, credit unions, and rural electric cooperatives and in so doing serves as a clearinghouse of information. Because of this CFA represents a wide constituency and range of interests versus some groups that are more focused. CFA is especially concerned about the needs of the least affluent and educated consumers who have little discretionary income and are especially vulnerable to deceptive or fraudulent sales. A partial list of other nongovernmental proconsumer groups and their primary functions are listed in Table 5.2. There are other organizations that are primarily academic in nature such as the American Council on Consumer Interests (ACCI) that publishes the *Journal of Consumer Affairs* and the Association for Financial Counseling and Planning Education that publishes *Financial Counseling and Planning*.

## CONSUMER PUBLICATIONS INCLUDING CONSUMER REPORTS

*The mission of media is to inform*. The **media mix** is the combination of media vehicles, nontraditional media, and marketing communication tools intended to reach the targeted audience (Wells, Burnett, and Moriarty, 2000). In consumer economics, the target is the consumer, and the messages could include how to stimulate shopping or search behavior or how to be more cautious and selective in purchasing behavior. A successful media campaign will deliver on its objectives which may be to:

- Increase sales
- Increase awareness
- Change attitudes

Consumers can be divided into two groups: those who buy the product or service and those who use the product or service. For example, parents buy baby food but the baby eats the food. In terms of consumer protection, a parent may be interested in putting screens or limiting Internet access to certain sites for their teenager, the users would be the teenager but the purchaser of the service or product would be the parent. In both cases, the parent is the targeted consumer.

A major source of consumer information are the many newspapers and magazines published about health or about personal finance such as *Money* or *Better Investing* or about the results of product tests, recalls, travel bargains, or other consumer news such as car testing results in *Motor Trend* magazine. These publications, combined with radio, the Internet, and television throughout the world, reach millions of consumers and perform a great public service. As mentioned previously, there are generalized consumer groups and sources of information and there are also specific publications with consumer in the title. The most famous of these is *Consumer Reports* magazine (and Consumer Reports Online and Consumer Reports on TV in the United States and Canada) published by Consumers Union, an independent, nonprofit testing and information organization. The magazine's subscribers number between 4 and 5 million. CU's mission since its inception in 1936 is to test products, inform the public, and protect consumers. CU has a president, a board of directors, and a staff of more than 450. Their Consumer Policy Institute and testing and research center is in Yonkers, NY. It is the largest nonprofit education and consumer product testing center in the world. All the products are tested off the shelf, meaning the staff buys them just as a consumer would. They send back free products sent by manufacturers. What do they test? In more than 50 labs, they test appliances, autos, chemicals, electronics, foods, home environment products, public service, and recreation and home improvement. Cars and trucks are tested at their auto-test facility in East Haddam, CT. They also survey readers to find out about repair reliability and to rate services. Their Policy Institute conducts research and education projects on such issues as air pollution, food safety, biotechnology, and right-to-know laws. It calls itself America's #1 Consumer Product Test Center. *Consumer Reports* does not take advertising, but it does engage in sales of its own services, products, and publications such the *Consumer Reports Travel Letter* and having inserts for new subscriptions or subscription renewals. Further, inside the magazines there are statements and advertisements that encourage subscribers to remember Consumers Union in their wills. The paper wrap on an issue mailed to a subscriber said,

> Your next issue will be your last issue! It's alarming, but true . . . unless you renew now! You're about to lose the money saving, safety preserving, rip-off preventing independent research results and recommendations compiled in every issue of Consumer Reports. So, quick! Check the term you prefer on the postage-free card and mail it today. (*Consumer Reports,* October 2002)

So, it could be said that *Consumer Reports* meets the three media objectives listed earlier: increased sales, changed attitudes, and increased awareness.

CU has three advocacy offices in Washington, DC, San Francisco, CA, and Austin, TX. Advocacy staff testify before federal and state legislative and regulatory bodies on issues such as health care, financial, food and product safety. They also petition government agencies and file lawsuits on behalf of consumers. This brings us back full circle to the beginning of the chapter that stressed that we are living in an information society; as consumers we need to know what is going on, what are the results of product tests, and how we can make the best choices.

# SUMMARY

Media is an important element in our information economy. The mission of media is to inform. *Consumer Reports* published by Consumers Union is an example of a nongovernmental, consumer-oriented publication. Government is one of the main gatherers, sorters, producers, and monitors of information. It produces useful publications such as the over 200 publications offered about everything from buying cars to making wills in the Consumer Information Catalog by the Federal Consumer Information Center.

The chapter began with a description of how to contact state and federal elected officials about issues and concerns. Then the chapter moved to explaining the workings of the main federal government agencies related to consumerism. Their jurisdictions differ, and it is not always easy to differentiate one from the other. For example, the USDA handles meat, poultry, and egg product testing whereas the FDA handles other food sources. Some agencies test products, others don't, and some have more investigation and enforcement powers than others. The different agencies also cooperate with each other and may each have a say in a particular part of a case or investigation. All are involved in providing consumer information to the public through their Web sites. State and local governments are also active in consumer protection as are some corporations, associations such as the Society of Consumer Affairs Professionals International, and nongovernmental proconsumer groups such as the Consumer Federation of America.

As the marketplace becomes more complex so does the need for more consumer protection. It was also pointed out that consumers often engage in injurious or risky behaviors. It is impossible to remove all risks, but reducing risks and providing better consumer information are goals of government agencies and consumer organizations.

# KEY POINTS

1. The Federal Trade Commission (FTC) established in 1914 is responsible for handling complaints of false advertising, fraud, and product safety and administering antitrust and consumer protection legislation. The FTC looks for patterns of noncompliance. It fosters free and fair business competition and prevents monopolies and activities that restrain trade.
2. As the name implies, the Consumer Product Safety Commission handles consumer product safety mainly in the areas of toys, baby and sports equipment, and household items.

3. The Food and Drug Administration's mission is to promote and protect the public health by helping safe and effective products reach the market in a timely way and by monitoring products for continued safety after they are in use.

4. The U.S. Department of Agriculture helps farmers and ranchers and leads in the Food Stamp, School Lunch and School Breakfast programs, researching human nutrition, encouraging stewardship of the land and conservation and community development, and monitoring the safety of meat, poultry, and egg products.

5. The Department of Justice enforces antitrust laws, promotes competition.

6. The Securities and Exchange Commission advocates for the investor and provides investor education. It looks out for fraud and deception in the securities markets.

7. The Department of Transportation looks out for highway safety and monitors seat belts and other safety devices.

8. State and local governmental units including police get involved in consumer protection.

9. There are pros and cons to deregulation. In theory, the pros may include lower prices, expanded choice, and enhanced services, but in practice this has not always been the case when industries are deregulated.

10. Thousands of nongovernmental proconsumer groups look out for the consumer interest.

11. The media including *Consumer Reports* magazine published by Consumers Union inform consumers about product quality, possible frauds, and recalls. Magazines and newspapers and their Web sites may also provide information on auto trends, cordless phones, running shoes, digital cameras and other products in the marketplace including up-to-date ratings.

## KEY TERMS

| | | |
|---|---|---|
| bunko | grifter | privatizing |
| claim rates | horizontal merger | product extension merger |
| confidence man (or con man) | information economy | regulation |
| conglomerate merger | injurious consumption | social marketing |
| corrective advertising | lobbyists | special interest groups |
| deregulation | market extension merger | vertical merger |
| extortion | media mix | |
| | merger | |

## DISCUSSION QUESTIONS

1. Why does the Department of Justice get involved in the violation of antitrust laws?

2. How do the police get involved in consumer protection? What sort of cases might they investigate? What is extortion and why would the police become involved in investigating extortion?

3. What is an example of injurious consumption? Why do consumers engage in activities that put themselves and others at risk?
4. Consumer advocacy comes in many forms. Go to the Consumer Federation of America Web site at www.consumerfed.org, and list the current issues that they are working on (click on What's New).

# E-RESOURCES

U.S. government Web site that leads to all others is www.firstgov.gov.

| | |
|---|---|
| FirstGov for Consumers<br>www.consumer.gov | Consumer information from over two dozen federal agencies |
| Federal Consumer Information Center (CIC)<br>www.pueblo.gsa.gov<br>Recalls posted, other consumer news<br>Pamphlets | Federal Government Center |
| Federal Trade Commission<br>www.ftc.gov<br>Click on consumer protection<br>Also, look for FTC's Consumer Sentinel,<br>a program to fight consumer fraud and scams | Federal Government Agency |
| Consumer Product Safety Commission<br>www.cpsc.gov<br>News updates, employment information | Federal Government Agency |
| Food and Drug Administration<br>www.fda.gov | Federal Government Agency |
| U.S. Department of Agriculture<br>www.usda.gov | Federal Government Agency |
| U.S. Department of Justice<br>www.usdoj.gov | Federal Government Agency |
| Securities and Exchange Commission<br>www.sec.gov<br>information on stocks and investing | Federal Government Commission |

| | |
|---|---|
| U.S. Department of Transportation National Highway Traffic Safety Administration www.htsa.dot.gov | Federal Government Agency |

| | |
|---|---|
| Nonprofits | |
| National Fraud Information Center www.fraud.org Look for Internet Fraud Watch, click on Internet tips | Nonprofit center exposing frauds |
| Center for Public Integrity www.public integrity.org | Nonprofit center reports on lobbyists |
| Consumer Reports ConsumerReports.org | Nonprofit, independent organization Has current consumer news, alerts, online shopping site e-ratings, and interactive product selectors |
| Consumer Federation of America (CFA) www.consumerfed.org | Washington-based advocacy organization, education |
| Society of Consumer Affairs Professionals International (SOCAP) www.socap.org | Nonprofit association addresses consumer concerns within the corporate structure |

# REFERENCES

Adams, S. (June 10, 2002). May I hold your watch? *Forbes,* p. 240.

Deregulated. (July 2002). *Consumer Reports,* pp. 30–35.

Drugmakers. (May 2002). *AARP Bulletin.* Washington, DC, pp. 13–14

Faber, R. (December 1985). Two forms of compulsive consumption. *Journal of Consumer Research,* pp. 296–304.

*Fourth Branch, The* (2002). Center for Public Integrity. Washington, DC.

GH Institute Report (August 2001). Shock away your wrinkles? *Good Housekeeping,* p. 16.

Hawkins, D., R. Best, and K. Coney (2001). *Consumer behavior: Building marketing strategy.* Boston: Irwin McGraw-Hill. Examples cited from I. Teinowitz, FTC faces test of ad power, *Advertising Age,* March 30, 1998, p. 26.

Hirschman, E. C. (1991). Secular mortality and the dark side of consumer behavior, in *Advances in Consumer Research XVIII,* ed. R. Holman and M. R. Solomon. Provo, UT: Association for Consumer Research, pp. 1–4.

Gasparino, C. and S. Craig (May 23, 2002). Broker watchdogs face scrutiny as investor complaints mount. *Wall Street Journal,* p. A1.

Jones, D. (December 17, 2002). More consumers give government services thumbs-up. *USA Today,* p. A1.

Kotler, P., and G. Armstrong. (2002). *Principles of marketing activebook.* Prentice Hall. www.prenhall.com/myactivebook, 19.

Landreth, H., and D. Colander. (2002). *History of economic thought,* 4th ed. Boston: Houghton Mifflin Company.

Lynch, P. (October 15, 2001). What's next? *Wall Street Journal,* p. A5.

Pope, E. (June 2002). 51 top scientists blast anti-aging idea. *AARP Bulletin,* pp. 3–5.

Simons, J. (July 30, 1999). FTC has a committed foe of Internet fraud. *Wall Street Journal,* p. A20.

Spencer, J. (June 11, 2002). Rejected! Rebates get harder to collect. *Wall Street Journal,* pp. D1–2.

Swann, J. P. (May 14, 2002). History of the FDA. From www.fda.gov. Adapted from George Kurian, ed. (1998). *A Historical Guide to the U.S. Government.* New York: Oxford University Press.

Wells, W., J. Burnett, and S. Moriarty (2000). *Advertising: Principles & practice,* 5th ed. Upper Saddle River, NJ: Prentice Hall.

# PART 3

# Consumers in the Marketplace

# Buying Process, Brands, and Product Development

*In commerce, bygones are forever bygones; and we are always starting clear at each moment, judging the values of things with a view to future utility.*

**William Stanley Jevons**

**Learning Objectives**

1. Know the six steps in the buyer decision process.
2. Understand firms' motivations, including consumer complaint handling and reactions to competition.
3. Know the four stages in product development.
4. Know population trends, including changes in families and households.
5. Identify the four stages in the household life cycle.

## INTRODUCTION

As was typical of early writers, Adam Smith (1723–1790) saw numerous connections between many areas of society—things that today are studied by economists, political scientists, philosophers, sociologists, marketers, family, and consumer scientists—particularly in consumer behavior. **Consumer behavior** refers to the buying behavior of consumers—the individuals, families, and households who buy goods and services for personal consumption. Our task in this chapter is to build on Smith's contribution, to continue to explore the interconnectedness of the economy with a particular emphasis on the connections among consumers, business, and the media. "One of the fundamental premises of the modern field of consumer behavior is that people often buy products not for what they do, but for what they mean. This principle does not imply that a product's basic function is unimportant, but rather that the roles products play in our lives go well beyond the tasks they perform. And the deeper meanings of a product may help it stand out from other, similar goods and services" (Solomon and Rabolt, 2004, p. 27). The chapter begins with the steps consumers go through in the buying decision.

## STEPS IN THE BUYER DECISION PROCESS

Consumers go through six steps in the buying process as shown in Box 6.1 that are part of prepurchase, purchase, and postpurchase behavior.

---

BOX 6.1    Steps in the Consumer Buying Process

Prepurchase:

1. Assessing need
2. Searching for information
3. Evaluating alternatives
4. Selecting

Purchase

1. Buying

Postpurchase

1. Evaluating after purchase through use and comparisons

---

## Prepurchase

In prepurchase, the consumer tries to determine how much pleasure or pain will be derived from a product or service. What is the anticipated performance? How much enjoyment can be expected? In prepurchase, the first step is *assessing need*. In this step problems or decision situations are recognized because people sense a discrepancy between their current state and a desired state. Need recognition can emerge internally such as "I am thirsty" or externally such as noticing that there is no milk in the refrigerator. The difference between needs and wants was presented in earlier chapters, including the discussion of Maslow's hierarchy of needs that begins with the importance of fulfilling our most basic physiological needs (hunger, thirst, shelter) before moving up to more advanced needs. Table 6.1 shows examples of needs and wants.

In terms of employment, most people need work skills, people skills, benefits, transportation, a gathering place and/or communication system, and, of course, pay. Wants can include nearly anything (the sky is the limit). Examples would be corner offices, special phones, designer clothing, boats, private jets, sports cars, state-of-the-art computers and sound systems, swimming pools, vacations, and fitness equipment.

Needs and wants can be complex. In marketing, the term **need set** is used to reflect the fact that most products satisfy more than one need. For example, a

Table 6.1    Differences between Needs and Wants

| Needs | Wants |
| --- | --- |
| Basic clothes for school, leisure, and work | Stylish clothes for special events |
| Transportation to get to class | A brand-new, high-end car |
| An apartment or room | A house with a pool, tennis court, and a view |
| Healthy, affordable food | 5 lb. Maine lobster and 16 oz. steak with loaded baked potato, cheese-cake for dessert |

house offers more than shelter. As a minimum, it offers storage for possessions and a place to sleep and eat besides serving as a shelter from the wind and weather. It also offers status and services as an extension of self. For instance, a homeowner told an interior designer who was suggesting a brown sofa and beige walls, "I need color, I cannot live without color." For the homeowner, color is a need—not simply a want—she cannot live in a brown world. Someone else may not care about color if they need a sofa right away and the price is right. Another way to look at needs are the types of relationships that individuals form with products. According to Susan Fournier (1998), these can include

1. *Self-concept attachment* wherein the products help establish the user's identity such as a professor carrying a briefcase or a student carrying a backpack.
2. *Nostalgic attachment* wherein the product serves as a link with one's past such as a favorite childhood brand of cereal. Kellogg's Frosted Flakes commercials show a middle-aged woman ashamed to admit that the bowl of Frosted Flakes is for her, not for her children.
3. *Interdependence* wherein the product is part of one's daily routine such as a soap or shampoo or a certain brand of orange juice. Another example is that most people have a favorite seat in the living room or family room; they are very interdependent with this chair or sofa.
4. *Love* wherein the product elicits warmth, passion, or another strong emotion. Examples would be stuffed toys or red roses at Valentine's Day. Expressions of love can be conventional like the red roses or a heart-shaped box of candy or more unique. One husband gave his wife a jar of honey every Valentine's Day.

Marketers take an individual's basic needs a step further by grouping consumers with similar need sets. They do not want to offer products that only appeal to one customer, but to many. Once this group or segment is determined through research and/or demographics, then they focus their attention on the **target market**—the largest, most likely group to purchase. Once this market is determined, then **marketing strategy** is formulated which addresses the question "How can we give excellent customer value to this target market?" The question is answered by providing the proper **marketing mix** which includes communications or information (to be discussed next) as well as product, price, distribution, and service.

The second step in the consumer buying process is *searching for information*. In this step information either internally or externally is accessed. Nonrisky behavior such as choosing what flavor of Snapple to buy requires less search behavior than a riskier purchase. Information search involves sorting behavior. Consumers search for information before they buy. They may conduct an **internal search** meaning going over in their minds what they know about a product based on past searches or personal experience or they may conduct an **external search** meaning they will look at advertisements, read articles, go on the Internet, or ask others what they think about a product. An internal search is easier and more common than an external search. External searches require activity such as talking with individuals or groups, reading marketing information, or experiencing the product itself such as through test driving cars or sampling foods at the grocery store.

Advertisers and businesses want to reach today's consumers who are actively conducting external searches and also they want to influence their internal

Convenience plays a large part in consumer decision making.

searches. This is a challenging task because consumers don't always have the time, energy, or the money to conduct extensive searches either internal or external. Have you ever heard someone say, "I just don't have time to think about that right now." They are saying that an internal search would take more time than they currently have. Regarding external searching, if a carload of people are running out of gasoline, they will drive into the nearest gas station regardless of cost or brand. But let's say they come to an intersection with two gas stations, then they may choose the one they prefer because of cost or brand preference or they may choose the one on the "right" side of the street. Convenience plays a large part in consumer decision making. This explains how two Starbucks (coffee shops) or convenience stores located only a block from each other can succeed.

To explain the concept further, external searches can include

- The opinions, attitudes, and behaviors of others such as friends, family members, neighbors, club members, television personalities, and even strangers, such as those contacted over the Internet.
- Direct experiences derived from product inspection, trial, or observation. For example, an attorney could observe that in her law firm the attorneys drive BMWs and the secretaries drive Toyotas or Saturns.
- Reading materials such as articles or professional publications.
- **Marketing communications** which include advertising, public relations, coupons, labels, packaging, billboards, in-store displays, and any other signal or message that the company provides about itself and its products. One of the newer forms is product placement in movies and television shows where the viewer sees a box of cereal or can of soda prominently displayed or used by a likable character. To reach the target market, the products and the communication mode should match. You wouldn't expect to see the giant purple Barney swigging down liquor or Spiderman eating prunes.

When consumers conduct a search, sometimes it is deliberate and sometimes nondeliberate. For example, if someone needs an airplane ticket immediately he or she will go on the Internet and search for airplane routes, availability, and prices. If there is more time, then the search may be less deliberate. The person may mentally say, I wonder what flights there are between New York and London and what they are going for and search the Internet out of curiosity or skim a full-page newspaper advertisement for discount fares. Another way to look at search behavior is to consider the ongoing searches that take place. An **ongoing search** is conducted to acquire information for possible later use. One person, for example, may enjoy paging through fashion magazines with an intention of future clothing purchases. Another individual may like going to open houses or looking at housing or building magazines for ideas. Camping equipment, cars, computers, boats, recreational vehicles, and trips may all be part of ongoing searches. Go to any bookstore, and you will see consumers paging through books and magazines mostly for recreational purposes.

Searching for information takes time and energy. The **information search rule** is that a consumer will search as long as the cost of the search is less than or equal to the expected savings from the search. Businesses help reduce search costs by locating near each other (i.e., auto dealerships). The cost of the information search should be mentally added to the total cost of the product. **Experience goods** refer to when the consumer gets relevant information after purchase such as food and entertainment. Until consumers eat the food or see the movie, how can they tell if it was a pleasurable experience or not? Often with these types of goods free samples or taste tests are given. In the case of movies, previews provide partial experiences. **Credence goods** are goods for which the consumer can never get relevant information such as drugs. Credence goods are often those where we find more government protection because consumers cannot evaluate the goods themselves.

Because so much consumer information exists and information overload is a distinct possibility, consumers make decisions about what types of information to access. They may use the following criteria:

- Attractiveness. Are they drawn to the information? For example, does the cover of a magazine attract? Does a movie preview look interesting?
- Appropriateness. Does the information fit their lifestyle? If they never travel, it is unlikely they will read travel books.
- Existence of various alternatives. Does one form of information fit better than another?
- Performance characteristics. What features are provided? This includes cost. Is the information free or readily available? If a magazine costs $4.95, is it worth buying for the information and entertainment value that it contains?
- Usefulness or caring. Do they care what the information is about? If an article is about foot care for diabetics, it is unlikely that a ten-year-old would be interested.

Information may be passively or actively acquired. **Passive information** is encountered when one is doing something else. For example, when most people have the radio on they are jogging, working at a desk, driving a car, reading a magazine, or doing housework. They do not sit and listen to the radio. Because of this radio ads have to break through the inattention. They have the advantage of sound effects and the human voice through the announcer or through songs that can be used to reach listeners. Another example of a source of passively acquired information is a **banner ad** that comes up at the top of a Web site. There is great debate in the marketing literature about how successful (or how irritating) banner ads are. Another example of a passive ad is a billboard by the side of the road. **Actively acquired information** is sought after for its own sake such as test driving a car or going to a fashion show. Another example of this would be if you were planning a Disneyland or DisneyWorld vacation you could go on the Disney.com Web site or call their phone number or go through a travel agent or travel Web site. You would be actively seeking information about the trip through a variety of sources, including books and travel magazines. Marketers are very interested in how an actively acquired, external search goes. They may want to find out through surveys ("how did you hear about us?"), how many stores or Web sites the person visited, the number of alternatives considered, the number of personal sources used, and the overall combination of measures and factors that influenced the final choice. Another way they can target their consumers is through asking for their zip code at the time of purchase. The zip code information will show them where to send circulars and catalogs.

The third step is *alternative evaluation*. Based on the information search, the person weighs the alternatives. Likes and dislikes, beliefs about the product or brand, and possibly going to several stores or Web sites, pricing, and availability help the consumer narrow the choices. In the case of Snapple, a consumer could eliminate all flavors with lemon in them if he or she doesn't like lemon, narrowing the field. Alternative search involves sorting behavior; picture someone looking at the products on the shelf or reading labels or warnings.

**Price**, the amount of money one pays to obtain the right to use a product, is very important in the alternative evaluation. An individual paying a price can own a product outright or may pay to rent or lease a product or service. One would assume that a lower price would sell more products, but price is also an indicator of quality. Would you feel comfortable paying $150 a month for a one-bedroom apartment? Or would you feel suspicious, thinking something must be wrong with an apartment that could be rented at such a low price? The same could be said for the pricing of sweaters or any other object or service. Retailers have witnessed the phenomena of a bin of the same sale-priced sweaters selling better at $39.99 than they did at $25.00. Setting a price requires a thorough knowledge of not only the product but also the potential market for that product.

Potential buyers will also consider the **consumer cost** which is the total cost involved in owning or using the product, also called the nonprice cost. For example, if one buys a car the consumer costs include the cost of gasoline, repairs, parking fees, depreciation, replacing tires, and so forth. A car that gets good mileage with regular gasoline will cost less to run than a car that uses a lot of premium gasoline. Sellers of products often will promote the cost savings.

Availability has an effect in the alternative evaluation. If the product is not readily available, a substitute product may be put in its place, or the purchaser may decide to wait until more selection is available. This relates to the marketing concept of **distribution** wherein products are available in places near target customers. A truckload of snow tires in Florida will just sit there, but in January they may be a "hot" item in Minnesota. This is an obvious example, but less obvious examples are differences in food preferences throughout the United States which successful grocers have to be aware of or they are stuck with slow moving merchandise.

Consumers will also evaluate **service**, activities that are performed to enhance and sustain the primary product or service. For example, consumers may inquire if they buy from a local distributor of appliances if the seller will also service the appliances when they break down. They may wonder, if they buy appliances over the Internet, who will install and service the appliances? Other service considerations may be free pickup and delivery. Will the company take away the old appliances at no cost and install the new appliances at no cost? With people's busy lives, convenience becomes more and more important.

Information is a key input into the alternative selection, but there are other factors or resources such as product characteristics. Resources include time, energy, money, and anything else that is useful to the decision and subsequent planning and action. Resources can be current or anticipated.

Since it would be impossible to taste every food in the grocery store, consumers narrow their selection by how much time they have to shop and by product characteristics such as sweet, sour, highly caloric or fatty, bitter, natural, or smooth. Does chunky peanut butter taste better than regular? What is your preference? Product characteristics include

Cost

Accessibility or availability

Features

Style

Perceived risk

All day long we make consumer decisions. We have to if we are to eat and drink and keep ourselves alive. We also consume to fulfill social functions since we as humans are social beings. For example, a mother may be baking a birthday cake from a mix at home that requires three eggs. When she opens the refrigerator she finds there are only two eggs—should she bake the cake using two eggs (taking a risk) or should she go to the store for more eggs? Or should she forget baking and go to the bakery? The final decision will rest on energy, time, money, availability of the store and bakery and a car to get there, features or style such as the type of cake desired, and so on. A connected decision is what about the candles? The candles are another resource as are the matches to light the candles. One consumer decision builds on another, forming a chain of decisions.

To return to the prebuying process, the fourth step is *selection*. The consumer takes the product off the shelf and carries it or puts it in his or her shopping basket, or if it is a large purchase tells the salesperson what they want delivered, or if on the computer, clicks the desired selection and puts it in his or her virtual shopping basket. What if consumers see something they like better on the way to the checkout? They may change their minds, put the object back, and proceed to the next step.

## Purchase

The fifth step is the *actual purchase*. The consumer buys the product. At purchase, consumers think they have made the best choice by weighing all the factors up to that point. The item or service is purchased in this step. Money is spent or a trade is made. Things usually go smoothly, and the consumer can relax unless the credit card isn't accepted or there isn't enough money to cover the purchase or "the computer is down."

## Postpurchase

After the purchase, buyers evaluate their purchase and seek reinforcement. Was the best decision really made? This sixth step is called *postpurchase behavior*. The consumer decides if it was a good or bad purchase by comparing the expected performance internally and externally. For example, internally a postpurchase consumer may decide that a food tastes good or bad. External reactions may include what others say or how they react to the new product. At a gas station pump, they may notice the other cars and talk to owners who own the same car that they do to see if they like the way their car is performing.

The tendency is to accentuate the benefits (in other words look for reinforcing information that the consumer made a good purchase) and downplay the deficits. This tendency is called **cognitive dissonance**. Consumers look for reinforcement. They will seek acknowledgment on the characteristics that are important to them. Being reassured brings pleasure to the decision-making process. A right decision removes doubt and uncertainty. It is generally more profitable for companies to retain customers than to replace them with new customers so it behooves them to be concerned with factors such as cognitive dissonance as part of overall **customer**

**satisfaction** which is a function of the prebuying, buying, and postbuying experience, including the satisfaction derived from the value of the product while it is in use.

Companies knowing all this seek to build loyalty in their customers. Ways to do this include frequent flyer programs, discounts on future purchases, gifts, discounts, and loyalty points such as those offered by Nordstrom. An example would be a woman being given a bottle of free shampoo at the salon she frequents or a 10 percent discount on her next beauty treatment. Another way to do this is to give the purchaser a consumer satisfaction survey at the time of purchase, such as at the end of a cruise or hotel stay or immediately upon their return home by a survey sent in the mail. Accompanying the survey may be a newsletter with discounts or other encouragements to shop again.

If things go wrong, the final evaluation of a product or service is an important step but many consumers choose to ignore it because they want to avoid pain or negative thoughts. They don't want to revisit bad clothing decisions so they will put ugly clothes at the back of their closet or get rid of them. The problem with an unworthy product may be its style or other characteristics, the brand, unrealistic expectations, or the place where purchased. In order to avoid wasting money again, the postpurchase step is a necessary part of the consumer process. The consumer may decide that the store or Web site should be avoided in the future and that alternative sources of products should be explored.

## MOTIVATIONS OF MARKETERS

In previous chapters we've introduced how businesses interact with consumers and government, but how do they operate internally? What are their motivations and concerns? Specifically in terms of marketing, what are their goals? We know that consumers want the best products at the best prices. Businesses want to participate in this process by bringing these sought-after goods to market and in so doing *maximize profits*. Marketing is key to this outcome.

Marketers want to:

*Effective consumer complaint handling is a way to keep customers and maintain good word-of-mouth.*

- *Maximize consumer awareness* of their goods and services. They want you to notice their promotions and advertisements.
- *Maximize consumption*. They want you to try their products and buy more the next time. From the business perspective, greater levels of consumption are seen as a way to better things for both the consumer and the seller. As covered in previous chapters, not everyone agrees with this perspective (i.e., the scornful indictment of consumerism expressed in *The Overspent American* by Juliet B. Schor), but this section of the chapter is about how firms view consumption and their place in it.
- *Maximize loyalty*. As mentioned in the last section, they want to see you again. An example, would be inviting you to join their loyalty club such as the Crown & Anchor Club for repeat Royal Caribbean International cruisers. You are a gold member after completion of one cruise and a platinum member after five cruises—the incentives go up with each category, and there are separate cruises just for repeat customers. Fund-raisers for universities, sorori-

ties, fraternities, and charities often use these levels to distinguish levels of givers and the names or titles provide prestige. The metals, gems, or whatever is used are geared to the levels so it is better to be gold than silver and platinum than gold. Often at the top are diamonds or categories of diamonds such as 5-diamonds.

- *Maximize consumer satisfaction*: Although they want repeat business, they want not only volume but they also want quality. They want customers to like what they buy; that their good satisfies a need in a style or way that is pleasurable or comfortable. This is less easily measured than the number of products sold, but it is important to the long-running success of a business. Handling consumer complaints promptly and efficiently falls under this category, as well as the previous one of maximizing loyalty.

## COMPANIES AND COMPETITION

In order to meet customer needs, companies have to efficiently manage their finances, production, research and development, delivery, human resources, facilities, technology, and image and reputation. Managing the image and reputation goes beyond producing effective advertising. Image and reputation include many avenues such as displays in stores or at conventions and news stories about managers and the health of the company, including present and future worth, growth, community leadership, treatment of employees, environmental friendliness, and so forth. If a scandal breaks out such as a tampered with consumer product, how does the company handle it? Do they act like nothing happened or do they quickly try to remedy the problem? Often positive news is sent out to counteract bad news. In a pharmaceutical company if one drug fails, they put out news about a promis-

---

**Case Study**

The following happened to the author of this book. I found a dead ladybug in a bag of prepackaged salad mix bought at the grocery store. The bug was found after half the salad mix had been eaten to which my family replied, "Oh, gross!" I called the manufacturer's toll free number and got the "Consumer Care" line. After explaining what happened and reporting that no one had gotten sick, I was offered a check for $15 or coupons worth about that much for future purchases. The Consumer Care person said that the salad mix is chlorinated in California and then shipped and so the bug was chlorinated as well and posed no health threat to anyone. However, they would report the bug to quality control and thanked me for providing the code on the label information so they could track the place of origin. She also said I could take the complaint further and possibly get more money, but she said that rarely works. She advised me to take the $15 which I did. The check arrived with an apology letter a few days after the call. The letter writer's title was "Consumer Response Specialist." In the second paragraph she wrote, "We are concerned when a product does not meet our high quality standards. Ready-to-use items, such as our pre-cut salads, are triple washed. The process should remove field debris or insect material. We informed our Quality Assurance staff of your report. The information will be helpful to prevent this in the future."

---

ing drug that is undergoing research and development. In a movie production company, a failed movie is pushed aside, and the promotion effort switches to the next upcoming film. Where to put time, human energy, and other resources is a continual problem for companies. It is what managers are paid to do.

Competition is a continual threat and stimulator. If companies are to succeed they need to keep up with, surpass, or anticipate competition. They respond to competition by:

- Reducing prices
- Increasing advertising or changing placement
- Introducing a new or improved product
- Buying out the competition through mergers
- Developing a new strategic plan
- Improving customer service, giving better value such as offering free gift wrap or delivery
- Improving product quality

Across the United States and in many other places in the world, a common phenomenon is when a large company such as Wal-Mart or Home Depot comes into a small community disrupting the existing mix. Since they deal in such large volumes, they often offer lower prices than smaller dealers can. In order to stay alive, the smaller stores have to make themselves distinctive by offering easier parking, more services, or unique products. In the long run, competition allows companies to grow to be more efficient and profitable and serve customers better. Government policy plays a part in this competition through changes in zoning and in treaties or trade agreements such as NAFTA (North American Free Trade Agreement) which greatly reduced trade barriers and increased the level of competition.

## Customers: Building Brand Loyalty

Companies use **product positioning** to give brands a specific and unique image or position in the minds of consumers within a target segment (Foxall, Goldsmith, and Brown, 1998). Their goal is to make their brand the most popular with the group they are trying to reach. It involves "creating the appropriate image of a product in the minds of consumers in the targeted markets" (Echtner and Ritchie, 1993). Generally, the greater match between a consumer's image of a product and the self-concept of the individual, the greater the likelihood the individual will have a favorable attitude toward the product and the more likely that he or she will purchase (Sirgy and Su, 2000). To do this a company such as Unilever makes many kinds of toothpastes such as Aim and Pepsodent that are positioned for different markets. As another example, tourist destinations can be marketed by product or image positioning (Sirgy and Su, 2000). Marketing managers determine the best product positioning through research, testing, and experience.

From a customer point of view, familiar brands make it easier to shop. A sure thing is easier than experimentation each and every time one shops. For example, if a family is on vacation looking for a place to stop for lunch, they know the menu, quality, and prices they can expect from a CrackerBarrel restaurant versus an unfamiliar local "home-cooking" restaurant. Another aspect of branding is that given economies of scale, widespread distribution of certain brands should save money for producers and sellers and the savings should be passed on to the consumers. A **brand** is a distinctive name identifying a product or a manufacturer usually talked about in terms of a popular brand of a product like Ivory or a popular company such as Coca-Cola or Gillette. Sometimes the product or object is so popular it becomes synonymous with a brand name such as Kleenex—someone may be more likely to say "hand me a Kleenex" rather than "hand me a tissue." Examples of famous brands besides those already named are Campbell's, Crayola, Hilton, Nabisco, Marriott, Chevrolet, Ford, Maytag, and Sears. As you can see from this list, brands can originate with manufacturers such as Nabisco or with dealers such as Sears. Sometimes manufacturers and dealers are one and the same or have a close relationship through a franchise. You can also see on this list competitive brands such as Hilton versus Marriott and Ford versus Chevrolet.

When the same brand name is given to several products, it is termed a **family brand**. Examples of family brands are Tom's Snack Foods and Frito-Lay. A family brand makes the most sense when the brands are of the same category such as a food or household cleaning product line. Unique packaging promotes and protects products. As mentioned in earlier chapters, the Federal Fair Packaging and Labeling Act of 1966 requires that consumer goods are clearly labeled in easily understood terms. There are ethical issues regarding packaging such as the picture on the label in the front of a can or package should be similar to the appearance of the product within and labels of competitive brands should be different enough so that consumers are not confused about what product they are buying. Another issue is that the size of the package should be similar to the amount of contents found inside. This is particularly a problem with potato chips and cereals that settle. Manufacturers remedy this by stating ounces and giving a warning on the label that contents may settle in transit.

**Generic products** usually have no brand at all and may be packaged in plain black and white paper such as generic (no name) bathroom tissue or table

Bright red Coca-Cola logo wrapped around a massive glass bottle, and large yellow M&M's bag, standing in front of the Showcase Mall on Las Vegas Boulevard. (Courtesy of Durling Kintersley Media Library. Photo by Alan Keohane.)

napkins. Because of the simplicity of these products and no markup for brand names or to cover advertising, they are usually less expensive than similar products on the same shelf. Generic products are common in chain grocery stores, discount grocery chains, and in less developed countries. This latter is because there is less exposure to advertising in less developed countries, branding may not be part of the consumer culture, and people are actively seeking low prices.

## How Products Are Developed

Products go through four stages in their development (see Box 6.2):

1. Introduction. In this stage, the product is developed and introduced to the market.
2. Growth. In this stage, easily recognized brands are aggressively marketed to keep sales growing such as product placement in movies or increased advertising. Gimmicks may be used such as coupons, games, add-ons, and giveaways. An example of an add-on is when a popular shampoo is bundled with a conditioner. A giveaway could be when a bank gives $500 to every 500th new customer.
3. Maturity. In this stage, the product is well known and accepted such as Crest toothpaste. It may be reenergized with new formulas or packaging.
4. Dormancy, decline, and possibly revitalization. A product in this stage may no longer be manufactured, for example, a book may be out of print and available only on the used market. But let's say a movie comes along that popularizes the book (an example would be *Forrest Gump*), then the book becomes in demand again and is reprinted. Likewise, cartoon characters, toys such as GI Joe, and jewelry can become popular again and remarketed.

To explain further, let's look at how new products in stage one are introduced:

- They could be totally new. An example of a totally new product would be chocolate-flavored french fries (although it could be said this is an off-shoot of chocolate-flavored or dipped potato chips or pretzels that already exist). It is difficult to have a totally new product.
- They could be a line extension such as Coke Vanilla (if it sells, will they try Coke Cinnamon?) or a new flavor of potato chip by an existing potato chip company.
- They could be a brand extension such as Mello Yellow Candy.

Since new product development is costly, it is critical that extensive consumer research take place before the product is introduced to the market. Research shows that certain individuals are more likely than others to quickly try something new—

---

**BOX 6.2     Four Stages of Product Development**

Introduction
Growth
Maturity
Dormancy and decline (possibly revitalization)

these people are called innovators. An **innovation** is something that is perceived as new or different. Those attracted to innovations are important from a company perspective because they are heavy users of new products often paying full price or a premium for newness. They may drive hours to see a car show or buy a new product. They may book an exotic trip to go somewhere none of their friends have gone. Usually people choose their categories to be innovative in such as computer equipment, software, cameras, music, clothes or restaurants. They give valuable feedback to companies through their buying habits and their reactions to specifics about product features. In the marketplace, they encourage future sales through good word of mouth. The consumer innovation curve was described in chapter 3.

Although so far the discussion has been about products, there can be innovators regarding:

- An idea
- A source
- A brand
- A practice, such as a new way of dusting furniture by using a pretreated cloth or making salad by opening a package of salad mix instead of washing a head of lettuce
- A strategy or plan, a set of actions

Following innovators there are early adoptors, then early majority, then late majority, and at the end the laggards. Laggards are the last people to adopt an innovation. They may want to wait until all the information is in before they make a decision. They may also be waiting for the price to fall before purchasing. Since people pick the category or categories they are innovators in, an individual can be a laggard in clothes but an innovator in electronics.

Innovativeness is linked to personality. A broad personality trait may be a likeness for trying something new versus having a more cautious outlook. Innovators are more likely to be risk takers than later adopters. Innovativeness is also linked to socioeconomic class since it takes discretionary income (extra money) to buy new products. Innovators are usually exposed to more media than laggards.

Everett M. Rogers, a leader in innovation theory, defined the innovation decision process as "the process through which an individual . . . passes (1) from first knowledge of an innovation; (2) to forming an attitude toward the innovation, (3) to a decision to adopt or reject, (4) to implementation of the new idea, and (5) to confirmation of this decision" (1995, p. 161). To put this into a list, think of the stages in the process as:

- Knowledge
- Persuasion
- Decision
- Implementation
- Confirmation (Foxall, Goldsmith, and Brown, 1998, p. 41)

To show how this works, take a fairly new magazine such as *Real Simple*. The first introduction may be through a friend, a newsstand, on an airplane, or a free offer for two issues. You would form an attitude of whether it is right for you or not, then decide to page through it or not. If you like it you may buy a copy or a subscription, if not put it back on the shelf, and, if purchased, after a while decide if it was a good decision or not.

## BRANDS, COUNTERFEITING, AND PIRATING

Brand names can be trademarked which means they can be protected by law. A **trademark** is a legal term that includes words, symbols, or marks that are legally registered for use by a company. An example of a trademark is Big Mac for McDonald's. No other competing fast-food restaurant uses the term Big Mac.

Counterfeiting refers to making a look-alike copy. Counterfeiters sell knockoffs, products that look like the real thing but aren't. Common examples are counterfeit copies of CDs, Gucci handbags, Levi's jeans, or Rolex watches. Most consumers know that if the item is being sold on the street or at an extremely low price then the item is probably a copy. If one buys the product with this understanding that is one thing, but if bought without this knowledge then a deception has taken place as well as a rip-off of the legitimate manufacturer, artist, singer, or designer.

Counterfeiting is especially common in countries that do not honor international trademark or copyright laws or who have a culture in which counterfeiting is not considered unethical. In recent history in China and South Korea, there were many counterfeit products and few protections for internationally known brands in such areas as clothing, music, and books including the popular Harry Potter books.

However, it is important to point out that low-income nations steal from other low-income nations so it is not a question of the products of richer nations being pirated by poorer ones. A case in point is the Ghana textile industry (the average annual income in Ghana is $400) that continually combats cheap knockoffs by China, Pakistan, Nigeria, India, and the Ivory Coast. These other countries make cheap copies of the most popular Ghana textiles, smuggle them back into Ghana, and snatch sales from potential customers of the original high quality fabrics (Phillips, 2002). "The fakes aren't hard to spot. They tend to be made of flimsier, less regular fabric, often synthetic such as rayon, instead of cotton. The colors don't always line up with the shapes" (Phillips, 2002, p. B1).

**Pirating** means stealing an original idea or product and selling it. Currently, "entertainment companies have a variety of techniques at their disposal to make it harder for people to share music, movies and software over the Internet" (Wingfield, 2002, p. D3). Examples of these techniques are:

- File-spoofing in which a song or movie is labeled as something else. The user experiences bursts of static or only part of a song's chorus.
- Redirection which happens when instructions are inserted into a bogus file; a possible outcome is the sending of the user to a commercial music site.
- Interdiction which overloads a computer, jamming the computer with traffic.

Obviously these techniques are controversial and could be considered extreme or anticonsumer. Pirating is not a new concept. Ever since the advent of tape recorders, music could be taped and copies shared and similarly with VCR equipment and cameras movies can be copied and so forth. Because only a few people were usually involved in these swapping activities, it was hard to prosecute or to work up much energy over the practice. But, the Internet has made it much easier and more pervasive through the file-swapping Web sites. Traditional industries are fighting back. "We think copyright owners ought to be able to do whatever they can that's lawful to protect their rights and their artists' careers," says Cary Sherman, president of the Recording Industry Association of America (Wingfield, 2002, p. D1).

# BRAND PERCEPTION AND IMAGE

**Brand perception** refers to how consumers rate or consider brands. How do they classify them? Do they think the brand is reliable or trustworthy or innovative or old-fashioned? "An **image** of a product, person, brand, or place is formed when people develop beliefs, ideas, perceptions, or impressions about a product person or place" (Deslandes, Goldsmith, and Bonn, 2002). An individual can have an image about a vacation destination, for example, without having ever been to the place. This image can come from the general media, educational sources, family, friends, travel agents, or brochures. It is widely assumed that an appropriate image can make or break a vacation destination; therefore, news of terrorism or civil unrest can wreak havoc with a country's tourist industry. On the other hand, visions of swaying palm trees, beautiful beaches, and cool drinks attracts tourists.

**Brand image** refers to the *set of perceptions* that consumers have formed about a brand such as this brand is for the young. MelloYello soft drink is marketed to young people as a good experience. The advertisements show shirtless teenage boys swinging on ropes off of cliffs and letting go and dropping into lakes and ponds. One would assume then that a brand extension such as Mello Yello candy would appeal to a similar group. Since consumers tend to resist change and keep buying the same brands or brand extensions, firms especially like to attract young people because once younger people like a brand they have a lifetime of buying ahead of them. It often takes a crisis such as nonproduction of a good or a true innovation to shake someone away from their established brand preferences.

Early brand perception is part of the socialization process in families. Usually one of the earliest consumer experiences outside the home is the child accompanying parents to the grocery store. Think of all the infants that you have seen in their carriers in grocery carts. This, among other reasons, is why it is important to turn our attention next to families and households and population trends.

# POPULATION TRENDS

The population is, of course, growing, but it is growing more in certain states and areas than others. Thus, population trends are of importance to those who study consumer economics because one has to know where the humans are now and where they are likely to be in the future. By 2050 the U.S. population could be more than 500 million—almost double the current population. Rather than being shocked by this number, it is important to remember that this country has been growing steadily since colonial times and that solutions are found to accommodate everyone. There are vast spaces in this country that are wilderness areas and other areas that are actually losing or barely maintaining population.

Here are population trends:

- The greatest growth is expected in the West—in states such as Nevada, Idaho, Alaska, Utah, New Mexico, Arizona, Colorado, and Wyoming.
- Rapid growth is also expected in Georgia, Florida, Tennessee, Texas, North Carolina, Washington, and Oregon.

- Slower growing states include those in the MidWest and New York, Pennsylvania, and Connecticut.
- Much of future growth will come from immigration.
- American families are having fewer children, that means more money can be spent per child and there will be more demand for smaller homes, out-of-home food and entertainment, travel, and smaller food packages in grocery stores. In the future, two-for-one may be a less popular sales ploy than another type of approach.
- The average age is rising, the average age now is about 36.
- There are more empty nesters (those between 50–64 whose children have grown up) and elders, senior citizens (those over age 65) affecting health care, cars, food services, finances, housing, and tourism.
- There are more teens. In 2010 there will be 30 million U.S. teens affecting clothing sales, recreation, cars, and music.
- Since World War II the most popular move has been to the suburbs affecting transportation, jobs, stores, and homes, making cars necessities. There is a countermove back into cities where people are renovating homes and getting rid of long commutes.
- Mobile markets are higher consumers than stay-put people, each move necessitates consumption of products and services.
- More people have middle-and upper-class incomes.
- Increased diversity. One in ten U.S. homes is non-English speaking (or a combined English and non-English), and the rates of this are much higher in certain areas than others, affecting education and all sorts of consumer preferences from food to entertainment.

## Changing Families and Households

The household is the most basic consumer unit. Households drive the consumer market in their selection of housing, food, transportation, entertainment, financial services, and clothing. The U.S. Census Bureau defines a **household** as comprised of all persons who occupy a "housing unit," that is, a house, an apartment or other group of rooms, or a single room that constitutes "separate living quarters." A household can contain related family members and unrelated persons such as foster children, lodgers, wards, or employees who share the same housing unit. A household may be made up of one person or many. The trend is for household size to be smaller.

A **family** by U.S. Census Bureau definition consists of two or more persons related by birth, marriage, or adoption and residing together in a household. It should be noted that some groups and family specialists do not like this definition of family because it does not include gay couples or other groups such as young heterosexual couples or nonmarried elderly couples who live together. The American Red Cross has a much broader definition of family which they used when they determined who was eligible for aid after the September 11 tragedy. As another example of a broader definition, an advertisement intoned that family is whoever's around the dinner table, and for many this is a better definition than the Census Bureau's. Numbers show that **nonfamily households** made up of householders who either live alone or with others to whom they are not related is, a growing group, accounting for almost 30 percent of all households in 2000. Another phenomenon

> A household may be made up of one or more persons, a family is made up of two or more persons. Since 1980 the percentage of households that are families has declined.

is extended families that may include a core family and aunts or uncles or grandparents or in-laws or other family members. Extended families living together are more common in China, South Korea, and India than they are in the United States.

Since 1980, the percentage of households that are families has declined and the percentage of people living alone has risen. There are more households than ever before, but household composition is changing. Less than half of all households have two parents and children under the age of 18 living at home. Americans are marrying later. Some cities such as Boston, New York, San Francisco, and Washington, DC, have large populations of singles.

What does all this mean for consumerism? For one thing, advertising has to reflect changes in households and families. If the marketer is trying to attract extended families, then a grandmother should be in the television advertisement and have lines to say as well as the two parents and children. A Holiday Inn advertisement about a family traveling to Las Vegas had just such an assortment. Appealing to families can be tricky because members of the same family have differing tastes and desires. For a family vacation destination or cruise line, the advertisement should show fun activities for children and adults. For example, the Disney and Carnival cruise lines advertisements show a variety of activities for the whole family.

Size and structure of the household affect products and advertising. In terms of housing the questions that arise include how many bedrooms and bathrooms should the featured home have? How large should the garage or the master bedroom suite be? Are supersize stainless steel refrigerators desired or smaller ones with more compartments and features?

The household can be segmented into four stages. Each stage in the household life cycle poses problems and opportunities.

Stage 1: This group consists of young under age 35 unmarried or married individuals. This can be further subdivided into those under age 25 and those between 25–35. In the younger group the person or persons may have recently graduated from high school or college, they are beginning work and setting up households. Movement is common in this age group. From 25–35 more stability sets in regarding employment, friends, and family. Marriage and divorce may occur in this stage, children may be born or adopted. In the United States, the average age for first marriage is 24.4 for women and 26.5 for men. Higher educated individuals tend to marry later than national averages. Whether married or not, young groups spend more money than other groups proportionally on movie tickets, take-out food, alcoholic beverages, and clothes.

Stage 2: Married or Single Parents with Young Children. Whether adopted or by birth or remarriage, adding children brings with it changes in lifestyle and consumption. Housing needs increase; baby clothes, furniture, and equipment are bought; televisions are tuned to kid shows; restaurant and food choices change. Cereal consumption goes up. Remember the slogan "Kix are for kids"? Hamburgers, pizza, macaroni and cheese, and spaghetti take the place of quiet romantic dinners. Noisy restaurants or restaurants with play spaces or overhead televisions are preferred. This is one of the most expensive stages in terms of what needs to be bought. If one parent does not work, reduced income is another outcome, and if they both work, child

care costs go up. This can be a time of high debt and other financial problems so you will see advertisements on television about consolidating debt
services directed at this age group that spills over into Stage 3. Since people
are having children later in life than earlier generations, it is difficult to separate Stages 2 and 3 and thus no age range is given for Stage 2.

Stage 3: Middle Aged Single or Married, with Children or Without. These individuals are between 36–64 and comprise the middle years of life although
some prefer to start the clock of middle age ticking at age 45 or 50. Putting
a number on an age or stage is not an exact science because age is not only
chronological but also a frame of mind or attitude. Since the midyears represent such a wide time span and remarriages or blended families are common from 35–64, there may be young children or children in the middle,
teen, or college years, or the family may be experiencing the empty nest
syndrome. Households with teens and children in their early twenties experience high costs associated with car insurance and college tuition.

Middle-aged singles without children generally live alone. They have
higher incomes and less expenditures than those with families yet they still
need dishwashers, appliances, and so forth. Single-person households tend
to have the same equipment as multifamily households. Singles' preferences
may include condominiums or homes with small yards, expensive restaurants and wine, luxury automobiles, jewelry, and travel. They tend to be
heavy gifters and purchasers of greeting cards. They also contribute to
groups and organizations.

Middle agers may also be part of the **sandwich generation**, meaning
they are supporting or taking care of children as well as aging parents. The
time and energy strain may be enormous. Vacations, maid services, or other
types of services may be targeted to them.

Middle-aged marrieds with no children travel extensively, prefer dining
out and buying time-saving services such as housecleaning, laundry, and
shopping, and luxury items such as expensive haircuts or spa treatments,
sports bikes, or fitness clubs. They may take up tennis or golf. They may be
interested in long-term care insurance because there are no children to take
care of them in their old age.

Stage 4: Older Marrieds and Singles. In the 65 and older group, most are now on
their own with the exception of grandparents that are taking care of grandchildren full time and those elders who are living with adult children. Most
are not working full time (although one in five men and one in ten women
work full time after the age of 65) and so they have extra time for travel and
recreation. They may be interested in part-time, volunteer, or seasonal work.
As long as their health holds out, they may favor retirement communities or
new multiage developments with walking paths or other recreational facilities, vacations, and recreational vehicles. Many elders are active Internet
users. The consumption patterns of young retirees (those 65–75) are quite
distinct from older retirees. Often the younger ones are heavier travelers
and users of recreation than the older ones. They tend to follow the news
more than younger groups. Since people are living longer and healthier
than ever before, the age range of active retirement keeps getting pushed
upward so what may be considered a young retiree could expand upward

into the eighties. In the later years, estate planning, rearranging insurance, health care, and assisted living and retirement homes become important.

## Groups and Market Segmentation

In the last section the discussion was mainly about households and families, but people belong to other groups as well. One of these is **reference groups** which are collections of people that influence your decisions and behavior. The family stands out as the most important reference group because of its longevity, emotional attachments, shared genetics, and intensity. Other than family members, reference group members can include teachers, neighbors, religious groups, political parties, racial or ethnic organizations, clubs, colleagues, and students. If there is frequent contact, then the reference group is considered *primary*. If contact is infrequent or from the past, it is considered *secondary*. In consumerism, reference groups exchange information, offer advice and guidance, provide identity, and serve as a measuring stick or as a means of comparing. Belonging to certain groups may require uniforms or other forms of appearance. For example, college students usually dress casually so if a student shows up for class in a suit the other students will assume that student is giving a presentation or going to a job interview.

Thus, groups engage in usual ways of behaving, and they may share other characteristics such as age, gender, education, social class, lifestyle, occupation, income, religion, and race and ethnicity. In terms of social class, it is estimated that about 14 percent of Americans are upper class, 70 percent are middle, and 16 percent are lower (Hawkins, Best, and Coney, 2001). The most widely used determinant of this is the **socioeconomic index (SEI).** This index is based on education level and occupation. For example, in the SEI bartenders and stevedores are rated lower than engineers and dentists (Stevens and Cho, 1985). Studies have shown that income does not cause direct consumption nearly to the extent that education and occupation do (Hawkins, Best, and Coney, 2001). Americans are becoming more educated and taking more white-collar positions.

The average American visits malls 3.2 times per month and spends 75 minutes each time.

Working women are the most important sales generators in malls, generating 42 percent of mall sales (Fetto, 2002). On average Americans visit the mall 3.2 times per month and spend an estimated 75 minutes each time (Fetto, 2002).

Companies as well as families have a social and cultural context. According to Charles Holliday, CEO of DuPont, "It's part of our culture to think about doing the right things and we're not going off on any short-term whims." He says he feels responsible to four distinct stakeholders: employees, investors, customers, and the public. He adds, "We're not changing our core values, including concern about the safety of our products and our people" (Hymowitz, 2002).

Businesses and the media study what groups exist and who belongs to which group. "A **market segment** is a portion of a larger market whose needs differ somewhat from the larger market. Since a market segment has unique needs, a firm that develops a total product focused solely on the needs of that segment will be able to meet the segment's desires better than a firm whose product or service attempts to meet the needs of multiple segments" (Hawkins, Best, and Coney, 2001). The segment has to be sizable enough to generate enough sales whether it be radio space time or toothpaste.

A couple shopping in a mall.
(Courtesy of Corbis Digital Stock.)

To determine a market segment, consumers are first grouped by similar need sets. For example, young families may be interested in backyard swing sets. In order to establish this need, a company may conduct focus groups, interviews, or surveys. Questions may be asked about what features are preferred such as how many swings, whether a slide is desired, building materials, and colors. Once this need set is delineated, then the attention turns to the most likely consumers. What is their lifestyle? Where do they live? What media do they use?

Everyone belongs to a dominant culture and subcultures. People identify with their core cultures and their subcultures each of which have values, norms, and customs. Holiday celebrations and foods are often connected up with cultures and subcultures. Ethnic subcultures include members with shared behaviors and beliefs based on a common language, background, or race.

In a directive from the federal Office of Management and Budget, all federal agencies are to report statistics according to the following recommended race and ethnicity categories: American Indian or Alaska Native, Asian, Black or African American, Native Hawaiian or Other Pacific Islander, White, and Hispanic or Latino. The different groups have different consumption patterns and store preferences. According to Simmons Market Research, whites shop at home improvement stores more than African Americans, Asians, or Hispanics (Frequent Shoppers, 2003). But for the most part profession or income may be more of an indicator of consumption than race or other criteria. For example, "African American, Hispanic and Asian American cable households are significantly more likely than their non-cable counterparts to be luxury car owners, homeowners, and college graduates with annual incomes exceeding $75,000, according to MRI research. . . . Consumers in these groups are also more likely to have professional/managerial jobs" (Karrfait, 2003, p. S4).

In the 2000 census, about 10 million Americans refused to pick a race or ethnicity category. Some people object to being classified in categories, others find making a selection difficult especially if they are of mixed heritage. *The three largest ethnic/racial categories are the Hispanic or Latino population, the African American population, and the Asian American population.*

**Hispanics/Latinos.**    Hispanic is used to describe an ethnic group with Spanish-speaking heritage. Hispanics constitute 13 percent of the U.S. population or nearly 35 million people, outnumbering African Americans (at 12 percent) for the title of the "largest minority group" in the nation. In the 2000 census, respondents were asked if they were Spanish/Hispanic/Latino. After responding yes, they could select a nationality group of Mexican/Mexican American/Chicano, Puerto Rican, Cuban, or Other. Hispanics are the largest ethnic group in areas of Texas, Florida, Arizona, and New Mexico and one of the fastest growing groups nationwide due to a high birthrate and immigration, making them an attractive consumer segment. Their households are larger, 3.5 people, than those of the general population at 2.7 people. By the year 2050 the U.S. Census predicts Hispanics will make up 23 percent of the nation's population.

Hispanic advertising is anemic compared with advertising to other groups, but given the results of the 2000 census advertising firms are rushing to catch up. According to Hispanic Business, the total ad budget for Hispanics is currently about $2.2 billion a year compared with $234 billion for the market mainstream (Raymond, 2002). The number of radio stations for Hispanics is much lower than the number for African Americans. One of the most well-known brands directed at the Hispanic market is the food powerhouse Goya. Its products include Mexican chilies, Caribbean fruit juices, and Spanish olive oil. It is the fourth largest Hispanic-owned company in the United States (Bianchi and Sama, 2002). Competitors include Unilevers's Iberia Foods and La Cena Fine Foods Ltd. and smaller companies. According to Marino Roa, vice president of sales at Le Fe Foods Inc., "Latinos are very loyal to their brands" (Bianchi and Sama, 2002). Latinos visit grocery stores an average of 4.7 times a week compared with 2.2 times for the average American. They also outspend other Americans $117 to $87 per week (Bianchi and Sama, 2002).

Since Hispanics are a growing market and high food spenders, grocery stores such as Albertson's Inc. are considering all-Hispanic stores. Kmart and Wal-Mart are considering similar initiatives. Meanwhile, retailers are expanding the number of products that they offer in their current stores that are attractive to Hispanics. This group is often called a sleeping giant because although retailers have been slow in the past to market to this group, this procedure is rapidly changing. Celebrities in this group used for advertising include Daisy Fuentes, Raquel Welch, and Rita Moreno.

Hispanics eat out less than most Americans. They average only 1.2 times per week. At home meal consumption is prepared mainly from scratch (Food Marketing Institute). Convenience foods are less important than foods made with care. In urban markets, there are television channels and magazines devoted to Hispanics. Their incomes and education levels are rising dramatically. The Hispanic market is not homogeneous, meaning that being Hispanic may be less important to the person than country of origin so care must be taken in how they are approached in terms of products such as foods and music and media messages. Hispanics also spend more on phone services, furniture, and apparel, and spend a higher proportion of their income on housing and transportation than the general population (Karrfait, 2003).

M. Isabel Valdes in her book *Marketing to American Latinos: A Guide to the In-Culture Approach, Part 2* emphasizes the "in-culture" approach which is a philosophy that encourages marketers to thoroughly understand consumers' culture and origin before attempting to court them. She says there are vast differences in spending power and consumer viability between Hispanics based on age, geographic distribution, and country of origin.

**African Americans.** When it comes to grocery shopping, African Americans spend slightly more per week than the total U.S. market but less than Hispanics. They constitute about 12 percent of the U.S. population with a concentration in the South and in urban areas. The U.S. Census estimates they will make up 14 percent of the population in 2050. Currently, they are somewhat younger than the general U.S. population. Their household incomes range run the gamut from low to high, but overall their incomes place them in the middle between Caucasians and Hispanics. Many of their consumer preferences are linked more to SEI than to race. Generally they spend less on housing and more on clothing, personal care items and services, and shopping trips to upscale malls and retailers (Fisher, 1996). On average, the African American woman spends three times as much as a Caucasian woman on hair-care products (Soloman and Rabolt, 2004). Companies such as Clairol, L'Oreal, and Alberto-Culver have extensive ethnic lines. Celebrity spokespersons include a wide range of singers, entertainers, sports figures, business leaders, models, athletes, educators, politicians, and political activists.

Magazines such as *Essence, Jet, Black Enterprise*, and *Ebony* are directed at the African American market. For example, *Jet* claims to reach 90 percent of the black mail market (Soloman and Rabolt, 2004). Advertisements in these magazines include product categories such as skin and hair care, cosmetics, and foods and beverages. Another marketing approach is to offer promotions or sponsor events targeted to African Americans such as sporting events or concert tours. African Americans tend to view shopping as more recreational than other groups and appreciate a pleasant and fun shopping environment. They have more buying power than any other ethnic group. They watch 40 percent more TV than the general market and what they watch differs from general audiences (Karrfait, 2003). "Because many more African American men love sports than any other group, they have purchased more large screen TV sets, with price tags of $500 or more," according to Willis Smith, principle researcher of the Urban Market Report (Karrfait, 2003, p. S4).

**Asian Americans.** As with all groups, sensitivity is needed when appealing to them. A mistake was made when an American company used a Chinese model in an advertisement for a Korean product. This brings up the notion that even though this section is discussing different racial and ethnic groups, within these groups there are vast differences. There is not a single Asian American market just as there is not one for Hispanics. Asian American children and adults are often seen in ads with groups of people especially for fashion, foods, or bars.

Asian Americans are more highly educated and have higher household incomes than the general population. *At 4 percent of the population they are smaller in number than Hispanics or African Americans, but they are slated to grow to 10 percent by the year 2050.* Their largest numbers are Chinese and Filipinos followed by Koreans, Vietnamese, and others. They are mostly concentrated in urban areas and in New York, California, and Hawaii. One of the challenges to reaching this group is the diversity of languages. The breakdown is Chinese (25 percent), Filipino (18 percent), Indian (17 percent), Vietnamese (11 percent), Korean (11 percent), and Japanese (8 percent). Seventy percent of the 12 million Asian Americans in the United States are foreign born compared with 44 percent Latino (Karrfait, 2003).

The largest percentage of Asian Americans are Chinese.

Grocery stores devote sections to foods used exclusively by Asian Americans and to those of the general population who like Oriental cuisine. Some Asian Americans (estimated at about 49 percent) strongly identify with their original culture and about half of these know their native language (Hawkins, Coney, and Best, 2001). Younger groups and those brought up in the United States have less traditional associations. Asian Americans are stronger savers than the general population. They are quality oriented in the goods that they seek. They are heavy users of computers and the Internet. Name brands and status appeal to a sizable number of Asian Americans. This would include BMW, Mercedes Benz, and other premium car brands, as well as designer handbags and clothes. They are generally affluent and the best educated of the major ethnic groups. Asian Americans and Hispanics spend more than other groups or the general population during visits to the mall (Fetto, 2002). Although their current numbers are small, this is a fast growing segment of the U.S. population. According to Simmons Market Research, they are more likely to shop in home electronics stores and home furnishings stores than whites, African Americans, or Hispanics (Frequent Shoppers, 2003).

"Young Asian Americans are also displaying a new ethnic pride in their heritage, helped by role models like the 7'6" Yao Ming of the Houston Rockets, who beat out Shaquille O'Neal in fan votes to start in this year's NBA All Star game (Ming appears in commercials for Visa and Apple Computers, and just signed a five-year deal to represent Gatorade). It's never been so hip to be Asian, as kids across all demographics are learning" (Karrfait, 2003, p.S5).

**Gays and Lesbians.**  Because many people are offended by or uncomfortable with images of gay lifestyles if they are portrayed in general audience publications, many companies such as American Express, Sony, and Subaru of America make specific advertisements designed for the gay media. Although someone may assume that these ads would be for sex-related products, actually many of them are for such prosaic products and services as financial planning. One reason this is a special concern for gays and lesbians is that employers may not provide benefits or coverage for partners to the extent that they do for heterosexual married couples. The ads may show same sex couples embracing, holding hands, or looking off into the future.

Research shows that homosexuals tend to be more highly educated than the general public; are dedicated to their careers; have more discretionary income; enjoy change, humor, and trends; and are more informed politically and socially. "A Simmons study of readers of gay publications found that compared to heterosexuals, these consumers are almost twelve times more likely to hold professional jobs, twice as likely to own a vacation home, and eight times more likely to own a computer notebook" (Solomon and Rabolt, 2004, p. 157). They are heavy users of the Internet. In terms of media, they:

> Prefer to read newspapers targeted at them and more upscale sections of the newspaper; the same is true for magazines. Prefer more intellectual and upscale TV and radio programs. Use catalogs, 800 numbers, and online forms of direct marketing" (Wells, Burnett, and Moriarty, 2000, p. 99).

High-profile figures in advertising include Martina Navratilova, k.d.lang, Melissa Etheridge, and Ellen DeGeneres. The television show *Will and Grace* has made homosexual lifestyles more acceptable to portions of the general public. Fashion advertisements even for general audience publications often show homosexual relationships so watch for changes in how this group is depicted and where. The exact proportion of the population that is gay or lesbian is difficult to say; the numbers vary based on source and by location. Gays and lesbians are more likely to be urban dwellers than rural dwellers.

## SUMMARY

This chapter explored the meaning of consumption. For example, it was shown that individuals have relationships with products that go beyond their mere functions. How functional are a dozen red roses? Consumer behavior refers to the buying behavior of individuals, families, and households who buy goods and services for personal consumption. Consumers go through six steps in the buying process—assessing needs, searching for information, alternative evaluation, selection, actual purchase, and postpurchase behavior. In this last step, companies or organizations want to build loyalty, relationships, and good word of mouth.

Companies compete with each other for consumer dollars. They use product positioning to give brands specific and unique images. Products go through four stages of development—introduction, growth, maturity, and dormancy/decline.

Some consumers are more innovative than others. Innovativeness is linked to personality.

Brand names can be trademarked. Counterfeit means look-alike copies. Pirating refers to stealing an original idea or product and selling it.

The household is the most basic consumer unit. The household life cycle can be broken down into four stages beginning with young adults and ending with older marrieds and singles.

## KEY POINTS

1. Consumers go through six steps in the buying process.
2. Businesses want to maximize profits by offering sought after goods.
3. A brand, such as Nike or Reebok, is a distinctive name identifying a product or manufacturer.
4. About 14 percent of Americans are upper class, 70 percent are middle, and 16 percent are lower. The most widely used determinant is the socioeconomic index (SEI).

5. Studies show that income does not cause or direct consumption nearly as much as education and occupation.
6. Media and business study market segments, groupings of people.
7. The three largest ethnic/racial groups in the United States are Hispanics/Latinos, African Americans, and Asian Americans. Each has individual characteristics and consumption needs that differentiate them from the general population. More and more marketers are aware of their consumption needs and market to them. New networks are springing up to serve a growing demand for multicultural fare.

## KEY TERMS

| | | |
|---|---|---|
| actively acquired information | family | nonfamily households |
| banner ad | family brand | ongoing search |
| brand | generic products | passive information |
| brand image | household | pirating |
| brand perception | image | price |
| cognitive dissonance | information search rule | product positioning |
| consumer behavior | innovation | reference groups |
| consumer cost | internal search | sandwich generation |
| credence goods | marketing | service |
| customer satisfaction | communications | socioeconomic index |
| distribution | marketing mix | (SEI) |
| experience goods | market segment | target market |
| external search | marketing strategy | trademark |
| | need set | |

## DISCUSSION QUESTIONS

1. What are the steps in the prebuying process? Why is so much time taken before purchase?
2. What are the stages in product development? Give an example other than those in the chapter for each stage.
3. Go to the Procter & Gamble web site (www.pg.com) and click on P & G Products. Find out the brand names of different laundry detergents or shampoos. Why would the same company offer different products that essentially perform the same function?

## E-RESOURCES

Thousands of company Web sites could be mentioned here, but for brevity's sake, here are two market leaders in consumer goods:

| | |
|---|---|
| Procter & Gamble www.pg.com | Leading maker of soaps, shampoos, detergents, diapers, and other household and personal care products |

| Wal-Mart Stores, Inc.<br>www.wal-mart.com<br>email: letters@wal-mart.com | Leading grocer in the United States, spreading internationally |

Government agencies mentioned in the chapter include:

| Federal Trade Commission<br>www.ftc.gov | Promotes fair trade, protects the public |
| Food and Drug Administration<br>www.fda.gov | Gives labeling and packaging requirements |

Data sources:

| CAB Multicultural Marketing Resource Center<br>www.cabletvadbureau.com/mmrc | Information and resources about ethnicity and consumption |
| International Data Corporation<br>www.idc.com | Provides market data |
| Simmons Market Research<br>www.simmonsmarketresearch.com | Multimedia research company with information on adults, teens, children, and Hispanics |

## REFERENCES

Bianchi, A., and F. Sama. (July 9, 2002). Goya foods leads an ethnic sales trend. *Wall Street Journal*, p. B4.

Deslandes, D., R. Goldsmith, R., and M. Bonn. (2002). *Measuring destination image: Do the existing scales work?* A working paper, Florida State University, Tallahassee, FL.

Echtner, C. M., J. R. B. and Ritchie. (1993). The measurement of destination image: An empirical assessment. *Journal of Travel Research* 31, no. 4, pp. 3–13.

Fetto, J. (March 2002). Mall Rats. *American Demographics*, p. 10.

Fisher, C. (September 1996). Black, hip, and primed to shop. *American Demographics*, pp. 52–59.

Fournier, S. (March 1998). Consumers and their brands: Developing relationship theory in consumer research. *Journal of Consumer Research, 24*, pp. 343–73.

Foxall, G. R., R. E. Goldsmith, and S. Brown. (1998). *Consumer psychology for marketing*, 2d ed.

Frequent shoppers (May 2003). *American Demographics*, p. 8.

Hawkins, D., R. Best, and K. Coney. (2001). *Consumer behavior: Building a marketing strategy*, 8th ed. Boston, MA: Irwin McGraw-Hill.

Hymowitz, C. (July 9, 2002). CEOs must work hard to maintain faith in the corner office. *Wall Street Journal*, p. B1.

Karrfait, W. (May 2003). A multicultural mecca. *American Demographics*, pp. S4–S6.

Phillips, M. (July 12, 2002). Pilfered patterns. *Wall Street Journal*, p. B1.

Raymond, J. (March 2002). ¿Tienen numeros? *American Demographics*, pp. 22–25.

Rogers, E. M. (1995). *Diffusion of innovations*, 4th ed. New York: Free Press.

Schor, Juliet B. (1998). *The overspent American*. New York: Harper.

Sirgy, J., and C. Su. (2000). Destination image, self-congruity, and travel behavior: Towards an integrative model. *Journal of Travel Research*, 38, pp. 340–52.

Solomon, M., and N. Rabolt. (2004). *Consumer behavior in fashion.* Upper Saddle River, NJ: Prentice Hall.

Stevens, G., and J. Cho. (1985). Socioeconomic indices. *Social Science Research* 14, pp. 142–68.

Valdes, M. I. (2002). *Marketing to American Latinos: A guide to the in-culture approach, Part 2.* New York: Paramount Market Publishing.

Wells, W., J. Burnett, J. and S. Moriarty (2000). *Advertising Principles & Practice*, 5th ed. Saddle River, NJ: Prentice Hall.

Wingfield, N. (July 11, 2002). Behind the fake music. *Wall Street Journal*, p. D1.

**CHAPTER**

**7**

# Decision Making and the Influence of Advertising

*In very few instances do people really
know what they want, even when they say they do.*
*Advertising Age*

**Learning Objectives**

1. Understand the role of decision making in consumer buying decisions.
2. Understand the role of advertising in relation to buying decisions.
3. Know the pros and cons of advertising in relation to consumers.
4. Explain the government agencies that affect advertising.
5. Know the steps the FTC can follow to stop deceptive advertising.
6. Understand the value of public service announcements.

## INTRODUCTION

This chapter builds on the last one on buying process, brands, and product development. It delves further into how consumers make decisions and how advertising influences those decisions. We discuss why people buy what they do and how they react to advertising. We also explore how advertising works and in particular why those irritating jingles stay in our minds. The secret is called "locking power." The chapter also discusses the influence of cultural or societal groups and lifestyles in relation to consumerism.

## DECISION MAKING AND TIME

In the last chapter, we discussed the steps that consumers go through in the buying process, including prepurchase, purchase, and postpurchase behavior. Another way to say this is that consumers are involved in preselection, selection, and post-selection. Consumers try to make good decisions, but this is becoming more difficult because (1) time is limited, (2) the number and complexity of products has increased, and (3) consumers have become farther and farther removed from the origin or basis of products. For example, rather than buying fruits and vegetables from a neighbor or nearby farmer, fruits and vegetables are bought in an impersonal grocery store, and the origins of the produce may be from anywhere in the world. Even local farmer's market today sell produce from nearly anywhere mixed in with local produce. The labels on the boxes near their stand reveal the distances that the produce may have traveled.

Regarding time as a scarce resource, we all have to make decisions about the best way to manage time. In consumption there are countless examples of time and consumption trade-offs, such as cooking a meal from scratch that would take several hours versus popping a preprepared frozen dinner in the microwave that will take minutes to heat. Another time saver is using the telephone or the Internet to search for products. A recent search for a certain brand of popcorn popper revealed that none of the local stores had one and the only way to get the popper was by ordering online direct from the company. The good part is that ordering online saved time and could be done at 11 o'clock at night when stores were closed; it also saved gasoline. The negative was the shipping charge versus buying in-person.

**Parkinson's law** states that a job expands to fill the time available to accomplish the task, such as finding and purchasing a product. A person who has all day to shop will view the shopping task differently than a person who has to buy something quickly on their lunch hour. Thus, Parkinson's law shows the elasticity of time and consumption behavior. It was named after an English historian, C. Northcote Parkinson, who studied the Royal Navy in 1977 and found that the more people hired, the more work was created without increasing output. So, in consumption the analogy would be that the more time spent in shopping does not necessarily mean there will be increased return for that effort. There is a point at which comparison shopping (and the time and energy that it involves) is wasteful, going to several stores a day could become a full-time occupation.

Another law or principle relevant to consumption is the **Pareto principle**, also known as the 80–20 rule, which states that 20 percent of the time expended produces 80 percent of the results and 80 percent of the time expended results in only 20 percent of the outcomes. Essentially this means that people waste a lot of time on nonproductive activities so again the message would be to use time wisely, to seek information and shop efficiently. This principle was named after Vilfredo Pareto, a nineteenth-century Italian economist and sociologist, who found that in any series of elements to be controlled, a select, small fraction of the elements accounted for a large fraction of effectiveness.

## TECHNOLOGICAL OBSOLESCENCE

As discussed in chapter three, technological obsolescence means that a product loses value even though it is not worn out yet because it can be replaced with a more technologically advanced product. Good examples are appliances, televisions, printers, cell phones, video cameras, calculators, and computers. The more rapid the advances, the more quickly the product will **depreciate**. Not only do you not want the product anymore, but also it is not worth very much to anyone else. New cars depreciate around $2,000 right after they are driven off the lot by the owner. Over time, the rate of depreciation slows or else the car could be worthless in a month. So, what should you do? First, accept technological obsolescence and depreciation as facts of life. Second, think before you purchase; ask yourself if it would be better to wait. Third, realize that sometimes you cannot wait, such as for a drug for a life-threatening disease or a business suit for an interview.

Computer companies are particularly aware of how rapidly computers are changing and have been very forthcoming with information about new releases to prospective buyers. For example, a college student ordered an Apple laptop and was called by the company to tell him that if he waited two weeks he could have a newer model at a similar price. Now, that is customer service, as a long-time Apple user they wanted to keep him happy. They gave him the choice of going with the model he ordered or getting the newer model with more bells and whistles—what would you do?

## RULES OF THUMBS AND STYLE PREFERENCE

One way consumers reduce the amount of options is to use **rules of thumb**. These are principles that guide purchases such as only buying certain brands or only shopping in certain stores or buying only certain styles. Regarding style, consumers have

1. A buying style (rational, slow, comparative versus impulsive, preferences such as bargains versus new merchandise at full price, small stores or large stores).
2. A preference for certain styles and colors. A person may like or dislike red, stripes, polka-dots, or plaids.
3. A desire for conformity or a desire for uniqueness. People vary in whether they want to stand out from the crowd or whether they want to fit in. The appeal of owning something one-of-a-kind is often the driving force behind auction bidding. Scarcity or uniqueness explains why someone would pay $145,000 at an auction for John Travolta's leisure suit from the movie *Saturday Night Fever*. When the auctioneer was asked later if the price seemed excessive, he remarked graciously, "Well, it certainly was a record for polyester" (Cialdini, 2001, p. 227).

Having a preference either in buying style or in styles of products or the desire to fit in or stand out eliminates a lot of wasted time and anxiety. A person who hates crowds would be well advised to avoid malls the day after Thanksgiving. An individual who hates used or damaged goods would be well advised to stay away from flea markets. If conformity is appealing, then the consumer can pick from a rack of dozens of the same blue shirts. When it comes to apparel the definition of **style** is "a particular combination of attributes that distinguishes it from others in its category" (Solomon and Rabolt, 2004, p. 6.). Examples would be styles of skirts, shirts, pants, and dresses—skirt length used to be a determinant of the latest style and a way of being fashionable.

**Impulse buying** means to walk in a store, or look at a catalog or webpage, see something attractive, and purchase it without taking the time to think about the ramifications such as cost, benefits, values, or needs. Sellers exploit impulse buying by putting displays at the front of the store or the checkout counter. Online or by catalog phone order, they may offer an add-on at the end. The add-on would be something like if you spend $10 more you will receive a bonus or slight discount.

Would you pay $145,000 for John Travolta's suit? Someone did.
(Courtesy of Corbis/Bettmann.)

Impulse items are often inexpensive or fun like a candy bar, magazine, or tabloid newspaper. Buying a refrigerator is rarely an impulse item, but a digital camera or a set of golf clubs may be. Style is often more important than substance in product categories such as clothing, restaurants, furniture, architecture, and certainly in packaging. This is why a hamburger ranges in price from $.59 to $20 or more depending on the restaurant, and of course, there are size and quality differences too. Packaging is a little more difficult to explain but again it comes down to image and branding. If you are going to throw out a package or display item anyway (such as a cardboard box for cosmetics or those tiny hangers that are used to display socks in stores), why would the style of it matter? Packaging does matter because it attracts your attention in the first place, helps you differentiate the brand from competitors (example, the light green boxes of Clinique cosmetics versus other brands), and is useful for other aspects of display. In many cases, part of image is aesthetic appeal and status, but beyond that it is personal expression. For example, no one really needs a $1,000 glass bathroom sink imbedded with copper, but it may be more pleasing to look at and certainly more unique than a typical $40 white porcelain sink. Both of the sinks function the same, the difference is in the style. Other examples are $600 antique door knobs and $7,000 custom-made copper range hoods when ordinary ones would cost much, much less.

If a product makes the consumer feel good and they can afford it, it can be thought of as a **consumer payoff**, a positive result from searching and making the best choice. The optimum behavior is to seek the highest quality at the lowest price (the essence of consumer economics), but as we have discussed this is not always the case and sometimes to get the highest quality one has to pay the highest price. There is no alternative such as when purchasing an art piece, an antique, or a collectible. To connect this with the decision making and time section at the beginning of the chapter, a consumer would seek the largest expected payoff from least time and energy expenditure especially given the price of the item. For example, one would assume a consumer would spend less time selecting a mouthwash than a computer. A truly busy person with a high income may send out a personal assistant to search for information. For example, an owner of a horse farm/estate sent her personal assistant to look at fabric for drapes; the assistant reported back what she had found and then the owner went to the store. Most of us do not have personal assistants, but we may have little time and find other ways to cut corners such as using shopping bots (sites on the Internet that gather shopping information and provide choices, outlets, and prices).

Consumers reach a point where the cost of searching further is greater than any possible benefit that can be derived from this practice. Comparison shopping for a single can of soda does not make financial sense past a point.

**Price variation** refers to when a single seller may charge different consumers different prices at different times for the same item. In the case of a heavy, large antique armoire, an antiques seller will probably be willing to sell it at a lesser price the last hour of a three-day antiques show than at the beginning—the reason being the problem and expense of packing it up and taking it to the next show. More common examples of **price discrimination** is the different prices charged by hotels, airlines, and cruise lines, depending on when the trip was booked, by whom (meaning a travel agent versus a private individual), and depending on the days the travel will take place. Price discrimination can be illegal if it is proven that an individual or a group is discriminated against in an unfair manner. For example, if a hotel charged a different price for the same room on the same day to people of different races or ethnicity that could be grounds for claiming discrimination.

Another rule of thumb is that people use seals of approval or trademarks as guides. Sometimes a new competitor will use only a slightly different brand name than a successful, established product. If it is too close, the established brand may sue over name rights. Quasi-fraud charities are notorious for using names that are very close to established legitimate charities. Another rule of thumb may be about price. If broccoli is being sold for $1.99 a bunch the consumer will buy, but if it is $4 a bunch then he or she will pass and substitute another vegetable and wait for the price on the broccoli to go down. Although as shown in earlier chapters, price is not the only guide.

Consumers will ignore a rule of thumb, for example, if they are in a hurry and really need a product such as disposable diapers. This explains why they will pay twice the normal price for milk at a convenience store than at a full-service grocery store or twice what they would normally pay for a hotel room if they are exhausted, they are in the middle of a snowstorm, and want to get off the road. Because of **budget constraints** (the relationship between what one can spend and what one will spend), most people can afford to pay double the price on a gallon of milk whereas they could not afford to pay double on a desired house. This is impacted by **ability to trade**, meaning trading one good for another. Let's say it is a new development of houses, all very similar, and the houses are lined up in a row. House A is right next to House B and is essentially identical; the prices differ by $5,000 so the preference will be for the less expensive house. Things get a little more complicated when the trade is between slightly dissimilar items such as lamb chops for pork chops or watermelon for cantaloupe or much more complicated between vastly dissimilar items such as a ham and chicken or rutabaga and lettuce. In the latter case, the consumer will have to decide how to maximize satisfaction given the conditions (price, quality, selection) that exist and trade or purchase accordingly. Information will be part of the transaction because a consumer will not buy a rutabaga if they do not know what to do with it or are unsure of the taste. A choice between iceberg lettuce and romaine lettuce may be easier to make.

*Price often serves as a rule of thumb guiding selection and purchase.*

Besides the purchase price of the item, there are added on costs such as cost of use, maintenance, or cost of end-result preparation. Examples of after-purchase prices are taxes, gasoline and repairs for cars, and even the added-on costs for simple things like food. Take for example the choice of buying a pound of hamburger: this could be a budget item or a mid- to high-priced meal, depending on what goes with it from tomatoes to truffles.

## READING CUSTOMERS' MINDS: CAN IT BE DONE?

So, consumers use rules of thumb (price, time, style, etc.) to guide decisions. But new research and testing is underway that may totally change how we think about and certainly how we measure the decision-making process. Gerald Zaltman, a marketing professor at the Harvard Business School, "uses brain scans, psychotherapy-like interviews and his patented Zaltman Metaphor Elicitation Technique (ZMET) to help the likes of Procter & Gamble, Pfizer, General Motors, and Coca-Cola get inside the consumer's head" (Useem, 2003, p. 48). He is the author of *How Customers Think*.

Zaltman says that at least 95 percent of the thinking that drives our behavior occurs unconsciously. Much of what we think were the steps that we went through are actually after-purchase constructions. In short, people are buying products for reasons they are not fully conscious of. The brain scans he or she uses involve monitoring the blood flows in the brain and seeing cortices light up. A new product can be shown to a subject, and the person experiences it negatively or positively; the brain scans pick up his or her reaction. To bring this out of the laboratory into a larger setting, new technologies are being developed, such as caps that people can wear. So far Zaltman and his colleagues have studied positive responses—joy and happiness—rather than disgust or turnoffs. In the long run, you have to know what repels consumers as well as what attracts. He sees applications of the new technology and testing particularly in certain industries such as cosmetics and personal appearance.

Another testing method that Zaltman uses involves asking people to bring in eight-by-ten pictures that represent their thoughts and feelings about something like snack foods. One person brought in a picture of someone covered with bees.

The trained interviewer asked what the bee picture meant and the woman responded that she had a lot of confidence that she wouldn't get strung—"that she could safely indulge in snack foods without running the risks of harm that everyone else talks about. So there was a bit of defiance to it" (Useem, 2003, 48). You can see from this example that this method is in the experimental stages and some would question the interpretation, but it is presented as a wave of the future, a consumer buying research area that will draw attention and grow. What Zaltman would say is that simply asking people why they buy what they do falls far short of what really happens.

# CONSUMERSPACE

Michael Solomon, director of a consulting firm called Mind/Share, an Auburn University professor, and author of *Conquering Consumerspace,* differentiates marketspace (a commercial system in which companies sell to us) from consumerspace (a commercial system in which they sell *with* us). His concept is that business no longer calls the shots, consumers do. He describes a trend called **identity marketing** that fuels the fire of consumerspace. In identity marketing, consumers wear or display in their homes product logos (i.e., T-shirts and shoes with Nike on them or lamp shades with a university name on them). In Great Britain, an ad agency paid students to wear temporary tattoos of product logos on their foreheads. Would you do this? And if so, at what price and for how long?

According to Solomon, branding provides security and clarity in a complicated world and nationalities are less important. To summarize, the bedrock of our identities is formed by allegiance to common value systems, often expressed concretely through affiliation with common product sets. In the preface, he writes "Welcome to consumerspace. Where reality is branded. Where we avidly search for the products and services that define who we are and who we want to be. Where we are what we buy—literally" (2003, p. xiii). Not everyone in consumer economics will be comfortable with this notion, feeling it is going too far, and believing that people are much more (their identities are much more) than what they purchase and use. But he is expressing a point of view that business listens to and anything of a trend nature is interesting to watch unfold. He wonders what consumerspace will look like and what firms will help build it and even control it? He posits that people will move seamlessly between offline and online worlds and in many ways this is already happening. Have you ever searched for a product online and then bought it at a store? Or have you found something in a store that you like but they do not have the right color or size or model so you went online to purchase or to find a lower price?

Solomon also says that "[p]eople hunger for unique products that help them express their individuality in an impersonal world. We have what psychologists call a *need for uniqueness*" (2003, p. 128). We can add that to the list of needs that Abraham Maslow posited in his hierarchy of needs. He says everyone needs to feel special, and perfumes are often marketed as smelling differently on each person. This leads us to our next section on advertising where mass marketed products boldly carry the messages "as individual as you are" or "making you feel your best."

# ADVERTISING

We discussed earlier the importance of the information search in the consumer buying process. The chapter, now, turns its spotlight on **advertising** defined as any paid form of nonpersonal communication about an organization, product, service, or idea by an identified sponsor (Alexander, 1965). Nonpersonal means that mass media forms are used that can transmit or reach large groups such as newspapers, radio, and television. The message is sent to an anonymous audience who does not respond back to the source of the message. Advertising is part of the promotional mix that sellers use to reach customers. It can be produced in-house or a separate advertising agency may be hired or the promotional mix could involve a combination of both.

Advertising, as a form of mass communication, can be classified as:

- National advertising—the biggest category. Some of the largest consumer brand advertising budgets are spent by Proctor & Gamble Co. and General Motors Corp.
- Retail or local advertising—examples would be fitness clubs and local restaurants.
- Political or cause-based, including public service announcements.
- Direct-response advertising—the customer reads the information and can choose to buy direct from the company through the mail, telephone, or Internet.
- Industrial advertising—includes business and health care publications.
- Professional advertising—targeted to groups such as doctors, teachers, and lawyers.

Advertising is based on the goals of the advertiser. What do they want to achieve? Most likely it is

- Increased sales.
- An attitude or perception change.
- Increased product and brand awareness.
- Provision of reminders and reinforcements. Familiar advertisements for familiar products reinforce past purchases and remind people to buy again.

To achieve these types of goals, the advertisements have to be attractive, creative, well executed, and placed in the right form of media. The message can be simple such as "Got Milk" from the American Dairy Association or complex and multileveled. Notice that simple messages have mental staying power. The message can be broken down into five parts: perception, awareness, understanding, persuasion, and retention/memorability (Wells, Burnett, and Morarity, 2000). In this way the message can be seen as a multilevel process, and it is only part of developing the total end-result advertisement. An effective advertisement has

- Memory
- Exposure—it gets to the consumer that the advertiser wants to reach
- Attention grabbing power
- Interpretation or understanding—the consumer gets the message

Advertisers can determine these factors in a number of ways from recall reports, recognition tests, diary reports, sales figures after an ad has shown, and more intrusive measures such as wiring people up or putting them in a special re-search room as they watch ads to measure eye pupil dilation and brain wave analysis or brain scans like in the Gerald Zaltman studies mentioned earlier in the chapter.

Usually there is a link between the cost of the advertisement space and the potential size of market. Thus, one Super Bowl ad during the Super Bowl game usually shown the last Sunday in January costs over a million dollars, but it has the potential of reaching over 500 million people because the game attracts not only the U.S. market but international viewers as well. Originality counts so many advertising firms and companies try to show off with their best talent to the point that many viewers remark that the ads are better than the game. About 48 percent of the viewers are women so it is not strictly a male market. Some start-up companies only advertise on the Super Bowl, putting their entire advertising budget on that one opportunity. They would be focusing on building awareness, making a first impression. Most companies such as a giant established beverage manufacturer and car makers would use the Super Bowl as only one venue among many. Their goal would be to keep the public interest alive in their brands and maybe push a new flavor, model, or version. Timing is important. The most expensive ads on the Super Bowl come at the beginning of the game when viewership is highest. Depending on how the game goes, viewership may sustain or drop off, a factor on which advertisers take a risk. Besides the large audience another reason that the Super Bowl is so popular as a showcase is because of **association**. Advertisers like to link up their products with a fun experience such as football; it has a pleasant association, a game, a contest that is all-American. Likewise, political candidates like to surround themselves with actors and other celebrities such as successful football coaches as a way build their popularity. Olympics sponsors also use association. A candy bar or a brand of sportwear may be the "official" product for the Olympics that particular year, boosting sales.

With the opening up of global markets advertisers have to address global markets as well as local markets. Naming products is difficult because an acceptable name in the United States may not be acceptable elsewhere. Similarly, settings or environments and types of models used have to be appropriate to the market. Advertising has to be adaptive and accountable or accurate to succeed.

Advertising push is uneven. Some product areas are heavily advertised such as food and beverages, goods that are used often and used up. Some other products are rarely advertised or, if so, only in small, targeted markets. Candy may be only advertised at Halloween and Easter. Because of economies of scale, large advertisers have an advantage—they are already known and accepted by markets. It is difficult for a new, smaller firm to break into established, heavily branded markets, such as cereals which are dominated by three major brands.

It is also necessary to point out that some ads don't work even if they are advertising a good product. The ad may be inappropriate or offensive. Have you ever watched an ad and wondered what it was about? Obviously, the sales point was not made. Probably the least effective advertising is direct mail that goes to mass markets. It is estimated that 98 percent of junk mail is thrown out. Examples of this are high-rise apartment dwellers receiving circulars for tires, middle-aged women without children receiving catalogs for children's clothes, and Midwest rural dwellers receiving reviews of the latest restaurants in Manhattan.

Advertisers use association to build or maintain images.

## Is Advertising Necessary?

Do you recall the discussion in chapter 2 of muckracker Vance Packard author of *The Hidden Persuaders?* At the beginning of his 1957 book, he wrote, "This book is an attempt to explore a strange and rather exotic new area of American life. It is about the large-scale efforts being made, often with impressive success, to channel our unthinking habits our purchasing decisions and our thought processes by the use of insights gleaned from psychiatry and the social sciences. Typically these efforts take place beneath our level of awareness; so that the appeals move us are often, in a sense, 'hidden'" (p. 1). There is no doubt that, as Packard suggests, advertising can be manipulative and that it uses psychology for profit advantage. He says some of the manipulating is amusing because it is so obvious. An example would be beautiful models draped on cars or pop stars drinking colas. But he says some of it is disquieting, intense, and potent. For example, the Weiss and Geller Advertising Agency became suspicious of the reasons people gave for buying home freezers because economically it didn't make much sense considering the initial cost, the added utility costs, and the amount of frozen leftovers thrown out. Researchers, whom Packard called probers, found that families filled freezers because they were trying to fill their inner anxieties brought on by the uncertainties in their lives. The probers concluded that a full freezer is reassuring. It means there will always be food in house and that means security, warmth, and safety. Economics had very little to do with the real reason for a home freezer purchase so the advertising and sales pitches were adjusted accordingly (Packard, 1957).

A home freezer may not be about keeping food cold or saving money, it may be about security, warmth, and safety.

Packard says probers have found out, "why we are afraid of banks; why we love those big fat cars; why we really buy homes; why men smoke cigars; why the kind of car we drive reveals the brand of gasoline we will buy; why housewives typically fall into a hypnoidal trance when they get into a supermarket; why men are drawn into auto showrooms by convertibles but end up buying sedans; why junior loves cereal that pops, snaps, and crackles" (p. 2). Of course, consumer behavior and advertising research has come a long way since the 1950s but the basic premise he puts forth has merit.

The industry would counter by saying that advertising is important for consumer information; it lets the consumer know what is out there and by doing this stimulates choices and competition. Advertising also communicates availability by saving consumers time from comparison shopping and needlessly shopping at stores that do not carry certain brands or products. For example, a television ad for a new movie says that it opens on March 3. This is useful information, saving the filmgoer the trouble of going to the theater in February.

Advertisers would also say they are primarily recommenders, for example, offering samples as a way to try something out. They would say they do not create needs, they help fulfill them. In the transaction process, then advertisers and marketers cannot create demand, so they try to fill the demand that is already there. *So, is advertising necessary? Yes, it probably is because it fulfills a function in the marketplace.*

The power of samples can be explained by the **rule of reciprocation**. In a classic psychology study, a university professor sent Christmas cards to perfect strangers. He was amazed at the number of people who sent holiday cards back addressed to him, and most did not inquire into his identity (Kunz and Woolcott,

1976). They appeared to be in some sort of automatic drive, get a card, send a card. The rule of reciprocation means that we try to repay what someone has given us. A free sample will often encourage someone to buy the full-size product. Individuals receiving samples may feel obligated to the salesperson or the company. Samples or free gifts are often for food or shampoo, but they also may be higher priced items such as certificates for free T-shirts or scarves, accompanied with a letter from the company president appreciating their business, given to frequent buyers at a national clothing chain. The rule of reciprocity has been tested and found to be true in many societies around the world. Sociologists and anthropologists theorize that our ancestors developed networks of sharing and learning and that this feeling of indebtedness is deeply ingrained in us.

The dark side to the rule of reciprocation is explained by Robert Cialdini in his book *Influence: Science and Practice*. What he says is that some people take this too far and may make a person feel uncomfortably indebted by expecting a favor in return. This could be a tactic of door-to-door salespeople or charities. For example, a common tactic is to receive unsolicited gifts such as address labels or notecards from charities or nonprofit organizations. Or a person may try to get someone to comply with a request. There are many approaches to dealing with unwanted samples, gifts, or favors and that is to reject them outright or to see the offers for what they are and not for what they are represented to be. Cialdini suggests, "We should accept initial favors or concessions in good faith, but be ready to redefine them as tricks should they later be proved as such. Once they are redefined in this way, we will not longer feel a need to respond with a favor or concession of our own" (2001, p. 50).

## Color in Advertising

Are you attracted to black-and-white photos of pizza? No, the advertisement or circular that comes in the mail or in your newspaper needs red for the tomato sauce and yellow for the cheese to be effective. Color has the power to create brand imagery, convey moods, and stimulate taste buds. Red is a common color in political advertising because it attracts attention and red, white, and blue are a popular combination for a patriotic appeal. The attractions of certain colors vary by intended message and targeted age and other groupings. Parkay margarine in electric blue and shocking pink targeted to children was a surprise to many doubting adults who asked, "Who would use that stuff?"

Blue is the most favored color overall, but the second-most popular color varies by ethnicity and race. Older people like sky blue much more than younger people. Blue and silver colored cars sell well. Whites like green. Hispanics and blacks lean toward purple. Asian Americans lean toward pink. It used to be there were more gender impacts, but increasingly men and women are agreeing on house paint colors and car colors (Paul, 2002). Reasons given for this trend is that gender roles have loosened up and men are being exposed through the world of sports to masculine men wearing uniforms of purple and teal. There are limits, for example, you can't put GI Joe in pink says Richard Brandt of Landor Associates (Paul, 2002, p. 33).

Another trend is toward brighter and more complex colors. Crayola crayons come in 120 different hues so children are exposed early to a wide range of colors.

When marketing to Hispanics the emphasis is on warmer tones with yellow and red according to Margaret Walch of the Color Association of the United States (Paul, 2002, p. 35). But even this generalization varies around the country since one's palette is dependent on light, temperature, where people live, and how they spend their time. Mexicans favor reds, blues, and blacks whereas Florida Hispanics like pastels, pinks, and salmons for fashions and interiors (Paul, 2002). African Americans experiment with color from chartreuse to brown; they are also attracted to yellows and reds. To be effective advertising needs to keep up with trends in ethnic and racial preferences. Although this section is on color, it should be pointed out that typeface, font, size, and legibility also affect how ads are perceived. Elderly people cannot and will not read small print. On television, advertising can use motion so for Gap, Old Navy, and Target ads you will often see people dancing while wearing the products.

## Vying for Your Attention: The Value of Repetition

A successful advertisement can stay in our heads for decades. The elderly remember jingles and slogans from their youth for products that no longer exist. Baby boomers can sing the Mickey Mouse Club song from their younger days. Memorability or **locking power** is a goal that advertisers strive for. Advertising plays on two forms of memory—recognition (seeing) and recall (more complex associations). For example, a shopper who sees hot dog buns realizes they do not need the buns, but seeing them is a cue that they need hot dogs or mustard or ketchup. Likewise, ads often provide a cue such as "oh yes, I need to remember to stop by and get donuts on the way to work tomorrow." The Krispie Kreme ad triggered this memory.

Repetition can be used as a memory jogging device over many years or over a short time span. For example, during the 2003 Super Bowl an advertisement for Anheuser-Busch, the world's largest brewery, featuring singer Tim McGraw promoting responsible drinking was shown in all four quarters of the game. Is it worth the expense to be repetitive? Usually, the answer to this is yes. Many people will ignore a first or second ad, but it is difficult to ignore the fourth ad shown during a single event or evening. And, when it comes to the major TV broadcasting advertising event of the year, the Super Bowl, the timing becomes even more complicated. "These days, PepsiCo releases its commercials about a week in advance of the game 'to capitalize' on the buzz surrounding Super Bowl, says Dave DeCecco, senior manager of public relations for Pepsi-Cola North America. The beverage and bottling concern got an estimated $10 million in free publicity for a 90-second Britney Spears performance it used to promote Pepsi soda last year" (Vranica and O'Connell, January 21, 2003, p. B1).

Memory devices include **jingles** (music), **slogans** (short phrases), and **taglines** (end messages). Repetition thrives on rhyme, catchy melodies, and repeating sounds. An example of a repeating sound is the sound of an Alka-Selter tablet dissolving in a glass of water and the jingle is "Plop, plop, fizz, fizz, Oh what a relief it is." Can you sing the Oscar Meyer Weiner song? Characters such as cartoon characters or animals can also assist in repetition and memory such as the AFLAC duck for insurance, a product that is difficult to visualize or make attractive.

## Economics and Advertising Pros and Cons

*Advertising is part of the free market system;* it encourages competition and fosters economic growth which is good for consumers. New products are developed and offered stimulating the economy. Volume sales can lead to lower production costs, and those savings should be passed onto consumers in the form of lower prices. These are all pros. The main negative is that advertising adds to the costs of marketing goods which is also passed down to consumers. The debate between the economic affects and values of advertising may never be resolved. Some economists take a negative view of advertising; others take an "it depends point of view," and still others are very positive. All agree that advertising is a powerful institution integral to the workings of the market. Consumer economists are not critical of advertising per se, but they may be critical of techniques or type of appeal.

From an economic standpoint, advertising provides information about alternatives and provides consumers with recall cues that help them make substitutes at the time of purchase. The more alternatives that consumers can think of, the greater the price elasticity. They may say I can't afford this product but I can afford another that will easily substitute. Advertising succeeds best in environments where choices exist and there is disposable income. The basic economic role of advertising is to let people know what is available that helps them make consumption decisions.

## Deceptive Advertising

Among other things advertising should be accountable. It should be accurate and give a fair portrayal of the product or service. But advertising can be deceptive or misleading. How much so is difficult to pinpoint. And it is also difficult to know where to draw the line between persuasiveness and manipulation. In political advertisements mud-slinging occurs, and misleading statistics are presented that alter people's perception of the truth. There have been studies that show decisively that purchases are consumer driven based on needs and advertising is simply an information source. Other studies show that consumers become aware of a new product and then the need or want follows. Critics say vulnerable groups, such as young children, teens, and the elderly, too easily succumb to marketing messages and that businesses take advantage of their vulnerability. Evidence to prove this is shaky except for very young children who cannot distinguish between an advertisement and a cartoon show.

Puffery is legal.

Accuracy or accountability refers to whether the advertising message, direct and subtle, is accurate. Most watchers of television know that a new face cream will not improve their social life, but where do you draw the line? **Puffery** refers to advertising that exaggerates the characteristics of a product. If an advertiser said their face cream would remove all wrinkles that would be puffery, but it is okay for them to say a moisturizer used as directed will reduce the "appearance of wrinkles." Puffery is legal. A common puffery phrase is the "world's best pizza." The Uniform Commercial Code (UCC) is a set of laws about sales and other commercial matters. In essence it says that it is okay for ads to make general statements praising a product or service. So it is all right for Silversmith's to advertise that it is the area's leading jeweler, but it is not okay for the store to advertise that "all our gold jewelry is 18 karat gold" when they also sell gold of a lesser quality.

The Federal Trade Commission (FTC) says an advertisement is unfair "if it causes or is likely to cause substantial consumer injury which is not reasonably avoidable by consumers themselves and is not outweighed by countervailing benefits to consumers or to competition." The FTC says it is deceptive if it contains misrepresentation or omission. It also uses the *average man rule* which means would an average person be deceived by the advertisement—if so, then it is ruled misleading. As has been discussed in other chapters, besides the FTC there are other groups that monitor advertising messages and images.

Here are more examples of deceptive advertising:

- A hamburger made to look large by putting it on a very small plate or in the hands of a small child.
- A toy racing car set and track that appears to go fast using camera tricks and angles when really the cars putter around a dull, oval-shaped track.
- Vegetables and beef added to vegetable beef soup for a TV ad so it looks like there is more there than in an actual can. An old trick was to put weights in the bottom of the bowl so that the vegetables and beef floated to the surface.
- Cars driven off-road by professionals, a practice that would actually wreck cars driven by ordinary people. In an effort to be more truthful, some television ads have small print on the bottom of the screen that says "driven by professional drivers."
- Using doctors as givers of testimonials/supporters of diet products when in fact they are not medical doctors or they are doctors whose specializations have nothing to do with diets.
- Saying a product is low in calories when it is indeed high in calories.

Examples of ethical (morals, principles or values) concerns include the sharing of buyer lists and personal information about consumers by companies, the promotion of harmful substances such as tobacco and alcohol to teens, and questionable or rigged sweepstakes and contests. When it comes to court action against companies, it often boils down to figuring out if the advertisers were deliberately untruthful or misleading. This can be proved by e-mails, letters, and the testimony of employees. Legitimate companies and advertisers want to rule out flagrantly deceptive advertising because shady advertising of any kind reflects poorly on the advertising industry as a whole.

Does advertising encourage materialism (a preoccupation with material things)? It is hard to argue that this is not the case. After all it encourages consumption. It also affects our sense of what constitutes status, success, and achievement. For example, a wine campaign could equate wine with elitism and elegance. Drinking wine could say, "I've arrived."

Does it create dissatisfaction? Many consumer economists would give a resounding yes in response to this question. They would say that advertising encourages the throwing out of the old in favor of buying something new. In the world of advertising, "new" is almost always better, the exception being eBay and similar Web sites. Advertisers say that they did not create materialism—they are simply providing information, a service. They think advertising has become a scapegoat for all of society's ills, as a maker of values rather than as a reflector of values. They will also say that no amount of advertising can sell a lousy product. Since products fail all the time, there is some merit to this argument. People will not buy what they don't like or can't use.

Does advertising portray an unreal world, a world of perfection? Yes, it often does. The models have perfect teeth and hair, everyone is happy and secure. Viewers or readers accept this because they want a better life, they like attractive people and settings.

Advertising also preys on people's insecurities such as fear of theft (to sell home security systems), of dying penniless (to sell funeral burial policies and financial products), and of smelling bad (deodorants, soaps, shampoos, body washes). Baldness remedies are sold on the basis of fears of public acceptance and fears of losing one's youth. The basic message is buy this product and you will feel or look better. Current events play into the type of advertising that is run and the products that sell. Following the September 11 tragedies in the United States, life insurance sales skyrocketed. War news curtails foreign travel and has the effect of increasing domestic travel, especially destinations within easy driving distance of home.

Does advertising pay for television and radio shows? The answer is yes—the commercials are the most overt on commercial television and radio. They are more subtle but nevertheless present on PBS when company names splash across the screen. PBS television and radio also rely on viewer and listener contributions and federal government support. According to the PBS Annual Report, leading corporate underwriters of shows that target kids such as *Sesame Street* include over $1 million Playskool, W. K. Kellogg Foundation, General Mills, Lego Co., and Look-Smart Ltd. In the next category of corporate underwriters at the $500,000 to $1 million level is KB Kids.com Inc., Libby's Juicy Juice, and Chuck E. Cheese. There are ethical issues involved in this level of corporate support; some feel it has gone too far. "It used to be 'the following program is brought to you with support from Mobil,' " says Robert Thompson, Director of the Center for the Study of Popular TV at Syracuse University in Syracuse, NY. "Now it is a moving video and some of it is pretty substantial—it's longer, it's a full-fledged commercial. It's no longer a mention. It's a commercial pure and simple and sometimes not so pure and not so simple" (Beatty, 2002, p. B1).

For television viewing in general, experiments have been conducted where people paid for television shows without commercials, but these experiments failed. We have become accustomed to "free" television and radio. With the advent of mute and fast forward buttons on remotes, we are paying less of a price. Not all advertisements are difficult to watch. Some are entertaining, using the latest music, or amusing as well as informative, especially on the first exposure; repeated exposure lessens the pleasurable effect. Curiously, though, some of the dullest commercials sell the most products.

Bait and switch as a fraudulent sales practice was discussed earlier in the book, but it needs to be added here because it is a common advertising fraud. A person reads an ad for a digital camera selling for $125, and since that is a very low price, they go to the store wanting to buy it. The store says they are sold out and tries to switch the customer to a $500 digital camera. State attorney generals' offices or other consumer affairs areas can look into bait and switch frauds, and consumers can file individual or class-action suits demanding compensation.

## Subliminal Advertising

We assume that advertising is seen and/or heard. **Subliminal advertising** refers to messages "transmitted in such a way that the receiver is not consciously aware of receiving it" (Wells, Burnett, and Moriarty, 2000, p. 41). The symbols or words may be too faint or too fast for the conscious mind to pick up. Many would say this is foul play whereas others would say this is like the creature "Big Foot," it does not exist. Comedian Steven Wright has a joke that goes something like this, "I saw a subliminal advertising executive the other day, but only for a second."

Subliminal advertising is a favorite topic of psychology and consumer classes. The question is: Is it possible to manipulate the mind of consumers with faint or hidden messages? In experiments when psychologists or communications experts have tested subliminal advertisements that they designed, it appears that it does not work. Consumers will not buy products they do not need regardless of overt or subliminal advertising messages. The advertising industry does not like the image that they would use subliminal advertising and say accusations of its use are damaging and false. Common accusations are that in movie theaters subliminal messages are given in premovie advertisements to increase popcorn or soda sales. Wilson Keys, an author, suggested that most embedded ads appeal to sexuality (Weir, 1984). An example is that of an attractive woman's body embedded in ice cubes in a print advertisement for an alcoholic beverage. Research indicates that an advertisement such as this may trigger a like or dislike response to the product, but it appears unlikely a subliminal advertisement will cause someone to drink whiskey if they do not normally drink whiskey. Although subliminal advertising may not exist or in experimental form it has been shown to be largely ineffective, it may be possible in the future for more sophisticated forms to exist that may be capable of manipulating consumers. This is the reason that this subject is worth a mention in a book on consumer economics, and given the previous section on the Zaltman research studies, perhaps there is more merit to studying unconscious thought regarding consumption than previously accepted.

Subliminal advertising has embedded images for a product that aren't noticed on a conscious level.

## Distasteful Advertising

Taste is about not only what is artistically pleasing but also what seems appropriate. Table 7.1 gives a list of ethical and/or taste issues facing advertisers. In Europe, an advertising firm painted advertisements on the sides of cows standing in fields (with the permission of and payment to the owners), and animal rights activists objected saying it was in bad taste because it took advantage of the cows. Do you agree or disagree? Also in Europe a baby carriage manufacturer had a contest, and the winners received expensive baby carriages with company advertising on the side of the carriage. People said this was in bad taste too. Do you agree or disagree?

Taste, as a value laden word, is in the eye of the beholder, and this includes where the viewer or consumer lives. Taste can refer literally to what tastes good. For example, cheese flavor is not appealing to most Chinese so to sell Frito-Lay's Cheetos in China the company tried out over 600 different flavors in taste tests. Although the end product is still called Cheetos, the flavor we are used to in the United States cannot be found in most of China. What flavors are they selling? American Savory and Japanese Steak were two of the favorites. In regard to advertising, what passes for bad taste in one country or area of the world may be considered appropriate in others. In Australia and Western Europe women's breasts are shown in television commercials, whereas in the United States this is considered poor taste and not allowed. In the United States, the time of day and types of shows that beer ads can appear on are regulated. Beer ads are not allowed on Saturday cartoon shows, but it is okay to have them on Saturday afternoon football

**Table 7.1**    Ethical and/or Taste Issues Facing Advertisers

| Issue | Types or Examples |
|---|---|
| Controversial products and ads | Alcohol, tobacco, lottery, gambling |
| Intimate products | Feminine hygiene, impotency cures, lingerie, underwear |
| Advertising to children | Type of ad, placement of ad, time of day |
| Bias or stereotyping | Offensive depiction of racial/ethnic groups, elderly, disabled, or other groups |
| Puffery | Legal exaggeration, the "best" |
| Social responsibility | Hurting or helping causes, going beyond legal lobbying rules |
| Use of models and spokespersons | Does the model or spokesperson really use the product? Is proof necessary? |
| Former public figures | Should former governors, presidents, legislators or generals endorse products? Which products are off-limits? |

game shows. Since children may be watching the games or playing in the room while their parents are watching the games, they are exposed to beer commercials. So although there are some guidelines to protect children, this example shows that they are exposed to adult product advertising on a regular basis. They also see roadside billboards for adult entertainment clubs and other adult fare.

Regardless of who it is directed to, U.S. consumers complain that much of advertising is in poor taste. They say it is irritating, repetitive, insulting to their intelligence, humorless, and degrading of certain individuals and groups. Beer ads and advertising for bars are often degrading to women. Asian Americans, African Americans, Hispanics, and the elderly have also been the target of stereotyping. The kinds of ads that are often said to be obnoxious have to do with personal care, such as deodorants, dandruff shampoos, and denture creams. Irritating ads can have close-ups of dogs crunching on dogfood or doorbells or telephones that ring and get people up off their couches to answer the phone or the door. Nauseating ads may have close-ups of people chewing with their mouths open, little children with food smeared all over their faces (some find this cute), or women spooning cat food from a can. Music or jingles can be especially irritating.

**Infomercials** are program-long advertisements that can run an hour or more for cooking products, cosmetics, tools, and diet programs/supplements. Traditionally, these were shown late at night when airtime was inexpensive, but increasingly infomercials are airing at noon during the week and on Saturdays. Some people find these irritating while others enjoy the advice, demonstrations, and comfortable conversational style. Infomercials go in and out of style, dropping off the air and being replaced with another.

## Marketing to Children

Monopoly and other games like Electronic Mall Madness by Milton Bradley encourage children to be acquisitive, aggressive, and shrewd in their spending decisions. The objects of the games are to make the most money or to have the money spread as far as it will go. In the case of the Electronic Mall Madness the object is to get the most stuff and get back to the parking lot first. It is quite an introduction to the world of credit cards, consumption, and competitiveness. Some would say this is too much for ten-year-olds, and others would say it is good life training since grown-ups are exposed to a continuous barrage of sales ads, credit card offers, and car salesman screaming at them from the television set about new, low prices.

Games involving money or gambling aimed at children are nothing new, nor are advertisements aimed at children. In 1912, Cracker Jack was offering a toy inside so that children would ask for it. Before television, children were saving box tops for prizes. The practice of putting toys in cereal boxes to attract children has been going on for decades, although lately coupons for products or discounts are becoming more common. McDonald's has had Happy Meals for years as have competitors using slightly different names for their meals with prizes marketed to children.

Children are exposed to about 200 television commercials a day, and the commercials have changed considerably from the ads that their parents viewed (De-Graaf, Wann, and Naylor, 2001). In earlier ads parents were shown as authority figures, someone who would help the children out by explaining how products worked or they could be relied upon to put products together. Newer ads often leave out parents and are more likely to show peers or cartoon-type characters showing how products work. In other words, mom and dad are no longer shown as the wise figures (value setters) that they used to be.

## Government Agencies Affecting Advertising

Table 7.2 lists the government agencies that most affect advertising. One of the agencies that has not been discussed extensively before is the Federal Communication Commission (FCC). It was formed in 1934 to protect the public in regard to broadcast communication. The FCC has limited control over broadcast advertising through its ability to revoke and issue licenses to stations. The FCC's concerns with radio and television stations and networks includes advertising that is perceived to be in bad taste or deceptive. As such, the FCC works closely with the FTC which is discussed in the next section.

As this chapter and previous ones have shown, often government and the advertising industry are at odds, but sometimes they cooperate and work together. For example on October 6, 2000, President Clinton signed an executive order at the White House that included language to establish the first multicultural advertising guidelines for federal government departments and agencies. The main point was to encourage inclusiveness and fairness throughout the marketing and advertising process from employment and career advancement to competition and compensation for creative services. The American Advertising Federation (AAF) and the AAF Foundation formed a committee that drafted the *Principles and Recommended Practices for Effective Advertising in the American Multicultural Marketplace*. Twenty-six companies, such as DaimlerChrysler and Kraft General Foods, and agencies have committed to adopting the principles laid out. For a complete report go to *www.aaf.org*.

**The Role of the FTC in Advertising.**   In an earlier chapter, there was a lengthy description of the oversight and powers of the Federal Trade Commission, but here is a brief review with the focus on advertising. The FTC receives complaints and in-

**Table 7.2**   Government Agencies That Affect Advertising

| Agency | Effect |
| --- | --- |
| Bureau of Alcohol, Tobacco, and Firearms (a division of the U.S. Treasury Department) | Regulates advertising of alcohol, can revoke permits for distillers, wine merchants, and brewers |
| Federal Communication Commission (FCC) | Issues and revokes licenses for radio and television stations, can eliminate deceptive or poor taste ads |
| Federal Trade Commission (FTC) | Regulates advertising, labeling, packaging, issues warnings, requires advertisers to validate claims |
| Food and Drug Administration (FDA) | Regulates labeling, packaging, and manufacture of food and drug products, safety and purity of cosmetics |
| Library of Congress | Watches over copyright protection such as coined phrases, slogans in ads that are well known |
| U.S. Patent Office | Watches over trademark registration |
| U.S. Postal Service | Controls advertising through the mail, handles complaints of unsolicited ads and products that come in the mail, i.e., obscenity, contests, fraud* |
| State agencies | Regulate unfair and deceptive trade practices within states, often includes advertising |

*Consumers who receive sexually offensive material in the mail can request that no more mail be delivered from that sender. The postmaster general has the power to stop offensive mail or questionable activities sent through the mail such as get-rich quick schemes.

quiries each month about advertising. The FTC investigates problems and may take action depending on the case. A first step is a **consent decree** in which the FTC notifies the advertiser that its ads are deceptive and asks the advertiser to sign a consent decree saying they will stop the deceptive practice. Most do sign it and thus avoid a possible fine of $10,000 per day and the bad publicity for refusing to do so.

For consumer redress, one of the strongest pieces of legislation is the **Magnuson-Moss Warranty-FTC Improvement Act of 1975**. It empowers the FTC to obtain consumer redress when a person or firm engages in deceptive practices such as false or misleading advertising. This includes the ad agency as well as the manufacturer of the product. For example, one case of misleading advertising of a shaving product ended with both the company and the agency paying $1 million each to the government, and they had to halt the advertising campaign. On behalf of consumers, the FTC can order any of the following:

- Cancellation or reformation of contracts
- Refund of money
- Return of property
- Payment of damages
- Public notification

One of the strongest actions that the FTC can take is **cease-and-desist orders**. A hearing, similar to a trial, takes place, in which the company presents their defense. An administrative law judge presides, and FTC staff attorneys represent the commission. If the FTC succeeds in proving that an ad is unfair or misleading, then it issues a cease-and-desist order requiring the ad to stop. If the company does not do so, they are given a stiff fine. The advertiser can appeal.

**Counteradvertising**, also called corrective advertising, is new advertising which is undertaken pursuant to a FTC order for the purpose of correcting false claims about the product. The new ad can be on radio, in print, or on television giving information to correct former misinformation. The purpose is not to punish the advertiser but rather to act in the best interest of consumers. A classic case was Warner-Lambert's Listerine campaign that ran for nearly 50 years. In this ad campaign, the claim was that the product prevented or reduced the severity of colds and sore throats. The cost of the corrective advertising was $10 million and ran for 16 months, mostly on television (Wells, Burnett, and Moriarty, 2000).

Whether counteradvertising works or not (changes consumer behavior) is questionable. For example, Warner-Lambert found that after the corrective advertising was over that 42 percent of Listerine users still believed that the mouthwash was being advertised as a remedy for sore throats and colds, and 57 percent of users rated cold and sore throat effectiveness as a key reason for purchasing the brand (Wilke, McNeil, and Mazis, 1984).

## THE ROLE OF PUBLIC SERVICE ANNOUNCEMENTS

It is fitting to end this chapter on a positive note. We have all benefited from **public service announcements (PSAs)** defined as messages on behalf of some good cause such as stopping drunk driving (Mothers against Drunk Driving) or preventing forest fires. A leader in creating these announcements is the Ad Council, a private, nonprofit organization, whose mission is to identify a select number of significant public issues and stimulate action. The Ad Council often teams up with government agencies or nonprofit organizations to get a message out to the public. For example, currently the Ad Council and the U.S. Department of Health and Human Services have a joint campaign to inspire healthier lifestyles. One of the first Ad Council campaigns was during World War II, using the slogan "Loose Lips Sink Ships." Here are some slogans that you were brought up with that were developed by the Ad Council:

- McGruff the Crime Dog's "Take a Bite Out of Crime"
- Smokey Bear's "Only You Can Prevent Forest Fires"
- "Keep American Beautiful"
- "A Mind Is a Terrible Thing to Waste"
- "Friends Don't Let Friends Drive Drunk"

According to the Ad Council's Web site, 68 percent of Americans exposed to the "Friends Don't Let Friends Drive Drunk" advertisements say they have personally stopped someone who had been drinking from driving. The United Negro College Fund's slogan "A Mind Is a Terrible Thing to Waste" has helped them raise more than $1.9 billion to graduate 300,000 minority students from college.

## SUMMARY

Time, technological obsolescence, and depreciation all affect buying decisions. Gerald Zaltman of Harvard University has conducted research that indicates that much of consumer decision making may be unconscious. More research is underway to determine the extent to which this is true. In 1957, Vance Packard in *The Hidden Persuaders* exposed the advertising industry and its manipulative ways. Government agencies and the advertising industry are often at odds with each other but sometimes they cooperate on social advances and initiatives. A positive side of the advertising industry is the public service announcements that they create often in cooperation with government agencies or nonprofit organizations to bring about positive social change.

Price often serves as a rule of thumb—a guide for narrowing down choices. A $200 cashmere sweater may be out of the question, but one marked down to $69 may be considered. Scarcity plays a part as well. It explains why at auctions famous oil paintings go for $75 million and John Travolta's leisure suit from the movie *Saturday Night Fever* sold for $145,000.

Another researcher, Michael Solomon, author of *Conquering Consumerpace,* suggests that the traditional way of doing business in which companies call the shots is obsolete. The trend is for businesses to work with consumers. He describes a world where boundaries between branded commodities and everyday life are blurred and nationalities are less important. More and more people will move seamlessly between the offline and online domains.

Advertising is part of the free enterprise system. It provides exposure to choice and competition, but in the long run it is added on to the price of consumer goods. There are many levels or steps in advertising—getting the message across is an underlying purpose. Advertisers like their goods to be associated with pleasant experiences (like football games) or lifestyles. Because of economies of scale, large advertisers have an advantage over smaller ones or beginners in a market. It is debatable whether subliminal advertisements exist or not, but there is no question that we are exposed to obnoxious or distasteful advertising. The Federal Communication Commission has the authority to issue and revoke licenses to broadcasting stations. It works closely with the Federal Trade Commission. The FTC is the government's main watchdog on deceptive advertising. They can issue consent orders, cease-and-desist orders, and request counteradvertising (also known as corrective advertising). Research studies question whether counteradvertising is effective.

## KEY POINTS

1. Consumers vary in their ability to trade, the amount of time, and the amount of money they have (budget constraints) which affect their decision making in the marketplace. Some seek bargains, others are content with full prices. Style matters to some and not to others; price is usually a strong guide, but not the only guide to purchasing.
2. Impulse buying is encouraged by sellers by various means such as check-out displays of candy or magazines or add-ons from catalog or Internet sales.

3. Advertising is part of the free market system. As such it encourages competition and fosters economic growth. It also ultimately costs the consumer. Consumers often find advertising irritating, objectionable, and in bad taste, but this varies by consumer and by country or region.
4. Puffery, exaggerated claims such as "the world's best pizza," is legal.
5. Children are exposed to about 200 television commercials a day.
6. Public service announcements (PSAs), developed on a volunteer basis by advertising and communications professionals, inform the public about critical social issues such as drunk driving and forest fires.

## KEY TERMS

| | | |
|---|---|---|
| ability to trade | infomercials | price discrimination |
| advertising | jingles | price variation |
| association | locking power | puffery |
| budget constraints | Magnuson-Moss | rule of reciprocity |
| cease-and-desist orders | Warranty-FTC | rules of thumb |
| consent order | Improvement Act of | slogans |
| consumer payoff | 1975 | style |
| counteradvertising | Pareto principle | subliminal advertising |
| depreciate | Parkinson's law | taglines |
| identity marketing | public service | |
| impulse buying | announcements | |

## DISCUSSION QUESTIONS

1. What have you bought on impulse? Was it a good or bad purchase? Explain why or why not.
2. What do you own that has depreciated in value? Do you accept this depreciation or not? Explain your answer.
3. Select two print ads and compare their messages. What are they selling? Who is their audience or target market? How effective are the ads in grabbing your attention?
4. Do you think there should be more or less government regulation of advertising? Support your answer with examples.
5. Go to the FTC Web site and see what it says about advertising. What are the particular current issues that they are involved in?

## E-RESOURCES

Advertising Industry

American Association
of Advertising Agencies
www.aaaa.org

Founded in 1917, a national trade association representing the advertising agency business.

| | |
|---|---|
| Advertising Age<br>AdAge.com | Trade publication |
| American Advertising Federation (AFA)<br>www.aaf.org | A trade association representing 50,000 professions in the advertising industry. |
| The Ad Council<br>www.adcouncil.org | Founded in 1947, a private, nonprofit organization that marshals volunteer talent from the advertising and communications industries and facilities of media to produce public service advertising to address critical social issues in America. |

Government Agencies

Federal Communications Commission
www.fcc.gov

Federal Trade Commission
www.ftc.gov

Food and Drug Administration
www.fda.gov

## REFERENCES

Alexander, R., ed. (1965). *Marketing Definitions,* Chicago, American Marketing Association, p. 9.

Beatty, S. (July 11, 2002). PBS and corporate underwriters: Too close for comfort? *Wall Street Journal,* p. B1.

Cialdini, R. (2001). *Influence: Science and practice.* Boston: Allyn and Bacon.

DeGraaf, J., D. Wann, and T. Naylor. (2001). *Affluenza: The all-consuming epidemic.* San Francisco, CA: Berrett-Koehler Publishers.

Kunz, P. R., and M. Woolcott. (1976). Season's greetings: From my status to yours. *Social Science Research, 5,* 269–278.

Packard, V. (1957). *The hidden persuaders.* New York: Pocket Books.

Paul, P. (February 2002). Color by numbers. *American Demographics,* 31–35.

Solomon, M. (2003). *Conquering Consumerspace.* New York: American Management Association.

Solomon, M., and N. Rabolt. (2004). *Consumer behavior in fashion.* Upper Saddle River, NJ: Prentice Hall.

Useem, J. (January 20, 2003). This man can read your mind. *Fortune,* p. 48.

Vranica, S., and V. O'Connell. (January 21, 2003). For immediate release! *Wall Street Journal,* p. B1.

Weir, W. (October 15, 1984). Another look at subliminal facts. *Advertising Age,* p. 46.

Wells, W., J. Burnett, and S. Moriarty. (2000). *Advertising principles & practice,* 5th ed. Saddle River, NJ: Prentice Hall.

Wilke, W., D. NcNeil, and M. Mazis. (Spring 1984). Marketing's "Scarlet Letter": The theory and practice of corrective advertising. *Journal of Marketing,* p. 26.

Zaltman, G. (2003). *How customers think.* Cambridge, MA: Harvard Business School Press.

# Food and Beverage Issues

*Eating is an art—the only art everyone can participate in.*
**Alice Waters**

## Learning Objectives

1. Discuss food and beverage consumption patterns and retailing.
2. Know agencies and laws that protect our food and water.
3. Know what organically grown means.
4. Know the different points of view regarding genetically altered foods.
5. Understand health and legal issues and government protection.

## INTRODUCTION

This chapter turns its attention to a specific area of consumer behavior, that of food and drink. As the second chapter showed, food is usually the first area of consumption that is government regulated because it is such a fundamental human need and people can die from contaminated food or get extremely ill. Since the first food and drug law was enacted in 1906, the federal government has taken an active role in ensuring the quality of our food supply. Food and drink are such integral parts of our daily lives that they are important areas to single out in terms of discussions about consumerism. We may buy only a few cars in the course of our lives, but we will buy countless foods and drinks.

Technology has provided the means for great advances in food and beverages. Did you know the Defense Department's combat-feeding program has come up with a barbecued-chicken sandwich that has a shelf life of three years? Military rations now called MREs (Meals Ready to Eat) have come a long way from the tinned foods and Spam of World War II. Speaking of Spam, did you know that the number one state in Spam consumption is Hawaii? Products sold to the general public like powdered milk, freeze-dried coffee, and processed cheese have their origin in GI rations. Currently, the military says they have found a way to keep lettuce and tomatoes fresh for 50 to 60 days at room temperature. One of the main MREs developers is combat-feeding director Gerald Darsch who has been described as a wry man with a great deal of intestinal fortitude. He is a modern-day example of the poison squad you read about in chapter 2. "His distinguished combat-food record includes taste-testing 12-year-old canned ham and lima beans. 'It was ugly' is all he'll say about it, apparently trying to forget" (Stipp, 2003, p. 46). Another technological advance is our ability to track tainted food through DNA matching. This advance, which has enormous health and legal implications, is covered in this chapter.

Although eating is one of life's greatest pleasures, nearly all Americans are on a diet or concerned about their weight. So people enjoy eating but worry about it at the same time. The concern about weight gain is so great that it has been called a national obsession. "The single most important issue in nutrition right now is gaining weight, and that's a matter of calories," says Marion Nestle, chairwoman of the department of nutrition and food studies at New York University. "It doesn't matter if they're healthy calories or unhealthy calories—calories are calories" (Parker-Pope, 2003, p. D1).

According to the Centers for Disease Control and Prevention (CDC), more than 60 percent of U.S. adults are either overweight or obese. But the question is what to do about it, if anything. Is it a problem government and business should get involved in or is it individual choice? At this point, consumers have to sort through lots of fads, misinformation, and downright fraudulent information coming from innumerable sources. Who should they believe? What should they do? What makes it even more complicated is that seemingly low-calorie, healthy-sounding foods by their names are often not either. For example, a Fresh City Chicken Teriyaki Wrap has 968 calories and 33 fat grams and Baja Fresh Ensalada Chicken is 857 calories and 57 fat grams. What drives up the calories and fat grams are the sauces and dressings. A ham sandwich at Fresh City only has 547 calories by comparison, but most consumers would assume this is higher in calories than a Chicken Teriyaki Wrap. Nutritionists would like calorie information available at the counter or on the packaging. "Nobody can tell how many calories are in food they haven't prepared themselves," says Dr. Nestle. "Even a trained nutritionist can't tell, not even a really good one" (Parker-Pope, 2003, p. D1). Restaurant chain owners such as Wendy's International that owns Baja Fresh say that consumers can always get wraps or salads without the sauces or dressings, and they offer low-cal items like Mahi Mahi tacos, with 216 calories and 11 fat grams. In short, nutritionists, consumer economists, and health advocates want to educate the public about food and health risks and encourage participation in healthy behaviors. They want to make sure that useful and valid information is available to the public.

Writing about food and beverage issues has its share of pitfalls because it is such a fast moving area it is difficult to be absolutely accurate and up-to-date. Every effort has been made to provide balanced and current coverage, but because of rapid discoveries the best advice is for readers to keep up with new developments from reliable sources and consult with their own physicians. Government sources were heavily relied upon for the information provided in this chapter, and the government Web sites in the E-Resources section near the end of the chapter should supply the latest updates. The chapter begins with a discussion of food and beverage consumption patterns.

## FOOD AND BEVERAGE CONSUMPTION

### Basic Terminology

**Foods** are products from plants or animals that can be taken into the body for energy and nutrients to sustain life and growth. The food and beverages consumed are one's diet. **Nutrition** is the science of foods and nutrients and their actions within the body. The six classes of nutrients are carbohydrates, lipids, minerals, proteins, vitamins, and water. Your body obtains nutrients through the digestive process in which foods are broken down in the gastrointestinal tract into compounds that the body can absorb. A kilocalorie is a measure of energy content in food.

## A Brief History

In early Colonial America, food often consisted of whatever came out of a large pot set above the flames of the fireplace. Food was plain except for the rich. Alcohol consumption (beer, wine, liquor, and cider) was high estimated at six gallons per year for Americans over the age of 15. Around the time of the American Revolution, the most common main dish served was ham, and in the South it was chicken. Accompanying these were breads and desserts, cheese and other dairy products. Vegetables, seafood, and fruits depended on location and season although importing was beginning from the Caribbean. By the 1820s finer dining and restaurants were in evidence in the cities. Manners, etiquette, and utensils improved. By the 1830s and 1840s extensive menus were available; dining out became high fashion from New Orleans to Boston. Railroads and ships brought fine cuisine to the West. A famous dinner at New York's Delmonico's held in 1868 to honor English author Charles Dickens involved nearly 40 sumptuous dishes (Mariani, 1991). By the end of the 1890s with advances in refrigeration and transportation nearly any food was available anywhere. Americans went oyster mad, with an average consumption of 660 oysters per year compared with 120 in the United Kingdom and only 26 in France (Mariani, 1991). This points out how consumption has changed over the years and how it varies by country. Do you normally eat 660 oysters a year?

In 1900 the hamburger patty on a bun was introduced, followed immediately by a hotdog in a bun. In the 1920s the widespread use of refrigerators revolutionized food and beverage storage. Dairy products including pasteurized milk became popular. In 1924 Clarence Birdseye sold the first frozen food, fish. Snack foods and candies prospered during the 1930s depression. The Twinkie was introduced in 1930.

The first TV dinner was introduced in 1954 by C. A. Swanson & Sons. The first affordable home microwave oven was introduced in 1965, and they became common household appliances in the 1980s. In 1990 Oscar Mayer launched Lunchables, packs of meat, cheese, and crackers, leading the way to more individualized servings. In 2000 Smucker's introduced Uncrustables, packaged frozen peanut-butter-and-jelly sandwiches. Throughout the century baking from scratch became less and less common. Prepackaged, prewashed salad mixes made their debut in the 1990s. Look in any large grocery store and notice how much space is devoted to salad mixes versus heads of lettuce. Changes in shelf space are good indicators of changes in American shopping habits. Another development in the twentieth century was the increase in snack food space. What once occupied a back corner of the store now has a whole aisle. Other changes are a wider variety of foods from other cultures and a greater variety of fruits and vegetables.

## Today's Practices and Habits

What are Americans eating and drinking today? Figure 8.1 shows the daily beverage consumption of Americans. Water is the highest category followed by coffee and bottled water then soft drinks and milk and on down the list. Probably most surprising in recent years is the explosive growth of sales in bottled water. This

TV dinners and a pot pie. Which would you select? (Courtesy of Getty Images, Image Bank.)

may seem like a new phenomenon, but water has been bottled and sold far from its source for thousands of years. *The Food and Drug Administration (FDA) regulates bottled water products* that are sold interstate under the Federal Food, Drug, and Cosmetic Act. Under this act, manufacturers are responsible for producing safe, wholesome, and truthfully labeled food products, including bottled water products (Buller, 2002). Box 8.1 gives the FDA classifications of bottled water.

Food and beverage choices and practices constantly change for individuals, families, households, communities, and nations. A good example of this is that carrying individually sized bottled water was a rarity until the 1990s in the United States. People decide what to eat to drink and when and where. Their choices are determined by:

- Personal preferences, tastes
- Habit
- Background, ethnicity, heritage, history
- Convenience, availability, location

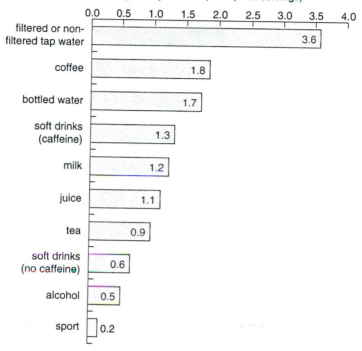

Source: International Bottled Water Association

**Figure 8.1**    What Americans Are Drinking. (Courtesy of International Bottles Water Association.)

---

**BOX 8.1    FDA Classifications of Bottled Water According to Its Origin.**

Artesian well water: Water from a well that taps an aquifer—layers of porous rock, sand, and earth that contain water. According to the EPA, water from artesian aquifers is often more pure.

Mineral water: Water from an underground source that contains at least 250 parts per million total dissolved solids. Minerals and trace elements must come from the source, not added later.

Spring water: Derived from an underground formation from which water flows naturally to the earth's surface.

Well water: Water from a hole bored or drilled into the ground, which taps into an aquifer.

In addition:

Tap water: Comes from municipal sources, usually treated.

Sparking water, seltzer water, soda water, tonic water, and club soda are not included as bottled water under the FDA's regulation; historically these have been considered soft drinks.

- Emotions (i.e., comfort foods, positive and negative associations)
- Values (i.e., religion, vegetarian, fresh vs. prepared)
- Cost (i.e., hamburger versus steak)
- Body image
- Nutrition and health benefits
- Innovation and marketing

As an example coffee consumption fell 50 percent over four decades until Starbucks Corp. made a brand out of a commodity. Coffee consumption has inched upward since 1995 (Killman, 2002). Another example of a food with a consumption history is chocolate. A nineteenth-century gourmet, Jean-Anthelme Brillat-Savarin, said that Spanish ladies in the New World were so enamored with hot chocolate, they sometimes had it brought to them in church. Chocolate consumption has been rising steadily in the United States. In 2000 total U.S. chocolate consumption rose to 3.3 billion pounds, up almost 7 percent from 3.1 billion pounds in 1996 which amounts to almost 12 pounds for every man, woman, and child (Constant Cravings, 2002). Other items increasingly consumed are salty snacks like chips, popcorn, and pretzels. According to a report released by Chicago-based Mintel Consumer Intelligence, 17 percent of Americans report they "can't help snacking on salty snacks" (Junk-Food Nation, 2001).

Different colors and taste combinations keep being developed. H. J. Heinz Co. introduced an Ore-Ida line extension called Funky Fries. The kid-oriented product found in the freezer section of grocery stores has new colors and flavors, including Cocoa Crispers, chocolate fries. This is on the heels of the success of neon-colored ketchup by the same company.

Unusual uses for foods also are on the horizon. Four football players at Sacramento State applied ConAgra Food's Pam nonstick cooking spray to one another during a game with the University of Montana. They lost the game, but the Big Sky Conference launched an investigation into the "slippery actions of the players."

Waiting for seasons for fruits and vegetables is a thing of the past. We get apples, grapes, and lettuce year round. When it is winter in the United States, it is summer in New Zealand and Chile. With transportation and shipping advances anything can be brought to market.

## Spending on Food

In the typical family's budget, the most expensive monthly item is housing, followed by transportation and then food. Low-income families spend a higher proportion on food than high-income families. So, *rising food prices hit low-income families harder than high-income families.* According to the USDA, food expenses consist of food and nonalcoholic beverages purchased at grocery, convenience, and specialty stores, including purchases with food stamps, dining at restaurants, and household expenditures on school meals. Consumer spending on food dropped 10 percent between 1990 and 2000 (Weiss, 2002). The Food Marketing Institute says that is because there are a lot more places to buy food so that means competitive pricing. But it is more complicated than that, for example, items such as health care are taking a larger share of the family income.

Those under the age of 25 spend more on fresh fruit than other age groups. Across the whole population, in the decade from 1990 to 2000, spending went up for poultry, fish, and seafood and down for beef, eggs, and dairy. Think of the appearance of sushi display counters in grocery stores in the 1990s; they weren't there in the 1980s. Beef consumption has been declining over the last 25 years, but the fresh meat counter is still a major money maker for grocery stores ringing in over $60 billion in sales each year (Kilman, 2002). New attempts are being made to remarket beef as precooked microwaveable roasts. In 2001, 474 new beef products were launched compared with 70 in 1997 (Kilman, 2002).

Over the next decade, the probable trends are

1. More convenience.
2. More healthy foods.
3. Smaller packages for smaller households.
4. More flavor. Watch for words like "zesty" and "spicy."
5. Increased safety.
6. More ethnic foods and regional distinctions, especially watch for more Hispanic foods.

## THE FOOD GUIDE PYRAMID CONTROVERSY

*The Food Guide Pyramid* (see Figure 8.2) *developed by the USDA is a graph depicting the recommended daily food guide.* It is controversial, and as this book went to press revisions of it were being discussed. The question is what to emphasize. In the 2003 version the emphasis was on grains, cereals, vegetables, and fruits. It assumed that people were meat eaters and dairy product eaters and that they don't drink alcohol. Naturally, people have to adapt the pyramid to their own food preferences, and many people (consumers, physicians, diet book authors, nutritionists) are critical of the pyramid. Revisions to it are constantly being considered. The pyramid was developed to help people choose a balanced, varied, and healthful diet. Studies have shown that people underestimate how much they eat of certain foods and overestimate others. The most commonly neglected areas are the fruit, milk, and bread groups with the most likely overindulgence at the tip—the fats, sweets, and oils (Whitney and Rolfes, 2002). Also be aware that serving sizes on the pyramid may not match serving sizes on labels. Lastly, many foods are not pure types, meaning much of what we eat falls into several categories such as the ingredients in a tuna salad sandwich or a burrito. This makes it a little harder to determine what levels in the pyramid are being met.

The Food Guide Pyramid provides a basis to build a healthy diet, but each population group faces unique challenges such as women, men, children and teenagers, college students, older adults, athletes, and people with special health concerns such as high blood pressure or diabetes. It takes a little planning, common sense, and a lot of information, including label reading, to find the right combination for individuals and their life stages.

## THE CROSSOVER BETWEEN FOOD AND DRUGS

We used to know what a food was and what was a drug, but that difference is blurring. Fresh fruits and vegetables are most likely to still be classified as foods, but what about a "healthy" flaked cereal which is a grain product that has been

# Food Guide Pyramid
## A Guide to Daily Food Choices

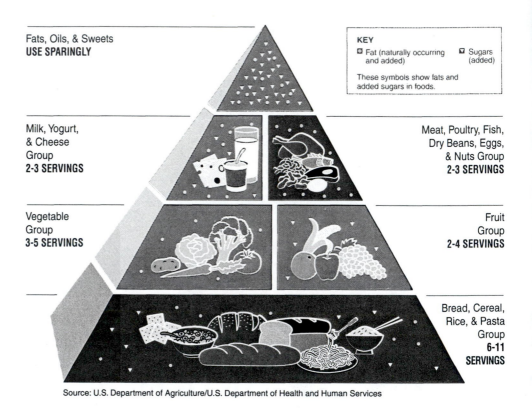

Source: U.S. Department of Agriculture/U.S. Department of Health and Human Services

**Figure 8.2** The Food Guide Pyramid. The base shows that bread, cereal, rice, and pasta deserve the most emphasis in the diet. Fats, oils, and sweets at the top deserve the least emphasis in the diet. (Courtesy of U.S. Department of Agriculture and Department of Health and Human Services.)

sprayed with vitamins or a prepackaged frozen lasagna with over 40 ingredients—many with lengthy chemical names on the label? Foods that have additives and supplements are more expensive and may fall somewhere between being a food and a drug. Manufacturers say that foods have been engineered to promote health, and if the alternative is rapid spoilage or fewer nutrients, they have a point. But consumers are very much on their own to determine, for example, if a candy bar full of sugar and fat is healthy because it also contains herbs.

## LABELS

Labels provide information about nutrient content and compare similar foods. They are useful up to a point. They do not tell the amounts in products, they simply give a list. The first item on the list is the one with the highest amount so that in a candy bar if the first ingredient listed is sugar then sugar is the leading ingredient, but the consumer will not know if it makes up 80 percent or 20 percent of the product. In soft drinks, the first ingredient is water. Consumer advocacy groups, weight-loss groups, and those suffering from certain diseases have been asking for years that amounts be put on labels, but manufacturers insist they have the right to have "secret formulas" or recipes and that lengthy labels are impractical and ultimately costly to the consumer.

The labels on food products should show the quantities per serving in the following easy to read format:

- Total food energy (kcalories)
- Food energy from fat (kcalories)
- Total fat (grams)
- Saturated fat (grams)
- Cholesterol (milligrams)
- Sodium (milligrams)
- Total carbohydrate, including starch, sugar, and fiber (grams)
- Dietary fiber (grams)
- Sugars (grams)
- Protein (grams)

Also, labels must present vitamin A, vitamin C, iron, and calcium information. Sometimes, the manufacturer chooses to add other nutrient content information. To encourage consumers to read labels, various campaigns have been launched through alliances with the food industry, government agency, consumer advocacy groups, and educational and health organizations. Notice that some foods such as fresh fruits and vegetables do not have labels. Part of this is practicality, it does not make sense to have a tiny label on every cherry or grape.

Can all labels be believed? No, is the answer. When nutrition experts heard about a product called Poi English Muffins that had only 70 calories each, about half the amount in other standard size brands, they did some testing. The muffins had taro root, a Hawaiian delicacy. Weight-loss magazines raved about the muffins as a speedy, low-calorie breakfast. The Good Housekeeping Institute sent two bags to an independent laboratory. The report came back that each muffin actually contained 160 calories and 30 grams of carbohydrates equivalent to two slices of bread (Low-Cal Muffins: Too Good to be True? 2001). The Poi English Muffins were definitely not a weight-loss food and should not be marketed as such.

## ACTIVITY, DIET, AND EATING

Dr. William Dietz of the Centers for Disease Control and Prevention says we should opt for smaller portions, turn off the TV, walk rather than drive, don't make cleaning the plate a requirement for kids, and if a child refuses a healthy meal, it's not up to the parents to prepare something else. The thinking here is that a hungry child learns to eat what is served; if they are not hungry, they should not be forced to eat.

About 27 percent of the American population is obese, and the percentage has more than doubled in the last 40 years. Obesity is the number two cause of preventable death in the United States (after smoking) and accounts for almost 10 percent of the money spent on health care. Some people blame the growing preference for fast food and snacking, but as Dietz mentions there is more to it than that. The solution in source after source is that it is not just about food, as inactivity and cultural practices play a part. As the next section points out, some are questioning the wisdom of our practices and preferences.

# FAST FOOD

About 14 percent of Americans consume a diet comprised almost entirely of fast food.

Fast food became in vogue in the twentieth century because of the frantic pace of life, multiple roles, and the need to pick up a quick meal. Today, about 50 percent of Americans visit a fast food restaurant each month and 30 percent go six to ten times (Addicted to Grease, 2002). It is estimated that about 14 percent of Americans consume a diet comprised almost entirely of fast food. The ones most likely to say this are between ages of 18 to 24 (Junk-Food Nation, 2001).

The term "fast food," popularized in the 1960s in the United States, referred to something quite specific—the preparation and service of hamburgers, french fries, milk shakes, fried chicken, and pizza at a chain restaurant where people order their meals from a cashier who sets the prepackaged order on a tray with a regimented, almost robotic quickness that send the customer on his or her way without further to-do (Mariani, 1991). The McDonald brothers led the way by firing carhops, cutting their 25-item menu to nine, minimizing the number of employees, getting rid of china and metal flatware, and passing their savings on to customers (Mariani, 1991). McDonald's hamburgers sold for 15 cents, french fries for ten cents, and milk shakes for 20 cents in the late 1940s and early 1950s. The first McDonald's with the trademark arches opened in 1953 in Phoenix, Arizona. In 1961, Ray Kroc bought out the McDonald brothers for $2.7 million and expanded the business, experimenting with drive-through windows that are the staple of many fast food restaurants today (Mariani, 1991).

> There is no question that McDonald's led the charge for fast food and that all other competitors—even those that had been in business before McDonald's—followed that lead. . . . There were fast-rising Mexican restaurants like Taco Bell of Irvine, California, and Chi'Chi's (Louisville), roast beef and steak restaurants like Arby's (Atlanta), Roy Rogers (Bethesda, Maryland), and Ponderosa (Dayton, Ohio), and pizzerias, which in the 1980s registered astounding growth, led by Pizza Hut (Wichita, Kansas), Little Caesar's (Farmington Hills, Michigan), Godfather's (Omaha), and Domino's (Ann Arbor, Michigan), whose selling point was the delivery of its pizzas to the customer's doors. And there were fried chicken restaurants like Bojangles (Charlotte, North Carolina), Popeye's (Jefferson, Washington), Church's (San Antonio), and the granddaddy of them all, Kentucky Fried Chicken." (Mariani, 1991, p. 172)

The cities of origin or headquarters are given to show how the fast food movement is spread across the United States; there is no one place or one corporation who owns it all. Also it is curious to see how Western-sounding restaurant names like Roy Rogers or Ponderosa are headquartered in the East and Midwest.

Coming back to the cultural changes that led to the popularity of fast food, Roxburgh (2002) found that high time pressures are related to the number of roles consumers occupied. In answer to the question "Who are the time pressured?" she found in a study of 734 full-time workers that they were the affluent, parents, caregivers, and those with high demands, low-control jobs. She concluded that time pressure is experienced by both men and women. Regarding home-related activities, Haas (1999) found that women spend more time than men engaged in activities considered traditionally female such as meal preparation, dishwashing, laundry, housecleaning, and grocery shopping while men spend their time in traditionally male activities such as minor household repairs, bill-paying, gardening, and car repairs.

## THE SLOW FOOD MOVEMENT

Social commentators have argued that life has accelerated as part of capitalism and the relentless pursuit of consumer goods to the point that the true pleasures of life, such as fine dining, have been all but ignored (Schor, 1992). Overloaded schedules and being busy have become cultural ideals that symbolize economic and social success (Daly, 1996; Hochschild, 1989).

In the twenty-first century people around the world began to question the value of this increased pace. The slow food movement started in Italy (now it is worldwide) as a way to defend endangered local foods and, as the name implies, it serves as a counterpoint to the trend toward mass produced fast foods and the range of foods offered in modern supermarkets. Slow food advocates favor local cheeses, wines, and meat products such as sausages and disdain the commercial overprocessing that is commonly done for shipping and storing purposes. Fresh is the emphasis, genetically modified food is reviled. The movement embraces organic methods of agriculture to produce foods more slowly even though it may cost more to do so. Many hail it as a return to taste and regional differences. *The slow movement supports authentic regional cuisine and the turning away from generic international cuisine.* Guides for tourists are published indicating local wines, restaurants, and food stores. The headquarters of the slow food movement is in Italy, and their Web site is *www.slowfood.com.*

The slow food movement can also be called the "buy local" movement. They both inspire consumers to get more of their food from local sources and resist an increasingly globalized agriculture industry. For example, a study by the Leopold Center for Sustainable Agriculture found that grapes make an average trek of 2,143 miles before arriving on Americans' plates. Produce shipped such long distances can lose freshness and flavor along the way, and there are also concerns about the environmental costs (electricity for cooling, gasoline for transportation). Driving the system is consumers' demand for a consistent marketplace where locally or even nationally out-of-season fruit is available year round. This is possible with worldwide growing and shipping.

## ORGANICALLY GROWN FOODS

Foods with the word organic on the label account for a $9.3 billion industry (de Lisser, 2002). The world's largest retailer of natural and organic foods with over 140 stores in the U.S. is Whole Foods Markets, based in Austin, TX. It is a growing company which is publicly traded on NASDAQ under the symbol WFMI.

The more accurate term is organically grown food, but often the word organic is used for simplicity's sake. **Organically grown foods** *are crops grown and processed according to USDA regulations.* Many of the foods have gone mainstream and are sold not only at a separate store such as Whole Foods Markets but also at the more conventional grocery chains such as Kroger, Albertson's, and Publix which have had organically grown sections for years. The recent trend is to offer organically grown throughout the store. For example, an advertisement for Publix promoted their "greenwise market" and a "naturally tasty night" complete with tastings and natural/organic foods gift basket door prizes. The copy on the ad read

> Publix knows you're trying to live healthier. By eating natural and organic foods. Using products that are environmentally sound. And taking a more wholesome approach to raising your family. Now we've made it easy, with our extensive selection of quality health products—in Produce and in Frozen Foods, on our Grocery aisles and in our Dairy case, in our Deli and our Seafood departments. If you know what's good for you—and especially if you don't—join us for our naturally tasty night, Thursday, January 16, 4 until 7 P.M. (*Tallahasee Democrat,* January 12, 2003 insert)

Manufacturers of conventional foods also sell organically grown versions. For example, Heinz sells an organic ketchup.

Why would someone choose organically grown foods? The main reasons are

1. improved taste
2. to avoid artificial ingredients (this includes synthetic colors and flavors)
3. to reduce "bad" foods from a diet (artery-clogging partially hydrogenated oils are not allowed in organic food)
4. to limit exposure to pesticides
5. to be more environmentally friendly

Under the USDA rules, organically grown produce cannot be treated with synthetic pesticides. But, this does not mean that organically grown foods are pesticide free because chemicals linger in the soil and the air. This can happen if an organic farm is next to a conventional farm that uses pesticides. One study found organically grown foods contain a third of the residues present on conventional produce. Another reason some consumers prefer organically grown foods is to protect the environment. Organically grown foods reduce spraying, water contamination, improve soil quality, and enhance wildlife habitats.

Many consumers are willing to pay more for organically grown foods. These foods typically cost 15 to 50 percent more than nonorganic. The potential for additional profit make them attractive to manufacturers, farmers, and grocery store owners. Examples of price comparisons between organic and conventional foods are given in Table 8.1. Why do consumers pay more for organically grown foods? The main answers have already been suggested, but in the end it comes down to individual choice. Cheryl Rezendes Rulewich became a big believer in organic foods when her five-year-old son's food allergies cleared up when she switched him to an organic diet (de Liser, 2002). She also believes organic foods are healthier and taste better for the whole family. "Conventional fruit and vegetables with their bright colors and waxy, unblemished surfaces, look unnatural to her eyes. 'They look like Play-Doh food,' she says" (de Lisser, 2002, p. D4). Not everyone would agree so the debate continues as to whether organic foods are truly healthier or even preferred given the greater price. "Nelda Mercer, a registered dietitian

**Table 8.1**   Organically Grown vs. Conventional Prices

|  | **Organically Grown** | **Conventional** |
|---|---|---|
| *Atlanta* | Whole Foods Market | Publix |
| Lettuce | $1.69 | $1.29 |
| Cottage cheese, 16 oz | $2.99 | $1.59 |
| Chicken | $2.09 per pound | $0.79 per pound |
| *Burlingame, CA* | Mollie Stone's | Safeway |
| Celery | $0.99 | $0.69 |
| Dozen Eggs | $3.78 | $2.19 |
| Whole Chicken | $2.99 per pound | $1.29 per pound |
| *New York City* | Perelandra Natural Food Center | Key Food |
| Lettuce | $1.69 | $0.99 |
| Gallon of milk | $4.99 | $2.69 |
| Steak, 8 oz. | $9.59 per pound | $7.89 per pound |

*Source:* Adapted from de Lisser, E. (August 20, 2002). Is that $5 gallon of milk really organic? *Wall Street Journal,* p. D4.

and spokeswoman for the American Dietetic Association, says there is no scientific evidence showing that organically produced foods are nutritionally better than their conventional counterparts" (de Lisser, 2002, p. D4).

USDA regulations define the use of synthetic fertilizers, herbicides, insecticides, fungicides, preservatives, and other chemical ingredients. Organic products cannot have been irradiated, genetically engineered, or grown with fertilizer made from sewer sludge (Whitney and Rolfes, 2002). Dairy and meat products may be called organic if the livestock have been raised according to USDA regulations. These regulations include grazing conditions and the use of organic feed, hormones, and antibiotics.

Foods that have met USDA standards may have a seal on their label. To get the green and white Department of Agriculture seal, a product must be at least 95 percent organic. Examples of products with the seal are fruits and vegetables and cereals that are 100 percent organic. If a product is at least 70 percent organic, the label can say, for example, "made with organic corn." Another label designation is contains "organic ingredients," which means that less than 70 percent of the product is organic. In this latter case, the word "organic" cannot be used on the front of the package. The manufacturer can list organic ingredients on the back.

Implied in the marketing of organically grown foods is that they are healthier than foods grown by conventional methods. This may or may not be the case. There are advantages and disadvantages to both, and consumers have to ask questions about pesticide and fertilizer use and other conditions. These can be difficult questions because the use of fewer chemicals is inherently appealing, but pesticides if used properly can yield more crops. If pesticides are used improperly they can be hazardous to human health. Organic fertilizers such as unprocessed animal manure can have ill effects. In the home, consumers can remove and reduce pesticide residues by peeling fruits and vegetables and washing fresh produce in warm water, using a scrub brush, and rinsing thoroughly. Further information can be obtained 24–7 from the EPA's National Pesticide Hotline at 800 858-PEST.

**Figure 8.3**    The USDA Organic seal tells consumers that a product is at least 95 percent organic. Organic food differs from conventionally produced food in the way it is grown, handled, and processed. (Courtesy of the U.S. Department of Agriculture and Department of Health and Human Services.)

## GENETICALLY ALTERED FOODS

One of the hottest controversies worldwide is the topic of genetically altered foods. Some consumers feel uneasy about the possible risks associated with genetically engineered foods, and others don't see the problem because foods have always been altered genetically either by nature or by man. "One theory of the origins of agriculture holds that domesticated plants first emerged on dump heaps, where the discarded seeds of the wild plants that people gathered and ate—already unconsciously selected for sweetness or size or power—took root, flourished, and eventually hybridized. In time people gave the best of these hybrids a place in the garden, and there, together, the people and the plants embarked on a series of experiments in co-evolution that would change them both forever" (Pollan, 2001, p. 186).

**Genetic engineering** is defined as the use of biotechnology to modify the genetic material of living cells so that they will produce new substances or perform new functions (Whitney and Rolfes, 2002). One of the first foods to be genetically engineered was the tomato introduced into the market in 1994. Prior to this development tomatoes did not last long on the shelf and being somewhat fragile many did not make it to market. More recently, experiments have been made on potatoes. "NewLeaf" is the name of a genetically engineered potato by the Monsanto Corporation (Pollan, 2001). This potato produces its own insecticide. What might the future hold? Possibilities include potatoes genetically modified to absorb less fat when fried, corn that can withstand drought, lawns that don't ever have to be mowed, "golden rice" rich in Vitamin A, and bananas that deliver vaccines (Pollan, 2001). **Biotechnology** is the use of biological systems or organisms to create or modify products. Examples of biotechnology is the use of bacteria to make yogurt, of yeast to make beer, and of cross-breeding to enhance crop production (Whitney and Rolfes, 2002). Plant engineering, a type of biotechnology, is being conducted worldwide. China's bioengineers have worked with more than 50 species of plants—adding genes for traits such as resistance to viruses and insects to everything from peanuts to papayas. As a consequence, they are reporting major fiscal and public health gains (The Shape of Biotech to Come, 2002, p. 130).

The reason that the controversy has heated up in recent years is that the twenty-first century has brought very rapid advances in agriculture and food production, and the public is more aware than ever before about these dramatic changes. Through genetic engineering scientists can introduce a copy of a specific gene that will produce a desired trait, their goal would be to improve crops or livestock. So the process has been speeded up, and this speed worries some people; it does not feel "natural." It is tampering with nature although others would argue that ever since crop rotation, selective breeding, and grafting that nature has been tampered with. The beginnings of agriculture and food production can be traced to before 8000 B.C. in Southwest Asia (the Fertile Crescent) and soon spread to Europe and North Africa (Diamond, 1999). But there is no question that genetic engineering is speeding up the changes in how farmers farm and how foods and drugs are processed. On the plus side genetic engineering improves the nutrient composition of foods, shelf life, can mean less use of pesticides, and makes land more usable. In terms of government control, much of the approval responsibility falls to the FDA, EPA, and the USDA.

Consumer advocacy groups want genetically altered foods labeled as such so consumers can know what they are buying. The problem with this is what to say and how much to say. In recent years, some foods have been pulled from the market when the public felt misled regarding contents. This dispute is not settled yet. For the most part, the scientific community (and this includes the FDA) contends that biotechnology can deliver a safe and better food supply and needs to continue. They contend that genetically altered food will serve more people and reduce hunger around the world. Today, one person in every five in the world suffers from persistent hunger and tens of thousands die everyday from starvation (Whitney and Rolfes, 2002). For more "pro" information, go to the USDA Biotechnology Information Center at *www.nal.usda.gov/bic*. For "con" points of view, go to Greenpeace at *www.greenpeaceusa.org* or *www.ucsusa.org*. According to Whitney and Rolfes (2002), the cons include worry about the

1. Disruption of the natural ecosystems
2. Introduction of diseases, newly created viruses
3. Creation of biological weapons
4. Ethical concerns, including furthering the gap between the haves and the have nots

## IRRADIATED FOODS

"**Food irradiation** is the treatment of foods with gamma rays, X-rays, or high-voltage electronics to kill potentially harmful pathogens, including bacteria, parasites, insects, and fungi that cause food-borne illness. It also reduces spoilage and extends shelf" (Insel and Roth, 2002, p. 348). For example, irradiated strawberries can last unspoiled in the refrigerator for up to three weeks versus the usual three to five days for untreated berries. Lengthening the shelf life of products has great value for grocers and ultimately consumers because it cuts down on the amount of food thrown out. Irradiated foods are very useful in situations such as camping, space exploration, and military operations when people are away from fresh sources of food for long periods of time. Since 1963, the government has allowed certain foods to be irradiated, starting with wheat and flour and now including fruits, poultry, herbs, vegetables, and meats. Irradiation is also used on contact lenses, medical supplies, teething rings, milk cartons, and plastic wrap. Although irradiation has been endorsed by the Centers for Disease Control and Prevention, the American Medical Association, and the World Health Organization, the general consuming public is skeptical. The concerns, legitimate or not, include that:

- Essential nutrients may be destroyed.
- Eating irradiated foods cause cancers or other ill effects.
- Employees exposed to irradiation or who live near factories that use irradiation will be hurt.
- Foods treated with irradiation taste different or odd.

The bottom line is that the foods are tampered with, and many consumers feel this is unnatural. Irradiated spices or ingredients embedded in complex products do not have to be labeled as irradiated. But primary goods such as fruits, vegetables, and meats that have been irradiated should carry a flowerlike radura symbol and a brief information label. Studies show that when consumers are given information about irradiation and its benefits, most want to try the foods (Insel and Roth, 2002).

## FOOD ADDITIVES

**Additives** are substances added to food either intentionally or by accident. Examples of "by accident" are bits of conveyer belts and packaging, soil, feathers, rocks, pesticide residues, or insects that can fall into products while in storage or processing. If, for example, rocks in food sounds absurd, notice the packaging on dry split peas or beans, often it will say to sort and rinse before use looking out for rocks and stones. Since rocks and stones can look and weigh very much like beans no machine can completely sort them out, the consumer must do this before making split pea or bean soup or forget the whole thing and buy already prepared or canned soups.

"Today, *some 2800 substances are intentionally added to foods* for one or more of the following reasons: (1) to maintain or improve nutritional quality, (2) to maintain freshness, (3) to help in processing or preparation, or (4) to alter taste or appearance" (Insel and Roth, 2002, p. 348). They make up less than 1 percent of our food. Most additives are preservatives that help prevent spoilage; others make food taste or look better.

**Preservatives** are antimicrobial agents, antioxidants, and other additives that retard spoilage or maintain desired qualities, such as softness in baked goods (Whitney and Rolfes, 2002). Regarding appearance, think of the colors in M&M candies—they are color additives that make the candy look better. Color is also added to margarine, cheeses, pastas, soft drinks, and baked goods. Nutrient additives include iodine in salt, Vitamins A and D in milk, calcium and Vitamin C in fruit juices, and thiamin in bread.

**Figure 8.4**  The flowerlike radura symbol signifies irradiated. (Courtesy of U.S. Department of Agriculture Food Safety and Inspection Services.)

Additives are approved by the FDA; the manufacturer has to show that the additives are effective (does what they are supposed to do), detectable and measurable in the final product, and safe. Additives have initial and periodic re-reviews. Regarding safety, the risk of cancer is not tolerated. The **Delaney Clause** (a clause in the Food Additive Amendment to the Food, Drug, and Cosmetic Act) states that no substance that is known to cause cancer in animals or human beings at any dose level shall be added to foods. This is a tough clause that has been difficult over time to administer. A case in point is the popular artificial sweetener saccharin. When tests in the 1970s revealed a possible cancer hazard in animal tests that led to talk of removing it from the market, there was a public outcry, and it is still on the market. The key problem is the phrase "at any dose level" because it has been shown in animal testing that huge amounts of a single additive may prove harmful, but very few people would drink, for example, 50 cups of coffee a day with saccharin in it. Instead of zero-risk, a more likely standard that the FDA uses is "negligible-risk" or minimal risk.

The food additives that have long been in use and are believed to be safe are on the **GRAS List** which stands for "generally recognized as safe." Examples are sugar, salt, and herbs.

## CALORIES, WEIGHT, AND DIETS

**Calories** are units by which energy is measured. Food energy is measured in kilocalories (1,000 calories equal 1 kilocalorie) abbreviated kcalories or more simply kcal. You can lose weight by eating fewer calories and increasing physical activity. Just because a product is fat-free does not mean it is calorie-free because it can be loaded with sugar and other sweeteners. There is also a tendency to eat more of a food that is low-fat or fat-free thinking this will save calories, but if the portion size is larger than normal, any potential calorie savings may be lost.

The surgeon general says that only one in five U.S. adults gets the recommended amount of physical activity. Thirty minutes on most days is recommended for various health reasons. Overweight and inactivity affects the rate of coronary heat disease and increases the risk of developing diabetes, hypertension, and colon cancer. About 30 to 40 percent of U.S. women and 20–30 percent of men consider themselves overweight, and about 5 percent of U.S. adults are underweight.

The market for weight-loss diets and books is estimated at $33 billion a year in the United States (Whitney and Rolfes, 2002). There is no doubt that some diets will provide short-term weight loss but improved health and long-term weight loss and maintenance of a preferred weight are rarer. Common fad diet claims to watch out for include

- You can lose weight by eating only at certain times of the day.
- Certain combinations of foods will help you lose weight.
- Diets that energize the brain.
- Products that will rewire your genetic code.
- Surefire remedies.
- Millions of people have been successful at permanent weight loss using this plan.

Also consumers should beware of programs that insist on large sums of money up front. Regarding the role of genetics, genes may not cause obesity, but genetic factors may influence the food intake and activity patterns that lead to it and the metabolic pathways that maintain it (Heitmann et al., 1997). Studies have shown that adopted children tend to be similar in weight to their biological parents, not to their adoptive parents. In experiments it has been shown that some people gain more weight than others even given the same energy intakes. Clearly, genes play a role in gaining and losing weight, but what can be done about this is still under investigation.

Although health and weight are linked, there are healthy overweight people and unhealthy normal-weight people. "The challenge for preventative medicine experts: getting people to focus on feeling better rather than looking thinner. . . . It likely will take years to dispel the myth that thin equals fit, and fat unfit. But there are signs of change. A 5-year old maker of fitness apparel for plus-size women, A Big Attitude, is posting double-digit growth" (Helliker, 2002, p. B1). Just as there is a slow food movement and an antigenetic food engineering movement, there is also a movement that is antidieting and weight fixation. Many hope for the day when our society can accept people of all shapes and sizes. Related to this is the concern about eating disorders that occur when dieting to lose weight progresses to a dangerous point.

To protect consumers, many states have adopted consumer bills of rights about weight-loss programs and products and have investigated cases of fraud. Most recently herbal remedies have come under attack.

## FEDERAL TRADE COMMISSION STEPS UP THE FIGHT AGAINST MIRACLE WEIGHT-LOSS PRODUCTS

The FTC in a study analyzed 300 ads for products and services that promised quick fixes for shedding weight and found more than half featured at least one claim that was very likely to be false or lacked adequate proof. Howard Beales III, director of the FTC's Bureau of Consumer Protection, said, " 'Lose weight while you sleep,' or 'Exercise in a bottle,' are claims that editors and publishers ought to be able to recognize as problematic. . . . Most newspapers don't run pornographic ads and it's not by accident. It's because they looked. That same level of looking should iden-

**Consumer Alert    Avoid "Fad" Diets and Magic Pills**

Examples of fad diets are those involving one particular food or type of food. The food may be cabbage or grapefruit or a group of foods, such as eating a high-protein diet. Although there is initial weight loss, these are hard diets to maintain for a lifetime, and there are potential negative health effects to concentrating on only one food or type of food for long periods of time.

So-called magic pills are to be avoided, but the FDA has approved prescription drugs that may help obese people who have difficulty losing weight through diet and exercise alone. Before trying any radical diet or medicine for weight reduction, a person should contact his or her doctor to discuss treatment, options, and possible side effects.

---

**Consumer Alert    Quackery and Communication**

The days when a wagon would wheel into town and the huckster would get up on the top and extol the virtues of his new food, miracle drink, or cooking device to anyone who would listen are long gone. In its place are other forms of misinformation and un-proven products: the Internet, glossy magazine advertisements and articles, "health" magazines, television infomercials, in-home sales, and so on. The Internet is a particu-lar problem because in many countries of the world there are few if any controls on what is sold and advertised in terms of health-related products. More than ever, re-member the words "may the buyer beware."

---

tify the kinds of [weight loss] claims that are clearly not true" (December, 2002, D7). In a magazine directed to the elderly, weight loss claims included foods that make you sleep sounder (if you are not awake, you can't eat). As a counterpoint to this argument, publishers and broadcasters would say that it is difficult to verify ad-vertisements. Newspapers and TV stations do not have scientific laboratories to con-duct experiments on advertised products.

There is also the question of profit incentives. Full-page ads for weight-loss products bring in a lot of revenue to magazines and newspapers as do infomercials on television. Publishers and broadcasters also hesitate to compromise freedom of speech. They think they have the right to run ads with the idea that the reader or viewer will be smart enough to read between the lines. The FTC is intent on pro-moting stricter media self-policing of obvious fraudulent claims.

Where are these ads placed? The FTC found fraudulent ads in broadcast and cable television, infomercials, radio, magazines, newspapers, supermarket tabloids, direct mail, commercial e-mail, and Web sites. When they compared current ads with ones from a decade earlier, they found weight loss ads not only appeared more frequently, but they also promoted 159 percent more products and carried a dramatically different tone. Box 8.2 shows some of the common advertising claims used by weight-loss ads.

As this book went to press, the FTC was considering holding media liable for disseminating products' false claims. This includes cable channels, newspapers, and magazines that run diet and health ads making dubious claims. The FTC could sue the media outlets for carrying the ads. From a legal standpoint there is prece-dence since regulators have used the argument that certain advertising has harmful effects such as in liquor, tobacco, and gambling ads. The FTC has gone after fraud-ulent marketers and manufacturers before. Some media outlets have said it is easier to determine what is wrong in liquor, tobacco, and gambling ads than it is in food and beverage ads—what is misleading and what isn't and that copyeditors are not trained in nutritional analysis.

## FOOD-BORNE DISEASES

It used to be when people got sick from tainted food it was difficult to trace the source. Although it is not foolproof, DNA analysis (genetic testing) is an objective way to link each sick person with a particular food or product. For example, the

---

**BOX 8.2     Questionable Ad Claims for Weight Loss**

Common advertising claims and techniques used by weight-loss ads. Here is a list of the FTC's examples of questionable ad claims:

"The fastest all-natural diet known for rapid weight loss without a prescription!"
"Amazing fat-fighting diet pill produces an extremely fast weight loss . . . even if you cheat or refuse to diet."
"It can make a delicious, juicy hamburger as low in fat as a lean turkey sandwich."
"Major weight loss breakthrough: New carb-killer lets you cheat and eat like crazy and still get skinny lightning fast!"
"Our amazing 'Herbal Bullet' blasts fat and flushes it out of your body!"

---

CDC found that a 68-year-old woman's death was caused by a strain of *E. coli* bacteria with a DNA fingerprint that matched a strain found 1,300 miles away at a meat-processing plant. Tainted ground beef was probably the culprit. "For epidemiologists, the genetic match was a powerful illustration of the role DNA fingerprinting can play in food safety and public health. Plaintiffs' lawyers, meanwhile, say the technique has become a formidable legal weapon in product-liability cases against food companies. The number of lawsuits stemming from food-borne illnesses is small, but the implications of using genetic fingerprinting are huge" (Abboud, 2003, p. B1). If an attorney can prove that a person became seriously ill or died from a food and the source is known, the only question is how much the settlement should be. Consumers will benefit because the food-industry will be even more aware than usual of the importance of food safety.

*A totally risk-free food supply is a goal to shoot for, but the reality is that the most that can be hoped for is increased risk-reduction.* Canned and packaged goods sold in grocery stores are largely controlled, and sources of problems can be traced through codes. Accidents occur, for example, when contaminated foods make their way to market or when seals or packages are broken, intentionally or unintentionally. Consumers should report any concerns they have immediately to the store where purchased and to the toll-free consumer complaint numbers on the package or can. Everyone from producers to suppliers to consumers—especially parents—should be involved in maintaining a safe food supply.

Food-borne diseases can cause illness or even death. *The estimates are that per year there are 76 million illnesses, 325,000 hospitalizations, and 5,200 deaths in the United States annually from food-borne illnesses* (Landro, 2002). Especially at risk are infants and small children and the elderly. The FDA's Food Safety and Applied Nutrition site (*www.cfsan.fda.gov*) has information on everything from the risk of bacterial infections from eating raw spouts to how to spot spoiled seafood. The other government Web sites and nutrition information groups listed in the E-Resources provide further information and warnings. The bugs to look out for according to the Partnership for Food Safety Education are

- Botulism caused by botulinum toxin. Found in canned goods and luncheon meats.
- Campylobacteriosis caused by *Campylobacter jejuni*. Found in meat, raw poultry, and unpasteurized milk.

- Listeriosis caused by *Listeria monocytogenes*. Found in cold cuts, seafood, and unpasteurized milk.
- Perfringens food poisoning caused by *Clostridium perfingens*. Found in foods not kept properly hot.
- Salmonellosis caused by salmonella bacteria. Found in raw meats, dairy products, shrimp, and poultry.
- Shigellosis (bacillary dysentery) caused by shigella bacteria. Found in milk and dairy products, poultry, and potato salad. The food becomes contaminated when hands aren't washed.
- Giardiasis caused by *Giardia lamblia*. Found mostly in contaminated water.
- Hepatitis A caused by hepatitis A virus. Found in oysters, clams, mussels, scallops, and cockles usually when their beds are polluted by untreated sewage.
- Staphylococcal food poisoning caused by *Staphylococcus aureus* bacteria. Found in bacteria that grows on food left at room temperature.

## OTHER FOOD CONCERNS

Another food issue is research conducted on animals. The degree to which animal testing is necessary is controversial. Some activists call for no further testing on animals. When shopping, their mission is to find foods that have not been tested on animals. They may frequent stores or Web sites that sell products that do not use animal testing. They may boycott companies and products that use animal testing. They may conduct protests at government or university laboratories that do tests on animals. Others would say that it is better to test on animals than on humans so the lesser of the two evils is to only conduct animal testing when absolutely necessary to protect human health. Some would differentiate between types of animals, feeling more comfortable with experimentation on mice and rats than larger animals. The general consensus is that animals should be treated in as humane a way as possible and that testing should be done only when absolutely necessary.

Food allergies are another issue. They are more severe than food intolerances such as lactose intolerance or reactions to food coloring or MSG. "A true **food allergy** is a reaction of the body's immune system to a food or food ingredient, usually a protein. The immune system perceives the reaction-provoking substance, or allergen, as foreign and acts to destroy it" (Insel and Roth, 2002, p. 349). The reaction (hives, swelled tongue, cramps, asthma, or in severe cases a loss of blood pressure called anaphylaxis) can occur in minutes. Trigger foods such as nuts, milk, eggs, wheat, fish, and shellfish must be avoided. People at risk should carry medications to treat their reactions. Many infants outgrow food allergies. *It is estimated that about 2 percent of the adult population has food allergies* (Insel and Roth, 2002). A good first step in determining whether you have a food allergy or an intolerance is to keep a diary or log of foods eaten and reactions to determine a pattern. Consultation with a physician is a next step.

A final food concern to discuss is the use of boycotts. A **boycott** is defined as "an attempt by one or more parties to achieve certain objectives by urging individual consumers to refrain from making selected purchases in the marketplace" (Friedman, 1999, p. 4, as cited in earlier works). No one knows when boycotts began, but there is evidence of them in history from boycotts in England and Ireland long ago to the Boston tea party to the beef boycotts in 1973 where protestors stood in front of selected grocery stores and asked people not to buy beef. There are commodity boycotts such as don't buy beef or boycotts against a company or a single product such as Starkist tuna. Boycotts can last a couple of days to several months. Techniques range from boycotters holding signs to sit-ins, to call-ins, mail-ins, and e-mails to signed petitions to more drastic measures such as obstructioning—using physical presence or obstacles, not allowing people into stores or to work at their jobs (such as harvesting grapes or unloading boats of fish). Examples of food companies that have been boycotted include Bumble Bee Seafoods and Heinz, the owner of Starkist tuna (the issue being Dolphin-safe tuna). The media is involved through coverage of events. The subject of consumer boycotts is much more comprehensive than food-only; for a complete guide to the subject read Milton Friedman's *Consumer Boycotts* (1999).

## SNACK POLICE/JUNK FOOD CRITICS/LAWSUITS

Food-and-beverage manufacturers are under fire from snack police—a group of consumer organizations, educators, and nutritionists calling for "sin taxes" on chips and soft drinks to combat the ever increasing waistline of the average American. Many consumer advocates are also fighting to keep snack and soft drink beverage vending machines out of elementary, middle, and high schools. The question is, does this work or do children bring snacks in their lunches from home or go off school grounds to buy snacks at neighboring convenience stores thus enhancing their risk of being hit by cars, being late for school, or skipping classes? These are not easy questions. It is all about freedom of choice and what children prefer to eat versus what they should eat. What were the rules in the schools you attended? Were vending machines available on school grounds?

One approach to lessening the availability of snacks and soft drinks is to bring lawsuits against the industry similarly to the way the antitobacco lobby conducted itself. A drawback is that snack food is less easily defined than tobacco products because a wide range of foods can be considered snacks. Most of the lawsuits have been directed at fast food restaurants rather than at food-and-beverage manufacturers. The most newsworthy was the July 2002 lawsuit in which a "272-pound New York City man sued four fast-food chains, alleging that their food contributed to his obesity, heart disease and diabetes" (McKay, September 23, 2002. A1). One of the restaurants in the lawsuit was KFC (Kentucky Fried Chicken). The national restaurant association came out with a statement dismissing the lawsuit as "senseless, baseless, and ridiculous" (McKay, September 23, 2002, p. A10). But ridiculous or not as a defensive maneuver, fast food chains are responding by using healthier oils in making french fries.

Steven Reinemund, chairman and chief executive officer of PepsiCo, says, "The trend is clear: More consumers are concerned about nutrition, and 'we need to be prepared to deal with it.' Already, low-fat snacks such as baked potato chips and pretzels account for 20% to 25% of Frito-Lay sales" (McKay, September 23, 2002, A10). In the case of PepsiCo, some of their less caloric products have succeeded and some like Wow! Chips and their unpleasant side effects were less successful.

Salt sprinkled on the surface of chips and pretzels helps with "flavor delivery" because it is one of the first elements to hit the tongue. Many products have less salt within than a lot of people think because the surface approach seems to taste best. Attempts to reduce salt have been less than successful, in some cases low-salt has sold but no-salt products have not.

Besides using better oils, what else can fast food or snack manufacturers do to produce healthier foods? PepsiCo is experimenting with adding broccoli, carrot, and tomato flecks to chips. More snacks may have oats, soy, and/or dairy products. It is tricky to find the right combinations because as Reinemund says, "The consumer wants a balance of indulgence, as well as 'better for you.' And if we overreact . . . in either direction, we won't get the balanced growth that we want" (McKay, September 23, 2002, p. A10).

## NAVIGATING THE GROCERY STORE

Grocery stores seek to develop and maintain long-term ties with their customers. They know loyal customers return again and again. Loyalty is often based on familiarity, availability of desired products, and good customer service. In a study of large format retailing, Morganosky and Cude (2000a) found that attending to the details of the food retail business (accurate pricing, product availability, continuity of personnel) are ways to improve the consumer experience. But there are problems such as misleading promotions and advertisements. Other problems include scanning errors at the checkout and coupons and rebates that don't always work.

**End-of-aisle displays** may feature products at a higher cost than similar products placed midaisle. For example, grape juice may be $3.99 on the end of the aisle and $2.99 on the shelves where there is a less expensive competitive name brand or a store brand. **Tie-ins** are common where complementary products are placed side by side with one price jacked up to compensate for the **loss-leader** (a very low-priced advertised special to bring shoppers in). For example, hamburger may be on sale, but the price on the buns or ketchup next to it may be jacked up. Food and wine samples also encourage sales as do the pleasant aromas circulating from the bakery. Sometimes, the aromas from the deli or bakery are piped out the front door so the sensory experience starts before entering the store.

Most stores are set up so that a consumer has to go around the perimeter to get the basics such as meat, milk, cheese, bread, and fruits and vegetables. There may be frozen food aisles in the middle of the store. The longer the customer stays in the store the more they will spend, hence the perimeter layout, encouragement to go up and down all the aisles, free samples, relaxing music, and aromas. The addition of precooked foods, pharmacies, in-store restaurants, floral, cards, magazines, paperback books, and deli areas also slows consumers.

At the checkout area, there are the last minute impulse items of candy (at child height), magazines, tabloids, small gadgets, gum, and other sundries. Checking the foods you have at home, reading the advertisements, clipping coupons, and making a list before shopping will save money in the store. Studies show that fewer and fewer people are doing these behaviors. One way stores are responding to this is by having coupons placed right on the products or in a coupon dispenser attached to the shelf.

**Unit pricing** refers to the presentation of price information on shelves on a common basis such as per ounce. This is valuable information for making price comparisons within brands and between brands. Sometimes unit pricing reveals that the middle-size box of cereal or size of toothpaste tube is actually less expensive per ounce than a larger size.

**Open dating** is a system of placing a date on perishable products and indicates when the product should be sold or consumed. Other dates are **pull dates** (the last day the product should be sold), **expiration date** (the last day the consumer should use the product), **quality assurance dates** (the last day when the product is at its peak), and **pack date** (when the product was packaged or manufactured). Quality assurance dates or statements may be found on bread wrappers such as "the quality of this product is best if purchased by September 1." Sometimes consumers know these dates such as an open date stamped on a gallon of milk and sometimes they do not. For example, a loaf of bread may have a green, blue, or a red twist tie that tells the person stocking the shelves when to remove the bread but the color means nothing to the consumer who doesn't know the code. The tendency is for shoppers to pick the freshest product, in other words, the one with the freshest date so that if milk is set out with dates of July 31 and August 1 shoppers will take the August 1 date even if it is July 24 and they intend to use the whole gallon that day.

Not everyone shops at large grocery stores; convenience stores do a lot of business and their prices are generally higher, but like anywhere else there are sales and deals to be had if one reads ads and compares shelf prices. Drug stores increasingly sell food and beverages.

A new technology called **radio frequency identification (RFID)** puts a tiny chip in products that allows for the automatic tracking of products. It was test marketed in a prototype grocery store in Germany and is spreading to other countries including the U.S. RFIDs would replace barcodes on products. RFID tags fall into three broad categories: passive, semi-active and active. Passive tags are the simplest, least expensive, and obtain power from the radio frequency field of the reader and therefore do not require an integrated power source. Semi-active and active tags use an on-board power source to achieve a greater range or the ability to record data from a sensor. There are several reasons why RFIDs are favored by grocery stores—the main one being faster, more detailed inventory, making stocking and ordering easier, others being more accurate pricing and less shoplifting. Consumers worry about a loss of privacy. Will their products be tagged all the way to their homes? Technology exists for consumers to have their goods detagged before leaving the store but this may involve standing in another line—not an attractive option. Since this is such a new technology all the pros and cons have not been worked out yet; but it is something to watch unfold.

The largest grocer in the United States is Wal-Mart Stores Inc. This is an amazing story of the growth of a business because Wal-Mart started selling food in 1988 and in 2002 became the nation's largest grocer with more than $53 billion in grocery sales.

Wal-Mart sells groceries in at least 1,258 supercenters, 180,000 square foot grocer/discount store combinations and in 49 small Neighborhood Markets. Most of the stores are in the South and Southwest. If Wal-Mart's supercenters continue to expand at their current pace, within this decade, more than three-quarters of the nation's Krogers and Albertsons Inc. stores and more than half the Safeway Inc. outlets could be within 10 miles of a Wal-Mart supercenter, according to Trade Dimensions, a market-data provider. (Callahan and Zimmerman, 2003, B1)

Wal-Mart pushes rivals to match its low costs. They do this by cutting down on excess labor, improving their inventory tracking systems, doubling or tripling discount coupons, and building customer loyalty with discount-card plans. "Studies show that items at Wal-Mart cost 8% to 27% less than at Kroger, Albertsons or Safeway including discounts from these competitors' loyalty cards and specials" (Callahan and Zimmerman, 2003, p. B1). When this book went to press, the second largest grocer was Kroger, followed by Albertsons and then Safeway and these companies and the other grocery store chains were fighting back with better prices, quality (especially meat), selection, and services. Neatness and cleanliness are issues too. With 100,000 people visiting an average supercenter each week, it is difficult to keep stocks shelved and displays orderly. In short, there is a grocery store war going on, and generally consumers fare well when companies actively compete for their business.

*The U.S. largest grocer is Wal-Mart.*

## GROCERY SHOPPING ONLINE

Various grocery stores in the United States, Canada, and Europe have experimented with online grocery sales. Some experiments have worked and some have failed. There are online retailers and online grocery shopping services. Some offer weekly home deliveries of groceries and other services such as picking up videos, dry cleaning, and UPS packages. Charges can be a percentage or a monthly flat rate or a minimum charge per delivery. Some services waive the delivery fee if the order is above an amount such as $75. Another way this can happen is for consumers to place their grocery order by computer and pick up the groceries all preselected and bagged on their way home. This works well for branded prepackaged foods such as crackers, cookies, and canned goods that are always the same, but not so well for meat, fruit, and vegetables where the shopper might like to see or feel the product before buying.

Regarding home delivery, the concerns are having someone there to receive groceries or having a unit in the garage or housing unit where a delivery person can leave frozen or refrigerated food. Naturally, there are security concerns.

Convenience is the most cited reason why a consumer uses online shopping (Morganosky and Cude, 2000b). Shopping online is also a boon to customers with physical constraints such as disabilities or injuries or lack of transportation. The future success of online grocery sales is not clear. Experiments are still going on, some services are making it and some have gone bankrupt.

## BOTTLED WATER CONSUMPTION

The difference in the quality (taste, consistency, safety) of tap water versus bottled water is controversial. Tap water may smell or look different from bottled water, but you can't always tell by that because most of the dangerous contaminants consumers cannot see, smell, or taste (Buller, 2002). Tap water is constantly tested for harmful substances. One of the controversies is the addition of fluoride to tap water. Fluoride is added to drinking water to promote strong teeth and prevent tooth decay. There is a concern that children who drink only bottled water will have more dental problems. Again, this is controversial, and if you are concerned, you should ask your dentist or your children's dentist. To complicate things, some bottled water contains fluoride. To find out if the bottled water you drink has fluoride in it, you need to contact individual companies directly.

Why do consumers, especially young, health-oriented people, buy bottled water? Jeremy Buccellato, 31, of Ramsey, Minnesota, says he's heard the arguments "that tap water is just as good if not better than bottled water. A glass from his own tap, however, provides water that's discolored, chlorinated, and tastes like 'pool water.' Buccellato says the extra money he spends on bottles of Dasani water is worth it" (Buller, 2002, 18).

Does bottled water ever go bad? No, according to the International Bottled Water Association, assuming that it has been treated by the bottler according to guidelines set by the Food and Drug Administration coupled with state and industry standards. Bottled water should contain nothing to attract and grow pathogens that pose a threat to human health. To preserve taste it is recommended that bottles should be stored in cool, dry places away from odors and toxic substances. Some bottles have two-year expiration dates stamped on them, but this has nothing to do with product safety. It is a number that store owners use to rotate bottles on the shelves.

"Generally, over the years, the FDA has adopted EPA standards for tap water as standards for bottled water," says Dr. Henry Kim, a supervisory chemist at the FDA's Center for Food and Safety and Applied Nutrition, Office of Plan and Dairy Foods and Beverages. "As a result, standards for contaminants in tap water and bottled water are very similar" (Bullers, 2002, 16). Box 8.1 shows the FDA classifications of bottled water based on origin.

*Bottled water sales are growing at a faster pace than soft drink sales, a new battleground for bottlers.*

In bottled water consumption there is the battle of the brands. As this book went to press, the top selling brand was Aquafina by PepsiCo Inc. followed by Dasani by Coca-Cola Co. These age-old rivals in the soda drink market have found a new battleground in the water wars. It makes sense that they would be major players because they have the water purifying and bottling plants and distribution systems already. Competitors include regional and imported bottled waters. In recent years bottled water has grown at a faster pace than soft drink sales. Annual supermarket sales are over $13 billion for soft drinks and over $3 billion for bottled water.

## AGENCIES AND LAWS

In an earlier chapter, you learned that the FDA regulates food, including foodborne illness, nutrition, and dietary supplements; drugs including prescription, over-the-counter, and generic, medical devices and biologics; and cosmetics including safety and labeling issues. The FDA monitors Web sites for products that may endanger the public health. In 1994, the Dietary Supplement Health and Education Act established specific labeling requirements and authorized FDA to promulgate good manufacturing practice regulations for dietary supplements. This act defines "dietary supplements" and "dietary ingredients" and classifies them as food. The act also established a commission to recommend how to regulate claims.

Box 8.3 lists the government agencies that monitor the food supply including the FDA. The USDA has a Food Safety and Inspection Service (FSIS) that inspects meat and poultry. It monitors slaughterhouses and processing plants. States also monitor parts of the food supply, particularly the wholesomeness of foods grown in their own state. Examples would be California and Florida who actively test and look out for problems in their citrus industries.

Both the FDA and USDA are active in consumer education, spending millions of dollars each year on education and in the case of USDA in promotion of agricultural products. The USDA has government-sponsored trade associations with the Egg Board, National Pork Board, Cattlemen's Beef Promotion and Research Board, and the National Dairy Promotion and Research Board. A consumer issue is whether using taxpayers dollars for promotional efforts is a good idea or not. It is an example of the crossover between government, industry, and media.

As we learned in previous chapters, the Federal Trade Commission is responsible for food advertising and industry competition. It does not distinguish between various claims and products (e.g., whether a substance is a food or a drug). So there is this gray area or confusing policy whereby food labels are more closely watched or

---

**BOX 8.3    Government Agencies that Monitor the Food Supply**

This is a very brief description of central activities. Each also is involved in consumer education, alerting the public to health concerns, and conducts research.

- Centers for Disease Control (CDC) *www.cdc.gov*
  About one-fourth of the U.S. population experiences food-borne illness each year. The CDC monitors food-borne diseases which are illnesses transmitted to humans through food and water. In homes, food-borne illnesses can be prevented by keeping a clean kitchen, avoiding cross-contamination, keeping hot foods hot, and keeping cold foods cold.
- Environmental Protection Agency (EPA) *www.epa.gov*
  Responsible for regulating pesticides and establishing water quality standards.
  Food and Agricultural Organization (FAO) *www.fao.org*
  This is part of the United Nations; its responsibilities include international monitoring of pesticides.
- Food and Drug Administration (FDA) *www.fda.gov*
  Responsible for ensuring the safety and wholesomeness of foods processed and sold in interstate commerce except meat, poultry, and eggs (which the USDA monitors). This includes inspection of food plants and imported foods. It cannot possibly sample all foods, it is a monitoring agency that sets standards. It samples regularly and acts promptly when problems occur or if there is suspicion of a potential problem.
- Department of Agriculture (USDA) *www.usda.gov*
  Enforces standards for the wholesomeness and quality of meat, poultry, and eggs produced in the United States.
- World Health Organization (WHO) *www.who.ch*
  International agency that adopts standards on pesticide use. Reports statistics on world food shortages.

BOX 8.4    Structure-Function Claims

These may be found in advertising, largely untested or regulated by government:

- Helps maintain body weight
- Builds strong bones and teeth
- Lifts your spirits
- Slows aging
- Improves memory
- Boosts your immune system
- Helps you relax so you can finally get some sleep
- Promotes heart health
- Reduces the risk of colds*
- Promotes relaxation and good karma
- Increases alertness
- Enhances mood

*This one is a borderline claim that has gotten some companies in trouble. A way around it is to mention the cold or flu season or have actors with red noses and holding tissues sneezing on each other and let viewers draw their own conclusions. Actions or settings are less easily regulated than words.

restricted than television commercials or magazine advertisements. Here is an example. A magazine advertisement may say that ketchup may reduce the risk of prostate and cervical cancer, but the label on the product will not say this even though ketchup contains cooked tomatoes that have pytochemical lycopene which is thought to reduce certain types of cancer. This brings us to the topic of **structure-function** claims. Health claims are fairly tightly regulated by FDA, but structure-function claims can be made without FDA approval. Products can be said to "improve memory" or "build stronger bodies" without proof. Advertisers are careful to skirt around the issue by not mentioning specific diseases. This is a fine distinction that is often lost on consumers. Here is an example: milk contains calcium which may reduce the risk of osteoporosis. These are health claims and nutrient content that need FDA approval. But an advertisement that goes further and has the structure-function claim of milk helping to promote bone health does not need FDA approval. The phrase "helps promote" is often the key; this is considered an easy way out. Box 8.4 gives more examples of structure-function claims.

The FTC does not have the resources to keep up with every U.S.-based Web site offering products with health claims. It certainly does not have the resources to keep up with foreign Web sites. Therefore, do not assume law-enforcement agencies can protect everyone from Internet food swindles.

## SUMMARY

Food and beverage consumption patterns in the United States have changed considerably since colonial times. Currently the top U.S. beverage is tap water followed by coffee and then bottled water. Coffee consumption was dropping considerably until it was reinvigorated in 1995 by StarBucks and competitors. Many innovations in food such as freeze-dried coffee have their origins in military research, specifically the development of MREs (Meals Ready to Eat).

The Food and Drug Administration regulates bottled water as well as the safety of most foods. The U.S. Dept. of Agriculture monitors the wholesomeness of meat, poultry, and eggs. The Federal Trade Commission is active in food labeling and monitoring advertising. Many frauds in the food and health industries exist especially in the areas of weight reduction and any product or service that promises a more attractive appearance.

The slow food movement also called the "buy local" movement is worldwide. It began in Italy as a reaction to the increased use of fast food and the toll the spread of fast food was taking on more unique and in many cases more flavorful regional cuisines. Advocates of slow food emphasize local and fresh foods as an alternative to global internationalized foods.

Consumer spending on food dropped 10 percent in the last decade. In the typical family budget, food is the third most costly item behind housing and transportation. Online grocery shopping is being experimented with, convenience being the main positive feature.

Organic foods may or may not be healthier than conventional foods, and they may cost more. The added health benefits of eating organically grown foods are controversial as is the eating of genetically altered or irradiated foods.

Genetically altered foods are controversial because in many people's minds it seems to go against what nature intended although advocates of the value of genetically altered foods would point out that man has been altering nature for centuries through a variety of food production and agricultural practices. Irradiated foods are also met with skepticism. Some people think we have gone too far; others think we have not gone far enough. Starvation still exists on this planet and advocates of genetically altered foods would suggest that higher crop yields and the reduction of hunger far outweigh "tampering with nature" worries. Everyone agrees that as the world population grows better methods of food production and land use are needed; the dispute is over the best way to do this.

# KEY POINTS

1. The USDA Food Pyramid was developed to help people choose a balanced, varied, and healthful diet. Certain individuals and population groups may need to alter it to meet their particular needs. Not everyone agrees with the structure and emphasis of the pyramid and discussions about revising it are underway.
2. Not all foods have labels, and not all labels are truthful.
3. It is difficult for consumers and even trained nutritionists to determine how many calories are in foods that they haven't prepared themselves. Many consumers think they are eating low-calorie, healthy foods in restaurants based on the name of the item, but many times that is not the case. Calorie information should be available on counters or packaging.
4. There are healthy overweight people and unhealthy normal-weight people.
5. Bottled water guidelines are set by the FDA.
6. The FDA regulates what is considered an organically grown food. These foods cost 15 to 50 percent more than conventionally grown foods.

7. The largest grocer in the U.S. is Wal-Mart and competitors are fighting back.
8. A number of government agencies monitor the U.S. food supply, most importantly, the FDA and USDA.
9. DNA matching (genetic testing) can be used to track tainted food. This has enormous health and legal implications.
10. Food allergies are rare, affecting about 2 percent of the adult population. Food intolerances, an adverse but not life-threatening reaction, are more common. Through trial and error, most people learn what foods their bodies will not tolerate.

## KEY TERMS

| | | |
|---|---|---|
| additives | foods | pull dates |
| biotechnology | genetic engineering | quality assurance dates |
| boycott | GRAS List | radio frequency |
| calories | loss-leader | identification (RFID) |
| delaney clause | nutrition | structure-function |
| end-of-aisle display | open dating | tie-ins |
| expiration date | organically grown foods | unit pricing |
| food allergy | pack dates | |
| food irradiation | preservatives | |

## DISCUSSION QUESTIONS

1. How have food preferences changed in the last 100 years? Give at least three examples.
2. What does the Delaney Clause refer to? What does negligible or minimal risk mean?
3. Why do people buy branded bottled water? What government agency regulates bottled water?
4. Select a Web site in the E-Resources section and report on what you find on a specific body-related issue such as food or beverages.

## E-RESOURCES

American Dietetic Association
www.eatright.org

American Medical Association
www.amaassn.org

Centers for Disease Control and Prevention
www.cdc.gov

Dietitians of Canada
www.dietitians.ca

Food and Drug Administration
www.fda.gov; if you have questions email webmail@oc.fda.gov

Healthfinder
www.healthfinder.gov

Tufts University Nutrition Navigator
www.navigator.tufts.edu

USDA Food and Nutrition Information
www.nal.usda.gov/fnic

U.S. Health and Human Services Office on Women's Health
www.4women.gov

American Journal of Clinical Nutrition
www.faseb.org/ajcn

# REFERENCES

Abboud, L. (January 21, 2003). DNA matching helps track tainted meat. *Wall Street Journal,* p. B1.

Addicted to grease (May 2002). *American Demographics,* p. 56.

Buller, A. C. (July–August 2002). Bottled water: Better than the tap? *FDA Consumer,* pp. 14–18.

Callahan, P., and A. Zimmerman. (May 27, 2003). Price war in aisle 3. *Wall Street Journal,* p. B1.

Constant cravings (May 2002). *American Demographics,* p. 56.

Daly, K. (1996). *Families and time.* Thousand Oaks, CA: Sage.

de Lisser, E. (August 20, 2002). Is that $5 gallon of milk really organic? *Wall Street Journal,* p. D1.

December, R. (September 18, 2002). New miracle weight-loss product? Fat chance! *Wall Street Journal,* p. D7.

Diamond, J. (1999). *Guns, germs, and steel.* New York: W. & W. Norton.

Friedman, M. (1999). *Consumer boycotts.* New York: Routledge.

Haas, L. (1999). *Families and work.* In *Handbook of Marriage and the Family.* M. Sussman, S. K. Steinmetz, and G. W. Peterson ed., New York: Plenum Press.

Heitmann, B. L., et al. (1997). Are genetic determinants of weight gain modified by leisure-time physical activity? A prospective study of Finnish twins. *American Journal of Clinical Nutrition,* 66, pp. 672–78.

Helliker, K. (July 23, 2002). Being heavy and healthy. *Wall Street Journal,* p. B1.

Hochschild, A. R. (1989). *The second shift: Working parents and the revolution at home.* New York: Viking.

Insel, P., and W. Roth. (2002). *Core concepts in health,* 9th ed. Boston: McGrawHill.

Junk-food nation (November 2001). *American Demographics,* p. 25.

Kilman, S. (February 2, 2002). A roast is a roast? Not in the new game of marketing meat. *Wall Street Journal,* p. A1.

Landro, L. (2002). The informed patient: Knowledge is half the battle in avoiding infectious diseases. *Wall Street Journal,* p. C2.

Low-cal muffins: Too good to be true? (October 2001). *Good Housekeeping,* p. 18.

Mariani, J. (1991). *America eats out.* New York: William Morrow.

McKay, B. (September 23, 2002). Fit to eat? PepsiCo challenges itself to concoct healthier snacks. *Wall Street Journal,* p. A1.

Morganosky, M., and B. Cude. (2000a). Large format retailing in the US: A consumer experience perspective. *Journal of Retailing and Consumer Services* 7, pp. 215–22.

Morganosky, M., and B. Cude. (2000b). Consumer response to online grocery shopping. *International Journal of Retail & Distribution Management* 28 (1), pp. 17–26.

Parker-Pope, T. (January 14, 2003). That veggie wrap you just chowed down is more fattening than a ham sandwich. *Wall Street Journal,* p. D1.

Pollan, M. (2001). *The botany of desire.* New York: Random House.

Roxburgh, S. (2002). Racing through life: The distribution of time pressures by roles and role resources among full-time workers. *Journal of Family and Economic Issues,* pp. 121–45.

Schor, J. B. (1992). *The Overworked American: The Unexpected Decline of Leisure.* New York: Basic Books.

Shape of biotech to come. (September 2, 2002). *Fortune,* p. 130.

Stipp, D. (January 20, 2003). Son of Spam. *Fortune.* p. 46.

Weiss, M. (April 2002). Inconspicuous consumption. *American Demographics,* p. 31–39.

Whitney, E., and S. Rolfes. (2002). *Understanding nutrition,* 9th ed. Belmont, CA: Wadsworth.

# Health and Body Issues

*Good health and good sense are two of life's greatest blessings.*

Publius Syrus (42 B.C.)

## Learning Objectives

1. Explain what it means to be well and the types of wellness.
2. Discuss the reasons why fraudulent health claims are rampant.
3. Discuss ways to reduce health care costs.
4. Discuss the issues and players involved in medical malpractice insurance.
5. Explain the market for cosmetics, why people use them.
6. Discuss addictions such as alcohol and tobacco and the consumer issues—health, safety, advertising, and costs thereof.

## INTRODUCTION

What is healthy is very subjective.

The last chapter focused on food and beverage issues. This chapter extends the discussion by turning its attention to the general topic of health and well-being. This is a more difficult topic than one would assume because "healthy is a very subjective definition," says Gene Cameron, vice president of marketing for Baja Fresh (Parker-Pope, 2003, p. D1). Health and body issues are important to study from a consumer economics standpoint because so much money is spent on health and body products, so much consumer protection legislation and regulation revolves around these issues, fraud is rampant, and, most important, individual and family health are critical. Subtopics to be covered include vaccines, brand-name versus generic drugs, cosmetics, and tobacco and alcohol use. The emphasis in this chapter is on legal drug use—not illicit drugs such as cocaine and marijuana. The Harrison Act of 1914 prohibited the use of cocaine, morphine, and opiates for non-medical purposes.

Prohibition began in 1919 and ended in 1933.

Throughout the twentieth century and into the present century, there has been an ongoing battle about defining what is a socially acceptable desire or habit and what is an addiction. The Eighteenth Amendment of 1919 (more commonly referred to as Prohibition) outlawed most alcohol use. The purpose was to eliminate or drastically reduce alcohol consumption. The amendment challenged the free market (protested by distillers, brewers, and importers and supported by the American Medical Association, reformers, and religious groups). In the end the experiment failed and the act was repealed in 1933 in the Twenty-First Amendment to the Constitution. Most of the enforcement efforts were directed at sellers rather than consumers. Prohibition introduced a new kind of criminal—the bootlegger—the most famous of whom was Al Capone. It also drove otherwise law-abiding citizens into a position of circumventing the law which made many people uncomfortable, and there was a concern that if they were illegal in this manner they were more likely to ignore the law in other areas as well. After Prohibition a few states continued to prohibit or control the sale of alcohol, but by 1966 liquor control became more a local control issue rather than a statewide or nationwide effort.

Life has gotten more complicated since the days of Al Capone and bootleg whiskey. Drugs, legal and illegal, have introduced a new set of health concerns. "Recent ads in newspapers and magazines claim that it's now legal to import drugs into the United States for personal use: In fact, some ads on the Internet and elsewhere claim that people can legally bring up to a 90-day supply of their prescription medications bought outside the United States home with them. Neither of these claims is true," says Ray Formanek Jr., editor of the *FDA Consumer* (October 2002, p. 2). Under the Federal Food, Drug, and Cosmetic Act, unapproved, misbranded, and adulterated drugs are prohibited from importation into the United States. This quote points out the interaction between the consumer, business, media, and government in the marketplace as shown in the circular flow model of consumerism. It also points out the importance of the Internet in terms of attaining drugs and information about drugs and medical treatment. Health information sites on the Internet get an incredible amount of traffic. For example, the Mayo Clinic reports over 2 million visitors a month.

Life improved during the twentieth century for most Americans because of:

- Availability of vaccinations for childhood diseases
- Fluoridation of drinking water
- Safer workplaces, homes, and schools
- The recognition that the use of tobacco caused severe health problems
- Healthier mothers and babies, improved obstetric care
- Increase in the life expectancy
- Control of infectious diseases
- Improved sanitation

It is assumed that the readers of this chapter have learned about the harmful short-and long-term effects of alcohol and drug abuse in previous classes and for individual health advice they will consult their physicians. The E-Resources section has Web sites with further information. The chapter begins with a discussion of wellness and well-being.

## WELLNESS AND WELL-BEING

"Everyone knows the feeling of waking up after a long illness and suddenly, miraculously, feeling full of life again! Being anxious to dive back into things that have been neglected, and try new things, too. Not feeling isolated, powerless, or estranged anymore" (De Graaf, Wann, and Naylor, 2001, p. 231). **Wellness** is the ability to live life fully with optimal health and vitality encompassing physical, emotional, intellectual, spiritual, interpersonal, social, and environmental well-being (Insel and Roth, 2002). Thus, wellness is an expanded idea of health beyond just the absence of physical disease. It can be said to transcend health, for example, when individuals with serious illnesses or disabilities rise above their physical or mental limitations to live rich, meaningful, and vital lives. **Well-being** is the state of being healthy, happy, or prosperous so that well-being is about both mental and physical health and having the finances to keep healthy, comfortable, and contented. The term "well-being," then, is about present health and the expectation of a good life, including excellent health in the future.

Why do we study health, wellness, and well-being in consumer economics? The answer is that *health is an asset;* in fact it is generally agreed that it is your greatest asset. "Some aspects of health are determined by your genes, your age, and other factors that may be beyond your control. But true wellness is largely determined by the decisions you make about how to live your life" (Insel and Roth, 2002, p. 2). According to Insel and Roth, wellness is made up six components or subtypes:

1. Physical wellness: including exercise, eating well, avoiding harmful habits, making responsible decisions regarding sex, getting regular dental and physical care
2. Emotional wellness: including the ability to share feelings, being optimistic, trusting
3. Intellectual wellness: including curiosity, having a sense of humor, openness to new ideas, love of learning, the capacity to question and think creatively
4. Spiritual wellness: including a set of guiding beliefs, values, or principles, adding meaning to life, thinking beyond oneself
5. Interpersonal and social wellness: including developing satisfying relationships
6. Environmental or planetary: including an appreciation for surroundings, natural and man-made, increasingly personal health depends on the health of the planet

Well-being is promoted by sensible behaviors such as attention to safety (wearing safety belts), eating well (good nutrition), and regular exercise. So, economists perceive maintaining good health and safety to be linked to personal behavior. The consumer of health care services is called the **principal** and the provider of health care is an **agent**. Apart from self-help such as wearing seat belts, the consumer as principal needs to find the right agent, the doctor or health services provider, and health insurance provider.

According to the AMA 90% of patients don't get good explanations of tests or treatments from their doctors.

**Consumer Alert**

Do you ever return from a doctor's visit and realize all the questions you should have asked? Or have you forgotten what the doctor said? There are several solutions including preparing ahead by going to the E-Resources section and looking up symptoms and treatment options, taking someone with you to take notes, or bringing paper to take your own notes. Patient advocates and medical professionals agree that patients need to become active advocates for their own care. Arming yourself with information and questions before the visit begins is a good start. During the exam, carefully frame the discussion about medical concerns. The American Medical Association reports that 90 percent of patients don't get good explanations of tests or treatments from their doctors.

Preventative health care includes careful driving, maintaining friendships and families, taking time to exercise and play, using a buddy system when swimming, and having smoke alarms installed in homes. Families are important socializing influences on teaching their children the do's and don'ts of safe behavior. Moderation is also important as a means to avoid overexertion and injury. Avoiding risk, another key economic concept, involves consumption behaviors such as heavy smoking and drinking.

**Consumer health** is an umbrella term encompassing the decisions consumers make about health care, including products and services that they buy or that their insurance covers and decisions made about their lifestyle that affects health care needs. Because health decisions are often made in a hurry, time is involved as well as money and information. Health information is available through many media, and consumers like buying over the telephone or computer in their own homes because of the privacy it provides. But because of the personal or privacy issues involved, consumers who are gypped are less likely to complain or ask for a refund about this area of consumption than they are about less personal areas. The result is that many **quacks** (unscrupulous individuals specializing in medical or health swindlers) and quasi-legitimate products and programs continue to exist because of the lack of complaints. This is worrisome because not only is there a money and esteem loss, but also there may be a health loss because the consumer did not seek legitimate advice or treatment.

## FRAUDULENT HEALTH CLAIMS VS. SCIENCE

Because health is so fundamental to our sense of well-being and people want to appear as well as feel healthy and well kempt, people are susceptible to products and services that offer a healthy glow or appearance. From Abraham Maslow's perspective, health and cosmetic products and services meet the full range of needs (see Figure 9.1).

Health frauds are perpetrated against all segments of the population, but certain age groups are particularly vulnerable to certain types of frauds. Teenagers are susceptible to acne cream, bust developers, and diet claims. The middle-aged are prone to products offering wrinkle reduction and perpetual youth. The elderly fall victim to fraudulent hearing aid schemes, medical quackery and gadgetry, and arthritis remedies. Usually the loss is of the person's time, money, and dignity. For example, consumers spend an estimated $2 billion a year on unproven arthritis remedies such as honey and vinegar mixtures, magnets, and copper bracelets. None of these remedies have been proven to offer long-term relief. Some products and treatments can cause serious harm and even death, and many are expensive because health insurance rarely covers unapproved treatments.

Consumers spend $2 billion a year on unproven arthritis cures.

Fraudulent health claims run the gamut from inflated claims about mouthwash to very serious life-threatening treatments. As noted in chapter 7, a classic case in the 1960s was when the Federal Trade Commission greatly stepped up efforts to regulate television advertising attacking the exaggerated health claims of Listerine mouthwash. Fundamental to a study of consumer behavior is the acceptance that there is always a market for products that will beautify or make consumers more socially acceptable.

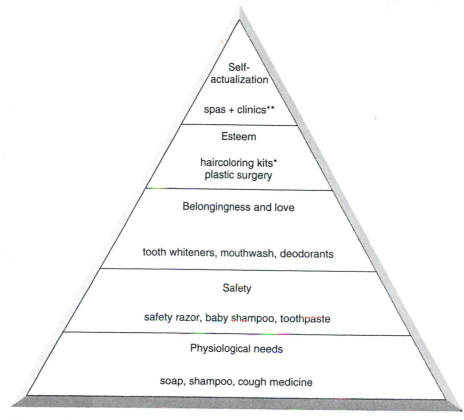

Self-actualization

spas + clinics**

Esteem

haircoloring kits*
plastic surgery

Belongingness and love

tooth whiteners, mouthwash, deodorants

Safety

safety razor, baby shampoo, toothpaste

Physiological needs

soap, shampoo, cough medicine

*For example, ads that say "I'm worth it."
**For example, ads that say "You have arrived."

**Figure 9.1**    Maslow's Hierarchy of Needs with examples of drugs or cosmetic products.

*The question is not why do they buy health-related or appearance-related products but why do they continue to buy obviously questionable products?* The simple answer is that healthy fraud trades on false hope, but as people become more educated and sophisticated shouldn't they be more skeptical of especially improbable product claims such as "lose 10 pounds while you sleep"? What can be done? Perhaps the answer lies in encouraging people to be less gullible (easily deceived or duped) by being more scientific in their approach to consumption such as asking for proof. Robert Park, professor of physics at the University of Maryland, frequent commentator on TV news programs, and author of *Voodoo Science: The Road from Foolishness to Fraud,* says,

> Of the major problems confronting society—problems involving the environment, national security, health, and the economy—there are few that can be sensibly addressed without input from science. As I sought to make the case for science, however, I kept bumping up against scientific ideas and claims that are totally, indisputably, extravagantly, wrong, but which nevertheless attract a large following of passionate, and sometimes powerful, proponents. I came to realize that many people choose scientific beliefs the same way they choose to be Methodists, or Democrats, or

Chicago Cub fans. They judge science by how well it agrees with the way they want the world to be. (2000, pp. viii–ix).

He makes a strong case in his book that the media plays a major role in promoting false health claims and that even the supposedly investigative shows or evening news shows have promulgated obviously fraudulent products. He wonders that if scientists can fool themselves and make mistakes, "how much easier is it to craft arguments deliberately intended to befuddle jurists or lawmakers with little or no scientific background? This is **junk science**." This term means there is little or no evidence or proof to support claims.

Here is a further question: Why is it that some people faced with the same set of facts choose to believe and others choose to doubt? Why do some people need more proof than others? Partly this has to do with the ability to discern patterns and accumulate observations and some people are stronger at this than others. It should also be understood that not everyone desires a world that is predictable and measurable through scientific reasoning and testing. They prefer a little adventure and mystery. It is more fun to believe that a $55 tiny jar of moisturizer will vanish wrinkles than to face up to the fact that you are old enough to have wrinkles.

"**Science** is the systematic enterprise of gathering knowledge about the world and organizing and condensing that knowledge into testable laws and theories" (Park, 2000, p. 39). When considering a new product or claim, scientists would apply two rules:

1. Expose the idea and/or result to independent testing and replication by other scientists.
2. Abandon or modify accepted facts, theories, or procedures in light of the new evidence.

What happens is that many inventors of new products or claims do not allow them to be tested by independent scientists or doctors. So, one of the first rules of determining whether a new health or cosmetic discovery is legitimate or not is to find out what sort of testing was done and by whom. Box 9.1 lists the various words in advertising or labeling that might lead one to believe that fakery is at hand or at least puffery. A way to lessen people being taken in by false claims is to encourage **scientific literacy**; the promotion of science education in the schools and in the community. Park adds that what is needed is a broader scientific worldview by that he means an understanding that we live in an orderly universe governed by natural laws that cannot be circumvented by magic or miracles.

In Box 9.1 it mentions that the consumer should beware of ads that use testimonials, especially full-page ads for such things as weight reduction and miracle cures. An example from *FTC Facts for Consumers* is "My husband has Alzheimer's disease]. He began eating a teaspoonful of this product each day. And now in just 22 days he mowed the grass, cleaned out the garage, weeded the flower beds and we take our morning walk again" (2003, p. 9).

To go back to the beginning of this section, the Federal Trade Commission continues to do everything they can to lessen misleading advertising. They are putting particular emphasis on advertising and products directed to children under the age of eight. For adults, a new concern is the marketing of brand-name prescription drugs on television and in magazines. The ads on evening television and in magazines suggest that consumers ask their doctor for a brand-name drug the next time

> Health fraud trades on false hope. It promises quick results and easy solutions.

---

**BOX 9.1    Health Fraud Buzz Words and Scams**

Look out for before and after photos, testimonials, limited supplies (so hurry!), and the following claims about a product:

- Shrinks tumors.
- Improves sex life. Cures impotency.
- Ancient remedy.
- Why the medical community is keeping this discovery secret.
- Fast/safe/easy.
- Guaranteed, works for everyone.
- Amazing.
- A new product breakthrough.
- A miracle.
- A secret formula.
- Exciting.
- Painless.
- Sleep well every night and awake refreshed.
- What primitive tribes can tell us.
- Improve your popularity.
- End baldness forever.
- Three out of four doctors recommend.

---

that they have an appointment. The problem is that these ads are designed for the general public and may not fit an individual's health status or symptoms. There is real potential of self-diagnosis which most likely will be off the mark. The counter-point to this is that someone may recognize symptoms in themselves for a disease like depression and know that there is help.

---

**Consumer Alert**

Beware of health frauds about cures for cancer. Because a diagnosis brings feelings of fear and hopelessness, people will try just about anything. They are susceptible to exotic cures or remedies. Cancer is a name given to a wide range of diseases, and each requires different forms of treatment that are best determined by a specialist, a health professional trained in that field.

The FTC turns up hundreds of Web sites touting unproven cures or treatments for cancer. One site pushes more than 100 alternative cancer treatments that it claims are safe, effective, and nontoxic. Some of these sites are by medical doctors so just because a product or treatment is endorsed by medical doctors does not mean it is safe. Types of cures include herbal teas and fish extracts—even electronic zappers. The FTC obtained "a $4.3 million judgment against BioPulse International Inc., for making unsubstantiated claims about two cancer 'treatments' it offered in Tijuana, Mexico. One of them, billed as 'hypoglycemic sleep therapy,' involved placing cancer patients in a series of insulin-induced comas over a seven-week period at a cost of nearly $40,000. Some patients, according to news accounts, died from their cancers soon after receiving the treatment" (Fleck, 2003, p.18). To learn more about quackery in cancer treatments go to www.quackwatch.org.

---

**Consumer Alert**

Beware also of health care frauds involving HIV and AIDS. According to the FTC, although legitimate treatments can extend life and improve the quality of life for people
with AIDS, there is, so far, no cure for the disease. People diagnosed with HIV, the virus
that causes AIDS, may want to try untested drugs or treatments. But trying unproven
products or treatments, such as electrical and magnetic devices and so-called herbal
cures, can be dangerous and may cause HIV-positive individuals to delay seeking
medical care. The government has information at *www.hivatis.org*.

---

## GOVERNMENT AGENCIES AND THEIR HEALTH CARE TASKS

As the Consumer Alert shows, the FTC is one of the active government agencies
engaged in guarding the public's health. Table 9.1 gives a partial list of key agencies and their main tasks. Figure 9.2 shows the different groups impacting on one
particular agency, the Food and Drug Administration. A goal of regulatory agencies
is to help people attain a high level of health at a reasonable cost. Another goal is
to protect them from being misled or taken in by outright fraud. Many issues surround the competency, credentialing, cost, and access to medical care.

## HEALTH CARE COSTS SKYROCKETING

*The United States has the most expensive health care in the world, and the costs are
rising.* "Medical costs increased 10 to 15 percent in 2001, after averaging 5 to 6 percent for a decade. Hospital spending accounted for about 45 percent of increased
health care costs in 2000. Unnecessary admissions and labor shortages are among

**Table 9.1**    Partial List of Government Agencies and Their Health Care Tasks

| Agencies | Tasks/Responsibilities |
|---|---|
| All agencies are involved in some form of education or public outreach; beyond that some of their main tasks and responsibilities are given below: | |
| National Institutes of Health (NIH) | Research |
| Internal Revenue Service (IRS) | Taxes and tax policy regarding deductions |
| Environmental Protection Agency (EPA) | Environmental protection, cleanup, disposal of toxic waste, protects water supply |
| Centers for Disease Control (CDC) U.S. Dept. of Health and Human Services State and County health departments Surgeon General's Office | Disease control and accident prevention, the search for cures, helping ill people, setting policy, overseeing nation's public health |
| Occupational Safety and Health Administration (OSHA) | Monitors the nation's workplaces for potential health hazards |
| Food and Drug Administration (FDA) | Testing, regulation |

**Figure 9.2** The Groups Impacting on the Food and Drug Administration.

the factors that make hospitals the primary driver of rising costs. Some hospitals have demanded increases of 40 percent to 60 percent for certain services" (Florida Blue State Edition, 2002). Health care premiums rise as medical costs and services rise. Hospitals are for the most part for-profit organizations that have to be enterprising to survive. Unprofitable hospitals close totally or close down unprofitable services. As of the writing of this book, the country's largest hospital chain is HCA, Inc. followed by Tenet Healthcare Corporation of Santa Barbara, California. Both of these compete in buying up smaller hospital chains and individual hospitals.

Because health insurance is so expensive about 40 million Americans do not have health insurance. In 2003, 17,500 employees of General Electric Co. (GE) went on a two day nationwide walkout to protest higher out-of-pocket health costs. It was the first national walkout at GE since 1969 which shows that employees of GE do not lightly make the decision to go on strike. This also illustrates that even employees with health insurance provided by their employers have to pay for part of the coverage. The GE workers were protesting an average copay increase of $300 to $400 annually. In an up-coming chapter, there will be more coverage on health insurance available through employers (HMOs and so on) but here are general points to follow to reduce health care costs:

1. Get good health care coverage from your employer. Find out about your health plan/program in terms of copayments, deductibles, and choice of physician. For example, find out if you can visit a non–network physician and, if so, what are the cost differences between a network and non–network physician.

2. Use generic drugs instead of a brand-name drug. A **generic drug** is a lower-cost copy of a brand-name drug that becomes available after the brand-name product's patent expires, typically after 15 years or more. The usual cost is 30 percent less than the brand-name drug, sometimes as much as 75 percent less. More information on generic drugs is given in the next section.

3. If you use a drug regularly, try a mail order program or shop around for the best price.

4. When traveling, choose a physician that participates in your health plan/program. If you choose a nonparticipating provider, your deductible and coinsurance amounts may be higher. One of the biggest plans, Blue Cross/Blue Shield has 400,000 providers in the United States that participate in the plans, and health providers can be reached at *www.bcbs.com* or by calling 800-810-BLUE.

5. Ask, How much is this going to cost me? Can the payments be stretched out?

6. Get free samples from the physician.

7. If your employer (or your spouse's) does not offer health care insurance, then you need to comparison shop for the best health care coverage at the best price. One suggestion is to check group policies offered by universities, credit unions, clubs, associations, and other groups which may offer better deals than you could find buying insurance as a nonaffiliated individual.

8. When getting a prescription filled, ask the pharmacist any further questions. Pharmacists are an underused resource.

One of the basic tenets of consumer economics is trying to get the best product at the lowest cost (time and money), but when it comes to your health perhaps this is not always the wisest course. For example, before agreeing to surgery you should seek a second opinion. Fortunately, most insurance companies will cover the cost of a second opinion. Peace of mind is worth a great deal.

## Medicare Fraud

Frauds and scams drive up the cost of health care for all of us. The federal government has been working for years to reduce the money loss through Medicare fraud. Recently, it instituted a volunteer program called the Senior Medicare Patrol sponsored by the U.S. Administration on Aging. **Medicare** is the federal health insurance program for people 65 or older and for many people with disabilities. It covers over 40 million Americans and is the nation's largest health-insurance program. By 2030 this number will double, and there are concerns about how to keep this program solvent. Fraud prevention will help. Medicare is subject to a number of errors and abuses, partly because it is so large. Someone who gets Social Security at age 65 is automatically enrolled in Medicare. It has two parts: hospital insurance and medical insurance that helps pay for doctors' services, outpatient care, tests, home health visits, and other services.

> Medicare is the nation's largest health insurance program.

Medicare fraud, abuse, and billing errors, which together cost taxpayers $12 billion a year, are being investigated through the Patrol by volunteers who are retirees (often retired medical doctors) looking into possible improper Medicare charges, based on tips from beneficiaries, or they serve as educators to other seniors about the potential for problems. As one example, after two days of training, volunteers worked one-on-one with beneficiaries to track down suspicious charges on the beneficiaries' monthly Medicare summary notices, or billing statements. Even when fraud is found, sometimes beneficiaries do not want to become involved in clearing it up, fearing bureaucracies and the time loss. Volunteers can help with this, making it easier for fraud victims to come forward by showing them the ropes and helping with the paperwork. Other volunteers may be trained to do educational programs because in the long run the biggest gains may come from prevention of fraud, abuse, and error rather than fixing things after they occur.

What kinds of frauds exist? Examples of fraud are Medicare payments for people long since dead, reconditioned wheelchairs billed as new, saline solutions sold as painkillers, and bills for home-health services never rendered. "Scam artists are really, really smart. There's a new gimmick every day," says Shirley Merner, state coordinator for Operation Restore Trust of Iowa, a Patrol project that has about 1,500 senior volunteers (Engstrom, 2002, p. R6).

## Brand-Name Drugs and Generic Drugs

The Food, Drug, and Cosmetic Act defines drugs by their intended use, as "(A) articles intended for use in the diagnosis, cure, mitigation, treatment, or prevention of disease . . . and (B) articles (other than food) intended to affect the structure or any function of the body of man or other animals" [FD&C Act, sec. 201(g)(1)]. A simpler way to say this is that **drugs** are any chemical other than food intended to affect the structure or function of the body (Insel and Roth, 2002, p. 227). Drugs are continually being changed from prescription to over the counter (OTC). An FDA committee decides whether to approve or disapprove the change from one category to another. Once approved, the agency is concerned about OTC labeling so that consumers know what they are buying, as well as any warnings. The FDA's purpose is to protect human health while at the same time providing freedom of choice in the marketplace. This isn't always easy to attain. Public participation is sought, and this is happening more often as consumers take an active role in acquiring health information.

According to the *FDA Consumer,* a bimonthly publication of the Food and Drug Administration, when the pain reliever acetaminophen was developed in the 1950s, it was only available under the brand name, Tylenol. Today, acetaminophen can be found in many generic and store-brand versions such as Pamprin, Midol, and Anacin. Similarly, many drug products, prescription and over the counter, have generic versions available. *An estimated 44 percent of all prescriptions in the United States are filled with generic drugs.* **Prescription drugs** are obtained by a written instruction usually from a physician for the preparation and use of a drug. It is illegal to write your own prescription or modify an existing prescription from a doctor. Since drugs have side effects, undesirable reactions and interactions, consumers are given warnings on labels and in advertising. Nonetheless it is estimated that nearly 200,000 people die every year from adverse drug reactions, making it one of the leading causes of death. Most of the medications sold are nonprescription or **over the counter (OTC)** because most people choose to self-medicate or are treating minor illnesses or discomfort such as headaches, stomachaches, or pain relief such as an analgesic. The biggest seller is aspirin which is acetylsalicyclic acid sold by nearly 500 companies. It may be mixed or coated with other substances. Anacin, Excedrin, and Bayer are common brand names. In using OTCs, the potential for misdiagnosis is very high, resulting in side effects, hospitalization, overuse, overdose, lack of efficacy, and failure to get professional care. **Lack of efficacy** means that the pill or treatment fails to produce the desired effect or outcome.

Given the savings possible, why doesn't everyone switch to generics? In an AARP study, 95 percent of respondents were aware of generics, but only 31 percent asked for them from their doctors (Generics May Be Cheaper, But Consumers Resist, 2002). About 28 percent of the respondents worried that the drugs would be

Drugs are chemicals other than foods intended to affect the structure or function of the body.

The biggest selling OTC drug is aspirin.

less effective or of inferior quality or in some other way different from brand-name drugs. As this section shows, this is not the case since generics must pass strict standards to earn FDA approval.

The way the approval process works for brand-name drugs is that companies develop new drugs, patent them, and in so doing, earn the right to sell them for a certain number of years. When the brand-name drugs near their expiration dates, manufacturers can apply to the FDA to sell generic versions. The Drug Price Competition and Patent Term Restoration Act of 1984 allows for this approval process. To summarize, generic drugs are safe, effective, and FDA approved (see Box 9.2). People can use them with total confidence according to Gary Buehler, M.D., director of the FDA's Office of Generic Drugs.

## Imported Drugs Raise Safety Concerns

"With an unapproved drug, you can't be sure that it has been shipped, handled, and stored under conditions that meet U.S. requirements" (Meadows, 2002b, p. 19). So, unapproved drugs that come into the United States carry innumerable health risks. The Internet, besides increased travel (much of it between Mexico and the United States), has made it easier for unapproved drugs to come into this country.

---

**BOX 9.2    Frequently Asked Questions about Generic Drugs (and Their Answers from the FDA)**

1. Are generic drugs as safe as brand name drugs?
   Yes. The FDA requires that all drugs be safe and effective.
2. Are generic drugs as strong as brand-name drugs?
   Yes. The FDA requires generic drugs to have the same quality, strength, purity, and stability as brand-name drugs.
3. Do generic drugs take longer to work in the body?
   No. Generic drugs work in the same way and in the same amount of time as brand-name drugs.
4. Why are generic drugs less expensive?
   Generic drugs are less expensive because generic manufacturers don't have the investment costs of the developer of a new drug. New drugs are developed under patent protection. The patent protects the investment—including research, development, marketing, and promotion—by giving the company the sole right to sell the drug while it is in effect.
5. Does every brand-name drug have a generic counterpart?
   No. Brand-name drugs are generally given patent protection for 20 years from the date of submission of the patent. This provides protection for the innovator.
6. If brand-name drugs and generics have the same active ingredients, why do they look different?
   In the U.S., trademark laws do not allow a generic drug to look exactly like the brand-name drug. However, a generic drug must duplicate the active ingredient. Colors, flavors, and certain other inactive ingredients may be different.

*Source: FDA Consumer,* September–October 2002, p. 24. For the sake of brevity, the key point of the answer is given, for additional information refer to this publication or the FDA Web site at www.fda.gov/cder/ogd/.

"We've found drugs that were stored in time containers and car trunks," says Daniel Hancz, a pharmacist with the Health Authority Law Enforcement Task Force (HALT) in Los Angeles (Meadows, 2002b, p. 18). Some criminals claim to have a medical background and not only do they illegally sell drugs but they also give injections. Some of the drugs are very old, others have side effects, some cause death. Through the FD&C Act, the interstate shipment of any prescription drug that lacks required FDA approval is illegal. Interstate shipment includes importation. The FDA works with the U.S. Customs Service. If a bag or package arouses suspicion, FDA or the Drug Enforcement Agency will be contacted. The U.S. Customs Canine Enforcement Team inspects arriving international mail for illegal pharmaceuticals. For information about the U.S. Customs Service, visit the agency's Web site at *www.customs.ustreas.gov.*

To summarize the potential health risk with imported drugs are:

1. Quality assurance concerns
2. Counterfeit potential
3. Presence of untested substances
4. Risks of unsupervised use
5. Labeling and language issues
6. Lack of information

**Crossing National Borders to Buy Drugs.**   On the evening news shows, there are segments showing elderly Americans going on bus trips to Canada to save money on prescription drugs. It is estimated that tens of thousands of Americans are going across the border on buying trips or are buying drugs online from Canadian pharmacies (Parker-Pope, 2002). There can be a real cost savings because drugs such as Celebrex (for arthritis) and Tamoxifen (for breast cancer) sell in Canada at less than half of American prices in U.S. dollars (Parker-Pope, 2003). Another example is the cholesterol-lowering drug Zocor. In 2002, it cost $327.86 for a three-month supply from U.S.-based drugstore.com, but at hometownmeds.com based in Manitoba, Canada, the price was $189.55 (Parker-Pope, 2003). Depending on the drug and shipping charges, savings may be more or less than this. When a married couple is using a dozen drugs between them, the savings can be $300 or more a month so it is worth shopping around. The Canadian and U.S. government regulators are looking into increased online shopping behavior. Canadian regulators are cracking down on unaccredited Canadian pharmacies who are staffed with unregistered pharmacists.

The FDA says people are taking a risk when they buy outside the United States, but not everyone sees it that way, including many physicians, congressmen, and

**Consumer Alert**

When buying drugs online from Canada or any other country, the U.S. consumer should deal only with a pharmacy that requires a prescription from a U.S. doctor. Also, the consumer should be able to speak to the pharmacist filling the prescription. To be really sure, the consumer should ask the pharmacy what country the drugs are from, request a copy of the pharmacy's license, and ask if the delivery date is guaranteed and, if so, in what manner.

senators. The concern according to the *FDA Consumer* is that some of the drugs may be exact and some may not. Consumers report that one problem is that certain doses carried in the United States aren't always available or are sold in quantities that do not match their prescription. The FDA does not have authority to approve drugs sold in Canada. Canada, who is cooperating with U.S. authorities, is having to deal with some of the same regulatory issues including their citizens buying from other countries over the Internet. Although this section has been primarily about Americans going to Canada, there are similar issues regarding Americans living in the Southwest going to Mexico to find less expensive drugs, and people in other countries traveling to neighboring countries around the world to save money. Crossing borders, physically or online, to buy drugs is an issue to watch, and more international agreements between countries in this regard are underway.

## Doctors Online

"Almost 30% of doctors have their own Web sites, according to the American Medical Association" (Reagan, 2002, p. D4). The functions of the sites are to:

- Provide information such as telephone numbers and office addresses.
- Attract new patients.
- Increase efficiency. An online feature allows patients to fill out their medical history before a visit, thus saving five minutes in the waiting room.
- Announce availability such as "we have flu shots available for $15 from October 1–Nov. 15."

A thorny issue is whether physicians should respond to patients' e-mail requests for information. Another issue is whether they should post warnings such as "the flu season has arrived." Many patients would like more interaction with their doctors, but doctors who are already overworked may have a hard time responding to individual e-mails or to keeping up-to-date information posted. Another issue is the privacy of e-mail exchanges because messages sent through unsecured servers can be intercepted. Under the Health Insurance Portability and Accountability Act of 1996, doctors can be fined for compromising the confidentiality of patients' records (Reagan, 2002). But the overall trend is toward more online consultations.

Medem Inc., of San Francisco, is the leading provider of Web sites for doctors. What it has found is that when major changes in medical news hit the media such as the June 2002 study results that showed potential risks of hormone-replacement therapy (HRT), thousands of women scrambled to Web sites for advice. Doctors pay Medem $2.50 per "online visit" and set their own fees for patients which averaged about $26 when this book was being written. A competitor, Medfusion, offers a secure message system and other features so as with any other new business there will be a back-and-forth between providers, charges, and consumers.

The bottom line is that what works on e-commerce sites may not necessarily work in health care, issues because their highly personal and individualistic nature require special thought and discretion. Clearly, there are ethical, technological, and cost issues to be worked out, but the trend is toward more doctors going online and to a national system where patients, parents, and doctors can easily access health records online such as vaccination records of children. A national system would save lives and reduce pain and suffering because X-rays, tests, and other records could be sent immediately to offices, emergency rooms, and operating

Almost 30 percent of doctors have Web sites and the trend is upward, including the development of a national system of health record access for patients, parents, and health care professionals.

rooms—the wait or float time while records are being found and sent would be erased. When doctors close their offices, there will be no more announcements or rushes to get records, they will automatically be in the system—they will never be lost. It would also be a boon to the majority of people in this country who move around a lot or are traveling—their records could be accessed immediately, anywhere. Eventually, there will be a worldwide system or at least cooperative relationships among a number of countries so that people who travel abroad can be assured of their records being available when needed.

# BIOLOGICS

Following a series of tragic deaths by tainted biological products, Congress enacted the Biologics Control Act in 1902. This law gave the FDA's Center for Biologics Evaluation and Research (CBER) authority to regulate biological products and ensure their quality. **Biologics** include vaccines, blood and blood derivatives, allergenic patch tests and extracts, tests to detect HIV and hepatitis, gene therapy products, cells and tissues for transplantation and new treatments for cancers and arthritis (100 Years of Biologics Regulation, 2002). Key developments since 1902 include the polio vaccine, measles vaccine, pertussis vaccine (for whooping cough), blood and plasma products, and the screening of the blood supply. A hundred years ago the average American could expect to die by age 47. Whooping cough, flu, pneumonia, and diphtheria could kill whole families. If someone got cancer, they did not usually live for long. Today four out of ten patients are alive five years after diagnosis, and we are near permanent cures. Life expectancy has greatly increased.

# HEALTH CHALLENGES

The main challenges are finding ways to reduce the three leading causes of death in the United States which are

1. Heart disease, 31 percent of total deaths
2. Cancer, 23.2 percent of total deaths
3. Stroke, 6.8 percent of total deaths

Other challenges include ethical issues surrounding tissue transplants and research on gene therapy and the growing costs of health care and prescription drugs. Another challenge is reducing the cost of health care and expanding services to underserved populations—the young, the elderly, rural dwellers, and the poor.

**Malpractice insurance** (insurance doctors or clinics have in case they are sued by patients) is one of the things driving up the costs of health care and the decisions doctors make about what specializations to go into and where to practice because malpractice insurance rates vary by specialization and by state. Many doctors pay over $100,000 a year for malpractice insurance. "An analysis by the American Medical Association finds that the escalating cost of medical-liability insurance is causing doctors to quit, relocate or abandon high-risk practices, creating a health-care crisis in 12 states," including Washington, Oregon, Nevada, Texas, Ohio, West Virginia, Pennsylvania, Florida, New York, New Jersey, Mississippi, and Georgia (Cummons, 2003, p. A4). Doctors have staged rallies in several of these states. On January 1, 2003, West Virginia surgeons walked "out of four hospitals to protest the rising insurance premiums that are driving some to quit and others to abandon high-risk specialties such as obstetrics, some surgeries and trauma treatment" (Cummings, 2003, p. A4). Generally, malpractice insurance premiums are highest for obstetricians and orthopedic surgeons. As this book went to press, physicians were pressuring Congress to cap damage awards as one means to bring down premiums (their payments to insurance companies). Several powerful groups oppose the doctors, including trial lawyers and patients' rights groups. These groups point out that:

1. Capping awards may not work (and may hurt consumers, especially families with young children who have had severe medical problems and face life-long care and medical expenses).
2. The medical profession could do a better job of policing their own physicians since only a small percentage account for most of the malpractice suits. They would say here is a good opportunity to root out less than adequate doctors. They would also say that government boards could do a better job of reprimanding or taking licenses away from errant physicians.

The end of this is not in sight. Two of the proposals being considered are limited noneconomic patient damages (i.e., legal and court fees) to $250,000 and shorten the statute of limitations for filing complaints (Cummings, 2003, p. A4). In a move toward political activism, in 2003 the American Medical Association moved all of its leadership meetings to Washington to give doctors plenty of opportunity to lobby and influence representatives. From the consumer point of view, what it really comes down to is doctor availability, and there are very critical health concerns connected with this. Patients in primarily rural states have died because the nearest available specialist was six hours or more away. Why? Because the specialists moved to states with better malpractice insurance rates. This is a many sided issue involving states, the federal government, the medical profession, attorneys and courts, patient's rights, and consumers.

Another factor driving up the cost of health care is the nursing shortage. Nurses are now being offered signing on bonuses, scholarships, more flexible hours, and significantly higher salaries than in the past.

Another substantial cost is the money poured into research and development— the search for cures. Pharmaceuticals commit a higher percentage to research and development (R&D) than any other industry. It costs an average of $500 million to discover and develop a single new medicine. Of the thousands of compounds screened for medical potential each year, only a few will pass enough hurdles to get to the human testing stage and be approved by FDA. If drug prices were lowered or more controlled, would it reduce R&D? Those representing pharmaceutical companies and researchers in the United States and Europe say "yes," those representing consumer groups are more likely to say "no." Some consumer advocacy groups argue that the companies should plow more of their profits into R&D. The industry replies that this is not realistic. The industry says price controls are harmful to innovation and discovery and that, in the long run, cutting back on R&D would be harmful to patients.

## VACCINES: CONSUMER SAFETY ISSUES

In the early twentieth century, many people died as a result of common infectious diseases and poor environmental conditions such as unrefrigerated food, poor sanitation, and air and water pollution. **Infectious disease** is defined as communicable from person to person; the causes are invading microorganisms such as viruses and bacteria. These are different from **chronic disease**, which is a disease that develops and continues over a long period of time. Chronic disease is usually caused by a variety of factors, including lifestyle. Examples of chronic disease are heart disease and cancer.

Bioterriorism threats in the twenty-first century has forced a reexamination of the nation's vaccine supply. Do we have enough vaccines? Vaccine shortages frustrate parents, patients, and doctors alike.

> There are many reasons for the shortages. A major reason is the fact that there are relatively few manufacturers in the vaccine business. It's also difficult to make vaccines; from start to finish, a particular batch of a given vaccine requires roughly a year of production time. Unlike most drugs, vaccines are produced from living cells and organisms. Most require growing the immunizing agent, whether its bacteria or viruses, in production facility where growth conditions are complex. (Meadows, 2002a, p. 12).

Of particular concern is smallpox vaccine, a possible tool in the war on bioterror. In its recorded 3,000-year history, smallpox has killed hundreds of millions of people. The problem with the vaccine is that it causes life-threatening reactions in 15 of every million people vaccinated, killing one or two of them (Chase and Hitt, 2002, p. A1). At highest risk of reaction are babies, pregnant women, people with the common skin rash eczema, and those with weakened immune systems. So doctors are wary to give the vaccine unless it becomes necessary, and government policy makers are tackling with who should get the vaccine first. One idea favored by federal health officials is to offer smallpox vaccinations to the 500,000 hospital workers viewed as most likely to come into contact with patients with smallpox should there be a widespread bioterrorism attack (Chase and Hitt, 2002, p. A1).

Vaccines that have been in short supply in the recent past are

1. Diptheria and Tetanus Toxoids and Acellular Pertussis (DTaP): The DTaP supply has returned to normal and is used the most for children six weeks to six years.
2. Measles, Mumps, Rubells (MMR): The first dose in the two-dose MMR regimen is at ages 12–15 months and the second between 4–6 years. Supply is at normal. This vaccine has been stockpiled since 1983.
3. Chickenpox (Varicella): Normally, the recommendation is one dose of varicella vaccine between 12 months and 18 months or at any age after 18 months if a child has not has had chickenpox or the vaccine. When this book was written, there was a shortage that was soon to improve.
4. Pneumococcal Conjugate: Infants normally receive a series of four shots with the final shot at age 12–15 months. According to manufacturer projections, supplies were low until 2003.
5. Tetanus and Diptheria Toxoids for Adults (Td): Given as booster shots to adolescents and adults; supply levels are adequate.

A number of government groups, in particular the FDA and the CDC, are working together to ensure a steady supply of vaccines. Discussions are underway regarding how to speed up production and how to stockpile more vaccines. Check with your health care provider about whether you need any of these vaccines and others such as flu (influenza vaccines) and Hepatitis B vaccine (HBV) which protects against hepatitis B virus. Hepatitis B is spread through contact with blood and body fluids of an infected person. To access the recommended schedule of adult vaccines, contact *www.cdc.gov/nip/recs/adult-schedule.htm.*

## HARMFUL EFFECTS OF TANNING

Moving to a different subject is a health issue that is, for the most part, under our control—how much or how little to tan. The darker side of tanning includes increased risk of skin cancer, eye damage, skin aging, and allergic reactions. **Tanning** is the body's response to skin exposed to ultraviolet radiation (UV) from the sun. Health problems can occur from using sunlamps and tanning beds, as well as from natural sunlight. If using artificial means to tan, the consumer should use goggles and other protective gear and watch timing carefully. Using a sunscreen appropriate to exposure and skin type is recommended. Another caution is that the consumer should be careful about any possible reactions that may occur from the use of certain medications while being exposed to the sun.

Besides the physical problems associated with excessive tanning, consumers should be careful before signing contracts with tanning salons. Tanning salons often go in and out of business so contracts may not be fulfilled. Individual questions about tanning salons, skin damage, and tanning from the sun should be directed to physicians.

Why do people spend time and money getting a deep tan given the negative health effects? Obviously, they do it to improve their appearance, but it goes beyond that. Getting a tan before going to the beach for the first time may provide freedom from ridicule—a strong motivator. Also, in consumer theory, there exists a dimension of the want-satisfying nature of products described as **hedonic**. This refers to the fact that many products and behaviors such as tanning provide sensory benefits—in short, because they taste, feel, look, or smell good to us. It is not difficult to understand why someone would want to escape a long snowy winter to find the sun in the Caribbean or Hawaii.

## BOTOX

Botox is a drug.

Is botox a cosmetic or a drug treatment? Advertisements to the contrary, *botox is a drug by FDA definitions.* **Botox** or "botulinum Toxin Type A is a protein complex produced by the bacterium Clostridium botulinum, which contains the same toxin that causes food poisoning. When used in a medical setting an injectable form of sterile, purified botulinum toxin, small doses block the release of a chemical called acetycholine by nerve cells that signal muscle contraction. By selectively interfering

A woman lies in a tanning bed. She is wearing protective goggles. (Courtesy of Omni-Photo Communications, Inc. Photo by Eric Kroll.)

with underlying muscles' ability to contract, existing frown lines are smoothed out, and in most cases, are nearly invisible in a week" (Lewis, 2002, p. 11).

The FDA approved the use of the drug under certain conditions. Drugs, including those used for cosmetic purposes such as botox, are subject to the FDA approval process. Part of the confusion is that the FDA regulates products, but not how they are used. Botox treatments have been given by nonmedical personnel, and this is against the law. Sometimes, a doctor oversaw a clinic or gave his or her name to be used in advertisements, but the actual injections were given by nonmedical personnel such as cosmetics/spa workers or beauticians. Unauthorized people who are caught giving injections are arrested and charged.

Botox gained public attention because it was marketed to groups of people in the form of a party. At the parties, adult men and women gathered, paid a fee, signed a consent form, ate snacks and had drinks, and one-by-one were led off to treatment rooms where they were sedated and the numbing treatments given. Common botox treatment side effects include headache, nausea, respiratory infection, and flu syndrome. Sometimes the numbing does not wear off easily. One of the main places for injections is the frown lines or wrinkles above the nose. It is not uncommon for someone to go in for botox treatments every three months. For more information on botox, see the E-Resources section.

## MEDICAL DEVICES, TREATMENTS, AND PROCEDURES

Since the beginnings of recorded time, people have been experimenting with various devices and procedures to restore health. Even today, there are so many fake devices and procedures it is difficult to put them into categories; many of them

**Consumer Alert**

Be careful when using health-related Web sites. There are thousands of them and not all are safe and surfable sites. Examples of reliable sites are given in the E-Resources section. When you are deciding about the worthiness of a site, consider:

- The source (who).
- Where the information comes from, who wrote it or what institution stands behind it, how old is the information.
- Why the source exists. Are they selling anything? Avoid sites that sell or have testimonials as a sales gimmick. Avoid sites with easy or "natural" cures for serious complex disorders.
- What the message is—look for names that you know and trust. And remember that a fraudulent name can be very close to a legitimate source name.

defy categorization because they claim to cure so many different kinds of ills. The best advice is that if it seems to be too good to be true, it probably is. Some products are harmful and others are merely ineffective. As an example, do warmed up fist-sized stones placed on your back give long-lasting health results? What do you think? Is the treatment worth the $150 spa charge?

The FDA cannot keep up with every device, treatment, or product sold in the marketplace, especially those from foreign countries advertised on the Internet or those cooked up in someone's kitchen and sold at in-home sales parties. They try to review products, especially those sold nationally, to see if they are effective and do not present unreasonable risk to patients. In short, not everything is thoroughly tested, and most medical devices are cleared through the premarket notification process, a less rigorous process. Examples of medical devices are contraceptives, defibrillators, lasers, heart devices, breast imaging devices, wart removal systems, contact lenses, and weight loss devices. The FDA Web site lists newly approved devices and procedures.

The FDA regulates prescription, over-the-counter, and generic drugs. They also regulate radiation-emitting products such as cell phones, lasers, microwaves, and mammogram machines. The Mammography Quality Standards Act passed in 1993 was reauthorized in 1998 and set to be revisited in the twenty-first century. Under this act, facilities are initially certified as meeting certain quality standards and then must continue to pass annual inspections. In 1994 a landmark Dietary Supplement Health and Education Act established specific labeling requirements, provided a regulatory framework, and authorized the FDA to promulgate good manufacturing practice regulations for dietary supplements. In 1999 the Food and Drug Administration Modernization Act mandated the most wide-ranging reforms in agency practices since 1918. Provisions included measures to accelerate review of devices and regulated advertising of unapproved drugs and devices. Examples of medical devices regulated by FDA include pacemakers, contact lenses, and hearing aids.

The challenge of preventative medicine is to get people to focus on feeling better rather than looking thinner or whatever other appearance change is desired. Many frauds in the health industries have their root in the promise of a more attractive appearance and an easy way to get it which leads us into the next section on cosmetics.

## COSMETICS

The Food, Drug, and Cosmetic Act (FD&C Act) defines **cosmetics** by their intended use, as "articles to be rubbed, poured, sprinkled, or sprayed on, introduced into, or otherwise applied to the human body . . . for cleansing, beautifying, promoting attractiveness, or altering the appearance (FD&C Act, sec. 20[i]). Among the products included in this definition are skin moisturizers, perfumes, lipsticks, fingernail polish, eye and facial makeup preparations, shampoos, permanent waves, hair colors, toothpastes, and deodorants, as well as any material intended for use as a component of a cosmetic product.

Famous name brands may be **aspirational** such as Chanel No. 5, meaning that consumers aspire to own them. A perfume or famous-brand cosmetic may fulfill a consumer's desire for acceptance, affiliation, esteem, achievement, prestige, and status. Another consumer may have no interest in what another individual or group thinks, but may aspire to own a certain fragrance or cosmetic to fulfill their own happiness, sense of beauty, or pleasure. Marketers try to satisfy different needs and may even position a product to fulfill several levels of needs. Thus, advertising for the same product may vary greatly from media outlet to media outlet. Depending on the **cues**—ads, signs, packaging, and other stimuli—the individual will respond positively, neutrally, or negatively. If there is a positive response, it is because the cue worked, that is, it somehow struck a nerve or a drive. When no one responds, the marketers or product manufacturers have missed their target.

A few years ago manufacturers and advertisers tried to get most of the American adult population interested in applying a special foot deodorant to their feet on a daily basis just as they apply deodorant under their arms. Consumers failed to pick up the cues because they didn't perceive foot odor to be an everyday kind of problem deserving their attention. This is a good example of consumers driving the marketplace; they will not buy a product if they do not perceive a need.

When it comes to cosmetics, some consumers are experimental, meaning that they like to try new brands and products, whereas others are brand loyal, preferring the tried and true. In fact, the latter type gets quite upset when their favorite lipstick or scent is no longer available. Cosmetics companies play into both experimental and stick-to-it types with promotions or samples of new products coupled with a few conventional products. Samples, as a type of cue, create the perception of a want or a need. Once tried, a certain percentage of customers will buy a full-size product—if not for themselves, then for someone on their gift list.

Can a product be both a drug and a cosmetic? Yes, some products meet both definitions. For example, a shampoo is a cosmetic because it is intended to clean hair, but an antidandruff treatment is a drug to treat dandruff. So, an antidandruff shampoo is both a drug and a cosmetic. Other examples of duo products are toothpastes with fluoride, deodorants that are also antiperspirants, and moisturizers and makeup with sun protection.

The FDA only regulates cosmetics after products are released to the marketplace. Ingredients or products are not reviewed or approved by FDA prior to being sold to the public. If the FDA wishes to remove a cosmetic from the market, it must first prove in a court of law that the product may be injurious to users, improperly labeled, or otherwise violates the law. The FDA inspects cosmetics manufacturing facilities, collects samples to check, and takes action through the Department of Justice. Foreign products may be refused entry into the United States.

## Labeling Including Hypoallergenic

Personal care products can produce unwanted effects such as skin irritations and allergies. About 10 percent of the population has adverse reactions to cosmetics and toiletries (The Hype in "Hypoallergenic," 2002). Fragrance is the most common irritant, but emulsifiers and preservatives can also be irritating. One of the ways consumers can minimize adverse effects is to know their skin type and read labels. The drawback to suggesting that consumers read labels is that they would have to be chemists to understand many of the ingredients.

About 10 percent of the population has adverse reactions to cosmetics and toiletries. Fragrance is the most common irritant.

According to the FDA Web site, federal regulations require ingredients to be listed on product labels in descending order by quantity. Consumers can check the ingredient listing to identify ingredients that they want to avoid. Based on the amount used, an ingredient such as water is usually found at the beginning of the product's ingredient list while color additives and fragrances usually in small amounts are normally seen at the end of the listing. These rules apply only to home use products. Professional use products are not required to have ingredient declarations. The FDA regulates the labeling directly on the product. Ads for cosmetics in magazines, newspapers, or on television are monitored by the Federal Trade Commission.

A common claim is that cosmetics are hypoallergenic. Consumers with sensitive skin are drawn to them, but in reality there are no federal standards or definitions governing the term "hypoallergenic." What consumers find on a list of ingredients on the product label are ingredients that usually are compatible with sensitive skin, but there are no guarantees. Manufacturers are not required to disclose the components of fragrances which as stated earlier are the most common irritants. To help fill in this gap in consumer information, Consumer Union has an Eco-Labels program and a Web site (*www.eco-labels.org*) that explains labels such as "hypoallergenic" and "unscented." So, if you want to know if a cosmetic is, for example, alcohol-free, then you can to the Web site and find the information about a specific product. Besides toiletries, this site also discusses cleaning products, food, and wood products.

## Organic Beauty: Natural or Environmentally Friendly Products

Certified organic beauty products must contain at least 70 percent certified organic ingredients which come from natural sources such as nuts, flowers, and fruits.

Just as there are organic foods, there are organic beauty products. Are they better? How much is hype? To be certified organic, a beauty product must contain at least 70 percent certified organic ingredients which means they come from natural sources such as nuts, flowers, and fruits. They should be cultivated in pesticide-free soil and be free of spraying. Regular and organic cosmetics are formulated to be irritation-free, but an individual may have a reaction. Differences may be found in scent, preservatives, color, and emollients (oils, essential fatty acids). Organic products may not last as long as regular cosmetics with preservatives. The rule of thumb is to use the product in a timely fashion and to throw out anything that smells, separates, or looks bad. There have been reports that organic cosmetics are more likely to have purity problems. Choosing organic or environmentally friendly products comes down to personal preference; they may be more compatible with your skin and your politics than conventional products. Connected to this are concerns about the use of animals in product testing. Many consumers prefer cosmetics that do not use animal testing in research and development so some companies put this on their label or manufacture whole lines of products in North American and in Europe that do not use animal testing.

## Tooth Whiteners: The Road to Glamour

It used to be that entertainers had to frequent a Hollywood dentist to get really white teeth. The treatments were done over several weeks or month's worth of appointments in the dentist's chair. But, with new technology and invention there are now more effective in-office dental treatments and home-based, do-it-yourself kits. Is there a market? Yes, a whopping 93 percent of Americans worry about their teeth being yellowed or stained according to a survey by Trident. The dental-bleaching business has gone from nearly nothing to billions of dollars in annual sales for oral care kits within the last few years. Sales for "tooth polishes" more than doubled in 2002, and Procter & Gamble alone had $1 billion in oral-care sales (De Lisser, 2003, p. D1). Teeth darken with age so treatments work best on those over 30 years of age and those with a history of coffee drinking and smoking.

Whiteners come in a variety of ways, including bottles, swabs, little brushes, strips, and tooth trays to collect the drool. Prices range from $15 to nearly a $1,000. Do they work? The answer is it depends on the product, the person's teeth, and how well the person follows the directions. Journalists and *Consumer Reports* have been testing the dental-bleaching products, and since these products are being perfected, it is best to continue watching for the best-performing products. To establish a baseline (what your teeth are like before treatment), a dentist can use a shade guide and then he or she can check your teeth to see much they have whitened after the treatment is completed. While at the dentist's office, ask what treatment may be right for you. When looking at whitening toothpastes, look for the ADA (American Dental Association) seal of approval. For more information, visit the ADA Web site at *www.ada.org.*

One of the most expensive treatments is the Zoom! Chairside Whitening System ($825 depending on dentist). In this treatment gel is applied to teeth and activated by a special light. The actual whitening takes close to 90 minutes, During this time, the patient sits in a chair, wears protective goggles, and the mouth is stretched open with a dental expander. Some people get panicky or experience claustrophobia while they wait, but the outcome of whiter teeth has been documented (De Lisser, 2003, p. D1). For much less expense, Colgate Simply White is a gel applied to individual teeth with a tiny brush, twice a day, for 14 days, at home. One of the most advertised products is Crest Professional Whitestrips that are plastic strips worn on top and bottom teeth for at least 30 minutes twice a day. It should be noted that most of the treatments involve some form of teeth pain afterward that tapers off.

The point of this section is that consumers are always interested in new health or cosmetic products, especially ones that have the promise of enhancing their appearance. Different generations tend to focus on different parts of the body such as the importance of shiny hair or in this case whiter teeth. Fads come and go, but the fact that consumers want to improve their appearance is a permanent human condition.

## ALCOHOL AND TOBACCO CONSUMPTION.

Now, the chapter turns its attention to the more serious topic of potentially addictive behavior—alcohol and tobacco consumption. **Addictions** are habits that have gotten out of control, resulting in a negative impact on one's health that often spills over into other aspects of life such as personal relationships or the ability to do work.

### Alcohol Consumption

**Alcohol** is the intoxicating ingredient found in fermented liquors: a colorless, pungent liquid (Insel and Roth, 2002, p. 258). The common use of the word alcohol refers to the intoxicating ingredients found in beer, wine, and distilled spirits (hard liquor). Chemists would use the term ethyl alcohol or ethanol. A drink is an alcoholic beverage that delivers one-half ounce of pure ethanol. Examples are 5 ounces of wine, 12 ounces of beer, and one-half ounce of distilled liquor (80 proof scotch, rum, vodka, or whiskey). People have different tolerance levels, so it is difficult to determine what would be a moderate amount. The generally accepted definition of moderation is not more than one drink per average-size woman and two drinks per average-size man a day (Whitney and Rolfes, 2002). Alcohol consumption has both short- and long-term effects. The most horrifying long-term effects are those of babies born to mothers who abused alcohol. This is called **fetal alcohol syndrome**.

Why is alcohol abuse a consumer issue? Society pays many prices for alcohol abuse, including the harm caused by drunken driving accidents, homicides, suicide, and unintentional injuries not to mention the health effects, insurance costs, lost workdays and lower productivity. The average American spends 61¢ a day on alcohol compared with 59¢ a day on prescription drugs and $1.26 a day on gasoline and oil. A 5-ounce glass of wine has about 100 calories, a 12-ounce regular beer about 150, and 1.5 ounces of 80-proof distilled spirits about 100 calories.

The liquor industry has voluntary advertising guidelines, including self-imposed bans, but according to George Hacker, director of the Center for Science in the Public Interest's alcohol policies project, the ads for fruit-flavored alcohol drinks are luring millions of teenagers. He says, "Those ads put liquor brand names right in kids' faces (Alcohol Ads Reaching Teens, 2002, p. 3A). An example is alcoholic lemonade that has the same amount of alcohol as beer, but the taste is masked by lemonade. Another category of product appealing to young consumers are the "malternative" beverages. Ads for these feature loud music and attractive young people laughing or dancing. In a survey taken by a polling firm for CSPI, an estimated 22 million teenagers—three out of four people ages 12 to 18—watch television after 9:00 P.M. on school nights when alcohol ads are typically run. Further, six in ten teens could name a specific company or brand that advertises during that time. Another product aimed at young people is "zippers," fruit-flavored gelatin cups containing 12 percent alcohol, roughly the same amount found in a glass of wine. In 2002, "zippers" were sold in at least 20 states, and the Community Anti-Drug Coalition of America spoke out against them. Grocery stores were selling "zippers" without proper labeling, making it easier for underage drinkers to buy them. The packaging looked like the type of dessert packs thousands of children eat every day so parents were unaware what their children were consuming.

About 30 percent of the American population is under age 21, but certain magazines that run alcohol ads draw a higher percentage of young readers.

About 30 percent of the American population is under age 21, but certain publications draw a higher percentage of young readers than others. For example, *Spin* magazine draws 48 percent of readers under the legal drinking age of 21 according to data used by ad executives. *Allure* has 44 percent underage readers, and *Rolling Stone,* 35 percent. Each of these magazines has alcohol ads, including products such as V. O. Seagram Co.'s Absolut Vodka (Wells, Burnett, and Moriarty, 2000).

Less than socially responsible ads have been removed from circulation, such as those showing people drinking while driving or boating. But generally liquor ads will show well-dressed young adults out as a group in an attractive setting, having fun while drinking so that drinking is portrayed as a social activity. In reality, a lot of excessive drinking takes place behind closed doors at home, alone—not an appealing image.

## Smoking and Nicotine Products

Three out of four smokers cannot quit.

**Tobacco** refers to the leaves of cultivated plants prepared for smoking, chewing, or use as snuff (Insel and Roth, 2002, p. 287). **Nicotine** is a poisonous, addictive substance found in tobacco and responsible for many of the effects of tobacco (Insel and Roth, 2002, p. 287). It is addictive because three out of four smokers want to quit but find they cannot (Insel and Roth, 2002, p. 286).

Cigarette smoking contains many toxic and carcinogenic (cancer-causing) chemicals that affect both the person smoking and the people breathing in tobacco smoke in the near environment. The debate about the use of smoking and nicotine products often circulates around the issue of *individual choice versus the rights of others* and leads to discussions of how much should be regulated or banned. In various states there are initiatives or laws that limit or ban smoking from restaurants. One state was experimenting with eliminating smoking from outside state buildings, requiring employees to smoke at least 50 feet away from state office buildings and further that no benches or other seating or shelters would be made available. In the debate, consumers may disagree with one another (smokers vs. nonsmokers). Generally consumer groups want more regulations because of the dangers inherent in secondhand smoke inhalation, and the industry (in it for the profit) wants fewer. Another issue is how high to tax smoking and nicotine products. Other issues are age restrictions, health warnings on labels, and advertising. There are related issues such as are candy cigarettes which are a bad idea because they encourage children to imitate smoking behaviors. Should tobacco-company advertisers be allowed to use cartoonlike characters in ads? How much risk disclosure is necessary on product labels and in advertising?

Many government groups actively set policies, taxation, and regulations on tobacco products. As one example, in 1995 the FDA declared cigarettes to be "drug delivery devices," and restrictions were proposed on marketing and sales to reduce smoking by young people. However some consumer groups feel there are double messages because tobacco farmers are given crop subsidies (money from the federal government to grow or not grow crops) while at the same time consumption of cigarettes is taxed. They wonder why the government is supporting the industry that has so many devastating effects on the health of the nation. In the United States more than 400,000 deaths a year are associated with cigarette smoking.

Nicotine products range from gums and chewing tobacco to bottled waters. Some are marketed as a smoking substitute so you drink when you can't light up, for example, on an airplane or in the office or as a way to lose weight. Others are marketed as a way to quit or reduce smoking. Nicotine addiction is considered a disease. The FDA has ruled that nicotine water is an unapproved drug under the Federal Food, Drug, and Cosmetic Act (FD&C Act) and therefore cannot be marketed without going through the approval process. The FDA has warned that nicotine lollipops and lip balm are illegal. These products had been selling over the Internet without a doctor's prescription. Children were getting a hold of the lollipops, lip balm, waters, and gums. Several groups have joined together, including the National Center for Tobacco-Free Kids, the American Medical Association, and the American Lung Association, to ban nicotine water marketed to children.

Cigarette smoking is declining in the United States.

The percentage of U.S. adults who smoke cigarettes is dropping. In 2002 the percentage was 23 percent compared with 28 percent in 1984.

## HEALTHY PEOPLE INITIATIVE

The U.S. government has a national Healthy People Initiative that seeks to prevent unnecessary diseases and disabilities and to achieve a better quality of life for all. The national goals for 2010 are

- Increase quality and years of healthy life.
- Eliminate health disparities among groups in the population. This is needed because health problems disproportionately affect certain populations such as ethnic minorities, less educated or wealthy people, and people with disabilities.

The federal government has a vital interest in the health of all citizens because a healthy population is the nation's greatest resource—the foundation of its vitality, creativity, and true wealth. Conversely, poor health is a drain on the nation's resources.

## SUMMARY

As in the last chapter on food and beverages, the Food and Drug Administration is the main regulator of health-related products and, as their name implies, of drugs. The emphasis in the chapter was on legal drugs such as those gained by prescription or over the counter. The Harrison Act of 1914 prohibited the use of cocaine, morphine, and opiates for nonmedical purposes.

Besides safety concerns there are cost maintenance concerns because health care costs are skyrocketing. On average, they are increasing faster than most other areas of consumer expenditure. What consumers seek is the best health care at a reasonable price. Preventative self-help is one way to reduce costs. Another way consumers reduce costs is by using generic drugs. It is estimated that 44 percent of all prescriptions in the United States are filled with generic drugs. Issues in the twenty-first century include the continued search for cures and the ethical issues surrounding tissue replacement, fertility treatments, and research on gene therapy. The threat of legal action (malpractice lawsuits) has driven up the cost of providing health care as have labor costs in general. To save money some American citizens are buying drugs by traveling to other countries or by ordering drugs over the Internet which raises quality-control issues.

About 30 percent of doctors have their own Web sites, and the trend is upward. More and more medical advice and information is being offered over the Internet, and there is a push to switch to e-records in the entire health industry. With this system, parents could look up their child's vaccination records online, and this type of information would be beneficial to schools and universities.

Consumers should be aware of quality issues, and guidelines for determining them were given in the chapter. Cosmetics were covered as well as alcohol and tobacco use. There are many health care and cosmetic products that are fraudulent. The chapter presented different reasons why consumers are so susceptible to this particular area of fraud (mostly false hope over reason) and why they may choose not to report fraud problems or why they may choose to ignore science. Some products are classified as both cosmetics and drugs such as dandruff shampoos.

The Federal Trade Commission is the main regulator of advertising of alcohol and tobacco/nicotine products. In the United States, more than 400,000 deaths a year are related to tobacco use. Studies have shown that teenagers are quite aware of the brand names of alcohol products that are advertised on television. National legislation to stop adult intake of alcohol (most specifically the Eighteenth Amendment to the Constitution passed in 1919 and repealed in 1933, more commonly referred to as Prohibition), has failed.

## KEY POINTS

1. Consumer health is an umbrella term encompassing the decisions consumers make about health care and their lifestyle.
2. Many health care frauds exist. Be especially wary of suspicious cancer cures and HIV-AIDS cures. The FTC has clamped down on fraudulent treatments. Other government agencies such as the FDA and the Centers for Disease Control are dedicated to protecting the public's health.
3. Health is your greatest asset.
4. Health care costs are rising significantly, and about 40 million Americans do not have health insurance.
5. Cigarette smoking is declining in the United States.
6. Congress enacted the Biologics Control Act in 1902, giving the FDA the authority to regulate biological products such as vaccines to ensure their quality.
7. Infectious disease is communicable from person to person; it is caused by invading microorganisms such as viruses and bacteria. One of the great advances of the twentieth century was a decrease in the percentage of deaths due to infectious diseases.
8. The top three causes of death in the United States are heart disease, cancer, and stroke.
9. Botox is a drug that is FDA regulated.

10. When it comes to cosmetics, there are no federal standards or definitions of "hypoallergenic."
11. Some cosmetics and scents are aspirational, meaning consumers aspire to own them.
12. Debates on limiting cigarette smoking usually revolve around individual rights versus the rights of others.

## KEY TERMS

| | | |
|---|---|---|
| addictions | drugs | prescription drugs |
| agent | fetal alcohol syndrome | principal |
| alcohol | generic drug | nicotine |
| aspirational | hedonic | quacks |
| biologics | infectious disease | science |
| botox | junk science | scientific literacy |
| chronic disease | lack of efficacy | tanning |
| consumer health | malpractice insurance | tobacco |
| cosmetics | medicare | well-being |
| cues | over the counter (OTC) | wellness |

## DISCUSSION QUESTIONS

1. In 1968 former Attorney General Robert Kennedy said, "The gross national product includes air pollution and advertising for cigarettes, and ambulances to clear our highways of carnage. It counts special locks for our doors, and jails for the people who break them. . . . It does not allow for the health of our families, the quality of their education, or the joy of their play." Why is health difficult to measure or quantify?
2. According to Robert Park, author and commentator, how does the media promote fraudulent products?
3. How long does it take before a patent usually runs out on an FDA-approved drug? Are all drugs available in generic form?
4. Why are people hesitant to use generic drugs?
5. How can a product be both a drug and a cosmetic? Give at least three examples of products that are both.
6. Select a Web site in the E-Resources section, and report on what you find on a specific body-related issue such as drugs, biologics, medical devices, or cosmetics.

## E-RESOURCES

General tip: If you are looking for someone who works for the government, there is a good chance you can locate that person through a Webpage called the U.S. Government Telephone and E-Mail Directories. This is sponsored by FirstGov; the page is a gateway for contacting elected officials, federal employees, and military personnel. This site links to the National Contact Center where there is information about health issues and Medicare, as well as other topics.

American Cancer Society
www.cancer.org

American Dental Association
www.ada.org

American Heart Association
www.americanheart.org

This site offers a personalized health program at www.onelife.americanheart.org

American Medical Association
www.amaassn.org

Centers for Disease Control and Prevention
www.cdc.gov

Federal Trade Commission
www.ftc.gov

Healthfinder
www.healthfinder.gov

Mayo Clinic
www.mayoclinic.com

National Cancer Institute
www.cancer.gov

PersonalPath.com
Created by doctors and nurses, the Web site covers health, illnesses, treatments, medications, benefits, costs, and finding help. Includes direct links to other Web sites, such as The Harvard Health Letter and Care Guides. You can research your symptoms or conditions and learn before your doctor visit about treatment options, tests, free clinical trials, prescriptions, and side effects.

WebMD
www.webmd.com

American Psychological Association
www.apa.org/psychnet

U.S. Health and Human Services Office on Women's Health
www.4women.gov

Medscape and CBS Healthwatch
www.medscape.com

Regarding botox and plastic surgery issues, sites to visit include:

American Academy of Dermatology

www.aad.org

American Society for Dermatologic Surgery
www.aboutskinsurgery.com

American Society for Aesthetic Plastic Surgery
www.asaps.org

New England Journal of Medicine
www.nejm.org

If you or someone you know needs guidance or someone to talk to regarding alcohol or drug use, contact your health care provider or a counselor. In addition to services on campus, the following organizations specialize in alcohol and other drug problems.

National Clearinghouse for Alcohol and Drug Information
www.health.org

Alcoholics Anonymous (for persons with alcohol problems)
www.alcoholics-anonymous.org

Narcotics Anonymous (for persons with other drug problems)
www.na.org

Alateen and Al-Anon (for family members and friends)
www.al-anon-alateen.org

National Council on Alcoholism and Drug Dependence
www.ncadd.org

American Society of Addiction Medicine
www.asam.org

Sites Related to Smoking and Disease:

World Health Organization
www.who.int

U.S. Centers for Disease Control and Prevention
www.cdc.gov

Sites Related to Smoking, Addiction and Quitting

U.S. Food and Drug Administration
www.fda.gov

U.S. Centers for Disease Control and Prevention
www.cdc.gov

National Center Institute
www.nci.nih.gov

QuitNet
www.quitnet.org

Sites Related to Secondhand Smoke

International Agency for Research on Cancer
www.iarc.fr

U.S. Environmental Protection Agency
www.epa.gov

# REFERENCES

Alcohol ads reaching teens (July 17, 2002). *Tallahassee Democrat*, p. 3A.

Chase, M., and G. Hitt. (October 21, 2002). Ugly side effects of smallpox vaccine color terror plans. *Wall Street Journal*, p. A1.

Cummings, J. (January 14, 2003). Doctors' activism revives malpractice bill. *Wall Street Journal*, p. A4.

De Graaf, J., D. Wann, and T. Naylor. (2001). *Affluenza: The all-consuming epidemic*. San Franciso, CA: Berrett-Koehler Publishers.

De Lisser, E. (January 14, 2003). The cranky consumer works on its smile. *Wall Street Journal*, p. D1.

Engstrom, P. (September 30, 2002). Medical sleuths. *Wall Street Journal*, p. R6.

Generic may be "equivalent," cheaper, but consumers resist. (July–August, 2002). *AARP Bulletin*, pp. 13–14.

Fleck, C. (January 2003). Cancer and snake oil. *AARP Bulletin*, p. 18.

*FTC facts for consumers: Miracle health claims: Add a dose of skepticism* (2003). Washington, DC.

Generics may be "equivalent," cheaper, but consumers resist (July-August 2002). *AARP Bulletin*, p. 13.

Huge profits in drug stocks. (July 2002). *Louis Rukeyser's Wall Street*, pp. 5–6.

Hype in "hypoallergenic," (June 2002). *Consumer Reports*, p. 6.

Insel, P., and W. Roth. (2002). *Core concepts in health, 9th ed.*, Boston: McGraw-Hill.

Lewis, C. (July–August 2002). Botox cosmetics: A look at looking good. *FDA Consumer*, pp. 11–13.

Meadows, M. (September–October 2002a). *FDA Consumer*, pp. 12–14.

Meadows, M. (September–October 2002b). *FDA Consumer*, pp. 18–23.

100 years of biologics regulation (July–August 2002). *FDA Consumer*, 36(4), pp. 8–10.

Park, R. L. (2000). *Voodoo science: The road from foolishness to fraud*. Oxford: Oxford University Press.

Parker-Pope, T. (January 14, 2003). That veggie wrap you just chowed down is more fattening than a ham sandwich. *Wall Street Journal*, p. D1.

Parker-Pope, T. (October 22, 2002). The ins and outs of getting drugs (the legal kind) from across the border. *Wall Street Journal*, p. D1.

Reagan, B. (October 21, 2002). Handle with care. *Wall Street Journal*, p. R4.

Wells, W., J. Burnett, and S. Moriarty. (2000). *Advertising: Principles & practice, 5th ed.* Upper Saddle River, NJ: Prentice Hall.

Whitney, E., and S. Rolfes. (2002). Understanding nutrition, 9th ed. Belmont, CA: Wadsworth.

# CHAPTER 10

# Ownership, Safety, and Repairs

There is no right to strike against the public safety
by anybody, anywhere, any time.
Calvin Coolidge

## Learning Objectives

1. Understand what satisfaction guaranteed means.
2. Know that many products cause injury and harm.
3. Explain what the U.S. Consumer Product Safety Commission does.
4. Know how to minimize the potential for home improvement and travel frauds.
5. Discuss sources of travel safety alerts and ways to stay safer when traveling.
6. Discuss the postpurchase life of products, including disposition.
7. Explain how to determine if charities are legitimate or not.

## INTRODUCTION

As you can see from the title, this is an eclectic chapter. The last one focused on health issues, this one covers a myriad of topics regarding home and vehicle repairs and the safety of consumer products. These are important areas to cover because many consumer complaints arise from faulty repairs and other services that don't live up to expectations. Severe injuries can result in death so safety concerns go beyond mere inconvenience and questions about restitution. The chapter focuses on how products are used after purchase, how they perform, and finally how they are disposed of. Public awareness of the hazards of everyday products are also discussed and the functions of the main consumer safety agencies that handle complaints.

Can consumers be sure of safety? Federal and state agencies have recalled many products because of defects or potential safety hazards ranging from lawn motors to toys. Products for infants and children are covered because child safety is paramount. Manufacturers should pretest toys, and parents should read product labels to determine if their child is old enough for a certain toy. Locking up household chemicals, drugs, and firearms are also important safety measures. Further, this chapter covers travel fraud and travel safety, including where to find sources of regular alerts about places of particular concern. If planning to travel or work abroad, this section and the E-Resources should not be missed. The chapter concludes with a discussion of charities and guidelines for separating the legitimate from the quasi-legitimate and the outright frauds. Keeping your money safe is part of the general topic of safety.

A recurring theme throughout the chapter is the importance of information gathering. For example, consumers should read and understand warranties. You may recall from the second chapter that the right to safety and the right to information are two of the four basic rights in President John F. Kennedy's Consumer Bill of Rights.

## CONSUMER RESEARCH ON NONUSE

Consumer research typically deals with three processes pertaining to individuals and families and their use of goods and services:

- Decision making
- Usage
- Disposal (Jacoby et al., 1977).

Of these processes the last two are the least researched. Within these categories is the rather peculiar one of items or services that are bought and never used or rarely used. In an earlier chapter we talked about how foods are bought and never used, but other items include membership in health and fitness clubs, in-home exercise equipment, small kitchen appliances, vitamins and supplements, crafts, sewing machines, high-tech goods, personal care items like hair gel, aftershave, and perfume, and clothes.

**Underutilization** is a condition where a consumer uses a product, but only to a small fraction of the extent for which they intended to use it (Trocchia and Swinder, 2002). Anger, embarrassment, and guilt may be associated with underutilization, or the buyer may simply have lost interest in the product or service. Interests change frequently with foods, books, workout equipment or clubs, and video games. A person may throw themselves into a new hobby or life change and buy everything associated with it and then change their minds. An individual may try to grow orchids, put in special growing lights, and in the process spend several thousand dollars and uncountable hours of work and when all the orchids die decide there must be an easier hobby. There may be concerns about physical injury or an illness may prevent or lessen use of clubs or equipment. Other life changes include changes in marital status, having children, educational or career goals, or geographic location.

A product may disappoint as well, perhaps it is not as much fun or smell as good or taste as yummy as hoped. The product or service may not transform the user into the popular or attractive person that they had hoped. When it comes to in-home products, there are storage and maintenance issues as well. A waffle iron, for instance, may be too much trouble to haul out and clean after use. A consumer may decide that a frozen waffle popped in the toaster is nearly as good and a lot less trouble that whipping up waffle mix, cooking, and cleaning up afterward.

To summarize, many products and services are purchased and rarely or never used. The reasons for underutilization or nonuse vary but include:

- Impulsiveness. One respondent in a survey said, "Even though I knew that the (high-heeled) shoes would hurt my feet, I bought them anyway" (Trocchia and Swinder, 2002, p. 191). As another example, after a cooking demonstration in a store someone may think they need a special gadget or ingredient where the one they have at home would suffice.

- Buying on sale. Examples are promotions such as three T-shirts for $10 when only one is needed. If it was inexpensive, people may shrug their shoulders and say, "Oh well it didn't cost much. If I get only a couple of wearings that is okay."
- Function problems such as maintenance difficulties, disappointing results, and difficulties using the product (Trocchia and Swinder, 2002). Examples are food preparation devices such as grills, juice machines, lawn mowers, and cosmetic/personal care treatments, and clothes that wrinkle easily or are difficult to care for such as requiring hand washing and drying flat.
- It doesn't fit or work.
- Self-consciousness—a person is not comfortable using or wearing the product. The product is not consistent with their self-image or with other people's image of them. An individual may feel like an idiot wearing the item, or a child may tell them the style is too young.
- Concern about personal injury such as in use of power tools or recreational equipment.
- Loss of interest or enthusiasm. The consumer may decide they don't need the product or service; examples include language tapes, humorous items or toys, and exercise equipment.
- Lifestyle changes.

It is true that businesses make money from products and services that are bought and never used, but nonuse is not good for repeat business. An unhappy buyer may spread bad word-of-mouth which further brings down sales. Money-back guarantees and generous return policies can reduce the number of disgruntled customers. Because of embarrassment or loss of interest, the consumer may not pursue getting a refund or returning a product, representing a waste of resources. Businesses and government agencies that handle complaints and recalls should do all they can to encourage use of products and services, and if the customer is not satisfied, they should do what they can to encourage redress. Presenting realistic views of products and services in the first place would reduce the incidence of nonuse.

Underutilization also points up the fact that *consumer behavior is imprecise*. Mistakes are made. In order to save money and heartache (guilt, anger, or whatever) consumers need to try to lessen nonuse perhaps by knowing themselves better and by spending more time on the decision end of the consumption process. Another remedy is to take advantage of the warranties and money-back or replacement guarantees to be discussed next.

## WARRANTIES AND GUARANTEES: PERCEPTIONS AND REALITIES

In previous chapters, we've covered the importance of price and brand name in consumer decision making, especially in determining quality. National brands are perceived by many as better than generic or store brands. As examples, consumers may think that a Band-Aid from Johnson & Johnson Inc. may be better than a store brand or that a higher priced sweater is better quality than a lower priced sweater. Other indicators of quality are country of manufacture and warranties. A lot of this has to do with perception. Would you think a camera or car from Japan is better than one manufactured in Russia? Do you think Egyptian cotton is better than Malaysian cotton? Research has shown that the longer and more inclusive the warranty, the better the quality of the product is assumed to be (Boulding and Kirmani, 1993). A product with a five-year warranty is assumed to be better than one with a three-month warranty. But what happens if the company goes out of business? Regardless of length the warranty may be worthless. Note the word inclusive because besides length consumers need to know what is covered, what types of repairs, replacement parts, and conditions are included.

In order to sell products, marketers extol the virtues of goods such as an extended warranty. They have found that the more variables or attributes presented, the greater the perception of reduction of risk. This is referred to as **attribute-based choices**. Warranties and guarantees are very important to risk reduction. One associates them with higher priced items, but they can apply to less expensive ones. For example, a shampoo can be guaranteed to give satisfaction, or your money is refunded in full. Some clothing stores will allow returns at any time for any reason, and others are more selective, perhaps having a three-month from purchase return policy or no-returns on sale items. Here is an example from Appleseed's (a company that sells women's fashions and accessories):

> "Satisfaction Guaranteed.
>
> Every Order. Every Time.
>
> You deserve the highest level of service and product quality we can provide. If something isn't right with your order, tell us. We'll work hard to keep your trust and make sure you're 100% satisfied. It's the way we've been doing business for over 50 years." (Fall 2002 catalog, p. 63)

Besides manufacturers and stores, service businesses such as dry cleaners or home inspection businesses provide warranties or guarantees. A checklist is given in Table 10.1. To complicate things, *attributes are not equally weighted*. Price may be by far the most important attribute in a product purchase or it may be brand or it may be quick service. A person may prefer a certain brand of deodorant and will not buy any other at any price. On the other hand, a product line may be eliminated as far too expensive, such as a $10,000 flat-screen television. In a competitive market, one product maker will emphasize price as a dominant evaluative

**Table 10.1**   Product or Service Comparison Checklist[*]

| Evaluative Criteria | Brand A (Name: ) | Brand B (Name: ) |
|---|---|---|
| Price<br>Size/Dimensions<br>Country of Origin<br>Warranty/Guaranty<br>Repairs/Service/Refunds<br>Reputation of Company | | |

[*]Suggested rating system: 1 being very poor and 5 being very good.

criterion in their advertisement, whereas a competitor will stress other aspects such as safety or warranties. Another example of attributes is features weighting. A person may want not only a safe car with a good warranty but also a car with automatic windows and air conditioning.

In economics, *rational choice theory assumes a rational decision maker has well-defined preferences.* Each option or alternative in a choice set is assumed to have a value to the consumer that depends on the characteristics of that option. Consumers are assumed to have sufficient skill to determine which options best suit their needs. They will maximize their value, getting the most for their money and needs. As we know from earlier chapters, rationality does not always exist. Consumers are said to have **bounded rationality,** meaning a limited capacity for processing information. What does this have to do with warranties and guaranties? In a word, "everything," because unless they are lawyers consumers cannot possibly understand every word in a lengthy tiny print warranty or guaranty nor are they inclined to take the time to read it. What happens is that most make a **constructive choice** which is a timely decision based on the situation at hand.

Many businesses now "guarantee" customer satisfaction with services. This may include free pizza if delivery does not take place in half an hour or a free lunch if not brought to the table in 14 minutes or less. These types of guarantees insure that service is timely and increases customer satisfaction. Regarding warranties and guarantees customer service is paramount. Not only does the product have to be fixed but also it has to be fixed or replaced quickly by courteous employees whether online, over the telephone, or in-person. So, customer-employee interaction is not only important at points of sale but also during service encounters. Consumers respond well not only to pleasant people but also pleasant environments while they wait. This is why car dealerships repair shops have comfortable waiting rooms with snacks, reading material, and chairs for customers.

The role of competition was covered in previous chapters, and one way firms compete is through guarantees. For example, United Parcel Service (UPS) competes with FedEx Corp. and the U.S. Postal Service. In a move to erase the service gap between UPS, the world's largest package hauler, and FedEx Corp., UPS rolled out money-back guarantees for U.S. residential shipments in the lower 48 states. About 20 percent of UPS shipments go to homes (Brooks, 2002). Regarding the announcement, "the consumer is the winner," said Satish Jindel, a transportation consultant at SJ Consulting Group Inc., in Pittsburgh. "Now, if they know when to expect it, it tells them when to be ready" (Brooks, 2002, p. D2).

## SERVICE CONTRACTS

When buying a new car, appliance, or computer you may be offered a **service contract** which provides repair and/or maintenance for a specific time period. They may also be called extended warranties. The length of warranty may differ. For a small appliance, the warranty may be for 90 days. For larger, more expensive items, the length of warranty is longer. For example, new cars come with a manufacturer's warranty, which usually offers coverage for 12,000 miles or at least one year or whichever comes first. A service contract would then extend the warranty, or pick up after 12,000 miles or after that first year. Many consumers buy a service contract for "peace of mind," and this is how the contracts are marketed. But are they necessary? Service contracts cost extra and are sold separately; they give extra protection, but are rarely worth the cost. For most consumer products, the chances are you will never use a service contract which can run from $20 to $600 depending on the length and amount of coverage provided. The problem may be that the service contract may cover only certain parts of the product or specific repairs. It could also be limited to repairs only at the local dealership in the case of a car or appliance. Read the contract carefully, ask questions. Labor is probably not included, for example, and there may be deductibles. From a financial standpoint, it may be better to set aside some money for emergencies, and when the rare breakdown occurs, use that cash to get things fixed or repaired.

True flaws show up quickly, and warranties should take care of most repairs.

Statistics show that costly consumer products do not break very often within the one- to three-year periods covered by service contracts. True flaws show up quickly and are covered by regular product warranties that should be included in the purchase price. Service contracts often exclude problems that are most likely to happen, and in many cases the warranties cost more than a repair or replacement would cost. If the car or appliance is sold, the service contract is probably ended because service contracts are rarely transferable to the next owner.

The Consumer Sentinel is a secure, online database about fraud information that is government operated and useful to law enforcement agencies.

If you have a complaint about a service contract, you should follow the usual procedure of starting with the dealer first. The Federal Trade Commission (FTC) gets many letters from consumers about service contracts. Although they cannot represent you in a dispute, it wants to know if companies are not meeting their obligations. To let the FTC know what is going on, use the complaint form available at *www.ftc.gov*. The FTC enters fraud-related complaints and also Internet, telemarketing, and identity theft fraud information into Consumer Sentinel, a secure, online database available to hundreds of civil and criminal law enforcement agencies in the United States and abroad.

## ARE CONSUMERS COMPLAINING MORE?

Yes, consumers are complaining more. The number of complaints each year rises, according to statistics keepers like the FTC and scores of law enforcement and consumer groups. Of course, some of this can be explained by the rise in population along with a greater public awareness of the problems. There is also a relationship between a downturn in the economy and an upswing in consumer complaints; people are more worried about their money. In addition, in a busier, sped-up world consumers expect better and faster service. Fortunately, registering a complaint with a company is getting easier because it can be done over the Internet. One example is that complaints about cleaning products jumped 33 percent in 2001 according to Planet Feedback.com, a company that tracks consumer behavior. Forrester Research, a marketing research company, found in a survey that 84 percent of people wished companies would make it easier to complain (Higgins, 2002, p. D1). Companies are increasingly viewing consumer complaints not only as a good source of feedback but also as an opportunity to sell more products. This is called **cross-selling**. If the person does not like a certain product, they may be given a refund or a coupon to buy another brand that the company sells. For example, if Unilever, which sells everything from Hellman's mayonnaise to Dove soap, finds out someone doesn't like a taste or a fragrance they suggest another one of their brands rather than lose a customer (Higgins, 2002, p. D1).

The cost of beefing up call centers to field complaints poses a dilemma for consumer-goods companies that are trying to cut costs, "but there's also a growing realization that consumers who aren't given a chance to vent can cause damage to a product's reputation by sending mass e-mails, a phenomenon that has become so common, it has a name: the viral effect. In one high-profile case, a businessman became so annoyed at a hotel chain, he designed a scathing PowerPoint slide show that eventually got forwarded from inbox to inbox around the world" (Higgins, 2002, p. D2).

## Changing Labels for Complaint Handling Information

Many old labels were out of date, making it difficult for consumers to find company addresses, toll-free complaint line numbers, or Internet addresses. It is expensive to redesign a whole line of labels so companies do it infrequently. A spokeswoman for Shop-Rite pitted olives said that the label for that product had not been redesigned since 1974, and the company was in the process of redoing it to include an 800-number and a Web address if there was room. They have found that many consumers like to talk to a person when they make complaints so the 800-number is still important (Higgins, 2002, p. D2).

Companies say they not only receive complaints but also compliments on these lines and through the Internet. "In fact, offering a compliment may be the quickest way to get what you want. John Schachter of Arlington, VA., says he has received everything from free coupons to a transistor radio in the shape of a Tropicana orange, in return for praising products to the manufacturer" (Higgins, 2002, p. D4).

## INJURIES

Each year about a quarter of the population is injured in some way, and about 150,000 Americans die from injuries. Disabling injuries, temporary or permanent, are other outcomes. Injuries can occur in a variety of places from cars to homes to leisure to work. Everyone is at risk, but injuries are most common among men, minorities, and people with low incomes due to a variety of factors, including social, environmental, and economic. According to Insel and Roth (2002), in a typical day in the United States the following occur:

- 58 homicides
- 85 suicides
- 265 deaths
- 3,200 suicide attempts
- 20,400 interpersonal assaults
- 100,000 unintentional injury-related emergency room visits

Besides loss of life, unintentional injuries are so common they account for more **years of potential life lost** than any other cause of death (Insel and Roth, 2002). This refers to the difference between an individual's life expectancy and his or her age at death.

Besides the emotional loss, the economic cost is high. More than $500 billion is spent each year for medical care and rehabilitation of the injured (Insel and Roth, 2002).

**Intentional injuries** are purposely inflicted like homicide, suicide, or assault. These can be inflicted by oneself or by another person. **Unintentional injuries** occur when no harm was intended, such as the results of falls, fires, or motor vehicle crashes. The fifth leading cause of death and the leading cause of death and disability among children and young adults are unintentional injuries. To lower injuries engineers and law enforcement can help with the use of safety belts and safety-related laws such as tamper-proof containers on OTC and prescription drugs.

*What causes most injuries? The answer is a combination of human and environmental error.* Slick roads, foggy conditions, defective tires, and undertow in the ocean are examples of environmental hazards. Human error involves risk taking and bad judgment and the following:

- Fatigue, stress, sleep deprivation.
- Distractions such as children yelling, pets jumping around, cell phones.
- Drugs and alcohol.
- Smoking in bed.
- Improper or nonuse of safety belts, child safety seats, and air bags. Since 1998, all new cars have been equipped with dual air bags (for driver and front-seat passenger).
- Not wearing helmets and other safety equipment when on motorcycles, mopeds, and bicycles.
- Not being careful when driving, crossing the street, exercising.
- In the home: falls, fires, poisoning (carbon monoxide poisoning is the most common type of poisoning by gases), suffocation and choking, firearms. Over 100,000 deaths and injuries are caused by firearms each year. To protect yourself in the home from unintentional injuries, remove or fix anything that causes tripping or falling, make sure smoke alarms and fireplaces work properly, use safety equipment, remove electrical cords in pathways, and store firearms appropriately.
- In leisure: boating, swimming and other sports, lack of skill or proper equipment. In-line skating accounts for more than 250,000 injuries a year in the emergency room (injuries to head and wrist are most common), scooter injuries accounted for 27,000 emergency room visits a year.
- At work: nearly 4 million Americans suffer disabling injuries on the job each year and many die. Possible causes include falls, exposure to toxic chemicals and radiation, burns, cuts, back sprains, loss of body parts in machinery, and electrical shocks. Back injuries are common. A common injury is **carpal tunnel syndrome** which is compression of the median nerve in the wrist, often caused by repetitive use of the hands such as cutting or computer use; it is characterized by numbness, tingling, and pain in the hands and fingers (Insel and Roth, 2002). This can be prevented or lessened by changes in behavior and workstations, the temporary wearing of a splint to stabilize the hand and wrist, and in extreme cases, by surgery. In the workplace, the main federal agency concerned with safety is the Occupational Safety and Health Administration (OSHA), created within the Department of Labor. It was established in 1970 through the Occupational Safety and Health Act.

## Product Safety

Children are often the victims of injuries from consumer products. The government and the public want to lessen the severity of accidents and reduce the incidence of accidents. So the question is how to improve product safety? The answers lie in better designed products, better labeling, removal of hazards and hazardous products, better industry standards, more government regulation where necessary, and increased consumer awareness. Another question is what is an appropriate amount of regulation or warnings? How many accidents happen from lack of common sense and preparedness? In the case of children, how many accidents occur because of parental neglect or ignorance?

Some hazards are known, some are hidden. For example, individuals would not know that a wheel is going to fall off a bicycle or that a pan on a stove would explode. They would also not know that someone's brakes on a car would fail and the car would plow through the front window of a restaurant injuring customers. On the other hand, known hazards include driving a faulty car or living in a house with a leaky roof.

Critics of safety regulations would say that:

1.  People should know better, look out for themselves. It is true that *many injuries are a result of misuse of a product.* An example is putting plastic ware on the stove and cooking in it. The problems can stem from ignorance, inexperience, and behavioral and environmental error. Examples of an environmental and behavioral error are riding in a boat during a lightning storm or playing golf in a lightning storm or surfing during a hurricane. Product manufacturers would say that behavioral and environmental conditions are beyond their control, and they should not be held responsible. Likewise, a product made for an adult that falls in the hands of a child such as a prescription drug container left on the sink with the cap off is primarily the responsibility of the supervising adult.
2.  Too much government costs too much money. Government-mandated safety standards cost manufacturers millions of dollars, and those costs are passed on to consumers.
3.  Too much government puts too much power into the hands of a few at the top.
4.  Too many regulations limit freedom. For example, in some states motorcycle riders have to wear helmets, in other states it is optional. Motorcycle riders argue that it is their lives that are at stake and if they don't want to wear helmets they should not have to. Federal, state, and local governments have passed laws and regulations regarding safety, but how much is too much? So all laws and regulations must be considered from several points of view, and the individual's right to freedom is one of them.

## Risk and Factors in Product Safety: The Consumer Product Safety Commission

What is an acceptable amount of risk? Everyone has to answer that question for him or herself. Is one accidental death too many, or do we just assume that a certain percentage of the public will be injured or die every year from consumer products?

To find out how many deaths and injuries occur each year from consumer products, one turns to the National Injury Information Clearinghouse. The Clearinghouse disseminates statistics and information relating to the prevention of death and injury associated with consumer products. It is part of the Consumer Product Safety Commission (CPSC). For their Web sites see the E-Resources section near the end of the chapter. The way the Clearinghouse gathers statistics is by data supplied by:

- A sample of hospital emergency rooms
- Health departments from death certificates where consumer products were involved
- From victim interviews
- From newspaper accounts
- Reports from medical sources besides hospital emergency rooms
- From consumer complaints and inquiries sent to the CPSC

Who uses the CPSC's Injury Data?

- Consumer groups
- Manufacturers and industry associations
- Media
- Educators, students, researchers, and attorneys

What can we learn from the Clearinghouse statistics? Studying Clearinghouse statistics reveals a myriad of problems people including young children can get into from using consumer products. Box 10.1 gives a list of categories of consumer product-related statistics categories (and subtopics) used by the Consumer Product Safety Commission in their Web site.

## Consumer Product Safety: Toys, Baby Equipment, Sports Equipment

As Box 10.1 indicates a lot of consumer product safety concerns revolve around infants and children. A large category of household consumption is in the area of toys, leisure or recreation or sports equipment, and baby equipment. Americans spend an estimated $25.7 billion on toys and games each year—half of which is spent in the last quarter of the year (Fetto, 2002). The prime toy market is children between the ages of two to 11. American children are more diverse racially and ethnically than the adult population. According to Census 2000, two in five children (39 percent) under the age of 18 are part of a minority group. Toy manufacturers are responding by adding Spanish-language Barbie Web sites and making phones and pull toys that use English and Spanish. Video games have expanded "toy" use into the teen years with teen boys being heavy users although 44 percent of the video game market is geared for children ages 12 and under (Fetto, 2002). In recent years, according to the London-based market research firm Mintel, sales of

**Consumer Alert**

The U.S. Consumer Product Safety Commission and the American Academy of Pediatrics have made recommendations for safe bedding practices for infants under 12 months of age. Among these are specific cautions on the use of soft bedding in cribs. Consult with pediatricians about the latest information.

BOX 10.1    Consumer Product-Related Statistics Offered by the Consumer Product Safety Commission.

—Children's Products
Toy-Related Deaths and Injuries
Nursery Products
Deaths Associated with Playpens
Asbestos Fibers in Children's Crayons
SIDS Awareness (Sudden Infant Death Syndrome)
Portable Youth Bed Rail Entrapments and Hangings
Hazards Associated with Children Placed in Adult Beds
—Child Poisonings
—CO (Carbon Monoxide) Poisonings
—Electrocutions
—Fires
Fires Caused by Children Playing with Lighters
Electric and Gas Clothes Dryers
Data Summary on Halogen Floor Lamps
Hazard Report for Candle-Related Incidents
—Fireworks
—Sports and Recreation
Amusement Rides
Children's Playground Equipment
Trampoline Related Injuries
ATV-Related Deaths and Injuries
Baby Boomer Sports Injuries
Helmets
Go-Cart/Fun-Kart Related Injuries and Deaths
Sports-related Injuries to Persons 65 years of age and older
—Other Products
Pool Alarm Reliability
Hazardous Products in Thrift Stores
Shopping Cart Injuries

*Source:* Consumer Product Safety Commission.

toys in the "play sports" category, including foam sports equipment, have grown the fastest, followed by infant/preschool toys, ride-ons like minijeeps, activity toys, and dolls. Sales of "plush" toys have declined.

## Toy-Related Injuries to Children and Causes

According to the CPSC, in 2000 an estimated 191,000 toy-related injuries were treated in U.S. hospital emergency rooms. There was a rise in estimated toy-related injuries from 1999 to 2000. The increase from 1999 to 2000 can be primarily attributed to a rise in injuries associated with unpowered scooters. The injury estimates for the years 1998 to 2000 are shown in Table 10.2. Seventy-nine percent (150,800) of the injuries in 2000 were to children under 15 and 37 percent (70,900) were to children under five. *Males are more likely to be injured than females.* Most of the victims (98 percent) are treated and released from the hospital.

**Table 10.2**   Estimated Toy-Related Injuries 1998 to 2000

| Year | Estimated Injuries |
|------|--------------------|
| 1998 | 153,400 |
| 1999 | 152,600 |
| 2000 | 191,000 |

*Source:* CPSC Web site.

The most likely area to be hurt is the head and face area followed by shoulders and fingers. Riding toys (including unpowered scooters) cause the most injuries.

## Injuries from Nursery Products

According to the CPSC, an estimated 69,500 children under age five were treated in U.S. hospital emergency rooms in 2001 for injuries associated with nursery products. From 1997 to 1999 there were 195 deaths from nursery product-related injuries. Table 10.3 shows the injuries and deaths by product. The number one cause of injury was infant carriers and car seats (excluding motor vehicle incidents). The number one cause of death was cribs.

## Advertising and Children's Products

Advertising plays a vital role in children's safety. Box 10.2 shows messages or images that should not occur in advertising because of potential harm to children. As mentioned in previous chapters, the Federal Trade Commission (FTC) is the main regulator of advertising. It works for the consumer to prevent fraudulent, deceptive, and unfair business practices in the marketplace and to provide information to help consumers spot, stop, and avoid them.

**Table 10.3**   Nursery Product-Related Injuries and Deaths to Children under Age Five by Product.

| Product Category | Estimated Injuries 2001 | Total Deaths 1997–1999 |
|------------------|-------------------------|------------------------|
| TOTAL | 69,500 | 195 |
| Infant Carriers and Car Seats | 15,370 | 18 |
| Strollers and Carriages | 13,070 | 5 |
| Cribs | 11,380 | 80 |
| High Chairs | 7,430 | 7 |
| Baby Walkers and Jumpers | 6,200 | 5 |
| Changing Tables | 1,990 | 3 |
| Baby Gates and Barriers | 1,670 | 2 |
| Playpens and Play Yards | 1,590 | 23 |
| Baby Bath Seats | 0 | 18 |
| Other | 10,140 | 34 |

The CPSC used National Electronic Injury Surveillance System (NEISS) for the CY 2001 injury estimates and In-depth Investigation File, Injury and Potential Injury Incident File, Death Certificate File and NEISS for 1997 to 1999 for reported deaths.
*Source:* CPSC Web site.

---

**BOX 10.2   Inappropriate Messages and Images in Advertising for Children**

1. Displaying products that they should not use such as alcohol, cigarettes, and drugs.
2. Showing adults and children using products in a way that they shouldn't and that may be misinterpreted, for example, a "miniaturized" adult in a toilet, refrigerator, washing machine, or dishwasher or a child alone in a swimming pool. Small children may imitate these behaviors.
3. Having young children playing with toys or sporting equipment or driving ATVs that are appropriate for teenagers or adults.
4. Showing children to be nonaccepted by their peers if they do not use or own a product. Messages implying increased popularity are inappropriate. Showing having fun is okay, but showing mockery, bullying, or loneliness of nonusers is not. An example is whether one owns a particular brand of shoes or clothing.
5. Eating less than healthy foods, food advertising directed at children shows foods within the context of a balanced meal, or if the food is a snack it should be clear that it is a snack and not a meal. Sugared and fast food products are especially controversial. Food advertising on Saturday mornings increased substantially over the last decade.
6. Showing items that do not perform as expected, as a child could use them. An example would be a boomerang thrown by an expert versus how well a seven-year-old could throw a boomerang.

*Note:* Advertisements during children's program hours such as Saturday morning and after school are heavily monitored, but increasingly children watch prime-time television (7:30–11:00 P.M.) so this places an additional responsibility on advertisers, marketers, and parents.

---

The regulation of advertising and marketing activities directed at children focuses primarily on the impact messages may have on children's health and safety and also on their values. In other words, physical harm is important but so is personal and social development. Advertising in a sense is an educator and part of the child's socialization process since children between two and 11 years old spent more than 25 hours per week watching televisions and are exposed to almost 25,000 commercials per year (Weisskoff, 1985). As discussed earlier in the book, television is primarily a one-way process, the viewer sits and watches. Web sites provide the opportunity for two-way interaction so children are not only being exposed to advertising but also they may provide information as well that marketers can use ('Many Kids' Web Sites Continuing to Collect Personal Information, 1999).

## VEHICLE SAFETY AND REPAIR

In an earlier chapter, we covered automobile safety in the discussion of Ralph Nader and his book *Unsafe At Any Speed* that condemned the auto industry's record on safety and brought about much needed vehicle safety legislation. Since then laws have been passed requiring the wearing of seat belts, for example. Earlier in the book we also covered the subject of recalls. An example of a recall was of the 1997 and 1998 Yamaha "Warrior" All Terrain Vehicles (ATVs) that sold for about $5,000. The problem was that a counting-bracket weld on the rear hub could come loose, resulting in rear brake failure and possible injury to operators. Yamaha received reports from consumers of the weld problems, including the injuries that resulted. State Departments of Consumer Services, the U.S. Consumer Product Safety Commission (CPSC), and Yamaha Motor Corporation, U.S.A. of Cypress, California, announced the voluntary recall of about 14,000 of the vehicles. In a nationwide newspaper announcement, consumers were told to stop using these ATVs immediately and call their local Yamaha ATV dealer to schedule a free appointment to have their units inspected and repaired if needed.

The Yamaha ATV example illustrates that vehicular safety, and repair is often a combination of industry and government cooperation. Recalls are expensive to the company, but not as expensive as bad publicity, loss of sales, lawsuits, and injuries or loss of human life. Likewise, government is charged to protect the welfare and lives of citizens. State governments register auto repair companies and resolve customer complaints. Repair shops have to follow certain rules. If they are in trouble, they have to get back into compliance and renew their licenses to operate. There are regulated and nonregulated complaints. Regulated complaints fall under the state's statutory authority to enforce such as a repair shop's failure to fill out forms or problems that are specifically listed in statutes. Nonregulated complaints may cover car accessories, towing charges, and other things that may not fall under statutes. Across the country, millions of dollars are refunded to consumers each year though consumer divisions in state government. These divisions send in undercover investigators who take in a car that has been prechecked for problems and then see if the repair shops find the correct problem and fix it at a reasonable price. If they add on extra charges or even go so far as to damage the car further and ask for more repair money, then they are in trouble.

How can you protect yourself from auto repair fraud? The best way is to go to companies or car dealerships that have existed for a long time and have a reputation for good service and quality work (see Box 10.3). Complaint records can be

---

**BOX 10.3    Vehicle Repairs: Steps to Follow**

Choose a reliable repair shop based on recommendations from family and friends.

If unsure, check out the repair shop's complaint record with a BBB or local or state consumer protection agency.

Describe the symptoms of the car (what it is doing) when you take it in.

If costly, get more than one estimate in writing.

Work should not begin until you authorize it and have an estimate.

Don't sign a blank repair order. Understand anything that you sign.

Check your warranty—should the repairs be covered?

Pay by credit card if the bill is over $50 because if there is a defect or problem with the repair, payment to the credit card company can be withheld until improvements are made.

Keep copies of all paperwork.

Report complaints to your local or state consumer protection office.

*Note:* These steps have been adapted and modified from The Consumer Action Handbook, U.S. General Services Administration, GSA Office of Communications, and Federal Consumer Information Center, 1800 F Street, NW, Washington, DC, 20405.

checked through Better Business Bureaus and motor vehicle divisions in states, most likely under the main consumer protection agency.

One of the worst consumer frauds in the auto repair market is the black market in used auto parts. In this scam auto parts are switched around and used ones are often sold to the consumer as new auto parts. A particularly bad practice is the black market on airbags, where used or damaged airbags are sold as new. Law officers in Florida made an arrest when a repair shop was putting cardboard in the slot for the air bag. If there was an accident, cardboard would fly out of the air bag compartment instead of an air bag. So, auto safety and repair is not just about cost or being gypped, it is about saving lives. Fly-by-night repair shops exist. In other words, someone does car repairs and also does other types of repairs going from one business to another. This is a good example of you get what you pay for—someone without an established business is someone to avoid or at least check out thoroughly.

The National Institute for Automotive Service Excellence (ASE) located in Herndon, Virginia, is an independent, national nonprofit organization that helps improve the quality of automotive service and repair through the voluntary testing and certification of automotive repair professionals. Nearly half a million ASE-certified technicians work in car dealerships, automotive repair services, auto parts stores, and service stations. The ASE also publishes consumer publications about auto repair.

## VEHICLE WARRANTIES

Standard car warranties are for three years or 36,000 miles (whichever happens first) and cover manufacturers defects. Labor and parts may be extra. To increase customer satisfaction and to encourage car sales, manufacturers are lengthening warranties and wrapping in new services such as free car washes with each checkup and free donuts and cappuccinos in the service area waiting rooms. As may be expected, luxury car dealers offer more services than the low-end dealers, including generous free loaner car policies, free wiper blade replacement, and 24-hour roadside service. Warranties that used to be limited to three years now go as high as 10 years for a Hyundai and five for a Ford Focus. Daimler-Chrysler introduced seven-year, 70,000 mile power-train warranties. Lengthy contracts are a way to distinguish brands. Whether they are a good idea or not depends on the features (likelihood that they will be needed) and the added price. Most are not transferable to a second buyer so the original purchaser should decide if they are going to keep the car from five to ten years or not. From the manufacturer's point of view, extended warranties can be moneymakers or they can be costly.

Consumers are more aware than ever before about the necessity for repairs because of the computer systems on dashboards on vehicles. Sometimes these systems malfunction, and the repair is not needed. This type of warning error wastes the consumer's and the dealer's time. However, usually these systems of blinking lights and warning signals are accurate and let the customer know when repairs are needed so they are useful safety features. Unquestionably the warning systems have saved lives as well as time and money. Volvos are particularly well known for safety features. Their Volvo S60 modules are "fitted with 26 censors that prompt six levels of warning messages, ranging from the mildly unsettling 'FIX NEXT SERVICE' to the more hysterical 'STOP SAFELY ASAP'" (Spencer, 2002, p. D2).

For warranties to remain in effect, it may be in the contract that you must follow all the manufacturer's recommendations for routine maintenance such as oil and spark plug changes and bring the car in for routine maintenance checks. Keep records and receipts to prove this although in most cases dealership service offices will keep records of work done on your car as well. There may be clauses in the contracts that say that taking your car to repair shops other than the dealership will not count.

According to a newspaper article, Alan Entin, a clinical psychologist in Richard, Virginia, says, "People who make heavy warranty demands may be seeking parental attention from their mechanics. It's 'Take care of me. You're bigger, you're stronger, you can make all things right in the world if you fix my car,' he says. The warranty represents approval or fixing from their daddy" (Spencer, 2002, p. D2). Entin's interpretation may seem reasonable or extreme depending on your point of view, but nevertheless the trend is toward more lengthy warranties and Box 10.4 explains how to get the most out of any car warranty.

According to the FTC's *Auto Service Contracts* "when shopping for a used car, look for a Buyer's Guide sticker posted on the car's side window. This sticker is required by the FTC on all used cars sold by dealers. It tells whether a service con-

---

**BOX 10.4    Vehicle Warranties: How to Get the Most from Them**

First:

- Keep up with the recommended maintenance schedule especially oil changes.
- Fill out all the necessary paperwork including service logs, save receipts.

When a repair is needed:

- Follow the recommended steps.
- Find out if other drivers have similar problems, go to *www.autosafety.org* for common problems by make of car. Visit *www.nhtsa.dot.gov* (National Highway Traffic Safety Administration site) for posted defect bulletins.
- If the dealer will not fix the problem when it is under warranty (to your satisfaction), appeal to the manufacturer by contacting the manufacturer's regional or national office. Ask for the consumer affairs representative or go to their Web site for this information.
- If still unsuccessful, consider contacting other organizations including *www.autosafety.org* for legal advice.

After warranties expire:

- Ask the dealer if policy adjustments/extensions are possible. A free fix is possible if the manufacturer has told dealers to authorize repairs.
- If the warranty has recently expired and the service log shows that the repair problem started before the warranty ran out, then there is a possibility of a free or lower cost repair.

Basic Advice: Car dealers want return customers so most will try to make the repairs needed in a timely fashion.

tract is available. It also indicates whether the vehicle is being sold with a warranty, with implied warranties only, or 'as is.' If the manufacturer's warranty is still in effect on the used car, you may have to pay a fee to obtain coverage, making it a service contract. However, if the dealer absorbs the cost of the manufacturer's fee, the coverage is considered a warranty" (2003, p. 3). Implied warranties are unspoken and unwritten and based on the principle that the seller stands behind the product. Sold "as is" means there is no warranty, you buy the car and must pay for all repairs even if the car breaks down on the street outside the dealership lot. Some states prohibit "as is" sales. Other states have lemon laws under which a consumer can receive a refund or replacement.

Buying a used car "as is" is risky business.

# NATIONAL HIGHWAY TRAFFIC SAFETY ADMINISTRATION (NHTSA)

According to their Web site, the mission of the National Highway Traffic Safety Administration (NHTSA) is to save lives, prevent injuries, and reduce traffic related health care and other economic costs, by facilitating the development, deployment, and evaluation of safety products and systems. Among other things, this involves research into the science of crash avoidance to enable the development of safety-enhancing products. The agency works with the automobile industry and other technology companies. The goal of the agency is to demonstrate improved capability of collision avoidance systems, ensure that systems are both effective and usable to consumers, and provide a basis for understanding the benefits (i.e., collisions, injuries and fatalities that will be avoided).

NHTSA wants to hear from consumers regarding potential car defects. NHTSA also has information on safety recalls, crash tests ratings, child safety seats, bicycles, air bags, and impaired driving prevention. Probably what the public knows best about the NHTSA is the results of the crash tests. Have you seen the dummies being tossed around in cars on television announcements or the nightly news? Those demonstrations and tests are part of what NHTSA does.

In 1978 the New Car Assessment Program was initiated with the purpose of providing consumers with a measure of the relative safety potential of vehicles in frontal crashes. NCAP supplies consumers with frontal- and side-crash results to help them in buying decisions. Ultimately the NCAP would like the industry to take up similar standards and provide better occupant protection in crashes. One thing the NCAP would really like to happen is a significant reduction in the number of rollovers.

If you want to check on the crash test results of a particular vehicle go to the Web site in the E-Resources and click on one of the icons: a car, truck, van, or SUV. Next, select your vehicle size and year, and keep clicking until you find the exact make, model, and year. The vehicles that are tested are purchased from dealerships so that they are the same vehicles that consumers would buy. The typical models tested are new vehicles that are predicted to have high sales volume or vehicles that have been redesigned with structural changes or have improved safety equipment for testing. Injury risk curves are obtained from the test dummy in the crash, demonstrating the probability of injury to a real person in that crash. The lower the injury number, the less chance an individual will be hurt in a crash.

An airbag inflates before a crash test dummy in the passenger side of a car with a cutaway door. (Courtesy of the National Highway Traffic Safety Administration.)

## FEDERAL AVIATION ADMINISTRATION

How safe are you when you fly? The Federal Aviation Administration, part of the Department of Transportation (DOT), is in charge of air safety for the general public and the aviation community. They investigate unsafe aviation practices. According to the FAA homepage, the DOT oversees consumer issues such as denied boarding, baggage, overbooking, and ticketing, as well as statistics on on-time performance. The FAA is in charge of civil aviation safety, including developing safety regulations, certifying pilots, and airport flight delay information. The Transportation Security Administration (TSA) is responsible for all modes of transportation (see *www.tsa.dot.gov*). At the FAA Web page there is a list of consumer rights and airline consumer obligations, including guides for traveling smart.

## HOME IMPROVEMENTS

Remodeling can range in price from a $15 can of paint to $100,000 additions. A wide range of minor repairs or upgrades cost under $3,000, and the do-it-yourself market is huge. An estimated 26 million Americans tackle home improvements each year, spending some $180 billion, according to the Remodelers Council of the National Association of Home Builders (Beck, 2002).

With repairs and upgrades also comes the potential for fraud or at least disappointment with the quality of end results. A huge area of consumer complaint is home repair and renovations and related items, such as pool construction and anything else having to do with yards, garages, and outbuildings. Small claims courts are filled with these types of complaints pitting the consumer against the contractor. Since in-ground swimming pools and kitchen remodeling can cost over $30,000, cases can go to higher courts. Similar to the advice for car repair, one should look for established businesses with good reputations, and the homeowner should be realistic in terms of the amount of time and inconvenience substantial renovations will cause. Contractors should be appropriately licensed. See Box 10.5 for more steps to follow in home improvements.

Certain behaviors should draw your attention. Avoid contractors who come door to door, especially those in unmarked vans with out-of-state license plates. Legitimate, busy contractors wait for you to call them. Very low bids should also be a warning sign as are exceptionally long guarantees. If you feel any kind of pressure to hurry up and pay up front, then that is another warning sign. If you are considering having a home painted, for example, get two or three bids from local services and check references. Not only the price but the availability and quality of materials and workmanship should be compared. To evaluate workmanship, according to Beck (2002) ask previous customers about these four critical measures of past work, was the contractor:

- On budget
- On time
- Agreeable (worked with homeowner)
- Capable of finishing the job to the homeowner's standards

---

**BOX 10.5    Home Improvements: Steps to Follow**

Choose a reliable contractor or company based on recommendations from family and friends.

Check your BBB or local or state consumer agency for information on contractors' licensing or registration requirements and complaint records. License requirements vary by state.

Get at least three written estimates and remember that the lowest one may not be the best.

Get references and talk with people who have had work done by the contractor.

Contact your local building inspection department to check for permit and inspection requirements.

Get a complete written contract, detailing work to be done, quality of materials, time tables, warranties, the names of subcontractors, and the total price of the job and payment schedules.

Do not pay completely upfront and try to limit your down payment. Don't make a final payment until you are satisfied.

You have cancellation rights (usually three business days) in home improvement contracts, meaning you can get out of the contract without penalty.

Pay by credit card because under most laws in most cases you have the right to refuse to pay the credit card company until any defects or problems are corrected.

*Note:* These steps have been adapted and modified from The Consumer Action Handbook, 2001 edition, U.S. General Services Administration, GSA Office of Communications, Federal Consumer Information Center, 1800 F Street NW, Washington, DC 20405.

## Home Improvement Professionals

Who do you hire? Home improvement professionals vary by complexity of projects. Choices include:

- *General contractors* who would manage all aspects of a project, including hiring and supervising subcontractors.
- *Subcontractors or specialty contractors* install particular products such as staircases, cabinets, or bathroom plumbing fixtures.
- *Architects* design homes, buildings, additions, and major renovations, especially those having to do with structural changes. A related specialty area is landscape architecture.
- *Designers* have expertise in design and layout, space planning, may specialize in kitchens and baths, contemporary or traditional, or they may do it all. Designers may work independently or with a firm, charge by the hour or by the project, or may work for free if you purchase items from the company they work for.
- *Design/builder contractors* may oversee projects from start to finish. Some firms have architects on staff, others use certified designers.

Contracts are well advised. These can range from a letter of agreement for a modest job to a full-blown contract. In each case the who, what, where, when, and cost of the project should be spelled out. The agreement should be clear, concise, and complete, including the contractor's or designer's name, address, phone, and license number. Hopefully this information should be on the person's letterhead stationary, but if not, request it. The kinds of information to be covered include costs, detailed lists of materials, warranties, how changes will be handled, estimated start and completion dates, payment schedules for all involved, cleaning up and trash hauling (a "broom clause"), and, for a major project, a written statement of your right to cancel the contract within three business days. The contract or letter should be dated. Keep all paperwork in one place and at the completion of the project, the homeowner and the home improvement professional should do a walk through and check that everything was done to expectation and as agreed upon.

## Where to Complain, Where to Find Help

First try to resolve differences with the home improvement professional, and then follow the other steps listed in the complaint section earlier in the book. Besides the usual sources of help, there are state and local Builders Associations and/or Remodelers Councils. The National Association of Home Builders Remodelers Council can be reached at *www.nahb.com*. The federal agency that has the most to do with housing is the Department of Housing and Urban Development located in Washington, DC. They have a home improvement branch, and their Web site is in the E-Resources section near the end of the chapter. The industry self-monitors itself to some extent. The state and National Homebuilders Associations would be the main groups interested in maintaining quality and good relations with the public. The Federal Trade Commission also investigates home improvement scams that are considered to be fraudulent, deceptive, or unfair business practices. They would especially check false or misleading advertising in this regard.

If a home has construction defects, there is a move afoot called **right-to-cure laws** that have passed in California, Washington, Arizona, and Nevada and are being considered in other states. Since this is changing rapidly, before buying a home or hiring a builder for major home improvements check the laws in your state. "The laws generally set up a procedure for homeowners to give builders a chance to repair their homes before they can file a lawsuit. But while the requirement sounds logical, some consumer advocates fear builders will gain an advantage over unsophisticated home buyers, who may sign away their rights to sue later if the problem isn't fixed properly. Tom Miller, a Newport Beach, Calif., lawyer who has built a national specialty in suing home builders, says "'right to cure' laws benefit builders more than consumers" (Perez, 2003, p. D2). The National Association of Home Builders, a Washington, DC, residential-builders lobby group, supports right to cure laws. The whole issue is similar to malpractice insurance for doctors. What has happened is that the lawsuits are affecting the insurance industry so that some builders cannot get insurance or are limited in the types of policies available and their premiums keep going up and up. *"The construction-defect problem is considered one of the most serious problems in the insurance market today,"* says Bob Harwig, chief economist for the Insurance Information Institute of New York (Perez, 2003, p. D2). Consumer advocates and plaintiff attorneys complain that builders are largely to blame for the increasing amounts of defects mainly because they are relying more and more on unskilled, cheap labor. The builders counter by saying it is getting more and more difficult to find reliable skilled labor. To give perspective to the whole issue of right-to-cure laws, building complaints are far down the list compared with complaints about car dealerships, for example. Nevertheless, the fact remains that building defects are moving up the list, indicating that potential and current homeowners should be especially cautious about the quality of construction and the reputation of builders.

## Home Improvements as Investments

Are home improvements good investments? The answer to that is it depends on several factors. If you rent out a house, then the monthly check from the renter can be considered a dividend. If you live in the house yourself, then it can be considered "imputed rent," which means you get to live in the house rent-free. A capital gain from housing on a national average is modest. According to Freddie Mac (a federal government mortgage program), over the past 27 years home prices have appreciated at 5.8 percent a year, that is, 1.2 percentage points a year faster than inflation (Clements, 2002, p. D1). This does not include regular costs of home maintenance (painting, fixing, replacing), and these usually come to 1 percent or 2 percent of the home's value each year. While owning a home, most people do not stop at simple maintenance. They begin to add on rooms, pools, air conditioning systems, and so forth. The bottom line is that usually home prices do not outplace inflation once maintenance and remodeling costs are figured in unless a person lives in a high growth area. Another way people make money on houses is to buy the worst house on the block and bring it up to comparable houses on the same street. A mistake (from a financial point of view) would be to upgrade the house so much that it is far grander than all the neighbors. Usually this type of investment will not be regained at resale.

Another way to look at the value of home improvements from a consumer point of view is that the consumer will save money if they add on to a cheaper house versus moving up to a much more expensive and bigger house. Staying in an existing neighborhood if it is a good one is usually cheaper than incurring the costs involved in buying and selling houses. Home improvements should not be made with an eye solely on resale unless the house is going up on the market within a year. Home improvements age just like any other consumer product or service and become worth less as time goes on. *Remodeling* magazine says that the most likely recoup on money spent on home improvements is 70 percent to 80 percent, and this is assuming the house is sold within one year of making improvements. Kitchen and bath remodeling historically provide the best return at resell. For example, according to *Remodeling* magazine you can get back 80 to 87 percent of what you spend on a kitchen upgrade. Perhaps how quickly remodeling ages is discouraging, but the biggest return on home ownership is the dividend discussed earlier, whether collected in rent or the ability to live rent-free. Fixing a place up gives a person the ability to express themselves, a more pleasant place to live, and comfort which also has value. Further, there are other paybacks, including immediate cost savings in home energy. For example, it is estimated that upgrading kitchen appliances will result in a significant energy savings. If the refrigerator, dishwasher, and range are updated, about $50 to $130 will be saved in energy a year. In the laundry, an Energy-Smart washer alone can save as much as $110 a year on utility bills depending on local rates and specific appliances.

Unless a homeowner is planning to sell soon, any remodeling should start with his or her needs first. A budget or spending plan may be set up to take care of short- and long-term goals. If doing-it-yourself, work safe and smart. Use safety goggles; protect yourself from splashes, spills, falls, scrapes, dropped tools and flying debris. Wear sturdy shoes (not sandals or slippers); add a dust mask if sanding, work gloves, long-sleeved shirts and so forth, in short, do what the professionals do.

*Historically, kitchen and bathroom remodeling provide the greatest return at resale time.*

## TRAVEL: WAYS TO SAVE MONEY, AVOID FRAUD, AND STAY SAFE

Numerous travel magazines and Web sites exist to help cost-conscious consumers compare services and prices and, in the end, sell products or services. Travel agencies can individualize consumer's wants and experiences and can provide advice tailor-made for the individual. Increasingly, consumers are booking airline tickets directly at sites like *www.delta.com* and *www.southwest.com*, making reservations by themselves to the hotel or cruise line and also to shopping bots or Internet travel Web sites. Examples of comprehensive sites include *www.bestfares.com*, *www.expedia.com*, *www.fodors.com*, *www.frommers.com*, *www.orbitz.com*, *www.sidestep.com*, and *www.travelocity.com*. The advantages of these sites are 24–7 service and the ability to rapidly compare prices.

Many hotels offer a variety of prices based on days of the week, occupancy rates, and discounts to government employees, students or faculty members, senior citizens or members of AARP, and members of AAA. People should seek the best discounts by inquiring about who qualifies for discounts. There may also be point systems such as Marriott Rewards or frequent flyer points that may serve as an incentive or offer upgrades or discounts or services. Most hotels are interested in increasing occupancy rates and would rather rent a room out for 70 percent of the "rack" rate rather than let it sit vacant. If the hotel is full or empty, they still have to pay maids, front desk workers, managers, wait staff, cooks, and so on.

Travel bargaining may be confusing to many U.S. travelers who are mostly used to a **one-price system**, meaning that you go in a grocery store or a Wal-Mart and you pay whatever is on the price sticker. So, if the advertised rate for a hotel room is $100 a night, they assume they will pay $100. Bargaining is less common in the United States than in many other countries in the world. Curiously, in the United States we are used to a system where high-priced items such as homes and new cars can be bargained for whereas small priced items such as toothpaste or fresh fruit have a set price. Some consumers enjoy bargaining and others find it distasteful. According to Meg Whitman, founder of EBay, over 150,000 people make their living, either full time or part time, by buying and selling on EBay, the online auction house with new and used items, so obviously a sizable portion of the population is reaping the benefits of people who enjoy bargaining. As this online auction house has risen in popularity so has the public's understanding of the pleasures of bargaining that should impact a number of industries and product sales.

Another pricing issue is whether airlines should charge an obese person more because he or she requires more space on the plane. Some airlines currently have a policy of charging for an extra seat. Some would argue that this is unfair. It could be reasoned that obesity is a health issue and that given the customs in our pricing system, oversized people should not have to pay extra for larger seats any more than they do for larger clothes (Stark, 2002). But what about the comfort and the rights of the person sitting next to the obese person? As with any issue, there are several perspectives to consider (the airline, the obese person, the other passengers) and related considerations such as individual rights, safety, and personal dignity.

Another issue in the travel industry is the extensive amount of fraud or deception that exists. Each year travel moves up higher on the list of consumer complaints. The list of steps to follow to avoid being ripped off is similar to the lists for auto repairs and home improvements. When going out of the country especially, start with reputable, established travel agencies or tour companies. Make sure that you understand the terms of the contracts and know that brochures are mostly marketing hype. Be wary of very low fares and any sweepstakes wins and off-season bargains that may not be bargains if one has to endure hurricanes and closed museums. One woman booked an August museum tour of Paris to arrive and find out that nearly every August museum workers go on strike and the museums are closed. Watch out for paying in advance and if the trip is a long time away you may want travel insurance. In some states, some travel agencies and tour operators have to be registered and insured; in others there is less regulation. Contact the attorney general in your state or where the company is located to see if any complaints have been lodged. Foreign travel is especially susceptible to fraud and problems. Again, the main protection is dealing with reputable companies. The American Society of Travel Agents helps resolve disputes with member agents, airlines have their own toll-free complaint lines, and state and local consumer protection agencies can help as well (see E-Resources).

Regarding travel safety, Australia, Japan, Denmark, Canada, Great Britain, and the United States regularly issue travel warnings. These are handy because they

**Consumer Alert**

College students are especially susceptible to travel fraud. Beware of ads in student newspapers and flyers posted on campus for extremely inexpensive trips at Spring Break and holiday times such as ski trips. Students have been stranded in Mexico and the Caribbean without hotels to stay at or have been sent to extremely low-quality hotels. In Europe, students are approached at railway stations and sometimes led to shoddy hotels or worse, mugged. Pickpocketing is much more common in Europe and other parts of the world than in the United States and Canada. There are fraudulent on-the-street ticket sales to Broadway and London plays. Group travel is usually safer than singles traveling alone, and groups can usually negotiate better prices. A tour guide or faculty member with a student trip can provide additional guidance and protection.

**Consumer Alert**

Be especially wary of a phone call, letter, unsolicited fax, e-mail, or postcard telling you that you have won a free or incredibly inexpensive trip. It is probably a trap. When you respond, the sales person will want your credit card number as a way of confirming, but they could use this to build up charges for something you do not want. A typical scam is when your first night is free, but subsequent nights are overpriced. Some offers do not include hotel taxes or service fees, transportation, or even basics like air conditioning and televisions that work. One family with young children found themselves in Nassau in a very seedy, bug-ridden hotel; they had to pay to get a decent room in another hotel and their "free" trip was ruined. Their return flight didn't leave for several days so they were stuck. They had been had and they knew it. Protect yourself by being wary of great deals, do not be pressured into buying, ask detailed questions, get all information in writing before buying, don't buy part of the package, don't give credit card numbers over the phone, and don't send money by messenger or overnight mail. The best protection is to make travel plans on your own. Beware of all unsolicited offers.

provide information pertaining to traveler safety, but they can wreak havoc on a country's tourism industry. One of the outcomes of the information provided is that whole countries are often shut down due to travel warnings when just a small area of the country is experiencing unrest. As a potential traveler to a certain country, it is difficult to tell from the news on television and in newspapers just how unsettled the country or region is or how much an infectious disease has spread so travel warnings issued by governments are useful. Usually, there is a lag time between the expiration of a threat, the reevaluation of the warning, and the return of tourists. During this lag time, adventuresome tourists find bargain prices. But, as with most purchases, consumers are taking a risk. They should weigh the risk factors and search for more information before making a decision about proceeding with travel plans.

To round out your perspective, visit several nations' travel warnings Web sites.

A useful Web site in this regard is the U.S. State Department which gives information on *travel.state.gov* for citizens traveling abroad. Box 10.6 gives a description of the types of information available on the site. This site is extremely popular for

BOX 10.6    U.S. State Department Travel Information Available at
*travel.state.gov*

- Travel Warnings:This includes reports of dangerous conditions in certain countries.
- Public Announcements:This lists warnings of significant risks to the security of travelers because of terrorist threats and short term conditions.
- Consular Information Sheets:These sheets give the locations of U.S. embassies and consulates in individual countries; information on health conditions, entry regulations, crime, security, and drug policies; and immigration policies.

This site also provides information about how to apply for jobs with the state department and foreign service, on international adoptions, on obtaining visas and passports, and offers travel publications.

tourists, business travelers, job seekers with the federal government, and those interested in world conditions; it receives 95 million hits a year (Neuman, 2002). To be really thorough, other nations' Web sites should be checked as well. Nations, given that they have different forms of intelligence gathering, don't always agree on where the risky places are and why. For example, in October 2002, Denmark and Great Britain reported on Web sites that they had received information that terrorists might target resorts in Phuket, Thailand. Basically, tourists were told to "exercise extreme caution."

At the same time the U.S. government sources did not report the need for extreme caution, but did issue a broad warning about Southeast Asia and fortunately, nothing of a terrorist nature happened in Thailand in the fall of 2002. However, tragedy did strike in Bali in October 2002 when more than 190 people, many of them foreign tourists, were killed in the deadly bombing of the Sari Club in Kuta Beach, Bali. This was not predicted or preannounced by the major Web sites; however, it is still recommended that it is worthwhile to gather advice from several governments (see E-Resources section) before traveling abroad. Several companies specialize in providing security advice, including medical aid and evacuation services, but they charge a price. If you work for a business that involves foreign travel or working abroad, the company may have in-house advice as to security and the safe conduct of business. As an added measure, many international businesses, resorts, and hotels are stepping up security measures. Travelers are encouraged to use common sense by avoiding standing out or appearing lost. They should be aware of surroundings, keep up with the news and changing events, and have an exit plan.

## UNORDERED MERCHANDISE

The Federal Trade Commission has ruled on merchandise sent through the mail directly to the consumer who did not order the merchandise. Only two kinds of merchandise may be sent legally in this way (without the consumer's consent):

1. Free samples that are clearly marked as such (besides arriving in the mail, these may appear also attached to newspapers).

2. Merchandise from charitable organizations such as address labels.

If you receive anything that does not fit these categories:

- Be wary of opening unexpected packages especially those unlabeled as to return address or with a return address you do not know, or
- Return the package to the post office, or
- You have the right to keep whatever is in the package if it is clearly addressed to you, the occupant, and you should not pay anything.

## CHARITIES: WHEN THE GIVING HELPS AND WHEN IT HURTS

Charities can be legitimate, quasi-legitimate, or outright frauds. Americans donate nearly $7 billion a year to the 400 largest charities in the United States Curiously, low-income people are often generous donors (some speculate it is because they can more easily relate to those in need) so donating is not for the rich only. For many years, the Salvation Army has received the largest donations. Following the September 11 disaster, donations to the American Red Cross skyrocketed. These are both legitimate charities not to be confused with ones that are not. An estimated $2 billion a year falls into the hands of fraudulent solicitors.

*Giving to legitimate charities can be satisfying, take the time to do it right.*

The problem is that there are so many charities that it is difficult to sort the goods ones from the bad ones. *Money* magazine estimates there are 626,226 charities vying for contributions, and 30,000 new ones join their rank every year (Stark, 1996). So how do you make good choices? Your first thought should be what causes or charities do I believe in. Your donation should be a reflection of your values and principles. This will narrow the field, and then the next guide should be how the charity ranks on the basis of how efficiently dollars are spent. For example, the American Red Cross ranks consistently high in the percentage of its income that goes to programs, directly to help those in need. *Money* magazine regularly reports the rankings of charities. Better Business Bureaus, other magazines, newspapers, state government consumer protection agencies, and consumer watchdog organizations also offer lists and rankings. See E-Resources for a list of charity watchdog Web sites. Go online, and investigate the charity itself; all large charities have Web sites with information.

The surest way to avoid fraud is to know about the charity and their activities, ask questions about how money is used making sure most of it gets to those who are in need, and to be sure the money will be spent where you want it spent. Do you want it to go to terrorist causes that blow up buildings? Do you want your hard-earned money to go to building mansions for fake religious leaders or adding to their fleet of luxury cars? Sometimes the surface organization seems okay, but the money is funneled to other organizations and people and causes that you would not normally support. Box 10.7 provides a charity checklist to ensure that your donation dollars benefit the people and organizations that you want. Be especially wary of charities or persons you do not know who ask for donations over the Internet.

Special care should be made when giving large donations, especially those made through trusts and wills. Donations of this sort should not be made without legal and tax advice from professionals.

BOX 10.7    Charity Checklist

1. Ask for written information. Do not go by what is said on the telephone or over e-mail. Be especially wary of unsolicited e-mails with sad stories from foreign countries.
2. Ask for identification. If solicitor refuses, call the local authorities.
3. Call the charity back to find out if the caller was legitimate.
4. Watch for similar sounding names. The fraudulent name may be only one word off a legitimate charity's name.
5. Be skeptical about being pressured to "pledge" money. Be wary if anyone says that you or someone in your family already pledged money.
6. Ask how the donation will be spent.
7. If there are special events or tickets, find out how much is tax exempt or tax deductible.
   If for your own taxes deductibility is important, ask for a receipt showing the amount of your contribution and stating that it is tax deductible. For security reasons, pay by check. Beware of any solicitor insisting on cash.
8. Discourage employers from pushing employees or schools from pushing school children to donate to legitimate charities. Donations should be individual choice.
9. Be wary of any gifts or sweepstakes offers connected with a contribution. To be eligible to win, a donation is not necessary.
10. Be wary of people who gather money at street corners or at traffic intersections, they may or may not be legitimate.
11. Be wary of fraudsters operating immediately after a crisis. They prey on your sympathy.
12. Let the attorney general, your local consumer protection office, and the FTC know of any organization that is making misleading solicitations.

**Consumer Alert**

For years, a common consumer charity fraud perpetuating on the Internet is for causes and persecuted individuals in Nigeria. The way it works is that you are first led to feel sorry for the charity or source and then it evolves into not only charity fraud but also mail and investment fraud. A particularly enduring and costly one is a proposal that asks individuals to assist government officials in transferring "tied-up" funds by establishing accounts in their country. The offer claims you can earn up to $7 million or 30 percent of the money that you help transfer into new accounts. All you have to do is provide a bank account where they can deposit millions of dollars that the Nigerian government has "tied-up" in bureaucracy. Initially, the proposal states that you need not invest any money up front. However, as time passes you begin receiving letters or faxes stating that the Nigerian government has snagged the transaction of depositing money into the account you set up. Then they ask you to provide your own money to complete the transaction, and afterward "millions" will be deposited into your account. Victims have been known to pump thousands of dollars into this scam. U.S. postal officials believe that this type of mail-fraud scheme has cost victims more than $100 million a year.

*Source:* The Florida Department of Consumer Services Web site, January 22, 2003.

# DISPOSITION

Some products are entirely consumed such as an ice cream cone; others are disposed of after use such as chewing gum. **Disposition** (disposal) of a product can occur before, during, or after its use. How can it occur before? It has been estimated that as much as 30 percent of the food brought into the home is disposed of before use. Examples of product waste include fruits and vegetables that spoil and milk and bread that go bad before use. Millions of pounds of packaging are disposed of each year. Think of the cardboard packaging in cereal boxes and foil on snack packages. So disposition is about not only the product but also the packaging around it. Manufacturers are concerned about disposition. The absence of a package or minimal packaging can be used as an attempt to attract environmentally oriented consumers.

Why do people get rid of things besides the obvious reason of spoilage? Other reasons may be that the product no longer functions in a manner that the consumer desires, wear and tear are visible, or a newer model or style may be better. There is a market for used products that still function or have value as the success of eBay and millions of garage sales attest. Dissatisfaction is caused by a failure of performance; the product does not live up to expectations or has worn out its welcome.

# SUMMARY

Good buying and ownership tactics were covered in this chapter. Even following all the tips and rules, consumers sometimes make mistakes and seek remedies or solutions. Sometimes bad purchases are buried in the back of closets or corners of basements or garages only to be faced during moving. Disposition (disposal) of a product can occur at any time, even before use. Warranties are included in the price of the product, while service contracts cost extra and are sold separately. Care should be taken before signing a service contract; often consumers pay for more protection than they need.

Home improvement scams are rampant. Investigating the credentials and past work of designers, architects, contractors, and subcontractors and other home improvement professionals can go a long way in reducing potential problems. Letters of agreement or contracts upfront are imperative.

The travel market responds to terrorist attacks or epidemic outbreaks. There are many ways to reduce risks, the foremost being informed before traveling, keeping aware of news and world events while traveling, changing itineraries when necessary, and using common sense.

Consumer safety is a serious issue. Most infant equipment injuries are caused by infant carriers and car seats, most infant deaths from cribs. Riding toys including unpowered scooters are associated with more injuries than any other toy category for older children. Almost 200,000 children a year end up in the hospital emergency room from consumer product-related injuries. Boys are more likely to be injured than girls. The most typical injury is to the head or face. The U.S. Consumer Product Safety Commission actively monitors injury statistics and tries to reduce the number of consumer product injuries through regulation, recalls, and education.

Americans are used to a one-price system for most things so that the sticker price is what they expect to pay at a grocery or discount store. However, bargaining and sliding price systems (price variation) are on the rise, and savvy shoppers seek to find out if they qualify for discounts on hotel rooms, airplane tickets, and so forth. Careful shoppers also look for warranties, read labels, pay cash when feasible to save credit card fees, keep records and receipts, and file complaints or send letters or online complaints when necessary. A first step in the buying process is to find out all one can before buying, making sure the product or service is truly needed and then finding the best supplier at the best price.

## KEY POINTS

1. Consumers underutilize products for a variety of reasons from impulse buying to change in lifestyle and interests.
2. Warranties are useful, but in most cases service contracts are unnecessary. The Federal Trade Commission keeps a database of fraud-related complaints and enters them into the Consumer Sentinel, a secure online database available to law enforcement agencies.
3. The U.S. Consumer Product Safety Commission assembles consumer product-related statistics not only for child-related products but also for other products such as fireworks, helmets, and candles.
4. The Federal Trade Commission regulates advertising and especially monitors advertising aimed at children.
5. Travel prices are increasingly negotiable. More than one price exists on the same flight and in the same hotel. Discount and frequent user programs are increasing.
6. Travel fraud especially at holiday and spring break is aimed at college students.
7. Before traveling abroad Web sites of several countries should be checked to find out if there are particular concerns or warnings.
8. Home improvement fraud is rampant. Right-to-cure laws set up a procedure for homeowners to give builders a chance to repair their homes before they file a lawsuit. Builder associations support these laws, but plaintiff attorneys and consumer advocates are skeptical.
9. Charities can be legitimate, quasi-legitimate, and downright fraudulent. Investigate before donating money to a cause or organization: For tax and safety purposes, donate by check.
10. Some products are totally consumed like an ice cream cone, but most have to be reused or disposed of.

## KEY TERMS

| | | |
|---|---|---|
| attribute-based choices | disposition | underutilization |
| bounded rationality | intentional injuries | unintentional injuries |
| carpal tunnel syndrome | one-price system | years of potential life |
| constructive choice | right-to-cure laws | lost |
| cross-selling | service contract | |

## DISCUSSION QUESTIONS

1. Why would someone buy a product and never use it? What is an example of a product that you have bought and rarely or never used? Describe the reasons why you underutilized the product.
2. Have you or a family member ever had a problem with car repairs? What happened as a result? What was the process from problem to the final fix-up?
3. Why is it said that information is the smart traveler's secret weapon? For safety purposes, what are information sources that a traveler could use before and during travel?
4. What is the Consumer Sentinel and why is it useful?
5. Select a Web site from the E-Resources list and report on what you find.

## E-RESOURCES

| Name/Web site | What it is/does |
| --- | --- |
| American Society of Travel Agents, Inc.<br>www.astanet.com | Travel clearinghouse, tips, education |
| Consumer Product Safety Commission (CPSC)<br>www.cpsc.gov<br>clearinghouse@cpsc.gov | National Injury Information Clearinghouse |
| Department of Housing and Urban Development Home Improvement Branch<br>www.hud.gov/homeimpr.html | Information on home improvements |
| Federal Aviation Administration (FAA)<br>www.faa.gov | Information on regulations, certifying pilots |
| Federal Trade Commission<br>www.ftc.gov | To file a complaint or get free information on consumer issues, including advertising |
| National Center for Injury Prevention and Control<br>www.cdc.gov/ncipc | Information about preventing unintentional injuries and violence |
| National Highway Traffic Administration<br>www.nhtsa.dot.gov | Education and safety regulations, crash test results, statistics on economic losses from crashes |
| National Institute for Automotive Service Excellence (ASE)<br>www/asecert.org | Training, certification, publications |

| | |
|---|---|
| National Safety Council www.nsc.org | Information about preventing unintentional injuries |
| World Health Organization www.who.int/violence_injury_prevention | Information and statistics about the consequences of intentional and unintentional injuries worldwide |

**For Travel Warnings and Advisories**

| | |
|---|---|
| The Bureau of Consular Affairs (U.S. Department of State) | Foreign travel, adoptions, passports, and career information |
| travel.state.gov www.travel.stat.gov/travel_warnings.html | |
| Great Britain's Foreign & Commonwealth Office www.fco.gov.uk/travel | Travel information |
| Canada's Consular Affairs Bureau www.voyage.gc.ca | Travel information |
| Australian Department of Foreign Affairs and Trade www.dfat.gov.au | Travel information |
| The Internet Public Library www.ipl.org/reading/news | Provides international news when traveling; also try BBC, CNN, local papers for news |

| | |
|---|---|
| Charity Watchdogs Council of Better Business Bureaus www.bbb.org | Charity scams reported Overall guide to consumer complaint filings |
| Money magazine Money.mag.com | Rankings of nation's largest charities |
| National Charities Information Bureau www.give.org | Monitors charities receiving $500,000+ per year |
| Internet Nonprofit Center www.nonprofits.org | Has an IRS database of 1.2 million nonprofits Use this to find out if a charity is registered |

# REFERENCES

Beck, E. (2002). Get with the remodeling boom. *Home Improvement: A Great Investment.* Lowes.com/investment.

Boulding, W., and A. Kirmani. (June 1993). A consumer-side experimental examination of signaling theory. *Journal of Consumer Research,* 11–23.

Brooks, R. (August 1, 2002). UPS guarantees home deliveries on time, following FedEx's lead. *Wall Street Journal,* p. D2.

Clements, J. (August 28, 2002). Skip the imported granite countertops: Home remodeling is a lousy investment. *Wall Street Journal,* p. D1.

Fetto, J. (October 2002). Babes in toyland. *American Demographics,* p. 14.

*FTC Facts: Auto Service Contracts,* 2003, Washington, DC.

Higgins, M. (August 28, 2002). 'My cookies are crumbled': The art of consumer griping. *Wall Street Journal,* pp. D1 and D4.

Insel, P., and W. Roth. (2002). *Core concepts in health, 9th ed.,* Boston: McGraw Hill.

Jacoby, J., C. K. Berning, and T. G. Dietvorst. (1977). What about disposition? *Journal of Marketing, 41,* 22–28.

Many kids' Web sites continuing to collect personal information. (July 19, 1999). Center for Media Education.

Neuman, S. (2002). Travel warnings pose threat to tourism in Asian countries. *Wall Street Journal,* p. D3.

Perez, E. (January 23, 2003). Builders push "right-to-cure" laws. *Wall Street Journal,* p. D2.

Spencer, J. (November 12, 2002). The best care deal around: Never paying for repairs. *Wall Street Journal,* p. D1.

Stark, A. (2002). Saving up for the lean times ahead. *Wall Street Journal,* p. D8.

Stark, E. (November 1996). Which charities merit your money. *Money,* pp. 100–102.

Trocchia, P., and J. Swinder. (2002). An investigation of product purchase and subsequent non-consumption. *Journal of Consumer Marketing, 19* (3), 188–204.

Weisskoff, R. (March 1985). Current trends in children's advertising. *Journal of Advertising Research,* 12–14.

# 11

# Being a Better Consumer of Housing and Vehicles

*A comfortable house is a great source of happiness.*
*It ranks immediately after health and a good conscience.*
**Sydney Smith**

## Learning Objectives

1. Explain the pros and cons of owning versus renting housing.
2. Explain the different types of home mortgages.
3. Discuss change points in people's lives and the effect on consumption.
4. Discuss the cost of utilities.
5. Explain the pros and cons of leasing versus owing vehicles.
6. Discuss how to buy new or used vehicles and what deceptive practices to avoid.

## INTRODUCTION

After the stock market bubble burst in the early part of this century, Americans worried that there was a real-estate bubble soon to follow, but home prices proved to be more stable. They are subject to different sorts of demands and flow than the stock market. People do not need stocks to survive, but they do need a roof over their heads. Also helping support the housing market was that while home prices rose, interest rates plunged on mortgages which helped to hold down mortgage payments for new home buyers. As this book went to press, the real estate market was holding up well.

Because homes and cars are the most visible high-ticket items that most consumers own, this chapter is devoted to how to become better consumers of both. *In the typical family's budget, housing represents 32 percent and transportation 18 percent, making homes the single most expensive purchase anyone makes.* The pie diagram in Figure 11.1 shows a typical family budget. Since the last chapter covered repairs such as vehicular repair and home improvements, the emphasis in this chapter is on the prebuying and purchasing part of these investments, starting with the decision of whether to buy or rent housing.

To provide historical perspective, it should be noted that "[no] century began with as much promise for change as the twentieth. The automobile and airplane, motion pictures and radio, the electric light and appliances, bottled soft drinks and canned soups, all so prosaic and common at the end of the century, were the new wonders of 1900" (Cross, 2000, p. 17). Can the same be said for the twenty-first

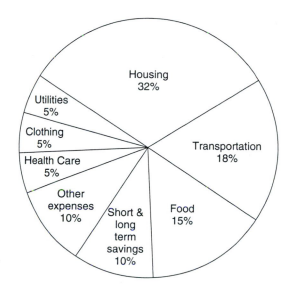

**Figure 11.1**  Typical Family Budget: each family differs; this is a general guide.

century? What developments bode well for our future? What can we expect from the automobile industry, for example? Is owning a home still the American dream? The numbers reveal that it is. *About 67 percent of households own their homes, and home equity accounts for 23.5 percent of household net worth.* With ownership comes responsibility and the need to make lasting choices. Before buying, nearly everyone rents so the chapter begins with a discussion of renting and leasing.

## RENTING

Millions of students sign their first leases while in college. Leases may be difficult to get out of so caution is recommended. There are month to month leases, school year leases, and yearly leases. Landlords give financial incentives or make improvements to keep the same renters year in and year out. **Rent** is payment for the use of property. Most students will continue to rent for the first few years out of college with the intention of buying housing. A great advantage of renting is that it is a temporary arrangement; you pay month to month so money is not tied up. Even with this advantage, increasingly people are buying homes at a younger and younger age because low mortgage rates make buying more affordable than or just as affordable as renting. As one 24-year-old said, why pay $700 a month for a small apartment when I can own a town house for the same price and then have something to sell when I move on? But one has to make these decisions weighing other parts of one's financial life. For example, in 1998 Tammy Hitchcock, 33, an Atlanta hospital administrative assistant, bought a $50,000 condominium whose $473 monthly mortgage and carrying charges she would easily meet, but trouble came after moving in. The problem was she already had about $12,000 in credit-card debt and student loans and then spent another $5,000 for bedroom and dining room furniture (Making Your House Pay Off, 2002). Tammy ended up in credit counseling to get things straightened out, a subject that is discussed in the next chapter.

# LEASING

Renting usually involves a **security deposit** which is a payment required by the landlord in advance to cover wear and tear of the unit and as the name implies to secure a unit for the renter. Most typically this is one month's rent on top of writing a check for the first month's rent. So a renter would probably pay $1,800 to move in if the rent was $900 a month plus the security deposit. There may also be a refundable or nonrefundable pet fee or deposit to take care of cleaning carpets and so forth when the renter moves out. Many landlord-tenant disputes are over the return of the security deposit at the end of the renting period.

Another part of renting is the signing of a lease. A **lease** is a legal document between the renter and the landlord, describing the rights and responsibilities of both. Part of the lease is a clause about subleasing. This clause describes what is allowed or what is not allowed and under what circumstances. **Subleasing** means the property can be leased by the original tenant to another person or persons.

## Landlord/Tenant Disputes

Disputes between landlords and tenants are common especially in college towns. Before moving in, renters should take photos showing the condition of the rental unit especially focusing on any damaged or substandard areas that may come into dispute later. If the landlord promises repairs such as retiling a bathroom or recarpeting, get that promise in writing. Upon leaving the unit, if it has been kept clean and undamaged, the tenants have the right to expect a prompt return of the security deposit. Tenants should give ample notice of vacating, usually at least a month, in order for the landlord to inspect the unit and line up another tenant. If there is a dispute about the return of the security deposit or over the conditions of subleasing, the tenant should try first to work something out with the landlord or leasing agent. If this does not work, most campuses offer free legal services to students to try to resolve issues such as landlord-tenant disputes. Locate this service through university student services. Another alternative is small claims court.

---

**Consumer Alert**

Before signing a lease:

- Review contents, know what you are signing.
- Features to look for are time, is it a one-year lease or a month-to-month lease? Are you liable for damages and what kind?
- Look over the property. How well maintained are the grounds and the interiors such as newer appliances?
- Find out about subleasing. Is there a fee for the privilege of subleasing?
- Landlords are not bound to anything they promise orally. If landlords make an oral promise, ask that it be written into the lease.
- Final advice, write everything down.

---

---

**Consumer Alert**

A common problem is bait and switch regarding the quality of the apartment rented. For example, two students may look at a model apartment in a large complex in the spring and sign a lease to rent an apartment similar to that apartment in the fall. When they arrive in the fall, their apartment is not of the same quality as the model apartment that they were shown. Perhaps the carpet is not new or the apartment has not been re-painted; if it is furnished, the furniture may be broken and so forth. As mentioned in the text, the students' first step is to try to resolve the issue with the landlord. Are there other apartments? Will the landlord agree in writing to fix the problems immediately?

---

## OWNING A HOME

As mentioned in the introduction, owning a home is often referred to as the American Dream. We have sentimental songs like Stephen Foster's "Home Sweet Home" that extol the virtues of home. Can you picture this as Apartment Sweet Apartment? According to the Census Bureau, record homeownership rate is taking place. Half of all Americans live in the suburbs, and nearly three-quarters (73 percent) of households are owner occupied. Between 1990 and 2000 the number of owner-occupied units rose 18 percent, while renter-occupied units edged up only 8 percent. The average age of a homeowner is 52 years old (Francese, 2003).

> Half of all Americans live in suburbs. Home owner-ship is up.

When buying a home what do most people want? Usually the answer for a middle-income family is a single-family detached house with three or four bedrooms, multiple bathrooms, central heating and air conditioning, an up-to-date kitchen, a two-car garage, and a yard. A starter home may be a town house, half of a duplex, condominium, small home in a new development, or a house that needs fixing up. Some people, especially dual-income couples, skip the starter home phase and head straight for the three bedroom, two bathroom house in the suburbs. "Minorities, immigrants and single people are buying homes in record numbers. They have transformed the housing market over the past 10 years and will likely be leading the charge in the decade to come" (The New "Starter" Home, 2002, p. 53).

> Minorities, immigrants, and single people are buying homes in record numbers.

Larger homes usually mean the purchase of more furniture and higher utility bills and property taxes so size and location of the home have financial implications beyond the home's price. "Credit counselors say that new homeowners often get into financial trouble by spending too much after they move in. The typical buyer of a new house lays out $9,000 for furnishings and improvements in the first year, according to Harvard's Joint Center for Housing Studies" (Making Your House Pay Off, 2002, p. 15).

> The typical buyer of a new house spends $9,000 on furnishings and improvements in the first year.

## LIFE CHANGE POINTS AFFECT CONSUMPTION

The discussion of people going from renting to owning a home is a good example of a visible change point in people's lives. It is a signal of settling down and putting down roots. Other change points in people's lives include going to college, getting married, having children, getting a first professional job, moving, and retiring. These usually involve increased expenses.

Marriage or having a first or second child or even getting a dog often signals the need for owning rather than renting. Families, friends, and work colleagues may help celebrate transitions with moving-in parties, baby showers, wedding showers, house warming parties, and retirement parties which involve presents for the changed family and/or household needs. Since life changes involve the spending of money, media and business are well aware of this and try to capitalize on it by sponsoring bridal shows or giving free sample gift packs at marriage license bureaus and at maternity wards in hospitals. The thinking is that a free magazine or Tide, Secret, or Pampers samples or coupons given at the right moment can set the mood for future sales. Conde Nast, publisher of *Bride's* and *Modern Bride,* estimates that U.S. newlyweds spend $70 billion in the first year after marriage on their households. *Consumers buy more in their first six months of marriage than a settled household does in five years* (Ellison and Tejada, 2003).

*Newlyweds are the ultimate consumer.*

> Corporate marketers say certain points in life make consumers especially vulnerable to sales pitches, with the soon-to-be married often being the most susceptible. It's a time when they aren't just choosing a marriage partner, but also are making brand decisions about toothpaste, detergent and appliances that could last even longer. Unless a couple has been living together for years, wedding represents a moment when two sets of habits and brand preferences meet and usually only one survives. "Newlyweds," says James Stengel, global marketing officer at Procter & Gamble Co. in Cincinnati, "are in some ways the ultimate consumer." (Ellison and Tejada, 2003, p. B1.)

Change points surge at certain times of the year. Graduations and weddings peak in June. One-fifth of wedding proposals occur in December, causing a huge spike in advertising in January bridal magazines. The ads are not just for wedding gowns and bridesmaid dresses, but for vacation destinations, household goods, shampoos, cosmetics, fragrances, and cars. American List Counsel, a marketing firm, gathers names of newlyweds from county clerk's offices and photographers and sells the names to marketers including realtors. "Newlywed names 'are like gold,' says Pete Hunsinger, president of Conde Nast's bridal group" (Ellison and Tejada, p. B3). House sales peak in the summer because people with children want to be settled before the new school year begins. Movers can charge more in the summer than they can during the rest of the year.

## HOMES AS INVESTMENTS

*Technically speaking, housing is considered a consumer good, not a pure investment; however, most people think of their homes as an investment. It is a consumer good because the house is typically used by the owners. Ninety percent of all single-family homes are owner occupied.* Homeowners typically stay in their homes for eight years, which is longer than most people hold shares of stock. Even with all that said, real estate investments are compared to investing in stocks. This is important to do to gain perspective even though they are not truly equivalent. As Federal Reserve Board Chairman Alan Greenspan said, "The transaction costs of homes are very high. You can't readily sell a home without a very large cost, and perhaps more importantly, you have to move. The type of underlying conditions that creates bubbles are very difficult to create in the housing market" (*The Freddie Mac Reporter Fact Book,* 2002–2003, p. 17). Home values fell nationally during the depression of the 1930s, but held up well for most the twentieth century and into the twenty-first century. Home values tend to hold up even during recessions. Predicted growth in the first decade of the 2000s is 4 to 5 percent. In terms of supply, the national housing market is well balanced.

Home values in recent years kept climbing, but there are upswings and slowdowns in surprising spots. Location, as always, matters greatly.

Investment-wise over the last 75-years, stocks have outperformed real estate. "Since 1968, the single-family house has risen in value by 6.3 percent a year. But, in today's razzle-dazzle housing market, people forget that houses can also fall in value. In the late 1980s, for example, house prices throughout Texas and Oklahoma were devastated by the oil industry's collapse" (Making Your House Pay Off, 2002, p. 13). When the economy dipped from 1999 to 2003 real estate held its own through low mortgage rates. It increased considerably in value in Greenwich, CT, Washington, DC, and Southern California, as only three examples. In fact, the housing market was so good that an article in *The Wall Street Journal* said, "Forget watching the stock market. The best—maybe the only—game in town these days is the remarkably resilient real-estate market. Last year alone, amid all the bad news, home prices still rose by 7% nationally—and some economists believe things will be almost as strong this year" (Fletcher, 2003, p. W1). In some parts of the United States, real estate values have declined or merely kept pace with inflation. So, land and/or a home may or may not be the best investment, depending on the location and interest rates. Realtors and wise buyers study the local market including comparing the house values on the street being considered.

## RENTING VS. BUYING: LENGTH OF TIME FACTOR

"The longer you stay in a house, the more you will benefit from the ability to live rent-free and the less you need to worry about short-term price dips. 'Over seven or eight years, you can be pretty sure that buying a house will financially dominate renting,'" according to Chris Mayer, a real estate professor at the University of Pennsylvania's Wharton School (Clements, 2003, p. D1). But if your time horizon is shorter than that, what should you do? The shorter the time horizon the more risk so more care should be taken in choosing type of housing and location. As a general rule, condominiums and high-end houses should be avoided because during market downturns these are hit harder than middle-income single-family homes. The cut-off point is three years so if you are going to be in an area less than three years renting may be a better option from a financial standpoint. The reasons are the high expense of buying and selling the house, including closing/financing costs and the possibility that the home will not rise significantly in value in a short amount of time. Of course, an area where housing prices are soaring would be an exception to this. Homes, can be **illiquid**, meaning they are difficult to sell readily and get the cash out. It is not unusual for homes to take more than a year to sell, and if they are vacant during that time, the homeowner is paying the mortgage and upkeep expenses while at the same time paying rent or mortgage payments in the new location.

If living in an area for less than three years, it may be wiser to rent rather than buy.

**Consumer Alert**

As stocks declined in the early 2000s and real estate rose in value, scam artists shifted their attention to the real estate market. Newlyweds can be a target since they are new to the housing market. State and federal regulators reported a decided increase in complaints regarding time shares and other types of real estate investments, including raw land in places like Texas. Part of the scam was the promise of oil on the land in Texas. The basic pitch was that because of unrest in the world, Texas oil was going to be worth more. As readers of this book know, geopolitical situations and the economy change, and fraudsters take advantage of whatever they can to prey on fear and uncertainty. Whether for personal use or as a way to build wealth, real estate investments should be carefully scrutinized. Ask yourself if the seller is legitimate (established), if the price is reasonable, and, in general, investigate before you invest. The best way to protect yourself is, as always, "If it sounds too good to be true, it probably isn't." Does the offer pass the sniff test?

# WHEN TO BUY, TYPES, AND FINANCING CHOICES

## Determining Readiness to Buy

After years of renting, individuals want to own. The main reason first-time homebuyers give for looking for a home is that they are *tired of paying rent,* according to the National Association of Realtors. So, the first determinant of readiness to buy is the feeling that it is time to buy. When asking people why they want to buy, the second most given reason is tax advantages and the third is a desire for a larger place. Box 11.1 gives other reasons why someone may prefer buying over renting. Owning a home has several advantages, including the most basic which is supplying the need for shelter. A home is an investment as well, an opportunity to build equity. When one buys one hopes the house will go up in value. **Appreciation** refers to the increase in the home's value. Emotional reasons include the need to lay down roots, pride, an opportunity for self-expression, security, and a sense of ownership.

Financially, how does one determine how much house one can afford? Several formulas exist to determine readiness to buy: The simplest is the *2½ times rule.* This would give a person a general idea of the maximum amount he or she could spend. To calculate this, multiply the annual household income by two and one-half. For example, a person earning $40,000 a year could afford a $100,000 house. A typical down payment is 10 to 20 percent of the purchase price so for the $100,000 house, a person should save up $10,000 to $20,000 before seriously looking to buy. Ads for new developments will often say no money down so in that case the person would not need a down payment, although it is usually a good idea so there are more choices and a higher down payment will diminish how much is owed. **Mortgages**, loans to purchase real estate in which the real estate serves as collateral, are what remains after the down payment is subtracted from the purchase price. Lenders such as banks can help a person determine how much house they can afford. Lenders estimate mortgages based on the down payment and the buyer's ability to handle monthly payments of principal, interest, taxes, and insurance (**PITI**). Another method for determining whether one is ready to buy or not is the *28/36 qualifying rule.* Monthly gross income is multiplied by .28 (28%)

BOX 11.1    Pros and Cons of Renting and Buying Housing

|      | Renting | Buying |
|------|---------|--------|
| Pros | Extras like swimming pools | Pride of ownership |
|      | Few responsibilities | Tax deductions |
|      | No yard work, no repairs | Build equity |
|      | Not tied down | Feeling of community |
|      | Close neighbors offer security | Can borrow against equity |
|      | Manager handles problems | Improved credit rating |
|      | Utilities may be included | Usually a garage and yard |
|      |  | More space |
| Cons | No tax deductions | Feeling tied down |
|      | Transient neighbors | Down payment |
|      | Can't make many changes | Closing costs |
|      | No pets policy | Repair bills |
|      | Not much storage | Yard work |
|      | Rents increase with little notice | Property taxes |
|      | Can't build equity | Homeowners assoc. dues |
|      | Lack of washer/dryer in unit | Money tied up |

or .36 (36%) to show the range that lenders would consider as appropriate. Here is an example if someone had a $4,000 monthly income.

|                | 28 Qualifying Rule | 36 Qualifying Rule |
|----------------|--------------------|--------------------|
| Monthly Income | $4,000 | $4,000 |
|                | × .28 | × .36 |
|                | $1120.00 | $1440.00 |

In this case the person could afford a mortgage of between $1,120 and $1,440 per month. This is assuming the person does not have high debt amounts owed on cars or on credit cards. The lender will look at the person's total **net worth** (assets−liabilities) to determine how much he or she can afford. **Assets** are what is owned. **Liabilities** are what is owed. The 2½ times rule or the 28/36 qualifying rule are starting points. An online tutorial that helps consumers determine if they are ready for homeownership and descriptions of the mortgage process and options is available at *www.freddiemac.com/homebuyers*. Through a congressional charter in 1970, **Freddie Mac** became a stockholder-owned corporation designed to increase the supply of money that lenders can make available to homebuyers and multifamily investors. Because of Freddie Mac, more people have access to better home financing and lower monthly mortgage payments. The goal is to make housing more accessible and affordable to a wide range of Americans.

## Types

The two main types are single-family dwellings which are unattached and multiunit dwellings such as duplexes, town houses, condominiums, and cooperatives. **Condominiums** and town houses are homes attached to one another. You own a unit, but you and neighbors share common areas such as swimming pools and lobbies. Condominiums can be found anywhere, but are most associated with beach, ski, golf, theme parks, or other types of resort, retirement, or recreational areas. The monthly maintenance or repair fees for common areas collected from single-family dwelling homeowners or from condominium owners are called **homeowner's fees**. **Cooperative apartments** are similar, except you own shares in the building as a whole with the right to lease a certain unit. Cooperative apartments are found mostly in big cities such as Boston and New York City. **Manufactured housing** includes units that are fully or partially assembled in a factory and moved to the living site.

## Quality

Regardless of housing type, care should be taken in assessing quality, availability of services, zoning laws, school zones, and covenants. Potential buyers should inquire about **home warranties** which provide additional protection for the buyer and **home inspections** to assess the condition of the home. States vary about how much is disclosed to the potential buyer before or at **closing**, the meeting in which real estate is transferred from seller to buyer. States also vary in how much is paid by the seller and how much is paid by the buyer at closing in terms of fees and add-ons. Many of these can be negotiated before going into the closing. An anxious seller is more likely to pick up extra costs and fees than a seller with many potential buyers. **Defect-disclosure forms** that describe the condition of the home are required in some states. Termite inspections are required in others. Before purchasing find out what the rules are in your area. Realtors should be upfront about a home's or a neighborhood's defects, but they are usually paid commission by the seller and therefore are more likely to be working in the seller's interest. Many realtors, however, take the long-term view and realize it is equally important to have satisfied buyers who may hire them again to buy or sell a house or because they give good word-of-mouth to other potential buyers and sellers. *About 90 percent of homes are sold by realtors.*

One would assume a new home bought direct from the builder would not require a home inspection, but today hiring inspectors for new housing is becoming more and more common. The potential buyer hires the home inspector and pays the fee. Investing in real estate is very much about the old adage "you get what you pay for," using highly recommended realtors and inspectors and buying well-built houses pays off in the long run.

## Mortgages

This section provides a quick overview of the main types of mortgages. The basic advice when shopping for a mortgage includes:

1. Educating yourself. Current interest rates are reported in the newspaper and over the Internet. Mortgages are available locally and over the Internet.
2. Knowing your lending institution.
3. Visiting Web sites providing home buying information. See E-Resources section for examples.

Most people get a fixed rate, fixed-term, fixed payment loan which is usually carried for 15 or 30 years and is called a **fixed-rate conventional mortgage**. When mortgage rates are low as they were in 2003 (around 6%), then this is a good choice because the housing costs are known, budgeting is easier, and the mortgage rate is set. If mortgage rates increase sharply, more people consider **adjustable rate mortgages (ARMs)** which allow the interest rates to fluctuate within a range, based on changes in the economy. Usually with ARMs, less is paid initially, as much as 2 percent less (a teaser rate) than the fixed-rate conventional mortgages so ARMs may be a good option for someone starting out as new hires or as newly-weds, assuming their incomes will build. At preset intervals the ARM would be re-visited and go up or down with a range, for example, between 5 and 10 percent.

See the E-Resources section for Web sites with mortgage quotes. Mortgage seek-ers can get mortgages, online or at mortgage companies, banks, or credit unions. A homebuyer can negotiate with the lender (online or in person) rather than assum-ing a published rate is final. If a person has a good credit rating, the amount may be reduced.

Sometimes, the seller offers help with financing. Potential buyers should weigh all the financial options and the state of the economy at the time of purchase.

Once owned, if mortgage rates drop considerably (at least two percentage points), then the homeowner can look into refinancing. For example, if the mortgage was 9 percent and the current fixed-rate conventional mortgage is at 5 percent, it would be worthwhile to look into refinancing. The problem is this change involves paperwork, time, and fees; the homeowner will have to weigh the costs and the benefits of chang-ing to a different mortgage. Usually refinancing makes the most sense if the home-owner is planning to stay several more years in the same home.

**Predatory Home Mortgage Abuses.**   Most people get their homes financed through legitimate mortgage companies and banks, but as in anything involving money and in this case large sums of money, the potential for fraud is enormous. May the borrower beware! **Predatory lending** lures people into loans that they re-ally can't afford, usually by borrowing against the equity in their homes or a rela-tive's home. The predatory practice could be about new mortgages or about home equity loans on homes already owned. Consumers' rights in this regard are par-tially protected by the Home Ownership and Equity Protection Act of 1994. Con-sumer advocates would like to strengthen this Act to provide further protection. This would include wider regulation of the high interest "subprime" lending market where predatory practices are common. Warning signs of predatory lenders are

1. Advertisements that say "We give credit to anyone" or "Poor credit, no prob-lem"
2. Rushes the person to sign immediately
3. Asks for a large fee up front to see if the potential homeowner qualifies for a loan
4. Offers an unusually low mortgage rate compared to the general market
5. Offers small monthly payments with a large balloon payment at the end

Older people or low-income people are prime targets for predatory home mort-gage sellers. Many people do not understand that they could lose their homes if they do not keep up payments. Loan origination fees are part of the problem. These may run as high as 10 to 25 percent of the total loan amount versus a more typical lender fee of around 2 percent. Advocacy groups such as AARP have suc-cessfully represented homeowners in suits against mortgage lenders in New York,

Washington, DC, and West Virginia. For copies of settlements go to the Federal Trade Commission Web site. Freddie Mac's information on predatory lending is available at *www.freddiemac.com/singlefamily/predlend.html*. For examples of beneficial lending practices and their predatory potential, see Table 11.1.

## Home-Based Loans: Pitfalls and Fraud Potential

Once an individual owns a home and starts building equity, they may take out a second mortgage, a home equity line of credit or cash-out refinancing or a reverse mortgage. Each financial instrument has pitfalls, the main one being that all forms of home-equity borrowing leeches value from the home. Here are the main types:

- In a second mortgage, a person pays a fixed rate of interest, usually around 6 or 7 percent for a set amount of money repaid over five to ten years to finance a single project such as renovations.
- The **home equity line of credit** carries a variable interest rate, usually around 4 percent (this varies so investigate current rates) and allows the homeowner to borrow up to a set amount. This can work well to finance home improvement projects.
- Cash-out refinancing allows the homeowner to replace the first mortgage with another, perhaps larger loan, and repocket the difference. The drawback here is that a person may be starting over with a new 30-year loan.

These are the basic three types, but there are new combinations being offered, including a combination first mortgage with a home equity line of credit. One of the features is that the credit line automatically increases as the borrower pays down the mortgage and the home's value grows.

The main advantages of home-based loans are that they offer low interest rates and that the interest paid is usually deductible from income tax. In January 2003, rates on home equity lines of credit were averaging 4.96 percent. Rates are usually

**Table 11.1**   Examples of Beneficial Lending Practices and Their Predatory Potential

| Lending Practice | Benefit | Predatory Potential |
|---|---|---|
| Allowing higher than market interest rates. | Enables relatively risky borrowers to obtain credit. | Excessive rates can financially ruin borrowers who lack financial capacity to repay the loan. |
| Ability to refinance | Enables borrowers to take advantage of lower interest rates | Can invite loan flipping, resulting in high loan fees and unnecessary credit costs. |
| Prepayment penalties | Provides borrower with lower rates | Prevents borrowers from refinancing, or unnecessarily drives up loan balance (as penalties are financed as part of a new loan) |

*Source: The Freddie Mac Reporter Fact Book 2002–2003, McLean, VA, p. 33.*

tied to the prime rate and move up when the prime rate increases. Popularity soared to the point that roughly one-quarter of homeowners with mortgages had a home equity loan in 2001. Here is an example:

> Chris Englin, an executive recruiter who lives near Seattle, took out a home equity line from Wells Fargo when she refinanced her $200,000 mortgage in December. Ms. Englin says her loan officer suggested the credit line when she mentioned she needed cash to buy a half-interest in a 24-foot fishing boat. Taking out the home-equity line "was really easy," she says. "We did the whole thing by e-mail." (Simon, 2003, p. D1)

The main drawback of home-based loans is that the home is at risk if the person does not keep up with the monthly loan payments. Before taking out a home equity loan, the homeowner should ask:

1. Do I really need the money?
2. Is there a minimum or maximum monthly payment?
3. What is the annual percentage rate? Is it set or is it adjustable? If rates are low, set is usually a better choice.
4. Are there any annual fees or transaction fees?
5. How long is the loan for? See the Consumer Alert for further advice.

Fraud abounds including advertisements on television and high sales pressure direct calls coming to the house from home salespeople. The elderly are often targeted because they have built up so much equity in their homes yet they may be cash poor. The best way to go about this is to apply for an equity loan through a local credit union or bank first or at least talk with a loan officer. This, at least, provides a sense of a baseline amount and terms. Do not sign anything unless it is completely understood. Home equity lines of credit, refinancings, and second mortgages may carry closing costs, fees, points, and taxes that may total up to 10 percent of the loan. So a $40,000 loan may end up costing $4,000 on top, and this is with a legitimate business.

**Reverse mortgages** pay the homeowner, usually an elderly person, in monthly advances or through a line of credit. Reverse mortgages convert home equity into cash with no repayment required for as long as the borrowers live in their homes. The main drawback is the person is taking value away from the home, when they move elsewhere or die, the home equity for the person or his or her heirs is reduced. It is prudent to consult an attorney or an accountant or another financial advisor before taking out a reverse mortgage. For further information, homeowners should gather information from their state office of consumer protection or the other sources listed in E-Resources.

As mentioned in an earlier chapter, in 1969 The Truth in Lending Act became a federal law as part of the Consumer Protection Act. It requires disclosure of a truth in lending statement on consumer loans, and this includes mortgages. The consumer has to know the total cost of credit such as the annual percentage rate and other specifics of the loan. The law was updated in 1980 as part of the Depository Institutions Deregulation and Monetary Control Act.

## Discrimination in Housing: Redlining and in Lending

**Discrimination** is an act based on prejudice or bias. In housing, it means that someone may not be treated fairly in terms of renting, buying, or financing. **Redlining**, prohibited by law, refers to the practice of drawing a red line or any

**Consumer Alert**

Banks are aggressively marketing home equity lines, but they are not for everyone.

- They make the most sense for short-term loans, two or three year, for example, for home improvements.
- If for longer terms, the borrower should seek fixed-rate loans.
- Pay attention to the interest rate. Compare rates. One source is Bankrate.com, a consumer finance Web site. The best home equity line may be from the same lender as the mortgage lender. Usually banks look favorably on someone they already know and have a relationship with.

other color around an area and that area is then marked as not receiving the same treatment as other areas regarding financing. Redlining can also exist for insurance and credit. Typically state laws protect consumers from being discriminated against regarding housing and financing; however, there are exceptions such as private clubs and religious organizations. There have been many lawsuits about discriminatory practices, including retirement living developments that have tried to keep out younger occupants. The Home Mortgage Disclosure Act requires the lenders to report where they make loans. No loans may be available in certain areas, usually low income or crime ridden, or if loans are available they may be significantly overpriced. Box 11.2 lists the protections against discrimination that the Equal Credit Opportunity Act (ECOA) and the Fair Housing Act (FHA) offer. These acts cover purchasing or refinancing homes or making home improvements.

Lenders cannot discourage individuals from applying for a mortgage or reject applications due to race, national origin, religion, sex, marital status, age, or because of public assistance. When a mortgage is denied, the lender has to give specific reasons. It is legal for lenders to factor in income, expenses, debts, and credit history. *Stable employment is an important factor* in how a lender will evaluate an application. Before applying for mortgages, potential homebuyers should check their credit report. Any errors should be corrected. Credit bureaus are required to investigate any errors in dispute.

**Consumer Alert**

If you or someone you know has been discriminated against, complain to the lender, then check your state consumer affairs department or attorneys general office to see if the creditor has violated state laws. Many states have their own equal credit opportunity laws. If a mortgage application is denied, the lender must provide the name and address of the appropriate government agency to contact. An option is suing the lender in federal district court. You can sue as an individual or join others to file a class action suit. Another source for advice is the National Fair Housing Alliance at *www.incacorp.com/nfba*). You can file a complaint with the U.S. Department of Housing and Urban Development (HUD) in Washington, DC. HUD will investigate the complaint and determine if there is reasonable cause to believe the Fair Housing Act has been violated.

BOX 11.2    Mortgage Discrimination

The ECOA and FHA protect against discrimination when an individual applies for a
    mortgage to purchase, refinance, or make home improvements.
Rights Under the Equal Credit Opportunity Act (ECOA)
Discrimination is prohibited in any aspect of a credit transaction based on:

Race or color
Religion
National origin
Sex
Marital status
Age (provided the applicant has the capacity to contract)
Applicant's receipt of income derived from any public assistance program and appli-
    cant's exercise, in good faith, of any right under the Consumer Credit Protection
    Act, the umbrella statute that includes ECOA

Rights Under the Fair Housing Act (FHA)
Discrimination is prohibited in all aspects of residential real-estate related transactions,
    including

Making loans to buy, build, repair, or improve a dwelling
Selling, brokering, or appraising residential real estate
Selling or renting a dwelling

FHA also prohibits discrimination based on:

Race or color
National origin
Sex
Familial status (defined as children under the age of 18 living with a parent or legal
    guardian, pregnant women, and people securing custody of children under 18)
Handicap

*Source:* Adapted from FTC Facts for Consumers, Mortgage Discrimination, *www.ftc.gov.*

## UTILITIES: COSTS AND ENVIRONMENTAL IMPACT

As shown in the pie chart at the beginning of the chapter, in the typical household
utilities take about 5 percent of the budget. Utilities include electricity, natural gas,
and water. Sometimes telephone services are included in a list of utilities, but because of the variety of new systems, most of them not tied to home use, telephone
services will be addressed in another chapter in this book. Consumers have
choices of energy suppliers and natural gas suppliers in most states. Choices include a local private or public utility company or from a cooperative. Costs should
be compared as well as services. Water comes from local water agencies, and the
main government protection comes from the Environmental Protection Agency. To
find out more about water quality go to their Safe Drinking Water Hotline at 1 800
426 4791 or visit their Web site.

When looking at national averages, the highest utility cost is for residential
space heating at 33 percent followed by water heating at 15 percent, next comes

space cooling at 10 percent. Of course, in warm climates the space cooling can run higher on a yearly basis than heating bills. Small appliances such as small motors, electric knives, DVD players, and sewing machines use very little energy and won't affect utility bills much one way or the other. Appliances, devices, or lights that are large and left on for long periods of time use more energy than appliances that are turned off and on and only used for a few minutes. For example, a blender uses far less energy than a refrigerator.

To address the new ways people cook and the reduced spaces in which they live, appliance manufacturers are developing refrigerators that are multifunctional, including a single appliance that looks like an oven but also has a refrigeration feature. The way this appliance works is that the homeowner puts meatloaf in the unit in the morning and it will stay cold, then at 4:00 P.M. the oven goes on and cooks the meatloaf. If the homeowner arrives later than expected after a certain amount of warming/holding time, the unit will go back into the refrigeration mode and cools the meatloaf. More multipurpose appliances are in development. Combination washer/dryers which are rare in the United States are common in Europe.

The ENERGYSMART program is a government program that requires appliance manufacturers to label the energy use of new appliances so the consumer will know how much energy the appliance uses in a typical year. A growing number of appliances and systems in the home are said to be getting smarter by communicating with each other, ascertaining workloads and so on. Microprocessors and computer networking have made these connections possible. New washing machines can measure how heavy a wash load is and how soiled clothing is and react accordingly. Over the next ten years, the majority of new appliances will have some type of electronics that make them smarter. For example, appliances can be put on timers that will have them run during off-peak energy times as an energy savings and potential money savings. As another way to reduce utility bills, most utility companies or government energy offices have inspectors or auditors who will provide free home energy audits so that the homeowner can learn how to save energy costs in their specific house.

In the long run, though, "There isn't a silver bullet," says David Garman, the U.S. Energy Department's assistant secretary for energy-efficiency programs. "There isn't a single 'gee whiz' technology that changes every thing. You usually have to try to do a lot of little things to achieve energy savings" (Moore, 2001). That said, builders and architects are working on this concept to the point that energy savings with fluorescent lighting and tankless water heaters can be as much as 75 percent compared with conventional homes. *Saving on utilities while saving on the environment is a good example of the crossover between consumerism and environmentalism* discussed in the second chapter. Environmentally friendly building practices have become increasingly popular in the custom building industry spurred by homebuyers' values, the cost savings derived from greater energy efficiency, and pressure from environmentalists.

## LEASING VEHICLES: PROS AND CONS

**Leasing** is a contractual arrangement outlining the terms of the lease, including monthly payments, security deposit, and condition of the vehicle on return. *It is estimated that about 30 percent of new cars are leased,* and some consumers lease a new car every three years. The *advantages* to leasing are

- Less money is needed upfront. Rather than a down payment, the car can be leased with a security deposit similar to renting an apartment. During promotions and in competitive markets, the security deposit may be waived.
- Monthly payments may be less than if the car was being bought.
- The lease may be paid by an employer or may be a tax deduction if the owner owns a business that uses the car.
- No trade-in worries or having to sell the car on one's own.
- People in businesses such as real estate where having a fairly new and presentable car is an asset may find that leasing is a good option.

The *disadvantages* of leasing are:

- You don't own the vehicle, hence it is not an investment with a return.
- Extra costs may be added when the vehicle is turned in, for example, if more than the recommended mileage has accrued or repairs are needed beyond average wear.

Before leasing read the contract thoroughly and focus on the number of miles recommended and determine if that meets your needs. *Contracts are usually written for 15,000 miles per year* which was figured as reasonable given that the average car is driven 15,100 miles. However, with commutes getting longer, it is expected that the average will increase. To figure total cost a leaser should find out what the additional per mile charge is for over the minimum—typically these run 20 to 25 cents a mile.

When reading the contract, be alert to other charges such as conveyance, disposition, and preparation fees. If there was a trade-in allowance, make sure the contract includes it.

## Types of Leases

Not all leases are created equal. The three main types are:

1. Closed-end or "walk-away" in which the leaser returns the vehicle at the end of the lease period (usually three years) and pays only for additional miles or repairs.

---

**Consumer Alert**

A lease covering 15,000 miles is typical, but big names in the luxury-car business are pushing low-payment leases to spur consumer traffic. Many of these deals allow motorists just 10,000 miles of driving a year before severe penalties occur. Here were two options for a BMW 325i three-year lease:

| Lease Miles | Monthly Payment |
|-------------|-----------------|
| 10,000      | $299            |
| 15,000      | $321            |

If mileage was exceeded by 5,000 miles/year the charge was $3,000. If the cost was added at the time of the lease (upfront), the 5,000 extra miles/year would be $792 (White, 2003). To win at this game the driver should be realistic about average number of miles that will be driven and pick the best option.

---

**Consumer Alert**

When leases first became available, some consumers did not understand that they were renting a vehicle versus owning it out right. When it came time to get a new model, they did not understand they could not sell it nor would they get any money back, in fact, they would most likely owe money. Others have been less than happy at the extra add-on charges when they brought the vehicles in to change for a new one. Still other consumers felt pressured to buy from the same dealership and found there were financial penalties involved in switching manufacturers so that they felt locked in to the same make for years—the only difference being a new color and updated features. On the other hand, some consumers have found a type of car that they want and get it over and over again and the leasing process makes this process easy.

2. Open-end or finance leases requiring the leaser to pay the difference between the expected value of the leased vehicle and the amount for which the leasing company sells it. There may be an end-of-lease payment.
3. Single-payment lease that allow the consumer to obtain a discount on the vehicle rental agreement if certain standards are met.

Consumer rights and responsibilities regarding leasing vehicles are given in Box 11.3.

## PRELEASING AND PREBUYING: INFORMATION SEARCH

Before buying or leasing a car, many consumers take a spin around the Internet. A search reveals makes, models, features such as color choices, upgrade packages, and dealer locations. Some individual dealers have put their whole inventory online so besides information from the manufacturer you can get direct information

---

**BOX 11.3   Know Your Right and Responsibilities When Leasing Vehicles**

The federal Consumer Leasing Act gives you the right to information that helps you understand and negotiate your lease.

When you lease a vehicle, you have the right to:

1. Use it for an agreed-upon number of months and miles.
2. Turn it in at lease end, pay any end-of-lease fees and charges, and "walk away."
3. Buy the vehicle if you have a purchase option.
4. Take advantage of any warranties, recalls, or other services that apply to the vehicle.

Responsibilities include

1. Excess mileage charges when you return the vehicle.
2. Excess wear charges when you return the vehicle.
3. Substantial payments if you end the lease early.

*Source:* Adapted from *Keys to Vehicle Leasing: A Consumer Guide* from the Board of Governors of the Federal Reserve System, Washington, DC 20551.

from the lot down the street. Before leasing or purchasing, most consumers are going to want to test drive a few cars to get a sense of how it feels and fits, but as a first step it is hard to beat an online search. Of course, Web sites vary: Some provide much needed information and others are more heavily into marketing and sales without the necessary concrete information. The best give energy-use figures and 360-degree photo tours of the interiors, including zoom-in features so that the dashboard and engine can be examined (see E-Resources section for a list of sites).

## BUYING VEHICLES: PROS AND CONS

*The main advantage of buying is that you own the vehicle. It is an asset.* Up-front costs include the cash price or a down payment, taxes, registration and other fees, and other charges. A drawback is that the monthly loan payments are usually higher than monthly lease payments because the total cost includes interest and other charges. If ending the loan early, there may be fees. Future value will be determined by the condition of the vehicle and the vehicle's market value at time of sell or trade. Another drawback is that a lot of money can be tied up in car payments that could be spent or invested otherwise. Another advantage to owning versus leasing is that there are no limits to how many miles that are driven or charges for excessive wear. Once the car is paid for in full or at the end of the loan term (typically 4–6 years), there are no further loan payments. Being debt free is a positive feeling, a goal many people hope to attain.

### Buying New Cars

Besides researching cars online, another option is to read *Consumer Reports, Popular Mechanics,* and *Motor Trend* for ratings, service, and safety. Information gathering of this sort can be pleasurable and useful since a new car is a major purchase, second only to a house in terms of expense. Once the make and model have been selected, suggestions include

- Comparison shopping at area dealerships or though online services or buying services such as AAA. Examples of sources of online price quotes are autoweb.com, autovantage.com, carpoint.com, or autobytel.com. Buy only from reputable dealers or services. Complaint records are available from state and local consumer protection agencies and Better Business Bureaus.
- Shop in advance for the best financing option. Local or online credit unions and banks often offer better interest rates than dealerships.
- Test drive cars to get a sense of how they handle and if they fit your size and shape and driving behavior. Get price quotes from several dealers. If buying from a dealer, test drive the specific car that you are going to buy. Do not allow a substitute or one that is coming in next week. If you order a car from a dealership, test drive it before buying it.
- Read the "Buyer's Guide" sticker required to be displayed in the window of the car.
- Don't buy on impulse or when being pressured by salespeople.
- Negotiate the price. Dealer profit margin is usually between 10 and 20 percent. The difference may be between the manufacturer's suggested retail

price and the invoice price. The **invoice price** is the manufacturer's initial charge to the dealer, in other words, what the car cost the dealer. The **sticker price or suggested retail price** is the price of the car, including options, transportation charges, and any "market adjustments." Look at the total price, not just the monthly payment.

- Find out if the manufacturer is offering rebates.
- Buying off the lot may bring the lowest price because that is in-stock inventory that has to move. On the other hand, ordering a car from a dealer or service will get the features that are desired and remove the ones not cared about. Volume tends to drive down prices, especially the cars sitting on the dealer's lots.

**Sales Techniques.**    A common sales technique is to polish up cars and put them under flattering lights in showrooms. Another technique is to encourage the buyer of a new car to become a loyal, repeat customer, and there are several ways of doing this, including offering good dealer repair services with free donuts in the waiting room. Another way is for the salesperson to build a relationship with the buyer. A usual first step is for the salesperson to call recent buyers and find out if they are satisfied with their car. But some salespeople go farther than that. Joe Girard, known as the "world's greatest car salesman" (how is that for puffery), says the secret of his success was getting customers to like him. He did this by sending every one of his more than 13,000 former customers holiday greeting cards every month (Happy New Year, Happy Thanksgiving, etc.) and each had the same printed message. "I like you." Joe explained, "There's nothing else on the card, nothin' but my name. I'm just telling 'em that I like 'em" (Cialdini, 2001, p. 152). Joe had learned that flattery worked. We tend to believe praise and like the people who give it (Cialdini, 2001).

A salesman shakes hands with a couple while handing them the keys to their new car at a car dealership. (Courtesy of Photo Edit, photo by Michael Newman.)

Another technique is pressure. This can work for selling cars (new and used) and houses. If the salesperson can convince the potential buyer that this is the one and only car or house for them that is a very hard pitch for buyers to resist. Making the buyer feel special (smart, unique, forward thinking) is a strong sales ploy.

## Buying Used Cars

As a potential buyer of a used car, the first step is to figure out how much you can afford. The next step is to narrow the choices by going online, researching the frequency of repair and maintenance costs on the models, knowing sellers, and checking the U.S. Department of Transportation's Auto Safety Hotline at 1 800 424 9393 to find out about recalls. Average prices can be located in *Edmund's Used Car Prices* and the *Kelley Blue Book* (see E-Resources section) as well as other guides and Web sites. For paying, there are two options: pay in full or finance over time. Financing will be more costly than paying cash because of the interest and other loan costs. Annual percentage rates (APRs) are usually higher and loan periods shorter on used cars than on new ones.

Where do you find used cars? Choices include dealers such as new car dealers selling trade-ins, used car dealers specializing locally in used cars, and dealers like Car Max with huge national inventories. There are also rental car companies, leasing companies, friends, relatives, coworkers, and strangers selling cars off the side of the road or out of driveways. The Federal Trade Commission's Used Car Rule requires dealers to post a Buyers' Guide in every used car that they sell. Note this rule applies only to dealers and specifically to dealers that sell six or more cars a year. There are fewer protections, if any, when buying from friends or off the side of the road. Box 11.4 shows the parts of the Buyers Guide. *Be especially careful of private sellers since generally they are not covered by the Used Car Rule. They will sell cars "as is."*

States vary on whether dealers can offer "as is—no warranty." State divisions of consumer services will know the laws in your state. They can also tell you about state requirements regarding implied warranties, warranty of merchantability, and warranty of fitness for a particular purpose (i.e., whether a dealer is liable if he or she says a car can haul a trailer and it turns out it can't). Basically what you want

---

**BOX 11.4    The Buyers Guide for Used Cars**

If a car is bought from a dealer, the Buyers' Guide must tell you:

- Whether the vehicle is being sold "as is" or with a warranty
- What percentage of the repair costs a dealer will pay under the warranty
- Spoken promises are difficult to enforce
- Get all promises in writing
- Keep the Buyers' Guide for reference after the sale
- The major mechanical and electrical systems on the car, including some of the major problems you should look out for
- Ask to have the car inspected by an independent mechanic before you buy.

*Source:* Adapted from *Buying a Used Car: A Consumer Guide from the Federal Trade Commission.* Bureau of Consumer Protection, March 2002, p. 3.

to find out is whether the used car has a full or limited warranty and what the warranty covers. Before buying the purchaser has the right to see a copy of the dealer's warranty. According to the FTC, warranties are included in the price of a product. Service contracts cost extra and are sold separately. As discussed in a previous chapter, service contracts provide extra protection at a price, and it is questionable whether a service contract is needed. Many used car service contracts only last 90 days, so the time limit should be noted as well as what it covers.

What is truly necessary is *to have a used car inspected by an independent mechanic, particularly if the used car is being purchased from a private seller.* The main concern is safety. Inspections may run $100 or less and are worth the expense. The inspection will indicate the mechanical condition of the vehicle and needed repairs. The mechanic should provide a written report. Mechanics can be found under "Automotive Diagnostic Service" in the Yellow Pages or by asking friends or relatives for referrals. The ASE seal, which stands for Automotive Service Excellence, is a certification to look for when choosing mechanics. Auto repair or diagnostic centers should be licensed or registered with the state.

To summarize, before buying a used car:

1. Examine the car yourself in daylight. Research the make and model, know prices and the seller.
2. Test drive over varied road conditions.
3. Inspect the car's maintenance record. Check with the dealership or the previous owner if the current owner's record is incomplete.
4. Hire a mechanic to inspect the car. Safety is the main concern.

*After the purchase, problems should be worked out first with the dealer.* The next step would be if the warranty is backed by a car manufacturer to contact the manufacturer. Then a consumer would go up to the next levels of dispute resolution as suggested in chapter 4, eventually going to small claims court if the amount falls within the dollar limit in a particular state. Suspected fraud should be reported to the state or the FTC. To file a complaint or to get information on consumer issues go to *www.ftc.gov*.

## Vehicle Laws Including Lemon Laws

Some states have **lemon laws** that allow owners of new vehicles that repeatedly break down to get their money back or get the car replaced. Rules vary by state regarding how many miles the car was driven, how long the person has had the car,

---

**Consumer Alert**

A common fraud is moving water damaged cars (from floods) to another state, drying them out, and selling the cars to unsuspecting consumers. A mechanic inspecting the engine will find this out. Stolen cars are another potential problem when purchasing from private sellers. Also there is the problem of dealers posing as private individuals. To avoid this problem look at the title and the registration to determine that the seller is the registered owner of the vehicle. Remember that private sellers have less responsibility than dealers to disclose defects.

---

**Consumer Alert**

When it comes to cars, all sorts of financial frauds can occur. In a real case in a state to be unnamed, the attorney general sued a dealership for damages and penalties under the state's Deceptive and Unfair Trade Practices Act according to courthouse records. The lawsuit alleges that a car dealership sent promotional mailings to residents promising, among other things, it would pay off their trade-ins. Instead, customers were obliged to pay off their former vehicles themselves, were enticed into unfavorable financing agreements, and denied the promised discounts. Customers filed complaints with the attorney general's office. This is an example of a classic bait-and-switch scheme in which the customer is lured in (the bait being the pay off of the trade-in) and once there the switch takes place.

and the amount of repair problems. A common rule of thumb is that the car has been out of service for 30 days within the first 12,000 miles/12 months. Another rule of thumb is that a car has been in the repair shop four or more times during the first year of ownership. The procedure to get the money back or replace the car is called **revocation of acceptance**. It takes place in writing and is usually handled between the buyer and the seller. Customers suspecting they have a lemon should follow a number of steps, including contacting their state or local consumer protection office, giving the dealer a list of symptoms, keeping repair order copies, and contacting the manufacturer as well as the dealer. Most states require dealers of used cars to label cars that have been returned as lemons so that future buyers know the car has had problems.

## Unfair Vehicle Pricing

When buying a car, the following unfair price setting practices may happen:

1. **High-balling** means a high amount is offered for a trade-in, but the extra amount is made up in an increased new car price. It is possible that car owners would be better off selling their old car themselves rather than going through the dealer.
2. **Low-balling** refers to a very low price that is quoted, but there are add-on costs at the end that drive the final price up.

On a more minor level, some dealers add on extra frills at the end that buyers don't want such as vinyl racing stripes or floor mats. This may have nothing to do with whether there is a trade-in so this practice is not necessarily high-balling. Buyers should mention that they do not want these extras and upon their removal they can save hundreds of dollars or use them as part of the negotiation. The best advice is to know the fair market price for new vehicles and for trade-ins. A little knowledge goes a long way in the car business. Because many people dislike the haggling part of car buying, they use auto brokers or car buying services or go through dealers such as Saturn who offer a no-haggling car-selling method.

## SUMMARY

If a person is going to live in an area less than three years, he or she should probably rent. The reason is that the longer one stays in a house, the higher the average return. The main exception to this is if people are living in an area where housing prices are rising rapidly and they could reasonably expect to make a profit in less than three years. One of the downsides to renting are the landlord/tenant disputes which are common, another is the lack of being able to change interiors to one's liking. A benefit to buying is that homeowners receive tax deductions for interest on mortgage and property taxes. The American Dream is still to own a house; 67 percent of American households own their own house. Housing represents 32 percent, transportation 18 percent, and utilities 5 percent of a typical family's budget. Environmentally friendly building practices reduce the cost of utilities and are examples of the crossover between consumerism and environmentalism.

People's lives go through change points that accelerate consumption, including the desire to own a home and buy new furnishings and appliances. Buying a house is the single most expensive purchase most people make, and a house is the most visible asset. There are a number of ways to determine how much house a person can afford. Two of the most common are the 28/36 qualifying rule and the 2½ times rule.

To pay for improvements or to get cash, four financial instruments based on home ownership include the second mortgage, the home-equity line of credit, cash-out refinancing, and reversible mortgages. Fraud potential or other problems, such as losing one's house or paying too much in fees, are rampant. The Truth-in-Lending Act, a federal law enacted in 1968, provides some protection. The lender must disclose in a truth in lending statement the total cost of a consumer loan, including those for mortgages. Redlining is illegal.

The discussion of the pros and cons of leasing cars and buying new and used cars included a number of steps to follow to avoid being fleeced. The Federal Trade Commission works to prevent fraudulent, deceptive, and unfair business practices involved in leasing and buying vehicles. Some states have lemon laws to cover new cars with repeated repair problems in the first year of ownership or the first 12,000 miles. Vehicle sales techniques include the use of flattery and praise, because repeat business is sought.

## KEY POINTS

1. A lease is a legal document.
2. Appreciation means the increase in the home's value.
3. Mortgages are loans to purchase real estate. Rates can be compared online and mortgages can be attained online.
4. Net worth is calculated as assets minus liabilities. Lenders will look at net worth before loaning money for a house because they are trying to determine ability to pay the mortgage.
5. Car leases are typically for 15,000 miles per year, and if the driver goes over that amount, there are financial penalties. Some luxury car dealers are offering

teaser rates for 10,000 miles to attract customers, but the average car is driven 15,100 miles per year. A downpayment may be required.

6. Buyers of used cars should hire their own independent mechanic to inspect the car they are interested in buying.

7. Car buyers should be aware of unfair pricing practices such as high-balling and low-balling.

8. Dealer profit margins on new cars are usually between 10 and 20 percent.

## KEY TERMS

| | | |
|---|---|---|
| adjustable rate mortgages (ARMs) | home equity lines of credit | mortgage |
| appreciation | home inspections | net worth |
| assets | homeowner's fees | PITI |
| closing | home warranties | predatory lending |
| condominiums | illiquid | redlining |
| cooperative apartments | invoice price | rent |
| defect-disclosure forms | lease | reverse mortgages |
| discrimination | leasing | revocation of acceptance |
| fixed-rate conventional mortgage | lemon laws | security deposit |
| Freddie Mac | liabilities | sticker price or suggested retail price |
| high-balling | low-balling | subleasing |
| | manufactured housing | |

## DISCUSSION QUESTIONS

1. Why have corporate executives called newlyweds the ultimate consumer? And why are their names like gold? How do companies get lists of newlyweds' names?

2. What are the pros of renting versus owning? What are the reasons people give for buying a home?

3. What are the pros and cons of leasing vehicles? What is the typical financial arrangement for a lease?

4. Go to the E-Resources list and select one from the housing or vehicle sites and report on what it offers.

## E-RESOURCES

U.S. Government Sites

Department of Housing and
Urban Development
www.hud.gov/places.html
800-347-3735 (fraud hotline)

| | |
|---|---|
| Environmental Protection Agency's Safe Drinking Water www.epa.gov/safewater | |
| Federal Trade Commission www.ftc.gov or | Predatory lending settlements. publications about buying cars, leasing, and warranties |
| write FTC Consumer Response Center, Rm. 130, 600 Pennsylvania Ave., NW, Washington, DC 20580 | |
| www.pueblo.gsa.gov | Gateway to home buying publications |

**Housing Sites**

| | |
|---|---|
| Bankrate.com | Comparisons of mortgage and home equity loan rates |
| Freddie Mac Freddiemac.com | Statistics on housing, mortgages Online fact book updates |
| Home Advisor Homeadvisor.msn.com | |
| HomePath www.homepath.com | |
| Homes.com www.homes.com | |
| National Association of Realtors www.realtor.com | |
| www.consumerworld.org | Gateway to housing/money advice |
| National Consumer Law Center (NCLU) www.consumerlaw.org | Represents low-income consumers, research, advocacy |

**More Mortgage Rates Sites**

| | |
|---|---|
| Loan.yahoo.com/m/ finance.html | National rate averages and articles about how to finance |
| Ditech.com Quickenloans.quicken.com LendingTree.com GetSmart.com | Each of these four sites offer mortgage rates; there are dozens more sites |

**Vehicle Sites**

| | |
|---|---|
| Autobytel.com | Side-by-side comparison chart of several vehicles This business has relations with thousands of dealers |
| CarPoint Carpoint.msn.com | Model car data, tours, "surround video" |
| Consumerguide.com | Packed with specs, prices, shopping tips, best buys |

| Consumerreports.org | Tips on narrowing choices, negotiating prices, saving money on leases |
| Edmund's Automobile Buyer's Guide Edmunds.com | Includes vehicle information, consumer chat, new and used car prices |
| Auto.msn.com | Gives history of makes and models, comparisons |
| Autos.yahoo.com | 360-degree views, side-by-side comparisons |
| Kelley Blue Book www.kbb.com | Used car prices, trade-in values |

Check out motor vehicle magazine Web sites such as roadandtrack.com and motortrend.com

# REFERENCES

Cialdini, R. (2001). *Influence: Science and practice, 4th ed*. Boston: Allyn and Bacon.

Clements, J. (February 5, 2003). Bubble? What bubble? Housing isn't that pricey, so go ahead and buy. *Wall Street Journal,* p. D1.

Cross, G. (2000). An all consuming century. NY: Columbia University Press.

Ellison, S, and C. Tejada. (January 30, 2003). *Wall Street Journal,* pp. B1 and B3.

Fletcher, J. (January 31, 2003). How's your town doing? *Wall Street Journal,* p. W1.

Francese, P. (May 2002). Horticulture is hot. *American Demographics,* p. 51.

Making your house pay off. (November 2002). *Consumer Reports,* pp. 12–18.

Moore, B. (September 17, 2001). Inventive answers. *Wall Street Journal.*

New "Starter" home, the (October 2002). *American Demographics,* p. 53.

Simon, R. (January 29, 2003). Getting a two-fer on a home loan. *Wall Street Journal,* pp. D1–D2.

*The Freddie Mac Reporter Fact Book 2002-2003.* Freddie Mac Corporate Communications, McLean, VA 22102-3110.

White, J. (February 10, 2003). Low lease price on luxury cars may cost you. *Wall Street Journal,* p. B1.

# PART 4

# Consumers in the Financial Marketplace

# CHAPTER 12

# Saving, Banking, Debt, and Credit Issues

*If one wants to harvest quickly, one must plant carrots and salads; if one has the ambition to plant oaks, one must have the sense to tell oneself: my grandchildren will owe me this shade.*

Leon Walras

## Learning Objectives

1. Identify the three steps in the financial management process.
2. Explain budget and net worth statements.
3. Describe banking and savings strategies, scams, and advances.
4. Discuss financial planner credentials and fees.
5. Explain credit, common pitfalls, and consumer rights.
6. Explain bankruptcy and how to avoid it.

## INTRODUCTION

In capitalism, economic decisions are made by individuals, households, and families mainly in their roles as consumers and owners of privately held goods and services such as houses, cars, and retirement plans. It takes money to have these things, and this section of the book explores how consumers can make the most of the money they have through wise planning.

We'll also go over common pitfalls and frauds related to finances. Through the life cycle we spend, save, borrow, and lend. As one ages the goal is to become more of a saver and a lender in order to build financial wealth and maintain stability. This chapter introduces the topic of personal finance and shows how it fits into life plans. **Personal finance** is an umbrella term that covers the spending, saving, investing, and protecting of financial resources. *Financial planning is a lifelong process.* No matter how much or how little money a person has, the principles of financial planning are useful.

According to Federal Reserve Chairman Alan Greenspan, "Making informed decisions about what to do with your money will help build a more stable financial future for you and your family" (1p, 2003, p. D3). Consumers are besieged by investment schemes on television and quasi-legitimate financial schemes over the Internet. To counteract these negative information sources, the Federal Reserve has stepped in with public service announcements (PSAs) with Chairman Greenspan and a Web site *(www.federalreserveeducation.org)* with links to dependable financial information sources.

The goal of this chapter is to make readers more aware of how money can be more successfully managed, including where to go for help and in so doing increase life satisfaction. Most consumption requires money—to get in the consumer game one needs money or something worth trading. An individual's or family's standard of living and future financial stability hinge on the ability to accumulate, save, invest, protect, and spend money wisely. Personal finance also takes place within the ups and downs of the general economy, and as covered earlier in the book, the way consumers spend, save, and invest affect the way the economy cycles so there is both cause and effect when talking about consumers and their behavior.

# THE FINANCIAL MANAGEMENT PROCESS

## Three Steps Described

Money management should be a no-brainer—you work, you earn money, you save, and you build an independent financial life. The 1.4 million personal bankruptcies filed each year indicate that this set of tasks is not so easy to accomplish. As further evidence, credit card debt is at an all-time high. In short, more and more people are having trouble making ends meet. As college students you are in a unique, positive position to begin a habit of good money management. The bottom line is being responsible, being a wise consumer, and handling income and expenditures in a prudent manner, avoiding debt, and putting your hard-earned money where you want it go, where it will do the most good. It is not simply about helping oneself, but helping others. Personal finance is a process involving three steps as shown in Table 12.1 and each of the steps is described next.

**Step 1:  Setting and Prioritizing Financial Goals and Creating Plans.**  The first question financial planners ask clients is, "What are your financial goals?" In other words, what are you saving for: a primary residence, a comfortable life, a vacation home, a secure retirement, or the college education of children? What are you striving for? Your answers may involve short-range goals such as paying bills each month. As mentioned in the first chapter, goals are end results, things worth striving for, things to be achieved. Goals are based on **values** (principles that guide behavior), **attitudes** (likes and dislikes), **resources** (what you have), and are affected by **decision making** (choice making between two or more alternatives). Table 12.2 provides a space for you to fill in your own financial goals based on time: short-term, intermediate, and long-range goals along with estimated prices and a place to rank their priority. A person in their forties may have the following long range goals (1) to college

**Table 12.1**    Three Steps in the Personal Finance Process

1. Setting Financial Goals and Creating Plans
2. Activating Plans
3. Evaluating and Revising Plans: Going Forward

**Table 12.2**   Setting Financial Goals

| Time | Example of a Goal | | Estimated Cost | Priority* |
|---|---|---|---|---|
| Short-Term (less than two months) | 1 | | $ | |
| | 2 | | $ | |
| Intermediate (2 months to 1 year) | 1 | | $ | |
| | 2 | | $ | |
| Long-Range (1 year or more) | 1 | | $ | |
| | 2 | | $ | |

*In each category select a or b, a = 1st priority. b = 2nd priority.

educate two children, (2) to move to a more expensive house, (3) to buy a vacation home, and (4) to retire at age 62. Not all of these goals will be held as equally important which is where prioritizing comes in. Financial planners (to be discussed later in this chapter) help people make informed decisions about their financial future.

*So, the first step in the financial process is setting and prioritizing goals and on the basis of goals, creating plans.* To be successful, goals should be flexible, action oriented, specific, and realistic. Financial goals are affected by risk. Risk is the possibility of experiencing loss or harm. Examples of risk are income risk (loss of income), investment risk, personal risk (health and safety), status risk, time risk, liquidity risk, interest rate risk, and inflation risk. Several of these were discussed in previous chapters, but as a recap inflation is a rise in prices and liquidity refers to how readily something can be turned into cash. Everyone varies in the amount of risk they can handle. This is referred to as risk tolerance. In regard to time, the longer one has until money is needed (the time horizon) the more chances or risks can be taken. Plans involve setting a course of action, making decisions about what to do such as continuing at the same pace, expanding (earning more, spending more, investing more), cutting back (saving more), or choosing an entirely new course of action.

**Step 2: Activating Plans.**   In this step, plans are actually carried out. Individuals make calls, go on appointments, open up a savings or brokerage account, or put a down payment on a house. Flexibility at this stage is important. Plans may need to change due to circumstances. For example, 20 houses may need to be looked at before the right one is found. And then the desired one may be more expensive, requiring a reworking of the budget. At this step there will be gains and losses, and learning takes place that will affect future decisions.

**Step 3: Evaluating.**   This step involves a looking back at how the plans went. Did they succeed or fail? Was the success total or partial? Evaluation is probably the least attractive of the steps, but in many ways the most important so one can learn what works and what doesn't. One's comfort level with risk is reassessed. Every day some level of assessment takes place, but a more formal once-a-year evaluation of financial plans is recommended. This usually takes place when one is filing taxes and has W-2 forms in hand and other records of earnings and expenditures. At the end of the evaluation, the person resets their course going back to step one and asking, For next year, what do I want to accomplish, what goals do I want to achieve, what plans do I need to make?

A deeper life evaluation may take place at the change points discussed in the last chapter such as graduations, weddings, births of children, and so forth. Another evaluation point may occur around a significant number birthday such as 30, 40, 50, or 60. The evaluation may not fall right on the birthday but in surrounding years. For example the 30th birthday can involve an evaluation anywhere from ages 29–32. Basically what happens is that people look back on the last decade of their lives and evaluate how it went. Career exploration is common in the twenties, and it is not until the ages of 45–54 that median income peaks. Self-evaluation involves an assessment of career, education, and personal and family progress. See the appendices for an example of a resume and a cover letter that may be of assistance in the beginning of a career or when redirecting career goals.

## DEVELOPING BUDGETS AND NET WORTH STATEMENTS

*If you don't know your net worth or where your money is going, you need to find out.*

A budget is a financial plan based on income and expenditures in a month. To develop a budget, one needs financial records that show consumption (i.e., bank and credit card statements) and organized paperwork. Budgets show how much money is flowing in (earnings, dividends, gifts) and how much is flowing out (rent, expenses). Budgets have **fixed expenses** such as rent and **variable expenses** such as food and entertainment. In the last chapter, net worth was defined as assets minus liabilities. Net worth statements are useful because they give an overall picture of financial worth. Lenders and creditors use them to determine whether to extend credit. Box 12.1 gives a budget, and Box 12.2 gives an example of a net worth statement. You can do budgets and net worth statements yourself or with the help of a financial advisor. A negative net worth is not unusual for college students. Your goal is to get going on the plus side (having more assets than debts).

## BUILDING SAVINGS

We all need cash for small immediate needs and savings for longer range needs. Savings provide a safety net and are also helpful for putting together money for future needs such as a down payment on a house. Savings provide a sense of comfort and security so they are useful from an emotional as well as from a fiscal point of view. Traditionally, an **emergency fund** of three to six months of salary set aside as savings is recommended as a financial goal. Emergency funds should be kept in a liquid interest-bearing account such as a money market fund or short-term certificates of deposit (CDs) or a savings account. During recessionary times

---

### BOX 12.1    Budget: Tracing the Flow of Income and Expenses

A budget is made up of cash inflows and cash outflows usually figured on a monthly basis.

Cash Inflows
| | |
|---|---|
| Net Salary | $ |
| Interest or dividends from savings accounts or investments | $ |
| Financial aid checks, scholarships | $ |
| Gifts | $ |
| Other sources of income* | $ |
| Total of cash inflows | $ |

Cash Outflows
| | |
|---|---|
| Housing (rent or mortgage payment) | $ |
| Utilities (electric, water, cable TV) | $ |
| Educational expenses, tuition and books | $ |
| Telephone | $ |
| Auto payments | $ |
| Gasoline, auto repairs | $ |
| Gifts | $ |
| Food including eating out | $ |
| Clothing | $ |
| Credit card payments | $ |
| Entertainment | $ |
| Medical/Dental/Prescriptions | $ |
| Personal Care | $ |
| Pet Care | $ |
| Savings | $ |
| Other expenses | $ |
| Total of cash outflows | $ |

Subtract outflow total from inflow total to determine what is
left over at the end of a typical month                    $

*Example: Josh, a college junior, gets $1,000 a month to live on from his mom while he is in college. His biggest expense is a combination of rent and utilities (he shares an apartment with a friend), followed by food. She pays for his tuition and books, and he drives an old, used car that is paid for. He noticed friends coming over and eating up all the food so he put an end to that. When he eats out he goes for the cheap, all-you-can-eat places. Josh eats over at his mom's house when he can. In exchange, he mows the yard and takes care of the pets when his mom travels. He had jobs in high school but is currently not working.

---

with higher than usual unemployment, six or more months is recommended for extra cushioning in case of job loss or other major setbacks or expenses such as unexpected auto or home repairs or medical bills. *Americans save less than 3 percent on average of disposable income per year,* and this rate is much lower than in most other industrialized countries. Savings accounts in banks and credit unions earn interest that is compounded continuously. The **Truth in Savings Act** requires financial institutions to reveal the annual percentage yield (the amount of interest earned on a yearly basis expressed as a percentage), fees charged, and information about rules regarding maintaining a minimum balance.

BOX 12.2    Net Worth Statement

Net Worth: Assets − Liabilities = Net Worth

Assets are what a person owns and liabilities are debts (what is owed).

Step 1: Figure out Total Assets

Current Assets
  Checking accounts        $
  Money market, savings accounts        $
  Cash value of life insurance        $

Investments
  Stocks, bonds, mutual funds (estimated worth)        $
  Individual retirement accounts        $
  Employer retirement accounts        $

Other Assets
  Worth of house, other real estate        $
  Value of car, appliances, computers        $
  Jewelry        $
  Other belongings such as furniture        $

Add together each category to get **Total Assets**        $

Step 2: Figure out Total Liabilities

Current liabilities
  Credit card bills        $
  Medical/dental bills        $
  Car payments        $
  Other        $

Total current liabilities        $

Long-term Liabilities
  Mortgage        $
  Student loans        $
  Other        $

Total long-term liabilities        $

Add together each category to get **Total Liabilities**        $

Step 3: Subtract total liabilities from total assets to determine net worth    $

*One of the best ways to build savings is to automate savings through payroll deduction* or transfers from a checking account to savings account. Young adults in their twenties and thirties should be developing an overall savings and investment plan and putting together an emergency fund. By the ages of 40 to 50, a goal should be to increase savings by holding on to money and making it grow. Middle-aged adults should be saving toward retirement based on estimates of how much they will need per year. Older adults are interested in trying to make savings last and in some cases, leaving a legacy.

# BANKS AND FINANCIAL PRODUCTS

The new financial marketplace has several features, including electronic banking, 24–7 access to accounts, ATMs, the electronic transfer of funds, stockbrokerages offering checking and savings accounts including money market funds, banks offering investment services, and deregulation. Overall, *in recent years there has been a crossover of services that has benefited consumers.* One of the few exceptions to this is that the wide variety of services has created some confusion as to safety and security. For example, today neighborhood banks offer mutual funds and other types of investments that are not protected by the FDIC (Federal Deposit Insurance Corporation) and so these offerings are subject to risk. This confused elderly consumers who assumed that everything offered by a bank was insured. The **Federal Deposit Insurance Corporation** *is government insurance of bank and savings and loan accounts up to $100,000 per account.* Credit unions are insured by the National Credit Union Administration.

Since there are so many kinds of financial professionals, Table 12.3 gives a list of providers and products and services. Box 12.3 gives a list of nonprofit organizations that can help with money management, including how to manage debt.

Banks and brokerage firms offer CDs with a maturity of at least seven days with penalties on early withdrawals. CDs, a type of **time deposit**, are usually safe ways to store money from seven days to several years. The longer the money is deposited and the larger the amount, the higher the interest rate offered. After the CD reaches maturity (the designated period of time has passed), the CD can be cashed

**Table 12.3**

| Financial Service Providers | Typical Products and Services |
| --- | --- |
| Accountants | Budgets, advice, prepare tax returns, perform audits, financial planning |
| Attorneys | Lawsuits, estate plans, trusts, legal matters regarding adoption or divorce, bankruptcy, wills, mediation, settle disputes |
| Banks, Credit Unions, S&Ls | Checking, share and savings accounts, money market accounts, CDs, loans, safe-deposit boxes, ATMs, debit and credit cards, trusts |
| Brokerage Firms (Financial Counselors) | Online or in-person stock purchases or sells, bonds, mutual funds, money market and asset management accounts including checking accounts, mortgages, individual retirement accounts, financial planning |
| Credit Counselors | Help clients manage debt, credit consolidation, set up budgets, 24-hour hotlines, sometimes free, sometimes sliding scale fees, bankruptcy |
| Financial Planners | Charge fees or commissions for financial planning services, such as setting up budgets, investing, life insurance, mutual funds |
| Insurance Companies | Annuities, retirement plans, sales of insurance |
| Real Estate Companies | Housing and land sales, investments, rentals |
| Tax Preparation Services | Help with income tax returns, advice |

---

**BOX 12.3    Nonprofit Organizations That Offer Information on How to Manage Money Wisely Including How to Manage Debt**

Consumer Action: A national consumer advocacy organization that directs consumers to complaint handling agencies and offers educational materials. *www.consumer-action.org*

Consumer Counseling Centers of America, Inc. offers free and low-fee counseling and services to help people manage their debts. *www.consumercounseling.org*

Consumer Federation of America is a proconsumer advocacy and educational organization. *www.consumerfed.org*

Debtors Anonymous is a national 12-step organization dedicated to helping people overcome debt problems. *www.debtorsanonymous.org*

National Foundation for Credit Counseling is a network of 150 member agencies at 1,300 locations that offer educational programs on money management, budgeting, credit, and debt counseling, including help arranging debt-repayment plans. *www.nfcc.org*

National Institute for Consumer Education is a professional development, training, and research institute that promotes personal finance education in workplaces, communities, and schools. *www.nice.emich.edu*

---

**Consumer Alert**

Although banks usually exercise good judgment, there are exceptions. Is your bank selling your secrets? In 1999 the U.S. Bancorp allegedly sold information on 930,000 account holders to a telemarketing firm called MemberWorks, who then pitched these customers "trial memberships" for a variety of services such as phones and discount travel. Even though some people said "no thanks" to these offers, their accounts were charged anyway (the bank received a commission). Allowing these kinds of withdrawals without the customers' permission is illegal and resulted in lawsuits totaling $6.5 million. Selling information is legal, so to stop it customers must tell banks to keep dealings confidential. Consumer groups are lobbying for tougher laws; for more information, go to *www.privacyrightsnow.com* (Stirland, 2001).

---

in or rolled over to a new CD, hopefully at a higher rate. Banks compete for CD business, and rates are compared in the newspaper or can be found by going online or making phone calls.

Money market deposit accounts are types of accounts that offer a higher rate of interest than most checking or savings accounts. Many require a minimum balance to be maintained.

Checking accounts are offered by banks and share accounts by credit unions. "Americans write about *42 billion checks each year,* and each one must be shipped from a bank to a central operations center to an intermediary (such as the Federal Reserve, a correspondent bank or a clearinghouse) before finally reaching the bank on which it's drawn. By the time a typical check lands back in your mailbox, it's been handled more than 15 times" (The Check is in the Air, 2003, p. 46). Since processing costs $1.25 to $5 a check, legislation is underway to streamline this process which typically takes five days per check. Fraud runs rampant. The current cost to banks/credit unions is about $700 million a year in processing and fraud investigations. When this book went to press, Congress was considering legislation that would involve banks sending images of each check electronically rather than by couriers coming to bank branches every afternoon. The savings in transportation alone would be $250 million and would slash fraud by 80 percent. The reason this is true is that the more float time involved and the more people who handle a check the greater the chance for fraud. Once the legislation passes, banks will need check-imaging technology, and while big banks have already done this, smaller community banks will have to come up to speed.

Banks or credit card companies offer **debit cards** issued to allow customers access to their funds electronically in places like grocery stores and **smart cards also called chip cards or stored value cards** that may be worth $20 or $50 to use in placing phone calls or buying sodas or snacks out of vending machines. Most retailers sell stored value cards in place of paper gift certificates. Some cards can be "reloaded" with additional value at a cash machine; other cards are disposable—when their value is gone you throw them away. Debit cards can be used to withdraw money from ATMs. Debit cards have no float like credit cards because debit card funds are withdrawn immediately. Cards may have combinations of these so the owner does not have to carry three separate cards.

---

**Consumer Alert**

Under the Electronic Fund Transfer Act (EFTA), if there is a mistake or unauthorized withdrawal from a bank account through the use of a debit card or other electronic fund transfers, the person must notify the financial institution of the problem or error not later than 60 days after the statement containing the problem or error was sent. If someone uses your debit card without your permission, you can lose from $50 to $500 or more, depending on when you report the loss or theft. If you report the loss within two business days after the discovery of the problem, you will not be responsible for more than $50 of unauthorized use. The longer you wait to report the loss the higher amount you could lose. If you do not report an unauthorized transfer or withdrawal within 60 days after your statement is mailed to you, you risk unlimited loss.

---

**Consumer Alert**

Be careful in selecting a **personalized identification number (PIN)** for use in ATMs and other forms of cash management. Usually you are better off using the one assigned to you by the bank. If you select one yourself, don't make it too easy. A number like 1111 or one that is too easily traced to you like your street address number, telephone number, or birthdate would be examples. Never keep the PIN number with your card: memorize it. When using an ATM, be careful of your surroundings and take your receipt. If the ATM card is lost or stolen, report it immediately to the financial institution. Watch out for ATM charges, especially if you use your bank card in another bank's machine. On the plus side, ATMs have made it possible to get cash anytime and nearly anywhere including abroad, reducing the need to carry traveler's checks and large sums of cash.

**Consumer Alert**

ATM thieves target customers in a variety of ways according to the Florida Division of Consumer Services Web site. A new scheme works like this: the ATM customer attempts to make an ATM withdrawal, and there is a malfunction resulting in their card being held by the machine. An official looking sign posted on the machine reads, "If for any reason your card gets stuck, punch in your PIN." The customer does as instructed, but the card is not returned. Later the customer learns money has been withdrawn from his or her account. Police investigators believe that the suspect inserts some type of plastic sleeve into the card slot and then waits for a customer to use the machine. When a customer arrives, they insert their ATM card and key in their PIN code. Investigators believe the suspect may be using binoculars to watch the victim enter their PIN. Then after the customer leaves, the suspect retrieves the card and starts making withdrawals. The advice to consumers is that if a ATM malfunctions, report it immediately to bank officials. In addition ignore all signs no matter how official looking, and report all suspicious looking persons or vehicles in the ATM vicinity to the bank and local police department immediately.

## Deregulation of Banking

With *deregulation,* there are different rules and more players in the financial market. For consumers, the good news is that the Depository Institutions Deregulation and Monetary Control Act of 1980 *opened up competition.* New forms of banking emerged, including banks without main offices or branches, which became even more popular with the advent of the Internet in the 1990s. Services opened up as well. Mergers took place more readily. So to recap regarding money and savings, with deregulation consumers have benefited by having more choices of financial institutions, including commercial banks, savings and loans associations (S&Ls), credit unions, and brokerage firms. Consumers should take advantage of this by comparing interest rates, features, risk, and convenience.

## Online Banking and E-Payments

*Online banking outpaces online auctions and stock trading.*

The Pew Internet and American Life Project survey revealed that online banking is the fastest growing Internet application, outpacing online auctions and stock trading. In 2003 there were more than 37 million online bank users in the United States versus 14 million in 2000. The best way to start banking online is with your current bank. Check its Web site to see what online banking services it offers and what the costs and fees are. These could be free or up to $10 a month. Also, investigate what your bank offers in terms of automatic bill paying. If you don't like what they offer, check out other local banks or consider using services like Yahoo! (Finance (*finance.yahoo.com*) and MSN Money (*billpay.msn.com*) which allow you to have all your online activities from banking, email, and stocks in one place.

The goal is to make handling finances, shopping, and bill paying simpler. Cards of any kind or the use of the Internet stimulates consumption. So financial institutions and retailers are motivated to provide cards for consumers in as many shapes and forms as they can. Most consumers use credit or debit cards to pay for online purchases, but other payment methods, such as "e-wallets" and automatic bill paying systems, are coming into vogue. The Federal Trade Commission wants these

---

**Consumer Alert**

The safety factors involved in online banking include:

- Making sure that your bank uses Secure Socket Layer (SSL) encryption technology or another such system.
- Looking for a liability guarantee against late payments and fraudulent activity.
- The ability to regularly log into your account and see what is happening.
- Securing your system with antivirus software and a firewall program.
- As stated earlier, picking a hard to trace PIN code.

---

payments and transactions to be as safe as possible by encouraging the use of secure browsers and care in using PINs. "**E-wallets**" are Internet-based payment systems that allow value to be transmitted through computers. You can use e-wallets to make "micropayments"—very small online or offline payments for things like books or fast food. The way it works is that when you buy something using your e-wallet, the balance on your online account decreases by that amount. E-wallets may be connected to your credit or debit card account. E-payments include authorizing your financial institution to pay recurring bills in regular amounts such as mortgages or rent and irregular amounts such as utility bills or credit cards. This is an especially useful service if a person is traveling or moving. If a biller does not accept e-payments, your bank can send a check instead. As explained earlier, check first with your bank to see what their policies are. New services are springing up daily. A company called Paytrust (**www.paytrust.com**) will process any bill you instruct to have sent there for a monthly fee.

## FINANCIAL PLANNER CREDENTIALS AND SCAMS

**Financial planners** look at a person's or a family's total financial picture, help that person or family define and prioritize goals, and then work out a plan to achieve those goals. Once the plan is in place, the financial planner may help implement or manage the plan, prepare tax returns, and obtain insurance coverage. A financial planner is really an asset manager which is different from a financial counselor who tries to reduce a client's debts.

Financial planning requires involvement and commitment from everyone in the family or household in order to succeed. Individuals availing themselves of financial planning help are trying to gain control over their money and move it in a better direction. *Over 500,000 people in the United States call themselves financial planners. This is an industry that is largely unregulated,* and hence the phrase "may the buyer beware" applies. The amount of regulation varies by state, by credentialing association, and by the Securities and Exchange Commission (SEC). It is not possible for the SEC to send investigators and auditors to visit every person claiming to be a financial planner. Better ways to regulate the industry are under discussion. That said, there are many financial planners who are legitimate and well trained. The most recognized credential is **Certified Financial Planner (CFP)** because of the rigorous examinations, three years of practical experience, and adhering to a code of ethics. New planners receive experience from established planners. Nationally, *there are more than 40,000 CFPs* (Hoffman, 2003). Other credentials are Chartered Financial Consultant (ChFC) and the Personal Financial Specialist (PFS). To search for a planner where you live, see the E-Resource section.

Often certified public accountants (CPAs) have taken the exams and are also CFPs—this is a strong set of credentials. After individuals check for these types of credentials, then they would interview two or three potential financial planners before final selection. Ten questions to ask a financial planner are given in E-Resources. The more that is known about the planner the better. Recommendations from several people whom you trust and a careful questioning of the financial planner's way of working should help screen out the fraudulent ones. The Consumer Alert gives other clues.

How much do they charge? *Most planners charge an hourly fee;* an initial consultation may be free. For example, Andy Claybrook, a CFP in Franklin, TN, a fee-only planner, charges $135 an hour (Hoffman, 2003). Others charge a flat fee such as $250 to do a net worth statement and write an initial plan. Still others charge commissions on products they sell such as mutual funds and life insurance. Others charge a combination fee and commission. Charles Schwab and other brokerage houses online or in-person may offer financial planning for free or at a reduced cost such as $99 if a person has an account with them—especially a sizable account.

If going with a CFP, generally it is accepted that the fee-only advisor brings the least biased advice (Clements, 2003). They may charge a yearly fee of 1 percent to maintain your records and update your investments once set up. With this set up the advisor has an incentive to manage money wisely because as the portfolio grows, the advisor will make more money. As might be expected, the more work that they do the more they will charge. Through commissions, the advisors make their money by selling life insurance or mutual funds or other investments that will pay them a commission. A lot of planners like the flexibility and the income derived from the combination fee and commission method. What it boils down to is matching the client's needs with what is being offered whether it be help with a particular problem that needs immediate attention (such as an impending divorce or sudden job loss) or more long-term planning. Some planners specialize in a certain type of client (widow, doctor, entertainer, executive, small business owner) and may not want to work with other types of clients.

See E-Resources for a list of financial planning services over the Internet that are free and also ways to find advisors who will help manage modest sums. Other sources of free financial advice include from bankers and credit union managers where one has accounts and human resource departments where one works.

## Divorce Planners: A New Breed of Financial Planner

A **certified divorce planner** is a specialist trained to focus on who gets the assets in divorces. They work alongside attorneys who handle legal documents and child-custody issues. Divorce planners help couples divvy up retirement accounts and stock options, divide up businesses, calculate alimony payments, and decide who keeps the primary house and vacation homes. "Nearly 70% of them have a financial title such as CPA or certified financial planner. About 1,000 divorce planners have been certified since 1993, with about 500 more in training right now. They generally charge between $100 and $200 and client work usually lasts about 12

---

**Consumer Alert**

Rapport, setting, Web sites, and materials give an indication of how a financial planner operates. Do the materials look professional or amateurish? Is the office nice but not over the top? Are calls returned promptly? Does the financial planner really listen? Remember that the courts are filled with horror stories about judges, bankers, relatives, and personal friends who acted as financial advisors and robbed others of everything they have. Be wary, be cautious, start small, and keep your eyes open. No matter which financial planner is selected, make sure to obtain a written estimate of what services are to be expected and at what price, then check records of purchases.

---

hours" (Silverman, 2003, D1). Most of the clients have been married at least ten years and have over $250,000 in assets. Clients are usually women who want help with dividing up the finances. The certifying bodies are the Institute for Certified Divorce Planners in Michigan and the College for Divorce Specialists in Boulder, CO. (see E-Resources for Web sites).

## FREE FINANCIAL SEMINARS AND BEST-SELLING "GET RICH" BOOKS

A popular mode of communication about financial matters involves free seminars at hotels, schools, churches, and libraries. These may be given by financial planners, stockbrokers, insurance agents, or motivational speakers. The worth of these has to do with who is sponsoring the talk or seminar and who is the speaker. Be wary of direct mailings or advertisements in newspapers offering free financial talks. In some cases, the quality of information is suspect, and in others the "free" seminar is really a sales presentation. There is nothing wrong with a sales pitch as long as it is clear from the beginning that is what the seminar is about. Scams occur when seminars are given in public places that are followed up by high pressure in-home one-on-one sales talks for a product or service.

A more dependable source of financial information is available from employers who offer it as a perk. For example, companies such as Honeywell, Dell, Pitney Bowes, and Procter & Gamble pay for reliable financial-service specialists to help executives prepare their taxes and set up estate plans and help lower ranked employees with college savings plans and retirement planning, including offering 800 numbers they can call for advice. The basic financial planning help may be one-on-one or full day seminars. The reasons employers are doing this is because of the growing role that workers assume in managing their personal finances and the knowledge that financial worries take employees' attention away from their work. As the 401(k) and 403(b) savings accounts for retirement and benefit plans become more employee controlled, workers are forced to make investment decisions that were normally made by higher management. About 28 percent of workers receive financial-planning advice through their employer, and the percentage is climbing (Higgins and Simon, 2003).

Regardless of source or sponsor, realize that no one speaker or author has the key to financial success; if they did, they would be on their yacht enjoying it and not sharing their secrets with the public. A speaker or author who supports diversification (a variety of investments) and is not selling any one way to get rich such as buying options or investing in foreign real estate is on the right track. Television programs on money management as well as in-person talks can be enjoyed as long as one realizes that a perspective is being given and this perspective is one among many. The best advice is tailored to individuals given their circumstances, goals, and changes in the economy and the financial marketplace which is why the one-on-one consultations or 800 numbers are beneficial. Because there are so many changes in tax rules and in investments including real estate, books and advice quickly outdate. Few things are more worthless than a five-year-old "how to get rich" book.

## CREDIT, LOANS, AND DEBT WARNING SIGNS

People borrow money through the use of credit and loans. The "buy now, pay later" philosophy is ingrained in American society. Credit can be used for luxury items or for longer term investments such as educational expenses. "The difference between using credit to purchase luxury products and using it to finance an education is that the former usage is more consumption-oriented, while the latter is more investment-oriented. The commonality is that both incur long-term financial obligation, or consumer debt. Although the growth of consumer credit has contributed to the expansion of the U.S. economy and raised the quality of life for millions of American consumers, it also has brought about extensive consumer debt" (Lee and Lee, 2001/2002, pp. 25–26). A study by Eun-Ju Lee and Jinkook Lee (2001/2002) found that consumers who approved of using credit for luxury purchases had more credit cards and greater credit card debt than consumers who disapproved of using credit for such purchases. They found this was not the case for using consumer debt to finance education. So they concluded that "learn now and pay later" is a reasonable credit choice for most consumers, but one should beware of "buy luxury now and pay later" since this strategy tends to lead to more serious financial burdens on households. Another reason using credit to finance education is a sounder choice is because higher education significantly enhances future earning potential, thus borrowing money for educational purposes can be viewed as an investment.

The cost of using money is called **interest**. The rate of interest is determined by supply (amount of money lenders are willing to lend) and demand (amount of money borrowers are willing to pay). Interest rates are expressed as percentages as in 4 percent per year. *You are a receiver of interest when you have a savings account that pays interest or you are a payer of interest if you use a credit card or take out a student loan.* Interest rates do not exist in a vacuum, they respond to changes in other parts of the financial market or the economy so they may change daily or weekly. Naturally, when borrowing one seeks the lowest interest possible with the best terms.

*Convenience is the main benefit of credit.* **Credit cards** are used to purchase something or to get cash now with the promise of future payment. The typical card holder carries eight to ten cards and owes over $4,000. Credit cards are also useful for identification purposes, rebates, emergencies, and the purchase of big ticket items. They came into being in 1973.

*Credit cards began in 1973.*

*The main deficit is overextension.* People overuse credit and go into debt. Other problems include loss of cards, loss of privacy, and loss of financial freedom as money becomes more and more tied up in past purchases and interest payments.

---

**Consumer Alert**

Use caution when signing for a loan or as a cosigner. As a cosigner, if the borrower defaults you will have to repay the loan. Not only would you lose money, but also failure to pay promptly will affect your credit rating.

---

**Loans** are sums of money lent at interest. A person considering taking out a loan should consider the source, the interest rate, and the terms, including the repayment schedule and any fees or penalties thereof. Loans can be divided up into two types either by what the loan is for (education, furniture, cash) or by the repayment schedule (monthly or yearly). Loans come from universities, stores, car dealerships, brokerage firms, banks, savings and loans, credit unions, consumer finance companies, sales finance companies, and life insurance companies. With the Internet, applying for a loan has never been easier, but that also causes problems because applying is easy, paying up is another matter. A **cosigner** agrees to repay the loan if the borrower does not (defaults). Property such as a car or recreational vehicle or boat used to secure a loan is called **collateral**. **Liens** are legal rights to take and hold property, if the person with the loan does not pay up. When the loan is paid off, the liens are removed. When someone buys a house, a title search will reveal if there is a lien on the property, and the buyer will not purchase the house until the liens are cleaned up. A mortgage is a lien against a house.

Different types of loans such as mortgages, home equity loans, and car loans have been covered in previous chapters. The main thing to focus on is the annual percentage rate (APR) known as the interest rate, such as 8 percent a year or 12 percent a year—obviously the lower the better. Most students are familiar with car or student loans. Regarding education loans, upon graduation students should schedule an exit counseling session with their lender or university financial aid office to determine rights and responsibilities and to set up a repayment schedule. Choices are going to include stretching out payments over ten years or having higher payments and getting them paid off faster, and there will also be choices about how soon the repayment begins. Some people never pay off their student loans, and lenders are getting more aggressive about getting their money back if not sooner, later. In some cases, lenders can get their money back when a person starts getting Social Security—they go through a process to remove a part of the amount each month until the student loan is paid off. Recent graduates should review loan statements, and if there is trouble making payments, then the lender should be contacted and a new repayment schedule developed.

## Credit and Your Consumer Rights

A good credit rating (and paying off student loans promptly is part of this) is important for a number of reasons, including the fact that potential employers may check your credit history before hiring you and landlords may check it to see if they would be wise to give you a lease or not. Sometimes things happen in the system that can cause credit problems so credit records should be checked. The FTC enforces credit laws and protects your rights to obtain, use, and maintain credit. They cannot guarantee that everyone will get credit, but they can require businesses to be fair and equal in their treatment of customers and resolve disputes.

---

**Consumer Alert**

Is it possible to be turned down for a new credit card because a person has no balance on another card because it is paid off each month? Yes. Lenders like people who borrow wisely and pay their bills; however, too much financial discipline can be a negative from their point of view which is making money off of you in finance charges. Is this fair for consumers? No, but if a person still wants a card, one option is to spend a moderate amount on the current card each month and make smaller repayments. After six months, reapply, and you should get a new card which you can then pay off each month. Or you can forget this credit card company and try another.

---

**Consumer reporting agencies (CRAs)** more commonly known as **credit bureaus** have files that contain information about income, debts, credit payment history and if you have been sued, arrested, or filed for bankruptcy. A **credit score** is given that includes all of this information plus assets, length of employment, and length of living in one place. Negative events such as bankruptcies or failure to pay bills impact heavily on the credit score. There are two types of credit scores:

1. The **FICO score** was developed by the San Rafael, CA-based firm named Fair, Isaac & Co. The three credit reporting centers listed next all provide a FICO score to lenders. FICO is the score most widely used by lenders and also the one you have to pay to see. The charge in 2003 was $12.95 from *www.myfico.com*, *www.equifax.com* and *www.transunion.com*. Experian was charging $14.95 because they had their own system and additional data.
2. Other scores available for free use factors that are similar to, but not the same as, those used by Fair, Issac. These scores are available online from such companies as FreeCreditReport.com and eLoan.com. However, in exchange for the free score, you may get e-mails from e-loan companies or other financial services.

The three credit reporting centers are

Equifax Information Service Center
PO Box 10596
Atlanta, GA 30348-5496
*www.econsumer.equifax.com*

Experian Consumer Assistance Center
PO Box 2104
Allen, TX 75013
*www.experian.com*

Trans Union LLC Consumer Disclosure Center
PO Box 1000
Chester, PA 19022
*www.transunion.com*

Your credit rights are protected under the *Fair Credit Reporting Act (FCRA)* which is designed to ensure that CRAs furnish correct and complete information to business when evaluating your application. According to the FTC, under FCRA your rights are as follows:

**Consumer Alert**

Each credit bureau keeps a separate file on each person with information supplied to them by creditors. It is possible one of the reports has serious inaccuracies that could damage credit while the other two could not have the error in the file. So if there are problems, some experts would suggest getting copies from all three bureaus. If everything is going okay, then a check may not be necessary, or it may be prudent to receive a copy of your credit report each year from one bureau to check for errors and to make sure you have not been a victim of identity theft. If there is a mistake, contact the credit bureau in writing or online and explain the situation. *The way to raise a FICO score is by paying down your current account balances and by paying bills on time.*

- You have the right to receive a copy of your credit report.
- You have the right to know the name of anyone who received your credit report in the last year for most purposes and in the last year for employment purposes.
- Companies that deny your application must supply the name and address of the CRA.
- You have the right to a free copy of your credit report when your application has been denied.
- If you disagree with the accuracy of information, you can file a dispute with the CRA and the company that furnished the information to them. Afterward, you should receive a summary explanation of the settling of the dispute.

Your credit rights are also protected under the *Equal Credit Opportunity Act (ECOA)* which prohibits credit discrimination. According to the FTC, under ECOA your rights are as follows:

- You cannot be denied credit based on your race, sex, marital status, religion, age, national origin, or receipt of public assistance.
- You have the right to reliable public assistance considered in the same manner as other income.
- If you are denied credit, you have a legal right to know why.

According to the FTC, your credit rights under the *Fair Credit Billing (FCBA)* and the *Electronic Fund Transfer Act (EFTA)* establish procedures for resolving mistakes on credit billing and electronic fund transfer statements, including:

- Charges or electronic fund transfers that you—or anyone you have authorized to use your account—have not made.
- Charges or electronic fund transfers that are incorrectly identified or show the wrong amount or date.
- Computation or similar errors.
- Failure to reflect payments, credits, or electronic fund transfers properly.
- Not mailing or delivering credit billing statements to your current address, as long as that address was received by the creditor in writing at least 20 days before the billing period ended.
- Charges or electronic fund transfers for which you request an explanation or documentation, due to a possible error.

Most credit laws apply to open end credit (up to a maximum like $5,000 or $10,000), revolving charge accounts such as department store accounts, and overdraft checking accounts. The EFTA applies to ATMs, debit transactions, and other electronic banking transactions.

To take advantage of consumer protection laws regarding incorrect charges, the person falsely charged must first write to creditors to straighten things out. The letter should be sent by certified mail, return receipt requested, so the person has proof that the creditor has received the letter. Copies of sales slips and other documents should be included. The sender should keep a copy of the dispute letter. An example of a sample dispute letter is given in Box 12.4.

## Students and Credit Cards

Credit card companies target students before freshmen year and hit them again before graduation. "When Laura Caccavone set off for her first semester of college last month she brought along her favorite stuffed animals, hot pink sheets—and a

---

**BOX 12.4    Sample Dispute Letter to Credit Card Issuers**

Date

Your Name
Your Address
Your City, State, Zip Code
Your Account Number

Name of Creditor
Billing Inquiries
Address
City, State, Zip Code

Dear Sir or Madam:
I am writing to dispute a billing error in the amount of $ _____ on my account. The amount is inaccurate because (describe the problem). I am requesting that the error be corrected, that any finance and other charges related to the disputed amount be credited as well, and that I receive an accurate statement.

Enclosed are copies of (use this sentence to describe any enclosed information, such as sales slips, payment records) supporting my position. Please investigate this matter and correct the billing error as soon as possible.

Sincerely,

Your Name

Enclosures: (List what you are enclosing.)

*Source:* ID theft: When bad things happen to your good name. Federal Trade Commission publication, February 2000, Washington, DC.

---

**Consumer Alert**

A person's liability for lost or stolen credit cards is limited to $50. If this happens, notify card issuers promptly upon discovery of loss. Most companies have toll-free numbers and 24–7 service. Companies will instruct on the next steps, if any.

---

Capital One Visa with a $300 credit limit. 'I know I have it if I need it,' says the 18 year old freshman at Drew University in Madison, N.J., who also uses the card to buy gas and the occasional must-have accessory" (Simon and Whelan, 2002, p. D1). The $300 limit won't get her into too much trouble, but overuse of credit can lead to substantial debt loads that affect students the rest of their lives. Percentages of students who have major credit cards in their own name are as follows: freshmen, 36 percent; sophomores, 55 percent; juniors, 51 percent; and seniors 64 percent (Simon and Whelan, 2002). The trend is upward. Students should shop carefully because rates and introductory credit limits vary widely. When this book went to press, examples of cards targeted to students included Discover Card (issuer Discover) with a minimum interest rate of 17.99 and a $1,000 credit limit and Blue for Students (issuer American Express) at 8.90 minimum interest rate and $500 introductory credit limit. The Senate Banking Committee has held hearings on the marketing of credit cards to college students because concerns have been raised about credit abuse.

Debit cards, ATM cards, and stored-value cards are other options that students can use. A growing number of colleges now give students identification cards that can be used to buy everything from books to pizza, with the school getting a share of the revenue. Alumni cards are also being used by schools as a source of revenue.

## Debt Collectors and Your Rights

**Debts** are what is owed. Examples of debts are bonds, notes, mortgages, and other forms of paper evidencing amounts owed and payable on specified dates or on demand. A debtor is a person who owes money. If a debtor does not keep up with their debts such as not keeping up with car payments or if there has been an error in the record or account, a debt collector may call. A debt collector is any person other than the creditor that collects debts. Lawyers can be debt collectors. The Fair Debt Collection Practices Act (FDCPA) prohibits debt collectors from using unfair, deceptive, or abusive practices while collecting debts. According to the FTC, your rights under the FDCPA include

- Debt collectors may contact you only between 8:00 A.M. and 9:00 P.M.
- Debt collectors may not contact you at work if they know your employer disapproves.
- Debt collectors may not harass, oppress, or abuse you.
- Debt collectors may not lie when collecting debts, such as falsely implying that you have committed a crime.
- Debt collectors must identify themselves to you on the phone.
- Debt collectors must stop contacting you if you ask them to in writing.

---

**BOX 12.5     How to Avoid Credit Card Scams**

- Beware of television or radio ads for "easy credit."
- Beware of the phrase "Anyone can qualify for a major credit card, even bankrupts!"
- Look out for calls to a "900" number for a credit card. This call may not be toll free and may not result in a credit card. The FTC has found calls can run from $2 to $50 or more.
- Watch out for credit repair companies or clinics. There are no tricks, only time and consistently paying bills will repair damaged credit. If someone advertises help consolidating debts into one check instead of several find out how much has to be paid and for how long.

---

## Solving Credit Problems

Your credit record or report influences your purchasing power, getting a job, renting or buying a house, and buying insurance. Negative information can stay on a report for seven years and bankruptcy for ten. Any problems paying bills should be reported at once to creditors and a modified payment plan worked out. In other words, be up front about problems and take care of them before creditors turn to debt collectors. Creditors want the money even if it takes a long time. It costs them to hire debt collectors, an expense they want to avoid. People who have been turned down for credit may get desperate and fall for credit card scams. See Box 12.5 for advice on how to avoid scams.

# CREDIT COUNSELING SERVICES

If after a person tries everything on their own to straighten out credit problems, an alternative is to turn to credit counseling services such as The National Foundation for Consumer Credit or the Consolidated Credit Counseling Service. They have offices throughout the United States and offer Web sites and toll free 24-hour hotlines. For services in your area, check the Yellow Pages of the phone book under credit counseling or refer to the E-Resources section at the end of the chapter. Services may be free or low cost. How can they afford to operate for free or by gathering low fees? The answer is that they are supported by local businesses and banks who want to help consumers be fiscally responsible and by foundations and groups such as the United Way. Also universities, military bases, credit unions, employers through employee as-

---

**Consumer Alert**

Women have often had trouble establishing a good credit history—a record of how bills were paid—because of name changes and because creditors report accounts shared by married couples in the husband's name only. Women should make sure all relevant information in the credit bureau's file is in their name. The credit bureaus should be informed of any changes in names and in marital status, including getting married, separated, divorced, or widowed.

sistance programs (EAPs), and housing or community authorities may offer free or low-cost money management or credit counseling services. Counselors look at the bills and try to arrange repayment plans that are acceptable to the person with credit problems and with their creditors. This may mean debt consolidation or the formation of a debt repayment plan. The Federal Consumer Information Center at 1 888 878 3256 offers publications on credit counselors and debt management and checklists of questions to ask when choosing a counseling agency.

Who has financial or credit problems? Nearly everyone has experienced a bounced check or problems with electric or telephone bills, but credit counseling services are primarily for people who really have gotten in over their heads. The average customer at The National Foundation for Consumer Credit is a woman, 35.4 years old, married or never married with children, with low to middle income, who owes several thousand dollars to over ten creditors. How do you know when things are getting out of hand? This typical profile provides a few indicators, such as having dependents and several creditors. Other signs include

- Routinely fighting about money with a spouse or partner.
- Being continually anxious about money, never feeling you have enough or worried about spending what you have.
- Not being able to save, feeling that spending is out of control, seeking instant gratification through shopping or rationalizing purchases such as the tenth pair of running shoes.
- Having no idea where money goes, not balancing a checkbook or looking at statements.
- Living paycheck to paycheck, especially running out of money before the next paycheck.
- Being turned down for credit cards.
- Bouncing checks regularly, having problems with bank accounts.
- Having trouble paying the rent and car payments.
- Having to regularly borrow money from family members and friends.
- Paying off the minimum each month on credit cards and never paying them off completely.
- Not wanting to hear about money problems, avoidance.
- Having a history of falling into debt, getting out of debt, and falling back in.
- Being attracted to people who have money problems, kindred souls.
- Having to have the best of everything even if not affordable such as the most expensive set of golf clubs or a showy car.

## DEBT AND RELATIONSHIPS/SELF-WORTH

Debt affects relationships. In a magazine article, a 31-year-old registered nurse revealed that she owed $57,000 and was afraid to tell her fiancé. When she told him, it turned out he had $27,000 in debt so they postponed the wedding. Later, they disagreed about money; for example, he bought a new car instead of paying his bills and eventually they broke up. Since then she has been paying off her debts each month and so far has reduced it by $5,000. Her goal is to be debt free in three years (Orman, 2001). In the same article, another woman age 34 who was in debt set a financial goal to save for a down payment of a house and eventually wanted to start a family. She gained control of her finances by paying off three credit cards which changed the dynamic between her and her husband for the better, and she reported they don't argue as much about money anymore.

**Self-worth** is a system of thoughts and feelings concerning or focused on self. Research indicates that self-worth is a driving force in people's perceptions of their financial situation and spending behavior. *"Some people spend because they have low self-worth.* This spending helps them feel better about themselves, at least momentarily. On the other hand, some people engage in excessive spending behavior and feel guilty, thereby diminishing their self-worth. The positive and significant relationship between self-worth and financial satisfaction is an important finding that has significant implications for educators and financial advisors" (Hira and Mugenda, 1999, p. 220).

# BANKRUPTCY

Credit counseling is encouraged, and bankruptcy is discouraged by credit counseling services. A person should try everything possible before they resort to **bankruptcy**, which is a form of legal recourse open to insolvent debtors. A debtor would petition a federal court for protection from creditors and arrange for the liquidation of assets. The bankruptcy rate is about 1.4 million Americans a year, and the number is rising. Some of it is caused by credit overextension, and other times it is caused by health crises, business failures, job loss, divorces, accidents, and natural disasters. Usually the debtors are under stress and unable to think clearly about the ramifications of bankruptcy which remains on credit reports for up to ten years. The person may get out from under debt, but they will be unable to buy a car, rent an apartment, buy a house, may not be able to get a job, or do other things most people take for granted. Over 25 percent of employers look into credit backgrounds before hiring, especially for jobs involving money and accounting such as retail, banks, and management positions. On an employment application, the potential employee authorizes the employer to do background checks including credit records.

*Most bankrupt individuals choose Chapter 7* of the federal bankruptcy code. **Chapter 7 bankruptcy** is known as "Straight Liquidation Chapter" because in return for eliminating debts, the debtor agrees to turn over nonexempt assets and pay as much as possible to creditors. However, the way it usually goes is that there are no nonexempt assets to sell so usually creditors receive nothing. Exempt items differ by state but usually include houses, tools of trade, cars, or farm animals. Chapter 7 is popular because if granted the court erases all dischargeable debt. In this situation assets are turned over to an appointed trustee who will sell the assets to pay debts, making partial payments to creditors. Usually the first one to be paid is the attorney that handles the bankruptcy, and it is suggested that people hire an attorney for these cases. Costs include the attorney fees, a filing fee, and trustee fees.

Another choice is **Chapter 13 bankruptcy** which allows debtors to repay some of the debt they owe, and in return they get to keep most of their property. Usually this type of debtor is a person with regular income. Through a court-approved plan, the debtor pays back some of the debt, and this looks better on the person's future credit report. Under Chapter 13 the debtor retains some of their assets, and debts have to be paid within five to seven years. States differ about what assets the debtor may keep. People also hide such assets as jewelry, cars, or boats at relatives' and friends' houses. The courts are quite shrewd about this and try to determine whether the debtor has given an honest accounting of assets and liabilities before final decisions are made.

Bankruptcy, then, represents an issue with several sides to it. The debtor may have been fiscally irresponsible and may be bilking creditors and lenders. In other cases, the debtor has been through an unfortunate set of circumstances, such as ill health or injuries and the laws are there to protect them from being harassed or unfairly treated. In recent years, Congress has considered bankruptcy legislation which would make declaring bankruptcy more difficult and might also include education requirements similar to traffic school for drivers with traffic tickets. Repeated or serial bankruptcies are not uncommon. Stopping the cycle for the debtors' sake and their families as well as for the economy and creditors is a goal. Ultimately, the cost of bankruptcy is passed down to the people who pay their bills and are responsible through higher interest rates, credit charges, and higher taxes. Somewhere along the line someone has to pay for other people's misfortunes and mistakes.

## Steps to Follow

When people declare bankruptcy, they file petitions and schedules with the clerk's office of the federal bankruptcy court. In the petition there will be a list of assets, income sources, liabilities including lists of creditors and amounts owed, and living expenses including number and ages of dependents. Proof will be needed in the form of deeds, mortgages, tax returns, credit card bills, medical bills, savings records, and loan papers. The process will take from four to six months to complete. One of the positive aspects is that debt collectors stop calling until things are settled, giving people breathing space. Attorneys also provide a buffer zone, debtors can refer creditors to them. Lenders may show up at the court case and will talk to the debtors and their attorneys immediately after the case trying to get their money first. The attorney will

- Advise the person of their rights and options in bankruptcy
- Complete the forms (or have someone in their office complete the forms) and file them
- Attend the "First Meeting of Creditors" with the debtor (this is also called the 341 meeting)
- Represent the debtor in the courtroom

A trustee appointed by a U.S. trustee, who works for the Department of Justice, administers the case, but cannot give legal advice. The trustee's job is to ensure that the debtor and creditors (people, banks, institutions, and stores to whom the debtor owes money) are treated in accordance to the rules and procedures established in the United States Bankruptcy Code. Even though someone goes bankrupt, they still have to pay taxes, alimony, child support, property settlements, and student loans. A judge decides disputes and usually debtors only see a judge if someone objects to their case.

## GOVERNMENT'S ROLE

Throughout this chapter, the government's role as defender of consumers' rights, regulator, law setter, holder of hearings, and mediator has been emphasized. The government also has a role in providing financial education and examples of this

**Consumer Alert**

People file for bankruptcy with the idea of being free from debt, but as noted in the chapter some debts such as student loans are not dischargeable, they keep going. Also, a Chapter 7 Bankruptcy only eliminates past debt, debt owed before the filing. So debtors are not absolved from future debt. They have to keep paying rent, telephone, electricity, and water bills or face losing services or being evicted even while they are in the process of filing for bankruptcy.

mentioned earlier, are the public service announcements and the Web site of the Federal Reserve. Since the 1970s, financial and credit rights have been at the forefront of the consumer movement. As this chapter has shown, there are many agencies and laws regulating the use of credit. *The leading agency is the Federal Trade Commission* that works for the consumer to prevent fraudulent, deceptive, and unfair business practices in the marketplace and to provide information to help consumers spot, stop, and avoid scams. Complaints against all kinds of creditors can be filed with the Department of Justice, Civil Rights Division, Washington, DC 20530.

An example in the chapter of government legislation aiding consumers and the banking business is the legislation being considered by Congress as this book went to press that would give electronic check images the same legal weight as paper checks. Instead of couriers arriving at bank branches to pick up checks to be processed, the checks would be sent electronically—this makes so much more sense from a time efficiency and cost and gasoline savings points of view. Technology in e-finance is one of the fastest growing areas of e-commerce.

Besides federal agencies and Congress, state agencies and legislators also work to protect consumers. Each state has usury laws that limit how high an interest rate pawnbrokers and other lenders can charge. State attorney generals prosecute creditors who have violated state equal credit opportunity laws. In state governments, the office of the attorney general has the muscle to stop anticonsumer practices.

## SUMMARY

It is never too soon or too late to work on improving finances. Financial planning is a lifelong process. Sound money management is a means, although not the sole means, to personal power, success, stability, esteem, and general well-being. Research indicates that self-worth, financial beliefs, behavior, and satisfaction are linked. Reaching financial goals requires setting realistic targets and creating a plan to reach them. The best strategy is to set short-, medium-, and long-term goals and to build savings. The sum that Americans save, as a percentage of their disposable income, has fallen sharply in recent years. Seeking financial advice will help, but the quality of financial advice varies. With the deregulation of financial institutions in 1980, the market opened up, mergers happened, and more choices were available to consumers. Americans write about 42 billion checks each year, and the antiquated processing system is being overhauled. Banks are offering products such as mutual funds that are not backed by the FDIC, and this is confusing to some investors who thought all bank products and services were secure and backed by the federal government.

Online banking is more popular than online auctions or stock trading. It is a very fast growing use of the Internet for bill paying and account checking. The chapter covered a number of ways to make sure that online banking is conducted in a safe way and that your liability is limited. Streamlining bill paying saves time and reduces clutter.

There are few controls or regulations over financial planners. The Certified Financial Planner (CFP) is the most recognized certification. Many different situations can trigger the need for professional help, such as significant changes in lifestyle or marital status. Certified divorce planners are financial planners who specialize in dividing assets in divorce cases.

The three main consumer report agencies (CRAs) also known as credit bureaus keep credit scores and records. Credit is used by many consumers to finance educations, buy houses, remodel homes, and buy cars. A number of acts ensure that consumers are given equal access to credit and are treated fairly. The list of uses for credit scores is growing from auto- to homeowners-insurance companies; every lender looks at credit scores to gauge the likelihood of customers' future claims, and sets premiums accordingly. More employers are using credit scores to screen job applicants, and landlords use them before renting. A credit score may be the earliest indication of an identity theft problem. Credit counseling is recommended for people with credit or bill paying problems. If the problems cannot be solved, an alternative is filing for bankruptcy which is a form of legal recourse open to insolvent debtors. The two main types of personal bankruptcy are Chapter 7 (the one most chosen) and Chapter 13 in which the debtor pays off some of the debts.

## KEY POINTS

1. Financial management is a three-step process.
2. Americans save less than 3 percent of disposable income on average each year.
3. An emergency fund is recommended as a fallback in case of job loss or other major setbacks.
4. With deregulation, money markets opened up, and consumers had more choice because of increased competition.
5. Four main kinds of financial institutions are commercial banks, credit unions, brokerage firms, and savings and loan associations.
6. Under the old paper check processing system, checks took five days to go through the system, and checks were handled more than 15 times. In the proposed electronic system, processing time and the chance for fraud will be reduced. Banks will know much faster whether a check is good and consumers will have increased security.
7. Online banking offers convenience.
8. There are over 500,000 financial planners in the United States; 40,000 have the CFP credential which requires three years of practical experience, passing exams, and adhering to a code of ethics.
9. Consumer credit can be used for a variety of reasons, including financing education or buying luxury items. Financing education is an investment in human capital.

10. A credit score is a key factor in determining access to credit and the interest rate a person may be charged. The FICO score is the credit industry standard. The FICO score allows lenders to rank loan applicants according to the likelihood they will repay on time.

11. Federal law sets procedures for correcting inaccurate information on credit reports.

## KEY TERMS

| | | |
|---|---|---|
| attitudes | credit score | loans |
| bankruptcy | debit cards | personal finance |
| Chapter 7 bankruptcy | debts | personalized |
| Chapter 13 bankruptcy | decision making | identification number |
| collateral | emergency fund | (PIN) |
| credit cards | e-wallets | self-worth |
| certified divorce planner | Federal Deposit | smart cards or chip |
| Certified Financial | Insurance | cards or stored value |
| Planner (CFP) | Corporation | cards |
| consumer reporting | FICO score | resources |
| agencies (CRAs), also | financial planners | time deposit |
| known as credit | fixed expenses | Truth in Savings Act |
| bureaus | interest | values |
| cosigner | liens | variable expenses |

## DISCUSSION QUESTIONS

1. Are you pleased or disappointed with your financial situation? What steps are you taking to get on sounder footing? What are your short-, medium-, and long range goals? Why does financial planning require flexibility?

2. Why is it true that it is never too soon or too late to start working on improving a financial situation?

3. What is your potential liability if your debit card is lost or stolen? What is your potential liability if your credit card is lost or stolen? In either case, what should you do first?

4. Look at the E-Resources list and select one Web site to investigate. Report what you find.

## E-RESOURCES

| Name/Website | Function |
|---|---|
| Banking and Savings Bonds sites: Federal Deposit Insurance Corporation www.fdic.gov | Insures bank accounts. |

| | |
|---|---|
| Federal Reserve www.federalreserve education.org | Government-based source of financial information on how the Federal Reserve operates and links to topics on banking and more |
| Treasury Department's Bureau of Public Debt www.savings-bonds.gov | Source for U.S. savings bond information and purchase |
| American Bankers Association www.aba.com | Provides general information on banking and loans |
| Bank Online Bankonline.com | Links to banks around United States |
| Gomez Advisors www.gomez.com | Ranks bank Web sites |

Financial Plans: Note that it has been estimated there are over 400 Web sites with financial calculators, and all of them produce different results, depending how they are set up and the depth of the information that the person seeking advice gives. So these are useful for a beginning stab at evaluating personal finance, but they are not the end word. Examples of some of the leading sources follow:

| | |
|---|---|
| John Hancock Mutual Life Insurance Company www.jhancock.com | Offers computer-generated financial plan |
| Citibank www.finance.com | Offers financial advise/plans |
| American Express www.americanexpress .com/advisors | Provides ways to calculate net worth, cash flow, etc. |
| Jump$tart Coalition for Personal Financial Literacy www.jumpstart.org | Educates K–12 students about financial matters |
| National Association of Personal Financial Advisors (fee-only) www.napfa.org | Aids in locating planners, will work with modest sums |
| Financial Planning Association www.fplanet.org | Aids in locating planners, fee and commission-based, will work with modest sums |
| Garrett Planning Network www.garrettplanning network.com | Aids in locating planners who charge by the hour, will work with modest sums |
| CFP Board of Standards www.cfpp-board.org click on "Consumers" | "10 Questions to Ask When Choosing a Financial Planner" and other consumer brochures |
| Institute for Certified Divorce Planners www.institutecdp.com | Search engine for divorce planners by zip code, state, or last name |

| | |
|---|---|
| The College for Divorce Specialists www.cdscollege.com | Search engine for divorce planners by keyword and geography |

**Credit/Bankruptcy**

| | |
|---|---|
| Federal Trade Commission www.ftc.gov | Information on credit, rights, frauds and scams |
| National Foundation for Consumer Credit www.nfcc.org | Information on credit and credit reporting centers |
| Consolidated Credit Counseling Services www.cccs.org | Credit counseling help |
| American Bar Association www.abanet.org | Legal information, lists of attorneys |
| West's Legal Dictionary www.wid.com | Legal terminology, definitions |
| American Bankruptcy Institute www.abiworld.com | Information on bankruptcy |
| National Association of Insurance Commissioners (NAIC) www.naic.org | Maintains links to all state insurance regulators. Credit scores are used in predicting future claims under auto and homeowner policies |

# REFERENCES

Check is in the air, The. (April 2003). *Smart Money,* p. 46.

Clements, J. (February 19, 2003). Finding a financial adviser who won't sneer at your little nest egg. *Wall Street Journal,* p. D1.

Higgins, M., and R. Simon (February 12, 2003). Getting stock picks from your boss. *Wall Street Journal,* p. D1.

Hira, T., and O. Mugenda. (1999). The relationships between self-worth and financial beliefs, behavior, and satisfaction. *Journal of Family and Consumer Sciences, 91* (4), 214–20.

Hoffman, E. (February 2003). Want some outside advice? *AARP Bulletin,* p. 26.

Ip, G. (May 20, 2003). New role for Greenspan: Pitching financial advice. *Wall Street Journal,* p. D3.

Lee, E., and J. Lee. (2001/2002). Credit choices: An examination of consumer approval for the financing of luxury items and education. *Journal of Consumer Education,* pp. 25–34.

Orman, S. (September 2001). Your net worth? Priceless. *O Magazine,* pp. 66–70.

Silverman, R. (February 12, 2003). How to plan the perfect divorce. *Wall Street Journal,* p. D1.

Simon, R., and C. Whelan. (September 3, 2002). The credo on campus: "Just Charge It," *Wall Street Journal,* p. D1.

Stirland, S. (October 2001). Is your bank selling the world your secrets? *Good Housekeeping,* pp. 229–30.

# Insurance and Investment Issues

You can fool some of the people all of the time, and all of the people
some of the time, but you cannot fool all of the people all of the time.
Abraham Lincoln

## Learning Objectives

1. Explain the purpose and types of insurance.
2. Describe the different parts of insurance contracts.
3. Explain the purpose and types of investments.
4. Describe frauds and scams involved in insurance and investments.
5. Discuss state and federal government agencies that look out for insurance and investment frauds.

## INTRODUCTION

Insurance and investments are little understood, yet important parts of our financial lives. They are multifaceted. As evidence of their role in the economy:

1. Over one-half of Americans own stocks through mutual funds and their retirement plans
2. One in twelve dollars in the United States is connected to the insurance industry

This chapter explains the basic forms of insurance and investments and the most common fraud problems. Since this is an ever-evolving area, readers need to keep abreast of changes in the general economy and the legislation that affects products and services.

As in all areas, the Internet brings with it increasing choices along with increasing opportunities for fraud. Since large sums of money are involved in insurance and investments, the attraction to swindlers is easily seen—swindlers go where the money is. But let's say you are a cautious person and unlikely to fall victim to obvious fraud, why should you care? Insurance fraud alone can inflate your premiums as much as 30 percent according to the National Insurance Crime Bureau. Whether you fall victim directly or not, you pay for the insurance fraud that occurs to others. The cost is passed down to all consumers.

The chapter begins with a brief overview of the purpose of and types of insurance because the frauds cannot be explained until the reader understands the way insurance works. Specifics on the different types of insurance will be given, leading to a discussion of consumer rights and responsibilities. After the insurance section, the chapter turns to a description of different types of investments and the frauds thereof. The purpose of this end section of the chapter is to give a thumbnail sketch of the main types of investments. Before putting money into either insurance or investments, the reader should investigate further.

# INSURANCE: PURPOSE AND TYPES

Insurance is for protection, it is a financial arrangement between consumers and insurers.

*The primary purpose of insurance is protection.* A secondary purpose is to use insurance as a form of investment. By buying insurance, individuals are trying to protect themselves, their families, and their assets such as homes and cars. **Insurance** is a financial arrangement between individuals and insurance companies to protect against loss or injury. It provides peace of mind.

College courses in insurance usually fall under the category of risk management taught in the business school. Individuals take out policies (contracts) and make premiums (payments) to insurers. The policies include agreements, **exclusions** (items not covered), conditions, deductibles, and endorsements (amendments or additions to the basic policy). An example of an exclusion would be excluding claims stemming from nuclear explosions or radioactive fallout. State Farm, the nation's largest auto and residential insurer, changed its car insurance policies to exclude such claims in the wake of heightened awareness over terrorism and the realization that there was no specific language in their existing contracts regarding nuclear-related claims. Letters were sent to 40 million auto policy holders saying that nuclear blasts or radioactive damage are not normal road hazards whether the incidents are accidental or intentional. In so doing, the company clarified that nuked cars are not covered. **Deductibles** are amounts policy holders pay toward a loss before insurance coverage begins. If there is a loss or injury, the insurer pays up.

Insurance is sold through agents in person, over the telephone, or online. Auto insurance is one type of insurance that is increasingly being sold online. **Exposures** such as driving are sources of risks. **Perils** are events such as car accidents that cause financial loss.

The buying of insurance can be thought of as a process beginning with awareness of need, moving through analysis and action (including purchase), to evaluation. Insurance policies should be revisited at least once a year and more often when there are significant lifestyle changes. The kinds of things that could change are peril exposure such as taking up skydiving or traveling extensively.

An insurer can turn down an applicant. If this happens, the applicant can ask the insurer why he or she was denied coverage and request a copy of one's medical information. The individual denied insurance can try other companies and check with the state department of insurance to find out about rights and responsibilities.

## Auto

*Many states, but not all, require auto insurance.* Most states require liability coverage. Since not all states require auto insurance, it is possible to get in an accident with an uninsured motorist. So what you may want to have as an individual is

**Consumer Alert**

Protect yourself when buying insurance on line by researching. Determine which insurance coverage best fits your needs, then shop around for companies, premiums, and coverage. In order to sell insurance in your state, the company and the agent must be licensed. You can link to your state insurance department's Web site by going to *www.naic.org*, click on "State Insurance Regulators Web Sites," then click on your state. Remember that security is important, protect your personal information, taking extra precautions when paying with credit cards. Keep detailed records, get all rate quotes, and print out forms and information. You should receive a copy (not a photocopy) of new policies within 30 to 60 days of purchase. If you do not, contact the company immediately.

*uninsured motorist coverage* which pays for bodily injury caused by an uninsured motorist or hit-and-run driver or negligent driver with an insolvent insurer. A driver may be underinsured as well. In the case of an accident whether a claim is paid or not depends on the insurance of the two drivers who were legally liable, agreements between the people involved, the amount of damage, and the amount of maximum limit on the policies.

In the last chapter it was discussed how banks and other institutions are crossing lines by adding more and more types of financial products. Similarly, a new twist in car insurance is in order to control cost, insurers such as Progressive Corporation, the nation's third largest auto insurer, has opened its own chain of one-stop auto claims centers. Customers make an appointment and bring in their cars and then the company takes it from there. At the centers, Progressive will inspect crashed vehicles,

People watch curiously from a sidewalk after witnessing an automobile accident in Las Vegas, Nevada. (Courtesy of Photo Edit, photo by Jeff Greenberger.)

hand customers keys to rental cars, take crashed cars to a body shop for repairs, and inspect them afterward before giving them back to customers. This hands-on approach is different from the usual procedure of crashed car owners finding their own repair shops and sending the paperwork to the company. From a convenience standpoint, this new service by Progressive is attractive, but critics are worried that the quality of repairs may suffer as insurers scrimp on costs. To save money generic auto parts may be used instead of brand-name auto parts, and this practice may be okay or may cause problems. In the past, the use of generic parts if deemed inferior has led to lawsuits. A pro argument to using insurer-repair shop combinations is that Farmers Insurance estimates that 40 percent of repair jobs found on the general market involve some type of fraud. According to one of them, "The next time you need to take your vehicle to the body shop, don't assume all the repairs were necessary or that the parts of work you were charged for were even used or completed" (Oster, 2003, p. D1). Since combined repair shops and insurance are limited in availability, it is too soon to tell if this service will dominate the marketplace. However, the trend appears to be underway. Other insurance companies such as AllState and Farmers are experimenting with similar services.

Regarding the differences between states in auto insurance coverage required, in Louisiana you must have liability coverage which pays for property damages or personal injury for which the driver is legally responsible. *Liability insurance covers bodily injury or property damage to the driver, family members, and others driving the vehicle with the driver's permission.* In Florida a driver has to carry a minimum of $10,000 of *personal injury protection (also called no-fault coverage)* and $10,000 of *property damage liability* if the motor vehicle is registered in Florida. *No fault insurance* (after an auto accident, each party collects from his or her insurer) *was available in seven states* when this book went to press. No fault insurance policies are rife with fraud and motorists paying too much for limited coverage. Other types of insurance include:

- *Bodily injury liability:* coverage pays for serious and permanent injury to death to others when you cause an accident involving your automobile.
- *Collision:* coverage pays for repair or replacement of your vehicle if it collides with another vehicle, flips over or crashes into an object, regardless of who causes the accident. People often drop collision coverage after their cars are over ten years old because the car is not worth much, and the cost of insurance does not make financial sense.
- *Comprehensive:* coverage pays for losses from incidents other than a collision, such as fire, theft, windstorm, vandalism, or flood.
- *Uninsured, underinsured motorist:* coverage pays for bodily injuries to you, your family members, and any other person occupying your covered vehicle, should they be caused by the negligence of others.
- *Medical payments:* coverage pays for medical expenses for accidental injury up to the limit of your policy.
- *Towing:* added towing and road service to basic auto insurance.

Actually there are more kinds of auto insurance, but they tend to be for unique situations. The point is that auto insurance is something that individuals buy on their own (not through an employer) and that the states vary in what they require. The factors that affect premiums include

---

**BOX 13.1     Types of Fraud Schemes and Scams Related to Auto Insurance**

*Agent sliding:* refers to an agent selling a consumer optional coverage or services without full consent.

*Deceptive claim:* refers to when an accident victim files for a claim for lost wages and medical bills following an accident. Investigators find out the injury was preexisting, had nothing to do with the accident.

*Fictional theft:* refers to a policy holder filing a phony claim for a stolen luxury car; the car is actually hidden in storage or at a friend's house.

*Repair-shop rip-offs:* refers to owners of shops offering to inflate the damage estimate as a "favor." The dishonest owner of the vehicle submits an inflated claim.

*Understatement of risk:* refers to dishonest applicants lying about number of miles frequently driven per year in order to get a lower premium.

Note that some of these scams and schemes are caused by the insurer and some by the consumer.

---

- Driving history, including past accidents or violations.
- Type of vehicle, model, year and value.
- Gender and age. Insurance companies typically charge higher premiums for males under the age of 25.
- Territory, including where you drive and where you keep your car. Urban drivers typically pay more than rural drivers. For example, insurance is higher in New York than it is in Wyoming or North Dakota.

Ways to reduce premiums include having a good driving record, being a nondrinker and nonsmoker, driving low-profile automobiles, aging, raising your deductible, getting good grades, having restraint systems, dropping collision on older cars, and antitheft devices. The price of insurance, average premium for full coverage, varies greatly by type of vehicle. *Consumer Reports* found that small sedans are usually the least expensive and midsize high-end sedans are the highest. Surprisingly SUVs were in the middle (What a Difference the Car Makes, 2002). Insurers base their rates on their claims experience. Box 13.1 lists the typical types of insurance frauds related to autos.

---

**Consumer Alert**

When applying for auto insurance policies, individuals must disclose past tickets or accidents; otherwise individuals risk policies being canceled, leaving them without coverage. Applicants must also be truthful about the number of drivers in their family. An insurance company can cancel the policy if the driver has been in three or more accidents in a three-year period. Failure to make premiums can also result in cancellation. As with any other major purchase, individuals should shop around. Companies are rated, see E-Resources. When receiving phone calls after an accident, it could be someone trying to involve you in a fraud scheme. Always carry auto and health insurance cards with you, and protect insurance identification numbers as you would credit card numbers.

## Credit

Credit insurance is one of the lesser known forms of insurance. It protects a loan or mortgage on the chance that a person cannot make their payments. Usually it is optional, meaning the lender will not demand it. The Federal Trade Commission says it is against the law for a lender to deceptively include credit insurance in your loan without your knowledge or permission. There are four types:

*Credit disability insurance*—pays off all or some of your loan if you become ill or injured and can't work.

*Credit life insurance*—pays off all or some of your loan if you die.

*Credit property insurance*—protects personal property used to secure a loan.

*Involuntary unemployment insurance*—makes loan payments if you lose your job due to no fault of your own, such as a layoff.

Several of these credit insurance types are covered by other types of insurance the individual may already have such as health or auto insurance, so before buying credit insurance this should be checked first. Alternatives may make more sense such as life insurance instead of credit life insurance. Before buying credit insurance, find out about these and the length of loan, as well as the usual questions about insurance such as coverage, cost of premiums, and ratings of companies.

## Homeowners (Property and Liability)

Homeowners' insurance helps pay to repair or rebuild your home and replace personal possessions lost to theft, fire, storms, or other disasters. Most states do not require the purchase of homeowners' insurance, but they may require it for specific purposes, for example, liability insurance if you have a swimming pool. **Property insurance** pays for losses to homes and personal property due to theft, fire, vandalism, natural disasters, or other causes such as trees falling on houses. **Liability insurance** pays for losses from negligence resulting in bodily injury or property damage to others for which the policy holder is responsible. All homeowners' policies provide liability coverage. From a consumer point of view, the main thing is to have replacement-cost coverage. If the home or apartment is destroyed by fire, a person wants to replace contents and, if owned, the structure as well. There are a variety of forms. The most popular of all homeowners' forms which covers the basics is HO-3. HO-4 is for renters. The policy seeker looks for a match between their needs and what the policy covers while keeping costs to a minimum. If a person only owns a beat-up bicycle, a three-year-old computer, and clothes, renters' insurance is probably not necessary. The more valuable possessions are, the more insurance is needed. To save money, homeowners and renters should raise the deductible, use security systems and smoke detectors, not smoke, and take advantage of discounts available such as those offered to groups.

Liability may be related to homes, autos, or other situations such as bodily injury, libel (a written, printed, or pictorial statement that damages a person by damaging his or her character or reputation), or other damages caused by the insured.

Three red flags that may prevent an insurer from covering a home include

- Water claims
- Wind/hail damage
- Burglaries

The insurance industry has been cracking down on houses with a past. The message from the insurer is "it is not you, it is your house."

Policies usually cover the basics. For extras such as jewelry, furs, and expensive computers, a person may need additional coverage that can be obtained as an **endorsement** or an addition to an insurance policy. "The truth is that homeowners insurance can be very limited in protecting valuable possessions. It's common to encounter special clauses that exclude fine art and antiques, or that cap payments on losses. . . . Standard policies also rarely protect against common causes of loss to fine art, like water damage and breakage" (Whitehouse, 2003, p. D2). Decisions about insurance should hinge on how losses are reimbursed. Some insurers use a method that gives replacement value minus depreciation. Usually sentimental value is not included so the policy holder has to decide how much coverage is appropriate. Cost is going to vary by part of the country. For example, in coastal areas of Florida endorsement or additions for breakables like china is going to be higher than it is in Utah. Box 13.2 gives a list of typical insurance frauds related to homeowners' policies. An **adjuster** is a person who determines the amount of claim, loss, or damage payable under a contract. Adjusters should be properly licensed. If there is a loss, insurers require that you notify them immediately.

---

**Consumer Alert**

If a housing unit is vacant for 30 days in a row, it may be considered abandoned, and insurance coverage may halt. If you are going to be gone for longer than 30 days, check your policy. A housesitter or someone checking your property regularly, including police, may take care of this problem. Also some policies do not cover floods or other disasters so if you live in a flood-prone area you may need extra insurance or you may take your chances.

---

> **BOX 13.2    Types of Insurance Fraud Related to Homeowner's Policies**
>
> *Arson for profit:* refers to financially strapped homeowners who intentionally set fires to destroy property in hopes of collecting the insurance claims.
> *Duplicate policies for profit:* refers to when consumers buy multiple policies on the same house or property (such as a piece of jewelry) hoping to collect when it is destroyed or lost.
> *Fictional theft:* includes exaggerating the value of missing items.
> *Unlicensed public adjuster:* refers to a public adjuster who lacks a license and who solicits distraught homeowners during claims-settlement processes after a disaster. The trick would include the homeowner paying more than 10 percent of the settlement and paying the money upfront.
>
> Note that some of these insurance frauds are caused by insurers and some by consumers.

## Health

*Of all the types of insurance, this one is the most costly and the most vital.* Understanding who health care consumers are and how they are changing are primary concerns of health insurance companies, hospitals, nurses, doctors, pharmaceutical companies, government policy makers, and the media. Health care is one of the nation's largest industries, and insurance is a big part of it. Some of the issues related to health insurance include the rapid rise of health care spending, the diversity of health care consumers, the Internet's growing importance to health care, the growing use of alternative medicine, the aging of the population, the deinstitutionalization of medical care, growth of outpatient care, and the change in attitudes toward disability, mental health, psychiatry, and even death.

*Health care costs are rising steeply.*

Health care costs are rising steeply, and this is affecting the cost of insurance. On a yearly basis, *health care costs are increasing 20 percent faster than the general inflation rate. The cost of prescription drugs is rising more than 20 percent per year.* People can have no insurance, private health insurance, or government-linked or managed care through employers. Increasingly, employers are cutting health care benefits or raising deductibles so employees pay more before health insurance kicks in. The annual percent increase in health care costs to U.S. employers was 12 percent in 2000, 13 percent in 2001, 14 percent in 2002, and 16 percent in 2003. This progression upward shows the burden employers are under. Private health insurance (meaning not obtained through an employer) is very expensive, and difficulties generally fall into the categories of cost-related, communications-based problems of convenience and serious medical concerns.

*An average doctor visit lasts seven to ten minutes.*

The number one problem people report having with their health care plan is payment or billing for services (Paul, 2002). Another major problem is that "*more than half of all Americans are not satisfied with the availability of their doctors* and the amount of information they receive in an office visit, which now averages seven to ten minutes. . . . Fifty-two million adults now use the Internet as their primary source of health-care information" (Zuboff and Maxmin, 2002, p. 6).

A criticism of health plans is that they do not cover a particular treatment or kind of care needed or the difficulty that exists getting someone from the plan on the phone to answer questions. The bottom line is that Americans want to feel in control of their health care services, and this includes more types of self-care such as at-home diagnostics and self-monitoring of benefits (Paul, 2002). A company has

---

**Consumer Alert**

Consumers with insurance from employers may think they are fully covered, but they may not be. Increasing copayments and deductibles are often not apparent until someone gets sick or disabled. According to The Commonwealth Fund's survey of people ages 19 to 64, 13 percent of insured consumers did not fill a prescription in the previous year due to cost, and 17 percent were unable to pay medical bills (The Unraveling of Health Insurance, 2002). The shift is away from employers to the employees being more responsible for their health care, including more financially responsible. As the survey results show, people are cutting corners by not filling prescriptions or are having trouble paying bills.

the right to refuse to sell coverage if a person is in ill health or if a person provides false information on the application.

*The majority of Americans are insured under governmental or managed plans.* An example of managed care is an HMO (health maintenance organization). Employers with at least 25 employees have to offer an HMO choice. In the past a lot of people were dissatisfied with managed care, but recent polls show the public is discontented with "the system" but not with their own health care plans. So despite a general atmosphere of frustration with the health care industry and with hassles with insurance companies, in a Harris Interactive survey two-thirds of Americans gave their plan a grade of A or B and three-fourths said they would recommend their plan to someone who is healthy and 68 percent would recommend it to friends or family with a serious or chronic disease. More Medicaid than Medicare beneficiaries gave their plans low marks (Paul, 2002). About one in five Americans has either Medicare or Medicaid. **Medicare** is the federal health insurance program for people 65 or older and many people with disabilities. The two main parts are hospital insurance and medical insurance. **Medicaid** is the federal health care program for low-income people who qualify.

So *Medicare and Medicaid are government programs. They are not forms of insurance that people buy in the for-profit market.* Because Medicare is mostly for elderly people, a lot of fraud and misconception is involved—padded bills are not unusual. Box 13.3 gives common red flags. The U.S. Administration on Aging and Social Security offices look out for Medicare fraud. There has been a crackdown on people who purposely make themselves poor so the government will pay for their nursing home care. "For years, thousands of middle class and even affluent retirees—terrified that long-term health care costs could wipe out their savings—have transferred their assets to relatives in order to qualify for Medicaid, the government health plan for the poor. Their goal is to make themselves poor by Medicaid's defi-

> People like their own health-care plans, but are less happy with "the system."

---

**BOX 13.3    Common Red Flags about Medicare Fraud**

Look out if someone says

- They represent Medicare.
- They have free service or equipment.
- They need your Medicare number or Social Security Number.
- They want to tell you how you can get more out of Medicare.
- They offer free tests or exams or consultations.
- They pressure you to buy Medigap insurance or use scare tactics.
- They show up at the front door or call over the phone.

It is illegal if they

- Bill for services not rendered or equipment not received.
- Bill twice for same services.
- Misrepresent a diagnosis or the place of diagnosis to get more payment.
- Falsify documents.
- Solicit, offer, or receive kickbacks, bribes, or illegal rebates.
- Seek to defraud Medicare or the government in any way other than those previously mentioned.

nition, generally meaning they have no more than $2,000 in assets, excluding their house and their car" (Higgins, 2003, p. D1). A whole industry has sprung up helping seniors to qualify, and often it is aided by children who are doing asset transfers for sick parents. This is a form of defrauding the government, if, indeed, the elder person is not poor. Therefore, guidelines are being looked into so this is not so easy to do. It is also unfortunate that people feel they have to do this to take care of sick parents; better solutions need to be found.

## Disability Income

**Disability income insurance** pays benefits to policy holders when they are incapable of working. It can be for temporary or long-term disability and typically policies pay 60 to 80 percent of one's paycheck. Most people get this coverage through employers, but it can be bought as an individual, for example, if one is self-employed or owns a small business. The policies have elimination periods, meaning a period of time that must elapse before insurance begins. Obviously, it is linked to employment so this type of insurance does not make sense for retirees or other nonworkers. Social Security also has disability insurance. In **workers' compensation**, money is paid if a disability is due to illness or injury received on the job. The upshot of this is that if one becomes disabled there are a variety of options. Benefits usually go to the injured or ill person, but there are situations in which the benefits go to the spouses or underage children if the person dies.

Employers and unions sometimes offer disability income insurance, and if it is offered for free or low cost, it should be considered especially if one travels to high-risk parts of the world or if one performs high-risk work. Even desk work can bring injuries such as carpal tunnel syndrome so a case could be made for every worker to have disability income insurance and/or workers' compensation. To keep premiums low, an employee should reduce coverage time, put in a high deductible, lower the monthly benefit, and lengthen the elimination period.

## Life

Seventy percent of American adults have life insurance policies.

Seventy percent of U.S. adults have life insurance policies. These can be bought on your own or through employers, some employers offer, for example, a $100,000 policy for free as a perk. **Life insurance** is a contract between a policy holder and an insurer that says what sum will be paid to beneficiaries on the insured's death. Most new policies are bought by people between the ages of 25 and 44. Most buy it when they have children because life insurance is a protection for survivors. Other reasons people have life insurance are to protect or make a more secure life for a surviving spouse or an aging or disabled relative or, in some cases, to protect a business and partners or to leave money to a charity or a cause. College students without dependents generally don't need it. If an employer provides it for free or at a low-cost this is a benefit to consider.

How much is needed depends on life circumstances such as age, income, and number and ages of children. One rule of thumb is the five to seven times rule so that a person earning $30,000 a year should have life insurance in the range of $150,000 to $210,000. Someone with several young children who is the main support of the family needs more than someone whose children are grown.

The two main types of life insurance are term (for five years, ten years, etc.) or whole which has a savings feature. With term, protection expires when the con-

---

**Consumer Alert**

**Churning** is an illegal practice of encouraging insureds (consumers) to switch policies often in order to generate commissions. Insurance agents make commissions when consumers purchase a policy, especially a whole life policy. When switching policies is not in the best interest of the client and is done solely to generate more commissions, then this is considered churning, a practice disdained by the legitimate insurance industry. Multimillion dollar class action suits about churning have been brought by bilked policy holders.

If an agent offers to replace your old life insurance policy, which has a high cash value, with a new "better"one, carefully review the premium schedule, benefits, and restrictions on benefits, such as preexisting conditions. Also if a life insurance pitch comes at a time when there is no apparent need to change insurance coverage, such as a marriage, a new child, or similar life change, be cautious. Do not buy insurance from a door-to-door salesperson or sign blank insurance claims forms.

---

tract expires so with five-year term insurance an individual would have to renew to keep it going. Term is considered pure protection; in other words, it only offers insurance—not a savings feature. It costs less than whole life insurance and is therefore recommended by most personal financial experts. Whole life insurance offers savings but at a very low rate of interest; most investors could make better money elsewhere. Policies should be reviewed every few years and changed if there are major life changes such as marriage, divorce, birth or adoption of children, a new house, change in employer, promotions, and retirements and if children have left the nest.

## Long-Term Care

"Advances in medical research and technology have exploded the numbers of people who will live longer lives than at any other time in human history. New treatments are also responsible for prolonging the lives of people with chronic illness, no matter what their age" (Zuboff and Maxmin, 2002, p. 200). **Long-term care insurance (LTC)** provides benefits for nursing home, assisted living, or in-home care not covered by Medicare insurance and for other types of long-term care. For example, a severe auto accident at age 40 could lay a person up for a month or more, and long-term care insurance could help with the bills. About 40 per cent of the people receiving long-term care today are younger than 65 (Greene, 2003). However, most people buy long-term care insurance with the intention of using it in old age. Most policies have the same basic features such as covering Alzheimer's disease or if you can no longer perform two of the six following daily living activities:

Bathing

Continence

Dressing

Eating

Transferring from one location to another

Using the toilet

The policies pay for a certain amount of care. The most important feature is the dollars-per-day that the policy will cover toward eventual care. The problem is that these costs keep going up, and no one knows if and when they will need assisted living or other help. Currently costs of care are estimated at from $130–$170 per day in a nursing home. According to the Health Insurance Association of America, the average nursing-home stay is two and one-half years at a cost of $130,000 (Greene, 2003). People buy LTC because the high cost of care could wipe out any savings they have accumulated. Some of the policies cost from $1,000–$6,000 a year, depending on the age of the person and the coverage offered.

A fundamental problem is if your personal finances decrease and you cannot keep up with premiums, you could lose the policy, or you may get a check for some of the residual value depending on the state that you live in and what the policy says. Policies may have riders (add-ons), as well and one of the most important of these is a compound-inflation option. This is a desirable feature because costs keep going up as the years pass.

Who sells long-term care insurance? Many insurance agents is the answer but they vary in their skills and credentials. A person seeking a policy should look for an agent that specializes in long-term care insurance. The letters after an agent's name refers to training programs, time, and testing. For example, the credential CLTC stands for certified in long-term care. It is awarded by the Corporation on Long-Term Care and requires two classroom days or 4–6 weeks' correspondence.

Most people buy LTC in their fifties or older as a protection in old age. Although some buy it as young as in their thirties. The decision to buy it or not rests on whether it is affordable and if one thinks it will be needed because of personal health problems or the lack of children who could provide care when parents age and a number of other factors. No one knows if they will absolutely need it, although statistics indicate that *60 percent of the U.S. population will need it*. Besides providing money for care it may be sought to preserve assets for children, grandchildren, or a spouse. So the point is that it is for more than nursing home care. It could be used for assisted living, hospice, or in-home care. Most seniors want to stay in their own homes as long as possible, and LTC can help with that.

The younger you are when you purchase it, the lower the premiums will be. Medicare or private health insurance does not cover all aspects of long-term care. Medicaid covers long-term care, but an elderly person has to "spend down" assets to at or near the federal poverty level in order to qualify. Another problem is that Medicaid-approved facilities have to be used and that narrows the choices which may be far from families and friends. Women are especially vulnerable because they outlive men by an average of seven years so they may more likely need LTC or other arrangements.

---

**Consumer Alert**

LTC is a fairly new form of insurance, and regulations between states vary widely. Low income people can rarely afford it and may be better off putting money to current care or other investments. Web sites of rating services where the financial strength of companies can be checked are given in the E-Resources section. This is important to know because especially in the case of long-term care insurance the company will have to last a long time. If the insurer goes bankrupt, you could be left with little or no coverage.

---

## OVERPRICED AND UNNEEDED INSURANCE

The previous sections listed some of the major kinds of insurance that consumers buy. There are rarer kinds that for the most part are not needed these include

- Private mortgage or mortgage life insurance. It would be better to pick other forms of investing or add on to existing life insurance policies rather than taking out a new one.
- Service contracts or extended warranties (described in previous chapters).
- Separate policies versus riders. When a rider is added to an existing policy, it usually costs less than buying a whole new policy. So a new boat or motorcycle could be added to an existing policy.
- Flight insurance. Statistics show an individual can fly on an airline every day for 26,000 years before that person would be involved in a plane crash. Even then the odds are in that person's favor that he or she would survive.
- Credit insurance (covered previously, remember that lenders cannot make you buy it).
- Short-term, cash value life insurance. If a policy holder does not keep cash value (whole life) insurance for a long time, the policies are a waste of money.
- Life insurance for children. Why? Children do not have debts or dependents so they do not need life insurance.
- Cancer or "disease specific" insurance. Unless the specific disease runs in your family, you don't need it. Conventional health insurance will cover most illnesses and diseases.
- Add-ons to homeowners' insurance such as "family protection." This latter type of insurance covers victims of home invasion, child abduction, and stalking threats. The policies pay medical bills, consulting, and other expenses, but not ransom payments. A wealthy, high-profile person may need this, but for the most part this is unneeded insurance.
- Short-term medical coverage usually for someone leaving one job for another. Under the federal COBRA law, an employee's old insurance policy can follow him or her if the employer has 20 or more employees for about 18 months after the end of employment, but there is a catch. The person has to pay the whole premium so the cost of coverage is high. A single healthy person may pass on this, but someone with a family may go ahead and get it. The idea is that employer-based insurance should be less expensive than having the former employee buy it in the open market as a private individual. This may or may not be the case so a former employee should comparison shop.

What to buy and what to pass on all goes back to the beginning of the chapter and the discussion of matching insurance to a person's needs and not paying for protection that is unnecessary. In terms of overpriced insurance, studies show that the poor pay more for goods and services mostly due to a lack of creditworthiness indicated by low credit scores (Lee, 2002). So, the poor are in a disadvantaged position in the financial market including insurance. Policy makers and regulators continue to evaluate how the poor are affected in the financial market and are on the look out for discrimination. This includes procedures such as redlining (not providing services in certain areas) addressed in the previous chapter.

# YOUR RIGHTS AND RESPONSIBILITIES

## Rights

Consumers have the right to:

> Choose insurance companies and agents.
>
> Obtain fair quotes for coverage.
>
> Receive policies in a timely manner.
>
> Receive proper and timely investigations of claims.
>
> Receive payments for repairs or whatever is necessary.
>
> Buy policies free of unfair discrimination due to age, gender, occupation, marital status, national origin, or a physical handicap that does not impair, for example, ability to drive.
>
> File complaints.
>
> Receive copies of all forms and applications signed by the applicant and insurer.

## Responsibilities

Consumers are responsible for:

- Evaluating their needs and choosing the policy or contract that meets those needs.
- Shopping around and comparing costs and services.
- Watching for exclusions and limitations.
- Investigating insurance salespeople credentials, finding out about licensure.
- Reading policies and contracts and understanding what is covered.
- Keeping insurance policies and records at home, keeping copies in safe deposit boxes or with a trusted friend or attorney.
- Telling beneficiaries about the kinds and amounts of health and life insurance owned and where policies are kept.
- Reviewing coverage periodically to make sure it is still meeting needs.
- Being truthful when applying, disclosing pertinent information.
- Contacting the insurance company or agent immediately after auto accidents.
- Keeping up with premiums and reviewing all bills.

# FRAUDS AND SCAMS

Remember the old expression "Oh, what a tangled web we weave, when first we practice to deceive"? The insurance industry is rampant with frauds and scams. Insurance scams are more subtle than the snake oil salesmen of old and thus more difficult to root out. The frauds and scams in the financial area feed on greed or fear rather than a quick cure sought from patent medicines and weight reduction pills. In financial fraud, victims fall prey to promises of large returns on their money. They are susceptible to things they do not understand. The area of insurance is particularly vulnerable because it is a subject few like to think about or discuss. The chance that something bad will happen—illness, disability, theft, destruction, death—makes it all the easier to perpetuate fraud. The sources for much of the following information are from state departments of insurance and the Coalition against Insurance Fraud Report. The next section covers scams by companies, and the section after that discusses how customers defraud companies.

## By Companies

Most agents are reputable professionals who have been trained in their area of expertise. Agents take classes and pass tests to be licensed. But there are **rogue agents** who are agents that are not associated with established companies and who are engaging in illegal activities. They will sell insurance and pocket the premiums so that when people try to file a claim they found out they have been had—there is no policy and there is no money. Naturally the industry wants to root out rogue agents and drive them from business because they give the whole industry a bad name. One trick is for an agent to drain the cash value of one policy to buy a new policy with the same insurer.

Another fraud is called *failure to forward premiums.* In this case an insurance agent convinces a consumer to pay each premium by a check written directly to the agent or in cash. The agent then pockets these payments, leaving the consumer without coverage.

*Understatement of risk or "cleansheeting"* is another type of fraud. In this case the agent omits pertinent health information from a consumer's application to make a sale which might not otherwise meet the insurance company's risk-management requirements.

*Overselling* refers to selling way too much insurance to one individual. For example, in a testimony at a National Association of Insurance Commissioners meeting in Atlanta in March 2003, an Alabama attorney said that an elderly woman with a house worth $19,000 had 17 homeowner's insurance policies on it—far too much coverage for the modest house. He said that she would sign anything that was put before her and unscrupulous agents took advantage.

## By Consumers

*"Nearly one in four Americans say it is acceptable to defraud an insurance company,* according to a survey by consulting firm Accenture Ltd. The results appear to confirm the worst suspicions of insurance companies, which say fraudulent claims are costing them—and honest policyholders—billions of dollars a year. The Insurance Services Office Inc., the main provider of claims data to the industry, estimates the annual cost of fraud to insurers at $24 billion" (Oster, 2003, p. D2). The kinds of fraud consumers engage in according to the survey are

- Overstating the value of a claim to an insurance agency
- Submitting claims for items that aren't actually lost or damaged
- Submitting claims for personal injuries that did not occur

Why do people do it? Nearly half of the survey respondents said it was because people could get away with it. Others said that people needed the money or that they paid too much to insurance companies and thought it was their due. The study subjects said it was important that insurers track down deceptive claims.

Another study found that "four out of ten Americans have tried to pad an insurance bill to cover the deductible" (Solomon, 2003, p. 234).

Another type of fraud is *applicant fraud.* In this case the applicant provides false information to a life insurance company in hopes of obtaining a lower premium or to prevent the application being rejected.

Another fraud called *deceptive claims* happens when a financially strapped consumer files false claims on credit disability and health insurance policies after staging an accident and exaggerating a preexisting injury. In other words, they are faking it. Insurance companies have investigators that can prove fraud by filming claimants with bad backs hauling lumber out of trucks or working out in gyms. One of the reasons states got rid of or altered no-fault auto insurance is because people would fake their own accidents (purposely run into a tree, have a friend's car nudge their car) and claim huge repair, emotional damage, or medical expenses. Along these same lines, people have faked accidents such as slipping and falling in theme parks and at hotels and tried to sue the park or hotel. The use of more security cameras should diminish these types of cases.

## STATE DEPARTMENTS OF INSURANCE: THEIR ROLE IN CONSUMER PROTECTION

*Insurance is largely regulated by states.* The objectives of state regulators are to protect consumers and to help maintain the financial stability of the insurance industry. Regarding health insurance, "most states impose only minimal regulation on benefits and premiums. Individual policies are also underwritten, meaning that premiums vary according to an applicant's health status, age, and gender. . . . Paying more doesn't always buy more. . . . To buy your own health-insurance policy, begin by investigating those sold by at least four or five carriers in your area, interview agents, and find one who offers policies from several different companies" (Shopping for Your Own Policy, 2002). Consumers should find out how their company is rated. Consumers residing in states that set minimum standards for coverage and limit how high premiums can go tend to have better protection. If a person is turned down for health insurance, they can investigate state requirements for obtaining a policy of last resort, and low-income people should find out if they qualify for Medicaid.

For over 50 years, the National Association of Insurance Commissioners (NAIC) and the states have enacted disclosure rules defining what insurers may and may not say to consumers about a variety of things, including pricing and product features. Over the course of time, policies have become more complex, and consumer advocates are calling for more fairness and transparency in information provided by insurers to consumers.

## INVESTING: PURPOSE AND GUIDING PRINCIPLES

The chapter switches gears now away from insurance to the subject of investment. Most simply stated, *the purpose of investing is to build and maintain wealth.* People invest to feel more secure or comfortable in retirement or in midlife and to acquire funds for vacations, for children's educations, and for homes. Investing should be based on goals. **Investment** is the commitment of funds (capital) to long-term growth. Investing is an important means to getting ahead, keeping ahead of inflation, and becoming independent and self-supporting.

Serious attempts at investing start after people have stabilized their lives, meaning they have a job and can meet basic life needs and their debt is under control. Retirement plans through employers or on one's own through individual retirement accounts (IRAs) are forms of investing. A guiding principle is that the sooner you start the greater the return (money needs time to grow) and that even a modest start (like $10 a week in a savings account) is better than no start at all. In investing, one assesses risk and return. The higher the risk (uncertainty) the greater the chance for return. "Your risk tolerance is your ability or willingness to endure declines in the value of your investments while you wait for them to return a profit that will help you meet your investment goal" (Your Risk Tolerance, 2001). A widely used risk assessment question from the Federal Reserve Board's Survey of Consumer Finances (SCF) is:

> Which of the following statements comes closest to the amount of financial risk that you are willing to take when you save or make investments?
>
> 1. Substantial financial risks expecting to earn substantial returns.
> 2. Above-average financial risks expecting to earn above-average returns.
> 3. Average financial risks expecting to earn average returns.
> 4. No financial risks.

According to Sung and Hanna (1996), 45.6 percent of respondents chose "no financial risk." This is not easy to do because there are no completely risk-free investments. For example, government bonds and savings accounts may guarantee principal, but they may fall behind in keeping up with inflation. Because principal is guaranteed, these are considered safer investments compared with ones such as stocks when much or all of the principal can be lost. Jean Lown, a Utah State University professor, in an article in the *Journal of Consumer Education,* suggested that educators can help investors adopt a more realistic view of risk tolerance and investment selection based on a time horizon (e.g., how many years until retirement) for financial goals. Further, she says **volatility** (the ups and downs of a security, commodity, or the stock market) should be of little concern to the long-term investor.

To be a successful investor a person has to:

- Keep perspective, stay in through the ups and downs
- Keep investing, even if small amounts
- Believe in the growth of business (stocks and corporate bonds) or the strength of government (bonds)

Some investments provide interest or **dividends** which are distributions of money from companies or government to investors. Most typically, dividends are paid twice a year and can come from stocks or bonds. Sometimes stocks and bonds can be bought in such a way (usually directly, e.g., bonds from the federal government) that there are no fees for transactions, and other times there are fees that vary greatly. Charges for transactions should be weighed against services rendered and probable returns. A consideration in investing is the tax implications of certain types of investing, such as tax-deferred retirement savings plans and municipal bonds or municipal bond funds.

**Consumer Alert**

Every investment has advantages and disadvantages. There are no "magic" investments that fit all of the people, all of the time. There is little hope of more than average returns without extraordinary luck or knowledge and of course, risk. A realistic approach works best, basing investments on goals, acceptable levels of risk, and one's personality and time horizon (how many years until the money will be needed). Knowledge is power. Find out everything you can about a potential investment from reliable sources.

Another guiding principle is that investors should **diversify**, meaning spreading money over several categories of investments such as bonds, blue-chip stocks, small and large companies, foreign shares, real estate, and real-estate investment trusts. In this way an investor will have a balanced **portfolio** which is a combined set of holdings to increase diversification and to reduce risk. At any given time, some of the holdings will be in favor and some will be out of favor, but in the long run this strategy should work versus putting all one's money into a single investment. To summarize, the least risk is involved in cash, government savings bonds, money market funds, and CDs. The most risk is associated with speculative investments such as options, commodities, and junk bonds. The Securities and Exchange Commission is a good source for information about investing wisely and avoiding fraud. In the next sections, the most widely used types of investing are discussed along with potential frauds and scams.

## TYPES OF INVESTMENTS

### Stocks

As noted in the introduction, more than half of Americans own stock. **Stocks** represent ownership in a company so that if you own one share of Microsoft stock you own part of Microsoft. Is the stock market rational (meaning reasonable, predictable)? The answer to this is no, it rises and falls and it is very difficult to predict how well an individual stock will do. It is useful to know a company's financial history and future prospects as a guide in choosing well. The best advice is to buy and hold, ride out the ups and downs, invest in quality companies, and keep transaction (buying and selling) costs low. Over the last 50 years, stocks have far exceeded inflation, but in the short run investing can be risky.

Investors may engage in **socially responsible investing**, meaning they invest in stocks that directly express their values. For example, they will not invest in companies involved in alcohol or tobacco or who have labor practices they do not believe in. "They seek to influence corporate decision-making by including social and ethical criteria in their investment choices. According to the Social Investment Forum, a nonprofit organization that promotes social investing, the total level of socially and environmentally responsible investing in the United States grew by 8 percent, from $2.16 trillion in 1999 to $2.34 trillion in 2001, despite a significant stock market decline during that period" (Zuboff and Maxmin, 2002, p. 110).

**Consumer Alert**

Millions of dollars worth of consumer lawsuits, for everything from faulty cell phones to stock fraud, are filed each year, but consumers are not always aware that money is owed to them. *More than half of people who are eligible for compensation never follow up* (Kalis, 2003). Fraud happens when companies charge substantial finder's fees (money to find out if you should be getting a consumer lawsuit settlement) when in reality you can check yourself for free. One place to look is *www.bigclassaction.com* for the latest settlements. Go to the "class action settlements" link. A site that charges for claim information is *www.classactionamerica.com*. Announcements of settlements are often given in the newspapers or information can be obtained from law enforcement agencies in your state. An example of a Web site that focuses on shareholder suits is *Securities.stanford.edu.* Be forewarned that the gains may be small. For example, one settlement had a maximum of $80 award for anyone who leased a phone from AT&T going back to 1984.

## Bonds

**Bonds** are investments involving the lending of money. If you have a bond for a corporation you have lent money to that corporation to build a new factory, for example.

Bonds can be for corporations or for government, state, local, or federal as in U.S. Savings Bonds. When the stock market took a downturn in the late 1990s and early 2000s, many investors switched to bonds because generally:

- They are considered safer than stocks.
- In many cases, the rate of return is guaranteed.
- There may be the added benefit of twice a year dividends paid to the bond-holder, so the bonds serve as a source of income.

Government bonds are more secure than corporate bonds. Bonds from corporations are rated, and these ratings should be used as a guide. The three types of U.S. Savings bonds are Series HH, Series EE, and Series I. For information about these go to **www.savingsbonds.gov.** By going to this Web site, you can buy bonds online direct from the government, or you can buy savings bonds at local banks or through your employer.

## Mutual Funds

American investors are increasingly turning to mutual funds to save for retirement and other financial goals. At last count, 93 million Americans owned mutual funds. There are 5,947 stock and bond mutual funds to choose from and they represent 21 percent of U.S. stocks. **Mutual funds** are groups of investments. If you buy one share of a mutual fund such as Capital Growth Fund, you are buying a small amount of several different holdings, thus spreading the risk which is a positive feature of mutual funds. Funds come in different types such as international, value, or growth. Growth is the largest category. Growth funds focus on stocks that have the potential for large capital gains. The name of the fund implies the type of fund that it is so that the Capital Growth Fund would be an example of a growth mutual fund. In 2001, rulings were passed calling for more alignment of fund names with fund holdings and requiring funds to include after-tax return data. Since each fund has to have a unique name, the names can get creative, including the Rydex Velocity 100 Fund, the Columbia Thermostat Fund, and the Amidex Cancer Innovations and Health-care Mutual Fund. Investors purchase fund shares from the fund itself or through a broker for the fund.

The main advantages are

- *Affordability:* some funds set relatively low dollar amounts for initial purchases and subsequent monthly purchases or both.
- *Diversification:* spreading investments across a wide range of companies and industry sectors.
- *Liquidity:* funds can be redeemed although there may be fees and charges at redemption time.
- *Professional management:* money managers research, select, and monitor funds.

Disadvantages include

- Front-end or management fees
- Taxes
- Lack of control (managers choose what stocks are in funds, not investors)

Also mutual funds are not guaranteed or insured by the FDIC or any other government agency—even if bought at a bank. A person can lose money investing in mutual funds, and past performance is not a totally reliable indicator of future performance. However, past performance is one factor to consider, it shows a pattern over time. The Securities and Exchange Commission offers a Mutual Fund Cost

---

**Consumer Alert**

Investment con artists thrive during times of uncertainty. Low-interest rates and poor investment returns in conventional markets, drive risk-taking consumers to look for something other than traditional investments. They are looking for excitement, being part of the action including investing in defense industries. Do not play this game. Protect yourself by:

1. Hanging up on aggressive cold-callers promoting investments in mutual funds, foreign currencies, precious metals such as gold, platinum, and silver, or oil and gas schemes.
2. Ignoring tips about tiny companies with great growth potential, especially those involved in war industries or bioterrorism.
3. Contacting state securities regulators or checking with the National Association of Securities Dealers (800 288 9999) when you suspect fraud.
4. Requesting written information about investments. Promotions with the words "safe," "secure," or "guaranteed" are usually rip-offs.

When it comes to investing, being rash or feeling pressured are warning signs. Don't do anything in a hurry. Use common sense, and do not succumb to confusion and fear. An example is that after the anthrax-laced mail tragedy in 2001, con artists began selling fake anthrax detectors and security enhancing technologies and stock in phony technology companies. Hucksters are surprisingly quick and resourceful at dreaming up schemes overnight.

Calculator to compare the costs of owning different funds before an individual makes a purchase (see E-Resources). Another source for mutual fund information is Morningstar.com.

## Real Estate Including Real Estate Investment Trusts

**Real estate** refers to a piece of land and everything related to it including the houses, landscaping, fencing, plus the right to the airspace above and the earth below (with limits, of course). In chapter 11, we covered how to be a better consumer of housing, including advice on buying homes. This chapter discusses real estate more from an investment angle. Seventy percent of American households own their own homes which is a type of **direct investment**. Other examples include owning apartment buildings, raw land, and other houses. One of the main disadvantages of real estate over other types of investments is illiquidity which means it is difficult to turn quickly into cash. **Indirect investments** refer to investing with a group of investors to own **real estate investment trusts (REITs)** and apartment buildings or office buildings. REITs are traded on the major stock exchanges so you can buy a share in them the same way that you can buy a share in a stock or mutual fund.

Owning a primary residence has tax advantages. The tax advantages of second homes or vacation homes are less attractive. **Time shares** are apartments, units, or homes usually for vacation purposes with several owners.

REITs are sold through stock brokerage firms or over the counter and are listed in *The Wall Street Journal* and other financial news sources. One of the main advantages is the pooling of money with others to buy into a bigger investment than one normally could. Another advantage is the professional management so that one could invest in apartments without having landlord worries. With any investment there is a risk of loss and tax consequences.

---

**Consumer Alert**

Do not buy time shares or vacation homes without investigating all the costs, rules, fees, taxes, and ease of resale. Many people have had trouble selling time shares and wish they had rented instead of tying up their money. Consumers are more satisfied if they purchase time shares in companies with cooperative arrangements across the country because this opens up more choices of places to visit and the types of units available. Remember that all buildings age—the model brand new time share unit will not look so good after a few years of wear and tear.

---

**Consumer Alert**

REITs fluctuate with the ups and downs of the market and with the quality of the investment. While some parts of the country are having marvelous success with new office buildings and shopping malls, others are overbuilt so care should be taken in selecting REITs. There are about 300 REITs that are traded publicly on the New York Stock Exchange.

### Buying a Franchise: Benefits, Responsibilities, Loss Potential

Another form of investing is franchises. Television infomercials and advertisements in newspapers suggest there is easy money to be had in franchises. *They play on people's dreams of being entrepreneurs,* their own boss. Although franchises can be legitimate such as a franchise for a McDonald's or Subway restaurant, many are investments with little or no guarantee of success. If you have never heard of the franchise before, this is a warning sign to slow down.

A **franchise** is a privilege to operate a business to sell the franchisor's products or services in a given area. This may or may not be an exclusive right. In other words, you could be the only franchisee at a certain intersection or the only one in a whole city. Arrangements are formalized in a franchisee agreement, a contract between the franchisee and the franchisor. The pro to this type of arrangement is that investment risk is reduced by being associated with an established company. Also the franchisor will often provide the right to use the company name for a limited amount of time and assistance, initial training, marketing, and so on. There will probably be ongoing technical support and training. The down side of being associated with an established company is that the franchisee has to conform to their standards and essentially he or she gives up a lot of individual control. In exchange for the name and the services, the franchisee will have to pay fees such as an initial franchise fee and other expenses (this can run from thousands to several hundred thousands of dollars) that include rent, building and equipment, signs, insurance, and licenses. Over time, the franchisee will pay royalty payments to continue to use the name. So, the startup costs are very high, and since most businesses fail in the first two years, many people lose money.

Before investing, the potential franchisee should consider their goals, abilities, experience, and how much this investment is going to cost as well as the current strength and potential growth of the parent company. Is the product or service in demand? What is the competition like? A common type of franchise is a janitorial service franchise. Before investing, find out how businesses, schools, or government agencies in your area hire janitorial services. If you had a franchise, would there be a demand for it? How much are locals willing to pay? Often figures given by franchisors are national and may be far higher than what you could charge locally.

Before attending a franchise exposition, investors should know how much they have to invest and what type of business is the best for them. Before investing, the franchisee should get a copy of the franchisor's disclosure document. Under the Federal Trade Commission's Franchise Rule, a potential franchisee must receive the document at least ten business days before being asked to sign any contract or paying any money to the franchisor. Things to look out for include business background, litigation history, bankruptcy, costs, restrictions, terminations, training, advertising, current and former franchisees, earnings potential, and financial history. Besides one's own research, before investing potential franchisees should talk with attorneys with franchise experience, accountants, banks, the Better Business Bureau, government departments that regulate the particular business (e.g., provide licenses), and the FTC. A bank or other financial institution can give an unbiased view of a franchise opportunity and can obtain a Dunn and Bradstreet report on a franchisor. If ever there was an area where the phrase "investigate before you invest" is true, it is in the franchise industry.

## All That Glitters: Precious Gems, Metals, and Collectibles

Diamonds are the most regulated gems and the ones most likely to hold their value. Most come from Botswana and Russia, but Canada is moving up the ranks. Canada has three diamond mines and hopes to have 12 percent of the world's rough gem–quality diamonds by the end of the decade. One of the questions is, Will consumers care where their diamonds come from? Some engaged couples have driven to Canada to purchase certified Canadian diamonds. Canada's diamond mines have strict environmental guidelines and pay miners well which makes them more politically correct. Some jewelers say people won't care about origin, but Oren Sofer, a New York wholesaler, says, "If you can put water in a bottle and sell it under a brand name, then trust me, you can brand a diamond. It just takes time" (Baglole, 2003, p. B1). Consider as examples Swiss watches, Idaho potatoes, and French wines—we associate certain products with places and other times we do not have a clue. How do you know the diamond is from Canada? Each diamond comes with a certificate of where it was mined, cut, and polished, and the certificate has a serial number engraved by laser on the diamond. A microscopically laser-engraved polar bear is sometimes put on larger Canadian diamonds.

Rubies are mined in Burma and sapphires from Tanzania, Madagascar, and Sri Lanka and flown into Thailand where they are sorted and treated for export.

The most precious metal available to consumers is platinum, followed by gold and silver. Gold is produced primarily in Russia and South Africa. It can be purchased as gold coins, gold certificates, gold mutual funds, bullion accounts, and stock shares in existing companies. People have lost and gained fortunes from investing in diamond and gold mines; it is not for amateurs. The price of precious metals usually rises when inflation rises and falls when inflation falls, but international events can disturb this. International incidents tend to drive up the price of gold, but it fluctuates widely. Before becoming an investor in precious metals, an investor should know the current price per ounce and the ups and downs in the last several years.

Over a third of Americans collects something. Collectibles include everything from books, stamps, coins, and athletic shoes to lunchboxes with cartoon characters on them to priceless antiques. In collectibles, knowledge is crucial, and this includes trusting one's source or dealer. There is no substitute for education and knowing prices and quality. Special care should be taken when buying valuables at auctions or over the Internet (see the next section). Generally speaking, gems, metals, and collectibles should be purchased first because the owner likes them or could use them and secondly as an investment.

Over a third of Americans collects something.

## Online Investing: Profit, Gloss, or Both?

The Internet has opened up a whole new world of investment opportunities—some legitimate and some not. Many of the schemes are the same that have been played out for centuries only in a glossy new format. Beware of promoters who make their companies look like venerable old established Wall Street firms. Look out for the usual promises of high profits in short amounts of time. Particular to the Internet may be a Web site asking for you to submit personal financial information online such as income level, bank accounts (never give pin numbers or account numbers), Social Security numbers (likewise, guard this), and other personal information. Read the site's privacy policy and consider the source. Do not invest in

---

**Consumer Alert**

Gemstone scandals include using heat treatments and additives to turn lesser sapphires and rubies into copies of better gems. In Chanthaburi, Thailand, the market was suddenly flooded with padparadschas—a rare orange-pink sapphire. Gem collectors swarmed in, some paying as high as $4,000 a carat, more than ten times the going rate. After a gem alert, the prices started falling. U.S. scientists charged that the gems had been altered with coloring agents which breaks no law but violates the ethics of the trade. "The degree to which gems are treated has spun out of control," says Stuart Robertson, research director of Gemworld, a U.S. company. He says, "Unless treatments are reined in . . . and disclosure taken seriously, the market will drop. . . . All color traits [that buyers] are led to believe occur in nature are being produced in ovens. All of the romance is taken out of the stone" (Mazurkewich, 2003, p. B1).

---

offshore investments or tax-free investments. Get a second opinion and learn about tax implications of offshore investments. For information about Internet investment sources, see the E-Resources section.

## Annuities: Supplementary Retirement Income

A common myth is that once one saves for retirement the need for financial planning is over. Nothing could be further from the truth. While in retirement investments have to keep growing to keep up with inflation. Often near retirement one considers **annuities** which are contracts in which the insurer promises the insured a series of periodic payments. Annuities are a type of investment that provides investors with tax-deferred growth. They do not limit how much can be contributed each year. They come in several forms, including fixed annuities that guarantee fixed payments for life or a specific number of years to variable annuities that provide returns based on the performance of the assets in the annuities. There are different payout options from lump sums to more periodic sums. They are purchased directly from insurance companies or indirectly from stock brokers. Fixed annuities are invested in financial securities which pay a fixed interest rate, like certificates of deposit, bonds, and treasury securities (safe investments). Money in variable annuities is more likely to be put into stocks and mutual funds. An investor could put money into both fixed and variable annuities and thus spread the risk and return.

Fixed annuities are being sold in record numbers as baby boomers retire. They can be an especially good hedge in a volatile market; still confusion, fraud, and deception are rampant. Consumers should use caution before buying annuities, making sure they understand what they are getting, the amount of risk involved, and how much it is going to cost. Annual expense fees vary by product. The major disadvantage of annuities is illiquidity, money is locked in for a long time.

## INVESTMENT SWINDLES: FEAR, GREED, AND EXCITEMENT

Investment swindles abound because people are drawn to high and quick returns on their money. They fall victim to various schemes and scams that can be nationally or internationally based.

Warning signs include

"A once in a lifetime opportunity"

"A secret of the wealthy"

"Invest now, quickly, low-risk, short-term offer"

"Only a few will be invited to participate"

"Get in on the ground floor"

"Assurances of display racks for things like greeting cards or vending machines for candy"

"Approved by a celebrity or a doctor or the IRS or IRA approved"

"The market is moving, don't be left behind"

You will notice from this list that a lot of the financial scams sound a lot like the come-on phrases used in weight-loss scams. The swindlers prey on the same emotions of fear, greed, and excitement. Swindlers also called con artists and fraudsters cheat people out of their money. They advertise in legitimate sources such as *USA Today* and campus newspapers.

## Multilevel Marketing Plans: Legal and Illegal Pyramid Including Ponzi Schemes

**Multilevel marketing plans** are ways of selling goods and services through distributors. The plans promise that if someone signs up as a distributor they will receive commissions from the person's own sales and from those of people who are recruited to become distributors. The Federal Trade Commission cannot tell anyone which plans are legal and which are illegal—you must decide yourself. They say that if a plan offers to pay commissions for recruiting new distributors to watch out. Most states outlaw this practice which is called **pyramiding**. It is legal to pay commissions for retail sales of goods or services, but not for recruiting new distributors. Why are they so cautious about pyramiding? Because in the past plans such as these invariably collapse when new distributors cannot be recruited—the people who begin the scam (at the top of the pyramid) often benefit—but the late recruits lose their money. An example of a pyramid scheme in the past was one in which an "investor" gave $100 to become a member which was passed on to the

---

**Consumer Alert**

Be wary of the sales pitches and products sold on infomercials which are half hour or longer, as well as radio and television commercials for gold, real estate, and other forms of investing. If it sounds too good to be true, it probably is. Common techniques are endorsements by actors and actresses (many of whom later regretted getting involved), motivational speakers, and by "satisfied" past investors. Often they are selling sets of 12 tapes or videos and books or asking $1,000 per person for an inperson investment seminar "coming to your area, soon!" Is someone really going to watch 12 videos about an investment technique and once past the first video, how much can one say that is new and original?

---

BOX 13.4    The Federal Trade Commission's Web Site Suggests That a Person Consider These Tips before Investing in Multilevel Marketing Plans

1.  Avoid any plan that includes commissions for recruiting additional distributors. It may be an illegal pyramid.
2.  Beware of plans that ask new distributors to purchase expensive inventory. These plans can collapse quickly—and also may be thinly disguised pyramids.
3.  Be cautious of plans that claim you will make money through continued growth of your "downline"—the commissions on sales made by new distributors you recruit—rather than through sales of products you make yourself.
4.  Beware of plans that claim to sell miracle products or promise enormous earnings. Just because a promoter of a plan makes a claim doesn't mean it's true! Ask the promoter of the plan to substantiate claims with hard evidence.
5.  Beware of shills—"decoy" references paid by a plan's promoter to describe their fictional success in earning money through the plan.
6.  Don't pay or sign any contracts in an "opportunity meeting" or any other high-pressure situation. Insist on taking your time to think over a decision to join. Talk it over with your spouse, a knowledgeable friend, an accountant, or a lawyer.
7.  Do your homework! Check with your local Better Business Bureau and state attorney general about any plan you're considering—especially when the claims about the product or your potential earnings seem too good to be true.

president of the scheme and then the investor had to sign up two more people and collect their $100. After ten people were recruited, the investor would become a president and form a new pyramid. The problem is finding new recruits to keep the money flow going. Pyramid schemes exist worldwide. Box 13.4 gives a list of sales pitches to avoid.

**Ponzi schemes** are a kind of pyramid scheme involving enticing come-ons that offer to make huge profits from a small investment in a very short time (Figure 13.1). They are named after Charles A. Ponzi, a dapper five-foot-two Italian immigrant, who in 1920 raked in an estimated $15 million in eight months by persuading tens of thousands of Bostonians that he had unlocked the secret to easy wealth (Darby, 1998). Ponzi claimed to have found a way to profit by speculating in international postal reply coupons, a form of prepaid return postage used in foreign correspondence. The first round of investors made money, and at the height of his success he had offices from Maine to New Jersey. The later recruits lost everything and half-a-dozen banks crashed. The problem was that there was no actual investing going on, just shuffling money from new investors to old ones. Ponzi was offering 50 percent interest in 90 days. Later he shortened the investment period to 45 days—no wonder people joined up, but these kinds of returns should raise any thinking person's suspicions.

Modern-day Ponzi swindlers explain losses by telling people that investments went sour and other times the swindlers just disappear. Ponzi schemes involve the idea that something is for sale whether it is coupons, foreign real estate, or race horses. *Legitimate multilevel plans involve the selling of actual products that one can see in-person and examine,* such as clothing, home furnishings, cookware, and cosmetics. These plans involve in-home or at workplace sales that do not differ too much from conventional store sales other than sellers are given incentives of free products or deep discounts on products and that any money they make is based

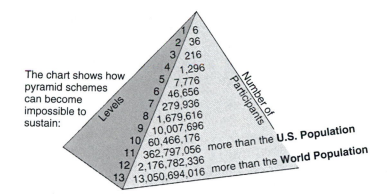

The chart shows how pyramid schemes can become impossible to sustain:

Levels / Number of Participants

| 1 | 6 |
| 2 | 36 |
| 3 | 216 |
| 4 | 1,296 |
| 5 | 7,776 |
| 6 | 46,656 |
| 7 | 279,936 |
| 8 | 1,679,616 |
| 9 | 10,007,696 |
| 10 | 60,466,176 |
| 11 | 362,797,056 more than the **U.S. Population** |
| 12 | 2,176,782,336 more than the **World Population** |
| 13 | 13,050,694,016 |

**Figure 13.1**   Ponzi scheme. (Courtesy of the U.S. Securities and Exchange Commission.)

on commission rather than salaries, for the most part. Examples of legitimate multi-level plans are Avon and Amway. As a customer you can purchase merchandise, as opposed to pyramid or Ponzi schemes where you walk away with nothing plus having to endure the hassle of trying to recruit new members.

## How to Avoid Swindles

The main ways to avoid swindles are to use common sense and to ask questions. Research is by far the best protection. Find the investment that meets your needs and goals, then shop around for companies and choices. Double-check the source and the seller. It is important to keep detailed records. Avoid high-pressure tactics

---

**BOX 13.5    Investment-Related Frauds to Avoid**

Coupon scams
Get-rich quick and self-employment schemes
Gifting clubs
Hoaxes aimed at the elderly or minority groups
International lottery scams
Investing in rare coins or stamps
Chain Letters*
Medical billing-at-home scams
Online investment opportunities
Patent scams—have an invention?
Publish your own book (for a price)
Work-at-home schemes
Learn-at-home schemes (is the school legitimate?)

Check out the source, the company's background, talk with previous owners or investors besides the ones the company recommends.

*These are violations of the mail fraud statute and can carry prison sentences and fines. Report chain letters (especially those involving money schemes or threats) to the U.S. Postal Service if the letter was received in the mail. They will go after the starters of the letters—not the recipients. See *www.usps.gov* for details.

---

and seek advice from attorneys, accountants, and banks as well as government agencies and consumer watchdog organizations. Do not be taken in by television infomercial hype or late night commercials when your sales resistance may be low. The Federal Trade Commission is a leader in alerting the public to investment fraud. Box 13.5 gives a list of types of frauds to avoid.

# SUMMARY

Hopefully, this chapter has provided a start toward understanding insurance and investments and the possible deceptions thereof. Those who wish to stay ahead of inflation (rising prices) need to invest, but they also need to protect what they have. Insurance buys protection for loved ones and assets such as homes and cars. It is a financial arrangement wherein individuals are concerned about potential hazards so they pay premiums (payments) to insurers who reimburse them in the case of loss or injury. Policies have different components, including exclusions. An example of an exclusion is excluding car insurance claims stemming from nuclear explosions or radioactive fallout.

Nearly all insurance is sold through agents. The trend is to buy insurance over the Internet. Group plans usually cost less than plans sold to individuals. Health insurance is the most expensive and the most vital, yet with growing costs many individuals and their families do not have health insurance. Employers are the main source of health insurance. The cost of providing health care costs rose from 12 percent in 2000 to 16 percent in 2004. Most Americans have either a government plan such as Medicaid or Medicare or a managed plan. To protect valuable possessions such as an engagement ring, art, or antiques, a homeowner may want to add an endorsement or rider to a basic homeowners' insurance policy. Life insurance is a contract between the policy holder and the insured. Some types of automobiles are less expensive to insure than others. Most states require liability coverage for vehicles. Seven states have no-fault auto insurance. In general, the poor are in a disadvantaged position in the insurance marketplace.

Today more and more employees are being asked to make investment decisions. Consumers are actively looking for ways to invest so that their money grows and lasts their lifetime. Investments are used to build or maintain wealth. They involve risk and return and should be based on goals. A guiding principle is that the greater the risk the higher the potential return. Diversification refers to reducing the risk by spreading investments around to different categories like bonds, blue-chip stocks, small and large companies, mutual funds, real estate, and real-estate investment trusts. Stocks represent ownership in a company whereas bonds are loans to the government or to companies. Mutual funds are groups of stocks or bonds. They are owned by 93 million Americans. Other forms of investing such as real estate, real estate investment trusts, franchises, gems, precious metals, collectibles and annuities were discussed in the chapter. Diamonds come from Botswana, Canada, and Russia. Gem scandals exist when rubies and sapphires are colored or treated in some way to imitate more expensive stones. Gold is mined in Russia and South Africa. When the world becomes less stable, investors often rush to buy precious gems and metals especially gold, but careful investors have an accurate knowledge of current and past prices and ride out the ups and the downs. Although there are legitimate precious-metals investment opportunities, this area tends to be risky and inappropriate for beginning investors.

Investors should be suspect of unknown companies that pop up overnight with new cures or security devices. Web-based technologies hold great potential for providing investment information.

Multilevel marketing plans are a way of selling goods or services through distributors. Some are legal, some are illegal. Pyramiding is prohibited. It is a type of multi-level marketing wherein most people lose money except for the people who started the plan. The Better Business Bureau is a useful source for checking into the complaint record of local businesses and of franchise opportunities. They can report if any consumers have complained about a company's products, services, or personnel.

The Federal Trade Commission and the Securities and Exchange Commission are sources of information on investments and ways to avoid frauds. The FTC works for the consumer to prevent fraudulent, deceptive, and unfair business practices in the marketplace. The SEC works specifically to prevent investment fraud.

# KEY POINTS

1. The primary purpose of insurance is protection. Most health insurance comes from employers or government programs such as Medicare and Medicaid.
2. Not everyone needs life insurance. The ones that do usually have dependents.
3. Term insurance is less expensive than whole life insurance.
4. Life insurance needs increase in midlife and decrease in old age.
5. Life insurance policies cannot be canceled because of an insured's poor health.
6. Credit insurance protects a loan or mortgage if a person cannot make their payments.
7. Homeowners' insurance pays to repair or rebuild a home and replace personal possessions.
8. Long-term care insurance provides for nursing homes, assisted living, hospice, and in-home care.
9. The purpose of investing is to build and maintain wealth. Successful investors are in it for the long term.
10. More than half of Americans own stock.
11. There is no one miracle, foolproof investment that fits everyone all of the time.
12. Con artists take advantage of times of confusion and fear by promoting bogus investment scams. Investors are vulnerable when traditional investment returns have dipped. Low interest rates and poor investment returns drive potential investors into uncertain markets—they take chances that they otherwise would not.
13. Socially responsible investing is based on the investor's values and beliefs of supporting or not supporting certain types of industries or business practices.
14. Franchises should be thoroughly investigated before investing.
15. Pyramid investment schemes, a type of speculation, are illegal. Ponzi schemes are a type of pyramid scheme.

## KEY TERMS

adjuster
annuities
bonds
churning
deductibles
disability income
    insurance
direct investment
diversify
dividends
endorsement
exclusions
exposures
franchise
indirect investment

insurance
investment
liability insurance
life insurance
long-term care insurance
    (LTC)
Medicaid
Medicare
multilevel marketing
    plans
mutual funds
perils
Ponzi schemes
portfolio
property insurance

pyramiding
real estate
real estate investment
    trusts (REITs)
rogue agents
socially responsible
    investing
stocks
time shares
uninsured motorist
    coverage
volatility
workers' compensation

## DISCUSSION QUESTIONS

1. One in four Americans, according to a survey, say it is acceptable to defraud an insurance company. Why would people say that? What is your opinion about falsely taking money from an insurance company?
2. Why do you think survey polls show that Americans are satisfied with their own health care plans, but critical of managed care in general?
3. The famous philosopher George Santayana (1863–1952) said, "Nonsense is so good only because common sense is so limited." Considering this saying, why do you think so many people fall prey to scams and frauds? List five financial phrases or scams that attract investors.
4. Why do people have collections? Do you or any of your friends collect anything? If so, what is it and how did the collection start? How can someone tell if a collectible is correctly priced?
5. Using the E-Resources section below, select one Web site and report on what it contains regarding insurance, investments, or frauds thereof.

## E-RESOURCES

| Insurance Sites: | Service Provided |
| --- | --- |
| Quotesmith www.quotesmith.com | Instant quotes for all kinds of insurance |

| | |
|---|---|
| InsWeb.com | Instant quotes for car insurance |
| Ecoverage www.ecoverage.com | Instant quotes for most types of policies |
| Insurance Information Institute www.iii.org/ | Explains how to cut costs |
| Insurance Regulatory Information Network www.irin.org | General information on the industry and links to state departments of insurance |
| American Lung Association www.lungusa.org | Data and statistics on deaths from lung disease, including asthma-related deaths |
| National Association of Insurance Commissioners www.naic.org | Consumer information on insurance NAIC is a voluntary organization of the chief insurance regulatory officials of the 50 states, DC, and four U.S. territories. Example of publication is "A Shoppers Guide to Long Term Care Insurance" |

Web sites of rating systems of the financial strength of insurance companies

A.M. Best Co.
www.ambest.com

Fitch Investors Services Inc.
www.fitchibca.com

Moody's Investor Service Inc.
www.moodys.com

Standard & Poor's Insurance Rating Service
www.standardandpoors.com

Weiss Ratings Inc.
www.weissratings.com

Investment information including Internet investments

| | |
|---|---|
| Federal Trade Commission www.ftc.gov | Provides information on investment frauds and scams |
| Securities and Exchange Commissionin www.sec.gov | Go to Investor Information section of Web site for formation about investing wisely and avoiding fraud |
| North American Securities Administrators www.nasaa.org | |
| Commodity Futures Trading Commission www.cftc.gov | |
| National Association of Securities Dealers www.nasd.com | |

| | |
|---|---|
| National Association of Investors Corporation www.better-investing.org | |
| Employee Benefit Research Institute www.ebri.org | |
| American Savings Education Council www.asec.org | |
| InvestorGuide www.investorguide.com | |
| InvestorWords www.investorwords.com | |
| The Motley Fool www.fool.com | General investing advice |
| Morningstar www.morningstar.com | Information on mutual funds |
| Alliance for Investor Education www.investoreducation.org | |
| The Online Investor www.theonlineinvestor.com | |
| National Fraud Information Center www.fraud.org | |
| Small Business Administration www.sba.gov | |

## REFERENCES

Baglole, J. (April 17, 2003). Political correctness by the carat. *Wall Street Journal,* pp. B1 and B3.

Darby, M. (December 1998). In Ponzi we trust. *Smithsonian* magazine.

Greene, K. (March 24, 2003). Buying a security blanket. *Wall Street Journal Reports,* pp. R1 and R3.

Higgins, M. (February 25, 2003). Getting poor on purpose. *Wall Street Journal,* p. D1.

Kalis, L. (February 18, 2003). Tracking consumer suits. *Wall Street Journal,* p. D1.

Lee, J. (2002). The poor in the financial market: Changes in the use of financial products, institutions, and services from 1995 to 1998. *Journal of Consumer Policy, 25,* 203–31.

Lown, J. (2001/2002). Educating consumers about investment risk. *Journal of Consumer Education, 19/20,* 1–8.

Mazurkewich, K. (April 17, 2003). Gemstone scandals. *Wall Street Journal,* pp. B1 and B3.

Oster, C. (February 12, 2003). Insurance-fraud survey confirms industry worries. *Wall Street Journal,* p. D2.

Oster, C. (April 8, 2003). Car insurers get into the repair business. *Wall Street Journal,* p. D1.

Paul, P. (July/August 2002). Managed care. *American Demographics,* p. 24.

Shopping for your own policy. (September 2002). *Consumer Reports,* pp. 38–41.

Solomon, M. (2003). *Conquering consumerspace.* New York: AMACOM.

Unraveling of health insurance, the. (July 2002). *Consumer Reports,* pp. 48–49.

What a difference the car makes. (October 2002). *Consumer Reports,* p. 22.

Whitehouse, K. (March 6, 2003). Is that Picasso covered by your home insurance? *Wall Street Journal,* p. D1.

Your risk tolerance. (2001). http://personal.vanguard.com/educ/inveduc.html. Select: Course 4: The basics of asset allocation: Your risk tolerance.

Zuboff, S., and J. Maxmin. (2002). *The support economy.* New York: Viking.

# PART 5

# Emerging Consumer Issues and the Global Perspective

# Identity Theft, Privacy Protection, Emerging Consumer Issues, At-Risk Consumers, and Developing a Global Perspective

*There is much of the past that is in the present, so also there is much of the present that will be in the future.*
**John Kenneth Galbraith**

## Learning Objectives

1. Describe the four drives impacting consumer behavior.
2. Discuss identity theft and privacy protection.
3. Know the federal agencies involved in resolving identity theft.
4. Discuss current consumer issues, at-risk consumers, and scams.
5. Explain globalization, the global perspective, and global ethics.

## INTRODUCTION

Controversy has always been part of consumer economics, and there is every indication that the future holds more of the same. Many of the controversies will surround the use and abuse of the Internet—the possibilities and the potential problems are endless. "E-commerce is to the Information Revolution what the railroad was to the Industrial Revolution—a totally new, totally unprecedented, totally unexpected development. And like the railroad 70 years ago, e-commerce is creating a new and distinct boom, rapidly changing the economy, society, and politics" (Drucker, 2002, p. 12). E-commerce has had the effect of eliminating geography or distance from the consumer-market exchange. "From a consumerism perspective, the Internet is more than a communication mechanism: it is an aid to consumer empowerment. The Internet has roles to play in each of the three stages of consumption: pre-purchase, purchase, and post-purchase" (Rha et al., 2001/2002, p. 61). Making decisions and choices after careful consideration of all that is available is not feasible. So how do consumers narrow the selection and in the process avoid as much fraud as possible? Unfortunately protecting oneself in the marketplace is becoming more and more difficult. Identity theft is the fastest growing crime in America. In 2000, the number of victims nationwide was estimated between 500,000 and 700,000. In 2003, the number was over a million and in 2004 estimates ran as high as 2 million. The good news is that prosecution of identity thieves is easier now than in the past due to a rash of laws, the work of law enforcement agents and bankers and other financial experts such as those in the credit industry, and, most important, the enlightened awareness of the public.

The essence of modern consumer economics is its eclectic approach. This chapter begins with a description of four drives affecting consumer behavior and proceeds with a discussion of identity theft and privacy protection. It then moves on to the special consumer needs of children and the elderly. The chapter also covers emerging consumer issues, including specific problems with gift cards and telephone services as well as broader global and environmental issues. It wraps up with a retrospective on the book and the consumer movement in general. What have we learned? Where are we going? Even though consumer fraud has been with us since the beginning of trade and exchange, there are always new wrinkles, new swindlers, and new issues. By this time in the course and the book, you should be far less gullible. The money and heartache that you will save and the increased peace of mind is beyond price, and in the process your knowledge of consumer economics should have increased tremendously.

## FOUR DRIVES IMPACTING CONSUMER BEHAVIOR

Before we leave the subject of consumer behavior, let's talk about one more set of constructs. Paul Lawrence and Nitin Nohria, two Harvard-based researchers, conclude that the way we act is a result of the conscious choices we make. These choices are fueled by an internal battle between four drives:

> "**The drive to acquire** objects and experiences that improve our status relative to others
>
> **The drive to bond** with others in long-term relationships of mutual care and commitment
>
> **The drive to learn** and make sense of the world and of ourselves
>
> **The drive to defend** ourselves, our loved ones, our beliefs, and our resources from harm." (2002, p. 5)

We will see in the course of this chapter each of these drives in action. The latter, the drive to defend, has a lot to do with the next section on identity theft and privacy protection. We want to defend ourselves, our loved ones, and our resources from unwanted intrusion. The drive to learn is inherent in consumer education and a section on that can be found near the end of the chapter. The second part of that drive, the needing to make sense of the world and of ourselves, is covered in the section on obtaining a global perspective. The drive to bond is part of what it means to be a consumer, as consumers we wonder how other consumers are far-ing and we care about their rights as well as our own. Further, on the subject of the drive to bond, customer loyalty, which is the bonding of customers to companies, is fundamental to such firms as Ben & Jerry's, whose Waterbury, VT, factory pumps out 190,000 pints of ice cream each day. "Their consumer affairs staff matches up the pint with the 225 calls and e-mails received each week, checking to see if there were any complaints, and if so, which supplier's milk, eggs, or cherries didn't meet the companies near-obsession with quality" (Schlosser, 2003, p. 114). Although Ben & Jerry's cultivates a down-home image it is a multimillion company that ships to 50,000 grocery stores in the United States and 12 other countries. Attention to detail, in particular to consumer complaints, has been one of the reasons for its success along with consistent quality, unusual flavors, and colorful names. Their number one seller is Cherry Garcia.

Another example of the drive to bond is the experience of giving and receiving gifts. **Gifting** is a symbolic act of bestowing voluntarily. It occurs in nearly every culture as a means of celebration. "Each American on average buys about six birthday gifts a year—about one billion gifts in total. Business gifts are used strategically to define and nurture professional relationships, to the tune of more than $1.5 billion per year" (Solomon, 2003, p. 204). Other gifting occasions include Hanukkah, Christmas, anniversaries, Easter, weddings, Mother's Day, Father's Day, and graduations.

The drive to acquire is crucial to the understanding of consumerism and was addressed in the first chapter in the discussion of needs versus wants. Here is further evidence of this drive: "When subjects are given the choice of living in two worlds, in which prices are the same, but in one they earn $90,000 and their neighbors earn $100,000 versus another in which they earn $110,000 but their neighbors earn $200,000, they are more likely to choose the former situation. Such behavior is at odds with standard utility-maximizing models of human behavior—in absolute terms subjects would be better off earning $110,000 instead of $90,000" (Lawrence

> Each American buys on average six birthday gifts a year.

The Ben & Jerry's factory offering public tours. They cultivate a down-home image. (Courtesy of Ben & Jerry's, Inc.)

Original names are a hallmark of Ben & Jerry's. (Courtesy of Ben & Jerry's, Inc.)

Ben & Jerry's is an example of a well-known consumer product company. At their headquarters in Vermont, they make, package, and market ice cream and handle customer complaints. (Courtesy of Ben & Jerry's, Inc.)

and Nohria, 2002, p. 66). What this experiment suggests is that humans compare themselves to others, they care about relative status. It sheds light on such concepts as competition, ambition, envy, and status.

Connected with the drive to acquire is the desire to use something we have paid for. This reluctance to waste a purchase is called the **sunk-cost fallacy**, a decision-making bias. An example given in Michael Solomon's book *Conquering Consumerspace* is that if there is a sudden snowstorm that makes it dangerous to go to a big football game, the person who paid for the ticket will more likely brave the storm and go than the person who was given a free ticket. As consumers, we are always weighing wins and losses, taking chances, and comparing costs and benefits. This example also illustrates the theory of mental accounting in which decisions are influenced by the way a problem is framed, meaning how it is posed. So that purchases should not be looked up solely in terms of price but in terms of circumstances or conditions. For example, someone may not balk at paying $50 for a haircut in a fancy salon but would object to this price at a CostCutters or Wal-Mart SuperCenter.

Another way to look at the drive to acquire is that employees may be perfectly happy with 5 percent raises until they find out that their colleagues received 7 percent raises. They will want to know why the difference exists and no explanation will appease them. They have a bad taste in their mouths. This reaction illustrates that drives are not always positive, they can lead to unhappiness, unsettling comparisons, and unproductive consequences. Reward systems cannot always live up to expectations. But it should be pointed out that the drive to acquire is counterbalanced with the other drives such as the need for more time. Most people would rather spend time relaxing at home than fighting for a parking space at the mall. Many report being more pressed for time than ever before, and they are actively seeking solutions to be less so, hence, the growth in the interest in prepared foods and in yoga and other relaxing, stretching forms of exercise. About a third of Americans report always feeling rushed, and the average American sleeps seven hours a night, ninety minutes less than people did a century ago (Solomon, 2003).

One-third of Americans report always feeling rushed. The average American sleeps seven hours a night.

Human relationships contain a mix of both competitive and cooperative elements (Lawrence and Nohria, 2002, p. 89). So, self-interest is not the only motivator, caring about others (extended family, friends, community, global) and a sense of fairness serve as counterbalances. Acts of selfless generosity or altruism abound in human affairs such as giving to charities, returning found wallets, helping strangers with flat tires, and doing volunteer work. The list is endless. But for now we have to leave that hopeful note and proceed to one of the darker sides of the marketplace—identity theft—beginning with background information on e-commerce.

## IDENTITY THEFT AND PRIVACY PROTECTION

**E-consumerism** is defined as actions of consumers or their agents to protect and promote consumer interest and seek empowerment in the context of the electronic marketplace (Rha et al., 2003). In order to participate in the marketplace, consumers have to provide codes or personal information as a way of identifying themselves to vendors. This is part of the transaction between consumers and producers.

E-commerce is still evolving. Ten years ago one of the leading car manufacturers conducted a study of car-buying habits and predicted that consumers might buy used cars via the Internet, but they would still want to touch and drive new cars before purchasing (Drucker, 2002). It is true that most consumers still want to test drive a new car before buying, but increasingly they are turning to the Internet for the final purchase. Dealers may soon serve as only deliverers of cars or as show-rooms rather than places of purchase. This has incredible implications for one of America's leading and most profitable industries. For years General Motors was the leading Fortune 500 company in the nation and was only recently surpassed by Wal-Mart in terms of revenue (sales).

Another aspect of e-commerce is that new distribution channels change who the customers are. "They change not only how customers buy but also what they buy. They change consumer behavior, savings patterns, industry structure—in short, the entire economy. This is what is now happening, and not only in the United States but increasingly in the rest of the developed world, and in a good many emerging countries, including mainland China" (Drucker, 2002, pp. 15–16).

Models of decision making that are based on economic considerations of utility, value maximization, and scarcity predict that consumers would evaluate the utility provided by each offering and choose the option that provides the maximum util-ity. Choice is narrowed by these considerations. Consumers want the best product at the lowest price with the maximum return or benefit. They also want ease of use which leads to the increased use of credit cards and the Internet as modes of pur-chase as opposed to in-person cash transactions where identity theft is not a prob-lem. No one is identified, the cash is exchanged, and that is the end. There is no paper trail. This is the starting point in our discussion. Times have changed, and with them the frauds have kept pace.

**Identity theft** refers to someone using your name or personal information, such as your Social Security number, driver's license number, credit card number or other account number, telephone number, or street address without your permis-sion. Essentially the identity thief is stealing your identity for personal gain such as using the information to open up credit accounts, bank accounts, take out loans, make long distance calls, or major purchases. Identity theft can result in the loss of money and the loss of reputation. An example of the latter would be the loss of a good credit rating.

**Privacy** is the right to be left alone, meaning not being bothered by unwanted intrusions such as unsolicited sales calls. The right to privacy is recognized by fed-eral and state law in the United States and by the laws of many other countries. Box 14.1 gives a list of U.S. federal privacy legislation. The question is how much government regulation is necessary. Some degree of regulation and author-ity is necessary, but not at the expense of individual freedoms and civil liber-ties. In the long run, self-regulation and discretion is the best defense against unwanted scam and other intrusions into one's life. This is done through aware-ness, choice, being careful about participation, learning about security, knowing rights, and seeking redress. According to Mason et al. (1995) ethical issues can be categorized as:

- *Privacy:* the collection, storage, and dissemination of information about indi-viduals. An issue in this category would be: What information about oneself should one have to reveal in order to get a product or service?

---

**BOX 14.1    Main U.S. Federal Privacy Legislation**

Privacy rights are built into many state and federal laws. Here is a list of representative federal privacy legislation acts.

Privacy Act of 1974
  Prohibits the government from collecting information secretly or if it is collected it must be for a specific purpose.
Privacy Protection Act of 1980
  Provides protection of privacy in computerized and related documents.
Electronic Communications Privacy Act of 1986
  Prohibits citizens from intercepting data communication without authority.
Computer Matching and Privacy Act of 1988
  Regulates the matching of computer files by federal and state agencies.
Video Privacy Protection Act of 1988
  Protects privacy in picture transmissions.
Fair Health Information Practices Act of 1997
  Gives a code of fair information.
Consumer Internet Privacy Protection Act of 1997
  Requires prior written consent before a computer service can disclose information about subscribers.
Federal Internet Privacy Protection Act of 1997
  Prohibits federal agencies from disclosing personal records from the Internet.
Communications Privacy and Consumer Empowerment Act of 1997
  Protects online commerce in terms of privacy rights.
Data Privacy Act of 1997
  Limits the use of personal information and regulates spamming.
Children's Online Privacy Act of 1998 (amendment to Internet Tax Freed Act)
  Requires companies to verify a person's age before showing online material that could be harmful to minors. This can be done through credit cards or access numbers.
Internet School Filtering Act
  Attempts to limit access to inappropriate material by controlling federal funds and grants to school and libraries. Schools provide blocking software.

---

- *Accuracy:* the authenticity, fidelity, and accuracy of information collected and processed. An issue in this category would be: Who is to be held accountable for errors in information?
- *Property:* the ownership and value of information and intellectual property. An issue in this category would be: Who owns the information?
- *Accessibility:* the right to access information and payment of fees to access it. An issue in this category would be: Who is allowed access to information? Should I be afraid to give information that may be sold, used, or revealed in an inappropriate manner? Research reveals that this issue comes up again and again and is one of the main reasons people refuse to buy over the Internet.

## It's the Law: Federal and State

Consumers are protected from identity theft by the Identity Theft and Assumption Deterrence Act of 1998.

The Identity Theft and Assumption Deterrence Act of 1998 makes it a federal crime if someone "knowingly transfers or uses, without lawful authority, a means of identification of another person with the intent to commit, or to aid or abet, any unlawful activity that constitutes a violation of federal law, or that constitutes a felony under any applicable state or local law." A Social Security number is considered a means of identification as are credit card numbers. The penalties are stiff. A conviction of identity theft carries fines and prison sentences of up to 15 years. States have passed laws related to identity theft, as well. To find out rules in your states contact the state attorney general's offices (**www.naag.org**) or local consumer protection agencies.

Many federal government agencies are involved in educating the public about identity theft and hunting down criminals. The E-Resources section lists many of the places consumers can turn to for information and help. The following agencies are particularly important in the fight to protect personal information:

- The Federal Trade Commission provides education and publications. The FTC has an electronic database called the Identity Theft Clearinghouse which is a system of records covered under the Privacy Act of 1974. The Privacy Act prohibits unauthorized use of these records, but the information may be shared with FTC attorneys and investigators or certain private entities such as credit bureaus if the FTC deems it necessary to resolve problems (see E-Resources).
- The U.S. Department of Justice and its U.S. attorneys prosecute federal identity theft cases.
- The Federal Bureau of Investigation (FBI) investigates cases connected with bank fraud, mail fraud, wire fraud, bankruptcy fraud, insurance fraud, fraud against the government, and terrorism. Field offices are listed in telephone directory Blue Pages.
- The U.S. Secret Service investigates financial crimes involving identity theft usually in cases of substantial dollar loss. Field offices are listed in telephone directory Blue Pages.
- The U.S. Department of the Treasury has a financial crimes division that specializes in identity theft problems.

*Stealing someone's identity is a federal crime.*

## How Identity Theft Occurs: Ways to Minimize Risk

Skilled identity thieves have a number of methods to gain access to personal information (see Box 14.2). Box 14.3 shows how the thieves use personal information.

Individuals cannot prevent identity theft entirely, but they can minimize the risk by:

- Watching credit card statements and ordering a copy of credit reports from each of the three major credit bureaus (Equifax, Inc., Experian, TransUnion, their contact information was given in chapter 12).
- Being careful with the following items: checkbooks, paystubs, receipts with credit card numbers, credit cards, ATM cards, palm pilots, business cards, driver's licenses, and health-insurance cards especially those with Social Security numbers. If you think you are safe because you have never lost any of these or put them in the wrong hands, think again. Anyone processing your credit card or taking information about you in a video-rental store, for example, can turn around and sell that information to a fraud ring. Be especially cautious when traveling.
- Using hard to figure out passwords on credit card, bank and phone accounts.

### BOX 14.2    Methods of Identity Thieves

The methods identity thieves use to get personal information:

1. They steal wallets and purses containing your identification and credit and bank cards.
2. They steal your mail, including your bank and credit card statements, preapproved credit offers, new checks, and tax information.
3. They complete a "change of address form" to divert your mail to another location.
4. They rummage through your trash, or the trash of businesses, for personal data in a practice known as "Dumpster diving."
5. They fraudulently obtain your credit by posing as a landlord, employer, or someone else who may have a legitimate need for, and legal right to, the information.
6. They find personal information in your home.
7. They use personal information you share on the Internet.
8. They scam you, often through e-mail, by posing as legitimate government agencies.
9. They get your information from the workplace in a practice known as "business record theft" by stealing files out of offices where you're a customer, employee, patient, or student; bribing an employee who has access to your files; or "hacking" into electronic files.

*Source:* Theft: When bad things happen to your good name. (September 2002). Washington, DC: Federal Trade Commission, p. 3.

### BOX 14.3    How Identity Theft Information Is Used

The ways identity thieves may use personal information:

1. They call your credit card issuer and, pretending to be you, ask to change the mailing address on your credit card account. The imposter then runs up charges on your account. Because your bills are being sent to the new address, it may take some time before you realize there's a problem
2. They open a new credit card account using your name, date of birth, and Social Security number. When they use the credit card and don't pay the bills, the delinquent account is reported on your credit report.
3. They establish phone or wireless service in your name.
4. They open a bank account in your name and write bad checks on that account.
5. They file for bankruptcy under your name to avoid paying debts they've incurred under your name, or to avoid eviction.
6. They counterfeit checks or debit cards, and drain your bank account.
7. They buy cars by taking out auto loans in your name.
8. They give your name to the police during an arrest. If they're released from police custody, but don't show up for their court date, an arrest warrant is issued in your name.

*Source:* Theft: When bad things happen to your good name. (September 2002). Washington, DC: Federal Trade Commission, p. 4.

- Securing personal information at home if there are roommates. At work be watchful of people in and out doing remodeling or repairs.
- Securing personal information at work.
- Updating virus protection software regularly on computers.
- Never clicking on hyperlinks sent from strangers nor downloading files.
- Taking special care with laptops, log off when finished.
- Taking mail with checks and personal information to the post office instead of putting mail in unsecured mailboxes.
- When disposing of a computer, delete personal information using a "wipe" utility program to overwrite the entire hard drive. For more information about how to do this go to *www.hq.nasa.gov/office/oig/hq/harddrive.pdf* from NASA or go to *www.ftc.gov*.

When filling out information cards in person or over the computer, choose the opt-out option as a way to reduce the number of people and organizations that receive personal information about you. Use work phone numbers and addresses rather than home phone numbers and addresses whenever possible. You can notify the three major credit bureaus that you do not want personal information about you shared for selling or promotional purposes.

## Recourse for Victims of Identity Theft

The four steps to follow if you are a victim of identity theft are

1. Contact the fraud departments of the three credit bureaus. Following an investigation there may be a dispute. If so a sample dispute letter is given in Box 14.4.
2. Close the accounts that you think may have been tampered with or opened fraudulently. In most cases, the Truth in Lending Act limits your liability for unauthorized credit card charges to $50 per card. The Fair Credit Billing Act establishes procedures for resolving billing errors, including fraudulent charges on accounts.
3. File a police report with your local police department and get a copy of the report and send it to Experian, Equifax, and TransUnion.
4. File a complaint with the Federal Trade Commission. This can be done online at **www.consumer.gov/idtheft**. The FTC does not bring criminal cases

**Consumer Alert**

The elderly are particularly at risk for identity theft when they are in nursing homes or assisted living centers. Seniors are vulnerable because they tend to have good credit, they are less likely to use their cards often, and they are unlikely to request their credit reports from credit bureaus. Their lack of use makes them easy targets. The cardholder's name can be used to open bank accounts and forge checks and even to take out bank loans for cars. Seniors' relatives can look out for them by lowering their credit card limit to $300–$500. Relatives should also be familiar with the security policies at the facility. Besides relatives, sheriff department detectives can look out for the elderly and give talks on what to notice. Nursing homes and assisted living centers should do background checks on potential employees before hiring.

BOX 14.4     Sample Dispute Letter—Credit Bureau

Date

Your Name
Your Address
Your City, State, Zip Code

Complaint Department
Name of Credit Bureau
Address
City, State, Zip Code

Dear Sir or Madam:
I am writing to dispute the following information in my file. The items I dispute also are circled on the attached copy of the report I received. (Identify item(s) disputed by name of source, such as creditors or tax court, and identify type of item, such as credit account, judgment, etc.)

The item is (inaccurate or incomplete) because (describe what is inaccurate or incomplete and why). I am requesting that the item be deleted (or request another specific change) to correct the information.

Enclosed are copies of (use this sentence if applicable and describe any enclosed documentation, such as payment records, court documents) supporting my position. Please investigate this (these) matter(s) and (delete or correct) the disputed item(s) as soon as possible.

Sincerely,

Your Name

Enclosures: (List what you are enclosing)

*Source:* Theft: When bad things happen to your good name (September 2002). Washington, DC: Federal Trade Commission.)

but can help victims by providing information to assist them in resolving the financial and other problems that can result from this crime, and reporting this information can help law enforcement officials track down identity thieves and stop them.

## BANK FRAUD

If an ATM or debit card is lost or stolen, report it immediately because the amount a person is held responsible for depends on the speed of report of loss. Banks are usually responsive to any problems with identity theft, but if someone is not satisfied with their treatment or wants to know more about rights they can go higher. For a general listing of banks and jurisdiction go to *wwww.ffiec.gov/enforcement.htm*. If an individual knows which government agency is in charge of a particular bank, then the list in the E-Resources will help. For example, the Federal Deposit Insurance Corporation

(FDIC) supervises state-chartered banks that are not members of the Federal Reserve System. The Federal Reserve System supervises state-chartered banks who are members. If the word "national" appears in the same of a bank then they may be Office of the Comptroller of the Currency chartered and supervised banks. Federal credit unions are under the National Credit Union Administration. The Office of the Comptroller of the Currency supervises banks with the word "national" in their title. The Office of Thrift Supervision is the main regulator of all federal and many of the state-chartered thrift institutions such as savings and loan institutions.

According to the Federal Trade Commission's Facts for Consumers, privacy notices from banks and other financial companies explain

- What personal financial information the company collects
- Whether the company intends to share your personal financial information with other companies
- What you can do, if the company intends to share your personal financial information, to limit some of that sharing
- How the company protects your personal financial information.

When you receive privacy notices the steps to follow include

Reading them

Getting answers to all your questions

Opt out, if you desire

If you opt out, follow the instructions, shop around to find a financial institution or seller that you like.

The two federal laws covering how companies share financial information are the Fair Credit Reporting Act and the Gramm-Leach-Bliley Act. As previously described the Fair Credit Reporting Act protects the privacy of certain information distributed by consumer reporting agencies (CRAs) commonly known as credit bureaus. The Gramm-Leach-Bliley Act requires financial companies to tell about their policies regarding the privacy of personal financial information such as to nonaffiliates, companies unrelated to a person's financial company. Examples of nonaffiliates are service providers such as those who print checks, joint marketers who sell other financial products or services, and other third-party nonaffiliates who may want a company's mailing list.

## BANKRUPTCY FRAUD

If someone files for bankruptcy using your name, you can write to the U.S. trustee in the region where the bankruptcy was filed. For information see the E-Resources section. You can complain to the U.S. trustee or to the U.S. attorney or to the FBI. You may need to hire an attorney to straighten this form of identity theft out.

## CRIMINAL VIOLATIONS

A person may also need to contact the police and hire an attorney, in this case a criminal attorney, if wrongful criminal violations are attributed to your name. In this case, someone is impersonating you, and you will want to clear your name.

## FAKE DRIVERS' LICENSES

If someone is using your name or Social Security number to get a driver's license, then you should contact the Department of Motor Vehicles.

## INVESTMENT FRAUD

In the last chapter, different types of investment frauds were introduced. This chapter emphasizes the frauds perpetrated over the Internet. When individuals invest it is necessary to give out personal information such as credit card numbers which an unscrupulous person (anyone from a broker to a person who cleans offices at night) could access. If someone tampers with securities investments or brokerage accounts, it should be immediately reported to the investment firm and to the Securities and Exchange Commission.

## MAIL FRAUD AND THEFT

Americans receive 500 pieces of junk mail a year.

Anything to do with fraud involving the mail should be reported to the U.S. Postal Service. For example, if mail has been stolen or tampered with this is the first line of defense. Americans receive 500 pieces of junk mail a year (Solomon, 2003). According to PlanetFeedback, 25 percent of consumers say they no longer open junk mail because of the threat of anthrax. Since many people are reluctant to open mail from sources they do not know the hope is that this practice should cut down on the amount of mail fraud. As a counterbalance, the amount of message fraud is increasing on the Internet.

## PASSPORT FRAUD

If a passport is stolen or lost, report it immediately to the U.S. Department of State. Field offices are listed in telephone directory Blue Pages.

## PHONE FRAUD

Unusual billing may be the result of an identity theft. Someone may be making unauthorized calls from a cellular phone or using a calling card or pin that is not theirs. In this case contact the phone company immediately and cancel the account or calling card and open new accounts. For cellular phones and long distance problems that persist, contact the Federal Communications Commission.

## SOCIAL SECURITY NUMBER THEFT AND MISUSE

The Social Security Administration wants to know if someone is using your number. If a card is stolen or lost or you suspect mischief, contact them.

## TAX FRAUD

This seems a rather remote possibility, but it is possible that someone would assume your identity to file federal income tax returns or commit other tax fraud. It has happened in the past. In this case, contact the Internal Revenue Service.

## ONLINE BUYING: SECURITY AND TRUST ISSUES

"**Trust** is the psychological status of involved parties who are willing to pursue further interactions to achieve a planned goal. A trading party makes itself vulnerable to the other party's behavior. In other words, both parties assume risk. In the **marketspace**, sellers and buyers do not meet face to face. The buyer can see a picture of the product but not the product itself" (Turban, et al., 2000, p. 86). The buyer must trust not only the seller but also the e-commerce infrastructure and environment. Can someone look in on the transaction and take information away from it? Security mechanisms can help solidify the trust between buyer and seller in the marketspace, the Internet realm in which buying and selling takes place.

Trust is also a basic expectation of brands so that customers are more likely to buy brand names online than unknown products. According to an article in *Advertising Age,* "When we ask consumers to tell us about those they believe are the best 'best brands,' the No. 1 attribute mentioned is 'it's a brand I trust.' Trust is the foundation for building relationships and for sustaining loyalty. Trust is critical when you introduce new ideas, products and benefits" (Keller, 2003, p. 28). According to this same article, trust was severely eroded in 2002 with all the corporate scandals including bloated CEO compensation and the continuing downturn of the economy in 2003. Not only did these factors affect stock valuations but also eroded people's confidence in business. In a survey, six in ten believed that the scandals resulted in a loss of trust that would take a long time to restore (Keller, 2003). Regulation is part of the solution, but businesses, through sound practices, must make a conscious effort to build trust.

According to Charles Hofacker, author of *Internet Marketing* (2000), trust is essential in facilitating exchange and consumers need three kinds of trust before buying:

Trust in the mechanics of the selling process.

Trust in the fairness and integrity of the specific people involved.

Trust in the firm or the institution and its ability to fulfill its delivery promise.

The benefits of shopping online is that the Internet is always open—seven days a week, 24 hours a day—and comparison shopping is easier. Good deals, convenience, and selection abound, but how do you make sure your online shopping experience is safe? Here are some rules to follow when buying online:

- Use a secure browser. Computers come with browsers installed, and you can download some browsers for free over the web.
- Shop with known brands, known companies. Determine refund and mailing policies.
- Keep passwords private. The most secure ones use a combination of numbers, letters, and symbols that have nothing to do with other parts of your life like mailing addresses, phone numbers, or birthdays.
- Pay by credit card so your transaction is protected by the Fair Credit Billing Act. In fact this is usually the only way you can pay online so it should be automatic.
- Keep a record by printing a copy of transactions.
- Pay bills online, and this is a great service as long as the company secures your financial and personal information. Many banks offer this service.
- Read the company's online privacy policy. The policy should disclose what information is being collected about you, how the company may use information, and as mentioned before, whenever possible opt-out of having your information passed on to others.

## Shopping Bots: Consumer Response

**Shopping bots** (or browser-based shopping assistants) are intelligent agent programs that scan the Internet and compile the information they are asked to locate in a format convenient to users. Most readers are probably familiar with Google, Yahoo! and Excite which are search programs that find and organize web information. Shopping bots, however, are specialized search engines that locate desired products and present a side-by-side comparison of online offerings, including the prices charged by each online merchant. Many of these services exist and one of the better known ones is MySimon.com. Other examples are IBuy.com, Shopper.com, and Pricewatch.com and the various travel sites that compare prices and deals. Since this is such a new and evolving phenomenon, many competitors will come and go. Shopping bots are essentially personal shoppers online that allow for quick comparison shopping.

As an example, the way the bots work is that shoppers type in a brand name such as Nike and then a specific model of athletic shoe and a maximum price they are willing to pay. Another example would be to ignore the brand name and enter a more open subject such as a man's oxford cloth blue dress shirt at less than $35. In both examples, the shopping bot would search and reveal sellers' names, prices, and further details, including links to sellers such as Lands' End or Kohl's. To be useful, search functions have to be adaptive (meaning responsive, able to make appropriate connections between buyers and sellers), organized, and communicative (understandable). With the link to the merchants, searchers can go direct to the company to find out more about the product and to buy from them.

A study by Goldsmith and Goldsmith (2003) revealed that users were more experienced and more innovative with regard to using the Internet for shopping than were nonusers. Users rated their experience with shopping bots as generally positive (easy, convenient, fast, enjoyable), and higher income and socioeconomic status were associated with higher ratings of the convenience, speed, and enjoyment of using bots.

Since a list of sellers and prices are given for a selected product such as a shirt or shoes, will the customer most likely select the first merchant on the list or will they go through the whole list and consider other details such as warranty and return terms, delivery date and conditions, price, name or brand recognition, and availability? An ethical question is whether retailers should pay to have their products listed first on the shopping bot's page, and if so, should the buyer be made aware of this fact? Future research will reveal answers to these questions.

## Online Auctions

Looking for signed baseball cards or a wooden sled from 1930? The Internet auction may be the place for you. Since it appeared in 1995, this has been a fast growing phenomena in the Internet marketplace. It is a global flea market with items going from dollars to millions of dollars. Usually sellers offer one item at a time although companies have started unloading large amounts of unsold merchandise. Typically the seller sells items at the price of the lowest successful bid; the seller may set a minimum acceptable price. The bidding closes at a scheduled time and the highest bidder wins. Afterward, the seller and the buyer communicate and arrange payment and delivery. This describes person-to-person sales, but there can also be business-to-person sales.

Buyers may pay by credit card, debit cards, personal check, cashier's check, money order, cash on delivery, and escrow services. Credit cards offer buyers the most consumer protection, and typically this is the form of payment that business-to-person sales want but person-to-person auctions often do not. A cashier's check or money order before shipping is more common. Some sellers use an escrow fee arrangement in which the buyer pays 5 percent of the cost of the item. The escrow service accepts payment from the buyer by check, credit card, or money order. Then, the service releases the money to the seller after the buyer receives and accepts the merchandise. This offers more protection to the buyer, but slows up the transaction process. Another option is when the seller agrees to send purchases COD (collect on delivery), and the buyer pays when the item is received.

The Federal Trade Commission receives complaints about auction fraud and most center on sellers who:

- Do not deliver the goods as advertised
- Deliver something far less valuable
- Do not deliver on time
- Fail to disclose relevant information (cracks, missing pieces, etc.)

Buyers can protect themselves by identifying the seller and checking the seller's feedback rating a telephone number is a way to confirm. They should also know product and prices and establish a top price and stick with it, avoiding getting caught up in bidding fever. Find out about payment options and who pays for shipping and delivery and return policies before bidding. Know all you can about the site itself. What protections does it offer buyers?

Sellers can protect themselves by providing accurate information, dealing with a reputable site, responding quickly to potential buyers' questions, contacting the highest bidder immediately, and shipping the merchandise as soon as possible.

---

**Consumer Alert**

Beware of "shill" testimonials that are put there by the seller themselves (using made up names) or by friends or relatives of the seller. Many people have been caught doing this. It is a technique used in live auctions as well where a seller's friend bids against potential buyers, driving up the price, and then the friend backs out at the last minute.

---

---

**Consumer Alert**

Beware of damaged goods, words like "refurbished," "flood sale," "close-out," "discontinued," or "off-brand." Take special caution when buying electrical or mechanical goods.

---

They cannot sell illegal goods or place "shill" bids or false testimonials. Sellers increase sales by offering photos of items. The chapter now turns its attention to current consumer issues outside of the Internet and identity theft.

# GIFT CARDS

Plastic gift cards have largely replaced paper gift certificates from stores and restaurants. Certificates typically allow customers to receive any change in cash, but some stores have challenged this. What usually happens is that customers leave a little money on the plastic cards and the stores keep the money. As a piece of advice, if you buy an $18.99 item from a $20.00 gift card and the store clerk offers you the change, take it, because the likelihood is that you couldn't find another item for a dollar or less or that you would forget about it and the card would expire or get mislaid. A significant problem is that people lose the cards. As a form of proof, companies should make a copy at the time of sale of the card.

Fights have broken out as retailers and consumers tussle over who should get the unspent money on cards and whether they should carry expiration dates. It sounds like small change but the sales of cards came to about $38 million in 2002 up about 20 percent from the year before. Besides making 5 percent to 10 percent of value stored on gift cards that are never spent, stores also profit because a customer with a card often spends over the amount, paying more. For example, with a $25 plastic gift card someone might spend $30 and pay for extra $5.

"Laws in most states require retailers to turn over unused gift-card value as lost property, so that state officials can try to return it to consumers. . . . But enforcement is spotty at best. Most merchants don't keep thorough records of gift-card sales, making returns difficult" (McCarthy, 2003, pp. A1 and A12). In some states they are trying to pass a ban on expiration dates. In 2002, New York Attorney General Eliot Spitzer's office and Home Depot reached an agreement on lost and stolen cards under which the chain will cancel them and reissue new cards to individuals who can prove they bought a card. His office was reaching similar agreements with other companies. The reason this came to a head in New York was over a complaint filed by Ann Becchina of Stony Brook, NY, who was trying to get a refund of a $1,879 balance on a $2,500 Home Depot card she had lost. She said, "I spent a frantic two days taking apart my home, cars, retracing my steps, checking lost-and-founds" (McCarthy, 2003, p. A12). She had bought the card herself and had a receipt for it, but her local store refused to replace it. The company has since revised its computer software to build in a way to repatriate the money to the holder. Before that, the company explained that losing the card was like losing cash. Once you lost the card you were out of luck. Until this issue is completely sorted out across all stores, consumers would be wise to treat the card as they would cash, but if the card is lost or stolen they should contact the store immediately and then follow steps like Ms. Becchina did.

## RENT-TO-OWN

**Rent-to-own (RTO)** is an industry of dealers who rent a variety of goods from furniture to electronics to appliances with an option to buy. RTOs have been around since the 1960s. Consumers can visit stores in person or look at their Web sites to see what is available. Typical rentals are for a week or a month, but if the consumer keeps up payments within a period of time such as a year they can become owners of the product. Most do not do this; they return the products within a few months. The problem with RTOs is that there are fees involved and high costs that consumers may not be aware of, and, hence, there are complaints. Often people who rent goods for a short time are in a transition state or have a poor credit history. State regulations vary on presale disclosures. Adrianne Vidrine and Frances Lawrence of Louisiana State University found that when they visited RTO stores the personnel were vague about total costs saying, "It depends on the actual items purchased" and "That's all in the computer—we won't know until we print up your agreement" (2001/2002, p. 110). So when it comes to RTOs, may the buyer beware. It is an alternative, but an expensive one. Knowing prices and models before shopping at RTOs is a beginning protection, another one is to comparison shop between RTOs since prices and fees vary widely.

## TELEPHONE SERVICES: COMPARING, PRICING ISSUES

Struggles with telephone billing charges rank high on consumer complaint lists. With deregulation came more consumer choice but also more consumer confusion. Advertising can be misleading about how bills will be figured and how much calls will actually cost. A case in point is Sarah Kalliney, a time-starved Manhattan executive, who bills out at roughly $200 an hour for her business services. She ended up spending nearly ten hours battling her cell phone company over $9 in late fees. Is such a battle worth her time? No, not from a purely economic sense, but she said it was worth it for the satisfaction. She finally won the battle but only after she tracked down the phone number for the president of the company (Spencer, 2003). The company says it has taken steps to improve customer service, including making it easier to reach operators.

## Prepaid Phone Cards

Telephone time paid for in advance can be put on prepaid phone cards. A person pays $10 or $20 upfront for the use of the card; the amount of time bought depends on the rate-per-minute charge. For most people, these cards are a convenience, used in travel. They are sold at post offices, travel agencies, retail stores, grocery and convenience stores, and book shops. Some of the prepaid cards can be recharged by billing the additional cost to credit cards. Some all purpose credit cards have a prepaid phone feature. The way they work is that most cards display a toll-free access telephone number and require a personal identification number (pin). The companies have computers that use the pin to keep track of card usage. Here are the key players:

- Carriers have the telephone lines that carry calls.
- Distributors get the cards to retailers so they can be sold.
- Issuers set the rates and the services.
- Resellers buy telephone minutes from carriers.
- Retailers sell the cards.

If things go wrong, here are the usual problems:

- PINs or access numbers do not work.
- Issuers go out of business or did not set up the cards right in the first place.
- Customer service numbers are overloaded, and consumers' needs are not met.
- Rates are higher than advertised; there may be hidden fees such as connection charges, taxes, and surcharges.
- Poor quality connections or services.

Consumers can protect themselves in several ways. First, they should know their issuer and retailer. Are they reliable? Second, the consumer should understand how the cards work, and if they do not function, what their avenues of recourse are. Customers should also note any extra fees that may be charged and expiration dates. If the card does not work and the customer service number is not responsive, further steps, including writing or calling state offices of consumer services, the Better Business Bureau, and the Federal Trade Commission, should be taken.

## Cramming and Slamming: Problems and Solutions

**Cramming** means unexplained charges on phone bills for services never ordered, authorized, received, or used. Most cramming schemes occur through the use of an 800 or other toll free number. Some are initiated by sweepstakes and contests; all are deceptive and to be avoided. Crooks can get your phone number and cram charges on your bill by the following:

- 800 number calls such as date lines, psychics, and adult entertainment. Your phone number is captured and billed, and your number can be sold to others. Be aware that 900 numbers cost money.
- Contests and sweepstakes come from filling out entry forms and sweepstakes promotions—be careful that the source is legitimate.
- Dating services set up to meet local people for free, but it turns out these are routed out of town and long-distance charges show up on the bill.

- Free minute deals have a come-on of free initial minutes, but the service puts you on hold until the charges start.
- International calls said to be local access but use unfamiliar area codes which may be international and costly. Usually these are linked to entertainment scams.

The main way to protect yourself or your family from cramming is to check the phone bill every month and look into unfamiliar charges. Sometimes there is an error on the bill and other times someone in the family has become entangled in a scam. Teenagers are particularly vulnerable. If there is an error on the bill, follow the instructions on the statement, and try to resolve the problem by contacting the telephone company, information provider, or billing agent. A call should be followed up by a letter. If unsatisfied, from there a consumer should follow the usual steps of complaint to the state office of consumer service and upward. The Federal Trade Commission has information about cramming at *www.ftc.gov.*

If a consumer's long distance telephone company switches to another company without his or her permission, it is called **slamming**. Victims' legal rights regarding this are covered by rulings in the Federal Communications Commission. Basically, a person has 30 days to rectify the situation without paying long distance charges and to switch back to the original carrier. This has been one of the most frustrating areas of consumer complaints and again, the best defense is to check phone bills carefully and to take the steps necessary for remedy.

## INTERNATIONAL GROUPS, TRADE AGREEMENTS, DEVELOPING A GLOBAL PERSPECTIVE

A U.S. worker averages 77 hours per month online. The most popular time is 11:00 A.M. to 2:00 P.M.

Technological and distribution advances are shrinking the distances within the world. The Internet and communications technology make it possible for global businesses to operate at far less cost in time and money than ever before. Consumers are responding, not only at home but also at work. The average number of hours that a U.S. worker spent logged onto the Internet at work per month was 77 with the most popular time to be online from 11:00 A.M. to 2:00 P.M. Some of this is

Consumerism is becoming increasingly globalized.

work activity and communication, but some of this is devoted to searching for consumer information and buying online. According to Nielsen/Net Ratings polls, in 2002, 41 percent of U.S. adults bought goods online, and 17% banked online.

New global markets have led to more affluence and more competition worldwide. The major competitors in the global market come from Europe, Asia, and North America. The largest economies in the world are the United States, Japan, and Germany. **Globalization** refers to the distribution of goods and services worldwide so that consumer goods eventually become universally accepted and homogeneous (Du Plessis and Rousseau, 1999, p. 132). It refers to an international marketing centrist approach with business at the center. It also implies a materialistic view of consumers. This is different from the term **"global perspective"** which "entails the challenging of materialism and commercialism and an examination of one's role as citizen. It further includes global ethics" (Erasmus, Kok, and Retief, 2001, p. 116). It is a philosophy or a way of thinking. The global perspective encourages and appreciates local, small business, including home-based businesses and the balance, creativity, and job opportunities they bring to the world economy. Even the bigger companies are increasingly expected to put money and support back into the communities that purchase from them or where their headquarters are located. There is a feeling of more of an obligation to those who generate profits to do something worthwhile with at least some of those profits. This is referred to as being **socially responsible**. To be truly socially responsible or to engage in **social marketing**, companies must address the needs of the masses as well as the needs of the few and balance individual quality with societal and environmental quality. It does not work to give money to charities while at the same time polluting the streams and rivers that run past the homes of the recipients of those charities. A more complete view of corporate responsibility is needed.

To go back to the concept of globalization, a very large scale economy, it is beyond the purview of one person or one company although James Bond and Austin Powers movies would lead us to believe that there are wealthy, power-hungry individuals out there who would like to rule the world. One of the leading management experts in the world, Peter Drucker, says, "When we talk about the global economy, I hope nobody believes it can be managed. It can't. There is no information on it. But if you are in the hospital field, you can know hospitals. If you were to parachute into some strange place and make your way to the lights in the valley, you would be able to identify the correct building as the hospital" (2002, p. 49). No one can completely manage the global economy, but a single person, an expert, can know how a specific industry or area of business operates. This is not to say that there are not some extremely powerful and pervasive businesses. The retail giant Wal-Mart is the biggest single employer in 21 states in the United States and the largest grocer in the United States, and its expansion in the U.S. and abroad is continuing. Carrefour is the first retailer in Europe and the second largest worldwide with 9632 stores in 30 countries including countries in Asia and South America. Their three leading formats are hypermarket, supermarket, and hard discount. They have nearly 400,000 employees and are the retail leader in nine countries. The company started in France in 1959 by two families.

Another way of discussing developing a global perspective is to think of it as a world attitude, an attitude shift away from self-interest to considering one's behavior within a greater context. According to Harman (1998, pp. 176–77), the United

Nations and the International Labour Organization came up with a list of universally felt human needs including:

- Basic human needs ("enough" food, shelter, health care, education, employment, and security of the person)
- A sense of the dignity of being human
- A sense of becoming (a chance to achieve a better life)
- A sense of justice or equity
- A sense of achievement, of being involved with something worth achieving
- A sense of solidarity—of belonging to a worthy group and of participating in decisions that affect the groups, and one's own, destiny

Besides all these needs, one of the greatest challenges that consumers face is knowing what outside information to access in order to make sound decisions. Who to believe? What to buy or not buy? The global economy has opened up the world to limitless possibilities. Customers are changing and distribution systems are changing. The effects on technology and competition are immeasurable. Drucker says, "Under e-commerce, delivery will become the one area is which a business can truly distinguish itself. It will become the critical 'core competence.' Its speed, quality, and responsiveness may well become the decisive competitive factor even where brands seem to be entrenched. And no existing multination and altogether very few businesses are organized for it" (2002, pp. 57–58). Examples of fast-growing e-commerce businesses are books (one in ten books were sold over the Internet in 2002 according to Forrester Research) and new cars through such businesses as CarsDirect, Autobytel.com, and CarPoint.com. Since there is no reason an e-seller must limit itself to one brand or make of car, for example, it opens up competitive pricing and styling and options possibilities beyond the traditional ways of selling cars such as Ford cars at a Ford dealership. In the New Economy, sales aren't necessarily linked to production, and this is a significant paradigm shift. Lest this section and chapter appear too positive about the benefits of e-commerce, it should be noted that certain goods and services cannot be sold online. There are limitations, for example, haircuts, manicures, and massages still require personal touch, and most brides would like to try on a wedding dress, in fact, several, before purchasing.

# CONSUMER TERRORISM

**Consumer terrorism** refers to a variety of activities conducted by individuals or groups whose purpose is to disrupt the marketplace. It includes threats and deliberately spreading misinformation and fear, as well as actually tampering with products. Product tampering is a form of bioterrorism that can cause great harm to individuals (such as those made ill by tampered with foods or drugs) and can ruin or temporarily cripple companies. The wise company addresses immediately any problems with its products by alerting the public and by handling recalls and rebates efficiently. The increased use of surveillance cameras in stores and in factories should reduce product tampering.

Another form of consumer terrorism is tampering with Web sites, company data, and personal computers through computer viruses. Sophisticated hackers can wreck company records and invade individual and government accounts and steal identities. This is such a new concept that it is difficult to envision all the ways consumer terrorism may take place, but suffice it to say that disruptions of financial, food, electronic, health, and supply networks are disconcerting, as well as potentially fatal. The main concern is the vastness of stretch, in other words, the large numbers of people who can be hurt given new modes, specifically through the use of the Internet.

## STEALTH MARKETING

Marketing strategies come and go, but one of the latest is called stealth marketing. Rather than being overt in offering new products and services, in **stealth marketing** the approach is to provide a unique service or product that is not too public. The company's intent is to "come in under the radar" by introducing something new without it being too obvious to competitors. Once established the company may keep new offerings or changes under wraps until the time to launch. *Stealth is used as a tool to gain competitive advantage.* This term is mentioned at this point in this chapter to show that both companies and consumers (including consumer terrorists) can engage in less than obvious behaviors or have less than obvious motivations. Attention may be drawn, for example, to a side product or event as a means to cover the main event. In stealth marketing a program or strategy may be targeted to a select group of customers or prospects (i.e., millionaires, yacht owners, urban teenagers) that is based on targeting criteria that are not obvious.

In the public's mind, mainstream marketing is often thought of as obvious, as being pushy, slick, and pressured, as being highly publicized in magazines and newspapers such as celebrity-filled product launches for new fashions, perfumes, or restaurant chains. Stealth marketing is the opposite of this. Stealth marketing is not illegal nor is it fully developed. It may be just a fad, but in any case the reader needs to be aware that it exists.

## ENVIRONMENTAL PROTECTION: BEING A PROENVIRONMENT CONSUMER

To move on to an entirely new topic, the relationships between environment and economics can be looked at from a variety of perspectives. The specialization in economics that focuses on these relationships is called **ecological economics** with a particular emphasis in changes in **natural capital**. "Natural capital is defined as the whole endowment of land and resources available to us, including air, water, fertile soil, forests, fisheries, mineral resources, and the ecological life-support systems that make economic activity, and indeed life itself, possible" (Harris, 2002). In ecological economics changes in these realms are viewed as important as changes in human-made capital. The gross national product (GNP) measures human production; it does not measure the state of the environment while the quality of our lives is a combination as well as the state of social issues of family, well-being, health, education, and harmony. "The economic indicators, such as the GNP, which measure how well the society is doing, are essentially measures of how rapidly resources are being used up—converted to economic product. The more economic the product, the 'healthier' the economy and, by implication, the society. Is that good, you ask, on a finite planet to place a premium on the maximum rate of using up resources" (Harman, 1998, p. 123)?

One way to determine if ecosystems are being strained is by noting the increased prevalence of large-scale or global environmental problems such as global climate change, ozone layer destruction, ocean pollution, soil degradation, and species loss (Harris, 2002). **Sustainable development** refers to "economic development that provides for human needs without undermining global ecosystems and depleting essential resources" (Harris, 2002, p. 28). Although it may seem like a contradiction in terms, abundance and affluence bring new forms of scarcity— "scarcity of natural resources, of fresh air and water, of arable land, of the waste-absorbing capacities of the natural environment, of resilience of the planet's life-support systems, of spirit-renewing wilderness. . . . The 'new scarcities' are of course also related to population growth, which in turn is a consequence of improved sanitation and public health measures" (Harman, 1998, p. 125).

The industrialized world places a high value on economic and financial signals, yet the public through the pollution problems caused by Eastern Europe in the

Curbside recycling—contributing to a better world. (Courtesy of Getty Images, Inc. Photodisc.)

1980s and the pervasive smog worldwide today has became more aware of the effects of production, transportation, and consumption on the environment. Many consumers feel that business, as mentioned earlier, has a social responsibility to look out for the quality of the environment as part of the consumer-market exchange. Consumers, likewise, have a responsibility to consume in environmentally friendly ways and to engage in recycling behaviors.

According to South African authors Alet C. Erasmus, Martha Kok, and Arda Retief (2001, p. 116), "Consumer behavior of the western world can generally be described as materialistic. . . . Driven by economic principles, the retail environment encourages and even promotes a materialistic value system. Although many consumers will deny being materialistic, every day consumer related behavior in the Western world unfortunately bears testimony of the opposite." Further they say that a global perspective results in an appreciation for voluntary simplicity and conservation and a respect for past and future generations.

**Voluntary simplicity** refers to a conscious effort to live more modestly with fewer possessions and at lower consumption levels. Erasmus, Kok, and Retief (2001) call for decisions to be based on these types of considerations, on the effect on interactive environments, rather than on a passion for consumption. Does anyone really need a 17-bedroom, 20-bathroom house? Many are calling for a "mind shift" away from indiscriminate consumption to a socially conscious and environmentally responsible consumer behavior where the consumer is regarded as a citizen (McGregor, 1999; McGregor, 1998a; McGregor, 1998b). "Voluntary simplifiers range from senior citizens who downsize their homes to young, mobile professionals who don't want to be tied down to their possessions . . . clearly, most mainstream consumers are not about to give up their Prada bags any time soon. However, many of us are overwhelmed by the profusion of stuff out there" (Solomon, 2003, p. 248). Voluntary simplifiers believe that once their basic needs are met there is no reason to keep consuming on top of that. They do not believe that more is better.

Environment can refer to so many things from energy alternatives to air quality to use of fuels to water quality. There is also the consumer right to a healthy environment. As mentioned in the history chapter, President John F. Kennedy, inspired by Rachel Carson's book *Silent Spring,* was an early advocate for better environmental protection. The Consumer Federation of America (CFA)—one of the most active consumer organizations advocating for a cleaner environment—believes that we must all reduce, reuse, and recycle more. The main government agency regarding environmental control is the Environmental Protection Agency (EPA). The CFA often says that the EPA is not doing enough, that more regulation and enforcement is needed, especially in regard to water quality and air pollution. It is a constant battle within the United States, within other countries, and cross-nationally. Polluted air and water do not stop at state or national boundaries. How does this relate to consumerism besides the obvious air that we breathe and water that we drink? Perhaps it would be useful to focus on one aspect of consumption such as packaging. The manufacture of packaging involves raw materials such as wood, energy, and water. First there can be an awareness of the negative effect of certain manufacturing procedures on the making of packaging materials on the environment with a consideration of redesign and acceptable alternatives. A next step could be eliminating unnecessary packaging such as double and triple layers of packaging. Have you ever noticed how much packaging you throw out? Recyclable or biodegradable packaging could be alternatives. **Biodegradable** means that material will decompose naturally through biological processes. In home use, packaging could be recycled into another use.

Another way to look at the environment/consumption interchange is to consider the environmental costs of producing goods from cradle to grave (from inception to disposal). How much electricity, raw materials, water, and gasoline (for transportation) are used? New methods and materials are needed as well as the support of consumers when they are offered more environmentally friendly goods. Consumers have to be informed about the larger part that they play and education is one of the keys to making informed decisions, more on this in a later section.

The discussion of caring about the environment harkens back to the beginning of the book when values (individual or collective beliefs that are considered desirable), standard of living, and the quality or quantity of goods and services were introduced. Values and standards of living impact economic life in the home. This approach is part of a far greater concept of life satisfaction, including the concept of buying wisely. This is in direct contrast to the concept that consumption just happens. On the contrary, consumption is far more complex and involves a set of behaviors, presumptions, and perspectives, including a global, environmental, or citizen-oriented approach.

## AT-RISK CONSUMERS

All of us are at some degree of risk in terms of consumption. For example, we can select a sandwich with bean sprouts that have been infected. It is estimated that a third or more of the American population gets sick each year from poorly prepared or handled food. Certainly low-income populations pay more and have more than their share of consumer problems. For example, individuals who use check-cashing outlets and other alternative financial services tend to have lower income, are less educated, and live in lower-income areas (Rhine et al., 2000). The Community and Reinvestment Act of 1977 encourages financial institutions to help meet the credit and banking needs of low- and moderate-income neighborhoods by offering services with safe and sound practices. The next sections address the especially vulnerable populations of children and the elderly.

### Children

Children are consumers of breakfast cereals, toys, games, entertainment, clothes, snack foods, and sports equipment and exert a great deal of influence on family purchases such as vacations and cars. They are also future consumers. Brands that are used in childhood are often preferred in adulthood, and this knowledge makes children a target for marketers. For example, Home Depot has workshops for parents and children to build birdhouses or other small items, and during the workshops the children wear orange Home Depot aprons. This is both cute and purposeful—the brand and the store are being mentally imprinted.

One study found that children were influenced by brand names and what the brands represented; hence, massive marketing campaigns exist for clothing and athletic shoe companies such as Tommy Hilfiger, Nike, and Adidas (Zollo, 1999). In this study, two-thirds of teens interviewed associated "cool" brands with quality. They assumed that a marketing campaign message of "cool" meant that the brands were of high quality—that the two characteristics go together. At any age, the meaning of quality is not easy to define. Characteristics of quality may include durability. Kadolph says that consumers hold a naïve notion of what constitutes quality, a kind of "you'll know it when you see it" attitude and that "quality is defined as the total of the characteristics that help describe the overall object or service" (1998, p. 13).

Children as young as four have made their first independent purchase, although eight is a more likely age (McNeal and Yeh, 1993). Consumers age 8–18 years spend over $30 billion a year mostly in these categories:

- food and beverage
- toys
- clothing, entertainment and personal care (Janof, 1999)

*The first independent purchase most likely takes place at age eight.*

It is during the preadolescent years, ages 8–12, that buying really takes off and purchasing behaviors are established. Countless media messages about consumption bombard children, parents, and teachers.

The Federal Communications Commission regulates children's TV programming to make sure that children are not deceived by advertising, but this is not so easy to do because children watch television more times than on Saturday mornings. Generally, the ads aimed at children are for toys, food, games, and clothing. The Internet is largely unregulated, and if children are on it is likely they are exposed to messages and images that parents consider inappropriate. This raises ethical issues about censorship in the home as well as in the greater society. **Censorship** is an attempt to control; it is the act, process, or policy of control. In the case of children, what might need to be censored are inappropriate materials such as pornographic, offensive, hate, and other potentially dangerous materials plus the solicitation of children for information about their parents or families or themselves. Approaches include training children how to be careful, getting parents involved, installing software that blocks, and having government and providers take steps to protect children.

The Children's Online Privacy Protection Act (COPPA), FTC, requires commercial Web site operators to get parental consent before collecting personal information from children under the age of 13. This act allows teachers to act on behalf of a parent during online school activities, but does not require them to do so. Many school districts have adopted Acceptable Use Policies to educate parents and children about Internet use and issues of online safety, privacy, and parental consent. The main cautions are about children's full names, addresses, and telephone numbers. Teachers are encouraged to notice the Web sites students are using and to steer them away from ones asking for personal information. Violators of COPPA should be reported to the FTC at *www.ftc.gov/kizprivacy.*

**Strong encryption** means the ability to achieve unbreakable confidentiality. This has good and bad aspects. For example parents could put strong encryption on messages coming into the home on their home computers thus protecting their children as much as possible. But, this same technology could be used by terrorists and child pornographers to protect the users of their sites. Should it be possible to essentially close out sites of any kind? This is an ethical question.

## Frauds Aimed at Elderly

"There are more people living into their seventh, eighth, and ninth decades than ever before. Although this longevity has been accompanied by improved health throughout the life course, eventually many older adults become frail and dependent on others" (Coleman and Ganong, 2003, p. 264). This dependency makes them vulnerable to frauds. Families can help them avoid trouble, but what if the family members live a thousand miles away or what if the elders keep the problems to themselves? Elders dislike reporting that they have been had or they may not even be aware that someone is taking advantage of them. They may be unaware of prices for things they have not bought in years and not realize that $2,500, for example, to recarpet a small bedroom is too much.

Skilled conmen and women know how to play on elders' loneliness and gain their confidence and in so doing gain access to financial accounts and belongings such as fine jewelry. Confidence is an important factor because "consumers' confidence in their existing information or knowledge may influence how much they search for additional information and the information sources they seek out" (Lee and Hogarth, 2000, p. 281). In this case, if the elderly person has confidence in the fraudster then he or she may not search for additional information or question what is happening.

The present chapter has already covered identity theft which can be a particular problem for the elderly who may be less aware of their finances and the location of their credit cards. The elderly are increasingly online and historically have devoted more time to television viewing and newspaper reading than the general public. They gather more information and embedded in that information are the frauds that exist. Also, because the elderly were raised to be polite they have a harder time hanging up on telemarketers and sales calls. In general, the elderly tend to be more trusting and therefore, more likely to fall victims to scams (see Box 14.5). They suffer from arthritis and other ailments more than other age groups and are thus susceptible to fake cures and treatments. They are also susceptible to work-at-home schemes.

A particularly disreputable practice called **youth peddling** refers to some for-profit companies using young salespersons to sell magazines and other items door-to-door. They trick the elderly into believing they are giving money to charity or to help youth programs. If solicited by a young person, the homeowner should ask for identification verifying the organization's name, address, and purpose. If anyone feels pressured or threatened by these sales tactics, they should contact the local police department.

The elderly portion of populations is growing, not only in the United States, but worldwide.

> By 2030, people over sixty-five in Germany, the world's third-largest economy, will account for almost half the adult population, compared with one-fifth now. . . . The German demographics are far from exceptional. In Japan, the world's second-largest economy, the population will peak in 2005, at around 125 million. . . . The figures are pretty much the same for most other developed countries—Italy, France, Spain, Portugal, the Netherlands, Sweden—and for a good many emerging ones, especially China. . . . Life expectancy—and with it the number of older people—has been going up steadily for three hundred years. (Drucker, 2002, pp. 242–43)

With this increase comes a myriad of consumer problems, including stress on health and welfare systems. Fewer working people may be in a position of supporting a burgeoning retirement class.

---

BOX 14.5    Frauds Aimed at the Elderly

Although the following frauds could happen to anyone, the elderly are particularly vulnerable.

Dance lessons frauds (elders have signed multiyear contracts for thousands of dollars)
Health spa frauds
Arthritis and other ailment cures and treatments such as impotence treatments (particularly susceptible are people searching for cures to multiple sclerosis, diabetes, Alzheimer's disease, cancer, HIV, and AIDS)
Money and investment scams, get rich-quick schemes
Charities that aim at the heartstrings (i.e., sick or undereducated children in foreign countries)*
In-home or door-to-door sales for knife sets, cleaning supplies, insurance, vacuum cleaners
In-home care in which the caregiver steals from the elderly person, taking over their finances
Mail fraud
Remodeling: roofs, landscaping, new carpet, additions (shoddy work or being overcharged)
Repairs to cars
Travel
Herb supplements, miracle foods, or diets
Prepaid funeral or cemetery plot sales, pressure or scare tactics used
Sweepstakes
Televised charity shows (beware of someone thanking you for a pledge that you don't remember)

*Before opening a checkbook, look into the charity being considered at *www.bbb.org* (Council of Better Business Bureaus) or *www.give.org* (National Charities Information Bureau). Do not give cash to a charity. For security and tax reasons, it is best to pay by check.

---

## FRAUDS AND UNETHICAL SERVICES AIMED AT JOB SEEKERS

*Beware of services offering to find the "hidden job market."*

It is a jungle out there, and unfortunately there are people willing and able to take advantage of job seekers. Consumer advocates observe that when the economy turns sour the rate of unethical firms that prey on vulnerable job seekers goes up. Be wary of any company that first presents itself as a recruiting agency. They may be present at job fairs or online. "They lure job seekers with the promise of contacts or access to a 'hidden job market,' but then try to sell other services. 'If anyone says anything is guaranteed, I'd run the other way,' says Margaret Dikel, author of online job-hunting manual The Riley Guide" (Maher, 2003, p. B6). One job seeker paid $700 to a firm for guidance, and they sent her resume out to potential employers but it did not result in a job. "'That was a real waste,' says the 51-year-old former marketing manager. 'You just get to where you'll do anything'" (Maher, 2003, p. B6).

Since most jobs are found through networking, money may be better spent in joining associations and groups with people in similar career fields. Career center services on campuses are free to students and often to alumni as well. They provide skills assessment tests, career advice, appointments with recruiters, and help with resumes, cover letters, and interview skills. If away from a college campus, a person who feels the need for an employment service should research the company or career coach before writing a check. This includes talking to former clients to learn about their experiences. Many who have used career-advisory services outside of college campuses have been burned, and some have alleged fraud. There are even Web sites set up by frustrated job seekers who vent their anger at career advisory services. A common complaint is that the service did not send out resumes as agreed or sent them to inappropriate places. As more and more job searches are conducted online, this type of fraud should decrease. Another warning sign of a fraudulent service is an offer of quick routes to employment. Job hunting takes personal effort, and there is no substitute for beating the pavement yourself once the resume and cover letter are in good shape and a career objective determined.

Interested in a career working with consumers? If so, look in the appendices for the section on careers in consumer affairs.

## CONSUMER EDUCATION

"The ability of consumers to make sound financial decisions has never been more challenged. . . . Educators, community leaders and policy makers face the challenge of bringing financial literacy and consumer education effectively to their constituencies" (Toussaint-Comeau and Rhine, 2001/2002, p. 9). As noted earlier in the chapter, changes in technology—most notably the Internet—have affected both the type and delivery of consumer goods and services, making the exchange process more complex and in other ways, speed, for example, easier. According to Edmonson, Flashman, and Quick, 1984, *the goal of consumer education is to provide a broad range of people the information, mechanisms and confidence that will give them a sense of control* over their individual and collective consumer decisions. Formal consumer education in K–12 varies by state and is usually part of several courses in high schools. Colleges vary in what they offer as well.

"**Consumer education** is concerned with the skills, attitudes, knowledge and understanding that individuals need to cope in an increasingly complex marketplace. The Internet has added to this complexity. Consumer education aims to protect consumers, inform them, promote an understanding between buyer and seller and contribute to society as a whole including providing a sense of economic well-being and fair play. The consumer experience relies on trust and dependability" (Goldsmith and McGregor, 2000, p. 126). Consumer education curricula requires a three-prong attack:

1. *Consumer decision making* (external and internal factors affecting consumer decisions as well as the stages of the decision making process)
2. *Resource management* (goal setting, personal finance, buying skills, technological developments, and conservation)
3. *Citizen and government participation* (including an awareness of economic conditions and legislative changes)

In modern consumer economics, there is an intense relationship between economic, social, and geopolitical forces. It focuses on how market forces operate and how individuals and families make choices in a complex society and diverse economy. Consumer education has its challenges in terms of getting students, at whatever level, to identify needs, allocate resources, and recognize the harsh reality of scarcity. Some needs are going to go unmet, and in the process of determining who gets what and who is left out of the loop, there are issues of equity, justice, and fairness. These all fall under the subject of economic education, as well as the more general category of character education. Discussions such as these are not for the faint of heart nor the perfectionist; it is the subject of debates with many sides represented. Legislators and governors constantly struggle with how to disburse tax dollars in a fair and effective way. Should budget money go to border control, education, or consumer protection? No matter which way they turn some program will have to do with less than in the past in order that other programs or new programs can thrive. Growth requires hard choices. Consumer education straddles between family and consumer sciences and other subjects within the social sciences such as economics and as such it sometimes falls through the cracks when money is being disbursed and programs set up.

The majority of high school seniors taking financial literacy tests fail to comprehend basic subjects such as banking products, credit cards, taxes, savings, and investments (Mandell, 1998). Further, the National Council on Economic Education has said that most high school students and adults score failing grades on their understanding of basic economics. A multiprong approach is suggested. The Jump$tart Coalition for Personal Financial Literacy is an example of an effective program aimed at high school students.

Besides school settings, it is clear that adult outreach programs are needed on consumer economics, including e-consumerism. Extension programs and Internet resources are available to those outside school environments. Consumer educators see their role as encompassing both the formal and informal learning environments. As more and more people become lifelong learners and since consumerism is a lifelong process, it makes sense that this topic transcends age and income groups. The Internet will increasingly play a bigger role in our consumption experiences and certainly in the search for information. Other delivery modes include information seminars, pamphlets and booklets, newspaper, magazines, radio, television, and videos. Scam alerts are part of the information exchange.

## CONSUMER ECONOMICS RETROSPECTIVE

Throughout the book, as we traced the unfolding of consumer economic thought we concentrated on economic thinking while keeping the welfare of the individual and the family in mind. In assessing economic ideas, it is important to remember that what we are seeing today has a history. "In an advanced industrial society, consumption is a necessity, not a luxury. It is what people must do to survive. It is the way that individuals take care of themselves and their families, much as hunting and gathering or growing crops were for people of earlier societies. For today's women and men, consumption decisions encompass everything from education to health care, insurance, transportation, and communication, as well as food, shelter, clothing and luxuries" (Zuboff and Maxmin, 2002, p. 7). We also consume experiences as well through such activities as travel and work.

Theories guide us on the right road. It is difficult to fully appreciate the development of economic thought as applied to consumerism without an examination of a variety of ideas and view points. The circular flow model of consumer economics introduced in the third chapter shows the interaction between various components such as media, consumers, business, government, and consumer organizations. We also learned about the less noble aspects of consumerism, namely, frauds and scams which each have a history and tend to repeat themselves in new and "improved" forms. Where money is concerned, fraud and deception are not far behind. As counterpoints, the concepts of citizenship and regulatory action were introduced.

"The search for better answers needs to go on at all levels—societal, organizational, family, local community, and individual—as people struggle with the difficult choices in their lives. . . . We have many reasons to be grateful that we, as members of the human species, come well equipped for these challenges. We are truly marvelous, adaptable creatures" (Lawrence and Nohria, 2002, pp. 283–84). This book provides the armor to protect yourself and those you care about from the unscrupulous and directs you toward the better parts of the marketplace, a place we all need. "No one can escape the centrality of consumption. There is no distinct class of consumers. Everyone is a consumer, no matter what their status or income level" (Zuboff and Maxmin, 2002, p. 7).

## SUMMARY

Consumer information processing is fundamental to the study of consumer economics. Greater access to information should lead to greater confidence in decision making. The downside to greater access is greater exposure to identity theft. In short, technology brings with it new opportunities and challenges. In this chapter two cases in point are the problems associated with redeeming gift cards and using telephone services.

The Identity Theft and Deterrence Act of 1998 makes it a federal crime for someone to steal your identity. The Internet creates numerous problems in the area of privacy, identity protection, sales, and children's issues. The risk to privacy can be minimized if the buyer trusts the mechanics of the selling process, the fairness and integrity of the people involved, and the firm or the institution and its ability to deliver as promised.

Two Harvard-based researchers have conceptualized human drives as being the drive to acquire, the drive to bond, the drive to learn, and the drive to defend. Identity theft and privacy problems fall under the category of the drive to defend. Thinking and caring about others relates to the need to bond and the drive to learn and make sense of the world and of ourselves. A global perspective is a way of thinking, a philosophy, in which small, local businesses are appreciated and seen as a part of the worldwide economy. Citizenship is an important consideration in the crossover between environmentalism and consumer behavior. Choosing wisely with an eye to the future generations takes present consumption into a higher realm, of thinking of others besides oneself. This requires a shift from individual consumer rights to an awareness of collective human responsibilities. The underlying principles of a global perspective require a mindshift to the greater good, an awareness of a greater role.

## KEY POINTS

1. Beware of services offering to find the "hidden job market."
2. Shopping bots are a type of intelligence agent used by e-shoppers to locate and compare products.
3. Establishing trust is fundamental to the consumer-market exchange. Identity theft has challenged that trust between consumers and between consumers and markets potentially resulting in a loss of money and reputation.
4. Consumer terrorism refers to activities whose purpose is to disrupt the marketplace.
5. Stealth marketing, engaged in to gain competitive advantage, refers to targeting an audience or market without being too obvious about it.
6. No one person or company manages the worldwide economy.
7. Globalization refers to international marketing, the distribution of goods and services worldwide. This is different from a global perspective that includes global ethics and challenges materialism. Educating consumers about the long-term effects of consumption, including environmental impacts and sustainable development, is part of building a global perspective.

## KEY TERMS

| | | |
|---|---|---|
| biodegradable | global perspective | social marketing |
| censorship | identity theft | stealth marketing |
| consumer education | marketspace | strong encryption |
| consumer terrorism | natural capital | sunk-cost fallacy |
| cramming | privacy | sustainable development |
| ecological economics | rent-to-own (RTOs) | trust |
| e-consumerism | shopping bots | voluntary simplicity |
| gifting | slamming | youth peddling |
| globalization | socially responsible | |

## DISCUSSION QUESTIONS

1. The case of Sarah Kalliney, an executive, spending nearly 10 hours trying to rectify a $9 late charge on a phone bill, brings up the question how much time should be spent following complaints and inconveniences. Have you or a friend or family member ever pursued getting your money back from a telephone company or had trouble getting a bill corrected? If so, what was the result and was it worth the effort?
2. Why are the elderly particularly vulnerable to identity theft? What steps can be taken to lessen the risk?
3. Since e-commerce is in process, it is not yet clear what kinds of goods and services will be bought and sold through e-commerce and what kinds will turn out to be unsuitable. In the chapter the success of books and cars being sold online was mentioned. What other types of goods and services do you think will succeed online and why? What goods and services cannot be accessed online?

# E-RESOURCES

For more information about identity theft contact:

Federal Trade Commission
www.ftc.gov

Library of consumer publications registering complaints

Please note that you have the option to submit information about identity theft or any other fraud problem anonymously. However, if you do this, law enforcement and other entities cannot contact you for further information to assist in identity theft investigations and prosecutions.

Department of Justice
www.usdoj.gov

Federal Bureau of Investigation
www.fbi.gov

U.S. Secret Service
www.treas.gov/usss

Banking fraud Web sites:

Overall banking issues
www.ffiec.gov/enforcement.htm

Federal Deposit Insurance Corporation
www.fdic.gov

Federal Reserve System
www.federalreserve.gov

National Credit Union Administration
www.ncua.gov

Office of the Comptroller of the Currency
www.occ.treas.gov

Office of Thrift Supervision
www.ots.treas.gov

Bankruptcy Fraud Web site:

U.S. Trustee
www.usdoj.gov/ust

Investment Fraud Web site:

Securities and Exchange Commission
www.sec.gov

Mail Theft Web site:

U.S. Postal Inspection Service
www.usps.gov

Passport Fraud Web site:

United States Department of State
www.travel.state.gov/passport_services.html

Phone Fraud Web site:

First contact local service, to go higher go to:

Federal Communications Commission
www.fcc.gov

---

Social Security Number Theft and Misuse Web site:

Social Security Administration
www.ssa.gov

---

Tax Fraud Web site:

Internal Revenue Service
www.treas.gov/irs/ci

---

For online buying information and privacy protection:

| | |
|---|---|
| American Express Company www.americanexpress.com | Full description of Web site security, how to decline email offers |
| Call for Action, Inc. www.callforaction.org | ABC's of privacy, international nonprofit |
| The Consumer Information Center www.pueblo.gsa.gov | Publications from federal agencies |
| The Direct Marketing Association www.the-dma.org | Trade association, acts as intermediary between consumers and companies |

# REFERENCES

Coleman, M., and L. Ganong. (2003). *Points & counterpoints: Controversial relationship and family issues in the 21st century.* Los Angeles, CA: Roxbury Publishing.

Drucker, P. (2002). *Managing in the next society.* New York: St. Martin's Press.

Du Plessis, R., and G. Rousseau. (1999). *Buyer behavior: A multi cultural approach,* 2d ed. Johannesburg: Thomson.

Edmonson, M., R. Flashman, and S. Quick. (1984). A successful consumer education model of informal learning designed for today's challenging economic climate. *Proceedings of the 30th Annual Conference of the American Council on Consumer Interests,* pp. 174–78.

Erasmus, A., M. Kok, and A. Retief. (2001). Adopting a global perspective in the discipline consumer science. *Journal of Family Ecology and Consumer Sciences, 29,* 116–23.

Goldsmith, R., and E. Goldsmith. (2003). The use of shopping bots by online buyers. *Proceedings of Marketing Theory and Practice Annual Meeting,* Hilton Head, SC.

Goldsmith, E., and S. McGregor. (2000). E-commerce: Consumer protection issues and implications for research and education. *Journal of Consumer Studies and Home Economics,* 24 (2), 124–27.

Harman, W. (1998). *Global mind change: The promise of the 21st century.* San Francisco, CA: Berrett-Koehler Publishers.

Harris, J. (2002). *Environmental and natural resource economics.* Boston: Houghton Mifflin.

Hofacker, C. (2000). *Internet Marketing, 3d ed.* New York: John Wiley.

Janoff, B. (1999). Targeting all ages. *Progressive Grocer Annual Report,* pp. 34–46.

Kadolph, S. (1998). *Quality assurance for textiles and apparel.* New York: Fairchild Publications.

Keller, E. (February 24, 2003). To regain trust, faking won't do. *Advertising Age,* p. 28.

Lawrence, P., and N. Nohria. (2002). *Driven: How human nature shapes our choices.* Cambridge: Harvard Business School.

Lee, J., and J. Hogarth. (2000). Consumer information search for home mortgages: Who, what, how much, and what else? *Financial Services Review, 9* 277–93.

Maher, K. (March 4, 2003). The jungle: Focus on recruitment, pay and getting ahead. *Wall Street Journal,* p. B6.

Mandell, L. (1998). *Our vulnerable youth: The financial literacy of American 12th graders.* Jump$tart Coalition for Personal Financial Literacy.

Mason, R. O. et al. (1995). *Ethics of information management.* Thousand Oaks, CA: Sage Publishers.

McCarthy, M. (February 26, 2003). Why merchants are so happy you lost that gift card. *Wall Street Journal,* pp. A1 and A12.

McGregor, S. (1998a). Reinterpreting economic theory in a global reality. *Journal of Family and Consumer Sciences, 90* (3), 35–40.

McGregor, S. (1998b). Towards adopting a global perspective in the field of consumer studies. *Journal of Consumer Studies and Home Economics, 22* (2), 111–119.

McGregor, S. (September 1999). Globalizing consumer education: Shifting from individual consumer rights to collective human responsibilities. *Proceedings of the 19th International Consumer Studies and Home Economics Research Conference,* pp. 43–52.

McNeal, J., and C. Yeh. (June 1993). Born to shop. *American Demographics,* pp. 34–39.

Rha, J., R. Widdows, N. Hooker, and C. Montalto. (2001/2002). E-consumerism as a tool for empowerment. *Journal of Consumer Education, 19/20,* 61–69.

Rhine, S., M. Toussaint-Comeau, J. Hogarth, and W. Greene. (2000). The role of alternative financial services in serving LMI neighborhoods. *Proceedings of the Changing Financial Markets and Community Development Conference,* 59–80.

Schlosser, J. (March 17, 2003). Looking for intelligence in ice cream. *Fortune,* 114–20.

Solomon, M. (2003). *Conquering consumerspace.* New York: AMACOM.

Spencer, S. (February 26, 2003). How much is your time worth? *Wall Street Journal,* pp. D1 and D2.

Toussaint-Comeau, M., and S. Rhine. (2001/2002). Delivery of financial literacy programs. *Journal of Consumer Education,* 9–17.

Turban, E., J. Lee, D. King, and H. M. Chung. (2000). *Electronic commerce: A managerial perspective.* Upper Saddle River, NJ: Prentice Hall.

Vidrine, A., and F. Lawrence. (2001/2002). Rent-to-own: Still costly for consumers. *Journal of Consumer Education,* 105–12.

Zollo, P. (1999). *Wise up to teens: Insights into marketing and advertising to teenagers.* Ithaca, NY: New Strategist Publications.

Zuboff, S., and J. Maxmin. (2002). *The support economy.* New York: Viking.

# Consumer Careers and Graduate School

## CONSUMER CAREERS AND GRADUATE SCHOOL OVERVIEW

If you have enjoyed this class and perhaps are majoring in consumer economics, financial planning, merchandising, housing, or a related field, you may be thinking about pursuing a consumer career or going on to graduate school. Consumer careers are many and varied; most exist in government, business, media, in organizations, and community development/education.

A popular Web site for college graduates seeking employment is monster.com. When this book went to press over 5,000 jobs were listed with the word "consumer" in the title. Most required a bachelor's degree although a few required advanced degrees and/or two or three years work experience. Once at monster.com click on search jobs. The types of employers listed included Pfizer, Pepsi, eBay, Inc., Bank of America, Countrywide Home Loans, Disneyland Resort, Sprint, Johnson & Johnson, Goody, Ashley Furniture Industries, Bank One, The Clorox Company, Wachovia, Toys Я Us, Inc., Federal Reserve System, and Bonne Bell. The job titles included consumer affairs manager, consumer promotions/marketing, consumer lending manager, consumer products sales, consumer fabrics, consumer insights manager, consumer researcher, and consumer services representative. For each job opening, click on it and find out more about the position and the employer. This Web site also lists jobs abroad. The term "consumer affairs" usually refers to careers that advocate for the consumer and involve activities in the public interest, specifically fairness in the marketplace and the improvement of consumer well-being.

## JOBS IN BUSINESS

Consumer positions in business may involve communicating with consumers, evaluating consumer applications for loans or mortgages or insurance, writing publications or press releases, representing the service or industry, designing exhibits or working at conventions, serving customers or clients, being a salesperson, or reporting consumer trends or consumer information gained from toll-free lines, consumer surveys, and other forms of research and communication to higher management. Consumer affairs departments may be called consumer care centers or consumer service or the consumer-related functions may be part of public relations, sales, management, or marketing. Monster.com suggests using related search terms such as banker, relationship banker, financial services officer, private banking officer and so on. So, when searching do not limit yourself to the word "consumer." You can also put in the area of the country you are interested in or the type of industry—consumer products, banking, and so on. Promotions can lead to jobs such as vice president of consumer affairs for Coca-Cola or another type of corporate officer.

At a recent consumer conference, representatives from Microsoft Corporation, Visa U.S.A., Inc, and AOL spoke on the issue of how to protect children in cyberspace. They were joined by representatives from the U.S. Federal Trade Commission and consumer organizations. So being a spokesperson is an option in a variety of settings. It is not unusual for consumer advocates from a number of employers to join together on a common theme or concern.

In a small company, the consumer services specialist may be a "jack-of-all-trades," performing a myriad of functions from product testing to proofreading advertisements and brochures to conducting survey research and responding to customer complaints. In a larger company, a consumer affairs professional (CAP) may specialize in one function. Another way the function may be specialized is that someone with course work or a major in consumer economics may become a stockbroker, a mortgage lender, a real estate developer, a product designer, an owner of a consumer services company, or a mutual fund manager. Forming a partnership is another way to go. More and more students like the idea of owning their own company or business, if not initially, in the long run.

Many companies belong to the Society of Consumer Affairs Professionals International (SOCAP) and their Web site *www.socap.org* could be used as a way to find potential employers. SOCAP has 2,600 members representing more than 1,500 companies, including multinational firms. The organization's goal is to improve the marketplace for consumers by addressing their concerns within corporate structures. An example is Mobil, Exxon Mobil Customer Relations in Exton, PA, can be reached at *www.exxonmobil.com*. Other sources of company names, addresses, and information include The Standard & Poor's Register of Corporation, Director and Executives; Trade Names Directory; Standard Director of Advertisers; and Dun & Bradstreet Directory. The Thomas Register of American Manufacturers lists the makers of thousands of products.

Trade associations offer other options where you would represent an entire industry or a group of industries. Examples would be the Soap and Detergent Association located in Washington, DC, the Toy Industry Association located in New York, and the Certified Financial Planner Board of Standards in Denver. Lobbying (for business, trade associations, or nonprofit organizations) would be another possibility.

## PERSPECTIVE

When reading job advertisements, be forewarned that not all jobs with "consumer" in the title require college degrees or even a course or two in the subject. And in many existing consumer positions one will find employees with all sorts of work experience and course work backgrounds. Often an employee starts out in human resources or accounting and finds they have great skill in consumer affairs or are drawn to the subject or are promoted to be head of a division. As another example, as discussed in the book anyone can say they are a financial planner, but to be a certified financial planner requires rigorous exams and training/apprenticeships. Another category that may be of interest is becoming a stockbroker. Do all stockbrokers have college degrees? The answer to this is no, but they must pass the Series 7 licensing examination, and sometimes a Series 63 exam too. The successful completion of the exams allows the broker to provide advice, solicit business, and execute transactions for clients/customers.

Perhaps this knowledge of the level of credentials necessary for some jobs in financial and consumer fields is disheartening, but really what it means is that as a job candidate it is a wide open field and that your credentials will be stronger than most. As mentioned previously each day monster.com lists over 5,000 openings with the word "consumer" in the title, this is a tremendously large job bank. And, then when you add on top all the related possibilities, not to mention what may be found on other search engines and all the jobs that are never listed, that are word of mouth, the number of potential jobs is astronomical. Because of the number of jobs, it also means that once employed it is not unusual for consumer specialists to work for one industry such as the airlines and then switch to a foods company and then work for a government regulatory agency. There are few fields as versatile as those in consumerism.

## JOBS IN GOVERNMENT

In government, the consumer specialist role may include designing educational programs, Web sites, and brochures, evaluating and setting policy, sculpting model laws, testing products, collecting and analyzing data, public speaking, writing reports, testifying, interviewing and giving interviews, and engaging in arbitration or mediation. Your goal would be to advance proconsumer views on a variety of issues. A person with consumer economics course work could become a leader in energy policy, tourism, or environmental protection or an expert on a state's lemon laws (for cars). Thus, the Environmental Protection Agency, as well as many other agencies or branches of the state and federal government, would be appropriate such as the Departments of Commerce. The E-Resource section at the end of each chapter can serve as a guide for finding government, as well as other types of jobs. Anything involving money, credit, or finances or the public welfare would have positions requiring consumer expertise. Military bases have positions in community and family services including financial counseling. This includes U.S. Military Family Centers (*http://mfrc.calib.com*) for the Navy, Air Force, Marine Corps, Coast Guard, and Army and Commissary and Exchange Offices.

America's Jobline, an audio version of the federal government's America's Job Bank, is available at no cost by telephone. Dial 800 414 5748 and follow the voice prompts. The Jobline also has information about employment services for the state you are calling from. Jobs are also available in the state attorneys general and other offices listed earlier in the chapter. Besides these counties and cities have openings.

The kind of places to look for include offices of consumer affairs, housing authorities or neighborhood community watches, human resources, departments of aging or community affairs, licensing, social services, energy administrations or public service utility commissions, insurance commissions or financial offices, legislative or congressional offices, departments of commerce or finance or motor vehicle regulation. The Consumer Price Index is compiled by the Bureau of Labor Statistics (*www.bls.gov*). The BLS regularly has openings for consumer analysts and economic assistants.

The Federal Trade Commission, the Consumer Product Safety Commission, the Food and Drug Administration, and any other agency mentioned in this book have positions and internships. Often the main way into state or federal jobs is through internships. A government job search may take six months or more. On government searches if you type in the word "consumer" you will find hundreds of matches or leads, but do not limit yourself to this word because as the list suggests consumer functions may fall under many bureaus and agencies.

Another specific example is the U.S. General Services Administration (GSA) in Washington, DC, which has many positions related to consumer economics. When this book went to press, GSA had a position available entitled Federal Citizen Information Center (FCIC) Information Program Manager for a recent graduate (BA/BS or masters) in consumer sciences, marketing, or a related field who is interested in educating citizens through a coordinated program of print publications, electronic information, and a national contact center. FCIC is known for promoting and delivering consumer information form Pueblo, Colorado. They also manage four award-winning Web sites and publish the annual Consumer Action Handbook, a 150-page compendium of the best consumer purchase and complaint advice. To receive a free copy of the current Consumer Action Handbook order through the FCIC Web site, *www.pueblo.gov*. It can also be viewed there. For information that is updated weekly, visit *www.consumeraction.gov*. This is a useful guide to all kinds of government, trade association, media, community/education, and corporate jobs; it lists names, addresses, and contact information.

Here is a list of other federal agencies with enforcement and/or complaint handling duties for products and services used by the general public not previously mentioned in this section.

Architectural and Transportation Barriers Compliance Board

Centers for Disease Control and Prevention

Commodity Futures Trading Commission

Department of Agriculture

Department of Defense

Department of Education

Department of Energy

Department of Health and Human Services

Department of Housing and Urban Development

Department of Justice

Department of Labor

Department of State

Department of the Interior

Department of the Treasury

Department of Transportation

Department of Veterans Affairs (Consumer Affairs Service)

Equal Employment Opportunity Commission

Federal Communications Commission (Consumer & Governmental Affairs Bureau)

Federal Deposit Insurance Corporation (Consumer Affairs Section)

Federal Emergency Management Agency

Federal Maritime Commission

Federal Reserve System (Division of Consumer and Community Affairs)

Government Printing Office

Immigration and Naturalization Service

National Archives and Records Administration

National Council on Disability

National Credit Union Administration

National Labor Relations Board

Nuclear Regulatory Commission (Office of Consumer Affairs)

Pension Benefit Guaranty Corporation (Customer Service Division)

Postal Rate Commission (Office of the Consumer Advocate)

Railroad Retirement Board

Securities and Exchange Commission

Small Business Administration

Social Security Administration

Surface Transportation Board

U.S. Postal Service (Office of Consumer Advocate)

U.S. Postal Inspection Service

## JOBS IN MEDIA

In media, the role may be that of consumer reporter on television or radio (common in bigger cities) or a writer for newspapers or magazines such as *Consumer Reports* or an Internet supervisor or designer of consumer Web sites. Newspapers such as *The Washington Post* and the *St. Petersburg Times* have consumer reporters. Smaller newspapers often have consumer news in their business sections. Magazines such as *Southern Living, Women's Day, Family Circle, Ladies Home Journal, Better Homes and Garden*, and so on are written for consumers. In the case of *Consumer Reports* published by Consumer Union located in Yonkers, NY, there are product tester positions, management and public relations positions, as well as writing and editing jobs.

Whole cable networks are devoted to consumer news and how-to shows such as HGTV (Home and Garden Television Network) and individual news shows such as the *Today Show* have segments on consumer related matters—financial, home, garden, nutrition, and health. NBC at 30 Rockefeller Plaza in New York has a consumer division. Go to their Web site or call 212 664 2333.

The Internet opens up vast new frontiers. Financial information is one of the main areas on the Web. Someone has to design Web sites, oversee them, update them, provide content, and respond to consumers' questions.

## JOBS IN NONPROFIT ORGANIZATIONS

In organizations, potential employers include all the organizations already listed in the book such as the Consumer Federation of America, Center for Auto Safety, American Association of Retired Persons (AARP), Better Business Bureaus, U.S. Public Interest Research Group, Legal Services, Public Citizen, and Common Cause. An example of an area within the Consumer Federation of America is their Food Policy Institute. Look for nonprofit or community action groups, legal service organizations, or policy/think tanks. For example, the Consumer Protection unit of AARP located in Washington, DC, is charged to examine those consumer problems and issues that impact the financial security of people 50 years of age and older, and to help its members protect themselves from marketplace fraud and deception (*www.aarp.org*). Another example is Public Citizen which has a division called Congress Watch in Washington, DC that works for consumer-related legislation, regulation, and policies in such areas as health and safety, and campaign financing (*www.citizen.org*). Other examples of organizations involved in consumer affairs are the Urban Institute, Heritage Foundation, Trial Lawyers for Public Justice, the American Council for an Energy-Efficient Economy, and the Center for Policy Integrity.

Better Business Bureaus (BBBs) are nonprofit organizations supported primarily by the business community to promote ethical marketplaces, to find locations in the United States and Canada go to *www.bbb.org*. Vehicle disputes are settled by several nonprofit groups, including an arm of the BBB, the Center for Auto Safety, and the RV consumer group.

## JOBS IN COMMUNITY DEVELOPMENT/EDUCATION

This is a crossover category since many consumer jobs in government or business involve education or community development. A prime example is the Cooperative Extension Service, a government agency under the U.S. Department of Agriculture, found in every county in the nation that serves rural and urban consumers (children and adults) through programs and information. Most jobs in K–12 require teaching certificates and most college instructors have master's or Ph.Ds degrees.

Community development jobs can also be found in nonprofit organizations such as those previously mentioned and also neighborhood revitalization programs, Habitat for Humanity, government-sponsored programs such as Vista and Peace

Corps, and church-sponsored programs. Nearly all government, media, nonprofit organizations, and business-based consumer positions involve some form of education or outreach.

## ADVANCED DEGREES

Consumer economics often serves as a launch pad for graduate school in family and consumer sciences (or human sciences or human ecology), law, public administration or business school among others. To find out more about graduate school in any of these fields go to the Web site of the specific school you are interested in or go to general search Web sites such as *www.abanet.org* for law school information from the American Bar Association. Books found in career planning areas of bookstores can also be useful resources for locating schools and programs. Many employers allow employees to take one or two classes during office hours or grant a leave of absence to enroll full time. Some pay tuition or have agreements with universities so that courses are free. Others set up on premises courses or encourage employees to enroll in night and weekend classes with the reward of a salary hike or promotion when a degree or certificate is completed.

# Journals

## ACADEMIC JOURNALS WITH CONSUMER ARTICLES*

Journals with word "consumer" in the title:

Advances in Consumer Research

Family and Consumer Sciences Research Journal

International Journal of Consumer Studies

International Review of Retail, Distribution and Consumer Research

Journal of Consumer Affairs

Journal of Consumer Behaviour

Journal of Consumer Education

Journal of Consumer Marketing

Journal of Consumer Policy

Journal of Consumer Psychology

Journal of Consumer Research

Journal of Consumer Satisfaction, Dissatisfaction and Complaining Behavior

Journal of Family and Consumer Sciences

Journal of International Consumer Marketing

Journal of Retailing and Consumer Services

The Forum for Family and Consumer Issues, an electronic journal

General journals:

Academy of Marketing Science Review

American Journal of Psychology

American Sociological Review

Asia Pacific Journal of Marketing and Logistics

Asian Journal of Marketing

Australasian Marketing Journals

*This is a partial list. New journals appear, and some on the list may be discontinued or re-named. In addition, there is a growing number of electronic journals. A few are listed and noted as such.

British Food Journal

Cambridge Journal of Economics

Canadian Home Economics Journal

Child Development

Clothing and Textile Research Journal

Consumption, Markets and Culture

Corporate Reputation Review

Developmental Psychology

Economic Journal

Educational and Psychological Measurement

European Journal of Marketing

Family Relations

Human Relations

Industrial Marketing Management

Interactive Marketing, an electronic journal

Marketing Science

Marketing Theory

Marketing, Zeitschrift fur Forschung und Praxis (in German)

Der Markt (in German)

Perceptual and Motor Skills

Personality and Social Psychology Bulletin

Psychology & Marketing

Psychological Bulletin

Psychological Reports

Public Opinion Quarterly

Qualitative Market Research

Quarterly Journal of Electronic Commerce

Recherche et Applications en Marketing (in French)

Review of Marketing Science, an electronic journal

Social Behavior

The Gerontologist

The New England Journal of Medicine

The Service Industries Journal

Utrecht Business Review

Journals beginning with the word "International" other than those previously listed:

International Journal of Advertising

International Journal of Bank Marketing

International Journal of Electronic Commerce

International Journal of Market Research

International Journal of Research in Marketing

International Journal of Retail and Distribution Management

International Journal of Retailing

International Journal of Wine Marketing

International Marketing Review

Journals beginning with the word "Journal" other than those previously listed:

Journal of Advertising

Journal of Advertising Research

Journal of Applied Psychology

Journal of Applied Social Psychology

Journal of Brand Management

Journal of Business Research

Journal of Current Issues and Research in Advertising

Journal of Database Marketing

Journal of Economic Issues

Journal of Environmental Systems

Journal of Experimental Social Psychology

Journal of Euromarketing

Journal of Family and Economic Issues

Journal of Fashion Marketing and Management

Journal of Financial Planning and Counseling

Journal of Financial Services Marketing

Journal of Food Distribution Research

Journal of Global Marketing

Journal of Hospitality and Leisure Marketing

Journal of International Marketing

Journal of Insurance Regulation

Journal of Marketing

Journal of Marketing Channels

Journal of Marketing Communications

Journal of Marketing Education

Journal of Marketing History

Journal of Marketing Management

Journal of Marketing Research

Journal of Marketing Theory and Practice

Journal of Marriage and Family

Journal of Nonprofit and Voluntary Sector Marketing

Journal of Personality and Social Psychology

Journal of Personal Selling & Sales Management

Journal of Product and Brand Management

Journal of Public Policy & Marketing

Journal of Promotion Management

Journal of Relationship Marketing

Journal of Retailing

Journal of Service Research

Journal of Social Behavior and Personality

Journal of Socio-Economics

Journal of Social Issues

Journal of Social Psychology

Journal of Strategic Marketing

Journal of the Academy of Marketing Science

Journal of Travel and Tourism Marketing

Journal of Vacation Marketing

# Presidents

## AMERICAN PRESIDENTS AND TERMS IN OFFICE

Washington
1789–1797

J. Adams
1797–1801

Jefferson
1801–1808

Madison
1809–1817

Monroe
1817–1825

J.Q. Adams
1825–1829

Jackson
1829–1837

Van Buren
1837–1841

Wm. H. Harrison
1841–1841

Tyler
1841–1845

Polk
1845–1849

Taylor
1849–1850

Fillmore
1850–1853

Pierce
1853–1857

Buchanan
1857–1861

Lincoln
1861–1865

A. Johnson
1865–1869

Grant
1869–1877

Hayes
1877–1881

Garfield
1881–1881

Arthur
1881–1885

Cleveland
1885–1889

B. Harrison
1889–1893

Cleveland
1893–1897

McKinley
1897–1901

T. Roosevelt
1901–1909

Taft
1909–1913

Wilson
1913–1921

Harding
1921–1923

Coolidge
1923–1929

Hoover
1929–1933

F. D. Roosevelt
1933–1945

Truman
1945–1953

Eisenhower
1953–1961

Kennedy
1961–1963

L. B. Johnson
1963–1969

Nixon
1969–1974

Ford
1974–1977

Carter
1977–1981

Reagan
1981–1989

G. H. Bush
1989–1993

Clinton
1993–2001

G. W. Bush
2001–

# Glossary

**ability to trade**   The trading of one good for another.

**actively acquired information**   Information sought after for its own sake.

**acquisitive**   Having a strong desire for things, ideas, and information.

**addictions**   Psychological and/or physiological dependencies on habit-forming substances or practices (i.e., gambling can be an addiction).

**additives**   Substances added to food either intentionally or by accident.

**adjustable rate mortgages (ARMs)**   Allows the interest rates to fluctuate within a range, based on changes in the economy.

**adjuster**   A person who determines the amount of claim, loss, or damage payable under a contract.

**advertising**   A paid communication of a product, service, or idea by a company/sponsor to a select group of people or the general public.

**agent**   The provider of health care.

**alcohol**   An intoxicating liquor containing various levels of alcohol.

**annuities**   Contract in which the insurer promises the insured a series of periodic payments.

**anti-trust laws**   Prevent business monopolies.

**appreciation**   Increase in value, usually referring to a home.

**arbitration**   The process by which the parties in the dispute submit their differences to the judgment of an impartial person or group appointed by mutual consent.

**aspirations**   Meaning that consumers aspire to own a brand name.

**assets**   What is owned.

**association**   Advertisers link up their products with a fun experience such as a sport or celebrity because it has a pleasant association.

**attribute-based choices**   The more variables or attributes presented, the greater the perception of reduction of risk.

**attitudes**   A person's likes and dislikes.

**banner ad**   Source of passively acquired information that comes up at the top of a Web site.

**bankruptcy**   A form of legal recourse open to insolvent debtors.

**behavioral economics**   A specialization within economics that emphasizes the impact of psychological or behavioral factors.

**biodegradable**   Material will decompose naturally through biological processes.

**biologics**   A broad category including vaccines, blood and blood derivatives, allergenic patch tests and extracts, tests to detect HIV and hepatitis, gene therapy products, cells and tissues for transplantation and treatments for cancers and arthritis.

**biotechnology**   The use of biological systems or organisms to create or modify products.

**bonds**   Investments involving lending money to governments or corporations.

**Botox**   A short name for Botulinum Toxin Type A which is used for a number of treatments including lessening of facial lines by injection.

**bounded rationality**   The limited capacity consumers have for processing information.

**boycott**   The act of refraining from or refusing to purchase certain items in protest to achieve a certain objective.

**brand**   A distinctive name identifying a product or a manufacturer usually talked about in terms of a popular brand of a product.

**brand extension**   The addition of a new product to an already existing brand to satisfy a consumer's need.

**brand image**   The set of perceptions that consumers have formed about a brand.

**brand perception**   How consumers rate or consider brands.

**bricks and clicks**   A store or business such as a bank that has a physical as well as an online presence.

**budget constraints**   The relationship between what one can spend and what one will spend, limitations.

**bunko**   Swindles in which an unsuspecting person or group of people are cheated.

**business cycle**   Illustrates the usual expansions and contractions in the economy.

**calories**   Units by which energy is measured.

**capitalism**   An economic system characterized by open competition in a free market.

**carpel tunnel syndrome**   Compression of the median nerve in the wrist causing numbness, tingling, and pain in hands and fingers caused by repetitive use of the hands such as computer use.

**caveat emptor**   Translated as "may the buyer beware."

**cease-and-desist order**   Administrative or judicial order, ordering a business to cease unfair or deceptive acts or practices.

**censorship**   An attempt to control, it is the act, process, or policy of control.

**certified divorce planner**   A specialist trained to focus on who gets the assets in divorces.

**certified financial planner (CFP)**   The most recognized financial planning credential, because of the rigorous examinations, three years of practical experience, and adhering to a code of ethics.

**Chapter 7 Bankruptcy**   A type of bankruptcy in which the court is asked to erase all dischargeable debt with a few exceptions which vary by state.

**Chapter 13 Bankruptcy**   Allows debtors to repay some of the debt they owe and in return they get to keep most of their property.

**chronic disease**   A disease that develops and continues over a long period of time; usually caused by a variety of factors, including lifestyle factors.

**churning**   An illegal practice of encouraging insureds (consumers) to switch policies often in order to generate commissions.

**civil cases**   Involve the settling of private conflicts between people or between businesses.

**claim rates**   The percentage of consumers who mail in rebate coupons.

**closing**   The meeting in which real estate is transferred from seller to buyer.

**cognitive dissonance**   The tendency to accentuate the benefits and downplay the deficits.

**collateral**   Property used to secure a loan.

**command or centrally controlled economy**   Most decisions about what, how, and for whom to produce are made by those who control the government.

**common law**   Unwritten system of law rights of buyers and competitors that is the foundation of both the U.S. and English legal systems.

**communism**   A social or an economic system in which nearly all capital is collectively owned.

**consent order**   The FTC notifies the advertiser that its ads are deceptive and asks the advertiser to sign a consent decree saying they will stop the deceptive practice.

**conciliation**   A type of dispute resolution program, meaning to reconcile, to make things pleasant again.

**condominiums**   Including townhouses, they are homes attached to one another, you can own a unit but you and neighbors share common areas such as swimming pools and lobbies.

**confidence men (or con men)**   A particular type of swindle in which victims are defrauded after their confidence has been won.

**conglomerate merger**   Combines companies, a conglomerate is a business corporation made up of a number of different companies in widely divergent fields.

**conspicuous consumption**   Paying an extremely high price for a product for its prestige value leading to a much higher demand.

**constitutional law**   Based on the U.S. Constitution, the fundamental law of the U.S. federal system of government.

**constructive choice**   A timely decision based on the situation at hand.

**consumer behavior**   The buying behavior of consumers—the individuals, families, and households who buy goods and services for personal consumption.

**consumer confidence**   A measure of consumer well-being measured by The Conference Board and the University of Michigan's Survey Research Center.

**consumer cost**   The total cost involved in owning or using the product, also called the nonprice cost.

**consumer durables**   Products bought by consumers that are expected to last three years or more including automobiles, appliances, and furniture.

**consumer economics**   The study of how people deal with scarcity, fulfill needs, and select among alternative goods, services, and actions.

**consumer education**   Referring to the skills, attitudes, knowledge and understanding that individuals need to cope in an increasingly complex marketplace.

**consumer expenditure survey**   Data collected by Bureau of Labor Statistics, provides detailed information on spending habits.

**consumer health**   An umbrella term encompassing the decisions consumers make about health care including products and services that they buy or that their insurance covers and decisions made about their lifestyle that affect health care needs.

**consumerism**   The belief that goods give meaning to individuals and their roles in society.

**consumer-market conflict**   When either side of a consumer-market exchange is not satisfied.

**consumer mediated environment**   Refers to buying and selling over the Internet.

**consumer movement**   Policies aimed at regulating products, services, methods and standards of manufacture, selling, and advertising in the interests of the buyer.

**consumer payoff**   A positive result experienced by the consumer from searching and making the best choice.

**consumer price index**   Measures prices each month of a fixed basket of 400 goods and services (durables and non-durables) bought by a typical consumer.

**consumer reporting agencies (CRAs), also known as credit bureaus**   Centers that have files that contain information about income, debts, credit payment history, and if you have been sued, arrested, or filed for bankruptcy.

**consumers**   Individuals or groups such as families who obtain, use, maintain, and dispose of products and services to increase life satisfaction and fulfill needs.

**consumer sovereignty**   The consumer is king, consumers decide which goods will survive, producers cannot dictate consumer tastes.

**consumer style**   Includes economics, history, culture, personality, biology or environment, technology, and politics or political climate.

**consumer terrorism**   Activities conducted by individuals or groups whose purpose is to disrupt the marketplace.

**consumption**   The using of goods by consumers.

**contracts**   Agreements or promises that are legally enforceable.

**cooperative apartments**   Type of housing unit in which the homeowner owns shares in the building as a whole with the right to lease a certain unit. Co-ops are most commonly located in large cities.

**corrective advertising**   Type of advertisement disclaiming previously false advertising claims, run by a firm to cause consumers to "unlearn" inaccurate information from prior advertisements.

**cosigner**   Agrees to repay the loan if the borrower does not (defaults).

**cosmetics**   Any substance applied to the body that is used to improve or alter the appearance.

**counteradvertising**   New advertising, which is undertaken pursuant to a FTC order for the purpose of correcting false claims about the product, also called corrective advertising.

**cramming**   Unexplained charges on phone bills for services never ordered, authorized, received or used.

**credence goods**   Goods for which the consumer can never get relevant information such as drugs.

**credit cards**   Used to purchase something or to get cash now with the promise of future payment.

**credit score**   A score or rating based on an individual's financial, workplace, and lifestyle information including assets, debts, length of employment, and length of living in one place. Bankruptcies or failure to pay bills on time impact heavily on the credit score.

**criminal cases**  Involve prevention, punishment, and rehabilitation. A violation is deemed to have taken place or an injustice against the government who brings charges against the person or persons who committed the crime.

**cross-selling**  Occurs when a company offers another one of their brands (coupons or samples) so that the customer remains loyal to the company.

**cues**  A reminder or a hint such as ads, signs, packaging and other stimuli that prompts a consumer to buy.

**customer satisfaction**  A function of the pre-buying, buying, and post-buying experience including the satisfaction derived from the value of the product while it is in use.

**debit cards**  Allow customers access to their funds electronically.

**debts**  What is owed.

**decision making**  Choice-making between two or more alternatives.

**deductibles**  Amounts policy holders pay toward a loss before insurance coverage begins.

**defect disclosure forms**  Describe the condition of the home, required in some states.

**defendant**  The party against which a legal action is brought.

**deflation**  Indicates falling prices.

**Delaney Clause**  States that no substance that is known to cause cancer in animals or human beings at any dose level shall be added to foods.

**demographics**  Data used to describe populations or subgroups.

**demography**  The study of human populations including characteristics such as size, growth, density, distribution, movement, and other vital statistics.

**depreciation**  The loss of value of an item over time.

**depression**  Characterized as a drastic and long-lasting decline in the economy with high unemployment, falling prices, and decreasing business activity.

**deregulation**  Removes or reduces government intervention.

**direct investment**  Owning your own house, apartment buildings, raw land, and other houses.

**disability income insurance**  Pays benefits to policyholders when they are incapable of working.

**discrimination**  An act based on prejudice or bias.

**disposition**  The process of disposing a product, can occur before, during, or after its use.

**distribution**  A marketing concept wherein products are available in places near target customers.

**diversify**  Spreading money over several categories of investments such as bonds, blue-chip stocks, small and large companies, foreign shares, real estate, and real-estate investment trusts. Diversifying diminishes risk.

**dividends**  Distributions of money from companies or government to investors.

**drugs**  Any chemical (not including food) that can affect the function of the body.

**ecological economics**  The specialization in economics that focuses on the relationships between environment and economics.

**e-consumerism**  The action of protecting, empowering, and informing consumers on the Internet.

**e-commerce**  Exchange transactions that take place on the Internet.

**economics**   The study of or science of production, distribution, and consumption.

**emergency fund**   Three to six months of salary set aside as savings in case of an emergency situation such as loss of job.

**end of aisle display**   Featured products, sometimes at a higher cost than similar products of another brand placed mid-aisle.

**endorsement**   Addition to an insurance policy that covers extra things such as jewelry or collections.

**endowment effect**   Theory that if someone is given a present (a sample) they will think it is worth more than someone who has not received the present, in other words they put a value on what is owned, they endow it with value.

**entrepreneurs**   Unique, industry changing leaders who relentlessly pursue new business opportunities. Inventors and small business owners can be entrepreneurs too.

**environmentalism**   Concern for the environment.

**equilibrium price**   Reached when supply and demand are equal.

**e-wallets**   Internet-based payment systems that allow value to be transmitted through computers.

**exchange process**   When people (as individuals or groups) negotiate with a goal of reaching an agreement.

**exclusions**   Items not covered under insurance.

**expansion**   The preferred stage in the business cycle, a period of prosperity, growth, higher output, low unemployment, increased retail sales and housing.

**experience goods**   When the consumer gets relevant information after purchase such as food and entertainment.

**expiration date**   The last day the consumer should use the product.

**exposures**   Sources of risks, such as driving.

**external search**   Occurs when consumers look at advertisements, read articles, go on the Internet, or ask others what they think about a product.

**extortion**   The illegal use of one's position, power, or knowledge to obtain money, goods, funds, or favors.

**family**   Consists of two or more persons related by birth, marriage, or adoption and residing together in a household (U.S. Census definition). Broader definitions exist that are more comprehensive, including other couples and groups who share resources.

**family brand**   The same brand name given to several products.

**Federal Deposit Insurance Corporation**   Government insurance of bank and savings and loan accounts up to $100,000 per account.

**fetal alcohol syndrome**   The long-term effects that babies suffer because of their mothers' alcohol abuse.

**FICO score**   Developed by California-based Fair, Isaac & Co., FICO is the score most widely used by lenders to determine who gets loans and for how much.

**financial planners**   Look at a person's or a family's total financial picture, help that person or family define and prioritize goals and then work out a plan to achieve those goals.

**fixed expenses**   Expenses that do not vary from month to month such as rent and car payments.

**fixed-rate conventional mortgage**   Fixed payment loans usually carried for 15, 20, or 30 years.

**food allergy**  A reaction of the body's immune system to a food or food ingredient, usually a protein.

**food irradiation**  The process of treating food with gamma rays, X rays, or high-voltage electronics to kill potentially harmful pathogens that cause food borne illnesses. It is also used to reduce spoilage and extend shelf life.

**foods**  Products from plants or animals that can be taken into the body for energy and nutrients to sustain life and growth.

**franchise**  The privilege to operate a business to sell the franchisor's products or services in a given area.

**fraud**  An intentional deception perpetrated to deprive another person of his or her assets.

**Freddie Mac**  A stockholder-owned corporation designed to increase the supply of money that lenders can make available to homebuyers and multifamily investors.

**generic drugs**  A copy that is the same as a brand-name drug in dosage, safety, and strength, how it is taken, quality, performance and intended use.

**generic products**  Products with no brand. (i.e. no logo or recognizable packaging) which are less expensive than brand name products.

**genetic engineering**  The modification of genetic materials to produce new substances or perform new functions through the use of biotechnology.

**gifting**  A symbolic act of bestowing voluntarily.

**globalization**  The distribution of goods and services worldwide so that they are more consistent and universally accepted.

**global perspective**  Challenges materialism and commercialism and asks citizens to examine their role in consumption and how it affects the world.

**GRAS List**  "generally recognized as safe," food additives that have long been in use and are believed to be safe.

**goals**  End-results, something you strive for.

**grifter**  Someone who uses his or her position to derive profit or advantages by unscrupulous means.

**hedonic**  The fact that many products and behaviors such as tanning provide sensory benefits—in short, because they taste, look, feel, or smell good to us.

**high balling**  A high amount is offered for a trade-in but the extra amount is made up in an increased new car price.

**home equity lines of credit**  Carries a variable interest rate and allows the homeowner to borrow up to a certain amount. Often used to finance home improvements.

**home inspections**  An assessment of the condition of a home, usually a home inspector is hired by the prospective buyer before purchasing a home.

**homeowner's fees**  Monthly maintenance or repair fees for common areas collected from single-family dwelling homeowners or from condominium owners.

**home warranties**  Provide additional protection for the home buyer.

**horizontal merger**  Combines direct competitors in the same product lines and markets.

**household**  The related family members and all the unrelated persons who share a housing unit.

**hucksterism**  Extreme promotion.

**Human Development Index (HDI)**  Quantifies well-being and compares the progress of nations by combining several measures of human well-being.

**identity marketing**   When consumers wear or display product logos.

**identity theft**   Someone using your name or personal information, such as your Social Security number, driver's license number, credit card number or other account number, telephone number, or street address without your permission.

**illiquid**   An asset that is difficult to turn readily into cash.

**implied warranties**   Not written but are inherently understood in the transaction.

**implied warranty of fitness**   The warranty holds for the *correct use* of the product.

**implied warranty of merchantability**   Implies that product should work, it is salable and fit for the market.

**impulse buying**   Purchasing an item without taking the time to think about the ramifications such as cost, benefits, values, or needs.

**indirect investment**   Joining in with a group of investors in a partnership or to own real estate investment trusts (REITs), investing in apartment buildings, commercial or office buildings.

**infectious disease**   Communicable disease from person to person; caused by invading microorganisms such as viruses and bacteria.

**inflation**   A steady increase in prices.

**infomercial**   Program long advertisements that can run an hour or more for cooking products, cosmetics, tools, exercise equipment, and diet programs/ supplements.

**information economy**   An economy where those who produce, have access to, and influence the spread of information have power in the global society.

**information search rule**   A consumer will search as long as the cost of the search is less than or equal to the expected savings from the search.

**injurious consumption**   Occurs when individuals or groups make consumption decisions that have negative consequences or misuse products in such a way as to cause injury to themselves or others.

**innovation**   A newly introduced method or product.

**innovators**   The people or group of people who created a newly introduced method or product.

**insurance**   A financial arrangement between individuals and insurance companies to protect against loss or injury.

**intentional injuries**   Purposely inflicted like homicide, suicide or assault inflicted by oneself or by another person.

**interest**   The cost of using money, the rate of interest is determined by supply.

**internal search**   Occurs when a consumer analyzes what they know about a product based on past searches or personal experience.

**investment**   The commitment of funds (capital) to long-term growth. Investing is an important means to getting ahead, keeping ahead of inflation, and becoming independent and self-supporting.

**invoice price**   The manufacturer's initial charge to the dealer, in other words, what the car cost the dealer.

**jingles**   Music memory device used by advertisers.

**junk science**   Term referring to when there is little or no evidence or proof to support a claim.

**lack of efficacy**   When a pill or treatment fails to produce the desired effect or outcome.

**law of demand**  As the price of a good or service rises, the quantity demanded of that good or service falls.

**law of supply**  As the supply of a good or service goes up, the price comes down.

**lease**  A legal document between the renter and the landlord, describing the rights and responsibilities of both.

**leasing**  A contractual arrangement outlining the terms of the lease including monthly payments, security deposit, and condition of the vehicle on return including number of miles.

**lemon laws**  Refers to laws that allow owners of new vehicles that repeatedly break down to get their money back or get the car replaced.

**level of living**  The way consumers are actually living.

**liabilities**  What is owed, a debt.

**liability insurance**  Pays for losses from negligence resulting in bodily injury or property damage to others for which the policyholder is responsible. All homeowners' policies provide liability coverage.

**liens**  Legal rights to take and hold property if the person with the loan does not pay up.

**life insurance**  A contract between a policyholder and an insurer that says what sum will be paid to beneficiaries on the insured's death.

**lifestyle**  How one lives, including patterns of time use, living space, what is thought to be important and how money is spent.

**litigants**  Consumers claiming damages or resolving disputes.

**loans**  Sums of money lent at interest.

**lobbyist**  Represents special interest groups.

**locking power**  When advertisers play on two forms of memory—recognition (seeing) and recall (more complex associations). *Also called memorability.*

**long term care insurance (LTC)**  Provides benefits for nursing home, assisted living, or in-home care not covered by Medicare insurance and for other types of long-term care.

**loss aversion**  Avoidance of risk, fear of loss.

**loss leader**  A very low-priced advertised special to bring in shoppers.

**low-balling**  A very low price that is quoted but there are add-on costs at the end that drive the final price up.

**Magnuson-Moss Warranty—FTC Improvement Act of 1975**  Empowers the FTC to obtain consumer redress when a person or firm engages in deceptive practices such as false or misleading advertising.

**malpractice insurance**  Insurance doctors or clinics have in case they are sued by patients.

**manufactured housing**  Units that are fully or partially assembled in a factory and moved to the living site.

**market economy**  Exchanges are controlled by marketplace forces of demand and supply rather than by outside forces such as government control.

**market extension merger**  Combines firms selling the same products in different markets.

**marketing communications**  Advertising, public relations, coupons, labels, packaging, billboards, in-store displays, and any other signal or message that the company provides about itself and its products.

**marketing mix**   Includes communications or information as well as product, price, distribution, and service.

**market segment**   Portion of a larger market whose needs differ somewhat from the larger market.

**marketing strategy**   There are many types of marketing strategies. One may be a plan or strategy created to give customer value to the target market.

**marketspace**   A term referring to when sellers and buyers do not meet face to face. For example, a buyer may see a picture of a product but not examine the product itself.

**mass consumption**   When millions of consumers make similar choices having a tremendous impact on the general economy.

**media**   A means of mass communications as in newspapers, magazines, television, or the Internet.

**media mix**   The combination of media and marketing communications used to reach a target audience.

**mediation**   The process of negotiating to resolve differences, an attempt to bring about a peaceful settlement or compromise between the consumer and the business through the intervention of a third party.

**Medicaid**   The federal health care program for low income people who qualify.

**Medicare**   The federal health insurance program for people 65 or older and for many people with disabilities.

**mental accounting**   Referring to when people frame or put into context their buying and selling.

**merger**   Occurs when two or more companies combine into a single unit.

**models**   Representations or schematics or illustrations of relationships.

**monopoly**   Exists when there is only one producer and there is no substitute.

**mortgage**   Loans to purchase real estate in which the real estate serves as collateral, what remains after the down payment is subtracted from the purchase price.

**muckraker**   Writers, politicians, journalists, and public speakers who search out and expose political or commercial corruption.

**multilevel marketing plans**   Ways of selling goods and services through distributors.

**mutual funds**   Groups of investments, usually stocks and/or bonds.

**nature capital**   The whole endowment of landed resources available, the natural environment that makes our lives possible.

**need set**   The term used to reflect the fact that most products satisfy more than one need.

**needs**   Things that are deemed necessary.

**net worth**   Someone's (assets—liabilities), determines how much can be borrowed or spent.

**nicotine products**   Any products containing nicotine such as cigarettes, cigars, and chewing tobacco.

**nonfamily household**   Householders who either live alone or with others to whom they are not related.

**nutrition**   The science of foods and nutrients and their actions within the body.

**ombudsperson**   Works with the court system to accelerate the bureaucratic process.

**one-price system**   Paying the price for a product that is stated on its price tag, not bargaining.

**ongoing search**   Conducted to acquire information for possible later use.

**open dating**   A system of placing a date on perishable products that indicates when the product should be sold or consumed.

**opportunity**   A favorable outlook, a chance for progress, advancement, and action.

**opportunity costs**   Exist when one alternative is selected over another and there is a cost attached to this choice.

**organically grown foods**   Crops grown and processed according to USDA regulations.

**over the counter (OTC)**   Medications sold that are non-prescription.

**pack dates**   When the product was packaged or manufactured.

**Pareto principle**   Also known as the 80-20 rule, which states that 20 percent of the time expended produces 80 percent of the results and 80 percent of the time expended results in only 20 percent of the outcomes.

**Parkinson's law**   States that a job expands to fill the time available to accomplish the task, such as finding and purchasing a product.

**passive information**   Encountered when one is doing something else.

**perils**   Events such as car accidents that cause financial loss.

**personalized identification number (PIN)**   Used for ATMs and other forms of cash management.

**personal finance**   An umbrella term that covers the spending, saving, investing, and protecting of financial resources.

**pirating**   Stealing an original idea or product and selling it.

**PITI**   Referring to how lenders estimate mortgages based on the down payment and the buyer's ability to handle monthly payments of principal, interest, taxes, and insurance.

**plaintiff**   The party bringing legal charges/a suit against the defendant.

**pollution**   Any undesirable change in biological, chemical, or physical characteristics of air, land, or water that harms activities, health, or survival of living organisms.

**Ponzi schemes**   A kind of pyramid scheme involving enticing come-ons that offer to make huge profits from a small investment in a very short time.

**portfolio**   A group of investments that an individual owns.

**predatory lending**   Lures people into loans that they really can't afford, usually by borrowing against the equity in their homes or a relative's home.

**prescription drugs**   Obtained by a written instruction usually from a physician for the preparation and use of a drug.

**preservatives**   Substances added to food to maintain a desired quality.

**price**   Amount of money a person pays to buy or use a product.

**price discrimination**   Different prices charged (a form of price variation). It can be illegal if an individual or group was treated unfairly, for example if charged a different price for no justifiable reason.

**price variation**   When a single seller may charge different consumers different prices at different times for the same item.

**principal**   The consumer of health care services.

**privacy**   The right to be left alone, meaning not being bothered by unwanted intrusions such as unsolicited sales calls.

**privatizing**   Turning over some of the functions of government to business.

**product**   Anything a consumer acquires or perceives to need.

**product extension merger**   Combines firms selling different but related products in the same market.

**product positioning**   Projecting a specific image of a brand to consumers within a target market.

**property insurance**   Pays for losses to homes and personal property due theft, fire, vandalism, natural disasters, or other causes such as trees falling on houses.

**property rights**   Legal rights over the use, sale, and proceeds from a good or resource.

**prospect theory**   People's degree of pleasure is more dependent on the change in their condition than on the absolute level.

**public policy**   A plan or decision by government to act in a certain way or direction.

**public service announcements**   A message sent out to the public usually arranged by the Ad Council who teams up with government agencies or non-profit organizations.

**puffery**   Advertising that exaggerates the characteristics of a product.

**pull dates**   The last day the product should be sold.

**pyramiding**   An illegal practice referring to plans that offer to pay commissions for recruiting new distributors.

**quacks**   Unscrupulous individuals specializing in medical or health swindlers.

**quality assurance dates**   The last day when the product is at its peak.

**quality of life**   Consumers' perception of and satisfaction with their lives.

**rational**   Having the ability to reason.

**rational self-interest**   Making choices that will give the greatest amount of satisfaction at a particular time based on known information.

**real estate**   A piece of land and everything related to it including the houses, landscaping, fencing, plus right to the airspace above and the earth below, with limits.

**Real Estate Investment Trust (REITs)**   Traded on the major stock exchanges so you can buy a share in them the same way that you can buy a share in a stock or mutual fund.

**real gross domestic products (real GDP)**   A measure of the value of all the goods and services newly produced in a country during some period of time, usually a year or a quarter, adjusted for inflation.

**reasonable person**   A person who is rational, attentive, knowledgeable and capable of making judgments in his or her best interest.

**recession**   A moderate and temporary decline or downturn in the economy.

**recovery**   The period in the business cycle when economic activity picks up, leading to expansion.

**redlining**   Prohibited by law, refers to the practice of drawing a red line or any other color around an area and that area is then marked as not receiving the same treatment as other areas regarding financing. It can also exist for insurance and credit.

**reference groups**   Collections of people that influence your decisions and behavior.

**regional subcultures**   Groups that have characteristic differences in environment, resource use, history, and traditions based on location.

**regulation**   An attempt by government to control the workings of the market-place.

**regulatory laws**   Laws or rules or regulations enacted to protect consumers through agencies of the federal or state government.

**rent**   Payment for the use of property.

**rent-to-own (RTOs)**   An industry of dealers who rent to individuals a variety of goods from furniture to electronics to appliances with an option to buy.

**resources**   Assets or what you have available to you.

**reversible mortgages**   Pays the homeowner, usually an elderly person, in monthly advances or through a line of credit, they convert home equity into cash with no repayment required for as long as the borrowers live in their homes.

**revocation of acceptance**   Referring to lemon laws, it is procedure to get the money back or replace a car.

**right-to-cure laws**   A procedure set up for homeowners to give builders a chance to repair homes before a lawsuit is filed.

**right to redress**   The right of consumers to seek and obtain satisfaction for damages incurred through the use of a product or service.

**risk**   The possibility or perception of harm, suffering, danger, or loss.

**rogue agents**   Agents that are not associated with established companies and who are engaging in illegal activities, usually used in reference to rogue insurance agents.

**rule of reciprocation**   The idea that we try to repay what someone has given us.

**rule of thumb**   Principles that guide purchases such as only buying certain brands or only shopping in certain stores or buying certain styles.

**sandwich generation**   Supporting or taking care of children as well as aging parents.

**scarcity**   A condition in which there is an insufficient amount or supply, a shortage.

**science**   The observation, identification, description, experimental investigation, and theoretical explanation of phenomena.

**scientific literacy**   The promotion of science education in the schools and in the community.

**second mortgages**   Often taken out by homeowners to get money in a lump sum for home improvements or other expenses.

**security deposit**   A payment required by the landlord in advance to cover wear and tear of the unit and as the name implies to secure a unit for the renter.

**self-worth**   A system of thoughts and feelings concerning or focused on self.

**service**   Activities that are performed to enhance and sustain the primary product or service.

**service contracts**   Contract which provides repair and/or maintenance for a specific time period.

**shopping bots**   Browser based shopping assistants.

**slamming**   When a consumer's long distance telephone company switches to another company without his or her permission.

**slogans**   Memory device used by advertisers by way of short phrases.

**small claims court**   A form of civil court that allows litigants claiming damages or resolving disputes that involve modest amounts of money (also called conciliation or magistrates court).

**Smart Card or chip cards, or stored value cards**   Cards embedded with computer chips for a prepaid amount of money, often used for phone calls or buying snacks out of vending machines.

**social marketing**   Marketing strategies and tactics are applied to alter or create behaviors that have a positive effect or try to reverse negative outcomes for individuals, society, and the environment.

**socialism**   An economic system in which the government centrally plans, owns, and controls most of the capital and makes decisions about prices and quantities.

**socialization**   The process of learning to interact with others, forming cooperative relationships, participating in society, and learning the ways of daily life.

**socially responsible**   Referring to the idea that companies must address the needs of the masses as well as the needs of the few and balance individual quality with societal and environmental quality.

**socially responsible investing**   Investments consistent with someone's values and attitudes.

**Society of Consumer Affairs Professionals (SOCAP)**   An international professional organization that offers training, conferences, and publications to encourage and maintain the integrity of businesses in their transactions with consumers and in communications with government regulatory groups and agencies.

**socio-economic index (SEI)**   An index (or measure) based on education level and occupation.

**special interest groups**   Units of two or more persons who have a common interest and seek to influence government policy and enforcement.

**standard of living**   The quality of life at which consumers aspire to live.

**statutory laws**   Laws enacted by the legislative branch of government.

**stealth marketing**   A marketing strategy, referring to providing a unique service or product that is not too public, "under the radar."

**sticker price or suggested retail price**   The price of the car, including options, transportation charges, and any "market adjustments."

**stocks**   Represent ownership in a company.

**strong encryption**   The ability to achieve unbreakable confidentiality.

**structure-function claims**   Health claims that can be made without FDA approval.

**style**   Individuality expressed by actions and tastes.

**subleasing**   The process that allows property to be leased by the original tenant to another person or persons.

**subliminal advertising**   Messages that are delivered in such a way that the person is not consciously aware of receiving the message.

**subpoena**   A written statement requiring appearance in court to give testimony.

**summons**   A notice summoning a person to appear in court.

**sunk-cost fallacy**   The desire to use something we have paid for.

**sustainable development**   Economic development that provides for human needs while not depleting global ecosystems and natural resources.

**taglines**   Memory device used by advertisers by way of end messages.

**tanning**   The body's response to skin exposed to ultraviolet radiation (UV) from the sun.

**target market**  The largest, most likely group to purchase.

**targeted advertising**  Advertising geared towards a specific group according to their environment or culture.

**technology**  The application of scientific knowledge to useful purposes.

**technological obsolescence**  Occurs when a product outdates soon after purchase or before it is worn out.

**theory**  Organized system of ideas or beliefs that can be measured.

**theory of reasoned actions**  This theory posits that actions are based on a combination of attitudes and beliefs and that motivations are linked to attitudes and beliefs.

**third-party complaint handling sources**  Used when the consumer involves someone besides themselves and the business in a complaint.

**tie-in**  Where complementary products are placed side by side with one price jacked up to compensate for the loss-leader.

**time deposit**  Safe ways to store money from seven days to several years, for example certificates of deposit.

**time shares**  Apartments, units, or homes usually for vacation purposes with several owners.

**tobacco**  A plant native to America, the leaves are processed for use in cigarettes, cigars, etc.

**tort**  A civil wrong that causes either (or both) emotional or physical injury, can be intentional or negligent.

**trademark**  Legal term, which includes words, symbols, or marks that are legally registered for use by a company.

**tradeoffs**  Something that is sacrificed (or traded) in order to obtain something else.

**transactions**  Exchanges leading to the exchange being fulfilled.

**trust**  The psychological status of involved parties who are willing to pursue further interactions to achieve a planned goal.

**Truth in Savings Act**  Requires financial institutions to reveal the annual percentage yield (the amount of interest earned on a yearly basis expressed as a percentage), fees charged, and information about rules regarding maintaining a minimum balance.

**under utilization**  When a consumer does not use a product to the full extent for which it was intended to be used.

**Uniform Commercial Code (UCC)**  A set standard by which merchants operating in more than one state can more easily comply with that state's laws.

**uninsured motorist coverage**  Pays for bodily injury caused by an uninsured motorist or hit-and-run driver, or negligent driver with an insolvent insurer.

**unintentional injuries**  Occur when no harm was intended such as the results of falls, fires, or motor vehicle crashes.

**unit pricing**  The presentation of price information on shelves on a common basis such as per ounce.

**values**  Principles that guide behavior.

**variable expenses**  Expenses that vary from month to month like food and entertainment.

**vertical merger**  Combines supplier and company or customer and company.

**volatility**  The ups and downs of a security, commodity, or the stock market.

**voluntary simplicity**   A conscious effort to live more modestly with fewer possessions and at lower consumption levels.

**wants**   Things wished for or desired.

**well-being**   The state of being healthy, happy, and/or prosperous. Well-being is about both mental and physical health and having the finances to keep healthy, comfortable, and contented.

**wellness**   The condition of good physical and mental health, which has been maintained by good diet and exercise.

**worker's compensation**   Money that is paid if a disability is due to illness or injury received on the job.

**written warranties**   Written promises that the character and quality of the product are as the manufacturer represent them.

**years of potential life lost**   The difference between an individual's life expectancy and his or her age at death.

**youth peddling**   The act of for-profit companies using young salespersons to sell magazines and other items door-to-door.

# Index